New Concise Maths 3

George Humphrey

Gill & Macmillan

Gill & Macmillan Ltd
Hume Avenue
Park West
Dublin 12
with associated companies throughout the world
www.gillmacmillan.ie

© George Humphrey 2003
0 7171 3345 1
Print origination by Mathematical Composition Setters Ltd, Salisbury, Wiltshire

The paper used in this book is made from the wood pulp of managed forests. For every tree felled, at least one tree is planted, thereby renewing natural resources.

CONTENTS

Revision Exercises

PREFACE

New Concise Mathematics 3 covers in one volume the complete course for Leaving Certificate Mathematics, Ordinary level.

Full analysis of the pattern and level of difficulty of the examination questions was taken into account. The book reflects the author's experience that students learn better from worked examples than from abstract discussion of principles. The emphasis is on clear and concise presentation of the material. Long explanations are avoided, on the principle that these are best left to the teacher. A comprehensive range of worked examples, with helpful comments highlighted in colour, is included. The author has carefully graded the exercises through testing them in class. Concepts are built up in a logical manner. Each chapter is broken down into short, manageable sections. A numbered, step-by-step approach, highlighted in colour, is used to help with problem solving. Key terms are defined simply, and highlighted. This has been found to save valuable class time sometimes spent copying notes from the board.

The last part of the book is a 'revision book' within the book. This provides a comprehensive range of graded questions. Each revision exercise contains an extensive selection of 'part a', 'part b' and 'part c' type questions similar in standard to the Leaving Certificate questions. Tackling these exercises is an excellent form of revision.

I would like to thank Stuart Scott and Geraldine Finucane, students in Trinity College, Dublin, who took on the task of checking my answers and making many valuable contributions to the text.

Finally, I wish to express my thanks to the staff of Gill & Macmillan for their advice, guidance and untiring assistance, and to Patrick Roberts in particular.

George Humphrey
St Andrew's College
Dublin

I would like to dedicate this book to the memory of my father-in-law
Liam O'Connell

COORDINATE GEOMETRY OF THE LINE

Distance Between Two Points

If (x_1, y_1) and (x_2, y_2) are two points, the distance d between them is given by the formula:

$$d = \sqrt{(x_2 - x_1)^2 + (y_2 - y_1)^2}$$

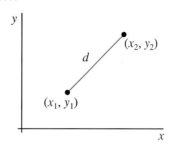

Note: Always decide which point is (x_1, y_1) and which point is (x_2, y_2) before you use the formula. The distance between the points a and b is written $|ab|$.

Example ▼

$a(5, 2)$, $b(8, 6)$, $c(6, -1)$ and $d(5, 7)$ are four points.

Calculate: **(i)** $|ab|$ **(ii)** $|cd|$

Solution:

(i) $a(5, 2)$ and $b(8, 6)$
          (x_1, y_1) (x_2, y_2)

$x_1 = 5, y_1 = 2$ $x_2 = 8, y_2 = 6$

$|ab| = \sqrt{(x_2 - x_1)^2 + (y_2 - y_1)^2}$
$ = \sqrt{(8 - 5)^2 + (6 - 2)^2}$
$ = \sqrt{(3)^2 + (4)^2}$
$ = \sqrt{9 + 16}$
$ = \sqrt{25} = 5$

(ii) $c(6, -1)$ and $d(5, 7)$
           (x_1, y_1) (x_2, y_2)

$x_1 = 6, y_1 = -1$ $x_2 = 5, y_2 = 7$

$|cd| = \sqrt{(x_2 - x_1)^2 + (y_2 - y_1)^2}$
$ = \sqrt{(5 - 6)^2 + (7 + 1)^2}$
$ = \sqrt{(-1)^2 + (8)^2}$
$ = \sqrt{1 + 64}$
$ = \sqrt{65}$

Exercise 1.1 ▼

Find the distance between each of the following pairs of points:

1. $(5, 2)$ and $(8, 6)$

2. $(1, 1)$ and $(7, 9)$

3. $(3, 4)$ and $(5, 5)$

4. $(1, -3)$ and $(2, 5)$

5. $(2, 0)$ and $(5, 0)$

6. $(3, -4)$ and $(3, 2)$

7. $(3, -6)$ and $(-3, -4)$

8. $(-2, 2)$ and $(-7, -3)$

9. $(-7, -2)$ and $(-1, -4)$

10. $(2, -4)$ and $(-4, 2)$

11. $(\frac{1}{2}, \frac{1}{2})$ and $(2, 1)$

12. $(\frac{3}{2}, -\frac{1}{2})$ and $(0, 1)$

13. Verify that the triangle with vertices $a(3, -2)$, $b(-2, 1)$ and $c(1, 6)$ is isosceles.

14. Find the radius of a circle with centre $(2, 2)$ and containing the point $(5, 6)$.

15. $x(2, 3)$, $y(-1, 6)$ and $z(1, 8)$ are three points.
Show that $|xy|^2 + |yz|^2 = |xz|^2$.

16. $a(5, -1)$ and $b(4, k)$ are two points. If $|ab| = \sqrt{10}$, find the two values of k.

Midpoint of a Line Segment

If (x_1, y_1) and (x_2, y_2) are two points, their midpoint is given by the formula:

$$\text{Midpoint} = \left(\frac{x_1 + x_2}{2}, \frac{y_1 + y_2}{2} \right)$$

In words: $\left(\dfrac{\text{add the } x\text{'s}}{2}, \dfrac{\text{add the } y\text{'s}}{2} \right)$

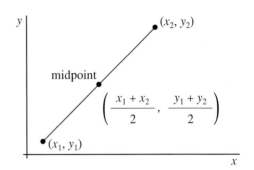

Example ▼

$p(5, 6)$ and $q(7, -4)$ are two points. Find the midpoint of $[pq]$.

Solution:

$p(5, 6)$ $q(7, -4)$ $x_1 = 5,$ $y_1 = 6$
(x_1, y_1) (x_2, y_2) $x_2 = 7,$ $y_2 = -4$

$$\text{Midpoint} = \left(\frac{x_1 + x_2}{2}, \frac{y_1 + y_2}{2} \right) = \left(\frac{5 + 7}{2}, \frac{-4 + 6}{2} \right) = \left(\frac{12}{2}, \frac{2}{2} \right) = (6, 1)$$

In some questions we will be given the midpoint and one end point of a line segment and be asked to find the other end point.

To find the other end point use the following method:

> **1.** Make a rough diagram.
> **2.** Find the translation that maps (moves) the given end point to the midpoint.
> **3.** Apply the same translation to the midpoint to find the other end point.

Example ▼

If $m(6, 5)$ is the midpoint of $[pq]$, and $p = (3, 7)$, find the coordinates of q.

Solution:

Step 1: Rough diagram.

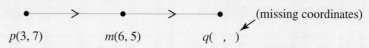

            $p(3, 7)$ $m(6, 5)$ $q(\ ,\ )$

Step 2: Translation from p to m. Rule: 'add 3 to x, take 2 from y'.

Step 3: Apply this translation to m.

$$m(6, 5) \rightarrow (6 + 3, 5 - 2) = (9, 3)$$

$$\therefore \text{ the coordinates of } q \text{ are } (9, 3).$$

Exercise 1.2 ▼

Find the midpoints of each of the following line segments:

1. $(3, 2)$ and $(5, 4)$ **2.** $(6, 8)$ and $(4, -2)$ **3.** $(10, 0)$ and $(8, -6)$

4. $(-3, 7)$ and $(-9, 3)$ **5.** $(-6, -5)$ and $(-10, -1)$ **6.** $(-8, 7)$ and $(4, -3)$

7. $(8, 8)$ and $(-2, -2)$ **8.** $(-7, 4)$ and $(9, -7)$ **9.** $(5, -1)$ and $(2, -3)$

10. $(3\frac{1}{2}, 1\frac{1}{4})$ and $(2\frac{1}{2}, \frac{3}{4})$ **11.** $(2\frac{1}{2}, -1\frac{1}{2})$ and $(1\frac{1}{2}, \frac{1}{2})$ **12.** $(5\frac{1}{2}, 7\frac{1}{4})$ and $(-2\frac{1}{2}, -2\frac{1}{4})$

13. If $m(3, 1)$ is the midpoint of $[pq]$ and $p = (1, 0)$, find the coordinates of q.

14. If $m(-3, -3)$ is the midpoint of $[ab]$ and $a = (-1, -5)$, find the coordinates of b.

15. The point $(4, -2)$ is the midpoint of the line segment joining $(-2, 1)$ and (p, q).
Find the values of p and q.

16. The point $(1, 6)$ is the midpoint of the line segment joining (a, b) and $(4, 7)$.
Find the values of a and b.

17. If $m(4, 5)$ is the midpoint of $[rs]$, where $r = (-2, 8)$ and $s = (h, k)$, evaluate $\sqrt{h^2 + k^2 - 23}$.

18. If the midpoint of (p, q) and $(-4, 7)$ is the same as the midpoint of $(4, -3)$ and $(-2, 7)$, find the values of p and q.

19. Find the coordinates of m, the midpoint of the line segment joining $p(7, 4)$ and $q(-1, -2)$.
Show that $|pm| = |qm|$.

20. $a(6, 2)$, $b(-4, -4)$ and $c(4, -10)$ are the coordinates of the triangle abc.
Find: **(i)**   the coordinates of p, the midpoint of $[a, b]$
           (ii) the coordinates of q, the midpoint of $[a, c]$.
Verify that $|pq| = \frac{1}{2}|bc|$.

Slope of a Line when Given Two Points on the Line

If a line contains two points (x_1, y_1) and (x_2, y_2), then the slope of the line is given by the formula:

$$m = \frac{y_2 - y_1}{x_2 - x_1}$$

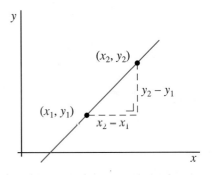

Example ▼

Find the slope of a line containing the points $(-2, 5)$ and $(3, 8)$.

Solution:

$(-2, 5)$	$(3, 8)$	$x_1 = -2$	$y_1 = 5$
(x_1, y_1)	(x_2, y_2)	$x_2 = 3$	$y_2 = 8$

$$\text{Slope} = m = \frac{y_2 - y_1}{x_2 - x_1} = \frac{8 - 5}{3 + 2} = \frac{3}{5}$$

Parallel lines

> If two lines are parallel, they have equal slopes (and vice versa).

Consider the parallel lines L_1 and L_2.
Let m_1 be the slope of L_1 and m_2 be the slope of L_2.
As $L_1 \parallel L_2$, then $m_1 = m_2$.

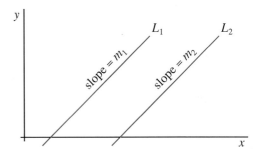

Perpendicular lines

> If two lines are perpendicular, when we multiply their slopes we always get -1 (and vice versa).

Consider the perpendicular lines L_1 and L_2.
Let m_1 be the slope of L_1 and m_2 be the slope of L_2.
As $L_1 \perp L_2$, then $m_1 \cdot m_2 = -1$.

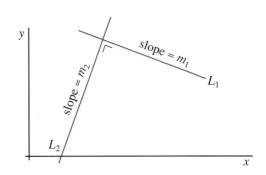

Note: If we know the slope of a line and we need to find the slope of a line perpendicular to it, simply do the following:

> Turn the known slope upside down and change its sign.

For example, if a line has a slope of $-\frac{3}{4}$, then the slope of a line perpendicular to it has a slope of $\frac{4}{3}$ (turn upside down and change its sign), because $-\frac{3}{4} \times \frac{4}{3} = -1$.

Example ▼

$a(2, 4)$, $b(7, 8)$, $c(2, 0)$, $d(7, 4)$ are four points. Show that $ab \parallel cd$.

Solution:

Let m_1 = the slope of ab and m_2 = the slope of cd.

$a(2, 4)$	$b(7, 8)$	$x_1 = 2$		$c(2, 0)$	$d(7, 4)$	$x_1 = 2$
(x_1, y_1)	(x_2, y_2)	$y_1 = 4$		(x_1, y_1)	(x_2, y_2)	$y_1 = 0$
		$x_2 = 7$				$x_2 = 7$

$$m_1 = \frac{y_2 - y_1}{x_2 - x_1} \qquad y_2 = 8 \qquad\qquad m_2 = \frac{y_2 - y_1}{x_2 - x_1} \qquad y_2 = 4$$

$$= \frac{8 - 4}{7 - 2} \qquad\qquad\qquad = \frac{4 - 0}{7 - 2}$$

$$= \frac{4}{5} \qquad\qquad\qquad\qquad = \frac{4}{5}$$

$$m_1 = m_2$$
$$\therefore ab \parallel cd$$

Example ▼

$p(2, 5)$, $q(6, 3)$, $r(0, 1)$ are three points. Verify that $pq \perp pr$.

Solution:

Let m_1 = the slope of pq and m_2 = the slope of pr.

$p(2, 5)$	$q(6, 3)$	$x_1 = 2$		$p(2, 5)$	$q(0, 1)$	$x_1 = 2$
(x_1, y_1)	(x_2, y_2)	$y_1 = 5$		(x_1, y_1)	(x_2, y_2)	$y_1 = 5$
		$x_2 = 6$				$x_2 = 0$

$$m_1 = \frac{y_2 - y_1}{x_2 - x_1} \qquad y_2 = 3 \qquad\qquad m_2 = \frac{y_2 - y_1}{x_2 - x_1} \qquad y_2 = 1$$

$$= \frac{3 - 5}{6 - 2} \qquad\qquad\qquad = \frac{1 - 5}{0 - 2}$$

$$= \frac{-2}{4} \qquad\qquad\qquad\qquad = \frac{-4}{-2}$$

$$= -\frac{1}{2} \qquad\qquad\qquad\qquad = 2$$

$$m_1 \times m_2 = -\tfrac{1}{2} \times 2 = -1$$
$$\therefore pq \perp pr$$

Find the slope of the line containing each given pair of points:

1. $(1, 2)$ and $(4, 5)$

2. $(2, 2)$ and $(6, 8)$

3. $(2, 0)$ and $(10, 8)$

4. $(0, 0)$ and $(3, 5)$

5. $(5, 7)$ and $(8, 4)$

6. $(-4, 6)$ and $(7, -2)$

7. $(-3, -6)$ and $(-5, -4)$

8. $(-2, 3)$ and $(-3, -7)$

9. $(\frac{3}{2}, 4)$ and $(\frac{7}{2}, -\frac{3}{2})$

10. $(0, 0)$ and $(\frac{3}{4}, \frac{3}{2})$

11. $a(-4, -3)$, $b(-1, 1)$, $c(2, 2)$ and $d(5, 6)$ are four points. Verify that $ab \parallel cd$.

12. $p(-4, 3)$, $q(-2, 0)$, $r(-5, 1)$ and $s(-2, 3)$ are four points. Show that $pq \perp rs$.

13. $x(8, -4)$, $y(7, -1)$ and $z(1, -3)$ are three points. Prove that $xy \perp zy$.

14. $a(-6, 2)$, $b(-2, 1)$ and $c(0, 9)$ are the vertices of triangle abc. Prove that $|\angle abc| = 90°$.

15. Show that the points $a(6, -4)$, $b(5, -1)$, $c(-1, -3)$ and $d(0, -6)$ are the vertices of a rectangle.

16. The line K has a slope of $-\frac{3}{4}$. Find the slope of L, if $K \perp L$.

17. The line M has a slope of $\frac{5}{3}$. Find the slope of L, if $M \perp L$.

18. The line T has a slope of $-\frac{1}{3}$. Find the slope of K, if $T \parallel K$.

19. The line L has a slope of $\frac{1}{4}$. Find the slope of M, if $L \perp M$.

20. The line K has a slope of -3. Find the slope of L, if $L \perp K$.

21. The slope of the line through the points $(3, 1)$ and $(6, k)$ is $\frac{7}{3}$. Find k.

22. $a(-1, -1)$, $b(5, 2)$, $c(2, -2)$ and $d(k, 0)$ are four points. If $ab \parallel cd$, find k.

23. $a(2, -3)$, $b(3, 1)$ and $c(-1, k)$ are three points. If $ba \perp bc$, find k.

Equation of a Line I

Let us plot the points $(-1, 8)$, $(0, 6)$, $(1, 4)$, $(2, 2)$, $(3, 0)$ and $(4, -2)$.

The points all lie on the same straight line. In this set of points there is the same relationship (connection, link) between the x coordinate and the y coordinate for **each** point.

If we double the x coordinate and add the y coordinate, the result is always 6.

That is:

$$2x + y = 6$$

This result will hold for every other point on the line. We say '$2x + y = 6$' is the equation of the line.

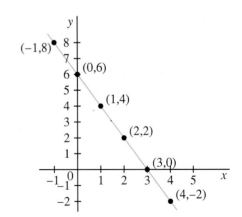

Note: $2x + y - 6 = 0$ is also the equation of the line.

To Verify that a Point Belongs to a Line

Once we have the equation of a line, we can determine if a point is on the line or not on the line. If a point belongs to a line, its coordinates will satisfy the equation of the line. We substitute the coordinates of the point into the equation of the line. If they satisfy the equation, then the point is **on** the line. Otherwise, the point is **not** on the line.

Example ▼

Investigate if the points $(2, -1)$ and $(5, -4)$ are on the line $5x + 3y - 7 = 0$.

Solution:

$(2, -1)$

$5x + 3y - 7 = 0$

Substitute $x = 2$ and $y = -1$

$5(2) + 3(-1) - 7$

$= 10 - 3 - 7$

$= 10 - 10$

$= 0$

Satisfies equation

$\therefore (2, -1)$ is on the line.

$(5, -4)$

$5x + 3y - 7 = 0$

Substitute $x = 5$ and $y = -4$

$5(5) + 3(-4) - 7$

$= 25 - 12 - 7$

$= 25 - 19$

$= 6 \neq 0$

Does not satisfy equation

$\therefore (5, -4)$ is not on the line.

Example ▼

The equation of the line L is $5x + 4y + 3 = 0$ and the equation of the line K is $3x + ty - 8 = 0$.
The point $(-3, k)$ is on L and the point $(2, -1)$ is on the line K.
Find the value of k and the value of t.

Solution:

$5x + 4y + 3 = 0$

Substitute $x = -3$ and $y = k$

$(-3, k):\quad 5(-3) + 4(k) + 3 = 0$

$-15 + 4k + 3 = 0$

$4k - 12 = 0$

$4k = 12$

$k = 3$

$3x + ty - 8 = 0$

Substitute $x = 2$ and $y = -1$

$(2, -1):\quad 3(2) + t(-1) - 8 = 0$

$6 - t - 8 = 0$

$-t - 2 = 0$

$-t = 2$

$t = -2$

Find which of the given points are on the corresponding line:

1. $(4, 1)$; $x + y - 5 = 0$
2. $(3, -1)$; $2x + 3y - 3 = 0$
3. $(2, 2)$; $5x - 4y - 1 = 0$
4. $(-3, -2)$; $6x - 7y + 4 = 0$
5. $(-4, 3)$; $3x + 2y - 8 = 0$
6. $(5, 2)$; $3x - 7y - 1 = 0$
7. $(-3, -1)$; $4x + y - 15 = 0$
8. $(2, \frac{1}{2})$; $x - 4y = 0$
9. $(\frac{5}{2}, \frac{3}{2})$; $6x - 2y - 12 = 0$
10. $(\frac{2}{3}, \frac{1}{3})$; $3x - 6y + 3 = 0$

11. L is the line $x - 4y - 5 = 0$. Verify that the point $p(1, -1)$ is on L.

12. The point $(1, 2)$ is on the line $3x + 2y = k$. Find the value of k.

13. The point $(t, 3)$ is on the line $4x - 3y + 1 = 0$. Find the value of t.

14. The point $(-3, k)$ is on the line $5x + 4y + 3 = 0$. Find the value of k.

15. The point $(1, -2)$ is on the line $4x + ky - 14 = 0$. Find the value of k.

16. The point $(-3, -4)$ is on the line $ax - 5y - 8 = 0$. Find the value of a.

Equation of a Line 2

To find the equation of a line we need:

1. The slope of the line, m

2. A point on the line, (x_1, y_1)

Then use the formula:

$$(y - y_1) = m(x - x_1)$$

In short: we need the **slope** and a **point** on the line.

Example ▼

Find the equation of the following lines:

(i) Containing the point $(2, -3)$ with slope 3

(ii) Containing the point $(-4, 2)$ with slope $-\frac{2}{3}$.

Solution:

(i) Containing $(2, -3)$ with slope 3:

$$x_1 = 2, \qquad y_1 = -3, \qquad m = 3$$
$$(y - y_1) = m(x - x_1)$$
$$(y + 3) = 3(x - 2)$$
$$y + 3 = 3x - 6$$
$$-3x + y + 3 + 6 = 0$$
$$-3x + y + 9 = 0$$
$$3x - y - 9 = 0$$

(ii) Containing $(-4, 2)$ with slope $-\frac{2}{3}$:

$$x_1 = -4, \qquad y_1 = 2, \qquad m = -\frac{2}{3}$$
$$(y - y_1) = m(x - x_1)$$
$$(y - 2) = -\frac{2}{3}(x + 4)$$
$$3(y - 2) = -2(x + 4)$$
(multiply both sides by 3)
$$3y - 6 = -2x - 8$$
$$2x + 3y - 6 + 8 = 0$$
$$2x + 3y + 2 = 0$$

Exercise 1.5 ▼

Find the equation of each of the following lines:

1. Containing $(4, 1)$ with slope 2

2. Containing $(-1, -4)$ with slope 3

3. Containing $(0, -2)$ with slope -1

4. Containing $(5, -3)$ with slope -5

5. Containing $(0, 0)$ with slope 4

6. Containing $(4, -7)$ with slope $\frac{3}{5}$

7. Containing $(-3, -1)$ with slope $-\frac{4}{3}$

8. Containing $(2, -5)$ with slope $\frac{5}{4}$

9. Containing $(3, -3)$ with slope $-\frac{1}{6}$

10. Containing $(-2, -1)$ with slope $-\frac{5}{7}$

11. Find the equation of the line K through $(2, -1)$, the slope of K being $\frac{2}{5}$.

12. Find the equation of the line L through $(3, -2)$, the slope of L being $-\frac{1}{2}$.

Equation of a Line 3

To find the equation of a line we need the **slope** and one point on the line.
However, in many questions one or both of these are missing.

Example ▼

Find the equation of the line which contains the points $(-4, 7)$ and $(1, 3)$.

Solution:

The slope is missing. We first find the slope and use **either one** of the two points to find the equation.

			Containing $(-4, 7)$ with slope $-\frac{4}{5}$:
$(-4, 7)$	$(1, 3)$	$x_1 = -4$	$x_1 = -4, \qquad y_1 = 7, \qquad m = -\frac{4}{5}$
(x_1, y_1)	(x_2, y_2)	$y_1 = 7$	$(y - y_1) = m(x - x_1)$
		$x_2 = 1$	$(y - 7) = -\frac{4}{5}(x + 4)$
$m = \dfrac{y_2 - y_1}{x_2 - x_1}$		$y_2 = 3$	$5(y - 7) = -4(x + 4)$
$= \dfrac{3 - 7}{1 + 4}$			(multiply both sides by 5)
$= \dfrac{-4}{5}$			$5y - 35 = -4x - 16$
$= -\dfrac{4}{5}$			$4x + 5y - 35 + 16 = 0$
$\therefore m = -\dfrac{4}{5}$			$4x + 5y - 19 = 0$

Exercise 1.6 ▼

In Q1–Q8, find the equation of the line containing the given pair of points:

1. $(2, 5)$ and $(6, 9)$ **2.** $(1, 8)$ and $(3, 4)$

3. $(4, -6)$ and $(5, -3)$ **4.** $(8, -3)$ and $(-6, 7)$

5. $(-6, -1)$ and $(-1, 2)$ **6.** $(1, -5)$ and $(3, -6)$

7. $(2, -2)$ and $(4, 3)$ **8.** $(\frac{1}{2}, -\frac{5}{2})$ and $(-\frac{3}{2}, \frac{3}{2})$

9. $a(3, -2)$, $b(2, 3)$ and $c(5, 7)$ are three points. Find the equation of the line containing a if it is:
   (i) parallel to bc **(ii)** perpendicular to bc.

10. Find the equation of the perpendicular bisectors of the line segments joining:
   (i) $(2, 3)$ and $(6, 1)$ **(ii)** $(-1, 2)$ and $(-3, -2)$.

11. Find the equation of the line L containing $(5, -1)$ and passing through the midpoint of $(6, 3)$ and $(-2, -1)$.

12. The line L contains the points $(2, 2)$ and $(-1, 4)$. The line K contains the point $(-4, 1)$ and $K \perp L$. Find the equation of K.

Slope of a Line when Given its Equation

To find the slope of a line when given its equation, do the following:

Method 1:

> Get y on its own, and the number in front of x is the slope.

Note: The number in front of x is called the **coefficient** of x.
In short, write the line in the form:

$$y = mx \qquad + c$$

$$y = (\text{slope})\, x + (\text{where the line cuts the } y\text{-axis})$$

Method 2:

> If the line is in the form $ax + by + c = 0$, then $-\dfrac{a}{b}$ is the slope.

In words: slope $= -\dfrac{\text{number in front of } x}{\text{number in front of } y}$

Note: When using this method, make sure every term is on the left-hand side in the given equation of the line.

Example ▼

Find the slope of the lines: (i) $3x - y - 5 = 0$ (ii) $5x + 4y - 12 = 0$

Solution:

Method 1:

(i)
$$3x - y - 5 = 0$$
$$-y = -3x + 5$$
$$y = 3x - 5$$

compare to $y = mx + c$

$\therefore$ slope $= 3$

(ii)
$$5x + 4y - 12 = 0$$
$$4y = -5x + 12$$
$$y = -\tfrac{5}{4}x + 3$$

compare to $y = mx + c$

$\therefore$ slope $= -\tfrac{5}{4}$

Method 2:

(i)
$$3x - y - 5 = 0$$
$$a = 3, \qquad b = -1$$
$$\text{slope} = -\frac{a}{b}$$
$$= -\frac{3}{-1}$$
$$= 3$$

(ii)
$$5x + 4y - 12 = 0$$
$$a = 5, \qquad b = 4$$
$$\text{slope} = -\frac{a}{b}$$
$$= -\frac{5}{4}$$

To prove whether or not two lines are parallel, do the following:

> **1.** Find the slope of each line.
>
> **2. (a)** If the slopes are the same, the lines are parallel.
>   **(b)** If the slopes are different, the lines are **not** parallel.

To prove whether or not two lines are perpendicular, do the following:

1. Find the slope of each line.

2. Multiply both slopes.

3. (a) If the answer in step 2 is –1, the lines are perpendicular.

   (b) If the answer in step 2 is **not** –1, the lines are **not** perpendicular.

Example ▼

$L: 3x + 4y - 8 = 0$ and $K: 4x - 3y + 6 = 0$ are two lines. Prove that $L \perp K$.

Solution:

$$3x + 4y - 8 = 0$$
$$4y = -3x + 8$$
$$y = -\tfrac{3}{4}x + 2$$
$$\therefore \quad \text{slope of } L = -\tfrac{3}{4}$$

$$4x - 3y + 6 = 0$$
$$-3y = -4x - 6$$
$$3y = 4x + 6$$
$$y = \tfrac{4}{3}x + 2$$
$$\therefore \quad \text{slope of } K = \tfrac{4}{3}$$

$$(\text{slope of } L) \times (\text{slope of } K) = -\tfrac{3}{4} \times \tfrac{4}{3} = -1$$
$$\therefore L \perp K$$

Note: To get the slopes we could have used: $m = -\dfrac{a}{b}$ in each case.

Exercise 1.7 ▼

Find the slope of each of the following lines:

1. $2x + y + 7 = 0$
2. $3x - y - 2 = 0$
3. $4x - 2y - 7 = 0$
4. $9x + 3y - 11 = 0$
5. $2x + 3y - 15 = 0$
6. $4x - 3y - 12 = 0$
7. $x + 4y - 3 = 0$
8. $x - 3y + 2 = 0$
9. $4x - 3y = 0$
10. $5x - 7y = 8$
11. $3x - 2y - 3 = 0$
12. $7x - 10y - 11 = 0$

13. $L: 5x - 2y - 10 = 0$ and $K: 2x + 5y - 15 = 0$ are two lines. Prove that $L \perp K$.

14. $L: 3x + 2y - 2 = 0$ and $K: 2x - 3y + 6 = 0$ are two lines. Prove that $L \perp K$.

15. $L: 3x + 4y - 11 = 0$ and $K: 6x + 8y - 5 = 0$ are two lines. Prove that $L \parallel K$.

16. If the line $3x + 2y - 10 = 0$ is parallel to the line $kx + 4y - 8 = 0$, find the value of k.

17. If the lines $5x - 4y - 20 = 0$ and $4x + ky - 6 = 0$ are perpendicular, find the value of k.

18. L is the line $5x + 2y - 10 = 0$. Find the slope of L.

    K is the line $ax + 10y + 3 = 0$. Find the slope of K in terms of a.

    Find the value of a if: (i) $K \parallel L$ (ii) $K \perp L$.

Equation of a Line, Parallel or Perpendicular to a Given Line

In some questions we need to find the equation of a line containing a particular point which is parallel to, or perpendicular to, a given line.

When this happens do the following:

> 1. Find the slope of the given line.
>
> 2. (a) if parallel, use the slope in step 1.
>   (b) if perpendicular, turn the slope in step 1 upside down and change sign.
>
> 3. Use the slope in step 2 with the point in the formula:
> $$(y - y_1) = m(x - x_1).$$

Remember: To find the equation of a line we need:

1. Slope, m
2. One point, (x_1, y_1)
3. Formula, $(y - y_1) = m(x - x_1)$.

Example ▼

L is the line $5x - 3y - 2 = 0$. The line K contains the point $(3, -1)$ and $K \perp L$. Find the equation of K.

Solution:

We have a point, $(3, -1)$. The slope is missing.

Step 1: Find the slope of L.

$$5x - 3y - 2 = 0$$
$$-3y = -5x + 2$$
$$3y = 5x - 2$$
$$y = \tfrac{5}{3}x - \tfrac{2}{3}$$

$\therefore$ slope of $L = \tfrac{5}{3}$

Step 2: Find the slope of K.

Perpendicular to L.

$\therefore$ slope of $K = -\tfrac{3}{5}$

(turn upside down and change sign)

Step 3: Containing $(3, -1)$ with slope $-\tfrac{3}{5}$

$$x_1 = 3, \qquad y_1 = -1, \qquad m = -\tfrac{3}{5}$$
$$(y - y_1) = m(x - x_1)$$
$$(y + 1) = -\tfrac{3}{5}(x - 3)$$
$$5(y + 1) = -3(x - 3)$$

(multiply both sides by 5)

$$5y + 5 = -3x + 9$$
$$3x + 5y + 5 - 9 = 0$$
$$3x + 5y - 4 = 0$$

The equation of the line K is $3x + 5y - 4 = 0$.

1. Find the equation of the line containing (2, 1) and parallel to $2x - y + 6 = 0$.

2. Find the equation of the line containing (3, −2) and perpendicular to $3x - 2y + 8 = 0$.

3. Find the equation of the line containing (−1, −4) and parallel to $5x + 4y - 3 = 0$.

4. Find the equation of the line containing (−2, 5) and perpendicular to $4x - 3y - 1 = 0$.

5. L is the line $3x + 5y - 10 = 0$. The line K contains the point (−2, 0) and $K \perp L$. Find the equation of K.

6. M is the line $x + 2y - 6 = 0$. The line L contains the point (−3, −1) and $M \parallel L$. Find the equation of the line L.

7. $a(3, -6)$ and $b(-1, -2)$ are two points. c is the midpoint of $[ab]$ and K is the line $2x + 5y - 5 = 0$. The line L contains the point c and $L \perp K$. Find the equation of L.

Point of Intersection of Two Lines

Use the method of solving simultaneous equations to find the point of intersection of two lines.

1. When the point of intersection contains whole numbers only

Example ▼

L is the line $2x - 5y - 9 = 0$ and K is the line $3x - 2y - 8 = 0$.
Find the coordinates of q, the point of intersection of L and K.

Solution:

Write both equations in the form $ax + by = k$.

$$2x - 5y = 9 \quad \text{(L)}$$
$$3x - 2y = 8 \quad \text{(K)}$$
$$\overline{6x - 15y = 27} \quad \text{(L)} \times 3$$
$$-6x + 4y = -16 \quad \text{(K)} \times -2$$
$$\overline{-11y = 11} \quad \text{(add)}$$
$$11y = -11$$
$$y = -1$$

Put $y = -1$ into (L) or (K)

$$2x - 5y = 9 \quad \text{(L)}$$
$$2x - 5(-1) = 9$$
$$2x + 5 = 9$$
$$2x = 4$$
$$x = 2$$

∴ the coordinates of q are (2, −1).

2. When the point of intersection contains fractions

If the point of intersection contains fractions, a very useful method is to:

> **Step 1:**   Remove the y's and get a value for x.
> **Step 2:**   Remove the x's and get a value for y.

Note: This method can be used even if the point of intersection contains whole numbers only.

Example ▼

$L: 6x + 3y - 11 = 0$ and $K: 5x + 2y - 8 = 0$ are two lines. $L \cap K = \{p\}$. Find the coordinates of p.

Solution:

Write both equations in the form $ax + by = k$.

Remove the x's:

$$
\begin{array}{ll}
6x + 3y = 11 & \text{(L)} \\
5x + 2y = 8 & \text{(K)} \\
\hline
30x + 15y = 55 & \text{(L)} \times 5 \\
-30x - 12y = -48 & \text{(K)} \times -6 \\
\hline
3y = 7 & \text{(add)} \\
y = \tfrac{7}{3} &
\end{array}
$$

Remove the y's:

$$
\begin{array}{ll}
6x + 3y = 11 & \text{(L)} \\
5x + 2y = 8 & \text{(K)} \\
\hline
12x + 6y = 22 & \text{(L)} \times 2 \\
-15x - 6y = -24 & \text{(K)} \times -3 \\
\hline
-3x = -2 & \text{(add)} \\
3x = 2 & \\
x = \tfrac{2}{3} &
\end{array}
$$

$\therefore$ the coordinates of p are $(\tfrac{2}{3}, \tfrac{7}{3})$.

Exercise 1.9 ▼

Note: Questions 10–15 have solutions that contain fractions.

Find the point of intersection of each of the following pairs of lines:

1. $2x + 3y - 7 = 0$
    $5x - 2y - 8 = 0$

2. $5x - 2y - 11 = 0$
    $3x - 4y - 1 = 0$

3. $3x - 2y - 3 = 0$
    $x + 4y - 1 = 0$

4. $4x - 3y + 25 = 0$
    $3x + 5y - 3 = 0$

5. $3x - y + 8 = 0$
    $x - 7y - 4 = 0$

6. $2x - 3y - 15 = 0$
    $5x - y - 5 = 0$

7. $x + 2y - 5 = 0$
    $2x - y = 0$

8. $x + 2y - 4 = 0$
    $4x - 5y - 29 = 0$

9. $5x + 2y + 1 = 0$
    $2x + 5y - 29 = 0$

10. $5x + 10y - 11 = 0$
     $2x + y - 2 = 0$

11. $3x - y - 6 = 0$
     $x - 7y - 12 = 0$

12. $x + 2y - 2 = 0$
     $2x - y - 2 = 0$

13. $2x - 3y + 2 = 0$
     $4x - y - 2 = 0$

14. $4x + 2y - 11 = 0$
     $3x - y - 7 = 0$

15. $3x + 3y - 20 = 0$
     $x + 2y - 10 = 0$

16. $L: x + 3y + 12 = 0$ and $K: 3x - 2y + 3 = 0$ are two lines. $L \cap K = \{p\}$.
     Find the coordinates of p.

17. $L: 5x - 4y - 6 = 0$ and $M: 2x - 3y - 8 = 0$ are two lines. $L \cap M = \{q\}$.
    Find the coordinates of q.

18. $L: 3x - 2y - 4 = 0$ and $K: 5x + 2y - 12 = 0$ are two lines. $L \cap K = \{a\}$.
    $M: x + 3y + 8 = 0$ and $N: 3x + 4y + 9 = 0$ are also two lines. $M \cap N = \{b\}$.
    Find the equation of the line ab.

19. $L: ax + 5y - 11 = 0$ and $K: 7x + by + 2 = 0$ are two lines. $L \cap K = (-2, 3)$.
    Find a and b.

Graphing Lines

To draw a line, only two points are needed. The easiest points to find are those where a line cuts the x- and y-axes.

This is known as the **intercept method**. We use the following facts:

> On the x-axis $y = 0$.   On the y-axis $x = 0$.

To draw a line, do the following:

> **1.** Let $y = 0$ and find x.
> **2.** Let $x = 0$ and find y.
> **3.** Plot these two points.
> **4.** Draw the line through these points.

Note: Any two points on the line will do; it is not necessary to use the points where the line cuts the x- and y-axes.

Example ▼

Graph the line $3x - 2y - 12 = 0$.

Solution:

1. and 2.

$$3x - 2y = 12$$

$y = 0$	$x = 0$
$3x = 12$	$-2y = 12$
$x = 4$	$2y = -12$
$(4, 0)$	$y = -6$
	$(0, -6)$

3. Plot the points $(4, 0)$ and $(0, -6)$.

4. Draw the line through these points.

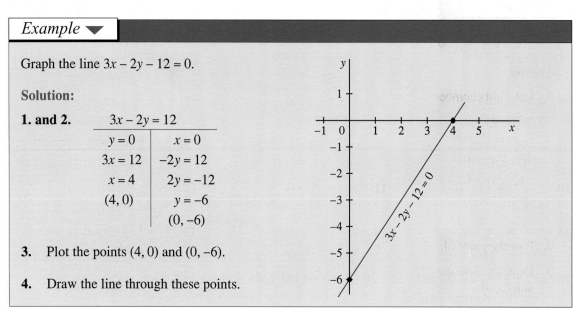

Graph each of the following lines:

1. $2x + 3y - 6 = 0$
2. $x + y - 5 = 0$
3. $3x - 5y + 15 = 0$
4. $4x - y - 8 = 0$
5. $x - y - 3 = 0$
6. $2x - 5y - 10 = 0$
7. $4x + 3y - 24 = 0$
8. $x - 3y - 12 = 0$
9. $4x - 5y - 40 = 0$
10. $2x - y - 6 = 0$
11. $3x - 2y + 12 = 0$
12. $x + 4y - 6 = 0$

13. Draw the line $2x + 3y - 12 = 0$. Show **(i)** graphically **(ii)** algebraically that the point $(3, 2)$ is on the line.

Lines that Contain the Origin

If the constant in the equation of a line is zero, e.g. $3x - 5y = 0$, or $4x = 3y$, then the line will pass through the origin, $(0, 0)$. In this case the **intercept method** will not work.

To draw a line that contains the origin, $(0, 0)$, do the following:

> **1.** Choose a suitable value for x and find the corresponding value for y (or vice versa).
> **2.** Plot this point.
> **3.** A line drawn through this point and the origin is the required line.

Note: A very suitable value is to let x equal the number in front of y and then find the corresponding value for x (or vice versa).

Example ▼

Graph the line $3x + 4y = 0$.

Solution:

1. Let $x = 4$ (number in front of y).

   $3x + 4y = 0$
   $\downarrow$
   $3(4) + 4y = 0$
   $12 + 4y = 0$
   $4y = -12$
   $y = -3$

2. Plot the point $(4, -3)$.

3. Draw the line through the points $(4, -3)$ and $(0, 0)$.

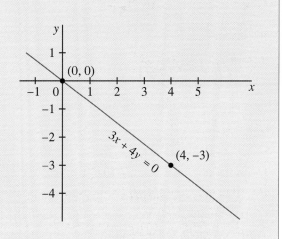

Graph each of the following lines:

1. $3x - 2y = 0$
2. $x + y = 0$
3. $3x - y = 0$
4. $5x = 3y$
5. $2x - 5y = 0$
6. $x = 4y$
7. $y = 3x$
8. $4x - y = 0$
9. $3x - 4y = 0$
10. $6x - 5y = 0$
11. $x - y = 0$
12. $2y = 3x$

Lines Parallel to the Axes

Some lines are parallel to the x- or y-axis.
$x = 5$ is a line parallel to the y-axis through 5 on the x-axis.
$y = -3$ is a line parallel to the x-axis through -3 on the y-axis.

Note:

> $y = 0$ is the equation of the x-axis.
> $x = 0$ is the equation of the y-axis.

Example ▼

On the same axes and scales, graph the lines $x = 2$ and $y = -1$.

Solution:

(i) $x = 2$
Line parallel to the y-axis through 2 on the x-axis.

(ii) $y = -1$
Line parallel to the x-axis through -1 on the y-axis.

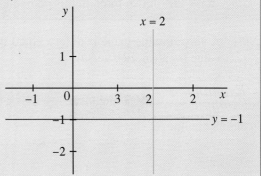

Exercise 1.12 ▼

Graph each of the following lines:

1. $x = 4$
2. $y = 3$
3. $x = -2$
4. $y = -1$
5. $x + 3 = 0$
6. $y - 5 = 0$
7. $x = -5$
8. $y - 4 = 0$
9. $x - 7 = 0$
10. $x = -4$
11. $2x = 1$
12. $2y = 3$

13. $x - 4 = 0$ is the equation of the line L and $y + 2 = 0$ is the equation of the line K.
    (i) On the same axes and scales, graph the lines L and K.
    (ii) Write down the coordinates of q, the point of intersection of L and K.

Area of a Triangle

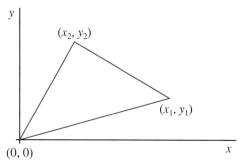

The area of a triangle with vertices $(0, 0)$, (x_1, y_1) and (x_2, y_2) is given by the formula:

$$\text{Area of triangle} = \tfrac{1}{2}\left| x_1 y_2 - x_2 y_1 \right|$$

Note:

1. The modulus symbol, $|\ |$, is included to make sure your answer is positive.
   Therefore, if the above formula gives a negative answer, simply ignore the negative sign.
   e.g. $\tfrac{1}{2}\left| -10 \right| = \tfrac{1}{2} \cdot 10 = 5$

2. If none of the vertices is at the origin, simply select one of the vertices and map (move) it to the point $(0, 0)$ by a translation. Then apply the same translation to the other two vertices to get (x_1, y_1) and (x_2, y_2).

Example ▼

Find the area of the triangle with vertices $(0, 0)$, $(-2, 5)$ and $(6, -3)$.

Solution:

$(-2, 5)$	$(6, -3)$	$x_1 = -2$	$y_1 = 5$
(x_1, y_1)	(x_2, y_2)	$x_2 = 6$	$y_2 = -3$

$$\text{Area of triangle} = \tfrac{1}{2}\left| x_1 y_2 - x_2 y_1 \right|$$
$$= \tfrac{1}{2}\left| (-2)(-3) - (6)(5) \right|$$
$$= \tfrac{1}{2}\left| -24 \right|$$
$$= \tfrac{1}{2} \cdot 24 = 12 \text{ sq. units.}$$

Example ▼

Find the area of the triangle with vertices $(-2, 4)$, $(1, -4)$ and $(2, -2)$.

Solution:

Map (move) the point $(-2, 4)$ to $(0, 0)$.

$(-2, 4)$	$(1, -4)$	$(2, -2)$	
↓	↓	↓	
$(0, 0)$	$(3, -8)$	$(4, -6)$	Rule: 'add 2 to x, take 4 from y'.
	(x_1, y_1)	(x_2, y_2)	$x_1 = 3 \qquad y_1 = -8$
			$x_2 = 4 \qquad y_2 = -6$

$$\text{Area of triangle} = \tfrac{1}{2}\left| x_1 y_2 - x_2 y_1 \right|$$
$$= \tfrac{1}{2}\left| (3)(-6) - (4)(-8) \right|$$
$$= \tfrac{1}{2}\left| -18 + 32 \right|$$
$$= \tfrac{1}{2}\left| 14 \right|$$
$$= 7 \text{ sq. units.}$$

Note: To find the area of a quadrilateral (4-sided figure), divide it into two triangles.

If the quadrilateral is a **parallelogram**, then the areas of both triangles are equal. Therefore, all that is needed is to find the area of one triangle and double it.

Exercise 1.13 ▼

Find the area of each of the following triangles whose vertices are:

1. $(0, 0), (5, 2), (3, 4)$

2. $(0, 0), (10, 8), (3, 5)$

3. $(8, 7), (0, 0), (2, -3)$

4. $(6, -3), (-2, 4), (0, 0)$

5. $(5, 0), (1, 3), (6, 2)$

6. $(-5, -3), (1, 5), (-2, 1)$

7. $(3, -2), (-5, 6), (7, -1)$

8. $(1, 3), (-4, 1), (5, -3)$

9. $(4, -5), (3, -2), (-4, -8)$

10. $(-1, -4), (2, -1), (-2, 3)$

Find the area of the parallelogram whose vertices are:

11. $(0, 0), (1, 3), (5, 5), (4, 2)$

12. $(5, 1), (3, 1), (5, 4), (7, 4)$

13. $(-2, 4), (2, 4), (2, 7), (-2, 7)$

14. $(-1, 3), (0, 2), (5, 4), (4, 5)$

Find the area of the quadrilateral whose vertices are:

15. $(1, 1), (1, 2), (9, 3), (6, 1)$

16. $(2, -4), (-1, 4), (-2, 2), (5, 5)$

17. $(5, -6), (5, -4), (0, 1), (-2, -9)$

18. $(-2, 2), (-5, -6), (8, -4), (9, 0)$

19. $a(-2, -5), b(1, -3)$ and $c(4, -1)$ are the vertices of triangle abc.
By finding the area of triangle abc, show that a, b and c are collinear (on the same line).

Exercise 1.14 ▼   (Revision of exercises 1.1 to 1.13)

1. $a(-2, 4), b(2, 2)$ and $c(5, 3)$ are three points. Find:
 (i) $|ab|$ **(ii)** the coordinates of m, the midpoint of $[ab]$
 (iii) the area of triangle abc **(iv)** the slope of ab
 (v) the equation of the line ab
 (vi) the equation of the line L, through the point c and $L \perp ab$
 (vii) the coordinates of p, the point of intersection of the lines L and ab.

2. **(i)** Verify that the point $(-2, -4)$ is on the line $2x - 5y - 16 = 0$.
 (ii) If $(k, -2)$ is also on the line $2x - 5y - 16 = 0$, find the value of k.

3. $a(2, -3), b(5, 1)$ and $c(1, 4)$ are three points. Verify that $|\angle abc| = 90°$.

4. The midpoint of the line segment $[ab]$ is $(1, -1)$.
 If the coordinates of a are $(-1, 3)$, find the coordinates of b.

5. The equation of the line K is $3x - 2y - 12 = 0$.
   K intersects the x-axis at a and the y-axis at b.
   (i) Find the coordinates of a and the coordinates of b.
   (ii) Graph the line K.
   (iii) Calculate the area of triangle aob, where o is the origin.

6. L is the line $x - 2y + 5 = 0$ and K is the line $3x + y - 6 = 0$.
   Find the coordinates of a, the point of intersection of L and K.
   L and K cut the x-axis at b and c, respectively. Find the coordinates of b and c.
   Find the area of triangle abc.

7. H is the line $3x + 2y - 4 = 0$.
   Verify that $c(2, -1)$ is on H.
   Points $a(-5, 1)$ and $b(1, 9)$ are on L. Find:
   (i) the equation of L
   (ii) the coordinates of d, the point of intersection of H and L
   (iii) the coordinates of the fourth point, m, of the parallelogram $dacm$
   (iv) the area of $dacm$
   (v) the value of k if the point $(-2, k)$ is on the line L.

8. $L: x + 2y + 2 = 0$ and $K: 4x - 2y + 18 = 0$ are two lines.
   (i) Verify that $p(4, -3)$ is on L.
   (ii) Prove that $L \perp K$.
   (iii) Find the coordinates of q, the point of intersection of L and K.
   (iv) Find the coordinates of r, the point where K cuts the y-axis.
   (v) Prove that $|pq| = |qr|$.
   (vi) Calculate the area of triangle pqr.

9. L is the line $x - 2y + 5 = 0$.
   (i) Find the coordinates of the point, r, where L intersects the y-axis.
   (ii) Find the equation of the line M, which contains the point $p(\frac{5}{2}, 0)$ and is perpendicular to L.
   (iii) Calculate the coordinates of q if $L \cap M = \{q\}$.
   (iv) Calculate the area of the quadrilateral $opqr$, where o is the origin.

10. $L: x + 2y - 11 = 0$ and $K: 2x - 5y + 5 = 0$ are two lines.
    (i) Verify that $a(1, 5)$ is on L.
    (ii) Find the coordinates of b, if $L \cap K = \{b\}$.
    (iii) Is $L \perp K$? Give a reason for your answer.
    (iv) Find the equation of the line M, containing $c(6, 2)$, if $L \perp M$.
    (v) M meets the x-axis at d. Find the coordinates of d.
    (vi) Calculate the area of the quadrilateral $abcd$.

11. K is the line $3x - y - 8 = 0$.

    (i) Verify that $(2, -2)$ is on K.

    (ii) Find the coordinates of the point where K crosses the y-axis.

    (iii) Find the equation of the line L containing the point $(-3, 3)$, if $K \perp L$.

    (iv) Find the coordinates of the point where L crosses the y-axis.

    (v) $K \cap L = \{p\}$. Find the coordinates of p.

    (vi) Find the area of the triangle formed by the lines L, K and the y-axis.

12. $p(1, 4)$, $q(x, 9)$ and $r(2x, x)$ are three points.

    If $|pq| = |qr|$, calculate the two possible values of x.

Transformations of the Plane

Translation

A translation moves a point in a straight line.

Note: The translation $a \rightarrow b$ is usually written $\vec{ab}$.

Example ▼

p$(-2, 4)$ and $q(1, -1)$ are two points. Find the image of the point $(3, -4)$ under the translation $\vec{pq}$.

Solution:

Under the translation $\vec{pq}$, $(-2, 4) \rightarrow (1, -1)$.

    Rule: add 3 to x, subtract 5 from y.

    $\therefore (3, -4) \rightarrow (3 + 3, -4 - 5) = (6, -9)$

    $\therefore$ the image of $(3, -4)$ is $(6, -9)$.

Translations are very useful in finding the missing coordinates of one of the vertices of a parallelogram when given the other three.

Example ▼

$a(1, -2)$, $b(-3, 1)$, $c(2, 3)$ and $d(x, y)$ are the vertices of a parallelogram $abcd$.

Find the coordinates of d.

$b(-3, 1)$ $c(2, 3)$

Solution:

Make a rough diagram (keep cyclic order).

Since $abcd$ is a parallelogram, $\vec{bc} = \vec{ad}$

(i.e., the movement from b to c is the same as the movement from a to d).

We find the rule that moves b to c.

$a(1, -2)$ $d(x, y)$

Then apply this rule to a to find d.

$\vec{bc}$: $(-3, 1) \rightarrow (2, 3)$

Rule: add 5 to x, add 2 to y

$\vec{ad}$: $(1, -2) \rightarrow (1 + 5, -2 + 2) = (6, 0)$

$\therefore$ the coordinates of d are $(6, 0)$.

Note: By 'cyclic order' we mean that the points are taken in clockwise, or anti-clockwise, order.

Central symmetry

Central symmetry is a reflection in a point.
The image of a point under a central symmetry in another point can be found with a translation.

Example ▼

Find the image of the point $p(-1, 3)$ under the central symmetry in the point $q(2, -1)$.

Solution:

Rough diagram:

$p(-1, 3)$ $q(2, -1)$ $p'(5, -5)$

Translation from p to q: Rule 'add 3 to x, subtract 4 from y'.
Apply this rule to q to find the image of p.

$\quad q(2, -1) \rightarrow (2 + 3, -1 - 4) = p'(5, -5)$

Therefore, the image of $p(-1, 3)$ under a central symmetry in $q(2, -1)$ is $p'(5, -5)$.

Axial symmetry in the axes and central symmetry in the origin

Note:

> S_x means 'axial symmetry in the x-axis'
> S_y means 'axial symmetry in the y-axis'
> S_o means 'central symmetry in the origin'

We will look at two methods of finding the images of points under axial symmetry in the axes and central symmetry in the origin.

1. Mathematical method:

The following three patterns emerge, and it is worth memorising them:

> 1. Axial symmetry in the x-axis $\rightarrow$ **change the sign of y**.
> 2. Axial symmetry in the y-axis $\rightarrow$ **change the sign of x**.
> 3. Central symmetry in the origin, $(0, 0) \rightarrow$ **change the sign of both x and y**.

2. Graphical method:

> Plot the point on the coordinated plane and use your knowledge
> of axial symmetry and central symmetry to find the image.

Find the image of $(3, 2)$ under: **(i)** S_x **(ii)** S_y **(iii)** S_o.

Solution:

1. Mathematical method

    (i) $S_x(3, 2) = (3, -2)$ (change the sign of y)

    (ii) $S_y(3, 2) = (-3, 2)$ (change the sign of x)

    (iii) $S_o(3, 2) = (-3, -2)$ (change the sign of both x and y)

2. Graphical method

    From the graph it can be seen that:

    (i) $S_x(3, 2) = (3, -2)$

    (ii) $S_y(3, 2) = (-3, 2)$

    (iii) $S_o(3, 2) = (-3, -2)$

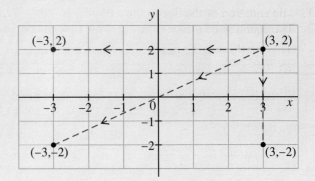

1. Find the image of $(3, 2)$ under the translation which maps $(5, 2) \to (7, 6)$.

2. Find the image of each of the following points under the translation which maps $(-3, 1) \to (-5, 4)$:

    (i) $(6, 2)$ **(ii)** $(3, -1)$ **(iii)** $(-4, -3)$ **(iv)** $(-6, 0)$

3. $a(1, -3)$ and $b(4, -5)$ are two points. Find the image of each point under the translation $\overrightarrow{ab}$:

    (i) $(4, -1)$ **(ii)** $(-2, 6)$ **(iii)** $(-5, -2)$ **(iv)** $(9, 5)$

    What is the image of $(1, 1)$ under the translation $\overrightarrow{ba}$?

4. Find the missing coordinates in each of the following parallelograms $pqrs$:

    (i) $p(1, 1)$, $q(4, 1)$, $r(4, 6)$, $s(x, y)$ **(ii)** $p(-2, -1)$, $q(2, -2)$, $r(x, y)$, $s(2, 3)$

    (iii) $p(-6, -3)$, $q(x, y)$, $r(1, 5)$, $s(-5, 1)$ **(iv)** $p(x, y)$, $q(2, 0)$, $r(-4, 3)$, $s(-7, 2)$

5. $a(-2, -2)$, $b(4, k)$, $c(7, 2)$ and $d(h, 1)$ are the coordinates of the parallelogram $abcd$.
    Find h and k.

6. Find the image of the point $(-1, 2)$ under the central symmetry in the point $(2, -3)$.

7. Find the image of the point $(4, 3)$ under the central symmetry in the point $(-2, 5)$.

8. Find the image of the point $(-4, 0)$ under the central symmetry in the point $(3, -1)$.

9. $a(2, -1)$ and $b(4, -5)$ are two points. Find:

    (i)   the image of a under a central symmetry in b

    (ii)   the image of b under a central symmetry in a.

10. $a(1, 1)$, $b(9, 2)$, $c(h, k)$ and $d(p, q)$ are the vertices of parallelogram $abcd$.
$x(6, 3)$ is the point of intersection of the diagonals $[ac]$ and $[bd]$.
Find the coordinates of c and d.

11. (i) $a(2, 1)$ and $b(x, y)$ are two points. The image of a under the central symmetry in b is $(8, -3)$.
Find the coordinates of b.

(ii) $(3, -1)$ is the image of (p, q) under the translation $(3, -2) \rightarrow (1, -3)$. Find (p, q).

(iii) Find the image of each of the following points under axial symmetry in the:

    (a) x-axis   **(b)** y-axis   and   **(c)** under central symmetry in the origin.

12. $(4, 3)$ **13.** $(5, 1)$ **14.** $(-2, -3)$ **15.** $(-1, 5)$ **16.** $(-3, 4)$

17. The equation of the line L is $x + 3y - 12 = 0$.
The equation of the line K is $3x - y + 14 = 0$.

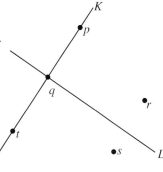

(i) Verify that the point $p(-2, 8)$ is on K.

(ii) Find the coordinates of q, the point of intersection of L and K.

(iii) Prove that $L \perp K$.

(iv) Find the coordinates of t, the image of p under the axial symmetry in L.

Given that s is the point $(0, 3)$ and that $pqsr$ is a parallelogram, find:

(v) the coordinates of r

(vi) the equation of the line rs.

18. The equation of the line L is $2x - 3y - 1 = 0$ and
the equation of the line K is $3x + 2y - 8 = 0$.

(i) Verify that the point $p(-4, -3)$ is on L.

(ii) Find the coordinates of q, the point of intersection of L and K.

(iii) Verify that $L \perp K$.

(iv) Find the coordinates of r, the image of p under axial symmetry in K.

(v) Name another transformation that maps p to r.

To Find the Image of a Line under a Translation or a Central Symmetry

The image of a line under a translation or a central symmetry is a line parallel to the original line. To find the image of a line under a translation or a central symmetry, use any of the following three methods:

> **1.** Select any two points on the given line. Find the image of each point under the translation or central symmetry. Find the equation of the line through these two image points.
>
> **2.** Select one point on the given line. Find the image of this point under the translation or central symmetry. Find the slope of the given line. Use this slope and the image point to find the equation of the image line.
>
> **3.** Say the line is $5x + 4y - 7 = 0$. Then a parallel line will be of the form $5x + 4y + k = 0$. All that is needed is to find the constant k. To find k, select one point on the given line. Find the image of this point under the translation or central symmetry. Substitute this image point into the second equation to find k and, hence, the equation of the line under the translation or central symmetry is found.

Verify that the point (2, 1) is on the line $3x + 2y - 8 = 0$ and find the equation of the image of the line $3x + 2y - 8 = 0$ under the translation $(3, 4) \rightarrow (7, 1)$.

Solution:

(using method 2)

$$3x + 2y - 8 = 0$$

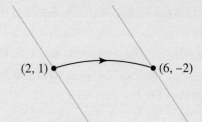

Substitute (2, 1): $3(2) + 2(1) - 8$

$$= 6 + 2 - 8 = 0$$

∴ (2, 1) is on the line $3x + 2y - 8 = 0$

Translation: $(3, 4) \rightarrow (7, 1)$ **Rule:** Add 4 to x, subtract 3 from y.
The image of (2, 1) under this translation will be a point on the image line.

$$(2, 1) \rightarrow (2 + 4, 1 - 3) \rightarrow (6, -2)$$

Slope of the image line will have the same slope as the line $3x + 2y - 8 = 0$.

$$3x + 2y - 8 = 0 \qquad \text{or} \qquad m = -\frac{a}{b}$$
$$2y = -3x + 8 \qquad\qquad\qquad = -\frac{3}{2}$$
$$y = -\tfrac{3}{2}x + 4$$

∴ slope $= -\frac{3}{2} \Rightarrow$ slope of the image line $= -\frac{3}{2}$.

Equation of image line: through (6, –2) with slope $= -\frac{3}{2}$

$$x_1 = 6, \qquad y_1 = -2, \qquad m = -\tfrac{3}{2}$$
$$(y - y_1) = m(x - x_1)$$
$$(y + 2) = -\tfrac{3}{2}(x - 6)$$
$$2(y + 2) = -3(x - 6) \qquad \text{(multiply both sides by 2)}$$
$$2y + 4 = -3x + 18$$
$$3x + 2y + 4 - 18 = 0$$
$$3x + 2y - 14 = 0$$

Exercise 1.16 ▼

1. (i) Verify that the points $a(2, 1)$ and $b(-1, -3)$ are on the line $4x - 3y - 5 = 0$.

Under the translation $(7, 5) \rightarrow (4, 6)$, a is mapped to p and b is mapped to q.

(ii) Find the coordinates of p and the coordinates of q.

(iii) Find the equation of the line pq.

(iv) Is $ab \parallel pq$? Give a reason for your answer.

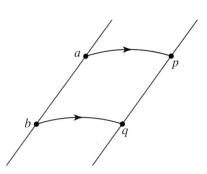

2. Verify that the point $(1, 3)$ is on the line $2x + 3y - 11 = 0$. Find the equation of the image of the line under the translation $(3, 4) \rightarrow (5, 5)$.

3. Verify that the point $(-1, 5)$ is on the line $5x - 2y + 15 = 0$. Find the equation of the image of the line under the translation $(-2, 4) \rightarrow (2, 1)$.

4. Verify that the point $(3, -4)$ is on the line $7x - 2y - 29 = 0$. Find the equation of the image of the line under the central symmetry in the point $(1, 1)$.

5. Verify that the point $(-4, 1)$ is on the line $3x + 5y + 7 = 0$. Find the equation of the image of the line under the central symmetry in the point $(-2, -1)$.

6. L is the line $3x - 4y - 12 = 0$. Find the equation of the image of the line under a central symmetry in the point $(1, -1)$.

7. L is the line $2x - 5y - 15 = 0$. Find:
    (i)   the slope of L
    (ii) the point of intersection of L and the y-axis
    (iii) the equation of the image of L under the translation $(3, 1) \rightarrow (-1, 4)$.

CHAPTER 2

COMPLEX NUMBERS

Imaginary Numbers, the Symbol i

The square root of a negative number is called an **imaginary** number, e.g. $\sqrt{-4}$, $\sqrt{-9}$, $\sqrt{-64}$, $\sqrt{-100}$ are imaginary numbers.

Imaginary numbers cannot be represented by a real number, as there is no real number whose square is a negative number.

To overcome this problem, the letter i is introduced to represent $\sqrt{-1}$.

$$i = \sqrt{-1}$$

Note: If $i = \sqrt{-1}$ then $i^2 = \sqrt{-1}\sqrt{-1} = -1$.

$$i^2 = -1$$

All imaginary numbers can now be expressed in terms of i, for example:

$$\sqrt{-36} = \sqrt{36 \times -1} = \sqrt{36}\sqrt{-1} = 6i$$
$$\sqrt{-81} = \sqrt{81 \times -1} = \sqrt{81}\sqrt{-1} = 9i$$

Exercise 2.1 ▼

Express each of the following in terms of i, where $\sqrt{-1} = i$:

1. $\sqrt{-9}$ 2. $\sqrt{-16}$ 3. $\sqrt{-25}$

4. $\sqrt{-4}$ 5. $\sqrt{-49}$ 6. $\sqrt{-64}$

7. $\sqrt{-100}$ 8. $\sqrt{-121}$ 9. $\sqrt{-144}$

Complex Numbers

A complex number has two parts, a **real** part and an **imaginary** part.
Some examples are $3 + 4i$, $2 - 5i$, $-6 + 0i$, $0 - i$.
Consider the complex number $4 + 3i$:

    4 is called the **real** part,
    3 is called the **imaginary** part.

Note: $3i$ is **not** the imaginary part.

$$\boxed{\text{Complex number} = (\text{Real Part}) + (\text{Imaginary Part})\ i}$$

The set of complex numbers is denoted by C.
The letter z is usually used to represent a complex number, e.g.

$$z_1 = 2 + 3i, \qquad z_2 = -2 - i, \qquad z_3 = -5i$$

If $z = a + bi$, then:

(i) $\quad a$ is called the real part of z and is written $\textbf{\textit{Re}}(z) = \textbf{\textit{a}}$

(ii) $\quad b$ is called the imaginary part of z and is written $\textbf{\textit{Im}}(z) = \textbf{\textit{b}}$.

Example ▼

Write down the real and imaginary parts of each of the following complex numbers:

(i) $\quad 3 + 2i$ $\qquad$ **(ii)** $-6 - 8i$ $\qquad$ **(iii)** 7 $\qquad$ **(iv)** $-5i$

Solution:

	Real Part	Imaginary Part
(i) $\quad 3 + 2i$	3	2
(ii) $\quad -6 - 8i$	-6	-8
(iii) $\quad 7 = 7 + 0i$	7	0
(iv) $\quad -5i = 0 - 5i$	0	-5

Note: i **never** appears in the imaginary part.

Exercise 2.2 ▼

Write down the real and imaginary parts of each of the following complex numbers:

1. $7 + 4i$	**2.** $4 - 5i$	**3.** $3 + 2i$	**4.** $-1 - 2i$
5. $-4 + i$	**6.** $2 - i$	**7.** 4	**8.** 6
9. $4i$	**10.** -2	**11.** $-7i$	**12.** $\sqrt{5} + \sqrt{3}i$

Operations on Complex Numbers
Addition and Subtraction of Complex Numbers

To add or subtract complex numbers do the following:

$$\boxed{\text{Add or subtract the real and the imaginary parts separately.}}$$

Example ▼

Write each of the following in the form $a + bi$:

(i) $(3 + 5i) + (4 - 9i)$

(ii) $(7 - 6i) - (3 + 8i)$

(iii) $(3 - 4i) + (-1 - i) + (4 - 2i)$

(iv) $(-3 - 7i) - (4i) - (6 - 2i)$

Solution:

(i) $(3 + 5i) + (4 - 9i)$
$$= 3 + 5i + 4 - 9i$$
$$= 3 + 4 + 5i - 9i$$
$$= 7 - 4i$$

(ii) $(7 - 6i) - (3 + 8i)$
$$= 7 - 6i - 3 - 8i$$
$$= 7 - 3 - 6i - 8i$$
$$= 4 - 14i$$

(iii) $(3 - 4i) + (-1 - i) + (4 - 2i)$
$$= 3 - 4i - 1 - i + 4 - 2i$$
$$= 3 - 1 + 4 - 4i - i - 2i$$
$$= 6 - 7i$$

(iv) $(-3 - 7i) - (4i) - (6 - 2i)$
$$= -3 - 7i - 4i - 6 + 2i$$
$$= -3 - 6 - 7i - 4i + 2i$$
$$= -9 - 9i$$

Multiplication by a Real Number

Multiply each part of the complex number by the real number.

Example ▼

If $z_1 = 3 - 2i$, $z_2 = 1 - 5i$ and $z_3 = -4i$, express in the form $x + yi$:

(i) $4z_1 - 3z_2$ **(ii)** $z_1 - 2z_2 + 3z_3$

Solution:

(i) $4z_1 - 3z_2$
$$= 4(3 - 2i) - 3(1 - 5i)$$
$$= 12 - 8i - 3 + 15i$$
$$= 12 - 3 - 8i + 15i$$
$$= 9 + 7i$$

(ii) $z_1 - 2z_2 + 3z_3$
$$= (3 - 2i) - 2(1 - 5i) + 3(-4i)$$
$$= 3 - 2i - 2 + 10i - 12i$$
$$= 3 - 2 - 2i + 10i - 12i$$
$$= 1 - 4i$$

Write each of the following in the form $a + bi$:

1. $(4 + 2i) + (5 + 6i)$ **2.** $(2 + i) + (6 + 4i)$

3. $(11 + 3i) - (5 - 2i)$ **4.** $(7 + 2i) - (4 - 2i)$

5. $2(4 + i) + 3(2 - i)$ **6.** $(-4 + 3i) + (3 + 2i) + (-2 + 3i)$

7. $(3 - 2i) - (4 + 3i) + (-2 + 2i)$ **8.** $3(1 - 3i) + 2(2 - 6i) + 3(5 - i)$

9. $2(2 - 3i) - 3(3 + i) - 3(4i)$ **10.** $-3(-3 + 2i) + 2(5 + i) - 4(2i - 3)$

If $z_1 = 2 + 3i$, $z_2 = 1 - 4i$, $z_3 = 5 - 2i$, $z_4 = 6$, and $z_5 = -3i$, express each of the following in the form $x + yi$:

11. $z_1 + z_2 + z_3$ **12.** $2z_1 + 3z_3$ **13.** $3z_2 + z_1 - z_4$

14. $3z_5 - 2z_4 + z_2$ **15.** $2z_5 - 3z_2 + 4z_3$ **16.** $5z_1 + 3z_4 - z_5$

17. $z_3 - (z_1 + z_2)$ **18.** $(z_5 + z_4) - (z_3 - z_2)$ **19.** $3(z_2 - z_1) - 2(z_4 + z_3)$

Multiplication of Complex Numbers

Multiplication of complex numbers is performed using the usual algebraic method, except:

$$i^2 \text{ is replaced with } -1.$$

Example ▼

Express: **(i)** $(2 + 3i)(-3 + 4i)$ and   **(ii)** $(3 + i)(-2 - 5i)$ in the form $a + bi$.

Solution:

(i) $(2 + 3i)(-3 + 4i)$

$= 2(-3 + 4i) + 3i(-3 + 4i)$

$= -6 + 8i - 9i + 12i^2$

$= -6 + 8i - 9i + 12(-1)$

(replace i^2 with -1)

$= -6 + 8i - 9i - 12$

$= -18 - i$

(ii) $(3 + i)(-2 - 5i)$

$= 3(-2 - 5i) + i(-2 - 5i)$

$= -6 - 15i - 2i - 5i^2$

$= -6 - 15i - 2i - 5(-1)$

(replace i^2 with -1)

$= -6 - 15i - 2i + 5$

$= -1 - 17i$

If $z_1 = 5 - 2i$, $z_2 = -2 - 3i$, and $z_3 = -1 - i$, express in the form $a + bi$:

(i) z_1^2 **(ii)** $iz_2 z_3$

Solution:

(i) z_1^2

$$= (5 - 2i)^2$$
$$= (5 - 2i)(5 - 2i)$$
$$= 5(5 - 2i) - 2i(5 - 2i)$$
$$= 25 - 10i - 10i + 4i^2$$

$$= 25 - 10i - 10i + 4(-1) \qquad \text{(replace } i^2 \text{ with } -1)$$
$$= 25 - 10i - 10i - 4$$
$$= 21 - 20i$$
$$\therefore \quad z_1^2 = 21 - 20i$$

(ii) $iz_2 z_3$

$$= i(-2 - 3i)(-1 - i)$$

First work out $i(-2 - 3i)$ and multiply your answer by $(-1 - i)$.

$i(-2 - 3i)$	$(3 - 2i)(-1 - i)$
$= -2i - 3i^2$	$= 3(-1 - i) - 2i(-1 - i)$
	$= -3 - 3i + 2i + 2i^2$
$= -2i - 3(-1)$	
$= -2i + 3$	$= -3 - 3i + 2i + 2(-1)$
$= 3 - 2i$	$= -3 - 3i + 2i - 2$
	$= -5 - i$

$$\therefore \quad iz_2 z_3 = -5 - i$$

Write each of the following in the form $a + bi$, where $a, b \in \mathbf{R}$ and $i^2 = -1$:

1. $(3 + 2i)(4 + 3i)$ **2.** $(2 + i)(3 + 5i)$ **3.** $(2 + 3i)(5 - 2i)$

4. $(-2 + i)(3 - 2i)$ **5.** $(6 - 2i)(4 - 3i)$ **6.** $(1 - i)(2 - i)$

7. $3 + 2i(3 + 4i) - i$ **8.** $5(1 + i) + i(6 - 2i)$ **9.** $i(-2 + 3i) - 5(i - 3)$

10. $i(3 - 5i)(4 + 2i)$ **11.** $4i(2 - 3i)(-2 - 4i)$ **12.** $-3i(-2 - 4i)(-5 - i)$

If $z_1 = 2 + 3i$, $z_2 = 3 + 4i$, $z_3 = 5 - i$, $z_4 = -1 + 2i$, $z_5 = 4$ and $z_6 = 2i$, express each of the following in the form $p + qi$, where $p, q \in \mathbf{R}$ and $i^2 = -1$:

13. $z_5 \cdot z_1$ **14.** $z_6 \cdot z_2$ **15.** $z_5(z_3 + z_4)$ **16.** z_1^2

17. $z_2^2 + 16$ **18.** $z_3^2 - 2z_1$ **19.** $z_5 \cdot z_2 - z_6 \cdot z_1$ **20.** $z_6 \cdot z_1 \cdot z_2$

21. If $u = 2 + 3i$, show that $u^2 - 4u + 13 = 0$.

22. Explain why $i^3 = -i$. If $w = 3i$, show that $w^3 - w^2 + 9w - 9 = 0$.

Complex Conjugate

Two complex numbers which differ only in the sign of their imaginary parts are called **conjugate complex numbers**, each being the conjugate of the other.

Thus $3 + 4i$ and $3 - 4i$ are conjugates, and $-2 - 3i$ is the conjugate of $-2 + 3i$ and vice versa.

In general, $a + bi$ and $a - bi$ are conjugates.

If $z = a + bi$, then its conjugate, $a - bi$, is denoted by $\bar{z}$.

$$z = a + bi \Rightarrow \bar{z} = a - bi$$

To find the conjugate, simply **change the sign** of the imaginary part only.

For example, if $z = -6 - 5i$ then $\bar{z} = -6 + 5i$.

Note: If a complex number is added to, or multiplied by, its conjugate the imaginary parts cancel and the result will **always** be a real number.

Example ▼

If $z = -2 + 3i$, simplify: **(i)** $z + \bar{z}$ **(ii)** $z - \bar{z}$ **(iii)** $z \cdot \bar{z}$

Solution:

If $z = -2 + 3i$, then $\bar{z} = -2 - 3i$ (change sign of imaginary part only).

(i) $z + \bar{z}$
$= (-2 + 3i) + (-2 - 3i)$
$= -2 + 3i - 2 - 3i$
$= -4$

(ii) $z - \bar{z}$
$= (-2 + 3i) - (-2 - 3i)$
$= -2 + 3i + 2 + 3i$
$= 6i$

(iii) $z \cdot \bar{z}$
$= (-2 + 3i)(-2 - 3i)$
$= -2(-2 - 3i) + 3i(-2 - 3i)$
$= 4 + 6i - 6i - 9i^2$
$= 4 - 9(-1)$
$= 4 + 9$
$= 13$

Find $\bar{z}$ for each of the following:

1. $z = 3 + 5i$ 2. $z = 4 - 3i$ 3. $z = -2 + 6i$ 4. $z = -3 - 7i$

5. $z = -3i$ 6. $z = 5i$ 7. $z = -i$ 8. $z = 4i$

Find: (i) $z + \bar{z}$ (ii) $z - \bar{z}$ (iii) $z \cdot \bar{z}$ for each of the following:

9. $z = 4 + 5i$ 10. $z = 3 - 2i$ 11. $z = -4 + 2i$ 12. $z = -1 - i$

13. $z = 5i$ 14. $z = 4$ 15. $z = -3$ 16. $z = -6i$

17. If $u = 3 - 4i$, show that $u^2 - 6u + u \cdot \bar{u} = 0$.

Division by a Complex Number

Multiply the top and bottom by the conjugate of the bottom.

This will convert the complex number on the bottom into a real number. The division is then performed by dividing the real number on the bottom into each part on the top.

Example ▼

Express $\dfrac{1 + 7i}{4 + 3i}$ in the form $a + bi$.

Solution:

$$\frac{1 + 7i}{4 + 3i} = \frac{1 + 7i}{4 + 3i} \cdot \frac{4 - 3i}{4 - 3i} \qquad \text{[multiply top and bottom by the conjugate of the bottom]}$$

Top by the top	Bottom by the bottom
$= (1 + 7i)(4 - 3i)$	$= (4 + 3i)(4 - 3i)$
$= 1(4 - 3i) + 7i(4 - 3i)$	$= 4(4 - 3i) + 3i(4 - 3i)$
$= 4 - 3i + 28i - 21i^2$	$= 16 - 12i + 12i - 9i^2$
$= 4 - 3i + 28i - 21(-1)$	$= 16 - 9(-1)$
$= 4 - 3i + 28i + 21$	$= 16 + 9$
$= 25 + 25i$	$= 25$

$$\therefore \frac{1 + 7i}{4 + 3i} = \frac{25 + 25i}{25} = \frac{25}{25} + \frac{25}{25}i = 1 + i$$

Express each of the following in the form $a + bi$, where $a, b \in \mathbf{R}$ and $i^2 = -1$:

1. $\dfrac{2 + 10i}{3 + 2i}$

2. $\dfrac{7 + 4i}{2 - i}$

3. $\dfrac{3 + 4i}{2 + i}$

4. $\dfrac{1 + 7i}{1 - 3i}$

5. $\dfrac{19 - 4i}{3 - 2i}$

6. $\dfrac{7 - i}{1 + i}$

7. $\dfrac{11 - 7i}{2 + i}$

8. $\dfrac{7 - 17i}{5 - i}$

9. $\dfrac{8 - 4i}{2 - i}$

10. $\dfrac{3 - 2i}{2 + 3i}$

11. $\dfrac{2 + i}{1 - i}$

12. $\dfrac{4 - 2i}{2 + i}$

13. If $a + bi = \dfrac{9 - 7i}{2 - 3i}$, find the value of a and the value of b.

14. If $p + qi = \dfrac{2 - i}{1 - 2i}$, evaluate $p^2 + q^2$.

15. $u = 1 + 2i$. Express $u + \dfrac{5}{\bar{u}}$ in the form ku, where $k \in \mathbf{N}$.

16. $z_1 = 9 + 7i$ and $z_2 = \dfrac{5 + i}{1 - i}$. Express in the form $a + bi$, where $a, b \in \mathbf{R}$ and $i^2 = -1$:

(i) z_2 (ii) $\dfrac{z_1}{z_2}$ (iii) $\dfrac{z_1 - 4(z_2 - 1)}{3 - z_2}$

Equality of Complex Numbers

If two complex numbers are equal then:
their real parts are equal and their imaginary parts are also equal.

For example, if $a + bi = c + di$,

then $a = c$ and $b = d$.

This definition is very useful when dealing with equations involving complex numbers.

Equations involving complex numbers are usually solved with the following steps:

> **1.** Remove the brackets.
> **2.** Put an R under the real parts and an I under the imaginary parts to identify them.
> **3.** Let the real parts equal the real parts and the imaginary parts equal the imaginary parts.
> **4.** Solve these resultant equations (usually simultaneous equations).

Note: If one side of the equation does not contain a real part or an imaginary part it should be replaced with 0 or $0i$, respectively.

If $3x + (7 - 2y)i = xi + 2(y + 3) - yi$, find $x, y \in \mathbf{R}$.

Solution:

$$3x + (7 - 2y)i = xi + 2(y + 3) - yi$$

Step 1: $\quad 3x + 7i - 2yi = xi + 2y + 6 - yi \qquad$ (remove the brackets)

Step 2: $\qquad R \quad I \quad I \quad I \quad R \quad R \quad I \qquad$ (identify real and imaginary parts)

Step 3:

Real parts = Real parts	**Imaginary parts = Imaginary parts**
$3x = 2y + 6$	$7 - 2y = x - y$
$3x - 2y = 6$ .... (A)	$-x + y - 2y = -7$
	$x + y = 7$ .... (B)

Step 4: Solve between the equations A and B:

$$\begin{array}{ll} 3x - 2y = 6 & (A) \\ \underline{x + y = 7} & (B) \\ 3x - 2y = 6 & (A \times 1) \\ \underline{2x + 2y = 14} & (B \times 2) \\ 5x = 20 & \text{(add)} \\ x = 4 & \end{array}$$

Substitute $x = 4$ into either A or B:

$$\begin{array}{ll} x + y = 7 & (B) \\ 4 + y = 7 & \\ y = 7 - 4 & \\ y = 3 & \end{array}$$

Solution: $\quad x = 4, y = 3$

$z_1 = 4 - 2i$, $z_2 = -2 - 6i$. If $z_2 - pz_1 = qi$, $\qquad p, q \in \mathbf{R}$, find p and q.

Solution:

$$z_2 - pz_1 = qi$$

The right-hand side has no real part, hence a 0, representing the real part, should be placed on the right-hand side.

Now the equation is:

$$z_2 - pz_1 = 0 + qi \qquad \text{(put 0 in for real part)}$$

$$(-2 - 6i) - p(4 - 2i) = 0 + qi \qquad \text{(substitute for } z_1 \text{ and } z_2\text{)}$$

Step 1: $\quad -2 - 6i - 4p + 2pi = 0 + qi \qquad$ (remove the brackets)

Step 2: $\qquad R \quad I \quad R \quad I \quad R \quad I \qquad$ (identify real and imaginary parts)

Step 3:

Real parts = Real parts	**Imaginary parts = Imaginary parts**
$-2 - 4p = 0$ .... (1)	$-6 + 2p = q$ .... (2)

Step 4: Solve between the equations 1 and 2:

$$-2 - 4p = 0 \ (1)$$
$$-4p = 2$$
$$4p = -2$$
$$p = -\tfrac{2}{4} = -\tfrac{1}{2}$$

Substitute $p = -\tfrac{1}{2}$ into equation 2:

$$-6 + 2p = q \ (2)$$
$$-6 + 2(-\tfrac{1}{2}) = q$$
$$-6 - 1 = q$$
$$-7 = q$$

Solution: $p = -\tfrac{1}{2},\ q = -7$

Exercise 2.7 ▼

In Q1–Q12, find x and y:

1. $3x + 2yi = 12 + 6i$

2. $2x + 5yi - 3 = 7 + 20i$

3. $4x + 3yi + 4i - 5 = 3 + 7i$

4. $(2x + y) + i(3x - y) = 7 + 3i$

5. $5(2 + i) = (x + yi) + (3 - 2i)$

6. $2 - 5i + 2(x + 2yi) = 4 + 3xi$

7. $(2x - yi) + i = (y - xi) + (4 + yi)$

8. $x(3 + 4i) + y(6i + 4) = 2i$

9. $x(2 + 3i) + y(4 + 5i) - 19i = 16$

10. $x(3 - i) + 8i + y(2 - i) - 9 = 0$

11. $(x + yi) + (3 - i) = 2(1 - 3i) - (y - xi)$

12. $3x - i(x + y + 5) = (1 + 3i)i + 2(3 - y)$

13. If $k(3 - 2i) + l(i - 2) = 5 - 4i$, find k and l.

14. If $3(a - 3i) - b(2 + 4i) = 7(a + i)$, find a and b.

15. If $2(h - 2) - k + i = i(2k - h)$, find h and k.

16. $2p - q + i(7i + 3) = 2(2i - q) - i(p + 3q)$, find p and q.

17. $z_1 = 4 - 3i,\ z_2 = 5(1 + i)$. If $z_1 + tz_2 = k$, find t and k.

18. $z_1 = 5 + 7i,\ z_2 = 3 - i$. If $k(z_1 + z_2) = 16 + (t + 2)i$, find t and k.

19. $z = 2 - 3i$. If $z + i + 3(a + bi) = iz - 5$, find a and b.

20. $z_1 = 2 + 3i,\ z_2 = -4 - 3i$. If $lz_1 - z_2 = ki$, find l and k.

21. $z_1 = 6 - 8i,\ z_2 = 4 - 3i$. If $pi = z_2 + lz_3$, find p and l where $z_1 - z_3 = z_2$.

22. If $(x + yi) - (xi - y) = (3 + 2i)^2 - 7i$, find x and y.

23. Find x and y if: **(i)** $(x + yi)(4 + 3i) = (1 + 7i)$ **(ii)** $(1 + 2i)(x + yi) = 5$.

Argand Diagram

An Argand diagram is used to plot complex numbers. It is very similar to the x- and y-axes used in co-ordinate geometry, except that the **horizontal** axis is called the **real axis** (**Re**) and the **vertical** axis is called the imaginary axis (**Im**). It is also called the **complex plane**.

If $z_1 = 3 + 2i$, $z_2 = 4 - 2i$, $z_3 = -2 + i$, $z_4 = 2$ and $z_5 = -3i$,
represent z_1, z_2, z_3, z_4 and z_5 on an Argand diagram.

Solution:

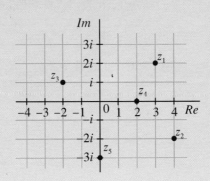

Construct an Argand diagram from −6 to 6 on the real axis and −5i to 5i on the imaginary axis. Represent each of the following complex numbers on it:

1. $5 + 4i$
2. $-3 - 2i$
3. $-6 + 5i$
4. $2 - i$

5. $4 + 2i$
6. $-1 + 4i$
7. -5
8. $-4 - 5i$

9. 6
10. $-3i$
11. i
12. $5 - 4i$

Note: To represent a complex number on an Argand diagram, it must be written in the form $a + bi$.

In questions 13–24, take:

$z_1 = 4 - 3i$, $z_2 = 1 + i$, $z_3 = -6 + 4i$, $z_4 = i$ and $z_5 = 2$.

13. $z_1 + z_2$
14. $z_5 \cdot z_2$
15. $z_1 + z_3$
16. $z_3 + 3z_1$

17. $z_4 \cdot z_2$
18. $z_5 \cdot z_4 \cdot z_2$
19. $z_4 \cdot z_1$
20. $z_1 - 4z_2 - iz_3$

21. $\dfrac{z_3}{z_5}$
22. $\dfrac{z_1}{z_4}$
23. $\dfrac{iz_3}{z_2}$
24. $\dfrac{z_1 - z_3 + 2z_4}{z_5 + z_4}$

Modulus

The **modulus** of a complex number is the distance from the origin to the point representing the complex number on the Argand diagram.

If $z = a + bi$, then the modulus of z is written $|z|$ or $|a + bi|$.

The point z represents the complex number $a + bi$.

The modulus of z is the distance from the origin, o, to the complex number $a + bi$.

Using the theorem of Pythagoras, $|z| = \sqrt{a^2 + b^2}$.

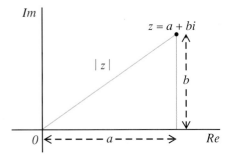

$$\boxed{\begin{array}{c} \text{If } z = a + bi, \text{ then} \\ |z| = |a + bi| = \sqrt{a^2 + b^2} \end{array}}$$

Example ▼

Find: (i) $|3 + 4i|$ (ii) $|2 - 5i|$ (iii) $|3i|$

Solution:

(i) $|3 + 4i|$

$= \sqrt{3^2 + 4^2}$

$= \sqrt{9 + 16}$

$= \sqrt{25} = 5$

(ii) $|2 - 5i|$

$= \sqrt{2^2 + 5^2}$

$= \sqrt{4 + 25}$

$= \sqrt{29}$

(iii) $3i = 0 + 3i$

$= \sqrt{0^2 + 3^2}$

$= \sqrt{0 + 9}$

$= \sqrt{9} = 3$

Notes:

1. i **never** appears when the modulus formula is used.
2. The modulus of a complex number is **always positive**.
3. Before using the formula a complex number must be in the form $a + bi$.

Example ▼

Let $z_1 = 4 - 3i$, $z_2 = -5 + 12i$ and $z_3 = k + 6i$.

(i) Investigate if $|z_1| + |z_2| = |z_1 + z_2|$.

(ii) For what two values of k is $|z_3| = 2|z_1|$, $k \in \mathbf{R}$?

Solution:

(i) $|z_1| = |4 - 3i| = \sqrt{4^2 + 3^2} = \sqrt{16 + 9} = \sqrt{25} = 5$

$|z_2| = |-5 + 12i| = \sqrt{5^2 + 12^2} = \sqrt{25 + 144} = \sqrt{169} = 13$

$z_1 + z_2 = (4 - 3i) + (-5 + 12i) = 4 - 3i - 5 + 12i = -1 + 9i$

$\therefore \ |z_1 + z_2| = |-1 + 9i| = \sqrt{1^2 + 9^2} = \sqrt{1 + 81} = \sqrt{82} \approx 9.06$ (correct to two decimal places)

$|z_1| + |z_2| = 5 + 13 = 18$ $|z_1 + z_2| = 9.06$

$\therefore \ |z_1| + |z_2| \neq |z_1 + z_2|$

(ii) $|z_3| = 2|z_1|$

$|k + 6i| = 2(5)$

$\sqrt{k^2 + 6^2} = 10$

$\sqrt{k^2 + 36} = 10$

$k^2 + 36 = 100$ (square both sides)

$k^2 = 64$

$k = \pm\sqrt{64}$

$k = \pm 8$

Evaluate each of the following:

1. $|4+3i|$ **2.** $|6+8i|$ **3.** $|12-5i|$ **4.** $|-8-15i|$

5. $|40-9i|$ **6.** $|0-7i|$ **7.** $|-3-5i|$ **8.** $|-5+6i|$

9. $|i(12-9i)|$ **10.** $|(3-2i)^2|$ **11.** $\left|\dfrac{2+i}{1+2i}\right|$ **12.** $\left|\dfrac{5+i}{1-i}\right|$

13. If z_1-2-3i and z_2-4-5i, verify that $|z_1|+|z_2|>|z_1+z_2|$.

14. If $z=3-4i$ and $w=5-12i$, verify that $|z|.|w|=|zw|$.

15. Let $w=1+7i$ and $u=1-i$. Investigate if $|2w|=|10u|$.

16. Let $z=(1+2i)(1-3i)$. Evaluate: **(i)** $|z|$ **(ii)** $|z\bar{z}|$.

17. Let $w=\dfrac{9-3i}{2+i}$. Express w in the form $a+bi$, where $a, b \in \mathbf{R}$ and $i^2=-1$.

   (i) Evaluate $|w|$ **(ii)** Verify that $|w+\bar{w}|=|w-\bar{w}|$.

   For what value of a is $\dfrac{w}{2i}=a\bar{w}$?

18. Let $z=1+7i$ and $w=-1+i$. Express $\dfrac{z}{w}$ in the form $a+bi$, $a, b \in \mathbf{R}$ and $i^2=-1$.

   Verify that $\dfrac{|z|}{|w|}=\left|\dfrac{z}{w}\right|$.

   Solve for real h and k: $hz=\left|\dfrac{z}{w}\right|kw+16i$.

19. **(i)** If $x^2=9$, verify that $x=\pm3$. **(ii)** If $|a+3i|=5$, $a \in \mathbf{R}$, find two possible values of a.

20. If $|8+ki|=10$, $k \in \mathbf{R}$, find two possible values of k.

21. If $|11+qi|=|10-5i|$, $q \in \mathbf{R}$, find two possible values of q.

22. If $|a+ai|=|1-7i|$, $a \in \mathbf{R}$, find two possible values of a.

23. Let $z_1=8+i$ and $z_2=k+7i$, $k \in \mathbf{R}$.
   If $|z_2|=|z_1|$, find two possible values of k.

24. Write down 4 complex numbers each having the same modulus as $|6+8i|$.

Quadratic Equations with Complex Roots

When a quadratic equation cannot be solved by factorisation the following formula can be used:

> The equation $ax^2 + bx + c = 0$ has roots given by:
> $$x = \frac{-b \pm \sqrt{b^2 - 4ac}}{2a}$$

Note: The whole of the top of the right-hand side, including $-b$, is divided by $2a$.
It is often called the **quadratic** or **$-b$** formula.

If $b^2 - 4ac < 0$, then the number under the square root sign will be negative, and so the solutions will be complex numbers.

Example ▼

Solve the equations: **(i)** $x^2 - 4x + 13 = 0$ **(ii)** $2x^2 + 2x + 1 = 0$.

Solution:

(i) $x^2 - 4x + 13 = 0$

$ax^2 + bx + c = 0$

$a = 1, b = -4, c = 13$

$x = \dfrac{-b \pm \sqrt{b^2 - 4ac}}{2a}$

$x = \dfrac{4 \pm \sqrt{(-4)^2 - 4(1)(13)}}{2(1)}$

$x = \dfrac{4 \pm \sqrt{16 - 52}}{2}$

$x = \dfrac{4 \pm \sqrt{-36}}{2}$

$x = \dfrac{4 \pm 6i}{2}$

$x = 2 \pm 3i$

∴ the roots are $2 + 3i$ and $2 - 3i$.

(ii) $2x^2 + 2x + 1 = 0$

$ax^2 + bx + c = 0$

$a = 2, b = 2, c = 1$

$x = \dfrac{-b \pm \sqrt{b^2 - 4ac}}{2a}$

$x = \dfrac{-2 \pm \sqrt{(2)^2 - 4(2)(1)}}{2(2)}$

$x = \dfrac{-2 \pm \sqrt{4 - 8}}{4}$

$x = \dfrac{-2 \pm \sqrt{-4}}{4}$

$x = \dfrac{-2 \pm 2i}{4} = \dfrac{-1 \pm i}{2}$

$x = -\tfrac{1}{2} \pm \tfrac{1}{2}i$

∴ the roots are $-\tfrac{1}{2} + \tfrac{1}{2}i$ and $-\tfrac{1}{2} - \tfrac{1}{2}i$.

Note: Notice in both solutions the roots occur in conjugate pairs. If one root of a quadratic equation, with real coefficients, is a complex number, then the other root must also be complex and the conjugate of the first.

i.e. if $3 - 4i$ is a root, then $3 + 4i$ is also a root;
       if $-2 - 5i$ is a root, then $-2 + 5i$ is also a root;
       if $a + bi$ is a root, then $a - bi$ is also a root.

Example ▼

Verify that $3 - 5i$ is a root of $x^2 - 6x + 34 = 0$ and find the other root.

Solution:

Method 1:

If $3 - 5i$ is a root, then when x is replaced by $3 - 5i$ in the equation, the equation will be satisfied, i.e.,

$$(3 - 5i)^2 - 6(3 - 5i) + 34 = 0$$

Check:

$$(3 - 5i)^2 - 6(3 - 5i) + 34$$
$$= (-16 - 30i) - 6(3 - 5i) + 34$$
$$= -16 - 30i - 18 + 30i + 34$$
$$= 0$$

$\therefore$ $3 - 5i$ is a root

and $3 + 5i$ is the other root

(the conjugate of $3 - 5i$).

Method 2:

$$x^2 - 6x + 34 = 0$$

$$a = 1, b = -6, c = 34$$

$$x = \frac{-b \pm \sqrt{b^2 - 4ac}}{2a}$$

$$x = \frac{6 \pm \sqrt{(-6)^2 - 4(1)(34)}}{2(1)}$$

$$x = \frac{6 \pm \sqrt{36 - 136}}{2}$$

$$x = \frac{6 \pm \sqrt{-100}}{2}$$

$$x = \frac{6 \pm 10i}{2}$$

$$x = 3 \pm 5i$$

$\therefore$ $3 - 5i$ is a root and $3 + 5i$ is the other root.

Example ▼

If $-3 - 2i$ is a root of $z^2 + pz + q = 0$, where $p, q \in \mathbf{R}$, find p and q.

Solution:

If $-3 - 2i$ is a root, then $-3 + 2i$ is also a root.

Method: Form an equation with roots $-3 - 2i$ and $-3 + 2i$.

Let $z = -3 - 2i$ and $z = -3 + 2i$

$z + 3 + 2i = 0$ and $z + 3 - 2i = 0$

$(z + 3 + 2i)(z + 3 - 2i) = 0$

$z(z + 3 - 2i) + 3(z + 3 - 2i) + 2i(z + 3 - 2i) = 0$

$z^2 + 3z - 2zi + 3z + 9 - 6i + 2zi + 6i - 4i^2 = 0$

$z^2 + 6z + 9 - 4(-1) = 0$

$z^2 + 6z + 9 + 4 = 0$

$z^2 + 6z + 13 = 0$

By comparing $z^2 + 6z + 13 = 0$ to $z^2 + pz + q = 0$,

$p = 6$ and $q = 13$.

Solve each of the following equations:

1. $x^2 - 6x + 13 = 0$ **2.** $z^2 - 2z + 10 = 0$ **3.** $x^2 + 4x + 5 = 0$

4. $x^2 + 10x + 34 = 0$ **5.** $z^2 + 4z + 13 = 0$ **6.** $z^2 - 10z + 41 = 0$

7. $z^2 + 2z + 2 = 0$ **8.** $z^2 - 2z + 5 = 0$ **9.** $x^2 + 14x + 53 = 0$

10. $x^2 + 8x + 17 = 0$ **11.** $x^2 + 16 = 0$ **12.** $z^2 + 25 = 0$

13. $2z^2 - 2z + 1 = 0$ **14.** $2z^2 - 6z + 5 = 0$

Verify in each of the following that:

15. $-1 + 2i$ is a root of $z^2 + 2z + 5 = 0$ and find the other root.

16. $3 - 2i$ is a root of $x^2 - 6x + 13 = 0$ and find the other root.

17. $2 - 5i$ is a root of $z^2 - 4z + 29 = 0$ and find the other root.

18. $-4 - 6i$ is a root of $x^2 + 8x + 52 = 0$ and find the other root.

19. $-5 - i$ is a root of $z^2 + 10z + 26 = 0$ and find the other root.

20. $-5 + 4i$ is a root of $x^2 + 10x + 41 = 0$ and find the other root.

Find the equations whose roots are:

21. $-2 \pm i$ **22.** $4 \pm 3i$ **23.** $-1 \pm 3i$ **24.** $1 \pm 2i$

25. $1 \pm i$ **26.** $-5 \pm 2i$ **27.** $\pm i$ **28.** $\pm 3i$

29. If $3 + 5i$ is a root of $x^2 + px + q = 0$, $p, q \in \mathbf{R}$, find p and q.

30. If $7 - i$ is a root of $z^2 + az + b = 0$, $a, b \in \mathbf{R}$, find a and b.

31. If $-3 - 3i$ is a root of $x^2 + mx + n = 0$, $m, n \in \mathbf{R}$, find m and n.

32. If $1 + 5i$ is a root of $x^2 + hx + k = 0$, $h, k \in \mathbf{R}$, evaluate $\sqrt{k + 2h^2}$.

33. If $-6 - 2i$ is a root of $z^2 + tz + 40 = 0$, $t \in \mathbf{R}$, evaluate t^2.

34. If $4 - i$ is a root of $x^2 - 8x + q = 0$, $q \in \mathbf{R}$, form an equation with roots $-2 \pm \sqrt{1 - q}$.

CHAPTER

3

STATISTICS

Averages

There are many types of average. Two that we will meet are called the **mean** and **median**. They are also known as **measures of central tendency**.

Mean

The **mean** is the proper name for what most people call the average.

> The mean of a set of values is defined as the sum of all the values divided by the number of values.

That is:

$$\text{Mean} = \frac{\text{Sum of all the Values}}{\text{Number of Values}}$$

The formula is often written as:

$$\bar{x} = \frac{\Sigma x}{n}$$

where:

(i) $\bar{x}$, read as 'x bar', is the symbol for the mean

(ii) Σ, the Greek capital letter sigma, means 'the sum of' (i.e., Σx means 'add up all the x-values')

(iii) n is the number of values of x.

Note: Strictly speaking, $\bar{x}$ should be called the '**arithmetic mean**'.

Median

> When the values are arranged in ascending, or descending, order of size, then the median is the middle value. If the number of values is even, then the median is the average of the two middle values.

Note: Half the values lie below the median and half the values lie above the median.

Find: **(i)** the mean **(ii)** the median of the array of numbers: 3, 7, 9, 5, 4, 2, 3, 8, 4.

Solution:

(i) Mean $= \bar{x} = \dfrac{\Sigma x}{n} = \dfrac{3+7+9+5+4+2+3+8+4}{9} = \dfrac{45}{9} = 5$

(ii) Median: First write the numbers in ascending order:

$\qquad$ 2, 3, 3, 4, 4, 5, 7, 8, 9

$\qquad$ The middle number is 4 $\therefore$ the median $= 4$

Find the median of the array of numbers: 11, 8, 10, 2, 3, 5

Solution:

First write the numbers in ascending order: 2, 3, 5, 8, 10, 11
Since there is an even number of numbers we take the average of the two middle ones, 5 and 8.

$\therefore \quad$ the median $= \dfrac{5+8}{2} = \dfrac{13}{2} = 6.5$

Note: The mean and the median need not necessarily be members of the original set of values.

Find the mean and median of each of the following:

1. 3, 7, 2, 5, 3
2. 4, 0, 2, 6, 8, 2, 6, 4
3. 10, 4, 5, 4, 12, 2, 8, 5, 4

4. 6.2, 9, 6.4, 7.4, 2.5
5. 2.8, 3.1, 6.7, 1.4, 5.6, 8.6

6. A waitress kept a record of her tips given to her each day for seven days.
The record read: €3.68, €10.11, €2.93, €5.42, €1.94, €6.19, €5.15.
Calculate: **(i)** the mean **(ii)** the median amount of tips given to her per day.

7. The mean of 5 numbers is 9. Find the sum of the numbers.

8. The mean of the six numbers 10, 7, 3, 4, 9 is 7. Find x and, hence, the median.

9. The mean of 8 numbers is 9. When one of the numbers is taken away the mean is increased by 1. Find the number that is taken away.

10. A footballer had an average of 3 points in his last 7 games. How many points must he score in his next match if he is to increase his average to 4?

11. Find the mean of $4a + 6$, $a - 3$, $7a + 12$, $3 - a$, $4a + 7$.

Frequency Distribution

> If the values in a distribution are arranged in ascending or descending order, showing their corresponding frequencies, the distribution is called a **frequency distribution**.

Note: If the values and frequencies are given in a table, it is called a **frequency distribution table**.

Mean and Median of a Frequency Distribution

Mean

To find the mean of a frequency distribution, do the following:

> **1.** Multiply each value by its corresponding frequency.
> **2.** Sum all these products.
> **3.** Divide this sum by the total number of frequencies.

That is:

$$\bar{x} = \frac{\Sigma fx}{\Sigma f}$$

(i) x is the value of each measurement
(ii) f is the frequency of each measurement
(iii) Σfx is the sum of all the fx values
(iv) Σf is the sum of all the frequencies.

Median

As the values are arranged in order of size, the median can be read directly from a frequency distribution table by looking for the middle value, or the average of the two middle values if there is an even number of values.

Example ▼

A test consisted of five questions. 1 mark was awarded per question for a correct solution and no marks for an incorrect solution. The following frequency distribution table shows how a class of students scored in the test:

Mark	0	1	2	3	4	5
Number of students	1	3	6	7	7	4

Calculate: **(i)** the mean **(ii)** the median mark.

Solution:

(i) Mean

$$\text{Mean} = \bar{x} = \frac{\Sigma fx}{\Sigma f} = \frac{1(0) + 3(1) + 6(2) + 7(3) + 7(4) + 4(5)}{1 + 3 + 6 + 7 + 7 + 4}$$

$$= \frac{0 + 3 + 12 + 21 + 28 + 20}{28} = \frac{84}{28} = 3$$

∴ the mean = 3 marks.

(ii) Median

There are 28 values altogether. Therefore, the median is the average of the 14th and 15th mark. The first mark is 0, the next 3 are each 1 mark, the next 6 are 2 marks each. The next 7 are 3 marks each and these include the 14th and 15th mark.

$$\therefore \quad \text{the median} = \frac{3 + 3}{2} = 3 \text{ marks.}$$

Exercise 3.2 ▼

Find: **(i)** the mean **(ii)** the median of each of the following frequency distributions:

1.

Value	1	2	3	4
Frequency	8	6	4	2

2.

Value	0	1	2	3	4	5	6
Frequency	1	7	6	5	2	6	3

3.

Value	1	3	5	7	9	11	13	15
Frequency	1	2	5	7	6	3	2	2

4.

Value	8	10	12	14	16	18	20
Frequency	4	6	9	10	9	6	4

5.

Value	0	1	2	3	4	5	6	7	8	9
Frequency	6	8	10	7	3	5	4	2	1	1

6.

Value	10	11	12	13	14	15	16
Frequency	4	7	9	5	6	8	1

7. A die was thrown 40 times and the frequency of each score was as follows:

Value	1	2	3	4	5	6
Frequency	7	7	8	9	5	4

    (i) Find the median score.

    (ii) Calculate the mean of these scores.

    The die was then thrown another 10 times. The mean of these 10 throws was 3.5.

    (iii) Calculate the overall mean for all 50 throws.

8. A test, consisting of 8 questions, was given to 40 pupils. One mark was awarded per question for a correct solution and no marks for an incorrect solution.
The results were as follows:

$$3, 2, 5, 6, 1, 3, 5, 7, 1, 4$$
$$2, 4, 3, 7, 4, 8, 6, 3, 2, 3$$
$$6, 5, 6, 1, 5, 5, 2, 4, 5, 4$$
$$5, 4, 2, 3, 4, 3, 4, 5, 3, 5$$

    (i) Represent the information on a frequency distribution table.

    (ii) Calculate the mean mark per pupil.

    (iii) Calculate the median mark.

    (iv) If the pass mark was 4, what percentage of the pupils failed the test?

    (v) 10 other pupils did the same test. The mean mark then for the 50 pupils was unchanged. Calculate the sum of the marks for the 50 pupils.

    (vi) A different 50 pupils did the same test and the mean for the 100 pupils was increased by one mark. Calculate the mean mark for the second set of 50 pupils.

Grouped Frequency Distribution

Sometimes the range of the values is very wide and it is not suitable to show all the values individually. When this happens we arrange the values into suitable groups called **class intervals**, such as 0–10, 10–20, etc. When the information is arranged in class intervals it is not possible to calculate the exact value of the mean. However, it is possible to estimate it by using the **mid-interval value** of each class interval. The easiest way to find the mid-interval value is to add the two extreme values and divide by 2.

For example, in the class interval 30–50, add 30 and 50 and divide by 2.

i.e., $\dfrac{30 + 50}{2} = \dfrac{80}{2} = 40$ $\therefore$ 40 is the mid-interval value.

Otherwise, the procedure for estimating the mean is the same as in the previous section.

> Use the formula: $\bar{x} = \dfrac{\Sigma fx}{\Sigma f}$, taking x as the mid-interval value.

The frequency distribution below shows the number of hours per week spent watching television by 37 people.

Hours	0–2	2–6	6–12	12–20	20–30
Number of people	5	9	12	6	5

(**Note:** 0–2 means 0 is included but 2 is not, and so on.)

(i) Estimate the mean number of hours spent per week watching television.

(ii) In which class interval does the median lie?

Solution:

We assume the data to be at mid-interval values.
It is good practice to rewrite the table using these mid-interval values.

New table:

Hours (mid-interval values)	1	4	9	16	25
Number of people	5	9	12	6	5

(i) Mean $= \bar{x} = \dfrac{\Sigma fx}{\Sigma f} = \dfrac{5(1) + 9(4) + 12(9) + 6(16) + 5(25)}{5 + 9 + 12 + 6 + 5} = \dfrac{370}{37} = 10$

∴ the mean number of hours spent watching television per week is 10 hours.

(ii) There are 37 people altogether. The middle one is the 19th person. Therefore, we require the class interval in which the 19th person lies.
By looking at the table, it is obvious that the time spent watching television by the 19th person lies in the 6–12 hour class interval.
∴ the median lies in the 6–12 hour class interval.

Exercise 3.3 ▼

Assuming that the data can be taken at mid-interval values, calculate the mean of each of the following grouped frequency distributions. In each case state in which class interval the median lies.

1.

Value	0–2	2–4	4–6	6–8
Frequency	12	9	6	3

2.

Value	1–5	5–9	9–13	13–17	17–21
Frequency	5	8	7	5	3

3.

Value	0–20	20–40	40–60	60–80	80–100
Frequency	2	5	8	6	4

4.

Value	0 2	2–6	6–12	12–20
Frequency	4	4	6	11

5.

Value	5–15	15–35	35–45	45–75
Frequency	15	37	14	9

6.

Value	0–5	5–10	10–20	20–35	35–40	40–50
Frequency	3	5	6	9	5	2

7.

Value	0–60	60–120	120–180	180–240
Frequency	18	35	31	16

8.

Value	0–5	5–15	15–25	25–50
Frequency	10	21	47	22

9. A survey of 80 students gave the amount of money spent per month in the school canteen:

Amount in €	0–8	8–16	16–24	24–32	32–40
Number of students	8	12	20	24	16

(**Note:** 0–8 means 0 is included but 8 is not, etc.)

Taking the amounts at the mid-interval values, show that the mean amount of money spent per student was €22.80.

10. A department store carried out a survey on the length of time a number of people spent shopping in their store. The table shows the length of time spent shopping, in 10-minute intervals:

Time interval in minutes	0–10	10–20	20–30	30–40	40–50	50–60	60–70
Number of shoppers	30	x	24	30	40	20	10

(**Note:** 0–10 means 0 is included, but 10 is not, etc.)

(i) If the average number of shoppers for the first, second and third intervals was 30, calculate the value of x.

(ii) Using mid-interval values, calculate the average shopping time in the store.

(iii) What is the least number of shoppers who completed their shopping within 35 minutes?

(iv) In which class interval does the median lie?

Weighted Mean

A weighted mean is one where the **frequencies** are replaced by **weights**. The weights are a **measure of importance** of a particular value, i.e., each value has a **statistical weight** attached to it.

Note: Calculating a weighted mean is exactly the same as finding the mean of a frequency distribution, except that the frequencies are replaced by weights.

We calculate the weighted mean using the formula:

$$\text{Weighted mean} = \bar{x}_w = \frac{\Sigma wx}{\Sigma w}$$

where:

(i) $\bar{x}_w$ is short for 'weighted mean'

(ii) x is the value of each measurement

(iii) w is the weight attached to each measurement.

(**Note:** The weights are often given in the form of a ratio or proportion.)

Example ▼

In an examination, two students, P and Q, obtained the following marks:

Subject		English	Irish	Maths	Economics
Marks	P	50	71	65	44
	Q	47	55	83	50

If weights of 4, 3, 3, 2, respectively, are assigned to English, Irish, Maths and Economics, find which of P or Q scored higher overall.

Solution:

Method: Obtain the weighted mean for each and compare.

Weighted mean for _P_:

Subject	English	Irish	Maths	Economics
Mark	50	71	65	44
Weight	4	3	3	2

Weighted mean for $P = \bar{x}_w = \dfrac{\Sigma wx}{\Sigma w}$

$$= \frac{4(50) + 3(71) + 3(65) + 2(44)}{4 + 3 + 3 + 2}$$

$$= \frac{200 + 213 + 195 + 88}{12} = \frac{696}{12} = 58$$

∴ _P_ had a weighted mean of 58 marks.

Weighted mean for _Q_:

Subject	English	Irish	Maths	Economics
Mark	47	55	83	50
Weight	4	3	3	2

Weighted mean for $Q = \bar{x}_w = \dfrac{\Sigma wx}{\Sigma w}$

$$= \frac{4(47) + 3(55) + 3(83) + 2(50)}{4 + 3 + 3 + 2}$$

$$= \frac{188 + 165 + 249 + 100}{12} = \frac{702}{12} = 58.5$$

∴ _Q_ had a weighted mean of 58.5 marks.

Thus we conclude that _Q_ did better than _P_ in this examination.

Exercise 3.4 ▼

1. The values 6, 2, 5, 4, 8 have, respectively, the weights 5, 4, 1, 2, 3. Calculate the weighted mean.

2. Calculate the weighted mean of the values 10, 6, 7, 3, given the respective weights 14, 6, 10, 9.

3. Calculate the weighted mean given:

Number	4	8	13	5	4	6	1
Weight	6	8	13	14	9	7	3

4. In an examination, two students, A and B, obtained the following marks:

Subject		French	Physics	Maths	Accounting
Marks	A	40	48	92	72
	B	68	76	44	48

Which student had the best average mark per subject?
If weights for the four subjects are, respectively, 3, 2, 1, 2, who, now, had the best average mark?
Give a reason for your answer.

5. A composite index number is constructed by taking the weighted mean.
The following table gives the index and weighting for each of four commodities:

Commodity	Food	Fuel	Mortgage	Clothing
Index	120	110	90	80
Weight	8	5	4	3

Calculate the composite index number.

6. Two supermarkets, S_1 and S_2, make reductions in prices, in cents, of four items, A, B, C, D, as shown in the table:

	A	B	C	D
S_1	11	2	6	5
S_2	8	3	7	10

Which supermarket had the best average reduction per item?
If the sales of the four items A, B, C, D, in each supermarket were in the ratio $4 : 2 : 3 : 1$, respectively, which, now, had the best average reduction?

7. In their Leaving Certificate, two students, A and B, obtained the following points:

Subject		Maths	Irish	English	Biology	French	Accounting
Points	A	5	2	1	3	4	2
	B	4	1	3	5	2	2

How many points had each student?
A university attached weights, 4, 3, 4, 2, 1, 1, respectively, to the six subjects as written above.
If there was only one place left in the university, which student obtained the place?
If the weights were 5, 4, 3, 2, 1, 5, respectively, who, now, obtained the place?

Standard Deviation

> The standard deviation is a measure of the spread of the values about the mean.

In other words, it gives us an indication of how the values we have are spread out. The higher the standard deviation, the more spread out around the mean is the data, and vice versa.
The Greek letter σ, sigma, is used to denote the standard deviation.

Standard Deviation of a Set of Values

To calculate the standard deviation, σ, of a set of values we use the following formula:

$$\sigma = \sqrt{\frac{\Sigma d^2}{n}} \qquad \text{where } d = x - \bar{x}$$

> x represents the values.
> d, the deviation, is the difference between a single value, x, and the mean, $\bar{x}$.
> n is the number of values of x.

There is no need to worry about the sign of d, because when it is squared it always becomes a positive number.

Note: When calculating σ, it is good practice to lay out the data in vertical columns in a table.

Example ▼

Calculate the standard deviation, correct to two decimal places, of the following array of numbers: 1, 3, 6, 7, 8.

Solution:

First calculate the mean, $\bar{x}$:

$$\bar{x} = \frac{1+3+6+7+8}{5}$$

$$= \frac{25}{5}$$

$$= 5$$

Now make out a table:

x	d	d^2	$d = x - \bar{x}$
1	4	16	
3	2	4	
6	1	1	
7	2	4	
8	3	9	$\Sigma d_2 = 34$

Standard deviation $= \sigma = \sqrt{\dfrac{\Sigma d^2}{n}} = \sqrt{\dfrac{34}{5}} = \sqrt{6.8} = \sqrt{2.61}$ (correct to two decimal places).

Calculate the standard deviation of each of the following arrays of numbers (answers correct to 2 decimal places):

1. 1, 2, 3, 4, 5

2. 2, 5, 6, 8, 10, 11

3. 4, 5, 6, 9

4. 1, 2, 2, 3, 4, 6

5. 4, 8, 10, 10, 11, 11

6. 5, 8, 11, 14, 17

7. 2, 4, 5, 7, 11, 13

8. 9, 12, 4, 6, 10, 7

9. 12, 4, 9, 8, 7, 11, 5

10. The standard deviation of the array of numbers 2, 8, 3, 7, 6, 4, 5 is k. Calculate the value of k.

11. Show that the following arrays of numbers have the same standard deviation:
   (i) 3, 4, 6, 8, 9   **(ii)** 7, 8, 10, 12, 13

12. The array of numbers, 1, 2, 4, 5, 8, 16 has mean $\bar{x}$ and standard deviation σ. Verify that $\bar{x} - \sigma = 1$.

13. The array of numbers, 1.8, 2.6, 4.8, 7.2 have mean $\bar{x}$ and standard deviation σ. Verify that $\bar{x} - \sigma = 2$.

14. Show that the mean of the array of numbers 3, 6, 7, 5.5, 3.5 is 5. Hence, calculate the standard deviation, correct to one decimal place.

Standard Deviation of a Frequency Distribution

To calculate the standard deviation, σ, of a frequency distribution we use the following formula:

$$\sigma = \sqrt{\frac{\Sigma f d^2}{\Sigma f}}$$ where $d = x - \bar{x}$

x represents the values, or mid-interval values, and f the frequency of the values.
d, the deviation, is the difference between a single value, x, and the mean, $\bar{x}$.

As before, when calculating σ set out the data in vertical columns in a table.

Example ▼

Calculate the mean and standard deviation, correct to two decimal places, of the frequency distribution:

Value	1	2	3	4	5	6
Frequency	7	8	4	4	3	4

Solution:

Mean

$$\bar{x} = \frac{\Sigma fx}{\Sigma f}$$

$$= \frac{7(1) + 8(2) + 4(3) + 4(4) + 3(5) + 4(6)}{7 + 8 + 4 + 4 + 3 + 4}$$

$$= \frac{7 + 16 + 12 + 16 + 15 + 24}{30}$$

$$= \frac{90}{30}$$

$$= 3$$

Standard deviation

Make out a table: $d = x - \bar{x}$

f	x	d	d	fd^2
7	1	2	4	28
8	2	1	1	8
4	3	0	0	0
4	4	1	1	4
3	5	2	4	12
4	6	3	9	36

$\Sigma f = 30$ $\Sigma d^2 = 88$

Standard deviation $= \sigma = \sqrt{\dfrac{\Sigma d^2}{\Sigma f}} = \sqrt{\dfrac{88}{30}} = 1.71$ (correct to two decimal places).

Note: For **grouped frequency distributions**, the standard deviation is calculated in exactly the same way, except that x stands for the mid-interval value.

Exercise 3.6 ▼

Find the mean and standard deviation, correct to two decimal places, of each of the following frequency distributions:

1.

Value	1	2	3	4	5
Frequency	2	3	5	3	2

2.

Value	2	6	8	9	10	13
Frequency	3	4	2	6	5	2

3.

Value	1	5	6	8	11	13	15
Frequency	7	4	7	3	2	2	1

4.

Value	13	14	15	16	17	18
Frequency	1	5	9	10	8	7

In questions 5–8, assume the data can be taken at the mid-interval values:

5.

Value	0–4	4–8	8–12	12–16	16–20
Frequency	2	3	9	7	3

6.

Value	0–20	20–40	40–60	60–80
Frequency	11	14	9	6

7.

Value	0–2	2–6	6–12	12–20
Frequency	6	14	18	10

8.

Value	0–20	20–30	30–60	60–80	80–120
Frequency	9	9	21	14	7

9. 20 pupils were given a problem to solve. The following grouped frequency distribution table gives the number of pupils who solved the problem in the given time interval:

Time (minutes)	0–4	4–12	12–24	24–40
Frequency	3	8	7	2

(**Note:** 0–4 means 0 is included but 4 is not, etc.)

(**i**) In which interval does the median lie?

(**ii**) Explain what is meant by **median** solving time.

Assuming the data can be taken at the mid-interval values, calculate:

(**iii**) the mean

(**iv**) the standard deviation, correct to two decimal places.

Histogram

A histogram is often used to display information contained in a frequency distribution. It is similar to a bar chart with no gaps between the bars, and the two are often confused. The essential characteristic of a histogram is that the **area of each rectangle represents the frequency** and the sum of the areas of the rectangles is equal to the sum of the frequencies. The drawing of a histogram is straightforward. However, be careful when the class intervals are unequal.

Procedure for constructing a histogram

A histogram is constructed with the following steps:

1. Let the base of the rectangle which represents the class interval of smallest width have a length of 1 unit (or of length 2 units, 3 units, etc.).

2. Express the bases of the other rectangles, depending on the width of the class intervals, in terms of this base (i.e. are they one and a half times the base? double it? treble it? etc.).

3. Divide each frequency by its corresponding base in Step 2 to find the height of each rectangle.

   That is: Height = $\dfrac{\text{Frequency}}{\text{Base}}$

4. With the values on the horizontal axis and the frequencies on the vertical axis, construct the rectangles beside each other.

When given a grouped frequency distribution and asked to represent the distribution with a histogram, it is good practice to rewrite the table again with extra rows to show the base and height of each rectangle.

Note: For the sake of drawing a histogram or using a histogram to work out frequencies, we say the area of the rectangle represents the frequency. However, mathematically we say that the **area of each rectangle is proportional to the frequency** of the corresponding class, i.e. if one class has a frequency twice that of another, then the area of the rectangle representing this class will have twice the area of the rectangle representing the other class, etc.

Example ▼

The following frequency distribution gives the number of marks obtained by students in an examination:

Marks	0–20	20–50	50–60	60–80	80–120
Number of students	8	21	8	10	24

(**Note:** Where 0–20 means 0 is included but 20 is not, etc.)

Represent the data with a histogram.

Solution:

The smallest interval is the 50–60. The rectangle that represents this interval will have a base of 1. The bases of the other rectangles are expressed in terms of this base. The rectangle representing the 0–20 interval will have a base of 2. The rectangles representing the 20–50, 60–80 and 80–120 intervals will have bases of 3, 2 and 4, respectively.

New Table:

Marks	0–20	20–50	50–60	60–80	80–120
Number of students	8	21	8	10	24
Base	2	3	1	2	4
Height	4	7	8	5	6

The last row, height, is simply obtained by dividing the base into the number of students.

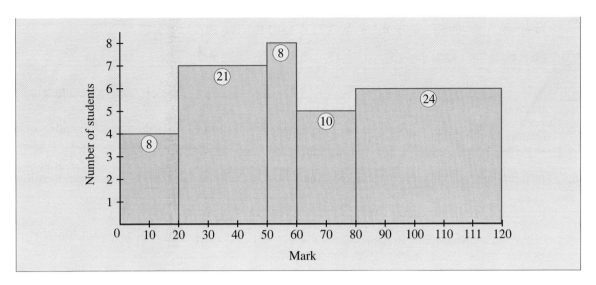

Note: It makes the distribution clearer if we label each rectangle with its frequency. A neat way to do this is to put the frequencies into each rectangle and put a circle around them. The horizontal axis is marked in units of the '**smallest class interval**'.

Exercise 3.7 ▼

Construct a histogram to represent each of the following grouped frequency distributions:

1.

Interval	0–20	20–30	30–50	50–80	80–120
Frequency	20	8	22	21	20

2.

Interval	0–4	4–12	12–16	16–28	28–32
Frequency	7	18	8	30	6

3.

Interval	0–10	10–30	30–60	60–100
Frequency	7	8	15	24

4.

Interval	0–200	200–300	300–600	600–700	700–1000
Frequency	12	8	30	9	15

5.

Interval	0–40	40–60	60–160	160–200
Frequency	32	24	100	36

6.

Interval	0–6	6–8	8–12	12–14	14–20
Frequency	12	5	12	3	15

7.

Interval	0–10	10–15	15–20	20–30	30–50
Frequency	10	6	4	12	20

8. The following frequency distribution gives marks, out of 20, obtained by students in an examination:

Marks	0–2	2–6	6–12	12–20
Number of students	4	4	6	11

  (i) Represent the data with a histogram.

  (ii) In which class interval does the median lie?

  (iii) Assuming the data can be taken at the mid-interval values, calculate the mean, $\bar{x}$, and standard deviation, σ, correct to one decimal place.

9. The distribution of the ages of people attending a meeting is shown in the following grouped frequency distribution table:

Ages (years)	20–25	25–35	35–50	50–70
Frequency	7	14	33	16

  (i) Represent the data with a histogram.

  (ii) Assuming the data can be taken at the mid-interval values, verify that the mean age is 42 years.

  (iii) Calculate the standard deviation, correct to two decimal places.

  (iv) What is the greatest possible number of people who are below the mean age?

Given the Histogram

Sometimes we are given the histogram already drawn and we need to calculate the frequencies represented by the rectangles. We are usually given the area of one of the rectangles (which represents the frequency) and its height (read directly from the diagram). From this we can work out the width of the base of the rectangle whose area we are given. We can then calculate the width of the bases of the other rectangles. The heights of the other rectangles can be read directly from the diagram.

> We then use the formula: Frequency = Area of rectangle = base × height

We use the following steps:

1. Divide the area of the rectangle whose area we are given by its height. This gives the base of the rectangle.

$$\text{Base} = \frac{\text{Area}}{\text{Height}}$$

2. Express the base of each of the other rectangles in terms of this base (i.e. is it half this base, double it, treble it, etc.?)

3. Multiply the given height of each rectangle by its base to find its area. The area of a rectangle is equal to the frequency it represents.

Example ▼

The distribution of the distances, in km, that a group of people have to travel to work each day is shown in the histogram:

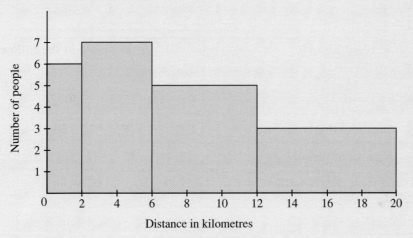

Complete the corresponding frequency distribution table:

Distances (km)	0–2	2–6	6–12	12–20
Number of people		28		

Solution:

Given:

1. Area of rectangle representing distances between 2 and 6 km is 28.

2. The height of this rectangle is 7.

$$\therefore \quad \text{Base} = \frac{\text{Area}}{\text{Height}} = \frac{28}{7} = 4$$

This rectangle uses two marked units on the horizontal axis

∴ each marked unit on the horizontal axis has a measurement of 2.

The bases of the rectangles representing the 0–2, 6–12 and 12–20 km are, therefore, 2, 6 and 8 respectively.

0–2 km : Area = frequency = height × base = 6 × 2 = 12
6–12 km : Area = frequency = height × base = 5 × 6 = 30
12–20 km : Area = frequency = height × base = 3 × 8 = 24

We could also work out the frequencies on the histogram.

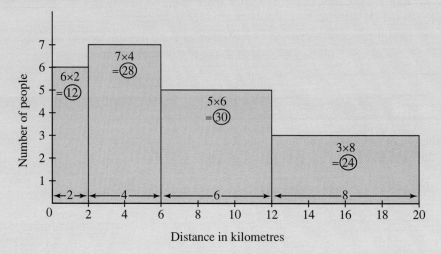

Distance in kilometres

Completed Table:

Distances (km)	0–2	2–6	6–12	12–20
Number of people	12	28	30	24

Exercise 3.8 ▼

1. The distribution of the ages of people at a meeting is shown in the histogram:

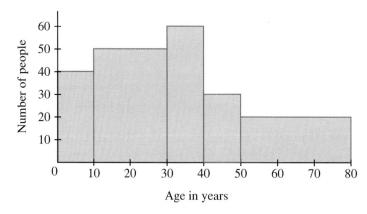

Age in years

Complete the corresponding frequency distribution table:

Age (years)	0–10	10–30	30–40	40–50	50–80
Number of people			60		

How many people were at the meeting?

2. A random selection of claims made against an insurance company for a certain year is shown in the histogram:

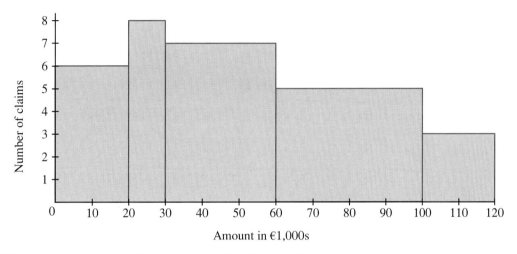

Amount in €1,000s

Complete the corresponding frequency distribution table:

Amount (€1,000s)	0–20	20–30	30–60	60–100	100–120
Number of claims			42		

In which interval does the median lie?

3. The histogram shows the distribution of the distances, in km, that some students have to travel to school:

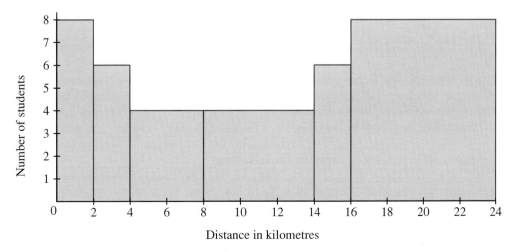

Distance in kilometres

Complete the corresponding frequency distribution table:

Distances (km)	0–2	2–4	4–8	8–14	14–16	16–24
Number of students		4				

Assuming the data can be taken at the mid-interval values, calculate:

(i) the mean   (ii) the standard deviation, correct to two decimal places.

4. The distribution of contributions, in euros, given to a charity by a number of people is shown in the histogram below:

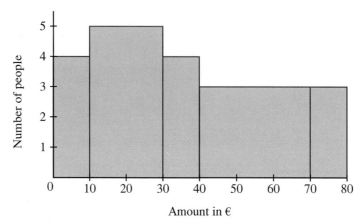

Amount in €

Complete the corresponding frequency distribution table:

Amount in €	0–10	10–30	30–40	40–70	70–80
Number of people		30			

By taking the data at the mid-interval values, calculate:

(i) the mean contribution   (ii) the standard deviation, correct to two decimal places.

Cumulative Frequency

In a cumulative frequency the frequencies are accumulated. Each accumulated frequency is the combined total of all the previous frequencies up to that particular value. If we fill in the accumulated frequencies in tabular form, we have what is called a **cumulative frequency table**. The graph of a cumulative frequency is called a **cumulative frequency curve** or **ogive**. It has a distinctively lopsided S-shape.

To draw a cumulative frequency curve do the following:

1. Construct a cumulative frequency table (if not given).
2. Put the values on the horizontal axis and cumulative frequency on the vertical axis.
3. Plot the points (value, cumulative frequency).
4. Join the points with a smooth curve.

Note: If the data is given as a grouped frequency distribution, always make sure that in step 3 the **upper class limits** (not the mid-interval value or lower class limit) are plotted against the cumulative frequencies.

Median and interquartile range

How to calculate the median and the interquartile range from a cumulative frequency curve is shown below:

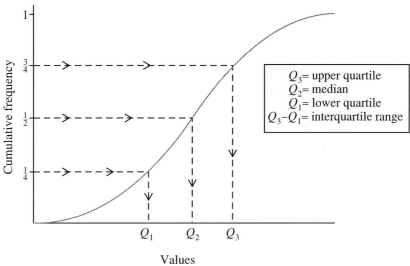

Q_3= upper quartile
Q_2= median
Q_1= lower quartile
Q_3-Q_1= interquartile range

Values

Quartiles, as their name suggests, are the quarter-way divisions of the data.
The **lower quartile**, Q_1, is the value one-quarter of the way through the distribution.
The **upper quartile**, Q_3, is the value three-quarters of the way through the distribution.
Therefore, half the values in a distribution must lie between the upper and lower quartiles.
The interquartile range is a single number and gives a measure of the spread of the values about the median.
The median is often referred to as Q_2.

Note: Readings from a cumulative frequency curve are only estimates.

Example ▼

40 students took an exam and their marks are shown in the table:

Marks	30–40	40–50	50–60	60–70	70–80	80–90	90–100
Number of students	2	3	4	8	15	6	2

(**Note:** 30–40 means 30 is included but 40 is not, etc.)

(i) Construct a cumulative frequency table.

(ii) Draw a cumulative frequency curve (ogive).

Use the curve to estimate:

(iii) the median

(iv) the lower and upper quartile marks

(v) the interquartile range.

Solution:

(i) **Cumulative frequency table:**

Marks	<30	<40	<50	<60	<70	<80	<90	<100
Number of students	0	2	5	9	17	32	38	40

(ii) **Cumulative frequency curve:**
Plot the points, (30, 0), (40, 2), (50, 5), (60, 9), (70, 17), (80, 32), (90, 38) and (100, 40) and join them with a smooth curve.

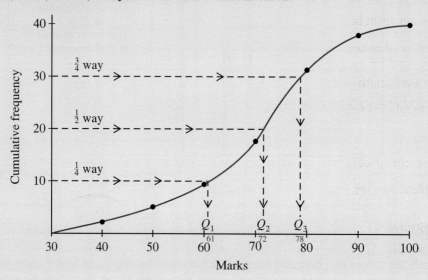

(iii) **Median:**
The middle value on the cumulative frequency axis is 20.
Draw a horizontal line from 20 to meet the curve and then straight down to the horizontal axis.
This line meets the horizontal axis at 72.
Thus, we estimate the median = Q_2 = 72.

(iv) **Upper quartile:**
The three-quarter-way value on the cumulative frequency axis is 30.
Draw a horizontal line from 30 to meet the curve and then straight down to the horizontal axis.
This line meets the horizontal axis at 78.
Thus, we estimate the upper quartile = Q_3 = 78.

(v) **Lower quartile:**
The quarter-way value on the cumulative frequency axis is 10.
Draw a horizontal line from 10 to meet the curve and then straight down to the horizontal axis.
This line meets the horizontal axis at 61.
Thus, we estimate the lower quartile = Q_1 = 61.

(vi) **Interquartile range:**
The interquartile range = $Q_3 - Q_1$ = 78 − 61 = 17.

Using Cumulative Frequency Curves

A cumulative frequency curve can be used to estimate the number of values that lie **below**, or **above**, a particular value or to estimate the number of values that lie **between** two values.

A shopkeeper recorded the amount of money spent by 50 customers on a certain day in the following cumulative frequency table:

Amount spent in €	<10	<20	<30	<40	<50	<60	<80
Number of customers	2	5	9	17	29	43	50

(i)   Draw a cumulative frequency curve to illustrate the data.

Use your cumulative frequency curve to estimate:

(ii)   the number of customers who spent less than €36

(iii)   the percentage of customers who spent between €47 and €65.

(iv)   Complete the corresponding grouped frequency table:

Amount spent in €	0–10	10–20	20–30	30–40	40–50	50–60	60–80
Number of customers							

Note: 0–10 means ⩾0 but less than 10, etc.

Solution:

(i)   Plot the points $(0, 0)$, $(10, 2)$, $(20, 5)$, $(30, 9)$, $(40, 17)$ $(50, 29)$, $(60, 43)$, $(80, 50)$ and join them with a smooth curve.

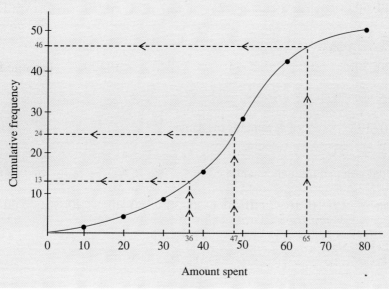

Note: $(0, 0)$ is plotted even though this is not a value in the cumulative frequency table.

(ii) Number of customers who spent less than €36
From 36 on the horizontal axis draw a vertical line to meet the curve and then straight across to the vertical axis.
This line meets the vertical axis at 13.
Thus we estimate that 13 people spent less than €36.

(iii) The percentage of customers who spent between €47 and €65
First work out the numbers.
From 47 and 65 on the horizontal axis draw vertical lines to meet the curve and then straight across to the vertical axis.
These lines meet the vertical axis at 24 and 46, respectively.

$$46 - 24 = 22$$

$$22 \text{ as a percentage of } 50 = \frac{22}{50} \times \frac{100}{1}\% = 44\%$$

Thus we estimate that 44% of the customers spent between €47 and €65.

(iv) Corresponding grouped frequency table
When the cumulative frequency table was constructed the frequencies were added.
Therefore, to construct a corresponding grouped frequency table we simply do the reverse:

Subtract the frequencies.

60–80	$50 - 43 = 7$

50–60	$43 - 29 = 14$

40–50	$29 - 17 = 12$

30–40	$17 - 9 = 8$

20–30	$9 - 5 = 4$

10–20	$5 - 2 = 3$

0–10	$= 2$, remains the same

Completed grouped frequency table:

Amount spent	0–10	10–20	20–30	30–40	40–50	50–60	60–80
Number of customers	2	3	4	8	12	14	7

Exercise 3.9 ▼

In the following cumulative frequency curves (ogives), estimate:

(i) the median   **(ii)** the upper quartile   **(iii)** the lower quartile   **(iv)** the interquartile range.

1.

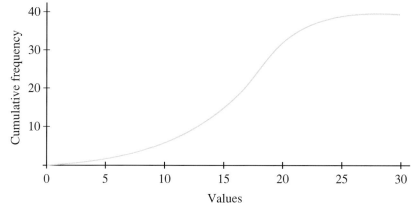

2.

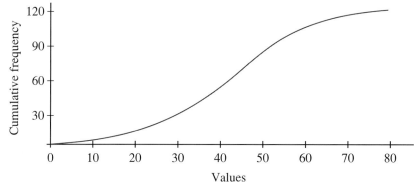

3.

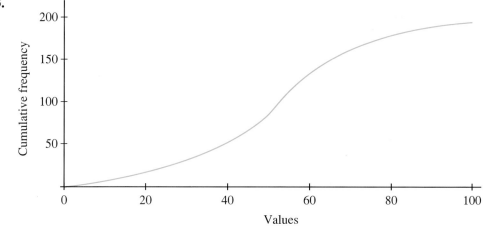

4.

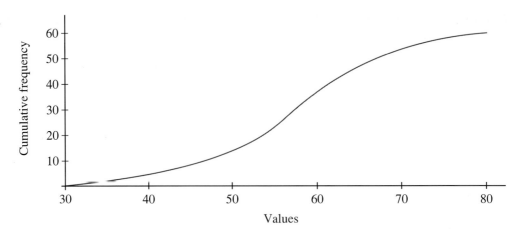

5. The times spent waiting at the checkout by 40 customers at a supermarket are represented by the cumulative frequency curve (ogive) shown.

Use the curve to estimate:

(i) the median waiting time

(ii) the interquartile range of waiting times

(iii) how many customers managed to get through in less than $2\frac{1}{2}$ minutes

(iv) how many customers took longer than $6\frac{1}{2}$ minutes to get through.

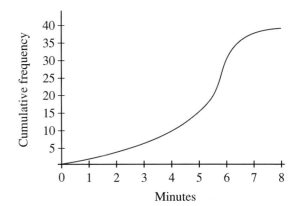

6. A garage owner recorded the amount of money spent by customers on petrol on a certain day in the following cumulative frequency table:

Value of petrol sales, €	<10	<20	<30	<40	<50	<60	<80
Number of customers	4	10	18	30	52	88	100

Draw a cumulative frequency curve to illustrate the data.

Use the curve to estimate:

(i) the number of customers who purchased less than €28 worth of petrol

(ii) the number of customers who spent between €36 and €52 on petrol.

(iii) Complete the corresponding frequency table:

Value of petrol sales, €	0–10	10–20	20–30	30–40	40–50	50–60	60–80
Number of customers					22		

(**Note:** 0–5 means $\geqslant 0$ but less than 5, etc.)

(iv) By taking the sales at the mid-interval values, verify that the mean sale was €45.40.

7 The following table shows the distribution of the arrival times at school by a group of 120 students:

Arrival time	08.20–08.30	08.30–08.40	08.40–08.50	08.50–09.00	09.00–09.10
Number of students	9	15	35	53	8

Complete the corresponding cumulative frequency table:

Arrival time	<08.20	<08.30	<08.40	<08.50	<09.00	<09.10
Number of students	0					120

Draw a cumulative frequency curve to illustrate the data. Use your curve to estimate:

(i) the median arrival time

(ii) the number of students who arrived between 08.35 and 08.45

(iii) the percentage of students who were late for school if arriving after 08.55 is considered as late.

8. A group of people form a club and over a period of time contribute to a fund to purchase equipment. The records showed the contributions as follows:

Contributions, €	0–10	10–20	20–30	30–40	40–60
Number of club members	5	10	25	40	20

(**Note:** 0–10 means 0 is included but 10 is not, etc.)

(i) Taking the contributions at the mid-interval values, calculate the mean contribution and the standard deviation, correct to two decimal places.

(ii) Represent the data with a histogram.

(iii) Complete the corresponding cumulative frequency table:

Contributions, €	<0	<10	<20	<30	<40	<60
Number of club members	0					100

(iv) Represent the data with a cumulative frequency curve (ogive).

Use your curve to estimate:

(v) the median contribution

(vi) the interquartile range of contributions

(vii) the number of contributions less than €18

(viii) the number of contributions between €45 and €55.

9. 60 students took a maths exam and their results are in the grouped frequency table below:

Marks	0–30	30–50	50–70	70–100
Number of students	9	18	24	9

(i) Represent the data with a histogram.

(ii) By taking the mid-interval values, calculate the mean mark.

(iii) Hence, calculate the standard deviation, correct to two decimal places.

(iv) Complete the corresponding cumulative frequency table:

Marks	<30	<50	<70	<100
Number of students		27		

(v) Represent the data on a cumulative frequency curve (ogive) putting the number of students on the vertical axis.

Estimate from your graph:

(vi) the median

(vii) the interquartile range

(viii) the pass mark, given that 38 of the students passed.

10. The grouped frequency table below shows the time, in minutes, that 100 students took to solve a maths problem:

Time (minutes)	0–20	20–40	40–60	60–80	80–100
Number of students	8	10	21	46	15

(**Note:** 0–20 means 0 is included but 20 is not, etc.)

(i) By taking the mid-interval values, verify that the mean time taken to solve the problem is 1 hour.

(ii) Complete the corresponding cumulative frequency table:

Time (minutes)	<0	<20	<40	<60	<80	<100
Number of students	0	8				

(iii) Represent the data with a cumulative frequency curve (ogive) putting the number of students on the vertical axis.

Use your curve to estimate:

(iv) the median time

(v) the interquartile range of times

(vi) the number of students who solved the problem:

    (a) in less than 35 minutes

    (b) between the mean and median times.

11. The grouped frequency table below refers to the ages of 28 people at a party:

Age (in years)	0–4	4–8	8–12	12–16	16–20
Number of people	2	6	12	6	2

(**Note:** 0–4 means ⩾ but less than 4, etc.)

Assuming the data can be taken at the mid-interval values, calculate:

(i)   the mean, $\bar{x}$ **(ii)**   the standard deviation, σ

(iii)   Evaluate the expression: $\sqrt{\bar{x} + 4\sigma} - 1$.

(iv)   Complete the corresponding cumulative frequency table:

Age (in years)	<4	<8	<12	<16	<20
Number of people					

and draw the cumulative frequency curve.

(v)   Use the curve to estimate the percentage of people in the range $\bar{x} - \sigma$ to $\bar{x} + \sigma$.

Given the Mean of a Frequency Distribution

Often we are given the mean of a frequency distribution and we need to find one of the values or frequencies. Essentially, we are given an equation in disguise and by solving this equation we can calculate the missing value or frequency.

Example ▼

The table below shows the ages of children in a creche:

Age	1	2	3	4	5
Number of children	4	7	9	x	5

If the mean age is 3, find the value of x.

Solution:

Equation given in disguise: mean = 3

$\therefore \quad \dfrac{4(1) + 7(2) + 9(3) + x(4) + 5(5)}{4 + 7 + 9 + x + 5} = 3$

$\dfrac{4 + 14 + 27 + 4x + 25}{x + 25} = 3$

$\dfrac{4x + 70}{x + 25} = 3$

$4x + 70 = 3(x + 25)$ [multiply both sides by $(x + 25)$]

$4x + 70 = 3x + 75$

$4x - 3x = 75 - 70$

$x = 5$

1. In the following frequency distribution the mean is 2.
   Find the value of x.

Number	1	2	3	4
Frequency	x	11	3	1

2. In the following frequency distribution the mean is 5.
   Find the value of x.

Number	3	4	5	6
Frequency	2	x	5	6

3. In the following frequency distribution the mean is 5.
   Find the value of x.

Number	2	4	6	8	10
Frequency	4	x	8	2	1

4. In the following frequency distribution the mean is 9.
   Find the value of x.

Number	5	7	9	11	13
Frequency	2	8	5	x	3

5. The result of a survey of the number of passengers carried by taxi in a town was recorded as follows:

Number of passengers	1	2	3	4	5
Number of taxis	3	t	9	6	4

   If the mean number of passengers carried per taxis was 3, find the value of t.
   How many taxis were in the survey?

6. The frequency distribution below shows the contributions, in euros, of a number of people to a charity:

Amount in €	1	2	3	4	5
Number of people	$x + 1$	x	7	1	5

   If the mean contribution was €3, calculate the value of x.

7. People attending a course were asked to choose one of the whole numbers from 1 to 12.
The results were recorded as follows:

Number	1–3	4–6	7–9	10–12
Number of people	4	7	x	8

Using mid-interval values, 7 was calculated as the mean of the numbers chosen.
Find the value of x.

8. The following grouped frequency distribution shows the sizes, in hectares, of a number of farms in a particular area:

Number of hectares	0–2	2–6	6–12	12–20	20–30
Number of farms	$m + 1$	4	2	m	1

(**Note:** 0–2 means 0 is included but 2 is not, etc.)
Using mid-interval values the mean size of a farm was calculated to be 8 hectares.
Find the value of m.

9. In the following frequency distribution the mean is 5.
Calculate the two possible values of p.

Number	1	5	$p - 1$	8	11
Frequency	p	4	p	3	2

10. Some of the marks received by a student are shown in the table:

Maths	English	Irish
80%	$x\%$	59%

If Maths, English and Irish have weights 4, 3, 2, respectively, calculate the value of x for this student to have a weighted mean of 74%.

ALGEBRA I

Evaluating Expressions (Substitution)

A **substitute** is used to replace something. In football, a substitute replaces another player. In algebra, when we replace letters with numbers when evaluating expressions, we call it **substitution**. When you are substituting numbers in an expression, it is good practice to put a bracket around the number that replaces the letter. (Remember: **BEMDAS**.)

Example ▼

(i) Evaluate $\dfrac{5(x - y)}{3(x^2 + y^2)}$ when $x = 2$ and $y = -1$.

(ii) Find the value of $3a - 4b$ when $a = \frac{2}{5}$ and $b = \frac{1}{3}$.

Solution:

(i)

$$\dfrac{5(x - y)}{3(x^2 + y^2)}$$

$$= \dfrac{5[(2) - (-1)]}{3[(2)^2 + (-1)^2]}$$

$$= \dfrac{5(2 + 1)}{3(4 + 1)}$$

$$= \dfrac{5(3)}{3(5)} = \dfrac{15}{15} = 1$$

(ii)

$$3a - 4b$$

$$= 3(\tfrac{2}{5}) - 4(\tfrac{1}{3})$$

$$= \tfrac{6}{5} - \tfrac{4}{3}$$

$$= \dfrac{3(6) - 5(4)}{15}$$

$$= \dfrac{18 - 20}{15} = -\dfrac{2}{15}$$

Exercise 4.1 ▼

Evaluate each of the following:

1. $3 + 4 \times 5$

2. $-5 + 3$

3. $4 - 7$

4. $-3 - 2$

5. $(-1 - 1)^3$

6. $2(-3) - 3(-3)$

7. $5(-1)^2$

8. $3(5 - 3)$

9. $\sqrt{\frac{4}{9}}$

10. $\sqrt{\frac{1}{4}}$

11. $\sqrt{\frac{25}{64}}$

12. $\sqrt{\frac{49}{16}}$

13. $\frac{1}{3} + \frac{1}{2} + \frac{5}{4}$

14. $\frac{1}{2} + \frac{2}{3} \times \frac{1}{5}$

15. $\sqrt{1\frac{7}{9}} + \frac{2}{3}$

16. $(\frac{3}{2} - \frac{2}{3})^2$

17. $\frac{1}{2} + (\frac{1}{2})^2 + (\frac{1}{2})^3$

18. $\sqrt{(\frac{1}{2})^2 + \frac{3}{4}}$

19. $(2)^2 - 3(2) + 3$

20. $2(-1)^3 - 6(-1)^2 - 2(-1) + 4$

21. $(-3)^3 + (-3)^2 - 6(-3) + 3$

22. $10 - 2\sqrt{13^2 - 12^2}$

23. $\sqrt{\frac{4}{3} + \frac{5}{4} + \frac{17}{12}}$

24. $\dfrac{1}{\frac{1}{2} + 1}$

Evaluate each of the following expressions for the given values of the variables:

25. $x^2 + 4x + 5$ when $x = 1$

26. $x^2 - 3x + 2$ when $x = -3$

27. $(x - y)^2$ when $x = 2$ and $y = -1$

28. $\sqrt{3a - 2b}$ when $a = 4$, $b = -2$

29. $\dfrac{p^2 + 4q}{2(q + 1)}$ when $p = -2$, $q = 3$

30. $\dfrac{5x - 3y^2}{4(y - x)}$ when $x = -1$, $y = 3$

31. $\dfrac{p(2p - q)}{q^2(p^2 + 2q)}$ when $p = 2$, $q = -1$

32. $\left(\dfrac{5a^2 - 1}{3b - 1}\right)^{1/2}$ when $a = -3$, $b = 4$

33. $\sqrt{\dfrac{2a^2(a - 2b)}{b^2(a^2 + 2b)}}$ when $a = 2$ and $b = -1$

34. $\dfrac{p(2p - q)}{q^p(p^p + pq)}$ when $p = 2$, $q = -1$

35. Evaluate $\dfrac{a + b - 1}{a - b + 1}$ when $a = \frac{1}{2}$ and $b = \frac{2}{3}$.

Simplifying Algebraic Expressions

Only terms that are the same can be added.

Example ▼

(i) Simplify $2(a^2 + 3a) - a(2a + 5) + a$

(ii) Simplify $(x + 1)(x^2 - x + 1) + (1 - x)(x^2 + x + 1)$

Solution:

(i) $2(a^2 + 3a) - a(2a + 5) + a$
$= 2a^2 + 6a - 2a^2 - 5a + a$
$= 2a^2 - 2a^2 + 6a + a - 5a$
$= 2a$

(ii) $(x + 1)(x^2 - x + 1) + (1 - x)(x^2 + x + 1)$
$= x(x^2 - x + 1) + 1(x^2 - x + 1) + 1(x^2 + x + 1) - x(x^2 + x + 1)$
$= x^3 - x^2 + x + x^2 - x + 1 + x^2 + x + 1 - x^3 - x^2 - x$
$= x^3 - x^3 + x^2 + x^2 - x^2 - x^2 + x + x - x - x + 1 + 1$
$= 2$

Simplify each of the following:

1. $5x + 3x$

2. $2x - 5x$

3. $-4x - 3x$

4. $-x + 4x$

5. $-x - 2x - 3x$

6. $5x^2 - 3x^2 - 6x^2$

7. $-2a^2 + 5a^2 - a^2$

8. $5x + 3 - 4x - 5 + 2x + 1$

9. $4x^2 - 3x + 8 - 3x^2 + 5x - 11$

Multiply these terms:

10. $(2x)(3x)$

11. $(-2x)(5x)$

12. $(3x^2)(-4x)$

13. $(-x)(-5x^2)$

14. $(3x)(-2x)(4x)$

15. $(2ab)(3ab)$

16. $(-2pq)(5p)$

17. $(-4a^2b)(-3ab^2)$

Expand each of the following (remove the brackets) and simplify:

18. $a(a - b) + b^2 + b(a - b)$

19. $a(b + c) - b(c - a) - c(a - b)$

20. $2(x^2 + 3x) - x(2x + 5) + x$

21. $2x(3x + 5y - 5) - 5y(y + 2x) + 5(2x + y^2)$

22. $2p(p - 4q) - 2p^2 - 5q^2 + 8q(p + q)$

23. $2a(b + c) - 2b(c + a) - 2c(a - b)$

24. $(x + 2)(x + 3)$

25. $(x + 4)(x - 3)$

26. $(x - 1)(x - 2)$

27. $(2x + 1)(x - 3)$

28. $(3x - 2)(2x + 5)$

29. $(5x - 1)(2x - 1)$

30. $(x + 3)^2$

31. $(2x - 1)^2$

32. $(3x - 2)^2$

33. $(2a - 3b)^2$

34. $(x + 1)(2x^2 + 3x + 6)$

35. $(2x + 1)(x^2 + 5x + 4)$

36. $(3x - 1)(2x^2 - 3x - 5)$

37. $(3x - 4)(x^2 - 5x + 4)$

38. $(x - 3)(x + 5) - x(x + 2) + 15$

39. $(x + 3)(x + 2) + (x - 4)(1 - x) + 5(1 - 2x)$

40. $(x - 3)(2x^2 - 3x + 4) - 2(x^3 - 5) + x(9x - 13)$

Single Variable Linear Equations

When solving an equation we can:

1. **add** or **subtract** the same quantity to both sides.
   (In practice this involves moving a term from one side to another side and changing its sign.)
2. **multiply** or **divide** both sides by the same quantity.

Rule: Whatever you do to one side of an equation, you must do exactly the same to the other side. Keep balance in mind.

Solve: **(i)** $4(x + 5) - 2(x + 3) = 12$ **(ii)** $\dfrac{x-1}{4} - \dfrac{1}{20} = \dfrac{2x-3}{5}$

Solution:

(i)

$$4(x + 5) - 2(x + 3) = 12$$

$4x + 20 - 2x - 6 = 12$ (remove brackets)

$2x + 14 = 12$ (simplify the left-hand side)

$2x = -2$ (subtract 14 from both sides)

$x = -1$ (divide both sides by 2)

(ii) The LCM of 4, 5 and 20 is 20. Therefore we multiply each part by 20.

$\dfrac{(x-1)}{4} - \dfrac{(1)}{20} = \dfrac{(2x-3)}{5}$ (put brackets on top)

$\dfrac{20(x-1)}{4} - \dfrac{20(1)}{20} = \dfrac{20(2x-3)}{5}$ (multiply each part by 20)

$5(x - 1) - 1 = 4(2x - 3)$ (divide the bottom into the top)

$5x - 5 - 1 = 8x - 12$ (remove the brackets)

$5x - 6 = 8x - 12$ (simplify the left-hand side)

$5x = 8x - 6$ (add 6 to both sides)

$-3x = -6$ (subtract $8x$ from both sides)

$3x = 6$ (multiply both sides by -1)

$x = 2$ (divide both sides by 3)

Exercise 4.3 ▼

Solve each of the following equations:

1. $7x - 5 = 16$ **2.** $2x - 5 = 1 - x$

3. $5(x + 4) - 3(x - 4) = 40$ **4.** $10(x + 4) = 3(2x + 5) + 1$

5. $2(7 + x) - 4(x + 3) = 15(x - 1)$ **6.** $2 - 6(2 - x) = 5(x + 3) - 23$

7. $5 + 2(x - 1) = x + 4(x - 3)$ **8.** $11 - 2(2x - 5) = 5(2x + 1) - 4(3x - 1)$

9. $\dfrac{x}{2} + \dfrac{x}{3} = \dfrac{5}{6}$ **10.** $\dfrac{3x}{4} = \dfrac{2x}{3} + \dfrac{5}{12}$

11. $\dfrac{x+2}{3} + \dfrac{x+5}{4} = \dfrac{5}{2}$ **12.** $\dfrac{x-1}{5} = \dfrac{17}{5} - \dfrac{x+3}{2}$

13. $\dfrac{x}{5} - \dfrac{11}{15} = \dfrac{x-3}{6}$ **14.** $\dfrac{3x-1}{2} = \dfrac{x}{4} + \dfrac{9}{2}$

15. $\dfrac{x-2}{6} + \dfrac{3x-7}{5} = \dfrac{x}{3}$

16. $\dfrac{x-1}{3} + \dfrac{x-3}{4} = x - 4$

17. $\dfrac{2x+3}{5} - \dfrac{x+3}{4} = \dfrac{x+1}{20}$

18. $\dfrac{x+5}{4} - 2 = \dfrac{x-3}{7}$

19. $\frac{1}{3}(4x+1) - \frac{1}{2}(2x+1) - 2 = 0$

20. $\frac{5}{6}(3x-4) - \frac{3}{2}(4x+2) = \frac{2}{3}$

Single Variable Linear Inequalities

The four inequality symbols:

1. $>$ means 'greater than'

2. $\geqslant$ means 'greater than or equal to'

3. $<$ means 'less than'

4. $\leqslant$ means 'less than or equal to'

Algebraic expressions that are linked by one of the four inequality symbols are called **'inequalities'**.
For example, $3x - 1 \leqslant 11$ and $-3 < 2x - 1 \leqslant 7$ are inequalities.

Solving inequalities is exactly the same as solving equations, with the following exception:

Multiplying or dividing both sides of an inequality by a **negative** number **reverses** the direction of the inequality.

That is:

$>$ changes to $<$ $\geqslant$ changes to $\leqslant$

$<$ changes to $>$ $\leqslant$ changes to $\geqslant$

For example, $4 > -7$ is true. If we multiply both sides by -1, it gives $-4 > 7$, which is **not** true.
Thus, $-4 < 7$ is true; multiplying both sides by -1 and reversing the direction of the inequality keeps the inequality true.

Solving an inequality means finding the values of x that make the inequality true.

The following rules apply to graphing inequalities on a number line:

Number line for $x \in \mathbf{N}$ or $x \in \mathbf{Z}$, use dots.

Number line for $x \in \mathbf{R}$, use a 'full' heavy line.

Example ▼

Find the solution set of $10 - 3x \geqslant 4$, $x \in \mathbf{N}$.
Graph your solution on the number line.

Solution:

$$10 - 3x \geqslant 4$$
$$-3x \geqslant -6 \qquad \text{(subtract 10 from both sides)}$$
$$3x \leqslant 6 \qquad \text{(multiply both sides by } -1 \text{ and reverse the inequality)}$$
$$x \leqslant 2 \qquad \text{(divide both sides by 3)}$$

This is the set of natural numbers less than or equal to 2.
Therefore, the values are 0, 1, 2.

Number line:

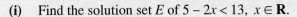

Example ▼

(i) Find the solution set E of $5 - 2x < 13$, $x \in \mathbf{R}$.

(ii) Find the solution set H of $\dfrac{2x}{5} + \dfrac{x}{3} \leqslant \dfrac{22}{15}$, $x \in \mathbf{R}$.

(iii) Find $E \cap H$ and graph your solution on the number line.

Solution:

We solve each inequality separately and then combine their solutions.

(i)
$$5 - 2x < 13$$
$$-2x < 8$$
$$2x > -8$$
$$x > -4$$

(ii)
$$\frac{2x}{5} + \frac{x}{3} \leqslant \frac{22}{15}$$
$$15\left(\frac{2x}{5}\right) + 15\left(\frac{x}{3}\right) \leqslant 15\left(\frac{22}{15}\right)$$
$$6x + 5x \leqslant 22$$
$$11x \leqslant 22$$
$$x \leqslant 2$$

(iii) Combining the two inequalities:

$$E \cap H\colon -4 < x \leqslant -2$$

Number line:

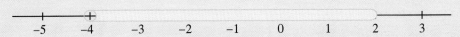

A circle is put around −4 to indicate that −4 is **not** part of the solution.

Solve each of the following inequalities, and in each case graph your solution on the number line:

1. $2x + 1 \geqslant 7$, $\quad x \in \mathbf{R}$.

2. $3x + 1 \leqslant 4$, $\quad x \in \mathbf{R}$.

3. $5x - 7 \geqslant 3x + 1$, $\quad x \in \mathbf{N}$.

4. $2x - 1 \geqslant 4x - 7$, $\quad x \in \mathbf{N}$.

5. $2(x + 4) < 2 - x$, $\quad x \in \mathbf{R}$.

6. $9(x + 1) \geqslant 1 + 2(5x + 6)$, $\quad x \in \mathbf{Z}$.

7. $3(x - 4) > 5(2x - 3) + 17$, $\quad x \in \mathbf{R}$.

8. $5(3x + 2) < 3(3x + 2) + 16$, $\quad x \in \mathbf{R}$.

9. $\dfrac{x + 2}{4} - \dfrac{x - 2}{2} < 3$, $\quad x \in \mathbf{R}$.

10. $\frac{2}{5}(x - 1) - \frac{3}{2}(1 - x) \leqslant \frac{19}{10}$, $\quad x \in \mathbf{N}$.

11. Find the solution set of: **(i)** $A: x + 2 \leqslant 5$, $\quad x \in \mathbf{R}$ **(ii)** $B: x + 3 \geqslant 1$, $\quad x \in \mathbf{R}$.
    Find $A \cap B$ and graph your solution on the number line.

12. Find the solution set of: **(i)** $H: 2x - 3 \leqslant 5$, $\quad x \in \mathbf{R}$. **(ii)** $K: 3x + 2 \geqslant -1$, $\quad x \in \mathbf{R}$.
    Find $H \cap K$ and graph your solution on the number line.

13. **(i)** Find the solution set P of $4x - 1 < 3$, $\quad x \in \mathbf{R}$.
    (ii) Find the solution set Q of $5 - x \leqslant 8$, $\quad x \in \mathbf{R}$.
    (iii) Find $P \cap Q$ and graph your solution on the number line.

14. **(i)** Find the solution set G of $3x - 1 \leqslant 9 - 2x$, $\quad x \in \mathbf{R}$.
    (ii) Find the solution set H of $1 - 3x \leqslant 8 - x$, $\quad x \in \mathbf{R}$.
    (iii) Find $G \cap H$ and graph your solution on the number line.

15. **(i)** Find the solution set M of $4 - x \leqslant 6$, $\quad x \in \mathbf{R}$.
    (ii) Find the solution set N of $3x - 1 \leqslant x + 9$, $\quad x \in \mathbf{R}$.
    (iii) If $M \cap N = a \leqslant x \leqslant b$, write down the value of a and the value of b.

16. Find the solution set H of $9 - 2x \geqslant 7$, $\quad x \in \mathbf{N}$.
    Find the solution set K of $3x - 4 \leqslant 5$, $\quad x \in \mathbf{N}$.
    Write down the elements of the set $K \setminus H$.

17. The solution of the inequality $11 - 2x \geqslant 3$, $\quad x \in \mathbf{N}$, is given as $\{a, b, c, d, e\}$.
    Write down the values of a, b, c, d and e where $a < b < c < d < e$.

    Hence, evaluate $\sqrt{\dfrac{b}{0.c} + de - 1}$

Simultaneous Linear Equations

Simultaneous linear equations in two variables are solved with the following steps:

1. Write both equations in the form $ax + by = k$ and label the equations ① and ②.
2. Multiply one or both of the equations by a number in order to make the coefficients of x or y the same, but of opposite sign.
3. Add to remove the variable with equal coefficients but of opposite sign.
4. Solve the resultant equation to find the value of the remaining unknown (x or y).
5. Substitute this value in equation ① or ② to find the value of the other unknown.

Example ▼

Solve for x and y: $\quad 2x + 3y - 8 = 0 \quad$ and $\quad \dfrac{3x}{2} + y - 1 = 0$

Solution:

First write both equations in the form $ax + by = k$ and label the equations ① and ②.

$2x + 3y - 8 = 0$

$\qquad 2x + 3y = 8 \qquad$ ① $\quad$ (in the form $ax + by = k$: label the equation ①)

$\dfrac{3x}{2} + y - 1 = 0$

$\qquad 3x + 2y - 2 = 0 \qquad$ (multiply each part by 2)

$\qquad\quad 3x + 2y = 2 \qquad$ ② $\quad$ (in the form $ax + by = k$: label the equation ②)

Now solve between equations ① and ②:

$2x + 3y = 8$ $\qquad$ ①	Put $x = -2$ into ① or ②:
$3x + 2y = 2$ $\qquad$ ②	$2x + 3y = 8 \qquad$ ①
$\overline{4x + 6y = 16} \qquad$ ① × 2	
$-9x - 6y = -6 \qquad$ ② × −3	$2(-2) + 3y = 8$
$\overline{\quad -5x = 10} \qquad$ (add)	$-4 + 3y = 8$
$5x = -10$	$3y = 12$
$x = -2$	$y = 4$

$\therefore$ the solution is $x = -2$ and $y = 4$.

Solution containing fractions

If the solution contains fractions the substitution can be difficult.
In such cases the following method is useful:

> **1.** Eliminate y and find x.
>
> **2.** Eliminate x and find y.

Example ▼

Solve the simultaneous equations $2x + 3y = -2$ and $3x + 7y = -6$.

Solution:

Both equations are in the form $ax + by = k$. Number the equations ① and ②.

1. Eliminate y and find x.

$2x + 3y = -2$	①
$3x + 7y = -6$	②
$14x + 21y = -14$	① × 7
$-9x - 21y = 18$	② × -3
$5x = 4$	(add)
$x = \frac{4}{5}$	

2. Eliminate x and find y.

$2x + 3y = -2$	①
$3x + 7y = -6$	②
$6x + 9y = -6$	① × 3
$-6x - 14y = 12$	② × -2
$-5y = 6$	(add)
$5y = -6$	
$y = -\frac{6}{5}$	

Therefore, the solution is $x = \frac{4}{5}$ and $y = -\frac{6}{5}$.

Note: This method can also be used if the solution does not contain fractions.

Exercise 4.5 ▼

Solve for x and y:

1. $3x + 2y = 8$
   $2x - y = 3$

2. $5x - 3y = 14$
   $2x + y = 10$

3. $2x + y = 13$
   $x + 2y = 11$

4. $x + y = 7$
   $2x + y = 12$

5. $4x - 3y = 1$
   $3x + 5y = -21$

6. $2x + y = 7$
   $3x - 2y = 0$

7. $x + y = 10$
   $x - y = 4$

8. $2x - 5y = 11$
   $3x + 2y = 7$

9. $2x + 3y = 12$
   $x + y = 5$

10. $2x - y = -3$
   $x - 2y = -3$

11. $2x - 3y - 14 = 0$
   $3x + 4y + 13 = 0$

12. $x - 4y - 3 = 0$
   $3x - y + 2 = 0$

13. $x - 2y = 0$
   $2(x + 3) = 3y + 5$

14. $5x + y = 19$
   $2x - y = 2(y - x)$

15. $3(x + y) + 2(y - x) = 4$
   $2(x - 2) = 3(y - 3)$

16. $3x + y = 9$

$\dfrac{x}{2} - y = -2$

17. $2x - 5y = 19$

$\dfrac{3x}{2} + \dfrac{4y}{3} = -1$

18. $3x - 4y = -3$

$\dfrac{x}{2} + \dfrac{y}{3} = \dfrac{5}{2}$

19. $2x + 7y = 3$

$x + y = \dfrac{x - 2y + 1}{2}$

20. $2(x - 5) = 3y$

$\dfrac{2x + 1}{5} + \dfrac{x + y}{2} = 1$

21. $3x - 2y = y - 6x$

$\dfrac{5x - 3y + 2}{2} = \dfrac{x - 2y + 4}{3}$

In questions 22 to 27, the solutions contain fractions:

22. $7x - 3y = 6$
$3x - 6y = 1$

23. $5x + y = 10$
$3x - y = 2$

24. $4x - 3y = 6$
$2x + 6y = 13$

25. $2x + y = 2$
$5x + 10y = 11$

26. $2x + 3y = 8$
$2x - 3y = 2$

27. $x - y = 1$
$3x + 5y = 7$

Factors Required to Solve Quadratic Equations

There are three types of quadratic expression we have to factorise to solve quadratic equations:

	Type	Example	Factors
1.	Quadratic trinomials	$2x^2 - 7x + 3$	$(2x - 1)(x - 3)$
2.	Taking out the HCF	$2x^2 - 5x$	$x(2x - 5)$
3.	Difference of two squares	$x^2 - 25$	$(x - 5)(x + 5)$

1. Quadratic trinomials:

Factorising quadratic trinomials
Quadratic trinomials can be broken up into **two** types:

1. Final term positive

When the final term is positive, the signs inside the middle of the brackets will be the **same**, either two pluses or two minuses. Keep the sign of the middle term given in the question.

Middle term plus: (number x + number)(number x + number)   (two pluses)

Middle term minus: (number x – number)(number x – number)   (two minuses)

2. Final term negative

When the final term is negative, the signs inside the middle of the brackets will be **different**.

(number x + number)(number x – number)   (different signs)

or

(number x – number)(number x + number)   (different signs)

In both cases the factors can be found by trial and improvement. The test is to multiply the inside terms, multiply the outside terms, and add the results to see if you get the middle term of the original quadratic trinomial.

Example ▼

Factorise fully each of the following:

(i) $2x^2 - 11x + 5$ **(ii)** $8x^2 + 2x - 15$

Solution:

(i) $2x^2 - 11x + 5$
The factors of $2x^2$ are $2x$ and x.
Final term + and middle term −,
∴ the factors are $(2x - \text{number})(x - \text{number})$

Factors of 5
1×5

1. $(2x - 5)(x - 1)$ middle term $= -5x - 2x = -7x$ (no)

2. $(2x - 1)(x - 5)$ middle term $= -x - 10x = -11x$ (yes)

$$\therefore \quad 2x^2 - 11x + 5 = (2x - 1)(x - 5)$$

(ii) $8x^2 + 2x - 15$.
The factors of $8x^2$ are $8x$ and x or $4x$ and $2x$,
∴   the factors are:

$(8x + \text{number})(x - \text{number})$ or $(4x + \text{number})(2x - \text{number})$
Note: The signs inside these brackets could be swapped.

Factors of 15
11×5
3×5

1. $(8x + 3)(x - 5)$ middle term $= 3x - 40x = -37x$ (no)

2. $(8x + 5)(x - 3)$ middle term $= 5x - 24x = -19x$ (no)

3. $(4x + 3)(2x - 5)$ middle term $= 6x - 20x = -14x$ (no)

4. $(4x + 5)(2x - 3)$ middle term $= 10x - 12x = -2x$ (no, wrong sign)

The fourth attempt has the wrong sign of the coefficient of the middle term.
Therefore all that is needed is to swap the signs in the middle of the brackets.

5. $(4x - 5)(2x + 3)$ middle term $= -10x + 12x = 2x$ (yes)

$$\therefore \quad 8x^2 + 2x - 15 = (4x - 5)(2x + 3)$$

2. Taking out the highest common factor (HCF):

Example ▼

Factorise: **(i)** $x^2 - 3x$ **(ii)** $2x^2 + x$

Solution:

(i) $x^2 - 3x$
   $= x(x - 3)$ (take out the highest common factor x)

(ii) $2x^2 + x$
   $= x(2x + 1)$ (take out the highest common factor x)

3. Difference of two squares:

We factorise the difference of two squares with the following steps:

> 1. Write each term as a perfect square with brackets.
> 2. Use the rule $a^2 - b^2 = (a - b)(a + b)$.
>   In words: $(\text{first})^2 - (\text{second})^2 = (\text{first} - \text{second})(\text{first} + \text{second})$.

Example ▼

Factorise: **(i)** $x^2 - 16$ **(ii)** $9x^2 - 25$

Solution:

(i) $x^2 - 16$
   $= (x)^2 - (4)^2$ [write each term as a perfect square in brackets]
   $= (x - 4)(x + 4)$ [apply the rule, (first − second)(first + second)]

(ii) $9x^2 - 25$
   $= (3x)^2 - (5)^2$ [write each term as a perfect square in brackets]
   $= (3x - 5)(3x + 5)$ [apply the rule, (first − second)(first + second)]

Exercise 4.6 ▼

Factorise each of the following quadratic trinomials:

1. $2x^2 + 5x + 3$

2. $3x^2 + 8x - 3$

3. $2x^2 - 7x + 6$

4. $3x^2 - 4x - 7$

5. $2x^2 - 9x - 5$

6. $5x^2 + 9x - 2$

7. $2x^2 + 7x - 15$

8. $3x^2 - 11x - 20$

9. $7x^2 + 5x - 2$

10. $x^2 - 7x + 12$ **11.** $x^2 - 2x - 15$ **12.** $x^2 - 10x + 21$

13. $3x^2 + 11x + 6$ **14.** $2x^2 + 11x + 14$ **15.** $3x^2 - x - 2$

16. $2x^2 + x - 6$ **17.** $3x^2 + 10x - 8$ **18.** $5x^2 - 21x + 4$

19. $4x^2 + 8x + 3$ **20.** $4x^2 - 11x - 3$ **21.** $6x^2 - x - 2$

22. $6x^2 - 13x + 2$ **23.** $8x^2 + 6x - 5$ **24.** $10x^2 - x - 3$

Factorise each of the following by taking out the highest common factor:

25. $x^2 + 2x$ **26.** $x^2 - 4x$ **27.** $x^2 + 5x$

28. $x^2 - 7x$ **29.** $x^2 + x$ **30.** $x^2 - x$

31. $2x^2 - x$ **32.** $2x^2 - 3x$ **33.** $3x^2 + 5x$

Factorise each of the following using the difference of two squares:

34. $x^2 - 9$ **35.** $x^2 - 4$ **36.** $x^2 - 1$

37. $x^2 - 49$ **38.** $x^2 - 100$ **39.** $x^2 - 36$

40. $4x^2 - 9$ **41.** $25x^2 - 36$ **42.** $9x^2 - 4$

43. $16x^2 - 25$ **44.** $4x^2 - 1$ **45.** $9x^2 - 1$

Quadratic Equations

> A quadratic equation is an equation in the form:
>
> $$ax^2 + bx + c = 0$$
>
> where a, b and c are constants, but $a \neq 0$.

Solving a quadratic equation means 'finding the two values of the variable which satisfy the equation'. These values are called the **roots** of the equation. Sometimes the two roots are the same.

There are three types of quadratic equation we will meet on our course:

> **1.** $3x^2 - 13x - 10 = 0$ (three terms)
> **2.** $2x^2 + 3x = 0$ (no constant term)
> **3.** $9x^2 - 16 = 0$ (no x term)

Quadratic equations are solved with the following steps:

Method 1:

> **1.** Bring every term to the left-hand side.
>   (If necessary multiply both sides by -1 to make the coefficient of x^2 positive.)
> **2.** Factorise the left-hand side.
> **3.** Let each factor $= 0$.
> **4.** Solve each simple equation.

Method 2:

The roots of the quadratic equation $ax^2 + bx + c = 0$ are given by the formula:

$$x = \frac{-b \pm \sqrt{b^2 - 4ac}}{2a}$$

Notes: **1.** The whole of the top of the right-hand side, including $-b$, is divided by $2a$.

2. It is often called the '$-b$' or 'quadratic' formula.

3. Before using the formula, make sure every term is on the left-hand side, i.e. write the equation in the form $ax^2 + bx + c = 0$.

Note: If $\sqrt{b^2 - 4ac}$ is a whole number, then $ax^2 + bx + c$ can be factorised.
The formula can still be used even if $ax^2 + bx + c$ can be factorised.

Type 1

Example ▼

Solve for x: $5x + 12 = 3x^2$

Solution:

Method 1:

$$5x + 12 = 3x^2$$
$$-3x^2 + 5x + 12 = 0 \qquad \text{(every term is on the left-hand side)}$$
$$3x^2 - 5x - 12 = 0 \qquad \text{(multiply each term by } -1\text{)}$$
$$(3x + 4)(x - 3) = 0 \qquad \text{(factorise the left-hand side)}$$
$$3x + 4 = 0 \qquad \text{or} \qquad x - 3 = 0 \qquad \text{(let each factor = 0)}$$
$$3x = -4 \qquad \text{or} \qquad x = 3$$
$$x = -\tfrac{4}{3} \qquad \text{or} \qquad x = 3 \qquad \text{(solve each simple equation)}$$

Method 2:

Use the formula: $x = \dfrac{-b \pm \sqrt{b^2 - 4ac}}{2a}$

$$5x + 12 = 3x^2$$
$$-3x^2 + 5x + 12 = 0 \qquad \text{(every term is on the left-hand side)}$$
$$3x^2 - 5x - 12 = 0 \qquad \text{(multiply each term by } -1\text{)}$$
$$a = 3, \qquad b = -5, \qquad c = -12$$

$$x = \frac{-b \pm \sqrt{b^2 - 4ac}}{2a}$$

$$x = \frac{5 \pm \sqrt{(-5)^2 - 4(3)(-12)}}{2(3)}$$

$$x = \frac{5 \pm \sqrt{25 + 144}}{6}$$

89

$$x = \frac{5 \pm \sqrt{169}}{6}$$

$$x = \frac{5 + 13}{6}$$

$$x = \frac{5 + 13}{6} \quad \text{or} \quad x = \frac{5 - 13}{6}$$

$$x = \frac{18}{6} \quad \text{or} \quad x = -\frac{8}{6}$$

$$x = 3 \quad \text{or} \quad x = -\frac{4}{3}$$

Type 2

Example ▼

Solve for x: $2x^2 + 5x = 0$

Solution:

$2x^2 + 5x = 0$		(every term is on the left-hand side)
$x(2x + 5) = 0$		(factorise the left-hand side)
$x = 0$ or $2x + 5 = 0$		(let each factor = 0)
$x = 0$ or $2x = -5$		
$x = 0$ or $x = -\frac{5}{2}$		(solve each simple equation)

Note: It is important **not** to divide both sides by x, otherwise the root $x = 0$ is lost.

Type 3

Example ▼

Solve for x: $x^2 - 1 = 0$

Solution:

We will use two methods to solve this quadratic equation.

Method 1:

$x^2 - 1 = 0$		(every term is on the left-hand side)
$(x)^2 - (1)^2 = 0$		(difference of two squares)
$(x - 1)(x + 1) = 0$		(factorise the left-hand side)
$x - 1 = 0$ or $x + 1 = 0$		(let each factor = 0)
$x = 1$ or $x = -1$		(solve each simple equation)

Method 2:
$$x^2 - 1 = 0$$
$$x^2 = 1 \qquad \text{(add 1 to both sides)}$$
$$x = \pm \sqrt{1} \qquad \text{(take the square root of both sides)}$$
$$x = \pm 1$$
$$x = 1 \quad \text{or} \quad x = -1$$

Note: The examples of type 2 and type 3 could have been solved using the formula.

Exercise 4.7 ▼

Solve each of the following equations:

1. $(x - 2)(x + 5) = 0$
2. $(3x + 2)(x - 7) = 0$
3. $x(x - 6) = 0$
4. $x(3x - 2) = 0$
5. $(x - 2)(x + 2) = 0$
6. $(3x - 5)(3x + 5) = 0$
7. $2x^2 - 11x + 5 = 0$
8. $3x^2 + 2x - 5 = 0$
9. $5x^2 + 4x - 1 = 0$
10. $2x^2 - x - 3 = 0$
11. $5x^2 + 3x - 2 = 0$
12. $3x^2 - x - 10 = 0$
13. $5x^2 - 17x + 6 = 0$
14. $x^2 + 2x - 15 = 0$
15. $x^2 - 6x - 27 = 0$
16. $x^2 - 3x = 0$
17. $x^2 + 2x = 0$
18. $x^2 - 5x = 0$
19. $x^2 + 7x = 0$
20. $2x^2 - 3x = 0$
21. $3x^2 + 4x = 0$
22. $x^2 - 4 = 0$
23. $x^2 - 25 = 0$
24. $x^2 - 36 = 0$
25. $4x^2 - 9 = 0$
26. $9x^2 - 16 = 0$
27. $4x^2 - 1 = 0$
28. $4x^2 - 11x - 3 = 0$
29. $4x^2 - 12x + 5 = 0$
30. $6x^2 + x - 2 = 0$
31. $6x^2 + 13x - 5 = 0$
32. $8x^2 - 14x + 3 = 0$
33. $9x^2 - 12x + 4 = 0$

34. Simplify $(2x - 1)(x + 1) - 2(x + 7)$ and factorise the simplified expression.
    Hence, solve $(2x - 1)(x + 1) - 2(x + 7) = 0$.

Solve each of the following equations:

35. $x(2x + 7) + 6 = 0$
36. $(x + 3)(x + 5) = 3 + x$
37. $(x - 1)^2 - 4 = 0$

Addition and Subtraction of Algebraic Fractions

Algebraic fractions can be added or subtracted in exactly the same way as in arithmetic, i.e., we express the fractions using the lowest common denominator.

Algebraic fractions are added or subtracted with the following steps:

1. Put brackets in where necessary.
2. Find the LCM of the expressions on the bottom.
3. Proceed in exactly the same way as in arithmetic.
4. Simplify the top (add and subtract terms which are the same).

Note: If a part of the expression is not a fraction, it can be changed into fraction form by putting it over 1.

For example, $\quad 7 = \dfrac{7}{1}, \qquad 3x = \dfrac{3x}{1}, \qquad 2x - 5 = \dfrac{2x - 5}{1}.$

Example ▼

Write $\dfrac{1}{x} - \dfrac{2}{x+1} + \dfrac{1}{3}$ as a single fraction.

Solution:

$$\dfrac{1}{x} - \dfrac{2}{(x+1)} + \dfrac{1}{3} \qquad \text{(put brackets on } x+1\text{)}$$
$$\text{(the LCM is } 3x(x+1)\text{)}$$

$$= \dfrac{3(x+1) - 3x(2) + x(x+1)}{3x(x+1)} \qquad \text{(do the same as in arithmetic)}$$

$$= \dfrac{3x + 3 - 6x + x^2 + x}{3x(x+1)} \qquad \text{(remove the brackets on top)}$$

$$= \dfrac{x^2 - 2x + 3}{3x(x+1)} \qquad \text{(simplify the top)}$$

Note: It is common practice **not** to multiply out the expression on the bottom.

Exercise 4.8 ▼

Express each of the following as a single fraction:

1. $\dfrac{3x}{2} + \dfrac{4x}{3}$

2. $\dfrac{5x}{4} - \dfrac{2x}{3}$

3. $\dfrac{2x+3}{5} - \dfrac{x+1}{4}$

4. $\dfrac{2}{x} + \dfrac{4}{3x}$

5. $\dfrac{6}{5x} - \dfrac{3}{4x}$

6. $\dfrac{2}{3x} + \dfrac{5}{2x} + \dfrac{1}{4}$

7. $\dfrac{2}{x+2} + \dfrac{3}{x+1}$

8. $\dfrac{3}{x+3} + \dfrac{2}{x+5}$

9. $\dfrac{1}{x-4} + \dfrac{2}{x+2}$

10. $\dfrac{1}{3x+4} + \dfrac{2}{2x+1}$

11. $\dfrac{5}{2x-1} + \dfrac{4}{2x+1}$

12. $\dfrac{2}{3x-2} + \dfrac{3}{2x+5}$

13. $\dfrac{4}{3x-1} - \dfrac{3}{2x}$

14. $\dfrac{3}{2x-5} - \dfrac{4}{x-3}$

15. $\dfrac{5}{3x-1} - \dfrac{3}{2x+1}$

16. $\dfrac{1}{x} + \dfrac{1}{x+4} + \dfrac{1}{4}$

17. $\dfrac{3}{x} + \dfrac{2}{x+1} + \dfrac{5}{2}$

18. $\dfrac{5}{x} - \dfrac{3}{x-2} + 4$

19. $\dfrac{3}{x+1} + \dfrac{4}{x-2} = \dfrac{px+q}{(x+1)(x-2)}$. Write down the value of p and the value of q.

Quadratic Equations in Fractional Form

Quadratic equations in fractional form are solved with the following steps:

> **1.** Multiply each part of the equation by the LCM of the expressions on the bottom.
> **2.** Simplify both sides (no fractions left).
> **3.** Proceed as in the previous section on solving quadratic equations.

Example ▼

Solve for x: $5 + \dfrac{4}{x-2} = \dfrac{8}{x+4}$, $x \neq 2, -4$.

Solution:

Multiply each by the LCM of the expressions on the bottom.

$$5 + \frac{4}{(x-2)} = \frac{8}{(x+4)}$$ [put brackets on $x-2$ and $x+4$]

$$5(x-2)(x+4) + (x-2)(x+4)\,\frac{4}{(x-2)} = (x-2)(x+4)\,\frac{8}{(x+4)}$$ [the LCM is $(x-2)(x+4)$]

[multiply each part by $(x-2)(x+4)$]

$$5(x-2)(x+4) + 4(x+4) = 8(x-2)$$ [simplify both sides]

$$5(x^2 + 2x - 8) + 4(x+4) = 8(x-2)$$ [multiply out $(x-2)(x+4)$]

$$5x^2 + 10x - 40 + 4x + 16 = 8x - 16$$ [remove the brackets]

$$5x^2 + 14x - 24 = 8x - 16$$ [simplify the left-hand side]

$$5x^2 + 6x - 8 = 0$$ [every term on the left-hand side]

$$(5x - 4)(x + 2) = 0$$ [factorise the left-hand side]

$$5x - 4 = 0 \quad \text{or} \quad x + 2 = 0$$ [let each factor $= 0$]

$$5x = 4 \quad \text{or} \quad x = -2$$

$$x = \tfrac{4}{5} \quad \text{or} \quad x = -2$$ [solve each simple equation]

Exercise 4.9 ▼

Solve each of the following equations:

1. $1 - \dfrac{6}{x} + \dfrac{8}{x^2} = 0$

2. $1 + \dfrac{5}{x} + \dfrac{6}{x^2} = 0$

3. $x = 2 + \dfrac{15}{x}$

4. $x = \dfrac{2}{x} + 1$

5. $x = 3 + \dfrac{x+5}{x}$

6. $x + \dfrac{2x}{2x-1} = 3$

7. $1 - \dfrac{x}{5} = \dfrac{1}{x+1}$

8. $\dfrac{3}{x} + \dfrac{5}{x+3} = 2$

9. $\dfrac{1}{20} = \dfrac{1}{x} - \dfrac{1}{x+1}$

10. $2 + \dfrac{3}{x+2} - \dfrac{5}{x-2} = 0$

11. $3 = \dfrac{1}{x} - \dfrac{2}{x-2}$

12. $1 + \dfrac{2}{x+1} = \dfrac{3}{x-1}$

13. $6 + \dfrac{4}{x-1} + \dfrac{5}{x+2} = 0$

14. $\dfrac{1}{2} = \dfrac{2}{x-1} - \dfrac{1}{x+2}$

15. $1 + \dfrac{5}{2x-1} = \dfrac{6}{x}$

16. $3 + \dfrac{5}{x+1} = \dfrac{4}{x-3}$

17. $\dfrac{3}{x-2} - \dfrac{1}{x} - \dfrac{5}{4} = 0$

18. $\dfrac{4}{x-1} - \dfrac{3}{x} = \dfrac{5}{x+2}$

19. $\dfrac{x+2}{4} = \dfrac{3}{x-5} + \dfrac{3}{2}$

20. $\dfrac{1}{x} + 1 = \dfrac{3x+3}{x-1}$

21. $\dfrac{x+5}{x} + \dfrac{6}{x+1} = 3$

Quadratic Formula

In many quadratic equations $ax^2 + bc + c$ cannot be resolved into factors. When this happens the formula **must** be used. To save time trying to look for factors, a clue that you must use the formula is often given in the question. When the question requires an approximate answer, e.g., 'correct to two decimal places', 'correct to three significant figures', 'correct to the nearest integer', or 'express your answer in surd form', then the formula must be used.

The roots of the quadratic equation $ax^2 + bx + c = 0$, are given by the formula:

$$x = \frac{-b \pm \sqrt{b^2 - 4ac}}{2a}$$

Notes: 1. The whole of the top of the right-hand side, including $-b$, is divided by $2a$.

2. It is often called the '$-b$' or 'quadratic' formula.

3. Before using the formula, make sure every term is on the left-hand side, i.e. write the equation in the form $ax^2 + bx + c = 0$.

Example ▼

Solve the equation, $5x^2 + 7x - 4 = 0$, giving your solutions correct to two decimal places.

Solution:

$5x^2 + 7x - 4 = 0$ (two decimal places ∴ use formula)

$a = 5,$ $b = 7,$ $c = -4$

$$x = \frac{-b \pm \sqrt{b^2 - 4ac}}{2a}$$

$$x = \frac{-7 \pm \sqrt{(7)^2 - 4(5)(-4)}}{2(5)}$$

$$x = \frac{-7 \pm \sqrt{49 + 80}}{10}$$

$$x = \frac{-7 \pm \sqrt{129}}{10}$$

$$x = \frac{-7 \pm 11.3578}{10} \qquad (\sqrt{129} = 11.3578, \text{ correct to four decimal places})$$

$$x = \frac{-7 + 11.3578}{10} \quad \text{or} \quad x = \frac{-7 - 11.3578}{10}$$

$$x = \frac{4.3578}{10} \quad \text{or} \quad x = \frac{-18.3578}{10}$$

$$x = 0.43578 \quad \text{or} \quad x = -1.83578$$

$$\therefore \quad x = 0.44 \quad \text{or} \quad x = -1.84, \text{ correct to two decimal places.}$$

Exercise 4.10 ▼

In questions 1 to 6, solve the equations **(i)** by resolving into factors **(ii)** by formula:

1. $x^2 - 2x - 8 = 0$

2. $x^2 - 7x + 12 = 0$

3. $2x^2 + 3x - 2 = 0$

4. $5x^2 - 7x - 6 = 0$

5. $3x^2 + 5x - 12 = 0$

6. $3x^2 + 10x - 8 = 0$

Solve, correct to two places of decimals, each of the following equations:

7. $2x^2 - 3x - 8 = 0$

8. $5x^2 + 6x - 3 = 0$

9. $x^2 + 7x - 4 = 0$

10. $3x^2 - 7x - 1 = 0$

11. $4x^2 + x - 1 = 0$

12. $3x^2 + 5x + 1 = 0$

13. $3x^2 - x - 1 = 0$

14. $4x^2 - 5x - 3 = 0$

15. $2x^2 - x - 5 = 0$

16. $5x^2 + 8x + 2 = 0$

17. $3x^2 + 10x + 4 = 0$

18. $3x^2 - 6x + 2 = 0$

Express each of the following equations in the form $ax^2 + bx + c = 0$ and, hence, solve each equation, giving your solutions correct to one place of decimals.

19. $x^2 + \dfrac{x}{2} = \dfrac{5}{2}$

20. $x + \dfrac{1}{x} = 3$

21. $2 + \dfrac{3}{x} = \dfrac{8}{x^2}$

22. $4 = \dfrac{1}{x+1} + \dfrac{2}{x}$

23. $2 + \dfrac{1}{x} = \dfrac{12}{x+2}$

24. $\dfrac{1}{x+2} - \dfrac{1}{x} = 3$

25. $\dfrac{1}{x-1} + \dfrac{2}{x} = \dfrac{1}{2}$

26. $\dfrac{5}{2x-1} - \dfrac{2}{x} = \dfrac{1}{9}$

27. $\dfrac{1}{x} + \dfrac{1}{x+1} = \dfrac{2}{3}$

28. (i) Write $\dfrac{1}{x+1} + \dfrac{2}{x-3}$ as a single fraction.

(ii) Hence, or otherwise, find, correct to one place of decimals, the two solutions of:

$$\frac{1}{x+1} + \frac{2}{x-3} = 1$$

Simultaneous Equations, One Linear and One Quadratic

The **method of substitution** is used to solve between a linear equation and a quadratic equation.

The method involves three steps:

> 1. From the linear equation, express one variable in terms of the other.
> 2. Substitute this into the quadratic equation and solve.
> 3. Substitute separately the value(s) obtained in step 2 into the linear equation in step 1 to find the corresponding value(s) of the other variable.

Example ▼

Solve the simultaneous equations $2x - y - 1 = 0$ and $xy = 6$.

Solution:

$$2x - y - 1 = 0 \text{ and } xy = 6.$$

1. $2x - y - 1 = 0$ (get y on its own)

$$-y = -2x + 1$$
$$y = 2x - 1$$

2. $xy = 6$

$$x(2x - 1) = 6$$ (put in $(2x - 1)$ for y)
$$2x^2 - x = 6$$
$$2x^2 - x - 6 = 0$$ (everything to the left)
$$(2x + 3)(x - 2) = 0$$ (factorise the left-hand side)
$$2x + 3 = 0 \quad \text{or} \quad x - 2 = 0$$ (let each factor = 0)
$$2x = -3 \quad \text{or} \quad x = 2$$
$$x = -\tfrac{3}{2} \quad \text{or} \quad x = 2$$

3.   Substitute separately, $x = -\tfrac{3}{2}$ and $x = 2$ into the linear equation.

$x = -\tfrac{3}{2}$	$x = 2$
$y = 2x - 1$	$y = 2x - 1$
$y = 2(-\tfrac{3}{2}) - 1$	$y = 2(2) - 1$
$y = -3 - 1$	$y = 4 - 1$
$y = -4$	$y = 3$
$x = -\tfrac{3}{2}, y = -4$	$x = 2, y = 3$

∴   the solutions are $x = -\tfrac{3}{2}, y = -4$ or $x = 2, y = 3$.

Note: Sometimes there is only one solution.

Write down the expansion of each of the following:

1. $(x + 1)^2$ **2.** $(y - 2)^2$ **3.** $(x + 3)^2$ **4.** $(y - 4)^2$

5. $(2x - 1)^2$ **6.** $(1 - 3y)^2$ **7.** $(2x + 3)^2$ **8.** $(2 - 5y)^2$

Solve for x and y:

9. $y = x + 1$
$x^2 + y^2 = 1$

10. $x = y - 2$
$x^2 + y^2 = 10$

11. $y = 3 - x$
$x^2 + y^2 = 5$

12. $x - 2y - 5 = 0$
$x^2 + y^2 = 25$

13. $x - 2y = 0$
$x^2 + y^2 = 20$

14. $x - y - 4 = 0$
$y^2 + 3x = 16$

15. $y = x - 1$
$xy = 2$

16. $x = y + 1$
$xy = 6$

17. $y = 4 - 3x$
$xy = 1$

18. $x = 3 - y$
$x^2 - y^2 = -3$

19. $y = x - 4$
$y^2 = 16 - 3x$

20. $x + y = 0$
$xy - y^2 + 8 = 0$

21. $2x - y + 1 = 0$
$2x^2 + x = y^2$

22. $2x + y - 1 = 0$
$x^2 + xy + y^2 = 7$

23. $x - 3y + 1 = 0$
$3x^2 - 7xy - 5 = 0$

ALGEBRA 2

Long Division in Algebra

Long division in algebra follows the same procedure as long division in arithmetic. The stages in dividing one algebraic expression by another are shown in the following examples:

Example ▼

Simplify: **(i)** $(x^3 - 6x^2 + 14x - 15) \div (x - 3)$ **(ii)** $(6x^3 - 13x^2 + 4) \div (2x + 1)$

Solution:

(i) $(x^3 - 6x^2 + 14x - 15) \div (x - 3)$

$$
\begin{array}{r}
x^2 - 3x + 5 \\
x - 3 \overline{\big)\, x^3 - 6x^2 + 14x - 15} \\
\end{array}
$$

$\quad\quad x^3 - 3x^2$ $[x^3 \div x = x^2,$ put x^2 on top$]$

$\quad\quad\quad x^3 - 3x^2$ $[x^2(x - 3) = x^3 - 3x^2]$

$\quad\quad\quad\quad -3x^2 + 14x$ $[$subtract, bring down $14x,\ -3x^2 \div x = -3x,$ put $-3x$ on top$]$

$\quad\quad\quad\quad -3x^2 + 9x$ $[-3x(x - 3) = -3x^2 + 9x]$

$\quad\quad\quad\quad\quad\quad 5x - 15$ $[$subtract, bring down $-15,\ 5x \div x = 5,$ put 5 on top$]$

$\quad\quad\quad\quad\quad\quad 5x - 15$ $[5(x - 3) = 5x - 15]$

$\quad\quad\quad\quad\quad\quad\quad\quad 0$ $[$subtract$]$

$\therefore\ \ (x^3 - 6x^2 + 14x - 15) \div (x - 3) = x^2 - 3x + 5$

(ii) $(6x^3 - 13x^2 + 4) \div (2x + 1) = (6x^3 - 13x^2 + 0x + 4) \div (2x + 1)$
It helps in setting out the division if we put in the '**missing term**', $0x$.
All missing terms should be included in this way.

$$
\begin{array}{r}
3x^2 - 8x + 4 \\
2x + 1 \overline{\big)\, 6x^3 - 13x^2 + 0x + 4} \\
\end{array}
$$

$\quad\quad 6x^3 + 3x^2$ $[6x^3 \div 2x = 3x^2,$ put $3x^2$ on top$]$

$\quad\quad\quad 6x^3 + 3x^2$ $[3x^2(2x + 1) = 6x^3 + 3x^2]$

$\quad\quad\quad\quad -16x^2 + 0x$ $[$subtract, bring down $0x,\ -16x^2 \div 2x = -8x,$ put $-8x$ on top$]$

$\quad\quad\quad\quad -16x^2 - 8x$ $[-8x(2x + 1) = -16x^2 - 8x]$

$\quad\quad\quad\quad\quad\quad 8x + 4$ $[$subtract, bring down $4,\ 8x \div 2x = 4,$ put 4 on top$]$

$\quad\quad\quad\quad\quad\quad 8x + 4$ $[4(2x + 1) = 8x + 4]$

$\quad\quad\quad\quad\quad\quad\quad\quad 0$ $[$subtract$]$

$\therefore\ \ (6x^3 - 13x^2 + 4) \div (2x + 1) = 3x^2 - 8x + 4$

Simplify each of the following:

1. $\dfrac{x^3}{x}$ 2. $\dfrac{2x^2}{x}$ 3. $\dfrac{5x^3}{5x}$ 4. $\dfrac{3x}{3x}$ 5. $\dfrac{8x^2}{2x}$

6. $\dfrac{-6x}{3}$ 7. $\dfrac{-8x^2}{-4x}$ 8. $\dfrac{15x^2}{-5x}$ 9. $\dfrac{-3x}{x}$ 10. $\dfrac{-2x}{-2x}$

11. $(x^3 + 6x^2 + 11x + 6) \div (x + 2)$ 12. $(x^3 + 4x^2 + 5x + 2) \div (x + 1)$

13. $(2x^3 + 7x^2 + 5x + 1) \div (2x + 1)$ 14. $(3x^3 + 7x^2 + 5x + 1) \div (3x + 1)$

15. $(2x^3 + x^2 - 16x - 15) \div (2x + 5)$ 16. $(3x^3 - 8x^2 - 41x + 30) \div (3x - 2)$

17. $(x^3 + x^2 + 4) \div (x + 2)$ 18. $(x^3 + 11x - 30) \div (x - 2)$

19. $(x^3 - 13x + 12) \div (x + 4)$ 20. $(2x^3 - 5x^2 + 1) \div (2x - 1)$

21. Divide $(x^3 + 6x^2 + 11x + 6)$ by $(x + 3)$ and verify your answer by letting $x = 1$.

22. Divide $(6x^3 - 19x^2 + 4)$ by $(2x - 1)$ and verify your answer by letting $x = 3$.

23. $(x^3 + 2x^2 - 5x - 6) \div (x - 2) = ax^2 + bx + c$.
    Write down the values of a, b and c and evaluate $\sqrt{bc(b - a)}$.
    Factorise $ax^2 + bx + c$.

24. $f(x) = x^3 - 3x^2 - 4x + 12$, $g(x) = x + 2$ and $\dfrac{f(x)}{g(x)} = ax^2 + bx + c$.
    Factorise $ax^2 + bx + c$.

Factor Theorem

A polynomial in x is a collection of powers of x added together.

For example, $2x^2 - 3x + 5$, $5x^3 + 6x^2 - x + 4$ are polynomials.

Note: **1.** There cannot be negative or fractional powers in a polynomial.
    2. A polynomial is often denoted by $f(x)$.

Factor Theorem

If an algebraic expression is divided by one of its factors, then the remainder is zero. The expression $(x - k)$ is a factor of a polynomial $f(x)$, if the remainder when we divide $f(x)$ by $(x - k)$ is zero.

Generalising this:

> **1.** If $f(k) = 0$, then $(x - k)$ is a factor of $f(x)$.
> **2.** If $(x - k)$ is a factor of $f(x)$, then $f(k) = 0$.

Here are some examples:

Factor	Put factor = 0 and solve	Factor Theorem
$x + 4$	$x = -4$	$f(-4) = 0$
$x - 3$	$x = 3$	$f(3) = 0$

The factor theorem can be used to factorise polynomials or to find unknown coefficients in a polynomial.

Example ▼

(i)   Verify that $x - 2$ is a factor of $3x^3 - x^2 + 5x - 30$.

(ii)   If $x + 3$ is a factor of $x^3 - 3x^3 + kx + 24$, find the value of k.

Solution:

(i)   Let $f(x) = 3x^3 - x^2 + 5x - 30$

If $x - 2$ is a factor, then $f(2) = 0$

Check: $f(x) = 3x^3 - x^2 + 5x - 30$

$f(2) = 3(2)^3 - (2)^2 + 5(2) - 30$

$= 24 - 4 + 10 - 30$

$= 34 - 34$

$= 0$

$\therefore$ $x - 2$ is a factor of $3x^3 - x^2 + 5x - 30$

(ii)   Let $f(x) = x^3 - 3x^2 + kx + 24$

If $x + 3$ is a factor, then $f(-3) = 0$

$f(-3) = 0$

$(-3)^3 - 3(-3)^2 + k(-3) + 24 = 0$

$-27 - 27 - 3k + 24 = 0$

$-3k - 30 = 0$

$-3k = 30$

$3k = -30$

$k = -10$

Example ▼

If $(x + 3)$ and $(x - 2)$ are factors of $x^3 + ax^2 + bx - 12$, find the value of a and the value of b, $a, b \in \mathbf{R}$.

Solution:

Let $f(x) = x^3 + ax^2 + bx - 12$

If $(x + 3)$ is a factor, then $f(-3) = 0$

If $(x - 2)$ is a factor, then $f(2) = 0$

$f(-3) = 0$

$(-3)^3 + a(-3)^2 + b(-3) - 12 = 0$

$-27 + 9a - 3b - 12 = 0$

$9a - 3b - 39 = 0$

$9a - 3b = 39$

$3a - b = 13$ ①

$f(2) = 0$

$(2)^3 + a(2)^2 + b(2) - 12 = 0$

$8 + 4a + 2b - 12 = 0$

$4a + 2b - 4 = 0$

$4a + 2b = 4$

$2a + b = 2$ ②

Now solve the simultaneous equations ① and ②:

$$3a - b = 13 \quad ①$$
$$\underline{2a + b = 2 \quad ②}$$
$$5a = 15 \text{ (add)}$$
$$a = 3$$

Put $a = 3$ into ① or ②

$$2a + b = 2 \quad ②$$

$$2(3) + b = 2$$
$$6 + b = 2$$
$$b = -4$$

$$\therefore \quad a = 3 \quad \text{and} \quad b = -4$$

Exercise 5.2 ▼

1. Verify that $x - 1$ is a factor of $x^3 - x^2 - 4x + 4$.

2. Verify that $x + 2$ is a factor of $x^3 + 2x^2 - x - 2$.

3. Verify that $x + 3$ is a factor of $2x^3 + 5x^2 - 4x - 3$.

4. Verify that $x - 4$ is a factor of $x^3 - 5x^2 - 2x + 24$.

5. Verify that $x + 5$ is a factor of $x^3 + 3x^2 - 13x - 15$.

6. Verify that $x - 2$ is a factor of $2x^3 + 5x^2 - 8x - 20$.

7. If $x - 1$ is a factor of $2x^3 - 3x^2 + kx + 3$, find the value of k.

8. If $x - 2$ is a factor of $2x^3 - 5x^2 + ax - 6$, find the value of a.

9. If $x + 2$ is a factor of $x^3 - 2x^2 - 5x + k$, find the value of k.

10. If $x + 2$ is a factor of $x^3 + mx^2 + 4$, find the value of m.

11. If $x - 5$ is a factor of $x^3 + px^2 - 13x - 10$, find the value of p.

12. If $x + 1$ is a factor of $ax^3 - 4x^2 - 5x + 2$, find the value of a.

13. If $(x - 1)$ and $(x - 2)$ are factors of $x^3 - 5x^2 + ax + b$, find the value of a and the value of b, $a, b \in \mathbf{R}$.

14. If $(x - 1)$ and $(x + 2)$ are factors of $x^3 + px^2 - 5x + q$, find the value of p and the value of q, $p, q \in \mathbf{R}$.

15. If $(x + 1)$ and $(x - 2)$ are factors of $x^3 - 6x^2 + hx + k$, find the value of h and the value of k, $h, k \in \mathbf{R}$.

16. If $(x + 1)$ and $(x + 3)$ are factors of $ax^3 + bx^2 + 2x - 3$, find the value of a and the value of b, $a, b \in \mathbf{R}$.

Solving Cubic Equations

Any equation of the form $ax^3 + bx^2 + cx + d = 0$, $a \neq 0$, is called a cubic equation.
For example, $2x^3 - 3x^2 - x + 2 = 0$ is a cubic equation.

We use the factor theorem to find one root, and hence one factor. We divide the cubic expression by this factor to get a quadratic factor. We then let this quadratic factor $= 0$, factorise it and solve it to find the other two roots. Sometimes we have to use the '$-b$' or 'quadratic' formula.

In mathematical terms, the steps in solving a cubic equation are:

> **1.** Find the root k by trial and improvement, i.e. try $f(1), f(-1), f(2), f(-2)$, etc. (Only try numbers that divide evenly into the constant in the equation.)
> **2.** If $x = k$ is a root, then $(x - k)$ is a factor.
> **3.** Divide $f(x)$ by $(x - k)$, which always gives a quadratic expression.
> **4.** Let this quadratic $= 0$ and solve by factors or formula.

Example ▼

Solve the equation: $x^3 + 3x^2 - 13x - 15 = 0$.

Solution:

We use the factor theorem to find the first root by trial and improvement. The first root will be a factor of 15. Thus, we try $\pm 1, \pm 3, \pm 5$.

(**Note:** There is no point in trying ± 2 or ± 4 as these are **not** factors of 15.)

1. Let $f(x) = x^3 + 3x^2 - 13x - 15$

$\quad f(1) = (1)^3 + 3(1)^2 - 13(1) - 15 = 1 + 3 - 13 - 15 \neq 0$

$\quad f(-1) = (-1)^3 + 3(-1)^2 - 13(-1) - 15 = -1 + 3 + 13 - 15 = 16 - 16 = 0$

2. $\therefore \quad x = -1$ is a root of $x^3 + 3x^2 - 13x - 15 = 0$

$\quad \therefore \quad x + 1$ is a factor of $x^3 + 3x^2 - 13x - 15$

Now divide $x^3 + 3x^2 - 13x - 15$ by $x + 1$ to get the quadratic factor.

3.
$$\begin{array}{r} x^2 + 2x - 15 \\ x+1\overline{\smash{\big)}\ x^3 + 3x^2 - 13x - 15} \\ \underline{x^3 + x^2} \\ 2x^2 - 13x \\ \underline{2x^2 + 2x} \\ -15x - 15 \\ \underline{-15x - 15} \\ 0 \end{array}$$

4. Now let the quadratic factor $= 0$ and solve.

$$x^2 + 2x - 15 = 0$$
$$(x - 3)(x + 5) = 0$$
$$x - 3 = 0 \quad \text{or} \quad x + 5 = 0$$
$$x = 3 \quad \text{or} \quad x = -5$$

$\therefore$ the roots of the equation $x^3 + 3x^2 - 13x - 15 = 0$ are $-5, -1$ and 3.

Note: If the question said factorise $x^3 + 3x^2 - 13x - 15$, then the answer would be $(x + 1)(x - 3)(x + 5)$.

1. **(i)** Verify that $x - 1$ is a factor of $x^3 + 2x^2 - 13x + 10$.
   (ii) Hence, solve the equation $x^3 + 2x^2 - 13x + 10 = 0$.

2. **(i)** Verify that $x + 2$ is a factor of $x^3 + 9x^2 + 26x + 24$ and find the other two factors.
   (ii) Hence, solve the equation $x^3 + 9x^2 + 26x + 24 = 0$.

3. **(i)** Find the three linear factors of $x^3 + 5x^2 - 2x - 24$.
   (ii) Hence, or otherwise, solve the equation $x^3 + 5x^2 - 2x - 24 = 0$.

4. **(i)** Find the three linear factors of $x^3 + 2x^2 - 5x - 6$.
   (ii) Hence, or otherwise, solve the equation $x^3 + 2x^2 - 5x - 6 = 0$.

5. **(i)** Find the three linear factors of $2x^3 - 15x^2 + 34x - 24$.
   (ii) Hence, or otherwise, solve the equation $2x^3 - 15x^2 + 34x - 24 = 0$.

6. **(i)** Find the three linear factors of $x^3 - 7x + 6$.
   (ii) Hence, or otherwise, solve the equation $x^3 - 7x + 6 = 0$.

Solve each of the following equations:

7. $x^3 - 4x^2 - x + 4 = 0$

8. $x^3 - 2x^2 - 5x + 6 = 0$

9. $x^3 - 8x^2 + 19x - 12 = 0$

10. $x^3 - 4x^2 - 7x + 10 = 0$

11. $x^3 - 9x^2 + 23x - 15 = 0$

12. $x^3 - x^2 - 14x + 24 = 0$

13. $2x^3 + 7x^2 + 7x + 2 = 0$

14. $3x^3 - 4x^2 - 5x + 2 = 0$

15. $4x^3 + 8x^2 - x - 2 = 0$

16. $6x^3 + 19x^2 + 11x - 6 = 0$

17. Verify that -2 is a root of the equation $2x^3 + x^2 - 10x - 8 = 0$.
    Find the other two roots, correct to two decimal places.

18. Find the value of k if the equation $x^3 - 9x^2 + kx - 24 = 0$ has 2 as a root, and find the other roots.

19. Find the value of k if the equation $x^3 + 6x^2 + kx - 12 = 0$ has -3 as a root, and find the other roots.

20. The equation $x^3 + 2x^2 + hx + k = 0$ has roots -1 and 2. Find the value of h and the value of k, where $h, k \in \mathbf{R}$, and the other root.

21. The equation $2x^3 - 5x^2 + ax + b = 0$ has roots -1 and 3. Find the value of a and the value of b, $a, b \in \mathbf{R}$.

Constructing an Equation when Given its Roots

This is the reverse process of solving an equation by using factors.

(i) Write down a quadratic equation with roots $\frac{1}{2}$ and -4.

(ii) Write down a cubic equation with roots -5, -1 and 3.

Solution:

(i) roots $\frac{1}{2}$ and -4

$\quad$ Let $x = \frac{1}{2}$ and $x = -4$

$\quad$ $2x = 1$ and $x = -4$

$\quad$ $2x - 1 = 0$ and $x + 4 = 0$

$\quad$ $\therefore \quad (2x - 1)(x + 4) = 0$

$\qquad\qquad 2x^2 + 8x - x - 4 = 0$

$\qquad\qquad\quad 2x^2 + 7x - 4 = 0$

(ii) roots, -5, -1 and 3

$\quad$ Let $x = -5$ and $x = -1$ and $x = 3$

$\quad$ $x + 5 = 0$ and $x + 1 = 0$ and $x - 3 = 0$

$\quad$ $\therefore \qquad (x + 5)(x + 1)(x - 3) = 0$

$\qquad\qquad (x + 5)(x^2 - 3x + x - 3) = 0$

$\qquad\qquad\quad (x + 5)(x^2 - 2x - 3) = 0$

$\qquad x^3 - 2x^2 - 3x + 5x^2 - 10x - 15 = 0$

$\qquad\qquad\quad x^3 + 3x^2 - 13x - 15 = 0$

Exercise 5.4 ▼

Write down a quadratic equation with roots:

1. $2, 3$ $\qquad$ **2.** $-2, 1$ $\qquad$ **3.** $-3, -5$ $\qquad$ **4.** $-1, 4$

5. $-5, 3$ $\qquad$ **6.** $-8, 2$ $\qquad$ **7.** $-3, 3$ $\qquad$ **8.** $-1, 1$

9. $-2, 0$ $\qquad$ **10.** $0, 4$ $\qquad$ **11.** $\frac{1}{2}, 3$ $\qquad$ **12.** $-\frac{1}{3}, 2$

13. The equation $x^2 + mx + n = 0$ has roots -3 and 7. Find the values of m and n.

14. The equation $ax^2 + bx + c = 0$ has roots $-\frac{1}{2}$ and 5.
Find one set of values of a, b, and c, $\quad a, b, c \in \mathbf{Z}$.

Write down a cubic equation with roots:

15. $-1, -2, -3$ $\qquad$ **16.** $-4, 1, 5$ $\qquad$ **17.** $-5, -1, 1$ $\qquad$ **18.** $-4, 2, 3$

19. $-2, 4, 5$ $\qquad$ **20.** $-4, -3, 2$ $\qquad$ **21.** $\frac{1}{2}, 1, -3$ $\qquad$ **22.** $\frac{2}{3}, -1, -5$

23. The equation $x^3 + ax^2 + bx + c = 0$ has roots -1, 2 and 5. Find the values of a, b and c.

24. The equation $ax^3 + bx^2 + cx + d = 0$ has roots $-\frac{1}{2}$, -3 and 4.
Find one set of values of a, b, c and d, $\quad a, b, c$ and $d \in \mathbf{Z}$.

Changing the Subject of a Formula

When we rearrange a formula so that one of the variables is given in terms of the others we are said to be '**changing the subject of the formula**'. The rules in changing the subject of a formula are the same as when solving an equation, that is we can:

1. **Add** or **subtract** the same quantity to both sides.
   (In practice this involves moving a term from one side to another and changing its sign.)

2. **Multiply** or **divide** both sides by the same quantity.

3. **Square** both sides.

4. Take the **square root** of both sides.

Note: Whatever letter comes after the word 'express' is to be on its own.

Example ▼

(i)   If $a + \dfrac{b}{c} = 1$, express b in terms of a and c.

(ii) If $p = \dfrac{3qr}{q+r}$, express r in terms of p and q.

Solution:

(i)
$$a + \frac{b}{c} = 1$$

$$ac + b = c \qquad \text{[multiply each term by } c\text{]}$$

$$b = c - ac \qquad \text{[subtract } ac \text{ from both sides]}$$

(ii)
$$p = \frac{3qr}{q+r}$$

$$p(q+r) = 3qr \qquad \text{[multiply both sides by } (q+r)\text{]}$$

$$pq + pr = 3qr \qquad \text{[remove brackets on the left-hand side]}$$

$$-3qr + pr = -pq \qquad \text{[terms with } r \text{ on the left-hand side]}$$

$$3qr - pr = pq \qquad \text{[multiply each term by } -1\text{]}$$

$$r(3q - p) = pq \qquad \text{[take out common factor } r \text{ on the left-hand side]}$$

$$r = \frac{pq}{3q - p} \qquad \text{[divide both sides by } (3q - p)\text{]}$$

Sometimes we have to remove a square root. We do this by squaring both sides.

If $t = \sqrt{\dfrac{x-y}{xz}}$, express z in terms of x, y and t.

Solution:

$$t = \sqrt{\frac{x-y}{xz}}$$

$$(t)^2 = \left(\sqrt{\frac{x-y}{xz}} \right)^2 \qquad \text{[square both sides]}$$

$$t^2 = \frac{x-y}{xz} \qquad \text{[square root sign disappears]}$$

$$t^2 xz = x - y \qquad \text{[multiply both sides by } xz]$$

$$z = \frac{x-y}{t^2 x} \qquad \text{[divide both sides by } t^2 x]$$

Exercise 5.5 ▼

Change each of the following formulae to express the letter in square brackets in terms of the others:

1. $2p - q = 4$ [p]
2. $3a + b = c$ [a]
3. $ab - c = d$ [b]

4. $u + at = v$ [t]
5. $3a + 2b = 5c$ [a]
6. $3q - 4p = 2r$ [q]

7. $2(p - r) = q$ [p]
8. $a(b - c) = d$ [b]
9. $\dfrac{b}{2} + c = a$ [b]

10. $p + \dfrac{q}{3} = r$ [q]
11. $\dfrac{a}{2} + \dfrac{b}{3} = c$ [a]
12. $\dfrac{p+q}{2} = r$ [p]

13. $a = \dfrac{b - 2c}{3}$ [c]
14. $r = \frac{1}{2}(p - q)$ [q]
15. $x + \dfrac{w}{y} = z$ [w]

16. $2p + \dfrac{3q}{r} = s$ [q]
17. $2(a - 3b) = c$ [b]
18. $t = a + (n - 1)d$ [n]

19. $V = \frac{1}{3}\pi r^2 h$ [h]
20. $u^2 + 2as = v^2$ [a]
21. $s = ut + \frac{1}{2}at^2$ [a]

22. $\dfrac{p}{q} + \dfrac{r}{q} = s$ [q]
23. $p = \dfrac{q}{r+s}$ [s]
24. $m = \dfrac{n}{x-y}$ [y]

25. $r = \dfrac{1}{s} + t$ [s]
26. $p + \dfrac{t}{q} = r$ [q]
27. $x - \dfrac{y}{z} = w$ [z]

28. $\dfrac{a}{b} = \dfrac{b}{c} + d$ [c]
29. $\dfrac{2a - b}{a} = c$ [a]
30. $\dfrac{2(a - c)}{b} = c$ [c]

31. $a = \dfrac{bc}{b+c}$ [c]
32. $p = \dfrac{2qr}{q-r}$ [q]
33. $\dfrac{p-q}{q+1} = r$ [q]

Questions 34 to 37 contain a square root:

34. $\sqrt{ab} = c$ $[a]$ **35.** $a = \sqrt{\dfrac{p}{q}}$ $[q]$ **36.** $\sqrt{pq - r} = s$ $[p]$ **37.** $v = \sqrt{\dfrac{u - s}{ut}}$ $[t]$

38. If $t = \sqrt{\dfrac{x}{y - 2}}$, express y in terms of t and x.

  Hence, determine the value of y if $x = 25$ and $t = 5$.

39. If $\dfrac{p}{2} = \sqrt{\dfrac{1}{x^2 - 4}}$, express x^2 in terms of p.

  If $p = 2$ and $x = \sqrt{k}$, determine the value of k.

Notation for Indices

We use a shorthand called '**index notation**' to indicate repeated multiplication.

For example, we write $2 \times 2 \times 2 \times 2 \times 2$ as 2^5.

This is read as '2 to the power of 5'.

> 2 is the **base**.
> 5 is the **index** or **power**.

The power or index simply tells you how many times a number is multiplied by itself.

Rules of Indices

1. $a^m . a^n = a^{m+n}$ Example: $2^4 . 2^3 = 2^{4+3} = 2^7$
Multiplying powers of the same number: **add** the indices.

2. $\dfrac{a^m}{a^n} = a^{m-n}$ Example: $\dfrac{3^9}{3^5} = 3^{9-5} = 3^4$

Dividing powers of the same number: **subtract** the index on the bottom from the index on top.

3. $(a^m)^n = a^{mn}$ Example: $(4^5)^3 = 4^{5 \times 3} = 4^{15}$
Raising the power of a number to a power, multiply the indices.

4. $(ab)^m = a^m b^m$ Example: $(2 \times 3)^5 = 2^5 \times 3^5$
Raising a product to a power, every factor is raised to the power.

5. $\left(\dfrac{a}{b}\right)^m = \dfrac{a^m}{b^m}$ Example: $\left(\dfrac{2}{5}\right)^3 = \dfrac{2^3}{5^3}$

Raising a fraction to a power, **both** top and bottom are raised to the power.

6. $a^0 = 1$ Example: $4^0 = 1$
Any number to the power of zero is 1.

7. $a^{-m} = \dfrac{1}{a^m}$ Example: $5^{-2} = \dfrac{1}{5^2}$

A number with a negative index is equal to its reciprocal with a positive index.

Note: If a term is brought from the top to the bottom of a fraction (or vice versa), the sign of its index is changed.

8. $a^{m/n} = (a^{1/n})^m$ Example: $32^{3/5} = (32^{1/5})^3$

Take the root first and then raise to the power (or vice versa).

$8^{1/3}$ means, the number that multiplied by itself three times will equal 8.

Thus, $8^{1/3} = 2$, as $2 \times 2 \times 2 = 8$

Similarly, $25^{1/2} = 5$, as $5 \times 5 = 25$ and $81^{1/4} = 3$, as $3 \times 3 \times 3 \times 3 = 81$.

Note: $\sqrt{a} = a^{1/2}$, for example, $\sqrt{16} = 16^{1/2} = 4$.

Also, $\sqrt{a}\sqrt{a} = a^{1/2}.a^{1/2} = a^{1/2+1/2} = a^1 = a$

Alternative notation: $a^{1/n} = {}^n\sqrt{a}$,   example $8^{1/3} = {}^3\sqrt{8}$
$a^{m/n} = {}^n\sqrt{a^m}$,   example $32^{2/5} = {}^5\sqrt{32^2}$

When dealing with fractional indices, the calculations are simpler if the root is taken first and the result is raised to the power.

For example, $16^{3/4} = (16^{1/4})^3 = (2)^3 = 8$

(root first)   (power next)

Using a calculator

A calculator can be used to evaluate an expression such as $32^{3/5}$.

(⌨ 32 y^x 2 $a\frac{b}{c}$ 5 $=$)

The calculator will give an answer 8.
However, there are problems when dealing with negative indices or raising a fraction to a power, as the calculator can give the answer as a decimal.

For example, $8^{-2/3} = \dfrac{1}{8^{2/3}} = \dfrac{1}{(8^{1/3})^2} = \dfrac{1}{(2)^2} = \dfrac{1}{4}$

Using a calculator,

(⌨ 8 y^x $+/-$ 2 $a\frac{b}{c}$ 3 $=$)   gives an answer 0.25

Note: $\frac{1}{4} = 0.25$

Also, $\left(\dfrac{8}{27}\right)^{2/3} = \dfrac{8^{2/3}}{27^{2/3}} = \dfrac{(8^{1/3})^2}{(27^{1/3})^2} = \dfrac{(2)^2}{(3)^2} = \dfrac{4}{9}$

Using a calculator,

(⌨ $($ 8 $a\frac{a}{b}$ 27 $)$ y^x 2 $a\frac{b}{c}$ 3 $=$)   gives an answer 0.444444444 ...

Note: $\frac{4}{9} = 0.444444444 \ldots$

So avoid using a calculator with negative indices or when raising a fraction to a power.

Example ▼

Simplify each of the following:

(i) $32^{3/5}$ (ii) $27^{4/3}$ (iii) $64^{-2/3}$ (iv) $16^{3/4}.27^{-2/3}$ (v) $(2\frac{1}{4})^{1\frac{1}{2}}$ (vi) $\left(\dfrac{25}{16}\right)^{-3/2}$

Solution:

(i) $32^{3/5} = (32^{1/5})^3 = (2)^3 = 8$

(ii) $27^{4/3} = (27^{1/3})^4 = (3)^4 = 81$

(iii) $64^{-2/3} = \dfrac{1}{64^{2/3}} = \dfrac{1}{(64^{1/3})^2} = \dfrac{1}{(4)^2} = \dfrac{1}{16}$

(iv) $16^{3/4}.27^{-2/3} = \dfrac{16^{3/4}}{27^{2/3}} = \dfrac{(16^{1/4})^3}{(27^{1/3})^2} = \dfrac{(2)^3}{(3)^2} = \dfrac{8}{9}$

(v) $(2^{1/4})^{1\frac{1}{2}} = \left(\dfrac{9}{4}\right)^{3/2} = \dfrac{9^{3/2}}{4^{3/2}} = \dfrac{(9^{1/2})^3}{(4^{1/2})^3} = \dfrac{(3)^3}{(2)^3} = \dfrac{27}{8}$

(vi) $\left(\dfrac{25}{16}\right)^{-3/2} = \dfrac{25^{-3/2}}{16^{-3/2}} = \dfrac{16^{3/2}}{25^{3/2}} = \dfrac{(16^{1/2})^3}{(25^{1/2})^3} = \dfrac{(4)^3}{(5)^2} = \dfrac{64}{125}$

Example ▼

(i) Express: (a) 243   (b) $\sqrt{27}$ in the form 3^n.

(ii) Express $\dfrac{\sqrt{3} \times \sqrt{27}}{3 \times 243}$ in the form 3^n.

Solution:

(i) (a) $243 = 3 \times 3 \times 3 \times 3 \times 3 = 3^5$

   (b) $\sqrt{27} = (27)^{1/2} = (3^3)^{1/2} = 3^{3 \times 1/2} = 3^{3/2}$

(ii) $\dfrac{\sqrt{3} \times \sqrt{27}}{3 \times 243} = \dfrac{3^{1/2} \times 3^{3/2}}{3^1 \times 3^5} = \dfrac{3^{1/2+3/2}}{3^{1+5}} = \dfrac{3^2}{3^6} = 3^{2-6} = 3^{-4}$

In each of the following, write down the value of n:

1. $2^3 \times 2^4 = 2^n$

2. $5^4 \times 5^6 = 5^n$

3. $7 \times 7^3 = 7^n$

4. $\dfrac{3^7}{3^5} = 3^n$

5. $\dfrac{4^{10}}{4^7} = 4^n$

6. $\dfrac{6^4}{6^6} = 6^n$

7. $5 \times 5^2 \times 5^3 = 5^n$

8. $(3^2)^5 = 3^n$

9. $(7^3)^6 = 7^n$

10. $3^n = \dfrac{1}{3^2}$

11. $4^n = \dfrac{1}{4^3}$

12. $5^{-2} = \dfrac{1}{5^n}$

13. $\sqrt{3} = 3^n$

14. $(\sqrt{5})^4 = 5^n$

15. $(\sqrt{7})^3 = 7^n$

Evaluate each of the following:

16. $9^{1/2}$

17. $25^{1/2}$

18. $100^{1/2}$

19. $8^{1/3}$

20. $27^{1/3}$

21. $64^{1/3}$

22. $125^{1/3}$

23. $32^{1/5}$

24. $81^{1/4}$

25. $1000^{1/3}$

26. $16^{3/4}$

27. $8^{2/3}$

28. $25^{3/2}$

29. $32^{3/5}$

30. $125^{2/3}$

31. $8^{4/3}$

32. $64^{2/3}$

33. $4^{3/2}$

34. $9^{5/2}$

35. $16^{5/4}$

Express each of the following in the form $\dfrac{a}{b}$, $\quad a, b \in \mathbf{N}$:

36. $4^{-1/2}$

37. $9^{-1/2}$

38. $27^{-2/3}$

39. $32^{-4/5}$

40. $64^{-2/3}$

41. $\left(\dfrac{8}{27}\right)^{1/3}$

42. $\left(\dfrac{8}{125}\right)^{2/3}$

43. $\left(\dfrac{27}{64}\right)^{-2/3}$

44. $\left(\dfrac{16}{81}\right)^{-1/4}$

45. $\left(\dfrac{16}{9}\right)^{-3/2}$

46. $(27^{-1/3})^2$

47. $\dfrac{16^{-3/4}}{81^{-1/2}}$

48. $\dfrac{27^{-1/3}}{8^{-2/3}}$

49. $\left(\dfrac{1}{25}\right)^{3/2}$

50. $\dfrac{4^{-1/2}}{64^{2/3}}$

51. Express: (i) $\dfrac{8^{2/3} \times 32^{4/5}}{2 \times 16^{1/2}}$ in the form 2^n (ii) $\dfrac{\sqrt{3} \times 81^{3/4}}{9}$ in the form 3^n

52. Express each of the following in the form 2^n:
   (i) 8 (ii) 16 (iii) 32 (iv) $\sqrt{2}$ (v) $\sqrt{8}$ (vi) $\sqrt{32}$

   (vii) $\dfrac{4}{\sqrt{2}}$ (viii) $\left(\dfrac{4}{\sqrt{2}}\right)^2$ (ix) $\dfrac{16}{\sqrt{8}}$ (x) $\left(\dfrac{\sqrt{8}}{16}\right)^2$ (xi) $\left(\dfrac{4}{\sqrt{32}}\right)^2$

53. Express each of the following in the form 3^n:
   (i) 9 (ii) 27 (iii) 81 (iv) 243 (v) $\sqrt{3}$ (vi) $\sqrt{27}$

   (vii) $\left(\dfrac{27}{\sqrt{3}}\right)$ (viii) $\left(\dfrac{27}{\sqrt{3}}\right)^2$ (ix) $\left(\dfrac{81}{\sqrt{27}}\right)^2$ (x) $\left(\dfrac{\sqrt{3}}{9}\right)^2$

54. Express each of the following in the form 5^n:

(i) 25   (ii) 125   (iii) $\sqrt{5}$ (iv) $\sqrt{125}$

(v) $\dfrac{1}{\sqrt{5}}$ (vi) $\left(\dfrac{1}{\sqrt{5}}\right)^2$ (vii) $\left(\dfrac{1}{\sqrt{125}}\right)^2$ (viii) $\left(\dfrac{\sqrt{5}}{25}\right)^2$

Exponential Equations

Exponent is another name for power or index.
An equation involving the variable in the power is called an '**exponential equation**'.
For example, $3^{2x+3} = 9$ is an exponential equation.

Exponential equations are solved with the following steps:

> **1.** Write all the numbers as powers of the same number (usually a prime number).
> **2.** Write both sides as one power of the same number, using the laws of indices.
> **3.** Equate these powers and solve this equation.

Example ▼

Find the value of x if: **(i)** $4^{x+1} = 128$ **(ii)** $5^{3x+1} = \dfrac{125}{\sqrt{5}}$

Solution:

(i) **1.** $4^{x+1} = 128$ [both 4 and 128 can be written as powers of 2]

        $(2^2)^{x+1} = 2^7$ [$4 = 2^2$ and $128 = 2^7$]

   2. $2^{2x+2} = 2^7$ [multiply the indices on the left-hand side]

   3. $2x + 2 = 7$ [equate the powers]

         $2x = 5$

          $x = \frac{5}{2}$

(ii) **1.** $5^{3x+1} = \dfrac{125}{\sqrt{5}}$ [both 125 and $\sqrt{5}$ can be written as powers of 5]

        $5^{3x+1} = \dfrac{5^3}{5^{1/2}}$ [$125 = 5^3$ and $\sqrt{5} = 5^{1/2}$]

   2. $5^{3x+1} = 5^{2\frac{1}{2}}$ [subtract index on the bottom from the index on top]

   3. $3x + 1 = 2\frac{1}{2}$ [equate the powers]

        $6x + 2 = 5$ [multiply both sides by 2]

         $6x = 3$

          $x = \frac{1}{2}$

Express each of the following in the form a^n, where a is a prime number:

1. 8 **2.** 9 **3.** 32 **4.** 27 **5.** 125 **6.** 81

7. 49 **8.** 64 **9.** 625 **10.** 243 **11.** 128 **12.** 343

13. $\dfrac{1}{16}$ **14.** $\dfrac{1}{32}$ **15.** $\dfrac{1}{243}$ **16.** $\dfrac{27}{\sqrt{3}}$ **17.** $\dfrac{\sqrt{5}}{25}$ **18.** $32^{3/5}$

19. $\sqrt{125}$ **20.** $\sqrt{3}$ **21.** $\dfrac{\sqrt{3}}{9}$ **22.** $\left(\dfrac{\sqrt{3}}{9}\right)^2$ **23.** $\dfrac{\sqrt{5}}{125}$ **24.** $\left(\dfrac{\sqrt{5}}{125}\right)^2$

Solve each of the following equations for x:

25. $3^{2x} = 3^8$ **26.** $5^{2x+1} = 5^7$ **27.** $2^{3x-1} = 2^5$

28. $2^x = 8$ **29.** $2^{x-2} = 16$ **30.** $3^{2x-1} = 27$

31. $9^{x+1} = 81$ **32.** $4^{x-1} = 32$ **33.** $16^{x+1} = 32$

34. $2^x = \frac{1}{8}$ **35.** $3^{2x} = \frac{1}{81}$ **36.** $5^{2x-1} = \frac{1}{125}$

37. $9^{x+1} = \frac{1}{27}$ **38.** $\dfrac{3^{3n-1}}{3^{n+1}} = 9$ **39.** $\dfrac{2^{3x+1}}{2^{x+2}} = 32$

40. Express $32^{4/5}$ in the form 4^n. Hence, or otherwise, solve $4^{2x-1} = 32^{4/5}$.

41. Solve for x: $2^{3x-5} = 2^5 - 2^4$

42. Write as a power of 5: **(i)** 125 **(ii)** $\sqrt{5}$ **(iii)** $\dfrac{125}{\sqrt{5}}$

Hence, solve for x the equation: $5^{2x-1} = \left(\dfrac{125}{\sqrt{5}}\right)^2$

43. Write as a power of 2: **(i)** $\sqrt{2}$ **(ii)** $8^{4/3}$

Hence, solve for x: $\dfrac{8^{4/3}}{\sqrt{2}} = 2^{2x-1}$

44. Write as a power of 3: **(i)** $\sqrt{3}$ **(ii)** 27 **(iii)** $\sqrt{27}$

Hence, solve for x:

(iv) $3^{4x-3} = \left(\dfrac{27}{\sqrt{3}}\right)^2$ **(v)** $\dfrac{3^{2x-1}}{\sqrt{3}} = \left(\dfrac{1}{\sqrt{27}}\right)^3$

6

COORDINATE GEOMETRY OF THE CIRCLE

Equation of a Circle, Centre $(0,0)$ and Radius r

On the right is a circle with centre $(0,0)$, radius r and (x, y) any point on the circle.
Distance between $(0,0)$ and (x, y) equals the radius, r.

$\therefore \ \sqrt{(x-0)^2+(y-0)^2}=r$ (distance formula)

$\qquad \sqrt{x^2+y^2}=r$

$\qquad\quad x^2+y^2=r^2$ (square both sides)

Hence, $x^2+y^2=r^2$ is said to be the equation of the circle.

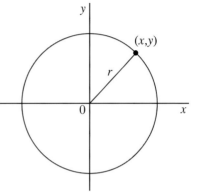

> Equation of a circle, centre $(0,0)$ and radius r, is
> $$x^2+y^2=r^2$$

Two quantities are needed to find the equation of a circle:

> **1.** Centre   **2.** Radius
> If the centre is $(0,0)$, the equation of the circle will be of the form $x^2+y^2=r^2$.

Example ▼

Find the equations of the following circles, each of centre $(0,0)$:

(i) K_1, which has radius 6

(ii) K_2, which contains the point $(3, -2)$.

Solution:

(i)   Centre is $(0,0)$, therefore K_1 is of the form $x^2+y^2=r^2$.

      Substitute $r=6$ into this equation:

$$x^2+y^2=6^2$$
$$x^2+y^2=36$$
$$\therefore \ \ K_1 \text{ is the circle } x^2+y^2=36.$$

(ii) Centre $(0, 0)$, therefore K_2 is of the form $x^2 + y^2 = r^2$.

The radius of K_2 needs to be found.

The radius is the distance from $(0, 0)$ to $(3, -2)$.

Using the distance formula:

$$r = \sqrt{(3 - 0)^2 + (-2 - 0)^2}$$

$$= \sqrt{3^2 + (-2)^2}$$

$$= \sqrt{9 + 4} = \sqrt{13}$$

$$x^2 + y^2 = (\sqrt{13})^2$$

$$x^2 + y^2 = 13$$

$\therefore$ K_2 is the circle $x^2 + y^2 = 13$.

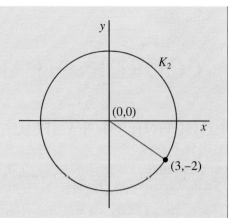

Alternatively, as the centre is $(0, 0)$, K_2 is of the form $x^2 + y^2 = r^2$

Thus, $x^2 + y^2 = (3)^2 + (-2)^2 = 9 + 4 = 13$

$\therefore$ K_2 is the circle $x^2 + y^2 = 13$.

Example ▼

Find the radius of each of the following circles:

(i) $x^2 + y^2 = 49$ **(ii)** $x^2 + y^2 = 10$

Solution:

Compare each to $x^2 + y^2 = r^2$

(i) $x^2 + y^2 = 49$

$\quad\quad x^2 + y^2 = r^2$

$\quad\quad\quad r^2 = 49$

$\quad\quad\quad\quad r = \sqrt{49} = 7$

(ii) $x^2 + y^2 = 10$

$\quad\quad x^2 + y^2 = r^2$

$\quad\quad\quad r^2 = 10$

$\quad\quad\quad\quad r = \sqrt{10}$

Example ▼

The circle C has equation $x^2 + y^2 = 25$.

(i)   Write down the centre and radius length of C.

(ii) Find the coordinates of the points where C intersects the x- and y-axes.

(iii) Draw a diagram of C.

Solution:

(i) $x^2 + y^2 = 25$

As the equation is in the form $x^2 + y^2 = r^2$, the centre is $(0, 0)$.

$$r^2 = 25$$
$$r = \sqrt{25} = 5$$

Thus, the radius length is 5.

(ii) $x^2 + y^2 = 25$

On the x-axis, $y = 0$

$$\therefore \quad x^2 = 25$$
$$x = \pm \sqrt{25} = \pm 5$$

Thus, C intersects the x-axis at $(5, 0)$ and $(0, -5)$.

On the y-axis, $x = 0$

$$\therefore \quad y^2 = 25$$
$$y = \pm \sqrt{25} = \pm 5$$

Thus, C intersects the y-axis at $(0, 5)$ and $(0, -5)$.

(iii) Diagram of C

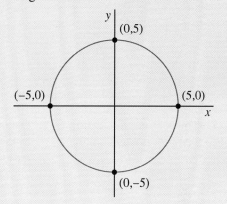

Note: When drawing a circle the scales on the x- and y-axes must be the same.

Exercise 6.1 ▼

In Q1 to Q14, find the equation of each of the following circles of centre $(0, 0)$ and:

1. radius 2
2. radius 3
3. radius 4
4. radius 10
5. radius $\sqrt{5}$
6. radius $\sqrt{13}$
7. radius $\sqrt{17}$
8. radius $\sqrt{23}$
9. containing the point $(4, 3)$
10. containing the point $(-3, -2)$
11. containing the point $(1, -5)$
12. containing the point $(0, -4)$
13. containing the point $(1, -1)$
14. containing the point $(-2, 5)$

Write down the radius length of each of the following circles:

15. $x^2 + y^2 = 16$
16. $x^2 + y^2 = 9$
17. $x^2 + y^2 = 1$
18. $x^2 + y^2 = 13$
19. $x^2 + y^2 = 5$
20. $x^2 + y^2 = 29$

Draw a graph of each of the following circles and write down the coordinates where each circle intersects the x- and y-axes:

21. $x^2 + y^2 = 9$
22. $x^2 + y^2 = 16$
23. $x^2 + y^2 = 49$

24. Find the equation of the circle which has the line segment joining $(3, -4)$ to $(-3, 4)$ as diameter.

25. $a(6, 1)$ and $b(-6, -1)$ are two points. Find the equation of the circle with $[ab]$ as diameter.

26. $(6, -3)$ is an extremity of a diameter of the circle $x^2 + y^2 = 45$. What are the coordinates of the other extremity of the same diameter?

27. What is the area of the circle $x^2 + y^2 = 40$? Leave your answer in terms of π.

Points Inside, On or Outside a Circle I

Method 1:

To find whether a point is inside, on or outside a circle, calculate the distance from the centre, $(0, 0)$, to the point and compare this distance with the radius. Three cases arise:

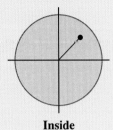
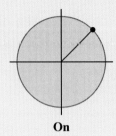
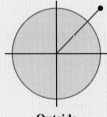

Inside	**On**	**Outside**
1. Distance from the centre to the point is **less** than the radius ∴ point inside the circle	2. Distance from the centre to the point is **equal** to the radius ∴ point on the circle	3. Distance from the centre to the point is **greater** than the radius ∴ point outside the circle

Method 2:

If the coordinates of a point satisfy the equation of a circle, then the point is **on** the circle. Otherwise, the point is either **inside** or **outside** the circle. By substituting the coordinates into the equation of the circle, one of the following situations can arise:

> **1.** $x^2 + y^2 < r^2$, the point is **inside** the circle.
>
> **2.** $x^2 + y^2 = r^2$, the point is **on** the circle.
>
> **3.** $x^2 + y^2 > r^2$, the point is **outside** the circle.

Example ▼

Determine whether the point $(3, 2)$ is inside, on or outside the circle $x^2 + y^2 = 10$.

Solution:

Using Method 1.

The radius of the circle is $\sqrt{10}$.

Distance from centre, $(0, 0)$ to the point $(3, 2)$:

$\sqrt{(3-0)^2 + (2-0)^2} = \sqrt{3^2 + 2^2} = \sqrt{9+4} = \sqrt{13}$

Distance from the centre to the point is greater than the radius, i.e. $\sqrt{13} > \sqrt{10}$.

∴ the point $(3, 2)$ is outside the circle $x^2 + y^2 = 10$.

Determine whether the points $(4, -1)$, $(5, 2)$ and $(3, \sqrt{5})$ are inside, on or outside the circle $x^2 + y^2 = 17$.

Solution:

Using Method 2.

$$x^2 + y^2 = 17 \implies r^2 = 17 \qquad \text{(by comparing with } x^2 + y^2 = r^2\text{)}$$

Substitute $(4, -1)$: $x^2 + y^2 = 4^2 + (-1)^2 = 16 + 1 = 17$

$$17 = 17$$

$\therefore \quad (4, -1)$ is on the circle.

Substitute $(5, 2)$: $x^2 + y^2 = 5^2 + 2^2 = 25 + 4 = 29$

$$29 > 17$$

$\therefore \quad (5, 2)$ is outside the circle.

Substitute $(3, \sqrt{5})$: $x^2 + y^2 = 3^2 + (\sqrt{5})^2 = 9 + 5 = 14$

$$14 < 17$$

$\therefore \quad (3, \sqrt{5})$ is inside the circle.

Exercise 6.2 ▼

In each of the following, determine whether the given point is inside, on or outside the given circle:

1. Point $(3, 1)$; circle $x^2 + y^2 = 10$
2. Point $(4, 2)$; circle $x^2 + y^2 = 17$
3. Point $(2, -1)$; circle $x^2 + y^2 = 5$
4. Point $(-2, 1)$; circle $x^2 + y^2 = 9$
5. Point $(7, -1)$; circle $x^2 + y^2 = 50$
6. Point $(-5, 2)$; circle $x^2 + y^2 = 29$
7. Point $(1, -9)$; circle $x^2 + y^2 = 100$
8. Point $(0, -4)$; circle $x^2 + y^2 = 16$
9. Point $(-2, -2)$; circle $x^2 + y^2 = 9$
10. Point $(-5, 1)$; circle $x^2 + y^2 = 25$
11. Point $(\frac{4}{5}, \frac{3}{5})$; circle $x^2 + y^2 = 1$
12. Point $(3, \sqrt{2})$; circle $x^2 + y^2 = 11$

13. Show that the point $(3, 2)$ is on the circle $x^2 + y^2 = 13$ and, hence, draw a graph of the circle.

14. The circle S has equation $x^2 + y^2 = 29$.
    The point $(5, p)$ lies on S. Find two real values of p.

15. Find the equation of the circle, centre the origin, which contains the point $(1, 7)$.
    The point $(1, k)$ is inside the circle. If $k \in \mathbf{Z}$, find the greatest and least values of k.

16. C is a circle with centre $(0, 0)$. It passes through the point $(1, 6)$.
    (i) Write down the equation of C.
    (ii) The point (k, k) lies inside C, where $k \in \mathbf{Z}$.
    Find all possible values of k.

Intersection of a Line and a Circle

To find the points where a line and a circle meet, the '**method of substitution**' between their equations is used.

The method involves the following three steps:

1. Get x or y on its own from the equation of the line.
   (Look carefully and select the variable which will make the working easier.)
2. Substitute for this same variable into the equation of the circle and solve the resultant quadratic equation.
3. Substitute **separately** the value(s) obtained in step 2 into the linear equation in step 1 to find the corresponding value(s) of the other variable.

Two Points of Intersection

Example ▼

Find the points of intersection of the line $x - 2y - 5 = 0$ and the circle $x^2 + y^2 = 10$.

Solution:

Line $x - 2y - 5 = 0$ and circle $x^2 + y^2 = 10$

Step 1: $x - 2y - 5 = 0$

$$x = 2y + 5 \qquad \text{[get } x \text{ on its own from the line equation]}$$

Step 2: Substitute $(2y + 5)$ for x into the equation of the circle.

$$x^2 + y^2 = 10$$

$$(2y + 5)^2 + y^2 = 10 \qquad \text{[substitute } (2y + 5) \text{ for } x]$$
$$4y^2 + 20y + 25 + y^2 = 10$$
$$5y^2 + 20y + 15 = 0 \qquad \text{[everything to the left]}$$
$$y^2 + 4y + 3 = 0 \qquad \text{[divide across by 5]}$$
$$(y + 3)(y + 1) = 0 \qquad \text{[factorise]}$$

$$y + 3 = 0 \qquad \text{or} \qquad y + 1 = 0$$
$$y = -3 \qquad \text{or} \qquad y = -1$$

These are the y coordinates.

Step 3: Substitute separately, $y = -3$ and $y = -1$ into the equation of the line in step 1 to find the x coordinates.

$$x = 2y + 5$$
$$y = -3$$
$$x = 2(-3) + 5$$
$$x = -6 + 5$$
$$x = -1$$
point $(-1, -3)$

$$x = 2y + 5$$
$$y = -1$$
$$x = 2(-1) + 5$$
$$x = -2 + 5$$
$$x = 3$$
point $(3, -1)$

Thus the two points of intersection are $(-1, -3)$ and $(3, -1)$.
The diagram illustrates the situation.

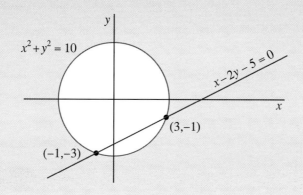

Exercise 6.3 ▼

Find the points of intersection of the given line and circle in each case:

1. Line: $x - y = 3$;   circle: $x^2 + y^2 = 5$.

2. Line: $x - y = 5$;   circle: $x^2 + y^2 = 17$.

3. Line: $x - y + 7 = 0$;   circle: $x^2 + y^2 = 25$.

4. Line: $x - 3y = 0$;   circle: $x^2 + y^2 = 10$.

5. Line: $x + 2y - 5 = 0$;   circle: $x^2 + y^2 = 10$.

6. Line: $x + 5y + 13 = 0$;   circle: $x^2 + y^2 = 13$.

7. Line: $x + y + 1 = 0$;   circle: $x^2 + y^2 = 13$.

8. Line: $2x + y - 10 = 0$;   circle: $x^2 + y^2 = 25$.

9. Line: $x + 3y - 5 = 0$;   circle: $x^2 + y^2 = 5$.

10. Line: $2x + y + 10 = 0$;   circle: $x^2 + y^2 = 40$.

11. The line $x - 2y + 5 = 0$ cuts the circle $x^2 + y^2 = 25$ at a and b. Calculate $|ab|$.

12. The line $x + 3y - 5 = 0$ intersects the circle $x^2 + y^2 = 5$ at p and q. Calculate $|pq|$.

13. The line L contains the point $(3, -1)$ and $(-1, -3)$. Find the equation of L.
Find, algebraically, the points of intersection of L and the circle K, $x^2 + y^2 = 25$.
Using the same axes and scales, graph L and K.

One Point of Intersection

Note: If there is only **one point of intersection** between a line and a circle, then the line is a **tangent** to the circle.

Example ▼

Find where the line $4x - y - 17 = 0$ cuts the circle $x^2 + y^2 = 17$ and investigate if this line is a tangent to the circle.

Solution:

Line $4x - y - 17 = 0$ and circle $x^2 + y^2 = 17$

Step 1: $4x - y - 17 = 0$

$$-y = -4x + 17$$
$$y = 4x - 17 \qquad \text{[get } y \text{ on its own from the line equation]}$$

Step 2: $\qquad\qquad x^2 + y^2 = 17$

$$x^2 + (4x - 17)^2 = 17 \qquad \text{[substitute } (4x - 17) \text{ for } y]$$
$$x^2 + 16x^2 - 136x + 289 = 17$$
$$17x^2 - 136x + 272 = 0 \qquad \text{[everything to the left]}$$
$$x^2 - 8x + 16 = 0 \qquad \text{[divide across by 17]}$$
$$(x - 4)(x - 4) = 0 \qquad \text{[factorise]}$$
$$x - 4 = 0 \quad \text{or} \quad x - 4 = 0$$
$$x = 4$$

Step 3: Substitute $x = 4$ into the equation of the line in step 1 to find y.

$x = 4$

$y = 4x - 17$

$y = 4(4) - 17 = 16 - 17 = -1$

point $(4, -1)$

$\therefore$ the line $4x - y - 17 = 0$ cuts the circle $x^2 + y^2 = 17$ at the point $(4, -1)$.

Since there is only **one point of contact** between the line and the circle, the line is a tangent to the circle.

The diagram on the right illustrates the situation.

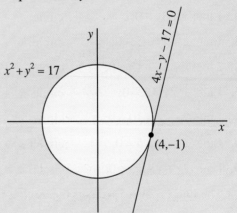

Verify that each line L is a tangent to the corresponding circle C in each of the following, and find the coordinates of the point of tangency in each case:

1. $L: x - y - 2 = 0$, $C: x^2 + y^2 = 2$
2. $L: x - y - 4 = 0$, $C: x^2 + y^2 = 8$
3. $L: 2x - y - 5 = 0$, $C: x^2 + y^2 = 5$
4. $L: x - 3y - 10 = 0$, $C: x^2 + y^2 = 10$
5. $L: 3x + y - 10 = 0$, $C: x^2 + y^2 = 10$
6. $L: x - 4y - 17 = 0$, $C: x^2 + y^2 = 17$
7. $L: 5x - y - 26 = 0$, $C: x^2 + y^2 = 26$
8. $L: x + 7y - 50 = 0$, $C: x^2 + y^2 = 50$

9. K is a circle with centre $(0, 0)$ and radius $\sqrt{5}$. Write down the equation of K.
   L is a line with equation $2x - y + 5 = 0$.
   Prove that L is a tangent to K and find the coordinates of the point of tangency.

10. $o(0, 0)$ and $p(3, \sqrt{11})$ are two points. Calculate $|op|$.
    C is a circle with centre $o(0, 0)$ and contains the point $p(3, \sqrt{11})$.
    Find the equation of K.
    L is the line containing the points $a(-4, 3)$ and $b(6, 8)$.
    Find the equation of L, verify that L is a tangent to C and find the coordinates of the point of tangency.

General Equation of a Circle, Centre (h, k) and Radius r

On the right is a circle with centre (h, k), radius r, and (x, y) is any point on the circle.
Distance between (h, k) and (x, y) equals the radius, r.

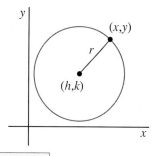

$\therefore \quad \sqrt{(x - h)^2 + (y - k)^2} = r$ (distance formula)
$\quad (x - h)^2 + (y - k)^2 = r^2$ (square both sides)

Hence, $(x - h)^2 + (y - k)^2 = r^2$ is said to be the equation of the circle.

> The equation of a circle, centre (h, k) and radius r, is
> $$(x - h)^2 + (y - k)^2 = r^2.$$

Two quantities are needed to find the equation of a circle:

        1. Centre, (h, k) **2.** Radius, r

Then use the formula $(x - h)^2 + (y - k)^2 = r^2$.

Note: If $(h, k) = (0, 0)$, the equation $(x - h)^2 + (y - k)^2 = r^2$ reduces to $x^2 + y^2 = r^2$.

(i) Find the equation of the circle, centre (2, 3) and radius 5.

(ii) Find the centre and radius of the circle, $(x + 1)^2 + (y - 4)^2 = 36$.

Solution:

(i) Centre (2, 3), radius 5

$h = 2, k = 3, r = 5$

Equation of the circle is:

$(x - h)^2 + (y - k)^2 = r^2$

$(x - 2)^2 + (y - 3)^2 = 5^2$

$(x - 2)^2 + (y - 3)^2 = 25$

(ii) $(x + 1)^2 + (y - 4)^2 = 36$

Compare exactly to:

$(x - h)^2 + (y - k)^2 = r^2$

$\downarrow \qquad\quad \downarrow \qquad\quad \downarrow$

$(x + 1)^2 + (y - 4)^2 = 36$

∴ $h = -1, k = 4, r = 6$

Thus, centre = (−1, 4) and radius = 6.

Find the equation of the circle which has the line segment from $a(-4, 3)$ to $b(2, -1)$ as diameter.

Solution:

The **centre** and **radius** are needed.
The diagram on the right illustrates the situation.

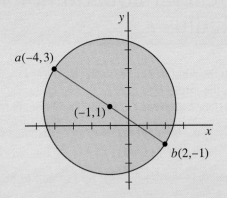

Centre
The centre is the midpoint of [ab].

$$\text{Centre} = \left(\frac{-4 + 2}{2}, \frac{3 - 1}{2}\right) = \left(\frac{-2}{2}, \frac{2}{2}\right)$$

$$= (-1, 1) = (h, k)$$

Radius
The radius is the distance from the centre (−1, 1) to either (−4, 3) or (2, −1).
Distance from (−1, 1) to (2, −1)

$$r = \sqrt{(2 + 1)^2 + (-1 - 1)^2} = \sqrt{3^2 + (-2)^2} = \sqrt{9 + 4} = \sqrt{13}$$

$$h = -1, k = 1, r = \sqrt{13}$$

Equation is $(x - h)^2 + (y - k)^2 = r^2$

$$(x + 1)^2 + (y - 1)^2 = (\sqrt{13})^2$$

$$(x + 1)^2 + (y - 1)^2 = 13$$

Find the equation of each of the following circles with given centre and radius:

1. Centre $(2, 3)$ and radius 4
2. Centre $(1, 4)$ and radius 5

3. Centre $(2, -1)$ and radius 2
4. Centre $(-5, 2)$ and radius 1

5. Centre $(-4, -3)$ and radius $\sqrt{17}$
6. Centre $(-3, 0)$ and radius $\sqrt{13}$

7. Centre $(0, 2)$ and radius $\sqrt{5}$
8. Centre $(-2, -6)$ and radius $\sqrt{29}$

9. Centre $(-1, -1)$ and radius $\sqrt{10}$
10. Centre $(-4, 2)$ and radius $\sqrt{12}$

Find the equation of the circle with:

11. centre $(1, 2)$ and containing the point $(2, 5)$
12. centre $(2, -1)$ and containing the point $(6, 4)$

13. centre $(4, -3)$ and containing the point $(0, 5)$
14. centre $(-2, -5)$ and containing the point $(3, 0)$

15. centre $(1, -1)$ and containing the point $(2, 4)$
16. centre $(-4, -2)$ and containing the point $(0, 0)$

Find the centre and radius of each of the following circles:

17. $(x - 3)^2 + (y - 2)^2 = 16$
18. $(x + 4)^2 + (y + 5)^2 = 9$

19. $(x - 1)^2 + (y + 3)^2 = 25$
20. $(x - 3)^2 + (y - 5)^2 = 4$

21. $(x - 2)^2 + (y - 2)^2 = 49$
22. $(x - 8)^2 + (y - 7)^2 = 1$

23. $(x - 5)^2 + (y + 2)^2 = 25$
24. $(x - 1)^2 + (y + 5)^2 = 36$

25. $x^2 + (y - 2)^2 = 64$
26. $(x - 3)^2 + y^2 = 4$

27. $a(5, 2)$ and $b(1, 4)$ are two points. Find the equation of the circle with $[ab]$ as diameter.

28. The end points of a diameter of a circle are $p(2, 4)$ and $q(-4, 0)$. Find the equation of the circle.

29. $a(-1, 5)$, $b(5, 13)$ and $c(-2, 12)$ are the vertices of triangle abc.
Show that the triangle is right angled at c.
Find the equation of the circle that passes through the coordinates
a, b and c.

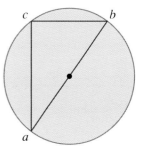

30. The circle C has equation $(x + 2)^2 + (y - 2)^2 = 13$.
Find the coordinates of the points where C intersects the x- and y-axes.

31. The circle C has equation $(x - 5)^2 + (y - 3)^2 = 18$.
C intersects the x-axis at p and q.
If $p < q$, find the coordinates of p and the coordinates of q.

32. The end points of a diameter of a circle are $(2, 3)$ and $(-6, -1)$.
(i) Find the equation of the circle.
(ii) The circle cuts the y-axis at the points p and q. Find $|pq|$.

33. $a(3, 5)$ and $b(-1, -1)$ are the end points of a diameter of a circle K.
(i) Find the centre and radius length of K.
(ii) Find the equation of K.
(iii) K intersects the x-axis at p and q, $p < q$. Find the coordinates of p and q.

Points Inside, On or Outside a Circle 2

Method 1:

To find whether a point is inside, on or outside a circle, calculate the distance from the centre, (h, k), to the point and compare this distance with the radius. Three cases arise:

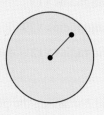 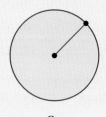 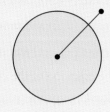

Inside	**On**	**Outside**
1. Distance from the centre to the point is **less** than the radius ∴ point inside the circle	**2.** Distance from the centre to the point is **equal** to the radius ∴ point on the circle	**3.** Distance from the centre to the point is **greater** than the radius ∴ point outside the circle

Method 2:

If the coordinates of a point satisfy the equation of a circle, then the point is **on** the circle. Otherwise, the point is either **inside** or **outside** the circle. By substituting the coordinates into the equation of the circle one of the following situations can arise:

1. $(x - h)^2 + (y - k)^2 < r^2$, the point is **inside** the circle.

2. $(x - h)^2 + (y - k)^2 = r^2$, the point is **on** the circle.

3. $(x - h)^2 + (y - k)^2 > r^2$, the point is **outside** the circle.

Example ▼

Determine if the points $(5, 3)$, $(-1, 4)$ and $(-2, -3)$ are inside, on or outside the circle

$$(x - 3)^2 + (y - 2)^2 = 20.$$

Solution:

$$(x - 3)^2 + (y - 2)^2 = 20 \qquad \text{(using method 2)}$$

Substitute $(5, 3)$: $(5 - 3)^2 + (3 - 2)^2 = (2)^2 + (1)^2 = 4 + 1 = 5 < 20$

∴ $(5, -3)$ is **inside** the circle.

Substitute $(-1, 4)$: $(-1 - 3)^2 + (4 - 2)^2 = (-4)^2 + (2)^2 = 16 + 4 = 20$

∴ $(-1, 4)$ is **on** the circle.

Substitute $(-2, -3)$: $(-2 - 3)^2 + (-3 - 2)^2 = (-5)^2 + (-5)^2 = 25 + 25 = 50 > 20$

∴ $(-2, -3)$ is **outside** the circle.

In each of the following, determine if the given point is inside, on or outside the given circle:

1. $(4, -1)$; $(x + 3)^2 + (y - 2)^2 = 16$ **2.** $(-1, 2)$; $(x - 2)^2 + (y + 3)^2 = 9$

3. $(3, 2)$; $(x - 1)^2 + (y + 2)^2 = 49$ **4.** $(-1, 5)$; $(x + 2)^2 + (y - 3)^2 = 36$

5. $(3, -4)$; $(x + 1)^2 + (y + 4)^2 = 1$ **6.** $(1, 2)$; $(x - 1)^2 + (y - 5)^2 = 4$

7. $(5, -1)$; $(x - 1)^2 + (y + 4)^2 = 25$ **8.** $(0, 0)$; $(x + 2)^2 + (y + 3)^2 = 64$

9. $(-7, 0)$; $(x - 2)^2 + (y + 1)^2 = 100$ **10.** $(-2, 1)$; $(x + 3)^2 + (y - 1)^2 = 16$

11. $(-1, 4)$; $(x + 5)^2 + (y - 3)^2 = 13$ **12.** $(4, 3)$; $(x - 2)^2 + (y + 1)^2 = 20$

13. $(2, -4)$; $(x - 6)^2 + (y + 5)^2 = 17$ **14.** $(1, -1)$; $(x + 1)^2 + (y - 2)^2 = 29$

15. The circle C has equation $(x + 1)^2 + (y + 1)^2 = 34$.
The point $(-4, k)$ lies on C. Find the two real values of k.

16. The circle S has equation $(x - 4)^2 + (y - 2)^2 = 13$.
The point $(p, 0)$ lies on S. Find the two real values of p.

Equation of a Tangent to a Circle at a Given Point

A tangent is perpendicular to the radius that joins the centre of
a circle to the point of tangency.

This fact is used to find the slope of the tangent.

In the diagram on the right, the radius, R, is perpendicular to the
tangent, T, at the point of tangency, p.

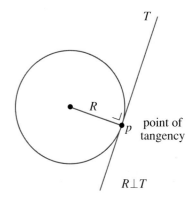

The equation of a tangent to a circle at a given point is found with the following steps:

Step 1: Find the slope of the radius to the point of tangency.

Step 2: Turn this slope upside down and change its sign.
This gives the slope of the tangent.

Step 3: Use the coordinates of the point of contact and the slope of the tangent at this point in
the formula:

$$(y - y_1) = m(x - x_1).$$

This gives the equation of the tangent.

A diagram is often very useful.

Find the equation of the tangent to the circle $(x - 2)^2 + (y - 3)^2 = 25$ at the point $(5, 7)$ on the circle.

Solution:

$$(x - 2)^2 + (y - 3)^2 = 25$$
$$\text{Centre} = (2, 3)$$

Step 1:

Slope of radius, R, $= \dfrac{7-3}{5-2} = \dfrac{4}{3}$

Step 2:

∴ Slope of tangent, T, $= -\frac{3}{4}$
(turn upside down and change sign)

Step 3: $x_1 = 5$ $y_1 = 7$ $m = -\frac{3}{4}$

$$(y - y_1) = m(x - x_1)$$
$$(y - 7) = -\tfrac{3}{4}(x - 5)$$
$$4(y - 7) = -3(x - 5)$$
$$4y - 28 = -3x + 15$$
$$3x + 4y - 28 - 15 = 0$$
$$3x + 4y - 43 = 0$$

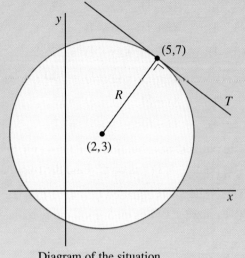

Diagram of the situation

Find the equation of the tangent to the given circle at the given point (make a rough diagram in each case):

1. Circle $x^2 + y^2 = 10$;   point $(3, 1)$.

2. Circle $x^2 + y^2 = 5$;   point $(2, -1)$.

3. Circle $x^2 + y^2 = 26$;   point $(-5, -1)$.

4. Circle $x^2 + y^2 = 13$;   point $(-3, 2)$.

5. Circle $x^2 + y^2 = 50$;   point $(-1, 7)$.

6. Circle $x^2 + y^2 = 17$;   point $(-1, 4)$.

7. Circle $x^2 + y^2 = 20$;   point $(4, 2)$.

8. Circle $x^2 + y^2 = 29$;   point $(-5, -2)$.

9. Circle $(x - 4)^2 + (y + 2)^2 = 13$;   point $(6, -5)$.

10. Circle $(x - 2)^2 + (y - 2)^2 = 20$;   point $(-2, 0)$.

11. Circle $(x - 4)^2 + (y + 3)^2 = 10$;   point $(7, -4)$.

12. Circle $(x - 5)^2 + (y + 2)^2 = 85$;   point $(-1, 5)$.

13. Circle $(x - 1)^2 + (y - 1)^2 = 2$;   point $(0, 0)$.

14. Circle $(x + 3)^2 + y^2 = 25$;   point $(0, 4)$.

15. Circle $x^2 + (y - 5)^2 = 29$;   point $(5, 3)$.

16. Circle $(x - 2)^2 + (y + 4)^2 = 10$;   point $(3, -1)$.

17. Circle $(x + 2)^2 + (y - 3)^2 = 29$;   point $(3, 5)$.

18. Show that the point $(1, -3)$ is on the circle $(x + 2)^2 + (y - 1)^2 = 25$.
    Find the equation of the tangent to the circle at the point $(1, -3)$.

Transformations

Under a central symmetry, axial symmetry or translation a circle will keep the **same** radius. Hence, all that is needed is to find the image of the centre under the particular transformation.

The equation of a circle under a transformation is found with the following steps:

> 1. Find the **centre** and **radius** of the given circle.
> 2. Find the image of the centre under the given transformation.
> 3. Use this new centre and the radius of the original circle in the equation:
> $$(x - h)^2 + (y - k)^2 = r^2.$$

As before, a diagram is very useful.

Example ▼

Find the equation of the image of the circle $(x - 3)^2 + (y - 4)^2 = 4$ under the translation $(2, 2) \rightarrow (4, -5)$.

Solution:

$(x - 3)^2 + (y - 4)^2 = 4$

Step 1: Centre $= (3, 4)$

Radius $= \sqrt{4} = 2$

Given circle has centre $= (3, 4)$ and radius 2.

Step 2: $(2, 2) \rightarrow (4, -5)$

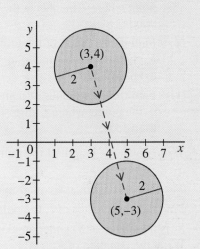

Rule: add 2 to x, subtract 7 from y.
Apply this translation to the centre, $(3, 4)$, of the given circle

∴ $(3, 4) \rightarrow (3 + 2, 4 - 7) = (5, -3)$

Thus the image circle has centre $(5, -3)$ and radius 2.

Step 3: $h = 5, k = -3, r = 2$

$(x - h)^2 + (y - k)^2 = r^2$

$(x - 5)^2 + (y + 3)^2 = 2^2$

$(x - 5)^2 + (y + 3)^2 = 4$

Exercise 6.8 ▼

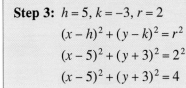

1. Find the equation of the image of the circle $(x - 2)^2 + (y - 3)^2 = 20$ under the translation $(1, 1) \rightarrow (3, -4)$.

2. Find the equation of the image of the circle $(x - 5)^2 + (y + 4)^2 = 25$ under an axial symmetry in the y-axis.

3. Find the equation of the image of the circle $(x + 2)^2 + y^2 = 9$ under a central symmetry in the centre of the circle $(x - 1)^2 + (y + 2)^2 = 1$.

4. $a(3, -1)$ and $b(0, 4)$ are two points. Find the equation of the image of the circle $(x - 2)^2 + (y + 3)^2 = 9$ under the translation $\vec{ab}$.

5. The equation of the circle S is $(x - 5)^2 + (y + 6)^2 = 64$. Find the centre and radius of S.

Find the equation of the image of S under an axial symmetry in the x-axis.

6. The circle K: $(x - 5)^2 + (y + 2)^2 = 36$ is the image of the circle C under an axial symmetry in the y-axis. Find the equation of C.

7. The equation of the circle C is $(x - 10)^2 + (y - 6)^2 = 20$.

    (i) Find the centre and radius of C.

    (ii) Verify that the point $s(6, 4)$ is on C.

    (iii) Find the equation of the tangent T to C at the point s.

    (iv) Find the coordinates of r, the point where T intersects the x-axis.

    (v) Find the equation of the circle K, the image of C under an axial symmetry in T.

    (vi) Find the coordinates of p and q, the points where K intersects the x-axis.

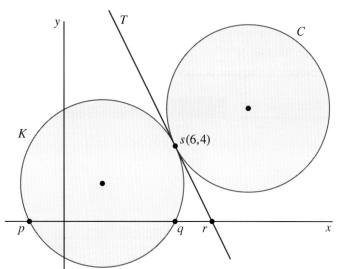

8. Write down the length of the radius of the circle S_1: $x^2 + y^2 = 20$.

T: $x - 2y + 10 = 0$ is the equation of a tangent to S_1.

Find the coordinates of r, the point of contact.

S_2 is the image of S_1 under an axial symmetry in T. Write the equation of S_2.

Find the coordinates of p and q, points in which S_2 intersects the y-axis.

S_3 is a circle through p and q with centre $(6, 8)$. Find the equation of S_3.

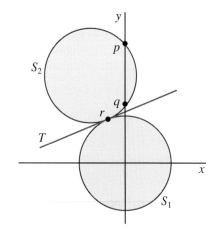

PERIMETER, AREA AND VOLUME

Perimeter and Area

Formulas required:

---

1. Rectangle

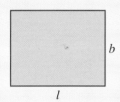

Area = lb

Perimeter = $2l + 2b = 2(l + b)$

---

2. Square

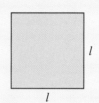

Area = l^2

Perimeter = $4l$

---

3. Triangle

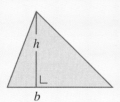

Area = $\frac{1}{2}bh$

---

4. Parallelogram

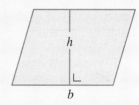

Area = bh

---

5. Circle (Disc)

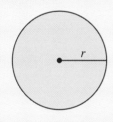

Area = πr^2

Circumference = $2\pi r$

---

6. Sector of a circle

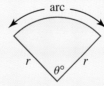

Area = $\dfrac{\theta}{360} \times \pi r^2$

Length of arc = $\dfrac{\theta}{360} \times 2\pi r$

$\left(\text{Similar to circle with } \dfrac{\theta}{360} \text{ in front of formulas}\right)$

The figure is made up of a semicircle and a triangle (all dimensions in cm).

Find the area of the figure in cm². (Assume $\pi = \frac{22}{7}$)

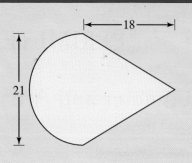

Solution:

Split the figure up into regular shapes, for which we have formulas to calculate the area.

Find the area of each shape separately and add these results together.

1. Area of semicircle

$= \frac{1}{2}\pi r^2$

$= \frac{1}{2} \times \frac{22}{7} \times \frac{21}{2} \times \frac{21}{2}$

$= 173.25 \text{ cm}^2$

(radius $= \frac{21}{2}$)

2. Area of triangle

$= \frac{1}{2}bh$

$= \frac{1}{2} \times 21 \times 18$

$= 189 \text{ cm}^2$

(base = 21, height = 18)

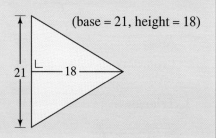

Area of figure = Area of semicircle + Area of triangle

$= 173.25 + 189 = 362.25 \text{ cm}^2$

The diagram represents a sector of a circle of radius 15 cm. $|\angle poq| = 72°$.
Find:

(i) the area of the sector *opq*, in terms of π

(ii) the perimeter of the sector; assume $\pi = 3.14$.

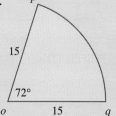

Solution:

(i) Area of sector

$= \frac{\theta}{360} \times \pi r^2$

$= \frac{72}{360} \times \pi \times 15 \times 15$

$= \frac{1}{5} \times \pi \times 15 \times 15$

$= 45\pi \text{ cm}^2$

(ii) Length of arc *pq*

$= \frac{\theta}{360} \times 2\pi r$

$= \frac{72}{360} \times 2 \times 3.14 \times 15$

$= \frac{1}{5} \times 2 \times 3.14 \times 15$

$= 18.84 \text{ cm}$

Perimeter $= 15 + 15 + 18.84 = 48.84 \text{ cm}$

Notes: 1. When using $\pi = \frac{22}{7}$, it is good practice to write the radius as a fraction.

For example, $21 = \frac{21}{1}$ or $4.5 = \frac{9}{2}$

2. If a question says 'give your answer in terms of π', then leave π in the answer: do **not** use 3.14 or $\frac{22}{7}$ for π.

Exercise 7.1 ▼

Unless otherwise stated, all dimensions are in cm and assume $\pi = 3.14$. All curved lines represent the circumference, or parts of the circumference, of a circle.

Find: **(i)** the perimeter **(ii)** the area of each of the following shapes:

1.
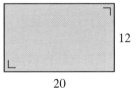
12
20

2.
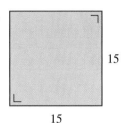
15
15

3.
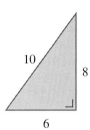
10
8
6

4.
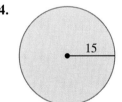
15

5.
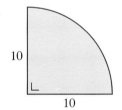
10
10

6.
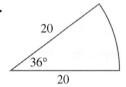
20
36°
20

7.
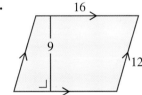
16
9
12

8.
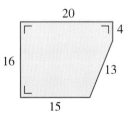
20
4
16
13
15

9.
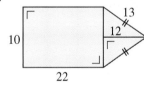
13
12
10
22

Find the area of each of the following:

10.
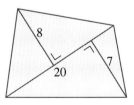
8
20
7

11.
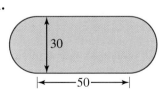
30
50

12.
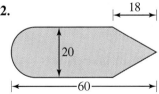
18
20
60

131

Calculate the area of the shaded region, where *abcd* is a rectangle and *pqrs* is a square:

13.

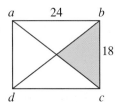

14.

15.

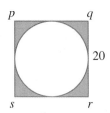

In questions 16–20, assume $\pi = \frac{22}{7}$.

16.

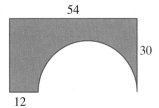

17.

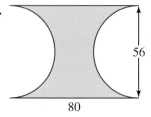

18.

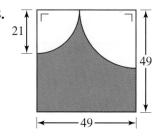

19.

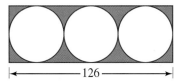

20.

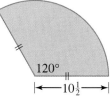

21. Two squares have sides of length 3 cm and 12 cm, respectively.
Find, in its simplest form, the ratio of their areas.

22. A square is inscribed in a circle.
The radius of the circle is 10 cm.
Find the area of the square.

23. A square is inscribed in a circle as shown in the diagram.
The length of the radius of the circle is 7 cm.
Calculate the area of the shaded region.
(Assume $\pi = \frac{22}{7}$)

24. A bicycle wheel, including the tyre, has a diameter of 56 cm. How far will it have travelled when it has made 200 revolutions? How many revolutions will the wheel complete in a journey of 924 m?
(Assume $\pi = \frac{22}{7}$)

25. A running track is in the shape of a rectangle with semicircular ends as shown:
  (i) Calculate the length of the track.
  (ii) Calculate the number of laps an athlete would have to complete in a 10 km race.
  (iii) Another athlete ran 3 laps in 5 minutes.
    Calculate her speed in km/h.
    (Assume $\pi = \frac{22}{7}$)

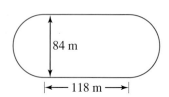

Given the Perimeter or Area

In some equations we are given the perimeter, the circumference, or the area and asked to find missing lengths. Basically we are given 'an equation in disguise' and we solve this equation to find the missing length.

Example ▼

The perimeter of a rectangle is 180 m. If length : breadth = 2 : 1, find the area of the rectangle.

Solution:

Let the length = $2x$ and the breadth = x.

Equation given in disguise:

Perimeter = 180

$\therefore \quad 2x + x + 2x + x = 180$

$6x = 180$

$x = 30$

$\therefore \quad$ breadth = 30 m

and length = $2x = 2(30) = 60$ m

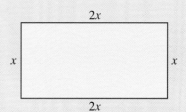

Area = $l \times b$

$= 60 \times 30$

$= 1800$

$\therefore \quad$ Area = 1800 m^2

Example ▼

The circumference of a circle is 37.68 cm. Calculate its area (assume $\pi = 3.14$).

Solution:

Equation given in disguise:

Circumference = 37.68 cm

$\therefore \qquad 2\pi r = 37.68$

$2(3.14)r = 37.68$

$6.28r = 37.68$

$r = \dfrac{37.68}{6.28} = 6$ cm

Area = πr^2

$= 3.14 \times 6 \times 6$

$= 113.04$

$\therefore \quad$ Area of circle = 113.04 cm^2

Exercise 7.2 ▼

If not given, drawing a rough diagram may help in solving the following problems.

1. The area of a rectangle is 320 cm^2. If its length is 40 cm, calculate:
    (i) its breadth   **(ii)** its perimeter.

2. **(i)** The perimeter of a square is 36 cm. Calculate its area.
    (ii) The area of a square is 25 cm^2. Calculate its perimeter.

3. The area of the triangle is 80 cm^2.
   The length of the base is 20 cm.
   Calculate its perpendicular height, h cm.

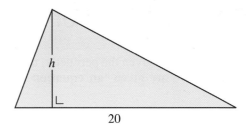

4. The triangle and the rectangle have equal area. Find h.

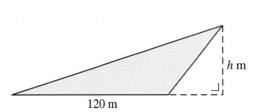

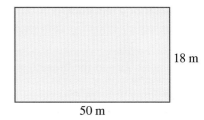

5. The length and breadth of a rectangle are in the ratio 3 : 2 respectively.
   The length of the rectangle is 12 cm. Find its breadth and its area.

6. The perimeter of a rectangle is 120 m.
   If length : breadth = 3 : 1, find the area of the rectangle.

7. The area of a rectangle is 128 m^2.
   If length : breadth = 2 : 1, find the length and the breadth of the rectangle.

The table below shows certain information on circles, including the value of π to be used. In each case write down the equation given in disguise, and use this to find the radius and complete the table.

	π	Circumference	Area	Radius
8.	π	$10\,\pi$		
9.	π		$9\,\pi$ m^2	
10.	π		$6.25\,\pi$ cm^2	
11.	$\frac{22}{7}$	264 cm		
12.	$\frac{22}{7}$		616 m^2	
13.	3.14	157 mm		
14.	3.14		1256 m^2	
15.	π		$30.25\,\pi$ cm^2	
16.	$\frac{22}{7}$		346.5 m^2	
17.	3.14		452.16 cm^2	

18. A piece of wire is 308 cm in length.

308 cm

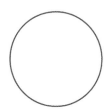

The wire is bent into the shape of a circle.

Calculate the radius of the circle.

(Assume $\pi = \frac{22}{7}$)

19. A piece of wire of length 66 cm is in the shape of a semicircle, as shown.

Find the radius length of the semicircle.

(Assume $\pi = \frac{22}{7}$)

66 cm

20. The diagram shows a small circle drawn inside a larger circle. The small circle has an area of 25π cm^2. The larger circle has a circumference of 16π cm.

Calculate the area of the shaded region, in terms of π.

21. The area of the sector shown is 31.4 cm^2.

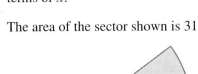

Calculate the value of r.

(Assume $\pi = 3.14$)

22. The area of the sector shown is 12.56 cm^2.

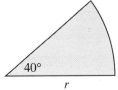

Calculate the value of r.

(Assume $\pi = 3.14$)

Volume and Surface Area

The **volume** of a solid is the amount of space it occupies.
Volume is measured in cubic units, such as cubic metres (m^3) or cubic centimetres (cm^3).
Capacity is the volume of a liquid or gas and is usually measured in litres.

Note: 1 litre = 1,000 cm^3 = 1,000 ml

The **surface area** of a solid is the '**total area of its outer surface**'.
It is measured in square units such as square metres or square centimetres.
To calculate the surface area of a solid you have to find the area of each face and add them together (often called the 'total surface area'). With some objects, such as a sphere, the surface area is called the 'curved surface area'.

Note: It is usual to denote volume by V and surface area by SA.

Rectangular Solids

Formulas required:

1. Rectangular solid (cuboid)	**2. Cube**

$$V = lbh$$

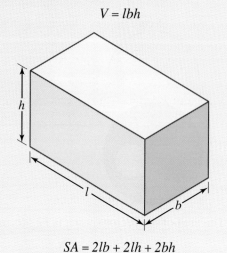

$$V = l^3$$

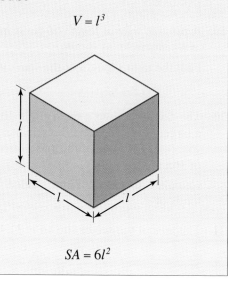

$$SA = 2lb + 2lh + 2bh$$

$$SA = 6l^2$$

Example ▼

The volume of a rectangular block is 560 cm^3.

If its length is 14 cm and its breadth is 8 cm, find:

(i) its height   **(ii)** its surface area.

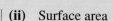

h

8

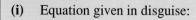

14

Solution:

(i) Equation given in disguise:

Volume = 560 cm^3

$(14)(8)h = 560$

$112h = 560$

$h = \frac{560}{112} = 5$ cm

(ii) Surface area

$= 2lb + 2lh + 2bh$

$= 2(14)(8) + 2(14)(5) + 2(8)(5)$

$= 224 + 140 + 80$

$= 444$ cm^2

Example ▼

The surface area of a cube is 96 cm².
Calculate its volume.

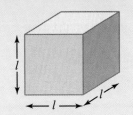

Solution:

Let the length of one side of the cube be l cm.
Equation given in disguise:

Surface area = 96 cm²

$$6l^2 = 96$$
$$l^2 = 16$$
$$l = 4 \text{ cm}$$

Volume = l^3
$$= 4^3$$
$$= 64 \text{ cm}^3$$

Thus, the volume of the cube is 64 cm³

Exercise 7.3 ▼

Find: **(i)** the volume **(ii)** the surface area of a solid rectangular block with dimensions:

1. 6 cm, 5 cm, 4 cm   **2.** 12 m, 8 m, 6 m   **3.** 20 mm, 9 mm, 7 mm

4. The volume of a rectangular block is 480 cm³.
   Its length is 12 cm and its breadth is 8 cm.
   Calculate:
   (i) its height   **(ii)** its surface area.

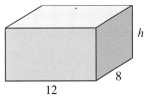

5. How many litres of water can be stored in a rectangular tank measuring 1.5 m by 70 cm by 50 cm?
   (**Note:** 1 litre = 1,000 cm³)

6. An open rectangular tank (no top) is full of water.
   The volume of water in the tank is 2.4 litres.
   If its length is 20 cm and its breadth is 15 cm, find:
   (i) its height   **(ii)** its surface area.
   (**Note:** 1 litre = 1000 cm³)

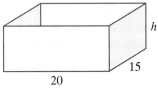

7. How many rectangular packets of tea measuring 12 cm by 4 cm by 4 cm can be packed into a cardboard box measuring 96 cm by 36 cm by 32 cm?

8. The volume of a cube is 27 cm³. Calculate its surface area.

9. The volume of a cube is 64 cm³. Calculate its surface area.

10. The surface area of a cube is 24 cm². Calculate its volume.

11. The surface area of a cube is 150 cm². Calculate its volume.

12. The sides of a rectangular block are in the ratio 2 : 3 : 7. If its volume is 2,688 cm³, find its dimensions and, hence, its surface area.

13. The surface area of a solid rectangular block is 258 cm². If its breadth is 6 cm and height is 5 cm, calculate: **(i)** its length   **(ii)** its volume.

Uniform Cross-section

Many solid objects have the same cross-section throughout their length.

Here are some examples:

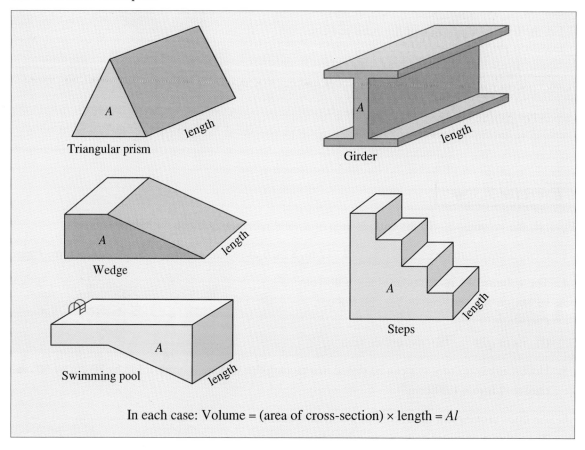

Triangular prism

Girder

Wedge

Steps

Swimming pool

In each case: Volume = (area of cross-section) × length = *Al*

The above objects are called prisms. A prism is a solid object which has the same cross-section throughout its length, and its sides are parallelograms.
A solid cylinder has a uniform cross-section, but it is not a prism.
So to find the volume of a solid object with uniform cross-section, find the area of the cross-section and multiply this by its length.

Example ▼

The diagram shows the design of a swimming pool.

Calculate the capacity of the pool in m³.

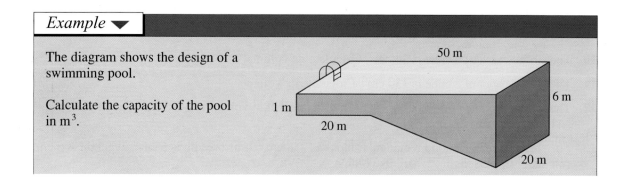

Solution:

The uniform cross-section is a combination of a rectangle and a triangle.

Area of cross-section

$$= l \times b + \tfrac{1}{2}bh$$

$$= 50 \times 1 + \tfrac{1}{2} \times 5 \times 30$$

$$= 50 + 75 = 125 \text{ m}^2$$

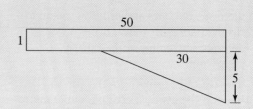

Volume = (Area of cross-section) × width

$$= 125 \times 20 = 2{,}500 \text{ m}^3$$

∴   The capacity of the pool is 2,500 m³.

Exercise 7.4 ▼

Calculate the volume of each of the following solids (all dimensions in cm):

1.

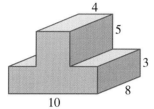

2.

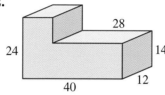

3.

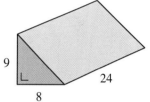

4.

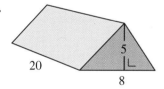

5.

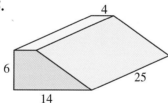

6.

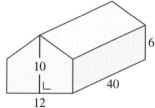

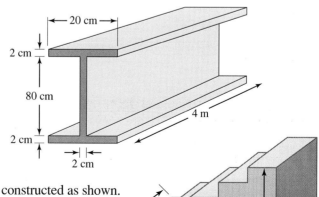

7. The diagram shows a steel girder. Calculate:

   (i)   the area of its cross-section (shaded region)

   (ii) the volume, in cm³, of steel used to manufacture it.

8. Five rectangular-shaped concrete steps are constructed as shown.

Each step measures 1.2 m by 0.4 m and the total height is 1 m, with each step having the same height of 0.2 m.

Calculate the volume of the solid concrete construction.

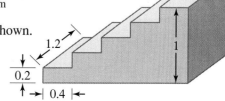

9. The diagram shows the design of a swimming pool.

Calculate:

(i) the capacity of the pool in m^3

(ii) the time, in hours and minutes, taken to fill the pool with water, if the water is delivered by a pipe at the rate of 10 m^3/min

(iii) the cost of heating the water for 15 hours if the average cost per cubic metre per hour is 0.08 c.

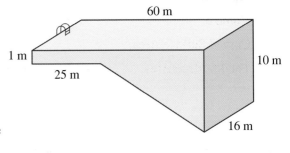

10. The diagram shows a triangular prism which has sloping sides that are perpendicular to each other.

(i) Calculate the area of its cross-section (shaded region).

(ii) If its volume is 120 cm^3, find x.

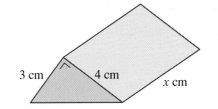

Cylinder, Sphere and Hemisphere

Formulas required:

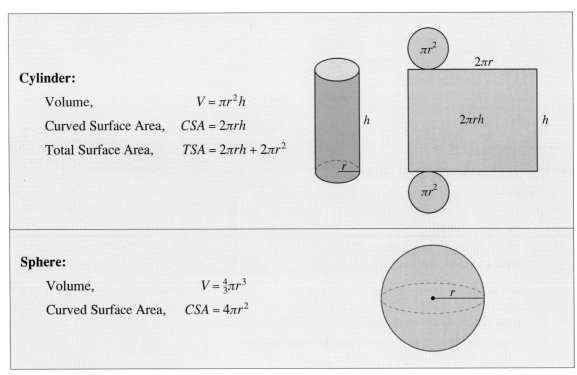

Cylinder:

Volume, $\quad\quad\quad\quad\quad\quad\quad V = \pi r^2 h$

Curved Surface Area, $\quad CSA = 2\pi rh$

Total Surface Area, $\quad\quad TSA = 2\pi rh + 2\pi r^2$

Sphere:

Volume, $\quad\quad\quad\quad\quad\quad\quad V = \frac{4}{3}\pi r^3$

Curved Surface Area, $\quad CSA = 4\pi r^2$

Hemisphere:

Volume, $\qquad V = \frac{2}{3}\pi r^3$

Curved Surface Area, $\quad CSA = 2\pi r^2$

Total Surface Area, $\quad TSA = 2\pi r^2 + \pi r^2 = 3\pi r^2$

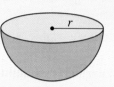

Example ▼

Find: **(i)** the volume **(ii)** the total surface area of a closed cylindrical can of radius 14 cm and height 10 cm (assume $\pi = \frac{22}{7}$).

Solution:

(i) $\quad V = \pi r^2 h$

$\qquad V = \frac{22}{7} \times \frac{14}{1} \times \frac{14}{1} \times \frac{10}{1}$

$\qquad V = 6160 \text{ cm}^2$

(ii) $\quad TSA = 2\pi rh + 2\pi r^2$

$\qquad\quad = \frac{2}{1} \times \frac{22}{7} \times \frac{14}{1} \times \frac{10}{1} + \frac{2}{1} \times \frac{22}{7} \times \frac{14}{1} \times \frac{14}{1}$

$\qquad\quad = 880 + 1232$

$\qquad\quad = 2112 \text{ cm}^2$

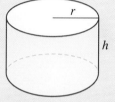

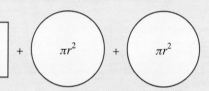

Example ▼

A solid sphere has a radius of 6 cm. Calculate: **(i)** its volume $\qquad$ **(ii)** its curved surface area. (Assume $\pi = 3.14$.)

Solution:

(i) $\quad V = \frac{4}{3}\pi r^3$

$\qquad = \frac{4}{3} \times 3.14 \times 6 \times 6 \times 6$

$\qquad = 904.32 \text{ cm}^3$

(ii) $\quad CSA = 4\pi r^2$

$\qquad = 4 \times 3.14 \times 6 \times 6$

$\qquad = 452.16 \text{ cm}^2$

Complete the following table, which gives certain information about various closed **cylinders**:

	π	Radius	Height	Volume	Curved Surface Area	Total Surface Area
1.	$\frac{22}{7}$	7 cm	12 cm			
2.	3.14	15 cm	40 cm			
3.	π	8 mm	11 mm			
4.	$\frac{22}{7}$	3.5 m	10 m			
5.	3.14	12 cm	40 cm			
6.	π	13 mm	30 mm			

Complete the following table, which gives certain information about various **spheres**:

	π	Radius	Volume	Curved Surface Area
7.	$\frac{22}{7}$	21 cm		
8.	3.14	9 m		
9.	π	6 mm		
10.	$\frac{22}{7}$	10.5 cm		
11.	3.14	7.5 cm		
12.	π	1.5 m		

Complete the following table, which gives certain information about various **hemispheres**:

	π	Radius	Volume	Curved Surface Area	Total Surface Area
13.	π	15 mm			
14.	π	$1\frac{1}{2}$ cm			
15.	$\frac{22}{7}$	42 cm			
16.	3.14	12 m			

17. A hollow plastic pipe has an external diameter 16 cm and an internal diameter 10 cm.

Calculate the volume of plastic in 2 m of pipe. (Assume $\pi = 3.14$.)

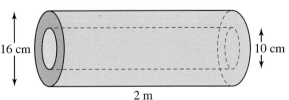

16 cm   10 cm

2 m

142

18. A cylindrical jug has dimensions radius 6 cm and height 40 cm. If the jug is full of lemonade, how many cylindrical tumblers, each with dimensions radius 4 cm and height 10 cm, can be filled from the jug?

19. A machine part consists of a hollow sphere floating in a closed cylinder full of oil. The height of the cylinder is 28 cm; the radius of the cylinder is 15 cm; and the radius of the sphere is $\frac{21}{2}$ cm.

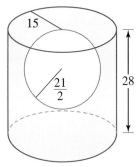

Taking π to be $\frac{22}{7}$, find the volume of:

(i) the cylinder

(ii) the sphere

(iii) the oil.

Cone

Formulas required:

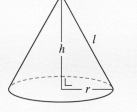

Volume, $V = \frac{1}{3}\pi r^2 h$

Curved Surface Area, $CSA = \pi r l$

Total Surface Area, $TSA = \pi r l + \pi r^2$

Pythagoras's Theorem: $l^2 = r^2 + h^2$

Notes: l is called the slant height.

A cone is often called a '**right circular cone**', as its vertex is directly above the centre of the base and its height is at right angles to the base.

Example ▼

A right circular cone has a height of 12 cm and a base radius of 5 cm.

Find: **(i)** its volume   **(ii)** its curved surface area (assume $\pi = 3.14$).

Solution:

(i) Volume of cone

$= \frac{1}{3}\pi r^2 h$

$= \frac{1}{3} \times 3.14 \times 5 \times 5 \times 12$

$= 314$ cm^3

(ii) Slant height is missing.

$l^2 = r^2 + h^2$

$l^2 = 5^2 + 12^2$

$l^2 = 25 + 144$

$l^2 = 169$

$l = 13$ cm

Curved surface area

$= \pi r l$

$= 3.14 \times 5 \times 13$

$= 204.1$ cm^2

Complete the following table, which gives certain information about various **cones**:

	π	Radius	Height	Slant Height	Volume	Curved Surface Area
1.	π	8 cm	6 cm			
2.	$\frac{22}{7}$		20 mm	29 mm		
3.	3.14	3 cm		5 cm		
4.	π	1.5 m		2.5 m		
5.	3.14		9 cm	41 cm		
6.	π	8 m		17 m		
7.	$\frac{22}{7}$	2.8 cm	4.5 cm			
8.	π	4.8 mm		5 mm		
9.	π	12 m	35 m			
10.	3.14	11 cm		61 cm		

11. A cone has a radius length 7 cm and height 2.4 cm.

Calculate: **(i)** its volume   **(ii)** its total surface area (assume $\pi = \frac{22}{7}$).

12. A cone has radius length 18 cm and height 16.25 cm.

Calculate: **(i)** its volume   **(ii)** its total surface area (assume $\pi = 3.14$).

Compound Volumes

Many of the objects of which we need to find the volume will be made up of different shapes.

When this happens do the following:

1. Split the solid up into regular shapes, for which we have formulas to calculate the volume or surface area.
2. Add these results together.

Example ▼

A solid object consists of three parts: a cone, A, a cylinder, B, and a hemisphere, C, each having a radius of 6 cm as shown. If the height of the object is 26 cm, calculate its volume, in terms of π.

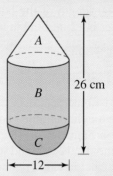

Solution:

A: Volume of cone $= \frac{1}{3}\pi r^2 h$

$\qquad\qquad = \frac{1}{3}\pi \times 6 \times 6 \times 8$

$\qquad\qquad = 96\pi \text{ cm}^3$

B: Volume of cylinder $= \pi r^2 h$

$\qquad\qquad = \pi \times 6 \times 6 \times 12$

$\qquad\qquad = 432\pi \text{ cm}^3$

C: Volume of hemisphere $= \frac{2}{3}\pi r^3$

$\qquad\qquad = \frac{2}{3}\pi \times 6 \times 6 \times 6$

$\qquad\qquad = 144\pi \text{ cm}^3$

Total volume = Volume of cone + Volume of cylinder + Volume of hemisphere

$\qquad\qquad = (96\pi + 432\pi + 144\pi) \text{ cm}^3 = 672\pi \text{ cm}^3$

Exercise 7.7 ▼

1. A glass container is in the shape of a cone surmounted by a cylinder, as shown. The height of the cylindrical part is 20 cm and the length of its radius is 8 cm. The slant height of the cone is 17 cm.

   Show that the volume of the container is $1{,}600\pi \text{ cm}^3$.

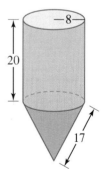

2. A test tube consists of a hemisphere, of diameter 3 cm, surmounted by a cylinder, as shown. The total height of the test tube is $16\frac{1}{2}$ cm.

   Calculate, in terms of π, the volume of the test tube.

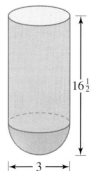

3. A boiler is in the shape of a cylinder with hemispherical ends (as shown in the diagram). The total length of the boiler is 30 m and its diameter is 12 m. Find in terms of π:

   (i) its volume

   (ii) its surface area.

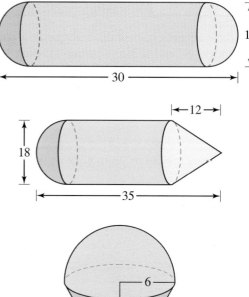

4. A solid object consists of 3 parts: a hemisphere, a cylinder and a cone, as shown, each having a diameter of 18 cm. If the height of the cone is 12 cm and the total height is 35 cm, calculate its volume, and surface area, in terms of π.

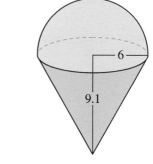

5. A buoy consists of an inverted cone surmounted by a hemisphere, as shown. If the radius of the hemisphere is 6 cm and the height of the cone is 9.1 cm, calculate, assuming $\pi = 3.14$:

   (i) the volume of the buoy

   (ii) the surface area of the buoy.

Given the Volume or Surface Area

In some questions we are given the volume or surface area and asked to find a missing dimension. As before, write down the '**equation given in disguise**', and solve this equation to find the missing dimension.

Example ▼

(i) A cylinder has a volume of 192π cm^3. If its radius is 4 cm, calculate its height.

(ii) The volume of a sphere is $\frac{32}{3}\pi$ cm^3. Calculate its radius.

Solution:

(i) Equation given in disguise:

$$\text{Volume of cylinder} = 192\pi \text{ cm}^3$$

$$\pi r^2 h = 192\pi$$

$$r^2 h = 192 \qquad \text{(divide both sides by } \pi)$$

$$16h = 192 \qquad \text{(put in } r = 4)$$

$$h = 12 \text{ cm} \qquad \text{(divide both sides by 16)}$$

(ii) Equation given in disguise:

$$\text{Volume of sphere} = \tfrac{32}{3}\pi \text{ cm}^3$$

$$\tfrac{4}{3}\pi r^3 = \tfrac{32}{3}\pi$$

$$4\pi r^3 = 32\pi \qquad \text{(multiply both sides by 3)}$$

$$4r^3 = 32 \qquad \text{(divide both sides by } \pi\text{)}$$

$$r^3 = 8 \qquad \text{(divide both sides by 4)}$$

$$r = 2 \text{ cm} \qquad \text{(take the cube root of both sides)}$$

Exercise 7.8 ▼

1. A cylinder has a volume of 720π cm^3. If its radius is 6 cm, calculate:
   (i) its height   (ii) its curved surface area, in terms of π.

2. The curved surface area of a sphere is 144π cm^2. Calculate:
   (i) its radius   (ii) its volume, in terms of π.

3. The volume of a cone is 320π cm^3. If the radius of the base is 8 cm, calculate its height.

4. The volume of a solid sphere is 36π cm^3. Calculate:
   (i) its radius   (ii) its surface area, in terms of π.

5. A solid cylinder has a volume of 96π cm^3. If its height is 6 cm, calculate:
   (i) its radius   (ii) its total surface area, in terms of π.

6. The curved surface area of a cylinder is 628 cm^2 and its radius is 5 cm. Calculate:
   (i) its height   (ii) its volume   (assume $\pi = 3.14$).

7. A solid cylinder has a volume of 462 m^3. If the height is 12 m, assuming $\pi = \tfrac{22}{7}$, calculate:
   (i) its radius   (ii) its total surface area.

8. The curved surface area of a cone is 60π cm^2. If the radius of its base is 6 cm, calculate:
   (i) its slant height   (ii) its volume, in terms of π.

9. A cone has a volume of $\tfrac{160}{3}\pi$ cm^3. If the radius of the base is 4 cm, find its height.

10. The radius of a cylinder is 2.8 cm and its volume is 49.28 cm^3. Calculate, assuming $\pi = \tfrac{22}{7}$:
    (i) its height   (ii) its curved surface area.

11. The volume of a solid cylinder is 401.92 m^3. If its height is 8 m, calculate, assuming $\pi = 3.14$:
    (i) its radius   (ii) its total surface area.

Equal Volumes

Many questions involve equal volumes with a missing dimension. As before, write down the '**equation given in disguise**' and solve this equation to find the missing dimension.

Notes:

1. Moving liquid

In many questions we have to deal with moving liquid from one container to another container of different dimensions or shape. To help us solve the problem we use the following fact:

> The volume of the moved liquid does not change.

2. Recasting

Many of the questions we meet require us to solve a recasting problem. What happens is that a certain solid object is melted down and its shape is changed. We use the following fact:

> The volume remains the same after it is melted down.

3. Displaced liquid

In many questions we have to deal with situations where liquid is displaced by immersing, or removing, a solid object. In all cases the following principle helps us to solve these problems:

> Volume of displaced liquid = volume of immersed, or removed, solid object

In problems on moving liquid or recasting or displaced liquid, it is good practice not to put in a value for π (i.e. do **not** put in $\pi = \frac{22}{7}$ or $\pi = 3.14$), as the π's normally cancel when you write down the equation given in disguise.

Example ▼

A sphere of radius 15 cm is made of lead. The sphere is melted down. Some of the lead is used to form a solid cone of radius 10 cm and height 27 cm. The rest of the lead is used to form a cylinder of height 25 cm. Calculate the length of the radius of the cylinder.

Solution:

Equation given in disguise:

Volume of cylinder + Volume of cone = Volume of sphere

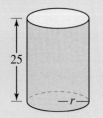 + 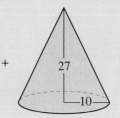 = 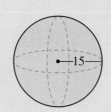   (diagram of the situation)

$$\pi r^2 h + \tfrac{1}{3}\pi r^2 h = \tfrac{4}{3}\pi r^3$$

$$r^2 h + \tfrac{1}{3}r^2 h = \tfrac{4}{3}r^3 \qquad \text{(divide each part by } \pi\text{)}$$

$$25r^2 + \tfrac{1}{3}(10)(10)(27) = \tfrac{4}{3}(15)(15)(15) \qquad \text{(put in given values)}$$

$$25r^2 + 900 = 4{,}500 \qquad \text{(simplify)}$$

$$25r^2 = 3{,}600 \qquad \text{(subtract 900 from both sides)}$$

$$r^2 = 144 \qquad \text{(divide both sides by 25)}$$

$$r = 12 \text{ cm} \qquad \text{(take the square root of both sides)}$$

Therefore, the radius of the cylinder is 12 cm.

Example ▼

(i) Find, in terms of π, the volume of a solid metal sphere of radius 6 cm.

(ii) Five such identical spheres are completely submerged in a cylinder containing water. If the radius of the cylinder is 8 cm, by how much will the level of the water drop if the spheres are removed from the cylinder?

Solution:

(i) Volume of sphere $= \tfrac{4}{3}\pi r^3 = \tfrac{4}{3}\pi(6)(6)(6) = 288\pi \text{ cm}^3$

(ii) Diagram:

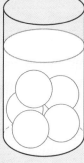

Old situation

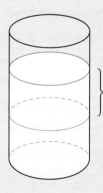

New situation   displaced water

Equation given in disguise:

Volume of displaced water = Volume of five spheres

Diagram:

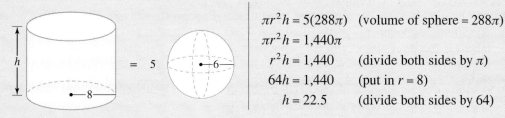

$$\pi r^2 h = 5(288\pi) \qquad \text{(volume of sphere} = 288\pi\text{)}$$
$$\pi r^2 h = 1{,}440\pi$$
$$r^2 h = 1{,}440 \qquad \text{(divide both sides by } \pi\text{)}$$
$$64h = 1{,}440 \qquad \text{(put in } r = 8\text{)}$$
$$h = 22.5 \qquad \text{(divide both sides by 64)}$$

Thus, the level of water in the cylinder would fall by 22.5 cm.

Find the missing dimensions. In each case the volumes are equal (all dimensions in centimetres):

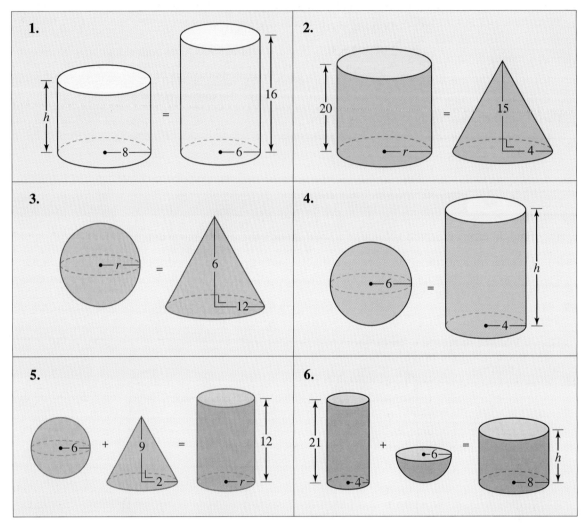

1. h, 8 = 16, 6

2. 20, r = 15, 4

3. r = 6, 12

4. 6 = h, 4

5. 6 + 9, 2 = 12, r

6. 21, 4 + 6 = h, 8

---

7. A solid lead cylinder of base radius 2 cm and height 15 cm is melted down and recast as a solid cone of base radius 3 cm. Calculate the height of the cone.

8. A cylinder of internal diameter 8 cm and height 18 cm is full of liquid. The liquid is poured into a second cylinder of internal diameter 12 cm. Calculate the depth of the liquid in this second cylinder.

9. A solid metal sphere has a radius of length 3 cm. Express the volume of the sphere in terms of π. A cylindrical container is partly filled with water. The sphere is completely submerged in this container. If the level of water in the container rises by 1 cm, calculate the radius of the base of the cylinder.

10. A solid metal rectangular block 30 cm by 24 cm by 15 cm is melted down and recast into cubes of side 3 cm. How many such cubes are made?

11. A solid metal hemisphere of radius 4 cm and a cone of height 10 cm and base radius 5 cm are completely immersed in water in a cylindrical can of diameter 12 cm. If both the hemisphere and cone are removed, calculate the drop in height of the water level.

12. A cylinder has diameter of 10 cm and contains water. A metal cone of base diameter 8 cm and height 15 cm is lowered into the cylinder so that it is completely immersed in the water. Find the rise in the level of the water.

13. A solid metal sphere, of radius 9 cm, is completely immersed in a cylinder containing water. The sphere is removed and the level of water drops by 3 cm. Calculate the diameter of the base of the cylinder.

14. A sphere of radius 15 cm is made of lead. The sphere is melted down. Some of the lead is used to form a solid cone of radius 10 cm and height 27 cm. The rest of the lead is used to form a cylinder of base radius 12 cm. Calculate the height of the cylinder.

15. A solid lead cylinder of radius 6 cm and height 24 cm is melted down and recast as 81 spheres. Calculate the radius of one of these spheres.

16. A solid cone is 24 cm in height and the diameter of its base is 12 cm. The cone is completely submerged in water in a cylindrical vessel of internal diameter 30 cm. Calculate the drop in depth of the water in the vessel when the cone is taken out.
A solid sphere is then completely submerged in the same cylindrical vessel and the water rises to the same level as before. Find the radius of the sphere.

17. A ladle in the shape of a hemispherical bowl of diameter 24 cm, attached to a handle, is full of liquid. Calculate, in terms of π, the volume of liquid in the bowl.
All the liquid is poured from the ladle into a glass cylindrical container with internal radius 8 cm. Calculate the height of liquid in the glass.

18. Find the volume of a solid sphere with a diameter of 3 cm. Give your answer in terms of π.
A cylindrical vessel with internal diameter of length 15 cm contains water. The surface of the water is 11 cm from the top of the vessel.
How many solid spheres, each with diameter of 3 cm, must be placed in the vessel in order to bring the surface of the water to 1 cm from the top of the vessel?
(Assume that all the spheres are submerged in the water.)

19. Water flows through a circular pipe of internal base diameter 6 cm at a speed of 10 cm/s. Calculate, in terms of π, the rate of flow of water from the pipe. The water flows into a cylindrical container of base diameter 36 cm and height 100 cm.
How long will it take to fill the container?

Note: Rate of flow $= \dfrac{\text{Volume}}{\text{Time}}$

20. A solid block, as shown, has a height of 12 cm and a base measuring 30 cm by 15.7 cm. Calculate the volume of the block. A solid cylinder is cut out of the block from top to bottom, as in the diagram. If the volume of the cylinder is $\frac{1}{6}$ of the volume of the block, calculate the radius of the cylinder (assume $\pi = 3.14$).

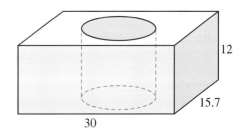

21. A small candle is in the shape of a cone which fits exactly on top of the cylinder as shown. The cylinder has a radius of length 2 cm. The slant length of the cone is 2.5 cm. Calculate:

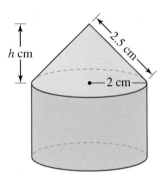

   (i) the height, h, of the cone

   (ii) the volume of the cone in terms of π.

   The volume of the cylinder is 5 times the volume of the cone. Calculate the total height of the candle.

22. (i) Soup is contained in a cylindrical saucepan which has internal radius 14 cm. The depth of the soup is 20 cm. Calculate, in terms of π, the volume of soup in the saucepan.

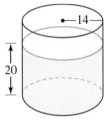

   (ii) A ladle in the shape of a hemisphere with internal radius of length 6 cm is used to serve the soup. Calculate, in terms of π, the volume of soup contained in one full ladle.

   (iii) The soup is served into cylindrical cups, each with internal radius of length of 4 cm. One ladleful is placed in each cup. Calculate the depth of the soup in each cup.

   (iv) How many cups can be filled from the contents of the saucepan if each cup must contain exactly one full ladle?

23. The base of a right circular cone has a radius of length 5 cm. The height of the cone is 12 cm. Calculate the volume in terms of π.

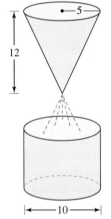

The inverted cone is filled with water. The water then drips from the vertex at the rate $\dfrac{\pi}{5}$ cm^3/s. Calculate the time in seconds until the cone is empty, assuming the volume of water to be the same as the volume of the cone.

If all the water dripped into a dry cylindrical can of diameter 10 cm in length, calculate the height of water in the can.

24. (i) Evaluate:

   (a) $8^{1/3}$ **(b)** $125^{1/3}$

   (c) $3.375^{1/3}$ **(d)** $15.625^{1/3}$

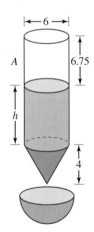

   (ii) A container, A (see diagram), is first filled to the top with a liquid which can flow through the cone's vertex. When the level of liquid is 6.75 cm lower than it was initially the hemispherical bowl is full. Calculate the radius of the bowl.

   A then contains 178.98 cm^3 of liquid, as shown. Find the height, h, of liquid in the cylindrical part.

Simpson's Rule

Simpson's rule gives a concise formula to enable us to make a very good approximation of the area of an irregular shape.

Consider the diagram below:

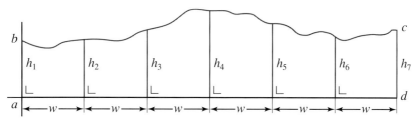

To find the area of the figure *abcd* do the following:

1. Divide the figure into an **even** number of strips of **equal** width, *w*.
2. Number and measure each height, *h*. There will be an **odd** number of heights.
3. Use the following formula:

$$\text{Area} = \frac{w}{3}\,[(h_1 + h_7) + 4(h_2 + h_4 + h_6) + 2(h_3 + h_5)]$$

$$\text{Area} = \frac{\text{width}}{3}\,[(\text{First} + \text{Last}) + 4(\text{Evens}) + 2(\text{Odds})]$$

Note: The greater the number of strips taken, the greater the accuracy.

Example ▼

Use Simpson's rule to estimate the area of the following figure:

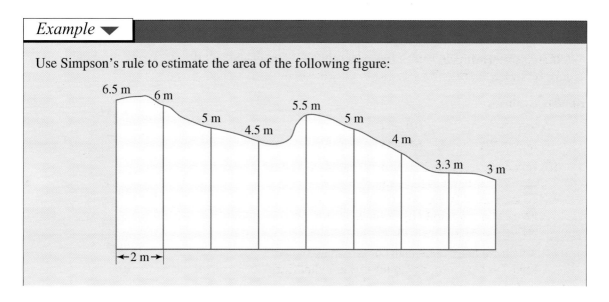

Solution:

$$A = \frac{\text{width}}{3} [(\text{First} + \text{Last}) + 4(\text{Evens}) + 2(\text{Odds})]$$

$$= \frac{w}{3} [(h_1 + h_9) + 4(h_2 + h_4 + h_6 + h_8) + 2(h_3 + h_5 + h_7)]$$

$$= \tfrac{2}{3}[(6.5 + 3) + 4(6 + 4.5 + 5 + 3.3) + 2(5 + 5.5 + 4)]$$

$$= \tfrac{2}{3}[9.5 + 4(18.8) + 2(14.5)]$$

$$= \tfrac{2}{3}[9.5 + 75.2 + 29]$$

$$= \tfrac{2}{3}[113.7]$$

$$= 75.8 \text{ cm}^2$$

$h_1 = 6.5$	(First)
$h_2 = 6$	(Even)
$h_3 = 5$	(Odd)
$h_4 = 4.5$	(Even)
$h_5 = 5.5$	(Odd)
$h_6 = 5$	(Even)
$h_7 = 4$	(Odd)
$h_8 = 3.5$	(Even)
$h_9 = 3$	(Last)

If an irregular shape has no straight edge it can be broken up into two regions, each with its own straight edge as in the diagram. We then apply Simpson's rule in the normal way, except we treat both heights on each side of the line as one height in using the formula (see the next example).

Sometimes we also have to deal with an equation in disguise.

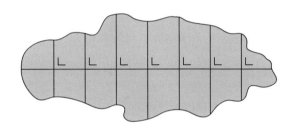

Example ▼

A surveyor makes the following sketch in estimating the area of a building site, where k is the length shown. Using Simpson's rule, she estimates that the area of the site is 440 m^2. Find k.

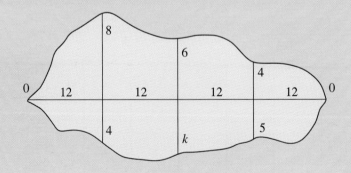

Solution:

Given: Estimated area of building site = 440 m^2

$\therefore \dfrac{\text{width}}{3}\left[(\text{First} + \text{Last}) + 4(\text{Evens}) + 2(\text{Odds})\right] = 440$

$$\frac{w}{3}\left[(h_1 + h_5) + 2(h_2 + h_4) + 2(h_3)\right] = 440$$

$$\frac{12}{3}\left[(0 + 0) + 4(12 + 9) + 2(6 + k)\right] = 440$$

$$4\left[0 + 4(21) + 2(6 + k)\right] = 440$$

$$4\left[84 + 12 + 2k\right] = 440$$

$$4\left[96 + 2k\right] = 440$$

$$384 + 8k = 440$$

$$8k = 56$$

$$k = 7$$

$h_1 = 0$	(First)
$h_2 = 8 + 4 = 12$	(Even)
$h_3 = 6 + k$	(Odd)
$h_4 = 4 + 5 = 9$	(Even)
$h_5 = 0$	(Last)

Exercise 7.10 ▼

Use Simpson's rule to estimate the area of the following figures (all dimensions in m):

1.

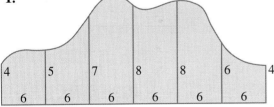

2.

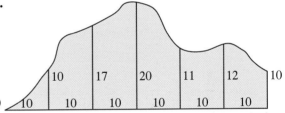

3.

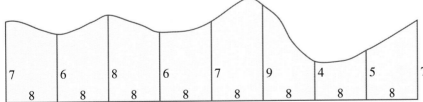

4.

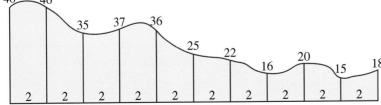

5.

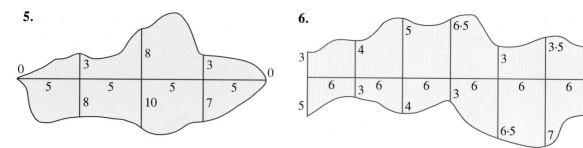

6.

7. A surveyor makes the following sketch in estimating the area of a building site. Using Simpson's rule, estimate the area of the site.

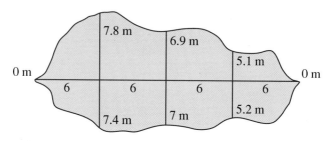

8. The depth of the water in a river of width 24 m was measured at intervals of 4 m, starting from one bank and ending at the other, and the results are recorded in the following table:

Distance from the bank (m)	0	4	8	12	16	20	24
Depth (m)	0.6	0.8	1.4	2.1	1.9	0.7	0.3

Use Simpson's rule to estimate the area of a cross-section of the water at this point.

9. The diagram shows a quadrant of a circle of radius 10. Using Simpson's rule, estimate the area of the quadrant (all dimensions in cm).

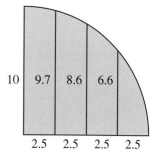

10. A sketch of a piece of land is shown. Using Simpson's rule, the area of the piece of land is estimated to be 276 m². Calculate the value of k.

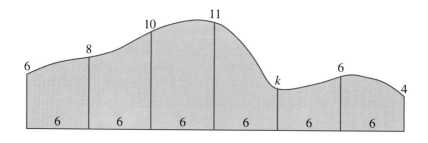

11. Surveyors make the following sketch in estimating the area of a building site, where k is the length shown. Using Simpson's rule, they estimate the area of the site to be 520 m^2. Calculate the value of k.

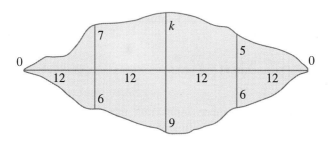

12. Using Simpson's rule, the area of the figure below was estimated to be 230 cm^2. Calculate the value of h.

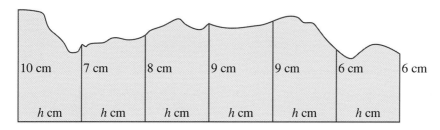

FUNCTIONS

Terminology and Notation

A function is a rule that changes one number (input) into another number (output). Functions are often represented by the letters f, g, h or k. We can think of a function, f, as a number machine which changes an input, x, into an output, $f(x)$.

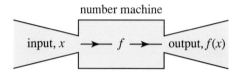

number machine

input, x ⟶ f ⟶ output, $f(x)$

$f(x)$, which denotes the output, is read as 'f of x'.

For example, let's represent the function 'double input and then add 5' by the letter f.

This can be written as:

$$f : x \longrightarrow 2x + 5 \qquad \text{or} \qquad f(x) = 2x + 5 \qquad \text{or} \qquad y = 2x + 5$$
$$(\text{input, output}) = (x, f(x)) = (x, 2x + 5) = (x, y)$$

Note: A **function** is also called a '**mapping**' or simply a '**map**'.

One number is mapped onto another number.
In the above example, x is mapped onto $2x + 5$, usually written $f : x \longrightarrow 2x + 5$.

Input number

If $f : x \longrightarrow 2x + 5$, then $f(3)$ means 'input 3 into the function',
i.e. it is the result of applying the function f to the number 3.

$$f(3) = 2(3) + 5 = 6 + 5 = 11 \qquad (\text{input} = 3, \text{output} = 11)$$
$$(\text{input, output}) = (3, f(3)) = (3, 11)$$

> A function does exactly the same to each input number, and
> produces only one output number for each input number.

The set of numbers that are put into a function is called the '**domain**'.
The set of numbers that comes out of a function is called the '**range**'.
A function connects **every** input in the domain to an input in the range.
A function is another way of writing an algebraic formula that links input to output.

The function g is defined as $g : x \rightarrow 3x - 2$, $x \in \mathbf{R}$.

(i)   Find: **(a)** $g(6)$ **(b)** $g(\frac{4}{3})$.

(ii)   Find the number k such that $kg(\frac{4}{3}) = g(6)$.

(iii)   Find the value of x for which $g(x) = 13$.

Solution:

$$g(x) = 3x - 2$$

(i)   **(a)** $g(6) = 3(6) - 2$
            $= 18 - 2$
            $= 16$

       (b) $g(\frac{4}{3}) = 3(\frac{4}{3}) - 2$
                 $= 4 - 2$
                 $= 2$

(ii) $kg(\frac{4}{3}) = g(6)$
       $k(2) = 16$
       $2k = 16$
       $k = 8$

(iii) $g(x) = 13$
       $3x - 2 = 13$
       $3x = 15$
       $x = 5$

$f : x \rightarrow x^2 - x$ and $g(x) = x + 1$.

(i)   Evaluate: **(a)** $f(-1)$ **(b)** $g(-\frac{1}{4})$.

(ii)   Find the two values of x for which $2f(x) = 3g(x)$.

Solution:

(i)   **(a)** $f(x) = x^2 - x$
          $f(-1) = (-1)^2 - (-1)$
               $= 1 + 1$
               $= 2$

       (b) $g(x) = x + 1$
          $g(-\frac{1}{4}) = -\frac{1}{4} + 1$
               $= \frac{3}{4}$

(ii) $2f(x) = 3g(x)$
      $2(x^2 - x) = 3(x + 1)$
      $2x^2 - 2x = 3x + 3$
   $2x^2 - 2x - 3x - 3 = 0$
     $2x^2 - 5x - 3 = 0$
   $(2x + 1)(x - 3) = 0$
   $2x + 1 = 0$ or $x - 3 = 0$
      $2x = -1$ or $x = 3$
      $x = -\frac{1}{2}$ or $x = 3$

Let $f(x) = \dfrac{1}{x+3}$, $x \in \mathbf{R}$.

Find: (i) $f(-\tfrac{10}{3})$ (ii) $f(-\tfrac{1}{2})$ (iii) $f(\tfrac{4}{5})$.

For what real value of $f(x)$ is $f(x)$ not defined?

Solution:

$$f(x) = \dfrac{1}{x-3}$$

(i) $f(-\tfrac{10}{3}) = \dfrac{1}{-\tfrac{10}{3}+3}$

$= \dfrac{3}{-10+9}$

(multiply top and bottom by 3)

$= \dfrac{3}{-1}$

$= -3$

(ii) $f(-\tfrac{1}{2}) = \dfrac{1}{-\tfrac{1}{2}+3}$

$= \dfrac{2}{-1+6}$

(multiply top and bottom by 2)

$= \dfrac{2}{5}$

(iii) $f(\tfrac{4}{5}) = \dfrac{1}{\tfrac{4}{5}+3}$

$= \dfrac{5}{4+15}$

(multiply top and bottom by 5)

$= \dfrac{5}{19}$

Division by 0 (zero) is not defined for real numbers.

When $x = -3$, $\dfrac{1}{x+3} = \dfrac{1}{-3+3} = \dfrac{1}{0}$ which is undefined.

∴ $x = -3$ is the real value for which $f(x)$ is undefined.

Exercise 8.1 ▼

1. The function f is defined as $f : x \to 3x + 4,$ $x \in \mathbf{R}$.
   Find: **(i)** $f(2)$ **(ii)** $f(5)$ **(iii)** $f(-1)$ **(iv)** $f(0)$ **(v)** $f(\tfrac{2}{3})$

2. The function g is defined as $g : x \to 5x - 2,$ $x \in \mathbf{R}$.
   Find: **(i)** $g(3)$ **(ii)** $g(-2)$ **(iii)** $g(0)$ **(iv)** $g(-1)$ **(v)** $g(\tfrac{2}{5})$
   Find the value of x for which $f(x) = 18$.

3. The function f is defined as $f : x \to x^2 + 3x,$ $x \in \mathbf{R}$.
   Find: **(i)** $f(3)$ **(ii)** $f(1)$ **(iii)** $f(0)$ **(iv)** $f(-2)$ **(v)** $3f(-4)$
   Find the two values of x for which $f(x) = 10$.

4. The function f is defined as $f : x \to 4 - 3x,$ $x \in \mathbf{R}$.
   (i) Find: **(a)** $f(-2)$ **(b)** $f(-\tfrac{1}{3})$
   (ii) Find the number k such that $f(-2) = kf(-\tfrac{1}{3})$.

5. The function f is defined as $f : x \rightarrow 7 - 4x, \qquad x \in \mathbf{R}$.
   Find the number k such that $kf(-\frac{3}{2}) = f(-8)$.

6. The function f is defined as $f : x \rightarrow x(x + 2), \qquad x \in \mathbf{R}$.
   Find: (i) $f(1)$ (ii) $f(-1)$ (iii) $f(2) + f(-2)$ (iv) $-2f(-3)$.
   Find the two values of x for which $f(x) = 15$.

7. The function f is defined as $f : x \rightarrow x^2 + 2x - 1, \qquad x \in \mathbf{R}$.
   Find the value of: (i) $f(0)$ (ii) $f(-1)$ (iii) $f(\frac{1}{2})$ (iv) $f(\frac{3}{5})$.
   Find the two values of k for which $f(k) = -1$.

8. The function f is defined as $f : x \rightarrow \dfrac{1}{x - 1}, \qquad x \in \mathbf{R}, x \neq 1$.

   Evaluate: (i) $f(3)$ (ii) $f(0)$ (iii) $f(\frac{3}{2})$.
   For what real value of x is $f(x)$ not defined?

9. The function f is defined as $f : x \rightarrow \dfrac{1}{x + 4}, \qquad x \in \mathbf{R}$.

   Evaluate: (i) $f(1)$ (ii) $f(-2)$ (iii) $f(-\frac{4}{5})$, writing your answers as decimals.
   For what real value of x is $f(x)$ not defined?
   Solve for x: $f(x) = \frac{1}{3}$.

10. The function f is defined as $f : x \rightarrow x^2 - 1, \qquad x \in \mathbf{R}$.
    (i)   Find: (a) $f(4)$ (b) $f(-3)$ (c) $f(2)$.
    (ii)   For what value of $k \in \mathbf{R}$ is $2k + 1 + f(4) = f(-3)$?
    (iii) Find the values of x for which $f(x) - f(2) = 0$.
    (iv)   Verify that $f(x - 1) = f(1 - x)$.

11. $f : x \rightarrow x^2 + 1$ and $g : x \rightarrow 2x$ are two functions defined on $\mathbf{R}$.
    (i)   Find $f(\sqrt{3})$ and $g(1)$.
    (ii)   Find the value of k for which $f(\sqrt{3}) = kg(1)$.
    (iii) Find the value of x for which $f(x) = g(x)$.
    (iv)   Verify that $f(x + 2) = g(x^2 + 2x + 1) - f(x) + f(\sqrt{3})$.

12. $f : x \rightarrow \sqrt{x}$ and $g : x \rightarrow \dfrac{x}{1 - x}$ are two functions defined on $\mathbf{R}$.
    Verify that $f(\frac{1}{4}) > g(\frac{1}{4})$.

Functions with Missing Coefficients

In some questions coefficients of the functions are missing and we are asked to find them. In this type of question we are given equations in disguise, and by solving these equations we can calculate the missing coefficients.

Notation

$f(x) = y$
$f(2) = 3$ means when $x = 2$, $y = 3$, or the point $(2, 3)$ is on the graph of the function.
$f(-1) = 0$ means when $x = -1$, $y = 0$, or the point $(-1, 0)$ is on the graph of the function.

$f : x \rightarrow 3x + k$ and $g : x \rightarrow x^2 + hx - 8$ are two functions defined on **R**.

(i) If $f(-2) = 1$, find the value of k.

(ii) If $g(-3) = -5$, find the value of h.

Solution:

(i) $f(x) = 3x + k$

$$\text{Given:} \qquad f(-2) = 1$$
$$3(-2) + k = 1$$
$$-6 + k = 1$$
$$k = 7$$

(ii) $g(x) = x^2 + hx - 8$

$$\text{Given:} \qquad g(-3) = -5$$
$$\therefore \quad (-3)^2 + h(-3) - 8 = -5$$
$$9 - 3h - 8 = -5$$
$$-3h + 1 = -5$$
$$-3h = -6$$
$$3h = 6$$
$$h = 2$$

$g : x \rightarrow ax^2 + bx - 3$ is a function defined on **R**.
If $g(2) = 15$ and $g(-1) = -6$, write down two equations in a and b.
Hence, calculate the value of a and the value of b.

Solution:

$$g(x) = ax^2 + bx - 3$$

Given: $\qquad g(2) = 15$
$\therefore \quad a(2)^2 + b(2) - 3 = 15$
$\qquad a(4) + b(2) - 3 = 15$
$\qquad 4a + 2b - 3 = 15$
$\qquad 4a + 2b = 18$
$\qquad 2a + b = 9$ ①

Given: $\qquad g(-1) = -6$
$\therefore \quad a(-1)^2 + b(-1) - 3 = -6$
$\qquad a(1) + b(-1) - 3 = -6$
$\qquad a - b - 3 = -6$
$\qquad a - b = -3$ ②

We now solve between equations ① and ②

$$2a + b = 9 \qquad ①$$
$$\underline{a - b = -3 \qquad ②}$$
$$3a = 6 \qquad \text{(add)}$$
$$a = 2$$

put $a = 2$ into ① or ②

$$2a + b = 9 \qquad ①$$
$$\downarrow$$
$$2(2) + b = 9$$
$$4 + b = 9$$
$$b = 5$$

Thus, $a = 2$ and $b = 5$.

The graph of the quadratic function

$f : x \rightarrow x^2 + px + q, \qquad x \in \mathbf{R}$, is shown.

Find the value of p and the value of q.

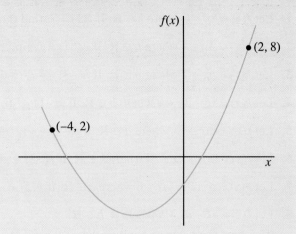

Solution:

$$f(x) = x^2 + px + q$$

The graph goes through the point $(-4, 2)$ | The graph goes through the point $(2, 8)$

∴   **Given:** $f(-4) = 2$ | ∴   **Given:** $f(2) = 8$

∴ $(-4)^2 + p(-4) + q = 2$ | ∴ $(2)^2 + p(2) + q = 8$

           $16 - 4p + q = 2$ | $4 + 2p + q = 8$

           $-4p + q = -14$ | $2p + q = 4$ ②

           $4p - q = 14$ ①

We now solve between equations ① and ②:

$$4p - q = 14 \qquad ① \qquad\qquad\qquad 2p + q = 4 \qquad ②$$
$$\underline{2p + q = 4} \qquad ② \qquad\qquad\qquad \downarrow$$
$$6p = 18 \quad \text{(add)} \qquad\qquad\qquad 2(3) + q = 4$$
$$p = 3 \qquad\qquad\qquad\qquad\qquad 6 + q = 4$$

put $p = 3$ into ① or ② | $q = -2$

           Thus, $p = 3$ and $q = -2$.

Alternatively, let $y = f(x)$, i.e., $y = x^2 + px + q$.

$(-4, 2)$ is on the graph of the curve | $(2, 8)$ is on the graph of the curve

∴ $2 = (-4)^2 + p(-4) + q$ | ∴ $8 = (2)^2 + p(2) + 1$

(put in $x = -4$, $y = 2$) | (put in $x = 2$, $y = 8$)

          $2 = 16 - 4p + q$ | $8 = 4 + 2p + q$

      $-14 = -4p + q$ | $4 = 2p + q$ ②

       $14 = 4p - q$ ①

Then solve the simultaneous equations ① and ② as before, to get $p = 3$ and $q = -2$.

1. Let $f(x) = 5x + k$ where $k \in \mathbf{R}$. If $f(1) = 7$, find the value of k.

2. Let $g(x) = 3x + h$ where $h \in \mathbf{R}$. If $g(-1) = 1$, find the value of h.

3. Let $h(x) = ax + 7$ where $a \in \mathbf{R}$. If $h(-3) = -2$, find the value of a.

4. Let $k(x) = x^2 - 3x + b$ where $b \in \mathbf{R}$. If $k(-1) = -6$, find the value of b.

5. Let $f(x) = ax^2 + 3x$ where $a \in \mathbf{R}$. If $f(-1) = -1$, find the value of a.

6. Let $f(x) = (x + k)(x + 3)$ where $k \in \mathbf{R}$. If $f(-2) = -6$, find the value of k.

7. Let $g(x) = a^2x^2 - 7ax + 6$ where $a \in \mathbf{R}$. If $g(2) = -6$, find two possible values of a.

8. Let $f(x) = x^2 + ax + b$ where $a, b \in \mathbf{R}$.
   (i)   Find the value of a, given that $f(2) = f(-4)$.
   (ii) If $f(-5) = 12$, find the value of b.

9. $f : x \longrightarrow 2x + a$ and $g : x \longrightarrow 3x + b$.
   If $f(2) = 7$ and $g(1) = -1$, find the value of a and the value of b.

10. $h : x \longrightarrow 2x + a$ and $k : x \longrightarrow b - 5x$ are two functions defined on $\mathbf{R}$.
    If $h(1) = -5$ and $k(-1) = 4$, find the value of a and the value of b.

11. $f : x \longrightarrow 3x + a$ and $g : x \longrightarrow ax + b$ are two functions defined on $\mathbf{R}$.
    If $f(2) = 8$ and $g(2) = 1$:
    (i)   find the value of a and the value of b
    (ii) find $f(-1)$ and $g(4)$
    (iii) using your values of a and b from (i), find the two values of x for which:

    $$ax^2 - (a - b)x + 2ab = 0.$$

12. $h : x \longrightarrow 2x - a$ and $k : x \longrightarrow ax + b$ are two functions defined on $\mathbf{R}$, where a and $b \in \mathbf{Z}$.
    $h(3) = 1$ and $k(5) = 8$.
    (i)   Find the value of a and the value of b.
    (ii) Hence, list the values of x for which $h(x) \geqslant k(x)$, $x \in \mathbf{N}$.

13. $g : x \longrightarrow ax^2 + bx + 1$ is a function defined on $\mathbf{R}$.
    If $g(1) = 2$ and $g(-1) = 6$, write down two equations in a and b.
    Hence, calculate the value of a and the value of b.

14. $g : x \longrightarrow px^2 + qx - 3$ is a function defined on $\mathbf{R}$.
    If $g(1) = 4$ and $g(-1) = -6$, write down two equations in p and q.
    Hence, calculate the value of p and the value of q.
    Find the two values of x for which $px^2 + qx - 3 = 0$.

15. $g : x \longrightarrow ax^2 + bx + 1$ is a function defined on $\mathbf{R}$.
    (i)   If $g(1) = 0$ and $g(2) = 3$, write down two equations in a and b.
    (ii) Hence, calculate the value of a and the value of b.
    (iii) Using your values of a and b from (ii), find the two values of x for which $ax^2 + bx = bx^2 + ax$.

16. $f : x \rightarrow ax^2 + bx + c$, where a, b and c are real numbers.
   If $f(0) = -3$, find the value of c.
   If $f(-1) = 6$ and $f(2) = 3$, find the value of a and the value of b.

17. $h : x \rightarrow x^2 + x + q$ is a function defined on **R**, where $q \in$ **Z**.
   (i)   If $h(-3) = 0$, find the value of q.
   (ii) Hence, solve the equation $h(x + 5) = 0$.

18. The graph of the linear function
   $f : x \rightarrow ax + b,$ $x \in$ **R** is shown.
   Find the values of a and b.

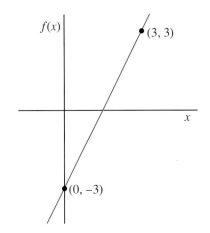

19. The graph of the quadratic function
   $f : x \rightarrow x^2 + bx + c,$ $x \in$ **R**, is shown.
   Find the values of b and c.
   Hence, find the value of k.

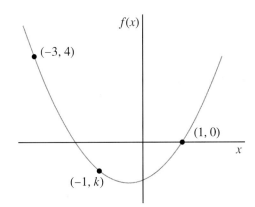

20. The graph of the quadratic function
   $g : x \rightarrow x^2 + px + q,$ $x \in$ **R**, is shown.
   Find the values of p and q.
   Hence, find the values of a, b and c.
   Solve the equation:

   $$\frac{c - 1}{b} = \frac{1}{x} + \frac{1}{x + p}$$

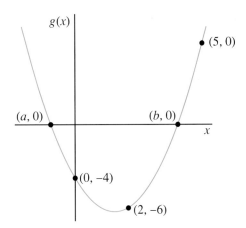

21. The graph of the quadratic function
$g : x \rightarrow ax^2 + bx - 3, \qquad x \in \mathbf{R}$, is shown.

Find the values of a and b.

Hence, calculate the value of h and k.

Solve the equation:

$$\frac{1}{x} + \frac{1}{x+k} + h = 0$$

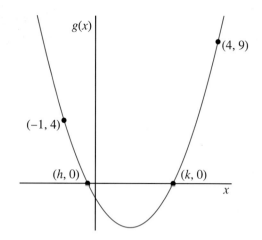

22. The graph of the quadratic function
$h : x \rightarrow c + bx - x^2, \qquad x \in \mathbf{R}$, is shown.

Find the value of b and c.

$k : x \rightarrow px + q$ is a function defined on $\mathbf{R}$.

If $k(0) = -1$ and $k(1) = 1$, find the value of p and the value of q.

Hence, find the two values of x for which $k(x) = h(x)$.

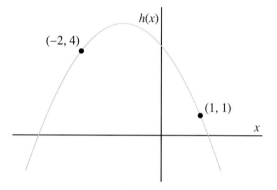

23. Let $f(x) = x^2 + bx + c, \qquad x \in \mathbf{R}$.

The solutions of $f(x) = 0$ are -5 and 2.

Find the value of b and the value of c.

If $f(-3) = k$, find the value of k.

Solve the equation $f(x) - k = 0$.

24. Let $g(x) = x^2 + bx + c, \qquad x \in \mathbf{R}$.

The solutions of $g(x) = 0$ are symmetrical about the line $x = -1$.

If $x = 1$ is one solution of $g(x) = 0$, find the other solution.

Find the value of b and the value of c.

GRAPHING FUNCTIONS

Notation

The notation $y = f(x)$ means 'the value of the output y depends on the value of the input x, according to some rule called f'. Hence, y and $f(x)$ are interchangeable, and the y-axis can also be called the $f(x)$-axis.

Note: It is very important not to draw a graph outside the given values of x.

Graphing Linear Functions

The first four letters in the word '**linear**' spell '**line**'. Therefore the graph of a linear function will be a straight line. A linear function is usually given in the form $f : x \rightarrow ax + b$, where $a \neq 0$ and a, b are constants. For example, $f : x \rightarrow 2x + 5$. As the graph is a straight line, two points are all that is needed to graph it. In the question, you will always be given a set of inputs, x, called the **domain**.

To graph a linear function do the following:

> 1. Choose two suitable values of x, in the given domain.
>   (Two suitable values are the smallest and largest values of x.)
>
> 2. Substitute these in the function to find the two corresponding values of y.
>
> 3. Plot the points and draw the line through them.

Note: $-3 \leqslant x \leqslant 2$ means 'x is between -3 and 2, including -3 and 2'.

Example ▼

Graph the function $f : x \rightarrow 2x + 1$, in the domain $-3 \leqslant x \leqslant 2$, $\quad x \in \mathbf{R}$.

Let $y = f(x) \Rightarrow y = 2x + 1$.

x	$2x + 1$	y
-3	$-6 + 1$	-5
2	$4 + 5$	5

Plot the points $(-3, -5)$ and $(2, 5)$ and join them with a straight line.

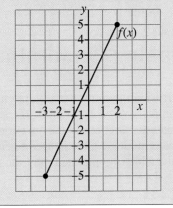

Graph each of the following functions in the given domain:

1. $f: x \rightarrow 2x + 3$ in the domain $-3 \leqslant x \leqslant 2$, $x \in \mathbf{R}$

2. $g: x \rightarrow 3x + 2$ in the domain $-2 \leqslant x \leqslant 3$, $x \in \mathbf{R}$

3. $f: x \rightarrow 4x + 3$ in the domain $-3 \leqslant x \leqslant 3$, $x \in \mathbf{R}$

4. $g: x \rightarrow 2x - 5$ in the domain $-1 \leqslant x \leqslant 5$, $x \in \mathbf{R}$

5. $h: x \rightarrow x - 2$ in the domain $-2 \leqslant x \leqslant 5$, $x \in \mathbf{R}$

6. $f: x \rightarrow 3x - 1$ in the domain $-3 \leqslant x \leqslant 3$, $x \in \mathbf{R}$

7. $g: x \rightarrow 5x - 2$ in the domain $-1 \leqslant x \leqslant 2$, $x \in \mathbf{R}$

8. $k: x \rightarrow x$ in the domain $-3 \leqslant x \leqslant 3$, $x \in \mathbf{R}$

9. $f: x \rightarrow 2x$ in the domain $-2 \leqslant x \leqslant 2$, $x \in \mathbf{R}$

10. $g: x \rightarrow 3x$ in the domain $-3 \leqslant x \leqslant 2$, $x \in \mathbf{R}$

11. $f: x \rightarrow -x$ in the domain $-3 \leqslant x \leqslant 3$, $x \in \mathbf{R}$

12. $h: x \rightarrow 2 - x$ in the domain $-4 \leqslant x \leqslant 4$, $x \in \mathbf{R}$

13. $k: x \rightarrow 3 - 2x$ in the domain $-3 \leqslant x \leqslant 4$, $x \in \mathbf{R}$

14. $f: x \rightarrow 4 - 3x$ in the domain $-2 \leqslant x \leqslant 4$, $x \in \mathbf{R}$

15. $g: x \rightarrow -1 - x$ in the domain $-4 \leqslant x \leqslant 3$, $x \in \mathbf{R}$

16. Using the same axis and scales, graph the functions:

$f: x \rightarrow x - 6$, $g: x \rightarrow -2x$, in the domain $-1 \leqslant x \leqslant 5$, $x \in \mathbf{R}$.

    (i)   From your graph, write down the coordinates of the point of intersection of f and g.

    (ii)   Verify your answer to part **(i)** by solving the simultaneous equations:

         $x - y = 6$ and $2x + y = 0$.

Graphing Quadratic Functions

A **quadratic** function is usually given in the form $f: x \rightarrow ax^2 + bx + c$, $a \neq 0$, and a, b, c are constants. For example, $f: x \rightarrow 2x^2 - x + 3$. Because of its shape, quite a few points are needed to plot the graph of a quadratic function. In the question, you will always be given a set of inputs, x, called the **domain**. With these inputs, a table is used to find the corresponding set of outputs, y or $f(x)$, called the **range**. When the table is completed, plot the points and join them with a '**smooth curve**'.

Notes on making out the table:

1. Work out each column separately, i.e. all the x^2 values first, then all the x values, and finally the constant. (Watch for patterns in the numbers.)

2. Work out each corresponding value of y.

3. The **only** column that changes sign is the x term (middle) column.
   If the given values of x contain 0, then the x term column will make one sign change, either from + to − or from − to +, where $x = 0$.

4. The other two columns **never** change sign. They remain either all +'s or all −'s.
   These columns keep the sign given in the question.

Note: Decide where to draw the x- and y-axes by looking at the table to see what the largest and smallest values of x and y are. In general, the units on the x-axis are larger than the units on the y-axis. Try to make sure that the graph extends almost the whole width and length of the page.

Example ▼

Graph the function $g : x \rightarrow 5 + 3x - 2x^2$, in the domain $-2 \leqslant x \leqslant 3$, $\quad x \in \mathbf{R}$.

Solution:

Let $y = g(x) \Rightarrow y = 5 + 3x - 2x^2$

x	$-2x^2 + 3x + 5$	y
-2	$-8 \ -6 \ +5$	-9
-1	$-2 \ -3 \ +5$	0
0	$-0 \ +0 \ +5$	5
1	$-2 \ +3 \ +5$	6
2	$-8 \ +6 \ +5$	3
3	$-18 \ +9 \ +5$	-4

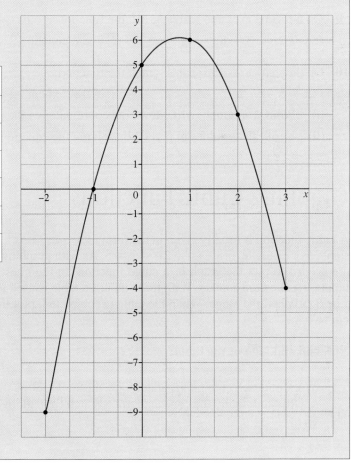

Graph each of the following functions in the given domain:

1. $g : x \rightarrow x^2 - 2x - 8,$ in the domain $-3 \leqslant x \leqslant 5,$ $x \in \mathbf{R}.$

2. $f : x \rightarrow x^2 + 2x - 3,$ in the domain $-4 \leqslant x \leqslant 2,$ $x \in \mathbf{R}.$

3. $f : x \rightarrow 2x - x^2,$ in the domain $-2 \leqslant x \leqslant 4,$ $x \in \mathbf{R}.$

4. $g : x \rightarrow 2x^2 + 3x - 2,$ in the domain $-3 < x < 2,$ $x \in \mathbf{R}.$

5. $f : x \rightarrow 2x^2 - x - 4,$ in the domain $-2 \leqslant x \leqslant 3,$ $x \in \mathbf{R}.$

6. $g : x \rightarrow 3 + 5x - 2x^2,$ in the domain $-1 \leqslant x \leqslant 4,$ $x \in \mathbf{R}.$

7. On the same axes and scales, graph the functions:
   $f : x \rightarrow x^2 - 2x - 4$ $g : x \rightarrow 2x + 1,$ in the domain $-3 \leqslant x \leqslant 5,$ $x \in \mathbf{R}.$

8. On the same axes and scales, graph the functions:
   $f : x \rightarrow 5 + 2x - x^2,$ $g : x \rightarrow 2 - x,$ in the domain $-2 \leqslant x \leqslant 4,$ $x \in \mathbf{R}.$

9. On the same axes and scales, graph the functions:
   $f : x \rightarrow 2x^2 - 3x - 8,$ $g : x \rightarrow 3x - 2,$ in the domain $-2 \leqslant x \leqslant 4,$ $x \in \mathbf{R}.$

10. On the same axes and scales, graph the functions:
    $f : x \rightarrow 5 - x - 2x^2,$ $g : x \rightarrow 1 - 3x,$ in the domain $-2 \leqslant x \leqslant 3,$ $x \in \mathbf{R}.$
    (i)   From your graph, write down the coordinates of the points of intersection of f and g.
    (ii)   Verify the x values in part (i) by solving the equation $g(x) = f(x)$.

Graphing Cubic Functions

A **cubic** function is usually given in the form $f : x \rightarrow ax^3 + bx^2 + cx + d,\ a \neq 0$ and a, b, c and d are constants. For example, $f : x \rightarrow x^3 - 2x^2 - 6x + 5$. As with graphing quadratic functions, quite a few points are needed to plot the graph of a cubic function. In the question, you will always be given a set of inputs, x, called the domain. With these inputs, a table is used to find the corresponding set of outputs, y or $f(x)$, called the range. When the table is completed, plot the points and join them with a '**smooth curve**'.

Notes on making out the table:

1. Work out each column separately, i.e. all the x^3 terms first, then all the x^2 terms, then all the x terms and finally the constant term. (Watch for patterns in the numbers.)

2. Work out each corresponding value of y.

3. Only **two** columns may change sign, the x^3 and x term columns. If the given values of x contain 0, then the x^3 and x term columns will make **one** sign change, either from + to – or – to +, where $x = 0$. So the only two signs to work out are the ones at the beginning of the x^3 and x term columns, which are changed at $x = 0$. The simplest way to find the first sign in these two columns is to multiply the sign of the first given value of x by the sign of the coefficient of x^3 and x.

4. The other two columns **never** change sign. They remain all +'s or all –'s. These columns keep the sign given in the question.

Note: Decide where to draw the x- and y-axes by looking at the table to see what the largest and smallest values of x and y are. In general, the units on the x-axis are larger than the units on the y-axis. Try to make sure that the graph extends almost the whole width and length of the page.

Example ▼

Graph the function $f : x \rightarrow x^3 + 3x^2 - x - 3$ in the domain $-4 \leqslant x \leqslant 2$, $\quad x \in \mathbf{R}$.

Solution:

Let $y = f(x) \Rightarrow y = x^3 + 3x^2 - x - 3$.

x	$x^3 + 3x^2 - x - 3$	y
-4	$-64 + 48 + 4 - 3$	-15
-3	$-27 + 27 + 3 - 3$	0
-2	$-8 + 12 + 2 - 3$	3
-1	$-1 + 3 + 1 - 3$	0
0	$0 + 0 + 0 - 3$	-3
1	$1 + 3 - 1 - 3$	0
2	$8 + 12 - 2 - 3$	15

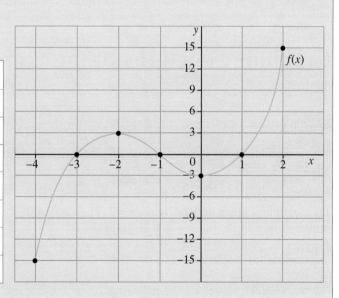

Exercise 9.3 ▼

Graph each of the following functions in the given domain:

1. $f : x \rightarrow x^3 + x^2 - 2x - 1$ in the domain $-3 \leqslant x \leqslant 2$, $x \in \mathbf{R}$.

2. $g : x \rightarrow x^3 - 4x^2 + x + 6$ in the domain $-2 \leqslant x \leqslant 4$, $x \in \mathbf{R}$.

3. $f : x \rightarrow 2x^3 - 3x^2 - 6x + 2$ in the domain $-2 \leqslant x \leqslant 3$, $x \in \mathbf{R}$.

4. $g : x \rightarrow 2x^3 - 2x^2 - 3x + 10$ in the domain $-2 \leqslant x \leqslant 2$, $x \in \mathbf{R}$.

5. $f : x \rightarrow 6 + 6x - x^2 - x^3$ in the domain $-3 \leqslant x \leqslant 3$, $x \in \mathbf{R}$.

6. $g : x \to 6 + 5x - 2x^2 - x^3$ in the domain $-4 \leqslant x \leqslant 3,$ $x \in \mathbf{R}.$

7. $f : x \to 4 + 8x + x^2 - 2x^3$ in the domain $-2 \leqslant x \leqslant 3,$ $x \in \mathbf{R}.$

8. $g : x \to 2x - x^2 - x^3$ in the domain $-3 \leqslant x \leqslant 2,$ $x \in \mathbf{R}.$

9. $f : x \to x^3 - 3x^2 - 2$ in the domain $-2 \leqslant x \leqslant 4,$ $x \in \mathbf{R}.$

10. $g : x \to 3 + 5x - x^3$ in the domain $-3 \leqslant x \leqslant 3,$ $x \in \mathbf{R}.$

11. On the same axes and scales, graph the functions:
    $f : x \to x^3 - 2x^2 - 4x + 1$ and $g : x \to 3x + 1$, in the domain $-2 \leqslant x \leqslant 4,$ $x \in \mathbf{R}.$

12. On the same axes and scales, graph the functions:
    $f : x \to x^3 + 3x^2 - x - 3$ and $g : x \to 3 - 2x - x^2$, in the domain $-4 \leqslant x \leqslant 2,$ $x \in \mathbf{R}.$
    From your graph, write down the coordinates of the points of intersection of f and g.

13. On the same axes and scales, graph the functions:
    $f : x \to x^3 - 2x^2 - 6x + 2,$ $g : x \to 2x^2 - 7x - 4,$ $h : x \to 2 - 3x$ in the domain $-2 \leqslant x \leqslant 4,$ $x \in \mathbf{R}.$
    From your graph, write down the coordinates of the points of intersection of f, g and h.

Graphing Functions of the Form $\dfrac{1}{x + a}$

Consider the graph of the function $f : x \to \dfrac{1}{x - 2}$.

It is impossible to draw the complete graph of the function because when $x = 2,$

$\dfrac{1}{x - 2} = \dfrac{1}{2 - 2} = \dfrac{1}{0}$ which is undefined.

There will be a break in the curve at $x = 2$. The curve will approach the line $x = 2$, getting closer without actually meeting the line $x = 2$ at any stage.

If a curve approaches a line, getting closer to it without actually meeting the line, the line is called an '**asymptote**' to the curve.

When you graph functions of the form $\dfrac{1}{x + a}$, there will be two asymptotes to the curve.

1. $x = -a$ (vertical asymptote)
2. $y = 0$ (the x-axis, horizontal asymptote)

On the right is a rough graph of the function $f(x) = \dfrac{1}{x - 2}$.

Notice that the curve **never** meets the line $x = 2$ and **never** meets the x-axis.

All functions of the form $\dfrac{1}{x + a}$ will have a similar shape to the graph on the right.

This curve is called a '**rectangular hyperbola**'.
From the graph we can see that as x increases, y decreases, and vice versa.

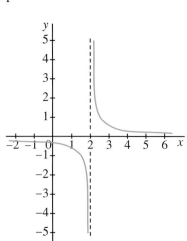

Method for Graphing Functions of the Form $\dfrac{1}{x+a}$

1. Let the expression on the bottom = 0, to find its vertical asymptote.
2. Represent this vertical asymptote with a broken line.
3. $y = 0$, the x-axis, will always be the horizontal asymptote.
4. Use a table to find suitable coordinates on the curve.
   Make sure to take some values of x very close to the vertical asymptote.
5. Join these points with a smooth curve.

Example ▼

Graph the function $f : x \rightarrow \dfrac{1}{x+1}$ in the domain $-4 \leqslant x \leqslant 2$, $\quad x \in \mathbf{R}, \quad x \neq -1$.

Solution:

Expression on the bottom = 0

$$x + 1 = 0$$

$$x = -1 \qquad \text{[this is the vertical asymptote (broken line on the graph)]}$$

The x-axis is the horizontal asymptote.

Let $y = f(x) \Rightarrow y = \dfrac{1}{x+1}$

x	$\dfrac{1}{x+1}$	y
-4	$\dfrac{1}{-4+1}$	$-\dfrac{1}{3}$
-3	$\dfrac{1}{-3+1}$	$-\dfrac{1}{2}$
-2	$\dfrac{1}{-2+1}$	-1
$-1\frac{1}{2}$	$\dfrac{1}{-1\frac{1}{2}+1}$	-2
$-\frac{1}{2}$	$\dfrac{1}{-\frac{1}{2}+1}$	2
0	$\dfrac{1}{0+1}$	1
1	$\dfrac{1}{1+1}$	$\dfrac{1}{2}$
2	$\dfrac{1}{2+1}$	$\dfrac{1}{3}$

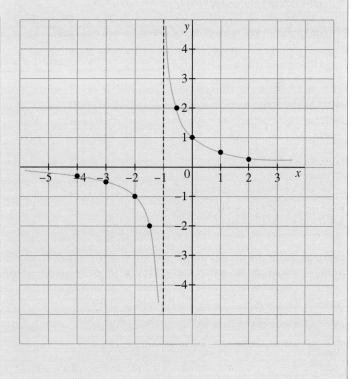

Graph each of the following functions in the given domain:

1. $f: x \rightarrow \dfrac{1}{x-1}$,   in the domain $-2 \leqslant x \leqslant 4$, $x \in \mathbf{R}$, $x \neq 1$.

2. $g: x \rightarrow \dfrac{1}{x-2}$,   in the domain $-1 \leqslant x \leqslant 5$, $x \in \mathbf{R}$, $x \neq 2$.

3. $f: x \rightarrow \dfrac{1}{x+3}$,   in the domain $-7 \leqslant x \leqslant 1$, $x \in \mathbf{R}$, $x \neq -3$.

4. $g: x \rightarrow \dfrac{1}{x-4}$,   in the domain $0 \leqslant x \leqslant 8$, $x \in \mathbf{R}$, $x \neq 4$.

5. $f: x \rightarrow \dfrac{1}{x+2}$,   in the domain $-6 \leqslant x \leqslant 2$, $x \in \mathbf{R}$, $x \neq -2$.

6. $g: x \rightarrow \dfrac{1}{x-3}$,   in the domain $-1 \leqslant x \leqslant 7$, $x \in \mathbf{R}$, $x \neq 3$.

7. $f: x \rightarrow \dfrac{1}{x}$,   in the domain $-4 \leqslant x \leqslant 4$, $x \in \mathbf{R}$, $x \neq 0$.

8. Let $f(x) = \dfrac{1}{x-5}$.

    (i)   Find $f(1), f(3), f(4\tfrac{1}{2}), f(5\tfrac{1}{2}), f(6), f(8)$.

    (ii)   For what real value of x is $f(x)$ not defined?

    (iii)   Draw the graph of $f(x) = \dfrac{1}{x-5}$ in the domain $1 \leqslant x \leqslant 9$, $x \in \mathbf{R}$.

9. On the same axes and scales, graph the functions:

    $f: x \rightarrow \dfrac{1}{x+1}$ and $g: x \rightarrow x+1$, in the domain $-5 \leqslant x \leqslant 3$, $x \in \mathbf{R}$.

Using Graphs

Once we have drawn the graph, we are usually asked to use it to answer some questions. Below are examples of the general types of problem where graphs are used.

Notes: **1.** $y = f(x)$, so $f(x)$ can be replaced by y.
         2. In general, if given x find y, and vice versa.

Examples of the main types of problem, once the graph is drawn:

1. **Find the values of x for which $f(x) = 0$.**
   This question is asking:
   'Where does the curve meet the x-axis?'

   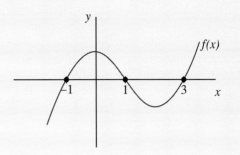

   Solution:
   Write down the values of x where the graph meets the x-axis.
   From the graph: $x = -1$ or $x = 1$ or $x = 3$

2. **Find the values of x for which $f(x) = 6$.**
   This question is asking:
   'When $y = 6$, what are the values of x?'

   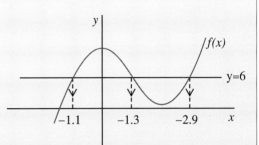

   Solution:
   Draw the line $y = 6$. Where this line meets the curve draw broken perpendicular lines onto the x-axis.
   Write down the values of x where these broken lines meet the x-axis.
   From the graph:
   When $y = 6$, $x = -1.1$ or $x = 1.3$ or $x = 2.9$

3. **Find the value of $f(-1.6)$.**
   This question is asking:
   'When $x = -1.6$, what is the value of y?'

   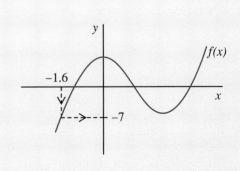

   Solution:
   From $x = -1.6$ on the x-axis draw a broken perpendicular line to meet the curve. From this draw a broken horizontal line to meet the y-axis. Write down the value of y where this line meets the y-axis.
   From the graph:
   $f(-1.6) = -7$

4. Local maximum and minimum points or the local maximum and minimum values

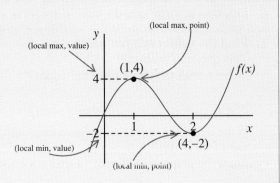

Often we are asked to find the local maximum and minimum points or the local maximum and minimum values. Consider the graph on the right. The local maximum and minimum points are where the graph turns, $(1, 4)$ and $(4, -2)$, respectively. The local maximum and minimum values are found by drawing a line from the turning points to the y axis and reading the values where these lines meet the y-axis. The maximum and minimum values are 4 and -2, respectively.

5. Increasing and decreasing

Graphs are read from left to right.

Increasing: $f(x)$ is increasing where the graph is **rising** as we go from left to right.

Decreasing: $f(x)$ is decreasing where the graph is **falling** as we go from left to right.

Find the values of x for which:

(i) $f(x)$ is increasing

(ii) $f(x)$ is decreasing.

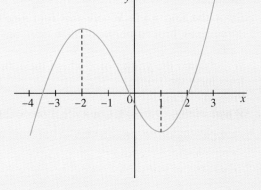

Solution:

(i) $f(x)$ increasing, graph rising from left to right.
The values of x are:
$-4 \leqslant x < -2$ and $1 < x \leqslant 3$

(ii) $f(x)$ decreasing, graph falling from left to right.
The values of x are: $-2 < x < 1$

Note: At $x = -2$ and $x = 1$, the graph is neither increasing nor decreasing.

6. Positive and negative

Positive, $f(x) > 0$: Where the graph is **above** the x-axis.

Negative, $f(x) < 0$: Where the graph is **below** the x-axis.

Find the values of x for which: **(i) $f(x) > 0$**   **(ii) $f(x) < 0$.**

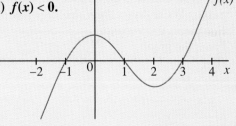

Solution:

(i) $f(x) > 0$, curve **above** the x-axis.
The values of x are:
$-1 < x < 1$ and $3 < x \leqslant 4$

(ii) $f(x) < 0$, curve **below** the x-axis.
The values of x are:
$-2 \leqslant x < -1$ and $1 < x < 3$

Note: If the question uses $f(x) \geqslant 0$ or $f(x) \leqslant 0$, then the values of x where the graph meets the x-axis must also be included.

7. Two functions graphed on the same axes and scales

The diagram shows the graph of two functions: $f(x)$, a curve, and $g(x)$, a line.

Find the values of x for which:

(i) $f(x) = g(x)$ (ii) $f(x) \leqslant g(x)$ (iii) $f(x) \geqslant g(x)$

Solution:

(i) $f(x) = g(x)$
(curve = line)
The values of x are: 0.4, 1.4 and 3.1

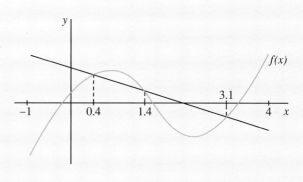

(ii) $f(x) \leqslant g(x)$
(curve equal to and below the line)
The values of x are:
$-1 \leqslant x \leqslant 0.4$ and $1.4 \leqslant x \leqslant 3.1$

(iii) $f(x) \geqslant g(x)$
(curve equal to and above the line)
The values of x are:
$0.4 \leqslant x \leqslant 1.4$ and $3.1 \leqslant x \leqslant 4$

Note: If the question uses $f(x) < g(x)$ or $f(x) > g(x)$, then the values of x where the graphs meet (0.4, 1.4 and 3.1) are **not** included in the solution.

8. Graph above or below a constant value (an inequality)

Find the values of x for which: (i) $f(x) \geqslant 2$ (ii) $f(x) \leqslant 2$.

These questions are asking:
'What are the values of x for which the curve, $f(x)$, is   (i) 2 or above   (ii) 2 or below?'

Solution:
Draw the line $y = 2$.

Write down the values of x for which the curve is:

(i)   on or above the line $y = 2$

(ii)   on or below the line $y = 2$.

(i) $f(x) \geqslant 2$, curve on or above the line $y = 2$.
The values of x are: $-0.8 \leqslant x \leqslant 0.4$ and $3.3 \leqslant x \leqslant 4$

(ii) $f(x) \leqslant 2$, curve on or below the line $y = 2$.
The values of x are: $-2 \leqslant x \leqslant -0.8$ and $0.4 \leqslant x \leqslant 3.3$

Note: If the question uses $f(x) > 2$ or $f(x) < 2$, then the values of x where the curve meets the line $y = 2$ (-0.8, 0.4 and 3.3) are **not** included in the solution.

9. **Using two graphs to estimate square roots and cube roots**

The diagram shows graphs of the functions:

$f : x \rightarrow x^3 - 3x + 4$ and $g : x \rightarrow 6 - 3x$, in the domain $-2 \leqslant x \leqslant 3$.

Show how the graphs may be used to estimate the value of $\sqrt[3]{2}$.

Solution:

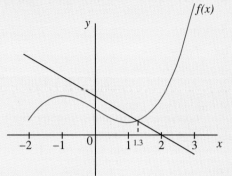

The values of x where two graphs meet is the most common way to use graphs to estimate square roots and cube roots.

    Let $f(x) = g(x)$ [curve = line]

$x^3 - 3x + 4 = 6 - 3x$

    $x^3 + 4 = 6$

       $x^3 = 2$

       $x = \sqrt[3]{2}$

Hence, where the two graphs meet can be used to estimate the value of $\sqrt[3]{2}$.
Where the two graphs intersect, draw a broken line to meet the x-axis.
This line meets the x-axis at 1.3.
Thus, using the graphs, we estimate the value of $\sqrt[3]{2}$ to be 1.3.

Note: A calculator gives $\sqrt[3]{2} = 1.25992104989$

---

10. **Number of times a graph meets the x-axis**

The number of times a graph meets the x-axis gives the number of roots of its equation. Often we need to find a range of values of a constant, which shifts a graph up or down, giving a graph a certain number of roots, e.g.:

For what values of k does the equation $f(x) = k$ have three roots?

Solution:

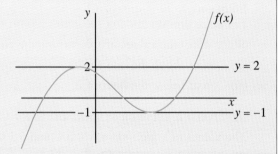

The equation $f(x) = k$ will have three roots if the line $y = k$ cuts the graph three times.
So we have to draw lines parallel to the x-axis that cut the graph three times.
The range of values of k will be in between the lowest and highest values on the y-axis, so that the line $y = k$ cuts the graph three times.

Question: Find the range of values of k for which $f(x) = k$ has three roots.

Solution:

The range of values of k is found by finding the range of the equations of the lines, parallel to the x-axis, which cut the graph three times.

Any lines drawn parallel to the y-axis between $y = -1$ and $y = 2$, will cut the graph three times
$\therefore$ k will lie between -1 and 2
$\therefore$ $f(x) = k$ will have three roots for $-1 < k < 2$.

Graph the function $f : x \rightarrow 2 - 9x + 6x^2 - x^3$, in the domain $-1 \leqslant x \leqslant 5$, $\quad x \in \mathbf{R}$.
Use your graph to estimate:

(i) the values of x for which $f(x) = 0$

(ii) $f(-0.5)$

(iii) the values of x for which $f(x) > 0$ and increasing

(iv) the range of real values of k for which $f(x) = k$ has more than one solution.

Solution:

Let $y = f(x) \Rightarrow y = 2 - 9x + 6x^2 - x^3$

x	$-x^3$	$+6x^2$	$+9x$	$+2$	y
-1	$+1$	$+6$	$+9$	$+2$	18
0	$+0$	$+0$	$+0$	$+2$	2
1	-1	$+6$	-9	$+2$	-2
2	-8	$+24$	-18	$+2$	0
3	-27	$+54$	-27	$+2$	2
4	-64	$+96$	-36	$+2$	-2
5	-125	$+150$	-45	$+2$	-18

(i) **Estimate the values of x for which $f(x) = 0$.**
This question is asking, 'Where does the curve meet the x-axis?'
The curve meets the x-axis at 0.3, 2 and 3.7.
Therefore, the values of x for which $f(x) = 0$, are 0.3, 2 and 3.7.

Note: 'Find the values of x for which $2 - 9x + 6x^2 - x^3 = 0$' is another way of asking the same question.

(ii) **Estimate the value of $f(-0.5)$.**
This question is asking, 'When $x = -0.5$, what is the value of y?'
From $x = -0.5$ on the x-axis draw a broken perpendicular line to meet the curve.
From this draw a broken horizontal line to meet the y-axis.
This line meets the y-axis at 7.9.
Therefore $f(-0.5) = 7.9$.

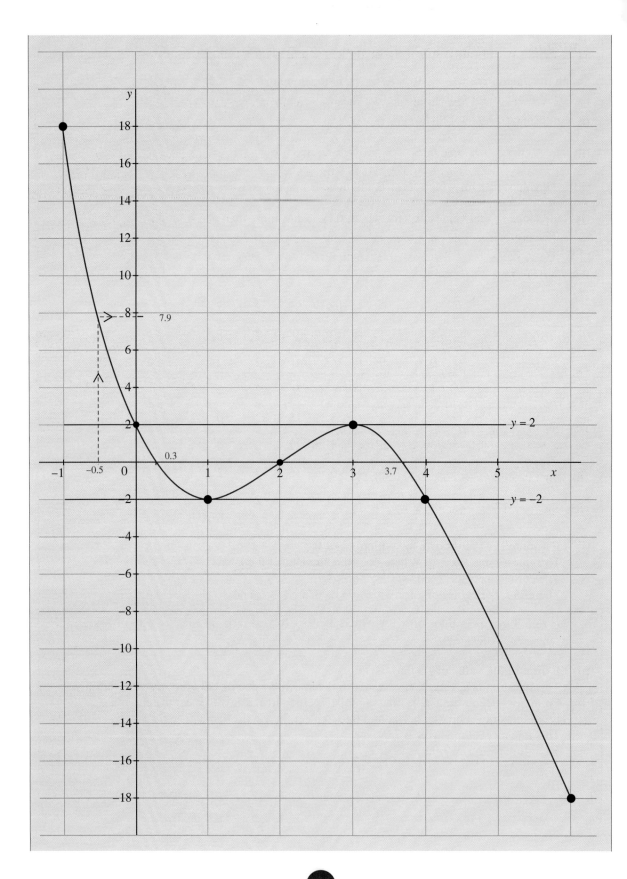

(iii) Estimate the values of x for which $f(x) > 0$ and is increasing.

This question is asking,
'Where is the curve above the x-axis and increasing as we go from left to right?'
From the graph, the curve is above the x-axis and increasing between 2 and 3.
Therefore, the values of x for which $f(x) > 0$ and increasing are $2 < x < 3$.

> **Note:** $x = 2$ is not included because at $x = 2$, $f(x) = 0$ and we are given $f(x) > 0$.
> $x = 3$ is not included because at $x = 3$ there is a turning point and $f(x)$ is not increasing.

(iv) Estimate the range of real values of k for which $f(x) = k$ has more than one solution.

The range of values of k is found by drawing lines parallel to the x-axis that meet the graph more than once.
Any lines drawn parallel to the x-axis between -2 and 2 will meet the curve more than once.
Therefore, k will lie between -2 and 2, including -2 and 2.
Therefore, $f(x) = k$ will have more than one solution when $-2 \leqslant k \leqslant 2$.

Example ▼

On the same axis and scales, graph the functions:
$f : x \rightarrow x^3 - 6x + 2$ and $g : x \rightarrow 2x - 2$, in the domain $-3 \leqslant x \leqslant 3$, $\qquad x \in \mathbf{R}$.
Use your graph to estimate:

(i) the values of x for which $f(x) = 2$.
Hence, estimate $\sqrt{6}$, giving a reason for your answer.

(ii) the range of values of x for which $g(x) > f(x)$

(iii) the roots of the equation $x^3 - 8x + 4 = 0$.

Solution:

Let $y = f(x) \Rightarrow y = x^3 - 6x + 2$

x	$x^3 - 6x + 2$	y
-3	$-27 + 18 + 2$	-7
-2	$-8 + 12 + 2$	6
-1	$-1 + 6 + 2$	7
0	$+0 + 0 + 2$	2
1	$+1 - 6 + 2$	-3
2	$+8 - 12 + 2$	-2
3	$+27 - 18 + 2$	11

Let $y = g(x) \Rightarrow y = 2x - 2$

x	$2x - 2$	y
-3	$-6 - 2$	-8
3	$6 - 2$	4

(using the smallest and largest values of x)

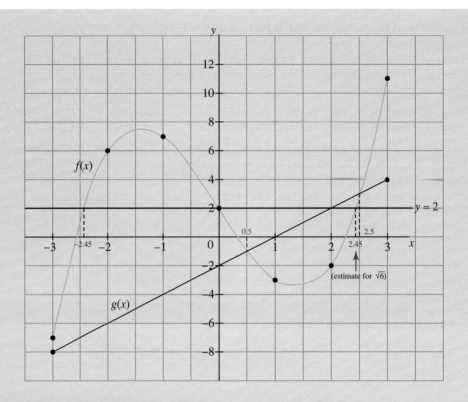

(i) **Estimate the values of x for which $f(x) = 2$.**
This question is asking, 'When $y = 2$, what are the values of x?'
Draw the line $y = 2$.
Where this line meets the curve draw broken perpendicular lines to meet the x-axis.
These lines meet the x-axis at -2.45, 0 and 2.45
Therefore, the values of x for which $f(x) = 2$ are -2.45, 0 and 2.45.

Note: 'Estimate the values of x for which $x^3 - 6x + 2 = 2$' is another way of asking the same
question.

Use $f(x) = 2$ to estimate $\sqrt{6}$.

Let $\qquad f(x) = 2$
$\qquad\qquad x^3 - 6x + 2 = 2$ $\qquad\qquad$ ($f(x) = x^3 - 6x + 2$)
$\qquad\qquad\quad x^3 - 6x = 0$ $\qquad\qquad$ (subtract 2 from both sides)
$\qquad\qquad\quad x(x^2 - 6) = 0$ $\qquad\qquad$ (factorise the left-hand side)
$x = 0 \qquad$ or $\qquad x^2 - 6 = 0$ $\qquad$ (let each factor $= 0$)
$x = 0 \qquad$ or $\qquad\quad x^2 = 6$
$x = 0 \qquad$ or $\qquad\quad x = \pm\sqrt{6}$

Therefore, when $f(x) = 2$, one of the roots is $\sqrt{6}$.
Thus, the line $y = 2$ can be used to estimate $\sqrt{6}$.
One of the values of x where the line $y = 2$ intersects the curve will give an estimate for $\sqrt{6}$.
From the graph, $\sqrt{6}$ is approximately 2.45.

(ii) **Estimate the range of values of x for which $g(x) > f(x)$.**

$f(x)$ is the curve, $g(x)$ is the line.

This question is asking, 'What are the values of x where the line is **above** the curve?'

First work out the values of x where the curve and line intersect.

Where the curve and line meet, draw broken perpendicular lines to meet the x-axis.

These lines meet the x-axis at 0.5 and 2.5.

Therefore, the values of x for which $f(x) = g(x)$ are 0.5 and 2.5.

From the graphs, the line is above the curve between 0.5 and 2.5.

Therefore, the values of x for which $g(x) > f(x)$ are $0.5 < x < 2.5$.

(iii) **Estimate the roots of the equation $x^3 - 8x + 4 = 0$.**

We have to use the graph to solve this equation.

$$x^3 - 8x + 4 = 0$$
$$(x^3 - 6x + 2) - 2x + 2 = 0 \qquad \text{(rearranging in terms of } f(x)\text{)}$$
$$f(x) - 2x + 2 = 0 \qquad (f(x) = x^3 - 6x + 2)$$
$$f(x) = 2x - 2$$
$$f(x) = g(x) \qquad (g(x) = 2x - 2)$$

$f(x) = g(x)$ is where the curve and the line meet.

Thus, the values of x where the curve and the line meet are solutions of the equation $x^3 - 8x + 4 = 0$.

From the graph, the values of x where the curve and line meet are 0.5 and 2.5.

Therefore, the roots of the equation $x^3 - 8x + 4 = 0$ are 0.5 and 2.5.

Note: There is another root, -3.1, of the equation $x^3 - 8x + 4 = 0$, but it is outside the given domain, $-3 \leqslant x \leqslant 3$, and thus we cannot use the graphs to find this root.

Exercise 9.5 ▼

1. Below is a graph of the function $f : x \rightarrow x^3 - 3x^2 + 4$, in the domain $-2 \leqslant x \leqslant 4$, $\qquad x \in \mathbf{R}$.

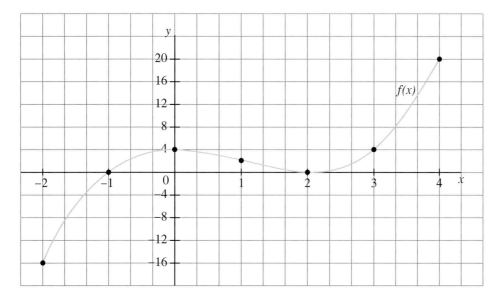

Use your graph to:

(i) find the values of x for which $f(x) = 0$

(ii) find the coordinates of the local maximum and minimum points of f

(iii) find the local maximum and minimum values

(iv) estimate the value of $f(3.5)$

(v) find the values of x for which $f(x)$ is decreasing

(vi) find the values of x for which $f(x)$ is increasing

(vii) find the values of x for which $f(x) < 0$ and increasing

(viii) find the values of k for which $f(x) = k$ has three solutions

(ix) estimate the values of x for which   **(a)** $f(x) = 2$ **(b)** $f(x) \geqslant 2$.

2. Graph the function $f : x \rightarrow x^3 + 4x^2 + x - 6$ in the domain $-4 \leqslant x \leqslant 2$, $x \in \mathbf{R}$.
Use your graph to find the values of x for which:

(i) $f(x) = 0$ **(ii)** $f(x) \geqslant 0$ **(iii)** $f(x) \leqslant 0$ and $x \leqslant 0$.

Estimate the value of $f(1.4)$.

3. Graph the function $f : x \rightarrow x^3 - 2x^2 - 5x + 6$ in the domain $-3 \leqslant x \leqslant 4$, $x \in \mathbf{R}$.
Use your graph to:

(i) find the values of x for which $f(x) = 0$

(ii) find the values of x for which: **(a)** $f(x) > 0$ **(b)** $f(x) < 0$.

(iii) estimate the values of x for which $f(x) = 5$.

4. Let $f(x) = 2x^3 - 3x^2 - 12x + 4$ for $x \in \mathbf{R}$.

(i) Complete the table:

x	-2.5	-2	-1	0	1	2	3	3.5
$f(x)$	-16							11

(ii) Draw the graph of $f(x)$ in the domain $-2.5 \leqslant x \leqslant 3.5$, $x \in \mathbf{R}$.

(iii) Write down the coordinates of the local maximum and the local minimum points.

(iv) Use your graph to find the values of x for which $f(x)$ is:

   (a) increasing   **(b)** decreasing   **(c)** positive, increasing and $x < 0$.

(v) Estimate the values of x for which $f(x) = 0$.

5. The function $f : x \rightarrow 2x^3 - 5x^2 - 2x + 5$ is defined on the domain $-2 \leqslant x \leqslant 3$ for $x \in \mathbf{R}$.
Verify that $f(-2) = -27$ and $f(-1) = 0$ and draw the graph of f.
Use your graph to solve the equation $2x(x - 1)(x + 2) = 7x^2 - 2x - 5$.
Use your graph to estimate:

(i) the value of $f(1.75)$

(ii) the values of x for which $2x^3 - 5x^2 - 2x = 0$.

6. Graph the function $g : x \rightarrow x^3 - 4x^2 + 5$, in the domain $-2 \leqslant x \leqslant 4$, $x \in \mathbf{R}$.

(i) Write down the coordinates of the local maximum point.

(ii) Estimate the values of x for which $f(x) = 0$.

(iii) Use your graph to solve the equation $x^3 - 4x^2 + 2 = 0$.

Find the range of values of h, in the given domain, for which $f(x) = h$ has only one solution.

7. Graph the function $f : x \rightarrow 12x + 3x^2 - 2x^3$, in the domain $-2 \leqslant x \leqslant 3.5$, $\qquad x \in \mathbf{R}$.
   Use your graph to estimate the values of x for which:
   (i) $f(x) = 0$ **(ii)** $f(x) = 2$ **(iii)** $f(x) \leqslant 0$ and $x > 0$.
   (iv) Write down the coordinates of the local maximum and local minimum points.
   (v) Find the range of values of k for which $f(x) = k$ has:
       (a) three real roots   **(b)** two real roots.

8. On the same axes and scales, graph the functions:
   $f : x \rightarrow x^3 - 3x^2 - 4x + 12$, $g : x \rightarrow 9 - 3x$, in the domain $-2 \leqslant x \leqslant 4$, $x \in \mathbf{R}$.
   Use your graphs to find the values of x for which:
   (i) $f(x) = 0$ **(ii)** $f(x) = 12$ **(iii)** $f(x) = g(x)$ **(iv)** $f(x) \geqslant g(x)$ **(v)** $f(x) \leqslant g(x)$.

9. On the same axes and scales, graph the functions:
   $f : x \rightarrow x^3 - 2x^2 - 6x + 4$ and $g : x \rightarrow 2x - 5$, in the domain $-2 \leqslant x \leqslant 4$, $x \in \mathbf{R}$.
   Use your graphs to find:
   (i) the two values of x for which $f(x) = g(x)$
   (ii) the range of values of x for which $f(x) \leqslant g(x)$
   (iii) the range of values of x for which $f(x) \geqslant g(x)$.

10. On the same axes and scales, graph the functions:
   $f : x \rightarrow 2x^3 - 3x^2 - 3x + 2$, $g : x \rightarrow 3x + 2$, in the domain $-2 \leqslant x \leqslant 3$, $x \in \mathbf{R}$.

   Use your graphs to estimate the values of x for which:
   (i) $f(x) = 0$ **(ii)** $2x^3 - 3x^2 - 6x = 0$ **(iii)** $2x^3 - 3x^2 - 6x \geqslant 0$.

11. Graph the function $f : x \rightarrow 2 + 3x^2 - x^3$, in the domain $-1 \leqslant x \leqslant 4$, $x \in \mathbf{R}$.
   (i) Write down the coordinates of the local maximum and local minimum points.
   (ii) Estimate the value of x for which $f(x) = 0$.
   (iii) Write the equation $-2x + 3x^2 - x^3 = 0$ in the form $2 + 3x^2 - x^3 = ax + a$.
   (iv) Using the value of a from part **(iii)**, and on the same axes and scales, graph the function $g : x \rightarrow ax + a$, in the domain $-1 \leqslant x \leqslant 4$, $x \in \mathbf{R}$.
   (v) Hence, use your graphs to find the solutions of the equation $-2x + 3x^2 - x^3 = 0$.

12. Let $f(x) = x^3 + 2x^2 - 7x - 2$ for $x \in \mathbf{R}$.
   (i) Complete the following table:

x	-4	-3	-2	-1	0	1	2	3
$f(x)$		10				-6		

   (ii) Draw the graph of f.
   (iii) Estimate the values of x for which $f(x) = 0$.
   (iv) Use the graph to find the least value of $f(x)$ in $0 \leqslant x \leqslant 3$.
   (v) If $g : x \rightarrow f(x) + k$, find the value of k when the x-axis is a tangent to the graph of g in $0 \leqslant x \leqslant 3$.
   (vi) By drawing an appropriate line, use both graphs to solve $x^3 + 2x^2 - 5x - 6 = 0$.

13. (i) Verify that $x = 2$ is a root of the equation $x^3 - 5x^2 + 2x + 8 = 0$ and find the other two roots.

Graph the function $f : x \rightarrow x^3 - 5x^2 + 2x + 8$ in the domain $-2 \leqslant x \leqslant 5$, $\quad x \in \mathbf{R}$.

(ii) Use your graph to find the values of x for which $f(x) = 0$ and verify your answers to part **(i)**.

(iii) Write the equation $x^3 - 5x^2 + 4x = 0$ in the form $x^3 - 5x^2 + 2x + 8 = a - bx$.

(iv) Using the values of a and b from part **(iii)**, and on the same axes and scales, graph the function $g : x \rightarrow a - bx$, in the domain $-2 \leqslant x \leqslant 5$, $\quad x \in \mathbf{R}$.

(v) Use your graphs to find the solutions of the equation $x^3 - 5x^2 + 4x = 0$.

(vi) Hence, or otherwise, write down the values of x for which $x^3 - 5x^2 + 4x \geqslant 0$, in the domain $-2 \leqslant x \leqslant 5$, $\quad x \in \mathbf{R}$.

14. Factorise $x^3 - 4x$ and hence solve the equation $x^3 - 4x = 0$.

Graph the function $f : x \rightarrow x^3 - 5x + 2$, in the domain $-3 \leqslant x \leqslant 3$, $\quad x \in \mathbf{R}$.

(i) Estimate from your graph the three values of x for which $f(x) = 0$.

(ii) Estimate from your graph the three values of x for which $f(x) = 2$ and hence, estimate $\sqrt{5}$, giving a reason for your answer.

15. Graph the function $f : x \rightarrow x^3 - 3x + 2$ in the domain $-3 \leqslant x \leqslant 3$, $\quad x \in \mathbf{R}$.

Use your graph to find the following:

(i) the local maximum and minimum values.

(ii) the coordinates of the local maximum and minimum points.

(iii) the range of values of x for which $f(x)$ is:

    (a) decreasing   **(b)** negative and increasing   **(iii)** positive and increasing.

(iv) the range of real values of k for which the equation $x^3 - 3x + 2 = k$ has three real and distinct roots.

Estimate from your graph the values of x for which $f(x) = 2$.

Hence, estimate $\sqrt{3}$, giving a reason for your answer.

16. Let $f(x) = x^3 + x^2 + x - 2$ for $x \in \mathbf{R}$.

(i) Complete the table:

x	-2	-1	0	1	2
$f(x)$	-8				

(ii) Draw the graph of $f(x)$ in the domain $-2 \leqslant x \leqslant 2$.

(iii) Use the same axes and scales, and in the same domain, graph the function $g : x \rightarrow x^2 + x - 6$, for $x \in \mathbf{R}$.

(iv) Use your graphs to estimate $\sqrt[3]{-4}$.

17. On the same axes and scales, graph the functions:

$g : x \rightarrow \dfrac{1}{x-1}$, $\quad h : x \rightarrow x + 1$ in the domain $-2 \leqslant x \leqslant 4$, $\quad x \in \mathbf{R}$.

Show how your graphs may be used to estimate the value of $\pm\sqrt{2}$.

Periodic Functions

A function whose graph repeats itself at regular intervals is called '**periodic**'.
For example, the graph below is a graph of a periodic function, $y = f(x)$.

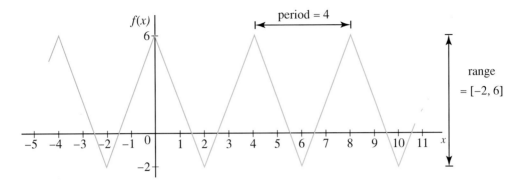

The '**period**' is the horizontal width it takes for a graph to repeat itself.
In this case the period = 4 (graph repeats itself after a distance of 4).
The '**range**' is the interval from the least value of y to the greatest value of y.
In this case the range = [−2, 6] (lower value is written first).
A feature of the graphs of periodic functions is that we can add, or subtract, the period, or integer multiples of the period, to the value of $f(x)$ and the value of the function is unchanged.
For example, using the graph above:

$$f(-4) = f(0) = f(4) = f(8) = 6 \qquad [f(-4) = f(-4+4) = f(-4+8) = f(-4+12) \dots]$$

$$f(10) = f(6) = f(2) = f(-2) = -2 \qquad [f(10) = f(10-4) = f(10-8) = f(10-12) \dots]$$

On our course we will be given the graph of a periodic function on scaled and labelled axes.
The period will be a positive whole number and the range will be a closed interval $[a, b]$, where a and b are whole numbers, positive or negative.

Example ▼

Part of the graph of the periodic function $y = f(x)$ is shown below.
State the period and range of the function.

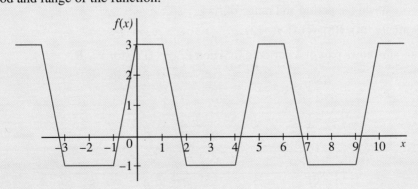

Evaluate: $f(1), f(4), f(20), f(23.5)$.

Solution:

Basic building block

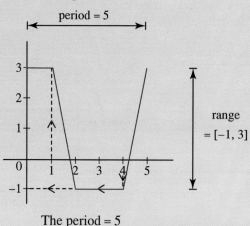

The period = 5

The range = [−1, 3]

$f(1) = 3$ and $f(4) = −1$

Basic building block

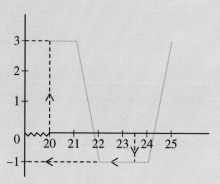

$f(20) = 3$ and $f(23.5) = −1$

Alternatively, by repeatedly subtracting the period 5:

$f(20) = f(15) = f(10) = f(5) = 3$

$f(23.5) = f(18.5) = f(13.5) = f(8.5) = f(3.5) = −1$

Exercise 9.6 ▼

1. The diagram shows part of a periodic function $f : x \rightarrow f(x)$, for $x \in \mathbf{R}$.

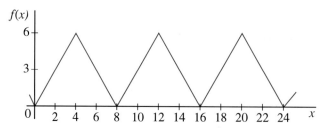

    (i)   Write down the period and range of $f(x)$.

    (ii) Evaluate $f(4), f(8), f(14), f(−12)$.

2. The diagram shows part of a periodic function $f : x \rightarrow f(x)$, for $x \in \mathbf{R}$.

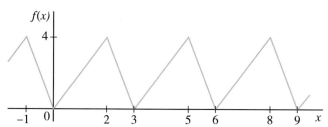

    (i)   Write down the period and range of $f(x)$.

    (ii) Evaluate: $f(2), f(3), f(−1), f(−6)$.

3. The diagram shows part of a periodic function $f : x \rightarrow f(x)$, for $x \in \mathbf{R}$.

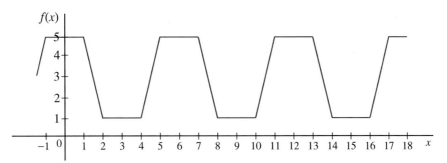

(i) Write down the period and range of $f(x)$.

(ii) Complete the following table:

x	1	2	3	8	11	−1	−6	−10	3.5	−6.5
$f(x)$										

4. The graph shows part of the graph of the periodic function $f : x \rightarrow f(x)$, for $x \in \mathbf{R}$.

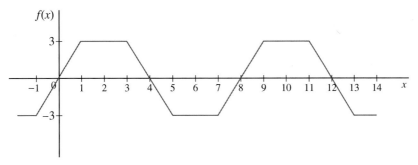

(i) Write down the period and range of $f(x)$.

(ii) Complete the following table:

x	1	4	6	8	20	−1	−8	−17	2.5	−1.5
$f(x)$										

5. The graph shows part of a periodic function $f : x \rightarrow f(x)$, for $x \in \mathbf{R}$.

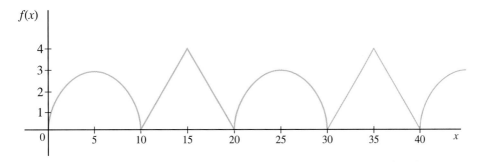

(i) Write down the period and range of $f(x)$.

(ii) Complete the following table:

x	5	10	15	20	45	60	−10	−25	−40	−50
$f(x)$										

(iii) Write down the three values of x in the domain $40 \leqslant x \leqslant 60$ for which $f(x) = 0$.

(iv) Write down the values of x in the domain $60 \leqslant x \leqslant 80$ for which:

    (a) $f(x)$ is a maximum   **(b)** $f(x)$ is increasing.

6. The diagram shows part of a periodic function $f : x \rightarrow f(x)$, for $x \in \mathbf{R}$.

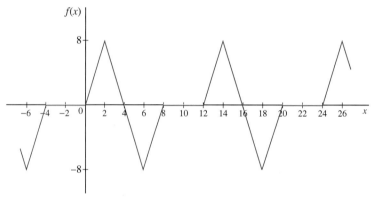

(i) Write down the period and range of the function.

(ii) Complete the following table:

x	0	2	4	6	8	10	12	30	41	−6	−10
$f(x)$											

(iii) Write down any four integer values of x in the domain $48 \leqslant x \leqslant 60$ for which $f(x) = 0$.

(iv) Write down the values of x in the domain $36 \leqslant x \leqslant 48$ for which:

    (a) $f(x)$ is a minimum   **(b)** $f(x)$ is decreasing   **(c)** $f(x)$ is positive and increasing.

7. The diagram shows part of the graph of the periodic function $f : x \rightarrow f(x)$ in the domain $0 \leqslant x \leqslant 6k$, $k \in \mathbf{R}$.

The period of $f(x)$ is 6 and its range is $[-2, 3]$.

Write down the values of k, a and b.

On separate diagrams draw sketches of $f(x)$ in the domain:

(i) $-3k \leqslant x \leqslant k$ **(ii)** $13k \leqslant x \leqslant 19k$.

Complete the following table:

x	1	4	6	7	−1	−10	−12	−16
$f(x)$								

If $f(k) = -2$, write down three values of k, $k \neq -1, 1, 7$.

Simpson's Rule and Graphs

Simpson's Rule can be used to calculate the area between the graph of a function and the x-axis.

Consider the graph of the function $f(x)$ in the domain $0 \leqslant x \leqslant 6$. Simpson's Rule can be used to calculate the area between the curve and the x-axis (shaded region). However, the negative y values must be taken as positive.

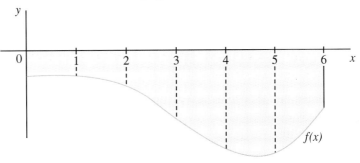

Exercise 9.7 ▼

1. The diagram shows the curve $f : x \rightarrow x^2 + 2$ in the domain $0 \leqslant x \leqslant 4$, $x \in \mathbf{R}$.

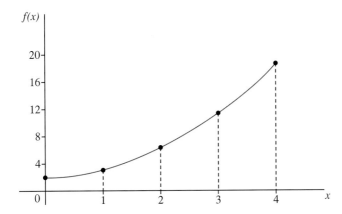

   (i) Complete the following table:

x	0	1	2	3	4
$f(x)$					

   (ii) Hence, use Simpson's Rule to calculate the area between the curve and the x-axis.

2. Graph the function $f : x \rightarrow 13 + 4x - x^2$, in the domain $0 \leqslant x \leqslant 6$, $x \in \mathbf{R}$.
   Use Simpson's Rule to calculate the area between the curve and the x-axis.

3. Graph the function $f : x \rightarrow 8 + 2x - x^2$, in the domain $-2 \leqslant x \leqslant 4$, $x \in \mathbf{R}$.
   Use Simpson's Rule to calculate the area between the curve and the x-axis.

4. Graph the function $f : x \rightarrow x^3 - 6x^2 + 9x + 6$, in the domain $0 \leqslant x \leqslant 4$, $x \in \mathbf{R}$.
   Use Simpson's Rule to calculate the area between the curve and the x-axis.

5. Graph the function $f : x \rightarrow x^3 + 3x^2 - x + 12$, in the domain $-4 \leqslant x \leqslant 2$, $x \in \mathbf{R}$.
   Use Simpson's Rule to calculate the area between the curve and the x-axis.

6. Graph the function $f : x \rightarrow -6 + 6x - x^2 - x^3$, in the domain $-3 \leqslant x \leqslant 3$, $x \in \mathbf{R}$.
   Use Simpson's Rule to calculate the area between the curve and the x-axis.

CHAPTER 10

DIFFERENTIATION

Differentiation from First Principles

Differentiation, or differential calculus, is the branch of mathematics measuring rates of change.

Slope of a line

On the right is part of the graph of the line $y = 3x$.
There is a relationship between x and y. For every increase in x, there is three times this increase in y.

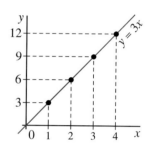

> Rate of change of $y = 3$ times rate of change of x

From coordinate geometry, the slope of the line $y = 3x$ is 3.

> Slope = 3

> Rate of change = Slope

The key word here is **slope**. The slope of a line will give **the rate of change** of the variable on the vertical axis with respect to the variable on the horizontal axis. Therefore, to find the rate of change we need only to find the slope.

Note: The y-axis is usually the vertical axis and the x-axis the horizontal axis. Therefore, the slope of a line will give the rate of change of y with respect to (the change in) x.

Slope of a Curve

Consider the curve below and the tangents that are constructed on it.

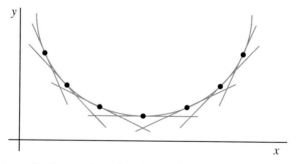

The slope of the curve at a point is equal to the slope of the tangent at that point. As we move along the curve the slope of each tangent changes. In other words, the rate of change of y with respect to x

changes. We need to find a method of finding the slope of the tangent at each point on the curve. The method of finding the slope of a tangent to a curve at any point on the curve is called **differentiation**.

Notation

We will now develop the method for finding the slope of the tangent to the curve $y = f(x)$ at any point $(x, f(x))$ on the curve.

Let the graph shown represent the function $y = f(x)$. $(x, f(x))$ is a point on this curve and $(x + h, f(x + h))$ is a point further along the curve.

S is a line through these points.

T is a tangent to the curve at the point $(x, f(x))$.

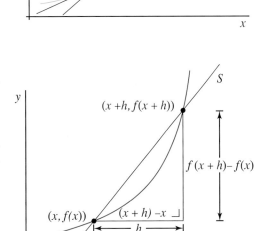

Slope of $S = \dfrac{y_2 - y_1}{x_2 - x_1}$

$\qquad = \dfrac{f(x + h) - f(x)}{(x + h) - h}$

$\qquad = \dfrac{f(x + h) - f(x)}{h}$

This would be a good approximation of the slope of the tangent T, at the point $(x, f(x))$, if $(x + h, f(x + h))$ is **very** close to $(x, f(x))$. By letting h get smaller, the point $(x + h, f(x + h))$ moves closer to $(x, f(x))$. The result is that the slope of S gets closer to the slope of T. In other words, as h approaches 0, the slope of S approaches the slope of T.

Mathematically speaking, we say that the slope of T is equal to the limit of the slope of S as h approaches 0. It is important to realise that h approaches 0, but **never** actually becomes equal to zero.

This is usually written $\lim\limits_{h \to 0} \dfrac{f(x + h) - f(x)}{h}$.

The process of finding this limiting value is called '**differentiation**'.

For neatness, this limit is written as $\dfrac{dy}{dx}$ (pronounced 'dee y, dee x') or $f'(x)$, pronounced 'f dash of x' or 'f prime of x'.

$\dfrac{dy}{dx}$ or $f'(x)$ is called the: '**differential coefficient**' or '**first derivative of y with respect to x**'.

The advantage of the notation $\dfrac{dy}{dx}$ is that it tells us which quantities are being compared.

$\dfrac{dy}{dx}$ is the derivative of y with respect to x.

$\dfrac{ds}{dt}$ is the derivative of s with respect to t.

$\dfrac{dA}{dr}$ is the derivative of A with respect to r.

Definition

The slope of the tangent to the curve $y = f(x)$ at any point on the curve is given by:

$$\frac{dy}{dx} = f'(x) = \lim_{h \to 0} \frac{f(x+h) - f(x)}{h}$$

Differentiation from first principles involves four steps:

Find:

1. $f(x + h)$

2. $f(x + h) - f(x)$

3. $\dfrac{f(x+h) - f(x)}{h}$

4. $\lim\limits_{h \to 0} \dfrac{f(x+h) - f(x)}{h}$

Example ▼

Differentiate $x^2 - 3x + 2$ from first principles with respect to x.

Solution:

$$f(x) = x^2 - 3x + 2$$

1. $f(x + h) = (x + h)^2 - 3(x + h) + 2$ [replace x with $(x + h)$]

     $f(x + h) = x^2 + 2hx + h^2 - 3x - 3h + 2$ [$(x + h)^2 = x^2 + 2hx + h^2$]

2. $f(x + h) - f(x) = \cancel{x^2} + 2hx + h^2 - \cancel{3x} - 3h + \cancel{2} - \cancel{x^2} + \cancel{3x} - \cancel{2}$

     $f(x + h) - f(x) = 2hx + h^2 - 3h$

3. $\dfrac{f(x+h) - f(x)}{h} = 2x + h - 3$ [divide both sides by h]

4. $\lim\limits_{h \to 0} \dfrac{f(x+h) - f(x)}{h} = 2x + 0 - 3 = 2x - 3$ [take the limit]

Exercise 10.1 ▼

Differentiate each of the following with respect to x from first principles:

1. $x^2 + 2x + 3$ 2. $x^2 + 3x - 2$ 3. $x^2 - 2x + 5$ 4. $x^2 - 5x - 3$

5. $x^2 - 4x - 4$ 6. $x^2 + 5x$ 7. $x^2 - 3x$ 8. $x^2 + 6x$

9. $3x + 2$ 10. $5x - 3$ 11. $2x^2$ 12. $2x^2 - 5x$

13. $3x^2 + 4$ 14. $3x^2 - 2x$ 15. $2x - x^2$ 16. $3x - 2x^2$

Differentiation by Rule

Differentiation from first principles can become tedious and difficult. Fortunately, it is not always necessary to use first principles. There are a few rules (which can be derived from first principles) which enable us to write down the derivative of a function quite easily.

Rule 1: General Rule

$$y = x^n \quad \text{then} \quad \frac{dy}{dx} = nx^{n-1}$$

$$y = ax^n \quad \text{then} \quad \frac{dy}{dx} = nax^{n-1}$$

In words: Multiply by the power and reduce the power by 1.

Example ▼

Differentiate each of the following with respect to x:

(i) $y = x^3$ (ii) $y = -5x^2$ (iii) $y = 4x$ (iv) $y = \dfrac{1}{x^5}$ (v) $y = 7$.

Solution:

(i) $y = x^3$ $\dfrac{dy}{dx} = 3x^{3-1} = 3x^2$

(ii) $y = -5x^2$ $\dfrac{dy}{dx} = 2 \times -5x^{2-1} = -10x^1 = -10x$

(iii) $y = 4x = 4x^1$ $\dfrac{dy}{dx} = 1 \times 4x^{1-1} = 4x^0 = 4 \quad (x^0 = 1)$

(iv) $y = \dfrac{1}{x^5} = x^{-5}$ $\dfrac{dy}{dx} = -5x^{-5-1} = -5x^{-6} \quad \text{or} \quad -\dfrac{5}{x^6}$

(v) $y = 7 = 7x^0$ $\dfrac{dy}{dx} = 0 \times 7x^{0-1} = 0$

Part (**v**) leads to the rule:

The derivative of a constant = 0.

Note: The line $y = 7$ is a horizontal line. Its slope is 0. Therefore its derivative (also its slope) equals 0. In other words, the derivative of a constant always equals zero.

After practice, $\dfrac{dy}{dx}$ can be written down from inspection.

Sum or Difference

If the expression to be differentiated contains more than one term just differentiate, separately, each term in the expression.

> ### *Example* ▼
>
> **(i)** If $y = 3x^2 - 5x + 4$, find $\dfrac{dy}{dx}$.
>
> **(ii)** If $f(x) - 4x^3 + x^2 - x - 6$, find $f'(x)$.
>
> **Solution:**
>
> **(i)** $y = 3x^2 - 5x + 4$
>
> $\dfrac{dy}{dx} = 6x - 5$
>
> **(ii)** $f(x) = 4x^3 + x^2 - x - 6$
>
> $f'(x) = 12x^2 + 2x - 1$

Exercise 10.2 ▼

Find $\dfrac{dy}{dx}$ if:

1. $y = x^4$ **2.** $y = x^6$ **3.** $y = 3x^2$ **4.** $y = -5x^4$ **5.** $y = 4x$

6. $y = -3x$ **7.** $y = 8$ **8.** $y = -5$ **9.** $y = \dfrac{1}{x^3}$ **10.** $y = \dfrac{1}{x}$

11. $y = x^4 + 2x^3$ **12.** $y = 2x^3 + 5x^2$ **13.** $y = 3x^2 + 4x$

14. $y = 2x^2 - 6x$ **15.** $y = 5x - 2x^2$ **16.** $y = 3x - 1$

17. $y = x^3 + 2x^2 + 5x$ **18.** $y = x - 3x^2 - 4x^3$ **19.** $y = 4 - 5x^2 - 6x^4$

Find $f'(x)$ if:

20. $f(x) = x^2 - x - 6$ **21.** $f(x) = x^3 - 3x^2 + 4$ **22.** $f(x) = 20x - 2x^2$

23. $f(x) = 2x^3 - 8x^2 + 7x - 6$ **24.** $f(x) = x^3 - 2x^2 + 4x - 1$ **25.** $f(x) = 8 + 2x - 3x^2 - x^3$

26. $f(x) = x^3 + \dfrac{1}{x^3}$ **27.** $3x^2 + \dfrac{1}{x^2}$ **28.** $f(x) = x^4 + 4 + \dfrac{1}{x^4}$

Evaluating Derivatives

Often we may be asked to find the value of the derivative for a particular value of the function.

(i) If $y = 2x^3 - 4x + 3$, find the value of $\dfrac{dy}{dx}$ when $x = 1$.

(ii) If $s = 4t^2 + 10t - 7$, find the value of $\dfrac{ds}{dt}$ when $t = -2$.

Solution:

(i)
$$y = 2x^3 - 4x + 3$$
$$\frac{dy}{dx} = 6x^2 - 4$$
$$\left.\frac{dy}{dx}\right|_{x=1} = 6(1)^2 - 4$$
$$= 6 - 4 = 2$$

(ii)
$$s = 4t^2 + 10t - 7$$
$$\frac{ds}{dt} = 8t + 10$$
$$\left.\frac{ds}{dt}\right|_{t=-2} = 8(-2) + 10$$
$$= -16 + 10 = -6$$

Exercise 10.3 ▼

1. If $y = 3x^2 + 4x + 2$, find the value of $\dfrac{dy}{dx}$ when $x = 1$.

2. If $y = 2x^3 + 4x^2 + 3x - 5$, find the value of $\dfrac{dy}{dx}$ when $x = 2$.

3. If $y = 4x^3 - 3x^2 + 5x - 3$, find the value of $\dfrac{dy}{dx}$ when $x = -1$.

4. If $s = 3t - 2t^2$, find $\dfrac{ds}{dt}$ when $t = 2$.

5. If $s = t^3 - 2t^2 - t + 1$, find $\dfrac{ds}{dt}$ when $t = -1$.

6. If $A = 3r^2 - 5r$, find $\dfrac{dA}{dr}$ when $r = 3$.

7. If $V = 3h - h^2 - 3h^3$, find $\dfrac{dV}{dh}$ when $h = 2$.

8. If $h = 20t - 5t^2$, find $\dfrac{dh}{dt}$ when $t = 4$.

9. If $A = \pi r^2$, find $\dfrac{dA}{dr}$ when $r = 5$, leaving your answer in terms of π.

10. If $V = \frac{4}{3}\pi r^3$, find $\dfrac{dV}{dr}$ when $r = 3$, leaving your answer in terms of π.

Rule 2: Product Rule

Suppose u and v are functions of x.

If $y = uv$,

then $\dfrac{dy}{dx} = u\dfrac{dv}{dx} + v\dfrac{du}{dx}$

In words: First by the derivative of the second + second by the derivative of the first.

Note: The word '**product**' refers to quantities being multiplied.

Example ▼

If $y = (x^2 - 3x + 2)(x^2 - 2)$, find $\dfrac{dy}{dx}$. Hence, evaluate $\dfrac{dy}{dx}$ when $x = -1$.

Solution:

Let $u = x^2 - 3x + 2$ and let $v = x^2 - 2$.

$\dfrac{du}{dx} = 2x - 3$ and $\dfrac{dv}{dx} = 2x$

$\dfrac{dy}{dx} = u\dfrac{dv}{dx} + v\dfrac{du}{dx}$ (product rule)

$= (x^2 - 3x + 2)(2x) + (x^2 - 2)(2x - 3)$

$= 2x^3 - 6x^2 + 4x + 2x^3 - 3x^2 - 4x + 6$

$= 4x^3 - 9x^2 + 6$

$\dfrac{dy}{dx}\bigg|_{x=-1} = 4(-1)^3 - 9(-1)^2 + 6 = -4 - 9 + 6 = -7$

Exercise 3.10 ▼

Use the product rule to find $\dfrac{dy}{dx}$ if:

1. $y = (2x + 4)(3x + 5)$

2. $y = (x^2 + 2)(2x^2 + 7)$

3. $y = (2x + 3)(x^2 + 3x + 4)$

4. $y = (x^2 + 3x)(x^3 - 3x + 4)$

5. $y = (3x^2 - 5x + 3)(3x - 2)$

6. $y = (x + 3)(x - 2)$

7. $y = (x^3 - 2x)(3 - 2x)$

8. $y = (x - 4)(x^3 - 5)$

9. $y = (x^2 + x + 1)(x - 2)$

10. $y = (2x - x^3 - x^4)(x^2 - 3)$

11. $y = (x^3 - x^2 - x)(x^3 + 2x)$

12. $y = (5x^3 - 6x)(x^2 - 3x - 1)$

13. Let $f(x) = (x^2 - 2x)(3x + 2)$. Find $f'(x)$, the derivative of $f(x)$.

14. Let $f(x) = (x^3 - 1)(2x - x^2)$. Find $f'(x)$, the derivative of $f(x)$.

15. If $y = (2x - x^2)(x^2 - x - 1)$, evaluate $\dfrac{dy}{dx}$ when $x = 0$.

16. If $s = (3t^2 - 4t)(t^2 - 4)$, find $\dfrac{ds}{dt}$ and evaluate it when $t = 1$.

17. If $x = (2h^2 - 3h + 5)(h - 2)$, evaluate $\dfrac{dx}{dh}$ when $h = 2$.

18. Find the coefficient of x^3 in the derivative of $(2x^2 - x - 3)(1 - 2x^2)$ with respect to x.

Rule 3: Quotient Rule

Suppose u and v are functions of x.

If $y = \dfrac{u}{v}$,

then $\dfrac{dy}{dx} = \dfrac{v\dfrac{du}{dx} - u\dfrac{dv}{dx}}{v^2}$.

In words:

$$\dfrac{\text{Bottom by the derivative of the top} - \text{Top by the derivative of the bottom}}{(\text{Bottom})^2}$$

Note: Quotient is another name for a fraction. The quotient rule refers to one quantity divided by another.

Example ▼

If $y = \dfrac{x^2}{x + 2}$ find $\dfrac{dy}{dx}$ and, hence, find the value of $\dfrac{dy}{dx}$ when $x = 2$.

Solution:

$$y = \dfrac{x^2}{x + 2}$$

Let $u = x^2$ and $v = x + 2$

$\dfrac{du}{dx} = 2x$ and $\dfrac{dv}{dx} = 1$

199

$$\frac{dy}{dx} = \frac{v\dfrac{du}{dx} - u\dfrac{dv}{dx}}{v^2} \qquad \text{(quotient rule)}$$

$$= \frac{(x+2)(2x) - (x^2)(1)}{(x+2)^2}$$

$$= \frac{2x^2 + 4x - x^2}{(x+2)^2}$$

$$= \frac{x^2 + 4x}{(x+2)^2}$$

Note: It is usual practice to simplify the top but **not** the bottom.

$$\left.\frac{dy}{dx}\right|_{x=2} = \frac{(2)^2 + 4(2)}{(2+2)^2} = \frac{4+8}{(4)^2} = \frac{12}{16} = \frac{3}{4}$$

Exercise 10.5 ▼

Find $\dfrac{dy}{dx}$ if:

1. $y = \dfrac{3x+2}{x+1}$

2. $y = \dfrac{2x+1}{x+3}$

3. $y = \dfrac{x}{x-1}$

4. $y = \dfrac{5x+2}{x+4}$

5. $y = \dfrac{1}{x+2}$

6. $y = \dfrac{1}{x-3}$

7. $y = \dfrac{3}{x+4}$

8. $y = \dfrac{x^2}{x-1}$

9. $y = \dfrac{2x+3}{5x-4}$

10. $y = \dfrac{2x-3}{x^2+1}$

11. $y = \dfrac{2x^2}{3x^2-1}$

12. $y = \dfrac{x^2+2}{4-x^2}$

13. If $y = \dfrac{3x+2}{x-2}$, evaluate $\dfrac{dy}{dx}$ at $x = 1$.

14. If $y = \dfrac{2x^2-1}{x+5}$, evaluate $\dfrac{dy}{dx}$ at $x = 2$.

15. If $y = \dfrac{x^2-4x}{5x-1}$, evaluate $\dfrac{dy}{dx}$ at $x = 0$.

Rule 4: Chain Rule

The chain rule is used when the given function is raised to a power, e.g. $y = (x^2 - 3x + 4)^4$.

To differentiate using the chain rule, do the following in *one* step:

> **(a)** Treat what is inside the bracket as a single variable and differentiate this (multiply by the power and reduce the power by one).
>
> **(b)** Multiply this result by the derivative of what is inside the bracket.

If $y = (\text{function})^n$,

then $\dfrac{dy}{dx} = n \, (\text{function})^{n-1}$ (derivative of the function).

Example ▼

Find $\dfrac{dy}{dx}$ if: **(i)** $y = (x^2 + 3x)^5$ **(ii)** $y = (2x^2 - 5x + 3)^{20}$.

Solution:

(i) $y = (x^2 + 3x)^5$

$\dfrac{dy}{dx} = 5(x^2 + 3x)^4(2x + 3)$

(ii) $y = (2x^2 - 5x + 3)^{20}$

$\dfrac{dy}{dx} = 20(2x^2 - 5x + 3)^{19}(4x - 5)$

Exercise 10.6 ▼

Find $\dfrac{dy}{dx}$ if:

1. $y = (2x + 3)^5$

2. $y = (5x - 1)^4$

3. $y = (x^2 + 3x)^3$

4. $y = (x^2 - 5x - 6)^7$

5. $y = (4 - 5x)^6$

6. $y = (3 - 2x)^5$

7. $y = (1 + x^2)^4$

8. $y = (5 - 2x^2)^7$

9. $y = (4 - 3x - x^2)^8$

10. $y = \left(x^2 + \dfrac{1}{x^2}\right)^5$

11. $y = \left(x^3 - \dfrac{1}{x^3}\right)^4$

12. $y = \left(1 + \dfrac{1}{x}\right)^{10}$

13. If $y = (x^2 - 1)^4$, evaluate $\dfrac{dy}{dx}$ when $x = 1$.

14. If $y = (2x^2 - 3x + 1)^{10}$, find the value of $\dfrac{dy}{dx}$ when $x = 0$.

15. If $y = (h^2 - h + 1)^2$, find the value of $\dfrac{dy}{dh}$ when $h = 1$.

16. If $y = (x^2 + 1)^3$, find the value of $\dfrac{dy}{dx}$ when $x = 1$.

17. If $y = (2t^2 + 3t - 1)^8$, find the value of $\dfrac{dy}{dt}$ when $t = -2$.

18. If $f(x) = (2x - 3)^4$, evaluate $f'(x)$ at $x = \frac{3}{2}$.

Finding the Slope and Equation of a Tangent to a Curve at a Point on the Curve

$\dfrac{dy}{dx}$ = the slope of a tangent to a curve at any point on the curve.

To find the slope and equation of a tangent to a curve at a given point (x_1, y_1), on the curve, do the following:

Step 1: Find $\dfrac{dy}{dx}$.

Step 2: Evaluate $\dfrac{dy}{dx}\bigg|_{x=x_1}$ (this gives the slope of the tangent, m)

Step 3: Use m (from step 2) and the given point (x_1, y_1) in the equation:

$$(y - y_1) = m(x - x_1)$$

Note: Sometimes only the value of x is given. When this happens, substitute the value of x into the original function to find y for step 3.

Example ▼

Find the equation of the tangent to the curve $y = 3 + 2x - x^2$ at the point $(2, 3)$.

Solution:

$$y = 3 + 2x - x^2$$

Step 1: $\dfrac{dy}{dx} = 2 - 2x$

Step 2: At the point $(2, 3)$, $x = 2$

$$m = \frac{dy}{dx}\bigg|_{x=2} = 2 - 2(2) = 2 - 4 = -2$$

Step 3: $m = -2$, $x_1 = 2$, $y_1 = 3$

$$(y - y_1) = m(x - x_1)$$
$$(y - 3) = -2(x - 2)$$
$$y - 3 = -2x + 4$$
$$2x + y - 3 - 4 = 0$$
$$2x + y - 7 = 0$$

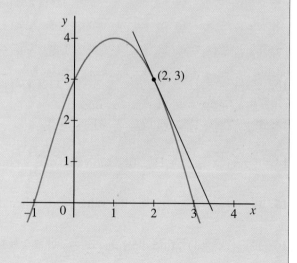

1. Find the slope of the tangent to the curve $x^2 - 3x + 2$ at the point $(1, 0)$.

2. Find the slope of the tangent to the curve $y = 3 - 3x - x^2$ at the point $(2, -7)$.

3. Find the slope of the tangent to the curve $y = x^2 - 2x - 3$ at the point $(1, -4)$.

4. Find the equation of the tangent to the curve $y = x^2 - x - 2$ at the point $(2, 0)$.

5. Find the equation of the tangent to the curve $y = x^3 - 2x^2 - 4x + 1$ at the point $(-1, 2)$.

6. Find the equation of the tangent to the curve $y = (2x + 3)^3$ at $x = -1$.

7. Find the equation of the tangent to the curve $y = \dfrac{2x - 4}{x - 4}$ at $x = 6$.

8. Verify that the point $(-1, -2)$ is on the curve $y = \dfrac{x - 1}{x + 2}$ and find the equation of the tangent to the curve at this point.

9. Show that the points $(2, 0)$ and $(3, 0)$ are on the curve $y = x^2 - 5x + 6$.
   Find the equations of the tangents to the curve at these points and investigate if these two tangents are at right angles to each other.

10. Show that the tangent to the curve $y = 3x^2 - 4x + 11$ at the point $(1, 10)$ is parallel to the line $2x - y + 5 = 0$.

11. Show that the tangent to the curve $y = \dfrac{6x - 3}{4x + 2}$ at the point $(1, \frac{1}{2})$ is parallel to the line $2x - 3y - 6 = 0$.

Given $\dfrac{dy}{dx}$, to Find the Coordinates of the Corresponding Points on a Curve

Sometimes the value of $\dfrac{dy}{dx}$ (slope of the curve at any point on it) is given and we need to find the coordinates of the point, or points, corresponding to this slope.

When this happens do the following:

Step 1:	Find $\dfrac{dy}{dx}$.
Step 2:	Let $\dfrac{dy}{dx}$ equal the given value of the slope and solve this equation for x.
Step 3:	Substitute the x values obtained in step 2 into the original function to get the corresponding values of y.

Find the coordinates of the points on the curve $y = x^3 - 3x^2 - 8x + 5$ at which the tangents to the curve make angles of $45°$ with the positive sense of the x-axis.

Solution:

$$y = x^3 - 3x^2 - 8x + 5$$

Step 1: $\dfrac{dy}{dx} = 3x^2 - 6x - 8$

Step 2: Angle of $45° \Rightarrow$ slope = 1   (as $\tan 45° = 1$)

$$\text{Let } \frac{dy}{dx} = 1 \qquad \text{(given slope in disguise)}$$

$$3x^2 - 6x - 8 = 1$$
$$3x^2 - 6x - 9 = 0$$
$$x^2 - 2x - 3 = 0$$
$$(x - 3)(x + 1) = 0$$
$$x - 3 = 0 \quad \text{or} \quad x + 1 = 0$$
$$x = 3 \quad \text{or} \quad x = -1$$

Step 3: Find the y values.

$y = x^3 - 3x^2 - 8x + 5$	$y = x^3 - 3x^2 - 8x + 5$
$x = 3$	$x = -1$
$y = (3)^3 - 3(3)^2 - 8(3) + 5$	$y = (-1)^3 - 3(-1)^2 - 8(-1) + 5$
$\quad = 27 - 27 - 24 + 5$	$\quad = -1 - 3 + 8 + 5$
$\quad = -19$	$\quad = 9$
point $(3, -19)$	point $(-1, 9)$

Thus the required points are $(3, -19)$ and $(-1, 9)$.

Note: $\tan 135° = -1$.

Find the coordinates of the point on the curve $y = x^2 - x$ where the tangent to the curve is parallel to the line $y = 3x - 5$.

Step 1: Curve: $y = x^2 - x$ Line: $y = 3x - 5$

$$\frac{dy}{dx} = 2x - 1 \qquad\qquad \frac{dy}{dx} = 3$$

Step 2: Slope of curve = Slope of line (given)

$$2x - 1 = 3$$
$$2x = 4$$
$$x = 2$$

Step 3: $y = x^2 - x$

$$x = 2$$
$$y = (2)^2 - 2$$
$$\quad = 4 - 2 = 2$$

Thus, the required point is $(2, 2)$

204

1. Find the coordinates of the point on the curve $y = 2x^2 - 3x + 2$ at which the tangent to the curve has a slope of 1.

2. Find the coordinates of the point on the curve $y = 3x^2 - 2x + 5$ at which the tangent to the curve has a slope of -10.

3. Find the coordinates of the point on the curve $y = x^2 - 5x + 3$ at which the tangent to the curve has a slope of 3.

4. Find the coordinates of the points on the curve $y = x^3 - 3x^2$ at which the tangents to the curve have a slope of 9.

5. Find the coordinates of the points on the curve $y = 2x^3 - 3x^2 - 13x + 2$ at which the tangents to the curve make angles of $135°$ with the positive sense of the x-axis.

6. Find the coordinates of the point on the curve $y = 2x^2 - 2x + 5$ at which the tangents to the curve are parallel to the line $y = 2x - 3$.

7. Find the coordinates of the points on the curve $y = 2x^3 - 3x^2 - 12x$ at which the tangents to the curve are parallel to the line $y = 24x + 3$.

8. Find the coordinates of the points on the curve $y = \dfrac{x}{1+x}$ at which the tangents to the curve are parallel to the line $x - y + 8 = 0$.
   Find the equations of the two tangents at these points.

9. (i) What is the slope of the x-axis?
   (ii) Show that the tangent of the curve $f(x) = x^2 - 2x + 5$, at the point where $x = 1$, is parallel to the x-axis.
   (iii) For what value of x is the tangent to the graph of $y = x^2 - 6x + 5$ parallel to the x-axis?
   (iv) Find the values of x for which the tangents to the graph of $y = \dfrac{x^2 + 2}{2x - 1}$ are parallel to the x-axis.

10. Find the value of a, if the slope of the tangent to the curve $y = x^2 + ax$ is 2 at the point where $x = 3$.

11. Let $f(x) = x^3 + ax^2 + 2$ for all $x \in \mathbf{R}$ and for $a \in \mathbf{R}$.
    The slope of the tangent to the curve $y = f(x)$ at $x = -1$ is 9. Find the value of a.

12. Let $g(x) = (x + 1)(x^2 - 4x)$ for $x \in \mathbf{R}$.
    (i) For what two values of x is the slope of the tangent to the curve of $g(x)$ equal to 20?
    (ii) Find the equations of the two tangents to the curve of $g(x)$ which have slope 20.

13. Let $f(x) = 2x^3 - 9x^2 + 12x + 1$ for $x \in \mathbf{R}$.
    Find $f'(x)$, the derivative of $f(x)$. At the two points, (x_1, y_1) and (x_2, y_2), the tangents to the curve $y = f(x)$ are parallel to the x-axis, where $x_2 > x_1$.
    Show that: (i) $x_1 + x_2 = 3$ (ii) $y_1 = y_2 + 1$.

Maximum and Minimum Points

$\dfrac{dy}{dx}$ can also be used to find the local maximum or local minimum points on a curve.

On the right is part of the graph of a cubic function. At the turning points, a and b, the tangents to the curve are horizontal (parallel to the x-axis). In other words, at these points the slope of the tangent is zero. These turning points are also called the **local maximum point**, point a, and the **local minimum point**, point b.

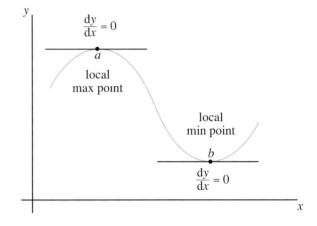

At a maximum or minimum point, $\dfrac{dy}{dx} = 0$.

To find the maximum or minimum points on a curve, do the following:

Step 1: Find $\dfrac{dy}{dx}$.

Step 2: Let $\dfrac{dy}{dx} = 0$ and solve this equation for x.

Step 3: Substitute x values obtained in step 2 into the original function to get the corresponding values of y.

Step 4: By comparing the y values we can determine which point is the local maximum or minimum point. The point with the greater y value is the local maximum point and vice versa.

Note: The graph of a quadratic function $f(x) = ax^2 + bx + c$ has only one turning point.

    1. If $a > 0$, the turning point will be a minimum.

    2. If $a < 0$, the turning point will be a maximum.

Example ▼

Find, using calculus, the coordinates of the local maximum point and the local minimum point of the curve $y = x^3 - 6x^2 + 9x + 4$.

Solution:

Step 1: $y = x^3 - 6x^2 + 9x + 4$

$$\frac{dy}{dx} = 3x^2 - 12x + 9$$

Graph of $y = x^3 - 6x^2 + 9x + 4$.

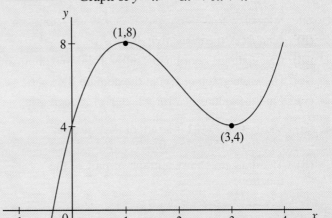

Step 2: Let $\frac{dy}{dx} = 0$.

$3x^2 - 12x + 9 = 0$

$x^2 - 4x + 3 = 0$

$(x - 3)(x - 1) = 0$

$x - 3 = 0$ or $x - 1 = 0$

$x = 3$ or $x = 1$

Step 3: Find the y values.

$y = x^3 - 6x^2 + 9x + 4$	$y = x^3 - 6x^2 + 9x + 4$
$x = 3$	$x = 1$
$y = (3)^3 - 6(3)^2 + 9(3) + 4$	$y = (1)^3 - 6(1)^2 + 9(1) + 4$
$= 27 - 54 + 27 + 4$	$= 1 - 6 + 9 + 4$
$= 4$	$= 8$
point $(3, 4)$	point $(1, 8)$

Step 4:   8 is greater than 4.

Thus, the local maximum point is $(1, 8)$ and the local minimum point is $(3, 4)$.

Exercise 10.9 ▼

Find, using calculus, the coordinates of the local minimum point of each of the following curves:

1. $y = x^2 - 4x + 3$ **2.** $y = x^2 + 6x + 1$ **3.** $y = 2x^2 - 8x + 3$

Find, using calculus, the coordinates of the local maximum point of each of the following curves:

4. $y = 7 - 6x - x^2$ **5.** $y = 5 - 4x - x^2$ **6.** $y = 1 - 12x - 3x^2$

Find, using calculus, the coordinates of the local maximum and the local minimum points of each of the following curves (in each case distinguish between the maximum and the minimum):

7. $y = x^3 - 3x^2 - 9x + 4$ **8.** $y = x^3 - 6x^2 + 9x - 1$ **9.** $y = 2x^3 - 9x^2 + 12x + 1$

10. $y = 8 + 9x - 3x^2 - x^3$ **11.** $y = 5 - 12x - 9x^2 - 2x^3 = 0$ **12.** $y = x^3 - 12x + 4$

13. Let $f(x) = x^3 - 9x^2 + 24x - 17$ for $x \in \mathbf{R}$.

    (i) Complete the following table:

x	0	1	2	3	4	5	6
$f(x)$		-1				3	

    (ii) Find $f'(x)$, the derivative of $f(x)$.

    (iii) Calculate the coordinates of the local maximum and the local minimum points of $f(x)$.

    (iv) Draw the graph of $f(x)$ in the domain $0 \leqslant x \leqslant 6$.

    (v) Find the values of x for which $f(x)$ is decreasing.

14. (i) Verify that $x = -1$ is a root of the equation:
$x^3 - 9x^2 + 15x + 25 = 0$.

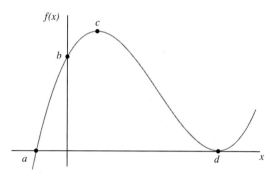

    (ii) The diagram shows a graph of part of the function:

$f : x \rightarrow x^3 - 9x^2 + 15x + 25$

There are turning points at c and d.

The curve intersects the x-axis at a and d and the y-axis at b.

Find the coordinates of a, b, c and d.

15. Let $f(x) = x^3 + ax^2 + 2$, for all $x \in \mathbf{R}$ and for $a \in \mathbf{R}$.

$f(x)$ has a turning point (a local maximum or a local minimum) at $x = 2$.

    (i) Find the value of a and the coordinates of the turning point at $x = 2$.

    (ii) Find the coordinates of the other turning point of $f(x)$.

    (iii) Draw the graph of $f(x)$ in the domain $-2 \leqslant x \leqslant 4$.

    (iv) Find the range of values of k for which $f(x) = k$ has three roots.

16. Let $f(x) = px^2 + qx + r$, for all $x \in \mathbf{R}$ and $p, q, r \in \mathbf{R}$.

Find $f'(x)$, the derivative of $f(x)$, in terms of p, q and x.

17. Let $f(x) = ax^3 + bx + c$, for all $x \in \mathbf{R}$ and for $a, b, c \in \mathbf{R}$.

Use the information which follows to find the value of a, of b and of c:

    (i) $f(0) = -3$

    (ii) the slope of the tangent to the curve of $f(x)$ at $x = 2$ is 18

    (iii) the curve of $f(x)$ has a local minimum point at $x = 1$.

Increasing and Decreasing

$\dfrac{dy}{dx}$, being the slope of a tangent to a curve at any point on the curve, can be used to determine if, and where, a curve is increasing or decreasing.

Note: Graphs are read from left to right.

Where a curve is increasing, the tangent to the curve will have a positive slope.

Therefore, where a curve is increasing, $\dfrac{dy}{dx}$ will be positive.

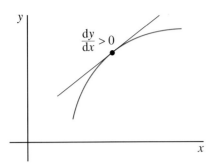

Where a curve is decreasing, the tangent to the curve will have a negative slope.

Therefore, where a curve is decreasing, $\dfrac{dy}{dx}$ will be negative.

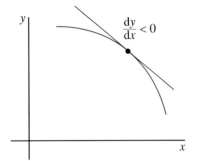

Example ▼

If $y = \dfrac{2x}{1-x}$, show that $\dfrac{dy}{dx} > 0$ for all $x \neq 1$.

Solution:

$$y = \frac{2x}{1-x}$$

$$\frac{dy}{dx} = \frac{(1-x)(2) - (2x)(-1)}{(1-x)^2} \qquad \text{(quotient rule)}$$

$$= \frac{2 - 2x + 2x}{(1-x)^2}$$

$$= \frac{2}{(1-x)^2}$$

$$\therefore \ \frac{dy}{dx} = \frac{2}{(1-x)^2}$$

$$(1-x)^2 > 0 \text{ for all } x \neq 1, \qquad 2 > 0 \qquad \text{(top and bottom both positive)}$$

$$\therefore \ \frac{2}{(1-x)^2} > 0 \text{ for all } x \neq 1.$$

$$\therefore \ \frac{dy}{dx} > 0 \text{ for all } x \neq 1.$$

Note: (any real number)^2 will always be a positive number unless the number is zero.

$\therefore$ $(1-x)^2$ must always be positive, unless $x = 1$ which gives $0^2 = 0$.

1. Let $f(x) = x^2 - 2x - 8$. Find the values of x for which $f(x)$ is: (i) decreasing   (ii) increasing.

2. Let $f(x) = 12 - 6x - x^2$. Find the values of x for which $f(x)$ is: (i) increasing   (ii) decreasing.

3. Let $f(x) = x^3 + 4x - 2$. Show that $\dfrac{dy}{dx} > 0$ for all $x \in \mathbf{R}$.

4. Let $f(x) = 5 - 2x - x^3$. Show that $\dfrac{dy}{dx} < 0$ for all $x \in \mathbf{R}$.

5. Show that the curve $y = x^2 - 3x + 5$ is increasing at the point $(2, 3)$.

6. Show that the curve $y = 10 - x - 2x^2$ is decreasing at the point $(3, -11)$.

7. If $y = \dfrac{x}{1 - x^2}$, show that $\dfrac{dy}{dx} > 0$ for all $x \neq \pm 1$.

8. If $y = \dfrac{x + 2}{x - 1}$, show that $\dfrac{dy}{dx} < 0$ for all $x \neq 1$.

9. If $y = \dfrac{4x + 1}{x - 3}$, show that $\dfrac{dy}{dx} < 0$ for all $x \neq 3$.

10. If $y = \dfrac{2x - 5}{x + 2}$, show that $\dfrac{dy}{dx} > 0$ for all $x \neq -2$.

11. An artificial ski-slope is described by the function $h = 2 - 8s - 4s^2 - \tfrac{2}{3}s^3$, where s is the horizontal distance and h is the height of the slope. Show that the slope is all downhill.

Rates of Change

The derivative $\dfrac{dy}{dx}$ is called the 'rate of change of y with respect to x'.

It shows how changes in y are related to changes in x.

If $\dfrac{dy}{dx} = 4$, then y is increasing 4 times as fast as x increases.

If $\dfrac{dy}{dx} = -5$, then y is decreasing 5 times as fast as x increases.

The derivative $\dfrac{dh}{dt}$ is called the 'rate of change of h with respect to t'.

The derivative $\dfrac{dR}{dV}$ is called the 'rate of change of R with respect to V'.

If s denotes the displacement (position) of a particle, from a fixed point p at time t, then:

> **1.** Velocity $= v = \dfrac{ds}{dt}$,
>
> the rate of change of position with respect to time.
>
> **2.** Acceleration $= a = \dfrac{dv}{dt} = \dfrac{d^2s}{dt^2}$,
>
> the rate of change of velocity with respect to time.

To find $\dfrac{d^2s}{dt^2}$, simply find $\dfrac{ds}{dt}$ and differentiate this.

In other words, differentiate twice.

Note: 'Speed' is often used instead of 'velocity'. However, speed can never be negative, whereas velocity can be negative.

If $\dfrac{ds}{dt} > 0$, the particle is moving away from p (distance from p is increasing).

If $\dfrac{ds}{dt} < 0$, the particle is moving towards p (distance from p is decreasing).

Example ▼

A particle moves along a straight line such that, after t seconds, the distance, s metres, is given by $s = t^3 - 9t^2 + 15t - 3$. Find:

(i) the velocity and acceleration of the particle in terms of t

(ii) the values of t when its velocity is zero

(iii) the acceleration after $3\frac{1}{2}$ seconds

(iv) the time at which the acceleration is 6 m/s² and the velocity at this time.

Solution:

(i) $\qquad s = t^3 - 9t^2 + 15t - 3$

$\qquad v = \dfrac{ds}{dt} = 3t^2 - 18t + 15 \qquad$ (velocity at any time t)

$\qquad a = \dfrac{d^2s}{dt^2} = 6t - 18 \qquad$ (acceleration at any time t)

(ii) Values of t when velocity is zero

$$\text{velocity} = 0$$

$$\therefore \qquad \frac{ds}{dt} = 0$$

$$\therefore \qquad 3t^2 - 18t + 15 = 0$$

$$t^2 - 6t + 5 = 0$$

$$(t - 1)(t - 5) = 0$$

$$t - 1 = 0 \qquad \text{or} \qquad t - 5 = 0$$

$$t = 1 \qquad \text{or} \qquad t = 5$$

Thus, the particle is stopped after 1 second and again after 5 seconds.

(iii) Acceleration after $3\frac{1}{2}$ seconds

$$\text{acceleration} = \frac{d^2 s}{dt^2} = 6t - 18,$$

When $t = 3\frac{1}{2}$,

$$\text{acceleration} = 6(3\tfrac{1}{2}) - 18$$

(put in $t = 3\frac{1}{2}$)

$$= 21 - 18$$

$$= 3$$

$\therefore$ Acceleration after $3\frac{1}{2}$ seconds $= 3 \text{ m/s}^2$.

(iv) Time at which acceleration is 6 m/s²

$$\text{acceleration} = 6 \text{ m/s}^2$$

$$\therefore \qquad \frac{d^2 s}{dt^2} = 6$$

$$\therefore \qquad 6t - 18 = 6$$

$$6t = 24$$

$$t = 4$$

After 4 seconds the acceleration is 6 m/s².

Velocity after 4 seconds

$$\text{velocity} = 3t^2 - 18t + 15$$

when $t = 4$,

$$\text{velocity} = 3(4)^2 - 18(4) + 15$$

(put in $t = 4$)

$$= 48 - 72 + 15$$

$$= -9 \text{ m/s}$$

After 4 seconds the velocity is –9 m/s.

The negative value means it is going in the opposite direction to which it started, after 4 seconds.

Example ▼

A ball is thrown vertically up in the air. The height, h metres, reached above the ground t seconds after it was thrown is given by $h = 8t - t^2$.

Find:

(i) the height of the ball after 3 seconds

(ii) the speed of the ball after 1 second

(iii) the height of the ball when its speed is 4 m/s.

(iv) After how many seconds does the ball just begin to fall back downwards?

Solution:

(i) Height at $t = 3$

$$h = 8t - t^2$$

When $t = 3$,

$$h = 8(3) - (3)^2$$

(put in $t = 3$)

$$h = 24 - 9$$

$$h = 15$$

∴ Height after 3 seconds = 15 m.

(ii) Speed after 1 second

$$h = 8t - t^2$$

$$\frac{dh}{dt} = 8 - 2t$$

(this is the speed in terms of t)

∴ speed after 1 second

$$= 8 - 2(1) = 8 - 2 = 6$$

(put in $t = 1$)

∴ Speed after 1 second = 6 m/s.

(iii) Height of the ball when the speed is 4 m/s

Given: speed = 4

∴ $\dfrac{dh}{dt} = 4$

∴ $8 - 2t = 4$

$$-2t = -4$$

$$2t = 4$$

$$t = 2$$

$$h = 8t - t^2$$

When $t = 2$,

$$h = 8(2) - (2)^2$$

(put in $t = 2$)

$$h = 16 - 4 = 12 \text{ m}$$

∴ When the speed is 4 m/s, the height of the ball = 12 m.

(iv) After how many seconds does the ball begin to fall downwards?

The ball begins to fall downwards when it has reached its maximum height.
It reaches its maximum height when its speed = 0.

speed = 0

∴ $\dfrac{dh}{dt} = 0$

∴ $8 - 2t = 0$

$$-2t = -8$$

$$2t = 8$$

$$t = 4$$

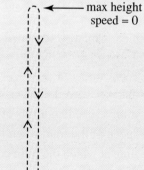

max height
speed = 0

∴ Ball begins to fall downwards after 4 seconds.

1. If $s = t^3 - 2t^2$, evaluate: (i) $\dfrac{ds}{dt}$ at $t = 3$ (ii) $\dfrac{d^2s}{dt^2}$ at $t = 2$.

2. If $h = 4t^3 - 12t + 8$, evaluate: (i) $\dfrac{dh}{dt}$ at $t = 1$ (ii) $\dfrac{d^2h}{dt^2}$ at $t = \frac{1}{2}$.

3. A ball bearing rolls along the ground. It starts to move at $t = 0$ seconds. The distance that it has travelled at t seconds is given by $s = t^3 - 6t^2 + 9t$.
   Find:

   (i) $\dfrac{ds}{dt}$ and $\dfrac{d^2s}{dt^2}$, its speed and acceleration, in terms of t

   (ii) the speed of the ball bearing when $t = 4$ seconds

   (iii) the acceleration of the ball bearing when $t = 3$ seconds

   (iv) the times at which the speed is zero

   (v)   the time at which the acceleration is zero

   (vi) the time at which the acceleration is 6 m/s^2

   (vii) the time at which the speed is 24 m/s.

4. A particle moves along a straight line such that, after t seconds, the distance s metres from a fixed point o is given by $s(t) = t^3 - 9t^2 + 24t$, $t \geq 0$.
   Find:

   (i) $\dfrac{ds}{dt}$ and $\dfrac{d^2s}{dt^2}$, its speed and acceleration, in terms of t

   (ii) the speed of the particle after 6 seconds

   (iii) the times when the speed is zero

   (iv) the acceleration of the particle after 4 seconds

   (v)   the time at which the acceleration is zero

   (vi) the time at which the acceleration is 6 m/s^2.

5. The distance, s metres, travelled in t seconds by a train after its brakes are applied is given by $s = 18t - 1.5t^2$.
   Find:

   (i)   the distance travelled when $t = 2$ seconds

   (ii) the train's speed, in terms of t

   (iii) the speed of the train when $t = 4$ seconds

   (iv) the time at which the train comes to rest

   (v)   the distance travelled by the train after it applied its brakes

   (vi) the constant deceleration of the train.

6. The distance, s metres, travelled by a car in t seconds after the brakes are applied is given by $s = 10t - t^2$. Show that its deceleration is constant. Find:

   (i)   the speed of the car when the brakes are applied

   (ii) the distance the car travels before it stops.

7. A ball is thrown vertically up in the air. The height, h metres, reached above the ground t seconds after it was thrown is given by $h = 16t - 2t^2$.

Find:

(i)   the height of the ball after 6 seconds

(ii) the speed of the ball in terms of t

(iii) the speed of the ball after 3 seconds

(iv) the height of the ball when its speed is 12 m/s.

(v)   After how many seconds does the ball just begin to fall back downwards? How far above the ground is it at this time?

8. A ball is thrown vertically up in the air. Its height, h metres, above ground level varies with the time, t seconds, such that $h = 1 + 30t - 5t^2$.

Find:

(i) $\dfrac{dh}{dt}$, its speed

(ii) its speed after $1\frac{1}{2}$ seconds

(iii) its acceleration.

(iv) After how many seconds does the ball just begin to fall back downwards? How far above the ground is it at this time?

9. The speed, v, in metres per second, of a body after t seconds is given by $v = 2t(6 - t)$.

(i)   Find the acceleration at each of the two instants when the speed is 10 m/s.

(ii) Find the speed at the instant when the acceleration is zero.

10. The speed, v, in metres per second, of a body after t seconds is given by $v = 3t(5 - t)$.

(i)   Find the acceleration at each of the two instants when the speed is 12 m/s.

(ii) Find the speed at the instant when the acceleration is zero.

11. An automatic valve controls the flow of gas, R cm^3/s, in an experiment. The flow of gas varies with the time, t seconds, as given by the equation $R = 8t - t^2$.

Find:

(i) $\dfrac{dR}{dt}$, the rate of change of R with respect to t

(ii) the value of $\dfrac{dR}{dt}$ after 6 seconds

(iii) the time when the rate of flow is a maximum.

(iv) After how many seconds is the rate of flow equal to:

(a) −4 cm^3/s   (b) 2 cm^3/s?

12. The volume, V, of a certain gas is given by $V = \dfrac{20}{p}$, where p is the pressure.

Find:

(i) $\dfrac{dV}{dp}$, the rate of change of V with respect to p

(ii) the value of $\dfrac{dV}{dp}$ when $p = 10$.

ARITHMETIC

Proportional Parts
(Dividing Quantities in a Given Ratio)

Ratios can be used to divide, or share, quantities.

To divide, or share, a quantity in a given ratio, do the following:

> **1.** Add the ratios to get the total number of parts.
> **2.** Divide the quantity by the total of the parts (this gives one part).
> **3.** Multiply this separately by each ratio.

Example ▼

Divide: **(i)** €300 in the ratio $2:5:8$ **(ii)** 56 g in the ratio $\frac{1}{2}:1:2$.

Solution:

(i)   Number of parts = $2 + 5 + 8 = 15$

$$1 \text{ part} = \frac{€300}{15} = €20$$

2 parts = €20 × 2 = €40

5 parts = €20 × 5 = €100

8 parts = €20 × 8 = €160

∴   €300 in the ratio $2:5:8$
   = €40, €100, €160

$\frac{1}{2}:1:2 = 1:2:4$

(multiply each part by 2)

Number of parts = $1 + 2 + 4 = 7$

$$1 \text{ part} = \frac{56 \text{ g}}{7} = 8 \text{ g}$$

2 parts = 2 × 8 g = 16 g

3 parts = 4 × 8 g = 32 g

∴   56 g in the ratio $\frac{1}{2}:1:2$
   = 8 g, 16 g, 32 g

Sometimes we are given an equation in disguise.

Example ▼

Copper and tin are mixed in the ratio $11:7$.
The amount of copper used is 187 kg. How many kilograms of tin are used?

Solution:

Equation given in disguise:

$$11 \text{ parts} = 187 \text{ kg} \qquad \text{(number of kg of copper} = 11 \text{ parts)}$$

$$1 \text{ part} = \frac{187 \text{ kg}}{11} = 17 \text{ kg} \qquad \text{(divide both sides by 11)}$$

Number of kilograms of tin = 7 parts = 7 × 17 kg = 119 kg.

Exercise 11.1 ▼

1. Divide: **(i)** €80 in the ratio 7 : 3   **(ii)** 450 g in the ratio 5 : 4.

2. Divide: **(i)** €480 in the ratio 3 : 4 : 5   **(ii)** €4,000 in the ratio 5 : 8 : 7.

3. Divide: **(i)** 238 g in the ratio 7 : 2 : 5   **(ii)** 162 cm in the ratio 4 : 3 : 2.

4. Divide: **(i)** €504 in the ratio 3 : 4 : 5   **(ii)** 336 cm in the ratio 2 : 5 : 7.

5. Divide: **(i)** €374 in the ratio 6 : 7 : 9   **(ii)** 1560 g in the ratio 8 : 1 : 4.

Write each of the following as the ratio of whole numbers:

6. $1\frac{1}{2} : 2$ 7. $\frac{1}{3} : 1$ 8. $\frac{1}{2} : \frac{1}{4} : 1$ 9. $\frac{3}{4} : \frac{1}{2} : 1$

10. Divide: **(i)** €42 in the ratio $1 : \frac{1}{2}$ **(ii)** 280 g in the ratio $\frac{1}{2} : 2$.

11. Divide: **(i)** €210 in the ratio $1 : 2 : \frac{1}{2}$ **(ii)** 585 cm in the ratio $\frac{1}{2} : 2 : 5$.

12. Divide: **(i)** 546 g in the ratio $1 : \frac{2}{3} : \frac{1}{2}$ **(ii)** €920 in the ratio $\frac{1}{2} : \frac{2}{3} : \frac{3}{4}$.

13. In a competition, team A scored $22\frac{1}{2}$ points and team B scored $17\frac{1}{2}$ points. The two teams share a prize of €28,000 in proportion to the number of points they scored. How much money does each team receive?

14. One town, A, has a population of 4,800 and a second town, B, has a population of 6,720. The two towns share a grant of €429,120 in proportion to their populations. How much does town A receive?

15. A and B share a sum of money in the ratio 2 : 3. If A's share is €80, calculate B's share.

16. Two lengths are in the ratio 7 : 5. If the larger length is 140 cm, calculate the other length.

17. The lengths of the sides of a triangle are in the ratio 4 : 3 : 2. If the shortest side is of length 36 cm, calculate the perimeter of the triangle.

18. P, Q and R share a sum of money in the ratio 2 : 4 : 5, respectively.
   If Q's share is €60, find: **(i)** P's share   **(ii)** the total sum of money shared.

19. The profits of a business owned by A, B, and C are shared in the ratio of their investments, €32,000, €16,000 and €20,000 respectively. If C received €6,350, how much did A receive?

20. A glass rod falls and breaks into 3 pieces whose lengths are in the ratio $8 : 9 : 5$. If the sum of the lengths of the two larger pieces is 119 cm, find the length of the third piece.

21. A woman gave some money to her 4 children in the ratio $2 : 3 : 5 : 9$. If the difference between the largest and the smallest share is €3,500, how much money did she give altogether?

22. €360 is divided between A and B in the ratio $3 : k$.
If A received €135, find the value of k.

23. When a cyclist had travelled a distance of 17 km she had completed $\frac{5}{8}$ of her journey.
What was the length of the journey?

Percentages

In many questions dealing with percentages we will be given an equation in disguise. The best way to tackle this type of problem is to write down the equation given in disguise. From this we can find 1% and, hence, any percentage we like.

Example ▼

A solicitor's fee for the sale of a house is $2\frac{1}{2}\%$ of the selling price.
If the fee is €10,500, calculate the selling price.

Solution:

Given: Solicitor's fee is €10,500.

$$2\frac{1}{2}\% = €10,500 \qquad \text{(equation given in disguise)}$$
$$5\% = €21,000 \qquad \text{(multiply both sides by 2)}$$
$$1\% = €4,200 \qquad \text{(divide both sides by 5)}$$
$$100\% = €420,000 \qquad \text{(multiply both sides by 100)}$$

∴ the selling price of the house was €420,000.

Example ▼

A bill for €127.05 includes VAT at 21%. Calculate the amount of the bill before VAT is added.

Solution:

Think of the bill before VAT is added on as 100%.

Given: $\quad 121\% = €127.05 \qquad$ (equation given in disguise, $100\% + 21\% = 121\%$)
$\qquad\quad 1\% = €1.05 \qquad$ (divide both sides by 121)
$\qquad 100\% = €105 \qquad$ (multiply both sides by 100)

∴ the bill before VAT is added is €105.

1. Calculate: **(i)** 8% of €120 **(ii)** 12% of €216 **(iii)** 21% of €124.

2. A musical store owner pays €2,800 for a set of drums and marks it up so that he makes a profit of 35%. Then 21% VAT is added on. Calculate the selling price.

3. A shopkeeper pays €240 for a bicycle and marks it up so that she makes a profit of 20%.
   Find the selling price.
   During a sale the price of the bicycle is reduced by 15%. Calculate: **(i)** the sale price **(ii)** the percentage profit on the bicycle during the sale.

4. One litre of water is added to four litres of milk in a container.
   Calculate the percentage of water in the container.

5. A tank contains 320 litres of petrol. 128 litres are removed.
   What percentage of the petrol remains in the tank?

6. A bill for €96.76 includes VAT at 18%. Calculate the amount of the bill before VAT is added.

7. A bill for €58.08 includes VAT at 21%. Calculate the amount of VAT in the bill.

8. When a woman bought a television set in a shop, VAT at 21% was added on. If the VAT on the cost of the set was €252, what was the price of the television set before VAT was added? What was the price including VAT?

9. A boy bought a calculator for €74.75, which included VAT at 15%. Find the price of the calculator if VAT was reduced to 12%.

10. When the rate of VAT was increased from 18% to 21%, the price of a guitar increased by €81. Calculate the price of the guitar, inclusive of the VAT at 21%.

11. When 9% of the pupils in a school are absent, 637 are present. How many pupils are on the school roll?

12. 15% of a number is 96. Calculate 25% of the number.

13. A salesperson's commission for selling a car is $2\frac{1}{2}$% of the selling price. If the commission for selling a car was €350, calculate the selling price.

14. A solicitor's fee for the sale of a house is $1\frac{1}{2}$% of the selling price.
    If the fee is €3,480, calculate the selling price.

15. In a sale the price of a piece of furniture was reduced by 20%. The sale price was €1,248.
    What was the price before the sale?

16. A salesperson's income for a year was €59,000. This was made up of a basic pay of €45,000 plus a commission of 4% of sales. Calculate the amount of the sales for the year.

17. A fuel mixture consists of 93% petrol and 7% oil. If the mixture contains 37.2 litres of petrol, calculate the volume of oil.

18. A book of raffle tickets sells for €10. The prizes in € are 2000, 1000, 500 and 250. If printing costs amount to €250, calculate the smallest number of books which must be sold to:
    (i) cover costs **(ii)** make a profit of €3,000.

19. A lottery had a first prize of 70% of the prize fund and a consolation prize of 30%. Six people shared the first prize and each received €3,500. If the consolation prize was divided between 450 people, how much did each receive?

20. A tanker delivered heating oil to a school. Before the delivery the meter reading showed 11,360 litres of oil in the tanker. After the delivery, the meter reading was 7,160 litres. Calculate the cost of the oil delivered if 1 litre of oil cost 36.5c.

When VAT was added to the cost of the oil delivered, the bill to the school amounted to €1,808.94. Calculate the rate of VAT added.

21. An antiques dealer bought three chairs at an auction. He sold them later for €301.60, making a profit of 16% on their total cost. Calculate the total cost of the chairs.

The first chair cost €72 and it was sold at a profit of 15%.

Calculate its selling price.

The second chair cost €98 and it was sold for €91.

Find the percentage profit made on the sale of the third chair.

Relative Error and Percentage Error

When calculations are being made errors can occur, especially calculations which involve rounding. It is important to have a measure of the error.

Definitions

Error = | true value – estimate value | and is always considered positive.

$$\text{Relative error} = \frac{\text{Error}}{\text{True Value}}$$

$$\text{Percentage error} = \frac{\text{Error}}{\text{True Value}} \times \frac{100}{1}$$

Example ▼

A distance of 190 km was estimated to be 200 km. Calculate:

(i) the error **(ii)** the relative error **(iii)** the percentage error, correct to one decimal place.

Solution:

True value = 190 km   Estimated value = 200 km

(i) error = | true value – estimated value | = | 190 – 200 | = | –10 | = 10 km

(ii) relative error = $\dfrac{\text{error}}{\text{true value}} = \dfrac{10}{190} = \dfrac{1}{19}$ (positive value)

(iii) percentage error = $\dfrac{\text{error}}{\text{true value}} \times \dfrac{100}{1} = \dfrac{10}{190} \times \dfrac{100}{1} = 5.3\%$ (correct to one decimal place)

The answer to 5.6 + 7.1 was given as 12.5.

What was the percentage error, correct to two decimal places?

Solution:

True value = 5.6 + 7.1 = 12.7   Estimated value = 12.5

error = | true value – estimated value | = | 12.7 – 12.5 | = | 0.2 | = 0.2

$$\text{Percentage error} = \frac{\text{error}}{\text{true value}} \times \frac{100}{1} = \frac{0.2}{12.7} \times \frac{100}{1} = 1.57\% \quad \text{(correct to two decimal places)}$$

Exercise 11.3 ▼

Complete the following table:

	True Value	Estimated Value	Error	Relative Error (as a fraction)	Percentage Error (correct to one decimal place)
1.	12	10			
2.	43	40			
3.	136	140			
4.	4.8	5			
5.	5.7	6			
6.	390	400			

7. The depth of a swimming pool was estimated to be 1.5 m.
   The true depth was 1.65 m.
   Find: **(i)** the error   **(ii)** the percentage error, correct to one decimal place.

8. The mass of a rock is estimated to be 65 kg. Its true mass is 67.5 kg.
   Find: **(i)** the error   **(ii)** the percentage error, correct to one decimal place.

9. A distance of 105 km was estimated to be 100 km. Calculate:
   (i) the error   **(ii)** the relative error   **(iii)** the percentage error, correct to one decimal place.

10. The estimate for building a wall was €3,325. The actual cost was €3,500. Calculate the percentage error.

11. The number of people estimated to be at a meeting was 400. The actual number who attended the meeting was 423. Calculate the percentage error, correct to two decimal places.

12. The value of $\dfrac{48.27 + 12.146}{14.82 - 3.02}$ was estimated to be 5.

Calculate the percentage error, correct to one decimal place.

13. The value of $\dfrac{30.317}{\sqrt{24.7009}}$ was estimated to be 6.

Calculate: **(i)** the error **(ii)** the percentage error, correct to two decimal places.

14. Calculate the volume of a solid cylinder of radius 6 cm and height 14 cm (assume $\pi = \frac{22}{7}$).

When doing this calculation a student used $\pi = 3$. Calculate the student's percentage error in the calculation, assuming $\pi = \frac{22}{7}$ is the exact value, correct to one decimal place.

15. Calculate the percentage error in calculating the total of $324 + 432 + 234$ if the digit 4 is replaced by a 5 each time.

Give your answer correct to one place of decimals.

16. Four items in a shop cost €7.70, €14.90, €16.80 and €23.10.

(i) Frank estimates the total cost of the four items by ignoring the cent part in the cost of each item. Calculate the percentage error in his estimate.

(ii) Fiona estimates the total cost of the four items by rounding the cost of each item to the nearest euro. Calculate the percentage error in her estimate.

Foreign Exchange

Currency is another name for money. In the European Union the unit of currency is called the euro (€). The method of direct proportion is used to convert one currency into another currency.

Note: Write down the equation given in disguise, putting the currency we want to find on the right-hand side.

Example ▼

A book cost €8.60 in Dublin and US$10.08 in New York. If €1 = US$1.20, in which city is the book cheaper and by how many European cents?

Solution:

Express the price of the book in New York in € and compare to the price in Dublin.

$\text{US}\$1.20 = €1$ (€ on the right because we want our answer in €)

$\text{US}\$1 = € \dfrac{1}{1.20}$ (divide both sides by 1.20)

$\$10.08 = € \dfrac{1}{1.20} \times 10.08$ (multiply both sides by 10.08)

$\$10.08 = €8.40$ (simplify the right-hand side)

Difference $= €8.60 - €8.40 = 20c$

∴ cheaper in New York by 20c.

A person changes €500 into Japanese Yen, ¥. A charge is made for this transaction. The exchange rate is €1 = ¥320. If the person receives ¥156,000, calculate the percentage charge.

Solution:

Express €500 in ¥.

$$€1 = ¥320 \qquad \text{(¥ on the right because we want our answer in ¥)}$$
$$€500 = ¥500 \times 320 \qquad \text{(multiply both sides by 500)}$$
$$€500 = ¥160,000 \qquad \text{(full amount due)}$$
$$\text{Amount received} = ¥156,000$$
$$\therefore \quad \text{Charge} = ¥160,000 - ¥156,000 = ¥4,000$$

$$\text{Percentage charge} = \frac{\text{Charge}}{\text{Full amount}} \times \frac{100}{1} = \frac{4,000}{160,000} \times \frac{100}{1} = 2.5\%.$$

Exercise 11.4 ▼

1. If €1 = $1.03, find the value of: **(i)** €250 in dollars **(ii)** $618 in euros.

2. A train ticket costs $54. If €1 = $1.08, calculate the cost of the ticket in euros.

3. If €1 = ¥304 (Japanese yen), how many:
   (i) yen would you receive for €240?
   (ii) euros would you receive for ¥115,520?

4. A part for a tractor costs €600 in France and the same part costs R1,368 in South Africa. If €1 = R2.4, in which country is it cheaper, and by how much (in euros)?

5. A tourist changed €5,000 on board ship into South African rand, at a rate of €1 = R2.2.
   How many rand did she receive? When she came ashore she found that the rate was €1 = R2.35. How much did she lose, in rand, by not changing her money ashore?

6. A person buys 167,400 Japanese Yen when the exchange rate is €1 = ¥310. A charge is made for this.
   How much, in €, is this charge, if the person pays €548.10? Calculate the percentage commission on the transaction.

7. When the exchange rate is €1 = $0.98, a person buys 3,430 dollars from a bank.
   If the bank charges a commission of $2\frac{1}{2}\%$, calculate the total cost in €.

8. A person buys 5,160 Canadian dollars when the exchange rate is €1 = $2.15.
   A charge (commission) is made for this service. How much, in €, is this charge if the person pays €2,448?
   Calculate the percentage commission on the transaction.

9. Dollars were bought for €8,000 when the exchange rate was €1 = $1.02. A commission was charged for this service. If the person received $7,956, calculate the percentage commission charged.

10. If €1 = $1.10 and €1 = R2.64, how many dollars can be exchanged for 2,112 rand?

11. A supplier agrees to buy 100 computers for $600 each. He plans to sell them for a total of €62,400.
   (i) Calculate the percentage profit, on the cost price, he will make if the exchange rate is €1 = $1.25.
   (ii) Calculate the percentage profit, on the cost price, if the exchange rate changes to €1 = $1.20.

Interest

> Interest is the sum of money that you pay for borrowing money, or that is paid to you for lending money. When dealing with interest we use the following symbols:
>
> P = the '**principal**', the sum of money borrowed or invested, at the beginning of the period.
> T = the '**time**', the number of years for which the sum of money is borrowed or invested.
> R = the '**rate**', the percentage rate per annum at which interest is charged.
> A = the '**amount**', the sum of money, including interest, at the end of the period.

Note: per annum = per year.

Compound Interest

Very often when a sum of money earns interest, this interest is added to the principal to form a new principal. This new principal earns interest in the next year and so on. This is called '**compound interest**'.

When calculating compound interest, do the following:

Method 1:

> Calculate the interest for the **first** year and add this to the principal to form the new principal for the next year. Calculate the interest for **one** year on this new principal and add it on to form the principal for the next year, and so on. The easiest way to calculate each stage is to multiply the principal at the beginning of each year by the factor:
>
> $$\left(1 + \frac{R}{100}\right)$$
>
> This will give the principal for the next year, and so on.

Method 2:

> Use the formula: $A = P\left(1 + \frac{R}{100}\right)^T$

Note: The formula does **not** work if:

> **1.** the interest rate, R, is changed during the period.
>
> **2.** money is added or subtracted during the period.

Example ▼

Calculate the compound interest on €10,000 for three years at 4% per annum.

Solution:

$$1 + \frac{R}{100} = 1 + \frac{4}{100} = 1.04$$

Method 1:

$P_1 = 10,000$	(principal for the first year)
$A_1 = 10,000 \times 1.04 = 10,400$	(amount at the end of the first year)
$P_2 = 10,400$	(principal for the second year)
$A_2 = 10,400 \times 1.04 = 10,816$	(amount at the end of the second year)
$P_3 = 10,816$	(principal for the third year)
$A_3 = 10,816 \times 1.04 = 11,248.64$	(amount at the end of the third year)

Compound interest $= A_3 - P_1 = $ €11,248.64 − €10,000 = €1,248.64

The working can also be shown using a table:

Year	Principal	Amount
1	10,000	$10,000 \times 1.04 = 10,400$
2	10,400	$10,400 \times 1.04 = 10,816$
3	10,816	$10,816 \times 1.04 = 11,248.64$

Compound interest $= A_3 - P_1 = $ €11,248.64 − €10,000 = €1,248.64.

Method 2:

Given: $P = 10,000, \quad R = 4, \quad T = 3, \quad$ find A.

$$A = P\left(1 + \frac{R}{100}\right)^T$$

$A = 10,000(1.04)^3$

$A = 11,248.64 \quad$ (🖩 10,000 ⊗ 1.04 y^x 3 =)

Compound interest $= A - P = $ €11,248.64 − €10,000 = €1,248.64.

€8,500 was invested for 3 years at compound interest. The rate for the first year was 6%, the rate for the second year was 8% and the rate for the third year was 5%.

Calculate: (i) the amount   (ii) the compound interest at the end of the third year.

Solution:

As the rate changes each year we **cannot** use the formula.

Year	Principal	Amount	
1	8,500	$8,500 \times 1.06 = 9010$	$(1 + \frac{6}{100} = 1.06)$
2	9,010	$9,010 \times 1.08 = 9730.80$	$(1 + \frac{8}{100} = 1.08)$
3	9,730.80	$9,730.80 \times 1.05 = 10,217.34$	$(1 + \frac{5}{100} = 1.05)$

(i)   The amount at the end of the third year is €10,217.34.
Alternatively, in one calculation:

$$A_3 = €8,500 \times 1.06 \times 1.08 \times 1.05 = €10,217.34$$

(ii)   Compound interest $= A_3 - P_1 = €10,217.34 - €8,500 = €1,717.34.$

Calculate the compound interest on €20,000 for 12 years at 3% per annum, correct to the nearest cent.

Solution:

As $T > 3$, it is easier to use the formula.

Given: $P = 20,000,$ $R = 3$ $T = 12,$ find A.

$$A = P\left(1 + \frac{R}{100}\right)^T$$

$$= 20,000 \, (1.03)^{12} \qquad \left(1 + \frac{R}{100} = 1 + \frac{3}{100} = 1.03\right)$$

$$= 28,515.21774 \qquad (\boxed{}\; 20,000 \;\boxed{\times}\; 1.03 \;\boxed{y^x}\; 12 \;\boxed{=}\;)$$

$$= 28,515.22 \text{ (correct to the nearest cent)}$$

Compound interest $= €28,515.22 - €20,000 = €8,515.22.$

Depreciation

For depreciation we multiply by the factor $\left(1 - \dfrac{R}{100}\right)$ for each year.

The formula for depreciation is:

$$A = P\left(1 - \frac{R}{100}\right)^{T}$$

P is the original value at the beginning of the period and A is the amount at the end of the period.

Example ▼

A machine depreciates at 15% per annum. It was bought for €40,000.
How much is it worth after four years?

Solution:

$$1 - \frac{R}{100} = 1 - \frac{15}{100} = 0.85$$

Given: $P = 40{,}000$, $R = 15$, $T = 4$,   find A.

$$A = P\left(1 - \frac{R}{100}\right)^{T}$$

$$= 40{,}000\,(0.85)^{4}$$

$$= 20{,}880.25 \quad (\boxed{}\ \ 40{,}000\ \boxed{\times}\ 0.85\ \boxed{y^{x}}\ 4\ \boxed{=})$$

Thus, after four years, the machine is worth €20,880.25.

Exercise 11.5 ▼

Calculate the compound interest on each of the following investments:

1. €12,000 for 2 years at 8% per annum.

2. €15,000 for 2 years at 7% per annum.

3. €18,000 for 3 years at 5% per annum.

4. €25,000 for 3 years at 8% per annum.

5. €40,000 for 3 years at 3% per annum.

6. €30,000 for 3 years at 4% per annum.

7. €750 for 3 years at 10% per annum.

8. €5,000 for 3 years at 2% per annum.

9. €12,400 for 2 years at 6.5% per annum.

10. €80,000 for 3 years at 2.5% per annum.

11. €4,000 was invested for two years at compound interest. The interest rate for the first year was 4% and for the second was 5%.

Calculate the total interest earned.

12. €6,500 was invested for three years at compound interest. The interest rate for the first year was 5%, for the second year 8%, and for the third year 12%.

Calculate the total interest earned.

13. €7,500 was invested for three years at compound interest. The rate for the first year was 4%, the rate for the second year was 3%, and the rate for the third year was $2\frac{1}{2}\%$.

Calculate the amount after three years.

14. €20,000 was invested for three years at compound interest. The rate for the first year was $3\frac{1}{2}\%$, the rate for the second year was 5%, and the rate for the third year was 4%.

Calculate the amount after three years.

15. A car depreciates at 15% per annum. It was bought for €30,000.

How much is it worth after three years?

16. A machine depreciates at 10% per annum. It was bought for €55,000.

How much is it worth after four years?

17. A machine cost €100,000 when new. In the first year it depreciates by 15%. In the second year it depreciates by 8% of its value at the end of the first year. In the third year it depreciates by 5% of its value at the end of the second year. By completing the table, calculate its value after three years. Calculate its total depreciation after three years.

New Price	**€100,000**
Value after 1 year	
Value after 2 years	
Value after 3 years	

Calculate, correct to the nearest cent, the compound interest on each of the following investments:

18. €18,000 for 10 years at 4% per annum.

19. €25,000 for 12 years at 5% per annum.

20. €40,000 for 15 years at 3% per annum.

21. €54,000 for 20 years at 4% per annum.

22. If $A = P\left(1 + \dfrac{R}{100}\right)^{T}$, express P in terms of A, R and T. Hence, or otherwise, find what sum of money will amount to €88,578.05 in 6 years at 10% per annum compound interest.

Repayments/Further Investments

In some questions money is repaid at the end of a year or a further investment is made at the beginning of the next year. It is important to remember that in these cases the **formula does not work**. In the next example, F_1 = a further investment at the beginning of the second year, F_2 = a further investment at the beginning of the third year.

A person invested €40,000 in a building society. The rate of interest for the first year was $3\frac{1}{2}\%$. At the end of the first year the person invested a further €6,000. The rate of interest for the second year was 4%.

Calculate the value of the investment at the end of the second year.

At the end of the second year a further sum of €4,704 was invested. At the end of the third year the total value of the investment was €55,350.

Calculate the rate of interest for the third year.

Solution:

$P_1 = 40,000$

$A_1 = 40,000 \times 1.035$ $\left(\left(1 + \dfrac{R}{100}\right) = \left(1 + \dfrac{3\frac{1}{2}}{100}\right) = 1.035\right)$

$A_1 = 41,400$ (amount at the end of the first year)

$F_1 = 6,000$ (further investment of €6,000)

$\overline{P_2 = 47,400}$ ($A_1 + F_1 = P_2$ = principal for the second year)

$A_2 = 47,400 \times 1.04$ $\left(\left(1 + \dfrac{R}{100}\right) = \left(1 + \dfrac{4}{100}\right) = 1.04\right)$

$A_2 = 49,296$ (amount at the end of the second year)

Therefore, the value of the investment at the end of the second year = €49,296.

$F_2 = 4,704$ (further investment of €4704)

$P_3 = A_2 + F_2$ ($A_2 + F_2 = P_3$ = principal for the third year)

$P_3 = 49,296 + 4,704 = 54,000$

Given $A_3 = 55,350$ (amount at the end of the third year)

Interest for the third year $= A_3 - P_3 = 55,350 - 54,000 = 1,350$

Interest rate for the third year $= \dfrac{\text{Interest for the third year}}{\text{Principal for the third year}} \times \dfrac{100}{1}$

$\phantom{\text{Interest rate for the third year}} = \dfrac{1,350}{54,000} \times \dfrac{100}{1}$

$\phantom{\text{Interest rate for the third year}} = 2\frac{1}{2}\%$

Example ▼

A person invested €20,000 for three years at 6% per annum compound interest.

(i) Calculate the amount after two years.

After two years a sum of money was withdrawn. The money which remained amounted to €22,260 at the end of the third year.

(ii) Calculate the amount of money withdrawn after two years.

Solution:

(i) $P_1 = 20,000$ (principal for the first year)

         $A_1 = 20,000 \times 1.06 = 21,200$ (amount at the end of the first year)

         $P_2 = 21,200$ (principal for the second year)

         $A_2 = 21,200 \times 1.06 = 22,472$ (amount at the end of the second year)

   $\therefore$ the amount after two years = €22,472.

(ii)   At this point a sum of money was withdrawn.

   What we do is '**work backwards**' from the end of the third year.

         $A_3 = 22,260$ (amount at the end of the third year)

   $\therefore$ $106\% = 22,260$ (increased by 6% during the year)

         $1\% = 210$ (divide both sides by 106)

         $100\% = 21,000$ (multiply both sides by 100)

   $\therefore$ the principal for the third year, P_3, was €21,000.

   But the amount at the end of the second year, A_3, was €22,472

   $\therefore$ the sum of money withdrawn at the end of the second year

   $= A_2 - P_3 = $ €22,472 − €21,000 = €1,472.

Exercise 11.6 ▼

1. A woman borrowed €30,000 at 6% per annum compound interest. She agreed to repay €5,000 at the end of the first year, €5,000 at the end of the second year and to clear the debt at the end of the third year.

   How much was paid to clear the debt?

2. A man borrowed €40,000 at 4% per annum compound interest. He agreed to repay €8,000 at the end of the first year, €9,000 at the end of the second year and to clear the debt at the end of the third year.

   How much was paid to clear the debt?

3. A man borrowed €15,000. He agreed to repay €2,000 after one year, €3,000 after two years and the balance at the end of the third year. If interest was charged at 8% in the first year, 5% in the second year and 6% in the third year, how much was paid at the end of the third year to clear the debt?

4. €4,000 was invested for one year. The interest earned was €120.
Calculate the rate of interest.

5. €2,500 amounts to €2,600 after one year.
Calculate the rate of interest.

6. €8,400 amounts to €8,694 after one year.
Calculate the rate of interest.

7. €6,500 amounts to €6,662.50 after one year.
Calculate the rate of interest.

8. €12,000 was invested for two years at compound interest.
    (i)   The interest at the end of the first year was €600. Calculate the rate of interest for the first year.
    (ii)   At the end of the second year the investment was worth €13,167. Calculate the rate of interest for the second year.

9. €60,000 is borrowed for two years. Interest for the first year is charged at 4% per annum.
    (i)   Calculate the amount owed at the end of the first year.
    (ii)   €7,400 is then repaid.
        Interest is charged at r% per annum for the second year. The amount owed at the end of the second year is €56,650. Calculate the value of r.

10. €40,000 was invested for three years at compound interest. The rate of interest was 4% per annum for the first year and $3\frac{1}{2}$% per annum for the second year.
    (i)   Calculate the amount of the investment after two years.
    (ii)   Then a further €2,444 was invested.
        If the investment amounted to €46,637.50 at the end of the third year, calculate the rate of interest for the third year.

11. A person invested €20,000 in a building society. The rate of interest for the first year was $2\frac{1}{2}$%. At the end of the first year the person invested a further €2,000. The rate of interest for the second year was 2%.
Calculate the value of the investment at the end of the second year.

At the end of the second year a further sum of €1,050 was invested. At the end of the third year the total value of the investment was €24,720.
Calculate the rate of interest for the third year.

12. €10,000 was invested for 3 years at compound interest.
The rate for the first year was 4%. The rate for the second year was $4\frac{1}{2}$%.
    (i)   Find the amount of the investment at the end of the second year.
    (ii)   At the beginning of the third year a further €8000 was invested.
        The rate for the third year was r%.
        The total investment at the end of the third year was €19,434.04.
        Calculate the value of r.

13. €75,000 was invested for 3 years at compound interest.
The rate for the first year was 3%. The rate for the second year was $2\frac{1}{2}\%$.

At the end of the second year €10,681.25 was withdrawn.

   (i)   Find the principal for the third year.

   (ii) The rate for the third year was $r\%$.
       The total investment at the end of the third year was €70,897.50.

       Calculate the value of r.

In questions 14 to 17 it may make the working easier to calculate the amount after two years, then work backwards from the end of the third year to find the sum of money withdrawn.

14. A person invested €30,000 for three years at 5% per annum compound interest.

   (i)   Calculate the amount after two years.

   (ii) After two years a sum of money was withdrawn. The money which remained amounted to €26,250 at the end of the third year.

       Calculate the amount of money withdrawn after two years.

15. A person invested €50,000 for three years at 4% per annum compound interest.
At the end of the first year, €11,500 was withdrawn.
At the end of the second year, another sum of money was withdrawn.
At the end of the third year, the person's investment was worth €36,400.

Calculate the amount of money withdrawn after two years.

16. €45,000 was invested for three years at compound interest. The interest rate for the first year was 6% per annum, the interest rate for the second year was 4% per annum and the interest rate for the third year was 3% per annum. At the end of the first year €7,700 was withdrawn. At the end of the second year €w was withdrawn. At the end of the third year the investment was worth €37,080. Find the value of w.

17. €60,000 was invested for three years at compound interest. The interest rate for the first year was $3\frac{1}{2}\%$ per annum, the interest rate for the second year was $2\frac{1}{2}\%$ per annum and the interest rate for the third year was 2% per annum. At the end of the first year €4,100 was withdrawn. At the end of the second year €w was withdrawn. At the end of the third year the investment was worth €56,100. Find the value of w.

Income Tax

The following is called the income tax equation:

$$\boxed{\text{Gross tax} - \text{Tax credits} = \text{Tax payable}}$$

Gross tax is calculated as follows:

Standard rate on all income up to the standard rate cut-off point	+	A higher rate on all income above the standard rate cut-off point

Example ▼

A woman has a gross yearly income of €48,000. She has a standard rate cut-off point of €27,500 and a tax credit of €3,852. The standard rate of tax is 18% of income up to the standard rate cut-off point and 37% on all income above the standard rate cut-off point. Calculate:

(i) the amount of gross tax for the year

(ii) the amount of tax paid for the year.

Solution:

(i) Gross tax = 18% of €27,500 + 37% of €20,500

$$= €27,500 \times 0.18 + €20,500 \times 0.37$$
$$= €4,950 + €7,585$$
$$= €12,535$$

> Income above the standard rate cut-off point
> $$= €48,000 - €27,500$$
> $$= €20,500$$

(ii) Income tax equation:

Gross tax	–	Tax credits	=	Tax payable
€12,535	–	€3,852	=	€8,683

Therefore, she paid €8,683 in tax.

Note: If a person earns less than their standard rate cut-off point, then they pay tax only at the standard rate on all their income.

Example ▼

A man paid €10,160 in tax for the year. He had a tax credit of €3,980 and a standard rate cut-off point of €26,000. The standard rate of tax is 17% of income up to the standard rate cut-off point and 36% on all income above the standard rate cut-off point. Calculate:

(i) the amount of income taxed at the rate of 36%

(ii) the man's gross income for the year.

Solution:

(i) Income tax equation:

Gross tax – Tax credits = Tax payable

17% of €26,000 + 36% of (income above cut-off point) – €3,980 = €10,160

€4,420 + 36% of (income above cut-off point) – €3,980 = €10,160

36% of (income above cut-off point) + €440 = €10,160

36% of (income above cut-off point) = €9,720

1% of (income above cut-off point) = €270

(divide both sides by 36)

100% of (income above cut-off point) = €27,000

(multiply both sides by 100)

Therefore, the amount of income taxed at the higher rate of 36% was €27,000.

(ii) Gross income = standard rate cut-off point + income above the standard rate cut-off point

$$= €26,000 + €27,000 = €53,000$$

1. A woman has a gross yearly income of €39,000. She has a standard rate cut-off point of €24,000 and a tax credit of €3,800. The standard rate of tax is 20% of income up to the standard rate cut-off point and 42% on all income above the standard rate cut-off point. Calculate:
   (i) the amount of gross tax for the year
   (ii) the amount of tax paid for the year.

2. A man has a gross yearly income of €37,000. He has a standard rate cut-off point of €20,500 and a tax credit of €2,490. The standard rate of tax is 18% of income up to the standard rate cut-off point and 38% on all income above the standard rate cut-off point. Calculate:
   (i) the amount of gross tax for the year
   (ii) the amount of tax paid for the year.

3. A man has a gross yearly income of €43,000. He has a standard rate cut-off point of €28,400 and a tax credit of €3,240. The standard rate of tax is 15% of income up to the standard rate cut-off point and 35% on all income above the standard rate cut-off point. Calculate:
   (i) the amount of gross tax for the year
   (ii) the amount of tax paid for the year.

4. A woman has a gross yearly income of €48,700. She has a standard rate cut-off point of €29,250 and a tax credit of €3,150. The standard rate of tax is 16% of income up to the standard rate cut-off point and 37% on all income above the standard rate cut-off point. Calculate:
   (i) the amount of gross tax for the year
   (ii) the amount of tax paid for the year.

5. A man has a gross yearly income of €26,000. He has a standard rate cut-off point of €28,000 and a tax credit of €1,800. If he pays tax of €3,400, calculate the standard rate of tax.

6. A woman has a gross yearly income of €27,500. She has a standard rate cut-off point of €29,300 and a tax credit of €2,115. If she pays tax of €2,835, calculate the standard rate of tax.

7. A woman paid €10,280 in tax for the year. She had a tax credit of €2,540 and a standard rate cut-off point of €29,000. The standard rate of tax is 18% of income up to the standard rate cut-off point and 40% on all income above the standard rate cut-off point. Calculate:
   (i) the amount of income taxed at the rate of 40%
   (ii) the gross income for the year.

8. A man paid €10,775 in tax for the year. He had a tax credit of €1,960 and a standard rate cut-off point of €28,500. The standard rate of tax is 15% of income up to the standard rate cut-off point and 36% on all income above the standard rate cut-off point. Calculate:
   (i) the amount of income taxed at the rate of 36%
   (ii) the gross income for the year.

Index Notation

Index notation is a shorthand way of writing very large or very small numbers.
For example, try this multiplication on your calculator: 8,000,000 × 7,000,000.

The answer is 56,000,000,000,000.

It has fourteen digits, which is too many to show on most calculator displays.

Your calculator will display your answer as $\boxed{5.6^{13}}$ or $\boxed{5.6\ 13}$ or $\boxed{5.6E13}$.

This tells you that the 5.6 is multiplied by 10^{13}.

This is written:

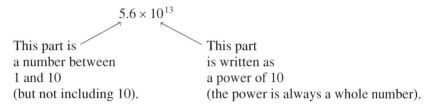

$$5.6 \times 10^{13}$$

This part is a number between 1 and 10 (but not including 10).

This part is written as a power of 10 (the power is always a whole number).

This way of writing a number is called **index notation** or **exponential notation**, or sometimes **standard form**. (It was formerly called '**scientific notation**'.)

Index notation gives a number in two parts:

Number between 1 and 10 (but not 10)	$\times$	power of 10

This is often written as $a \times 10^n$, where $1 \leqslant a < 10$ and $n \in \mathbf{Z}$.

Example ▼

Express the numbers: **(i)** 3,700,000 **(ii)** 0.000846 in the form $a \times 10^n$, where $1 \leqslant a < 10, n \in \mathbf{Z}$.

Solution:

(i) 3,700,000. (put in the decimal point)

3.700 000 (move the decimal point six places to the left to give a number between 1 and 10)

$\therefore$ $3,700,000 = 3.7 \times 10^6$

(ii) 0.000846 (decimal point already there)

8.46 (move the decimal point four places to the right to give a number between 1 and 10)

$\therefore$ $0.000846 = 8.46 \times 10^{-4}$

Example ▼

(i) Express $\dfrac{1456}{0.28}$ in the form $a \times 10^n$, where $1 \leqslant a < 10, n \in \mathbf{Z}$.

(ii) Find n if $\dfrac{441}{0.007} = 6.3 \times 10^n$.

Solution:

(i) $\dfrac{1456}{0.28} = 5{,}200 = 5.2 \times 10^3$

(ii) $\dfrac{441}{0.007} = 63{,}000 = 6.3 \times 10^4$

By comparing 6.3×10^n to 6.3×10^4, $n = 4$.

Express each of the following in the form $a \times 10^n$, where $1 \leqslant a < 10$ and $n \in \mathbf{Z}$:

1. 8,000
2. 54,000
3. 347,000
4. 470

5. 2,900
6. 3,400,000
7. 394
8. 39

9. 0.006
10. 0.0009
11. 0.052
12. 0.000432

13. $\dfrac{1,512}{0.36}$
14. $\dfrac{624}{0.008}$
15. $\dfrac{0.0048}{0.15}$
16. $\dfrac{0.0099}{2.2}$

In each of the following calculate the value of n:

17. $\dfrac{2,856}{0.42} = 6.8 \times 10^n$

18. $\dfrac{73,080}{1.74} = 4.2 \times 10^n$

19. $\dfrac{0.0624}{2.6} = 2.4 \times 10^n$

Addition and Subtraction

Numbers given in index notation can be keyed into your calculator by using the 'exponent key'. It is marked EXP or EE or E .

To key in a number in index notation, do the following:

> 1. Key in 'a', the 'number part', first.
> 2. Press the exponent key next.
> 3. Key in the index of the power of 10.

To enter 3.4×10^6, for example, you key in 3.4 EXP 6.

Note: If you press = at the end, the calculator will write the number as a natural number, provided the index of the power of 10 is not too large.

To add or subtract two numbers in index notation, do the following:

> 1. Write each number as a natural number.
> 2. Add or subtract these numbers.
> 3. Write your answer in index notation.
>
> Alternatively, you can use your calculator by keying in the numbers in index notation and adding or subtracting as required.

Example ▼

Express: **(i)** $2.54 \times 10^4 - 3.8 \times 10^3$ **(ii)** $2.68 \times 10^{-2} + 1.2 \times 10^{-3}$ in the form $a \times 10^n$, where $1 \leqslant a < 10$ and $n \in \mathbf{Z}$.

Solution:

(i) $2.54 \times 10^4 - 3.8 \times 10^3$

$2.54 \times 10^4 = 25,400$

$3.8 \times 10^3 = \underline{3,800}$

$21,600$ (subtract)

$= 2.16 \times 10^4$

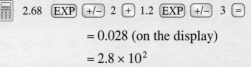 2.54 (EXP) 4 (−) 3.8 (EXP) 3 (=)

$= 21,600$ (on the display)

$= 2.16 \times 10^4$

(ii) $2.68 \times 10^{-2} + 1.2 \times 10^{-3}$

$2.68 \times 10^{-2} = 0.0268$

$1.2 \times 10^{-3} = \underline{0.0012}$

0.0280 (add)

$= 2.8 \times 10^{-2}$

2.68 (EXP) (+/−) 2 (+) 1.2 (EXP) (+/−) 3 (=)

$= 0.028$ (on the display)

$= 2.8 \times 10^2$

Multiplication and Division

To multiply or divide two numbers in index notation, do the following:

1. Multiply or divide the 'a' parts (the number parts).

2. Multiply or divide the powers of 10 (add or subtract the indices).

3. Write your answer in index notation.

Alternatively, you can use your calculator by keying in the numbers in index notation and multiplying or dividing as required.

Example ▼

Express:

(i) $(3.5 \times 10^2) \times (4.8 \times 10^3)$

(ii) $(4.86 \times 10^4) \div (1.8 \times 10^7)$

in the form $a \times 10^n$, where $1 \leqslant a < 10$ and $n \in \mathbf{Z}$.

Solution:

(i) $(3.5 \times 10^2) \times (4.8 \times 10^3)$

$= 3.5 \times 10^2 \times 4.8 \times 10^3$

$= 3.5 \times 4.8 \times 10^2 \times 10^3$

$= 16.8 \times 10^{2+3}$ (add the indices)

$= 16.8 \times 10^5$

$= 1.68 \times 10^1 \times 10^5$

$= 1.68 \times 10^6$

(▦ 3.5 [EXP] 2 [×] 4.8 [EXP] 3 [=])

$= 1{,}680{,}000$ (on the display)

$= 1.68 \times 10^6$

(ii) $(4.86 \times 10^4) \div (1.8 \times 10^7)$

$= \dfrac{4.86 \times 10^4}{1.8 \times 10^7}$

$= \dfrac{4.86}{1.8} \times \dfrac{10^4}{10^7}$

$= 2.7 \times 10^{4-7}$ (subtract the indices)

$= 2.7 \times 10^{-3}$

(▦ 4.86 [EXP] 2 [÷] 1.8 [EXP] 7 [=])

$= 0.0027$ (on the display)

$= 2.7 \times 10^{-3}$

Exercise 11.9 ▼

Express each of the following in the form $a \times 10^n$, where $1 \leqslant a < 10$ and $n \in \mathbf{Z}$:

1. $2.4 \times 10^3 + 8 \times 10^2$

2. $2.52 \times 10^6 + 2.8 \times 10^5$

3. $5.48 \times 10^5 - 2.8 \times 10^4$

4. $48.2 \times 10^3 - 2.52 \times 10^4$

5. $8.45 \times 10^{-3} - 6.5 \times 10^{-4}$

6. $3.48 \times 10^{-4} - 5.4 \times 10^{-5}$

7. $(1.8 \times 10^3) \times (4 \times 10^4)$

8. $(2.25 \times 10^4) \times (1.6 \times 10^3)$

9. $(2.2 \times 10^3) \times (3.4 \times 10^2)$

10. $(5.3 \times 10^2) \times (1.8 \times 10^4)$

11. $(3.91 \times 10^5) \div (1.7 \times 10^2)$

12. $(5.04 \times 10^7) \div (3.6 \times 10^2)$

13. $(8.64 \times 10^5) \div (3.6 \times 10^2)$

14. $(9.86 \times 10^5) \div (1.7 \times 10^2)$

15. $(3 \times 10^3) \div (2 \times 10^{-2})$

16. $(12.6 \times 10^3 \div (4.5 \times 10^7)$

17. $(5.4 \times 10^2) \times (6.5 \times 10^3)$

18. $(1.35 \times 10^7) \div (2.5 \times 10^3)$

19. $\dfrac{(2.4 \times 10^4) \times (1.5 \times 10^2)}{1.2 \times 10^3}$

20. $\dfrac{(3.2 \times 10^5) + (8.5 \times 10^4)}{8.1 \times 10^2}$

21. $\dfrac{2.45 \times 10^5 - 1.8 \times 10^3}{1.6 \times 10^3}$

22. $\dfrac{1.4 \times 10^3 + 5.6 \times 10^2}{7 \times 10^{-1}}$

23. Calculate the value of $8.45 \times 10^{-2} - 6.5 \times 10^{-3}$.

Write your answer as a decimal number.

Say whether this number is greater than or less than 0.08.

24. Calculate the value of $\dfrac{2.8 \times 10^4 + 4.2 \times 10^5}{2.24 \times 10^6}$.

Write your answer as a decimal number.

Say whether this number is greater than or less than 0.19.

25. $\sqrt{\dfrac{3.64 \times 10^5 - 1.7 \times 10^3}{9.0575 \times 10^2}} = k$. Find the value of k.

PERMUTATIONS, COMBINATIONS AND PROBABILITY

Operations

The result of an operation is called an '**outcome**'.
For example, if we throw a die one possible outcome is 5.
If we throw a die there are 6 possible outcomes, 1, 2, 3, 4, 5 or 6.

Fundamental Principle of Counting 1

> Suppose one operation has m possible outcomes and that a second operation has n outcomes. The number of possible outcomes when performing the first operation **followed by** the second operation is $m \times n$.

Performing one operation **and** another operation means we **multiply** the number of possible outcomes.

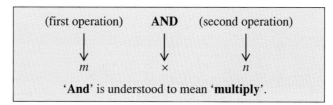

Note: We assume that the outcome of one operation does not affect the number of possible outcomes of the other operation.

The fundamental principle 1 of counting can be extended to three or more operations.

Fundamental Principle of Counting 2

> Suppose one operation has m possible outcomes and that a second operation has n outcomes. Then the number of possible outcomes of the first operation **or** the second operation is given by $m + n$.

Performing one operation **or** another operation means we **add** the number of possible outcomes.

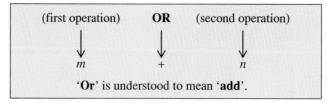

Note: We assume it is not possible for both operations to occur. In other words, there is no overlap of the two operations.

The fundamental principle 2 can be extended to three or more operations, as long as none of the operations overlap.

Permutations

> A permutation is an arrangement of a number of objects in a definite order.

Consider the three letters P, Q and R. If these letters are written down in a row, there are six different possible arrangements:

$$PQR \text{ or } PRQ \text{ or } QPR \text{ or } QRP \text{ or } RPQ \text{ or } RQP$$

The first letter can be written down in 3 ways, the second letter can then be written down in 2 ways and the third letter can be written down in only 1 way.
Thus the three operations can be performed in $\boxed{3} \times \boxed{2} \times \boxed{1} = 6$ ways.
The boxes are an aid in helping to fill in the number of ways each choice can be made at each position.
In an arrangement, or permutation, the order of the objects chosen is important.

Example ▼

(i) If a die is thrown and a coin is tossed, how many different outcomes are possible?

(ii) Write out all the possible outcomes.

Solution

(i) Represent each operation with an empty box: $\quad$ Die $\quad$ Coin $\quad$ $\square \times \square$

　　1. There are 6 possible outcomes for a die: 1, 2, 3, 4, 5 or 6.
　　2. There are 2 possible outcomes for a coin: H or T.

　　Hence, the number of different outcomes $= \boxed{6} \times \boxed{2} = 12$.

(ii)

T	•	•	•	•	•	•
H	•	•	•	•	•	•
	1	2	3	4	5	6

　　$(1, H), (2, H), (3, H), (4, H), (5, H), (6, H)$
　　$(1, T), (2, T), (3, T), (4, T), (5, T), (6, T)$

Note: It can help to write down one possible outcome above the box.

	Die		Coin
One possible outcome:	5		T
Number of outcomes:	$\boxed{6}$	$\times$	$\boxed{2}$ $= 12$

This is very useful when trying to decide the number of possible outcomes at a particular stage, especially when certain choices are restricted. For example, the letter v cannot be in the second place, or the number must be even.

In the following examples the choices available at each position are shown in a table on the right-hand side. A line through a letter or digit means it has already been used, whereas a circle around a letter or digit means it is unavailable for that position but can be used later.

Example ▼

(i) How many arrangements can be made of the letters P, Q, R, S, T, taking two letters at a time, if no letter can be repeated?

(ii) The digits $0, 1, 2, 3, 4, 5$ are used to form three-digit codes. A code cannot begin with 0 and no digit is repeated in any code. How many three digit codes can be formed?

Solution:

(i) Represent each choice with a box:

	1st	2nd	
Possible outcome:	S	T	
Number of ways:	$\boxed{5}$ ×	$\boxed{4}$	= 20

Explanation for the number of choices at each position:

choices available

1st: no. of outcomes = 5 (choose S)

P	Q	R	S	T

2nd: no. of outcomes = 4 (S used, choose T)

P	Q	R	~~S~~	T

(ii) Represent each choice with a box:

	1st	2nd	3rd	
Possible outcome:	3	2	5	
Number of ways:	$\boxed{5}$ ×	$\boxed{5}$ ×	$\boxed{4}$	= 100

↑
(0 cannot be used here)

Explanation for the number of choices at each position:

choices available

1st: No. of outcomes = 5 (0 unavailable, choose 3)

⓪	1	2	3	4	5

2nd: No. of outcomes = 5 (3 used, 0 back in, choose 2)

0	1	2	~~3~~	4	5

3rd: No. of outcomes = 4 (2 and 3 used, choose 5)

0	1	~~2~~	~~3~~	4	5

How many different arrangements can be made from the letters V, W, X, Y, Z, taking all the letters at a time, if V must be second and Z can never be last?

Solution:

Represent each choice with a box:

	1st	2nd	3rd	4th	5th
Possible outcome:	W	V	Z	Y	X
Number of ways:	$\boxed{3}$ ×	$\boxed{1}$ ×	$\boxed{2}$ ×	$\boxed{1}$ ×	$\boxed{3}$ = 18

(most restrictive, must be V)   (second most restrictive, cannot use V or Z)

Start with the choice that has most restrictions and choose a possible letter each time.

Explanation for the number of choices at each position:

choices available

2nd: No. of outcomes = 1 (must choose V)

5th: No. of outcomes = 3 (V used, Z unavailable, choose X)

1st: No. of outcomes = 3 (V, X used, Z back in, choose W)

3rd: No. of outcomes = 2 (V, W, X used, choose Z)

4th: No. of outcomes = 1 (V, W, X and Z used, must choose Y)

V	Ⓦ	Ⓧ	Ⓨ	Ⓩ
~~V~~	W	X	Y	Ⓩ
~~V~~	W	~~X~~	Y	Z
~~V~~	~~W~~	~~X~~	Y	Z
~~V~~	~~W~~	~~X~~	Y	~~Z~~

How many even numbers greater than 2,000 can be formed from the digits 1, 2, 3, 4, if each digit is used only once?

Solution:

Represent each choice with a box:

	1st	2nd	3rd	4th
Possible outcome:	2	1	3	4
Number of ways:	$\boxed{2}$ ×	$\boxed{2}$ ×	$\boxed{1}$ ×	$\boxed{2}$ = 8

(second most restrictive, must be 2 or greater) (most restrictive, must be even)

Start with the choice that has most restrictions and choose a possible digit each time.

Explanation for the number of choices at each position:

choices available

4th: No. of outcomes = 2 (1 and 3 unavailable, choose 4)

1st: No. of outcomes = 2 (4 used, 1 unavailable, choose 2)

2nd: No. of outcomes = 2 (2 and 4 used, choose 1)

3rd: No. of outcomes = 1 (1, 2 and 4 used, must choose 3)

①	2	③	4
①	2	3	~~4~~
1	~~2~~	3	~~4~~
~~1~~	~~2~~	3	~~4~~

1. How many different arrangements can be made from the letters *P, Q, R, S, T*, if no letter can be repeated and taking:

   (i) five letters   **(ii)** four letters   **(iii)** three letters   **(iv)** two letters, at a time?

2. How many different arrangements can be made using all the letters of the word *SEAT*?
   (i)   How many arrangements begin with *T*?
   (ii) How many arrangements end with *A*?

3. How many different arrangements can be made using all the letters of the word *VOWEL*?
   (i)   How many arrangements begin with *W*?
   (ii) How many arrangements begin with *V* and end in *L*?

4. How many different arrangements, taking three letters at a time, can be made from the word *TAKE*, if the first letter must be a vowel?

5. Six children are to be seated in a row on a bench.
   (i)   How many arrangements are possible?
   (ii) How many arrangements are possible if the youngest child must sit at the left-hand end and the oldest child must sit at the right-hand end?

6. Two boys and three girls are to be seated in a row on a bench.
   (i)   How many different ways can they be arranged?
   (ii) How many different ways can they be arranged if they must sit:
      (a) Girl–Boy–Girl–Boy–Girl   **(b)** Boy–Girl–Girl–Girl–Boy?

7. How many different arrangements can be made using all the letters of the word *DUBLIN*?
   (i)   How many arrangements begin with the letter *D*?
   (ii) How many arrangements begin with *B* and end in *L*?
   (iii) How many arrangements begin with a vowel?
   (iv) How many arrangements begin and end with a vowel?
   (v)   How many arrangements end with *LIN*?
   (vi) How many arrangements begin with *D* and end in *LIN*?

8. Tickets in a raffle have a code printed on them. The code is a letter followed by a digit.

   | **X 7** | (example)

   How many different codes are possible?
   How many different codes are there if no vowels are allowed and the digit 0 is not used?

9. A permutation lock has four rings which can be rotated about an axle.
   There are 10 digits (0, 1, 2, …, 8, 9) on each ring.

   If no digit can be repeated and 0 can never be first, find the maximum number of such locks that could be manufactured if no two locks have the same code and the lock will open only when a certain code of 4 digits is in line (see diagram).

10. How many four-digit numbers can be formed from the digits 1, 2, 3, 4 and 5, if no digit can be repeated and:

    (i)   there are no restrictions on digits

    (ii) the number is odd

    (iii) the number is even

    (iv) the number is greater than 3,000

    (v) the digit 5 is always second?

11. A number-plate is to consist of three letters of the English alphabet and two digits. If no letter or digit can be repeated and 0 can never be used as the first digit, how many different plates can be manufactured?

> **BAT 45**
>
> (an example)

12. A PIN number, Personal Identification Number, for an ATM machine consists of four digits. A number cannot begin with 0 and no digit is repeated in any code.

    (i)   Write down the largest PIN number.

    (ii) Write down the smallest PIN number.

    (iii) How many four-digit PIN numbers can be formed?

    (iv) How many four-digit PIN numbers are greater than 7,000?

13. **(i)**   How many different numbers, each with 3 digits or fewer, can be formed from the digits 2, 3, 4, 5, 6? Each digit can be used only once in each number.

    (ii) How many of the above numbers are odd?

14. How many different arrangements can be made using all the letters of the word *NAME*?

    (i)   How many arrangements end with a vowel?

    (ii) How many arrangements end with *NM*?

    (iii) In how many arrangements are the two vowels together?

        (**Hint:** Think of $\boxed{AE}$ or $\boxed{EA}$ as one letter.)

15. How many different arrangements can be made using all the letters of the word *ORIEL*?

    (i)   How many arrangements have the three vowels first?

    (ii) How many arrangements do not begin or end with a vowel?

    (iii) In how many arrangements are the three vowels together?

    (iv) In how many arrangements are the three vowels not together?

Factorials

Definition:

> The product of all the positive whole numbers from n down to 1 is called '**factorial n**' and is denoted by $n!$
>
> $$\text{Thus, } n! = n(n-1)(n-2) \ldots \times 3 \times 2 \times 1.$$

The shorthand used is to write an exclamation mark after the number.
For example:

$$1! = 1$$
$$2! = 2 \times 1 = 2$$
$$3! = 3 \times 2 \times 1 = 6$$
$$4! = 4 \times 3 \times 2 \times 1 = 12$$
$$5! = 5 \times 4 \times 3 \times 2 \times 1 = 120$$

As you can see, the values of the factorial increase in size at a very fast rate, e.g. $10! = 3,628,800$.

Note: $\quad 10! - 10 \times 9! - 10 \times 9 \times 8!$ (and so on) $\qquad n! - n(n-1)! - n(n-1)(n-2)!$ (and so on)

$\qquad\qquad 7 \times 6! = 7!$ $\qquad\qquad\qquad\qquad\qquad (n+1)n! = (n+1)!$

Example ▼

Evaluate: **(i)** $\dfrac{9!}{6!}$ $\qquad$ **(ii)** $4! + 2 \times 3!$

Solution:

(i) $\dfrac{9!}{6!}$

Method 1:

$$\dfrac{9!}{6!} = \dfrac{9 \times 8 \times 7 \times \cancel{6} \times \cancel{5} \times \cancel{4} \times \cancel{3} \times \cancel{2} \times \cancel{1}}{\cancel{6} \times \cancel{5} \times \cancel{4} \times \cancel{3} \times \cancel{2} \times \cancel{1}}$$
$$= 9 \times 8 \times 7$$
$$= 504$$

(🖩 9 $\boxed{n!}$ $\boxed{\div}$ 6 $\boxed{n!}$ $\boxed{=}$)

Method 2:

$$\dfrac{9!}{6!} = \dfrac{9 \times 8 \times 7 \times 6!}{6!}$$
$$= 9 \times 8 \times 7$$
$$= 504$$

(Start with the larger factorial and work down to the smaller factorial).

(ii) $4! + 2 \times 3!$

$$4! = 4 \times 3 \times 2 \times 1 = 24$$
$$3! = 3 \times 2 \times 1 = 6$$
$$\therefore \quad 4! + 2 \times 3! = 24 + 2 \times 6 = 24 + 12 = 36$$

Exercise 12.2 ▼

Evaluate each of the following:

1. $5!$ $\qquad$ **2.** $6!$ $\qquad$ **3.** $8!$ $\qquad$ **4.** $9!$ $\qquad$ **5.** $12!$

6. $\dfrac{6!}{4!}$ $\qquad$ **7.** $\dfrac{8!}{5!}$ $\qquad$ **8.** $\dfrac{10!}{6!}$ $\qquad$ **9.** $\dfrac{8!}{2! \times 6!}$ $\qquad$ **10.** $\dfrac{10!}{3! \times 7!}$

11. $(4!)^2$ $\qquad$ **12.** $(2! + 3!)^2$ $\qquad$ **13.** $(5! - 3!)^2$ $\qquad$ **14.** $5 \times 4! + 3 \times 2!$

15. $4.5! - 5.4!$ $\qquad$ **16.** $\dfrac{6!}{(3!)^2}$ $\qquad$ **17.** $\dfrac{6! - 4!}{3!}$ $\qquad$ **18.** $\dfrac{15!}{4! \times 11!} - \dfrac{9!}{2! \times 7!}$

19. If $k(5!) = 7!$, find the value of k.

20. By letting $n = 6$, verify that:

(i) $\dfrac{(n+1)!}{n!} = n + 1$

(ii) $\dfrac{(n+1)!}{n+1} = n!$

(iii) $\dfrac{(n+1)!}{(n-1)!} = n^2 + n$

Combinations

> A combination is a selection of a number of objects in any order.

In making a selection of a number of objects from a given set, only the contents of the group selected are important, not the order in which the items are selected.

For example, AB and BA represent the same selection.
However, AB and BA represent different arrangements.

Note: What is called a 'combination lock' should really be called a 'permutation lock', as the order of the digits is essential.

The $\binom{n}{r}$ Notation

> $\binom{n}{r}$ gives the number of ways of choosing r objects from n different objects.
>
> It's value can be calculated in two ways:
>
> **1.** $\binom{n}{r} = \dfrac{n!}{r!(n-r)!}$ \qquad (definition)
>
> **2.** $\binom{n}{r} = \dfrac{n(n-1)(n-2) \dots (n-r+1)}{r!}$ \qquad (in practice)

Both give the same result; however, the second is easier to use in practical questions.
For example:

1. $\binom{6}{2} = \dfrac{6!}{2!(6-2)!} = \dfrac{6!}{2!4!} = \dfrac{720}{2 \times 24} = 15$

2. $\binom{6}{2} = \dfrac{6.5}{2.1}$ $\rightarrow$ start at 6, go down two terms
$\rightarrow$ start at 2, go down two terms

$= 15$

Note: $\binom{n}{r}$ is pronounced '*n-c-r*' or '*n*-choose-*r*'.

Notes:

1. $\binom{n}{0} = 1$, i.e., there is only one way of choosing no objects out of n objects.

2. $\binom{n}{n} = 1$, i.e., there is only one way of choosing n objects out of n objects.

3. $\binom{n}{r} = \binom{n}{n-r}$; use this when r is greater than $\dfrac{n}{2}$.

Explanation for note 3:

Let's assume you have 13 soccer players and you can pick only 11 to play.

The number of ways of choosing 11 from 13 is given by $\binom{13}{11}$.

$$\binom{13}{11} = \frac{13.12.11.10.9.8.7.6.5.4.3}{11.10.9.8.7.6.5.4.3.2.1} = 78$$

However, every time you choose 11 to play, you choose 2 who cannot play.

Thus $\binom{13}{11} = \binom{13}{2} = \dfrac{13.12}{2.1} = 78$ (same as before).

Notice that $11 + 2 = 13$

Similarly, $\binom{20}{17} = \binom{20}{3}$ as $17 + 3 = 20$

and $\binom{100}{98} = \binom{100}{2}$ as $98 + 2 = 100$

If r is large, your calculator may not be able to do the calculation: thus use $\binom{n}{r} = \binom{n}{n-r}$.

Note: $\binom{n}{r}$ is sometimes written as $^{n}C_r$ or $_{n}C_r$.

Example ▼

Calculate: **(i)** $\binom{8}{3}$ **(ii)** $\binom{10}{4}$ **(iii)** $\binom{9}{1}$ **(iv)** $\binom{7}{0}$ **(v)** $\binom{30}{28}$

Solution:

(i) $\binom{8}{3} = \dfrac{8 \times 7 \times 6}{3 \times 2 \times 1} = 56$ (▦ 8 (nCr) 3 (=))

(ii) $\binom{10}{4} = \dfrac{10 \times 9 \times 8 \times 7}{4 \times 3 \times 2 \times 1} = 210$ (▦ 10 (nCr) 4 (=))

(iii) $\binom{9}{1} = \frac{9}{1} = 9$ ($\boxed{\ }$ 9 $\boxed{nCr}$ 1 $\boxed{=}$)

(iv) $\binom{7}{0} = 1$ ($\boxed{\ }$ 7 $\boxed{nCr}$ 0 $\boxed{=}$)

(v) $\binom{30}{28} = \binom{30}{30-28} = \binom{30}{2} = \frac{30 \times 29}{2 \times 1} = 435$ ($\boxed{\ }$ 30 $\boxed{nCr}$ 28 $\boxed{=}$)

Exercise 12.3 ▼

Calculate:

1. $\binom{5}{2}$ **2.** $\binom{8}{2}$ **3.** $\binom{7}{3}$ **4.** $\binom{10}{3}$ **5.** $\binom{7}{4}$ **6.** $\binom{9}{4}$

7. $\binom{6}{0}$ **8.** $\binom{4}{1}$ **9.** $\binom{8}{1}$ **10.** $\binom{9}{3}$ **11.** $\binom{20}{18}$ **12.** $\binom{30}{27}$

13. $5\binom{4}{2} + 3\binom{7}{2}$ **14.** $10\binom{8}{2} - 6\binom{5}{3}$ **15.** $\binom{6}{2} \times \binom{7}{2}$

Verify each of the following:

16. $\binom{10}{8} = \binom{10}{2}$ **17.** $\binom{7}{3} + \binom{7}{4} = \binom{8}{4}$ **18.** $\binom{9}{3} - \binom{8}{2} = \binom{8}{3}$

19. $\left[\binom{8}{2}\right]^2 = 4\binom{9}{4} + 5\binom{8}{3}$ **20.** $\sqrt{\binom{8}{2} - \binom{3}{2}} = 5$

21. If $\binom{8}{5} = \binom{8}{k}$, $k \neq 5$, find the value of k.

22. If $\binom{10}{2} = \binom{10}{k}$, $k \neq 2$, find the value of k.

23. If $n = 8$ and $r = 3$, verify each of the following:

(i) $\binom{n}{r} + \binom{n}{r-1} = \binom{n+1}{r}$ **(ii)** $r\binom{n}{r} = n\binom{n-1}{r-1}$

Equations Involving $\binom{n}{r}$

Sometimes we have to solve an equation involving $\binom{n}{r}$.

When this happens, the following are very useful:

$$\binom{n}{1} = n \qquad\qquad \binom{n}{2} = \frac{n(n-1)}{2 \times 1} = \frac{n(n-1)}{2}$$

Example ▼

Find the value of the natural number n such that $\binom{n}{2} = 28$.

Solution:

$$\binom{n}{2} = 28$$

$$\frac{n(n-1)}{2} = 28 \qquad\qquad \left(\binom{n}{2} = \frac{n(n-1)}{2 \times 1} = \frac{n(n-1)}{2} \right)$$

$$\frac{n^2 - n}{2} = 28 \qquad\qquad \text{(remove the brackets on top)}$$

$$n^2 - n = 56 \qquad\qquad \text{(multiply both sides by 2)}$$

$$n^2 - n - 56 = 0 \qquad\qquad \text{(quadratic equation)}$$

$$(n - 8)(n + 7) = 0$$

$$n - 8 = 0 \quad \text{or} \quad n + 7 = 0$$

$$n = 8 \quad \text{or} \quad n = -7$$

Reject $n = -7$, as -7 is not a natural number.

$$\therefore \quad n = 8$$

Note: Guessing values for n and substituting them into the equation is **not** an acceptable method.

Solve each of the following, where n is a positive natural number:

1. $\binom{n}{2} = 10$

2. $\binom{n}{2} = 15$

3. $\binom{n}{2} = 28$

4. $\binom{n}{2} = 45$

5. $\binom{n}{2} = 6$

6. $\binom{n}{2} = 55$

7. $\binom{n+1}{2} = 21$

8. $\binom{n}{2} = n$

9. $\binom{n+1}{2} = \binom{n}{1} + 4\binom{7}{1}$

Practical Application of Combinations

$\binom{n}{r}$ gives the number of ways of choosing r objects from n different objects.

Thus, n = the number of different objects we have to choose from (upper number),
and r = the number of different objects we choose at a time (lower number).
Before attempting a practical problem on combinations, it is good practice to write down the value of n (number of different objects to choose from) and the value of r (the number of objects chosen at a time).

Example ▼

Eight people take part in a chess competition. How many games will be played if each person must play each of the others?

Solution:

We **have** 8 people to choose from, of whom we want to **choose** 2 (as 2 people play in each game).
Thus, $n = 8$, $r = 2$

$$\text{Number of games} = \binom{8}{2} = \frac{8 \times 7}{2 \times 1} = 28$$

Example ▼

(i) How many ways can a committee of 4 people be chosen from a panel of 10 people?

(ii) If a certain person must be on the committee, in how many ways can the committee be chosen?

(iii) If a certain person must not be on the committee, in how many ways can the committee be chosen?

Solution:

(i) We **have** a panel of 10 people to choose from, and we need to **choose** a committee of 4.

$$\therefore \quad n = 10, r = 4$$

$$\binom{10}{4} = \frac{10 \times 9 \times 8 \times 7}{4 \times 3 \times 2 \times 1} = 210$$

Thus, from a panel of 10 people, we can choose 210 different committees of 4 people.

(ii) One particular person **must** be on the committee.
Thus, we **have** a panel of 9 people to choose from, and we need to **choose** 3 (as one person is already chosen).

$$\therefore \quad n = 9, r = 3$$

$$\binom{9}{3} = \frac{9 \times 8 \times 7}{3 \times 2 \times 1} = 84$$

Thus, from a panel of 10 people, we can choose 84 different committees of 4 people, if one particular person of the 10 must be on every committee.

(iii) One particular person **must not** be on the committee.
Thus, we **have** a panel of 9 to choose from (as one person cannot be chosen), and we need to **choose** 4.

$$\therefore \quad n = 9, r = 4$$

$$\binom{9}{4} = \frac{9 \times 8 \times 7 \times 6}{4 \times 3 \times 2 \times 1} = 126$$

Thus from a panel of 10 people, we can choose 126 different committees of 4 people, if one particular person of the 10 must not be on the committee.

Exercise 12.5

1. In how many ways can a committee of 3 be chosen from 8 people?

2. A set of 12 pupils exchange handshakes once with each other. Calculate the number of handshakes among the 12 pupils.

3. A class of 20 students wins a prize. Two members of the class are chosen to receive the prize. How many different pairs of students can be chosen?

4. In how many ways can four books be chosen from a shelf containing twelve different books?

5. A committee of 7 people is to be chosen from 11 people. If two people must always be on each committee, how many different committees can be formed?

6. A maths exam consists of 8 questions. A candidate must answer question 1 and any four others. In how many different ways can a candidate select his five questions?

7. **(i)** In how many ways can a team of 5 players be chosen from a panel of 9 players?
   (ii) If a certain player must be on the team, in how many ways can the team be chosen?
   (iii) If a certain player cannot play, in how many ways can the team be chosen?

8. There are 15 pupils in a class. How many teams of 11 can be selected from the class? If one person in the class is made captain and must always be included in each team, how many teams can now be selected? If 2 pupils in the class refuse to play, how many teams can now be selected, if the captain must be on every team?

9. In how many ways can a party of 6 children be chosen from a group of 10 children if:
   (i) any child may be selected?
   (ii) the oldest child must not be selected?
   (iii) the youngest child must be selected?
   (iv) the youngest and the oldest must both be selected?

10. A fifth-year student has to choose 4 subjects from the following list: Accounting, Biology, Chemistry, Physics, French, Applied Maths and Classical Studies.
   (i) How many different choices are possible?
   (ii) How many choices include French?
   (iii) How many choices do not include French?
   (iv) How many choices include Accounting and Biology?
   (v) How many choices include Applied Maths but not Chemistry?

11. Ten points are taken on the circumference of a circle (as shown). A chord is a line segment joining any two of these points. Calculate the number of such chords that can be drawn. With these points as vertices, how many triangles can be drawn?

Practical Applications from Two Different Groups of Objects

Sometimes we have to deal with problems choosing objects from two different groups.
This involves choosing a number of objects from one group **AND** then choosing a number of objects from the other group.

Note: There are two key words when applying the fundamental principle of counting:
   1. 'And' is understood to mean 'multiply'. Thus, and = ×.
   2. 'Or' is understood to mean 'add'. Thus, or = +.

Example ▼

There are 5 women and 4 men in a club. A team of four has to be chosen. How many different teams can be chosen if there must be exactly one woman or exactly two women on the team?

Solution:

| And = × | | Or = + |

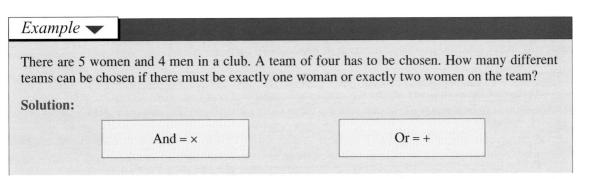

253

A team must consist of 4 people.

Thus, exactly one woman on the team means '1 woman **and** 3 men';

and exactly two women on the team means '2 women **and** 2 men'.

Thus, we need to choose '1 woman **and** 3 men' **or** '2 women **and** 2 men'.

Let W stand for women and let M stand for men.

We have 5 women and 4 men and these are **always** the upper numbers.

$$
\begin{array}{ccccc}
\text{1W and 3M} & & \text{or} & & \text{2W and 2M} & \text{(lower numbers in each case)} \\
\downarrow \quad \downarrow \quad \downarrow & & \downarrow & & \downarrow \quad \downarrow \quad \downarrow \\
\binom{5}{1} \times \binom{4}{3} & & + & & \binom{5}{2} \times \binom{4}{2} \\
\end{array}
$$

$$= \quad 5 \quad \times \quad 4 \quad\quad + \quad\quad 10 \quad \times \quad 6$$

$$= \quad 20 \quad + \quad 60$$

$$= \quad 80$$

Thus, 80 teams can have either one woman or two women on the team.

Exercise 12.6 ▼

1. In how many different ways is it possible to choose a group of 2 men and 3 women from 4 men and 5 women?

2. A mixed hockey team containing 6 men and 5 women is chosen from 8 men and 7 women. In how many different ways can this be done?

3. In how many ways can a committee of three men and four women be formed from seven men and eight women?

4. A Leaving Certificate Maths Paper 2 has a section A with seven questions and a section B with four questions. A student must do exactly five questions from section A and exactly one question from section B. In how many ways can a candidate select the six questions?

5. There are 5 women and 5 men in a club. A team of four has to be chosen. How many different teams can be chosen, if there must be exactly one woman or exactly two women on the team?

6. In how many ways can a group of four people be selected from 6 men and 4 women if:
   (i)   there are no restrictions?
   (ii) there must be two women and two men?
   (iii) there must be exactly three men or exactly two men?

7. There are five third-year students and six fourth-year students in a running club in a school.
   A team of three students are to represent the school at a meeting. How many different teams are possible? In how many of these teams are there more fourth-year students than third-year students?

8. A group consists of 5 men and 7 women. A committee of 4 must be chosen from the group. How many committees can be chosen in which there are an odd number of men?

9. From 6 teachers and 4 pupils, a committee of 5 is to be formed.
   In how many different ways can the committee be formed if it contains:

   (i) exactly 2 pupils   **(ii)** more pupils than teachers?

10. How many bundles of 3 different books can be made from 8 Maths books and 6 Physics books, if
    the number of Maths books must always be greater than the number of Physics books?

Probability

Probability involves the study of the laws of chance. it is a measure of the chance, or likelihood, of
something happening.

| toss coins | throw dice | spin a spinner | draw a card |

If you carry out an operation, or experiment, using coins, dice, spinners or cards, then each toss, throw,
spin or draw is called a **trial**.
The possible things that can happen from a trial are called **outcomes**. The outcomes of interest are
called an **event**. In other words, an event is the set of successful outcomes.
For example, if you throw a die and you are interested in the probability of an even number, then the
event is 2, 4, 6, the successful outcomes.
If E is an event, then $P(E)$ stands for the probability that the event occurs.
$P(E)$ is read 'the probability of E'.

Definition

> The measure of the probability of an event, E, is given by:
>
> $$P(E) = \frac{\text{number of successful outcomes}}{\text{number of possible outcomes}}$$

The probability of an event is a number between 0 and 1, including 0 and 1.

$$0 \leqslant P(E) \leqslant 1$$

The value of $P(E)$ can be given as a fraction, decimal or percentage.

Note: $P(E) = 0$ means that an event is **impossible**.

$P(E) = 1$ means that an event is **certain**.

An unbiased die is thrown once. Find the probability that the number obtained is:

(i) 2   **(ii)** odd   **(iii)** greater than 4.

Solution:

When an unbiased die is thrown there are 6 possible outcomes, 1, 2, 3, 4, 5 or 6.

(i)   There is only one 2

$$\therefore \quad P(2) - \tfrac{1}{6}$$

(ii)   There are three odd numbers, 1, 3 and 5

$$\therefore \quad P(\text{odd number}) = \tfrac{3}{6} = \tfrac{1}{2}$$

(iii)   There are two numbers greater than four, 5 and 6

$$\therefore \quad P(\text{number greater than four}) = \tfrac{2}{6} = \tfrac{1}{3}$$

A pack of cards consists of 52 cards divided into four suits: Clubs (black), Diamonds (red), Hearts (red) and Spades (black). Each suit consists of 13 cards bearing the following values 2, 3, 4, 5, 6, 7, 8 9, 10, Jack, Queen, King and Ace. The Jack, Queen and King are called 'picture cards'.
So the total number of outcomes if one card is picked is 52.

Notes: The phrase 'drawn at random' means each object is **equally likely** to be picked.
           'Unbiased' means 'fair'.

A card is drawn at random from a normal pack of 52 playing cards.
What is the probability that the card will be:

(i) an ace   **(ii)** a spade   **(iii)** black   **(iv)** odd numbered?

Solution:

(i) $P(\text{ace}) = \dfrac{\text{number of aces}}{\text{number of cards}} = \dfrac{4}{52} = \dfrac{1}{13}$

(ii) $P(\text{ace}) = \dfrac{\text{number of spades}}{\text{number of cards}} = \dfrac{13}{52} = \dfrac{1}{4}$

(iii) $P(\text{black card}) = \dfrac{\text{number of black cards}}{\text{number of cards}} = \dfrac{26}{52} = \dfrac{1}{2}$

(iv)   Each suit has four odd numbers, 3, 5, 7 and 9. There are four suits.
Therefore, there are 16 cards with an odd number.

$$P(\text{odd–numbered card}) = \dfrac{\text{number of cards with an odd number}}{\text{number of cards}} = \dfrac{16}{52} = \dfrac{4}{13}$$

In a class, there are 21 boys and 15 girls. Three boys wear glasses and five girls wear glasses. A pupil is picked at random from the class.

(i) What is the probability that the pupil is a boy?

(ii) What is the probability that the pupil wears glasses?

(iii) What is the probability that the pupil is a boy who wears glasses?

A girl is picked at random from the class.

(iv) What is the probability that she wears glasses?

A pupil wearing glasses is picked at random from the class.

(iv) What is the probability that it is a boy?

Solution:

It is good practice to represent the information in a table (including the totals for each column and row).

	Boy	Girl	Total
Does not wear glasses	18	10	28
Wears glasses	3	5	8
Total	21	15	36

There are $21 + 15 = 36$ pupils in the class.

(i) $P(\text{boy}) = \dfrac{\text{number of boys}}{\text{number of pupils in the class}} = \dfrac{21}{36} = \dfrac{7}{12}$

(ii) $P(\text{pupil wears glasses}) = \dfrac{\text{number of pupils who wear glasses}}{\text{number of pupils in the class}} = \dfrac{8}{36} = \dfrac{2}{9}$

(iii) $P(\text{boy who wears glasses}) = \dfrac{\text{number of boys who wear glasses}}{\text{number of pupils in the class}} = \dfrac{3}{36} = \dfrac{1}{12}$

(iv) We are certain that the pupil picked is a girl. There are 15 girls in the class. 5 of these wear glasses.

$P(\text{when a girl is picked she wears glasses})$

$= \dfrac{\text{number of girls in the class who wear glasses}}{\text{number of girls in the class}} = \dfrac{5}{15} = \dfrac{1}{3}$

(v) We are certain that the pupil picked wears glasses. There are 8 pupils who wear glasses. 3 of these pupils are boys.

$P(\text{when a pupil who wears glasses is picked, the pupil is a boy})$

$= \dfrac{\text{number of boys in the class who wear glasses}}{\text{number of pupils in the class who wear glasses}} = \dfrac{3}{8}$

1. A box contains 36 coloured balls. 12 are red, 15 are blue, 3 are yellow and the rest are white. One ball is selected at random from the box. Calculate the probability of selecting a:

   (i) red ball   **(ii)** blue ball   **(iii)** yellow ball   **(iv)** white ball.

2. A letter is chosen at random from the word '*SIMULTANEOUS*'. What is the probability that the letter is:

   (i) O **(ii)** S **(iii)** a vowel   **(iv)** a consonant?

3. From a class of 40 students with 25 boys, one student is chosen at random to read a poem. What is the probability that a girl is chosen?

4. In a raffle, a total of 500 tickets are sold. A girl bought 25 tickets. What is the chance of her winning the only prize?

5. The numbers 1 to 30 inclusive are written on 30 identical slips of paper, placed in a box and thoroughly mixed. One slip of paper is chosen at random from the box. Find the probability that the number printed on the slip is:

   (i) odd   **(ii)** less than 7   **(iii)** divisible by 5   **(iv)** divisible by 9

   (v) a two-digit number   **(vi)** a perfect square   **(vii)** a prime number.

6. A fair spinner has eight sides as shown. The sides are labelled A, B, B, C, C, C, C and F. The spinner is spun once. What is the probability that the spinner lands on:

   (i) A   **(ii)** B   **(iii)** C?

7. A card is drawn at random from a normal pack of 52 playing cards. What is the probability that the card will be:

   (i) the nine of spades   **(ii)** a red card   **(iii)** a club

   (iv) a King   **(v)** a picture card   **(vi)** a black picture card

   (vii) an even number   **(viii)** not a Queen   **(ix)** a joker?

8. A die is thrown 120 times. How many times would you expect the die to land on six?

9. 1,000 tickets are sold in a raffle. There is only one prize. How many tickets does a person need to buy to have exactly 1 chance in 5 (i.e. $\frac{1}{5}$) of winning?

10. A bag contains 3 red, 3 green and 4 blue discs. A disc is selected at random from the bag. What is the probability of selecting a blue disc?

    The selected disc is to be put back into the bag, plus a certain number of red discs. This causes the probability of selecting a red disc to equal $\frac{1}{2}$.

    Find the number of extra red discs that were placed in the bag.

11. The table shows the way that 150 first-year pupils travel to school.

	Walk	Bus	Car	Train	Bike
Boy	15	10	7	30	8
Girl	20	24	8	12	16

A first-year pupil is chosen at random.
What is the probability that the pupil:

(i)   is a boy   **(ii)** walks to school   **(iii)** does not use the train

(iv) is a girl who travels by bus   **(v)** is a boy who travels by train?

A first-year student who travels by bike is chosen at random.

(vi) What is the probability that the pupil is a boy?

A girl from the first year is chosen at random. What is the probability that she:

(vii) walks to school   **(viii)** does not travel by car?

12. A box contains 20 blue counters and 30 green counters. Each counter is numbered with an even or odd number. 5 of the blue and 20 of the green counters are odd.
Complete the table opposite.

	Even	Odd	Total
Blue			20
Green			
Total			50

One of the counters is chosen at random.
What is the probability that the counter is:

(i)   blue   **(ii)** green   **(iii)** blue and even   **(iv)** green and odd?

A green counter is chosen at random.

(v)   What is the probability that it is odd?

An odd-numbered counter is chosen at random.

(vi) What is the probability that it is blue?

13. There are 80 members in a club, 32 male and 48 female. 4 of the males and 8 of the females wear glasses. A club member is selected at random.

What is the probability that the club member is a:

(i)   male   **(ii)** female   **(iii)** person wearing glasses

(iv) female not wearing glasses   **(v)** male wearing glasses?

A male from the club is selected at random.

(vi) What is the probability that he wears glasses?

A member who wears glasses is selected at random.

(vii) What is the probability that it is a female?

Combining Two Events

There are many situations where we have to consider two outcomes. In these situations all the possible outcomes, called the **sample space**, can be listed in a sample space diagram (often called a '**two-way table**')

Example ▼

A fair coin is tossed and an unbiased die is thrown.

Calculate the probability of obtaining:

(i) a head and an odd number   **(ii)** a tail or a number less then 3.

Solution:

Represent each situation with a sample space diagram and indicate a successful outcome with a dot.

(i)

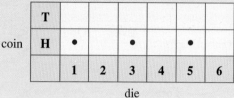

sample space diagram

P(head and an odd number)

$= \frac{3}{12} = \frac{1}{4}$

Note: The word '**and**' indicates we only count the outcomes where both a head and an odd number occur together.

(ii)

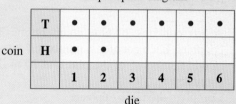

sample space diagram

P(tail or a number less than 3)

$= \frac{8}{12} = \frac{2}{3}$

Note: The word '**or**' indicates we count the outcomes with either a tail or a number less than 3, including a tail and a number less than 3 together.

Example ▼

Two dice are thrown, one red and the other black.

(i)   How many outcomes are possible?

(ii)   If the scores are added together, calculate the probability that the sum of the scores is:
   (a) less than 6   **(b)** 7   **(c)** greater than 10.

Solution: Represent the situation with a sample space diagram.

sample space diagram

black die						
6	7	8	9	10	11	12
5	6	7	8	9	10	11
4	5	6	7	8	9	10
3	4	5	6	7	8	9
2	3	4	5	6	7	8
1	2	3	4	5	6	7
	1	**2**	**3**	**4**	**5**	**6**

red die

(i)   There are $6 \times 6 = 36$ possible outcomes

(ii)   **(a)** P(sum less than 6) $= \frac{10}{36} = \frac{5}{18}$

   (b) P(sum is 7) $= \frac{6}{36} = \frac{1}{6}$

   (c) P(greater than 10) $= \frac{3}{36} = \frac{1}{12}$

A bag contains 3 red and 2 yellow discs only. When a disc is drawn from the bag, it is returned before the next draw. What is the probability that two draws will yield both discs the same colour?

Solution:

Make out a sample space diagram. Let R stand for a red disc and Y stand for a yellow disc.

sample space diagram

second selection					
Y				•	•
Y				•	•
R	•	•	•		
R	•	•	•		
R	•	•	•		
	R	R	R	Y	Y

first selection

There are 25 possible outcomes.
(5 for the first draw and 5 for the second draw)
The dots indicate where the colours are the same, successful outcome, either two reds or two yellows. There are 13 dots.
P(both discs the same colour) $= \frac{13}{25}$

Exercise 12.8 ▼

1. Two dice are thrown, one red and the other black. Calculate the probability that:
  (i) the outcomes are the same on each die
  (ii) the sum of the outcomes is 9
  (iii) the sum of the outcomes is greater than or equal to 5
  (iv) the sum of the outcomes is divisible by 3
  (v) the sum of the outcomes is 6 or 10
  (vi) the product of the outcomes is 12
  (vii) the outcome on the red die is exactly three more than the outcome on the black die.

2. Two unbiased five-sided spinners are labelled with the numbers 1, 2, 3, 4, 5. An experiment consists of spinning them together and the score is calculated by subtracting the smaller number from the larger number. When the numbers are equal, the score is 0.

  (a) Copy and complete the following sample space diagram to show all the possible scores.

Number on second spinner

Number on first spinner	1	2	3	4	5
1	0				
2					3
3					
4		2			
5					

  (b) Calculate the probability of a score of:
  (i) 0   **(ii)** 5   **(iii)** 3 or more.

3. A game is played with two fair spinners, as shown. Both are spun at the same time and the outcomes are added to get a score. How many scores are possible?

Calculate the probability of a score:

(i) of 4   **(ii)** of 6

(iii) greater than 6   **(iv)** less than or equal to 5.

4. A bag A contains 6 blue discs and 2 yellow discs. A bag B contains 4 blue discs and 2 yellow discs. A disc is drawn from bag A and then a disc is drawn from bag B.

Calculate the probability that:

(i) both discs are yellow   **(ii)** both discs are the same colour

(iii) the disc from bag A is blue and the disc from bag B is yellow.

5. A box contains 4 discs numbered 1, 3, 3, 4. A disc is drawn from the box and replaced. Then a second disc is drawn. A score is the sum of the two numbers drawn.

Calculate the probability that:

(i) the sum of the numbers is 4   **(ii)** the sum of the numbers is 6 or 7

(iii) the numbers drawn are the same   **(iv)** the difference between the numbers is less than 2.

6. A bag contains 4 red and 2 blue discs only. When a disc is drawn from the bag, it is returned before the next draw. What is the probability that two draws will yield:

(i) both disks red   **(ii)** both discs the same colour   **(iii)** discs with different colours?

7. A game consists of spinning an unbiased five-sided spinner which can land on A, B, C, D or E, and throwing an unbiased die. List all possible outcomes of the game, that is, of spinning the spinner and throwing the die.

Find the probability that in any one game the outcome will be:

(i) an A and a 6

(ii) a C and an odd number

(iii) a B and an even number or a D and an odd number

(iv) an E and a number greater than 4 or an A and a number less than or equal to 2.

8. A bag contains five discs numbered 1, 2, 3, 4 and 5. A disc is drawn from the bag and not replaced. Then a second disc is drawn from the bag.

How many outcomes are possible?

Calculate the probability that:

(i) the sum of the outcomes is less than 5

(ii) one outcome is exactly 3 greater than the other

(iii) the difference between the outcomes is 2.

Addition Rule (OR)

The probability that two events, *A* or *B*, can happen is given by:

$$P(A \text{ or } B) = P(A) + P(B) - P(A \text{ and } B)$$

(removes double counting)

It is often called the **or** rule. It is important to remember that *P*(*A* or *B*) means *A* occurs, or *B* occurs, or both occur. By subtracting *P*(*A* and *B*), the possibility of double counting is removed.

Probability of an event not happening

If *E* is any event, then 'not *E*' is the event that *E* does not occur. Clearly *E* and 'not *E*' cannot occur at the same time. Either *E* or not *E* must occur. Thus, we have the following relationship between the probabilities of *E* and not *E*:

$$P(E) + P(\text{not } E) = 1$$

or

$$P(\text{not } E) = 1 - P(E)$$

Example ▼

A fair spinner with ten sides, numbered 1 to 10, is spun.
What is the probability of a number divisible by 2 or 3?

Solution:

The possible outcomes are 1, 2, 3, 4, 5, 6, 7, 8, 9 or 10.

Numbers divisible by 2 are 2, 4, 6, 8 or 10   ∴ *P*(number divisible by 2) = $\frac{5}{10}$

Numbers divisible by 3 are 3, 6 or 9   ∴ *P*(number divisible by 3) = $\frac{3}{10}$

Number divisible by 2 and 3 is 6   ∴ *P*(number divisible by 2 and 3) = $\frac{1}{10}$

P(number divisible by 2 or 3)

= *P*(number divisible by 2) + *P*(number divisible by 3) − *P*(number divisible by 2 and 3)

= $\frac{5}{10} + \frac{3}{10} - \frac{1}{10}$ (removes the double counting of the number 6)

= $\frac{7}{10}$

The number 6 is common to both events and if the probabilities are added then the number 6 would have been counted twice.
An alternative to using the rule is to write down all the successful outcomes and not include any twice.

P(number divisible by 2 or 3) = *P*(2 or 3 or 4 or 6 or 8 or 9 or 10) = $\frac{7}{10}$

(6 included only once)

A single card is drawn at random from a pack of 52. What is the probability that it is a king or a spade? What is the probability that it is not a king or spade?

Solution:

The pack contains 52 cards.

There are 4 kings in the pack, $\therefore P(\text{king}) = \frac{4}{52}$

There are 13 spades in the pack, $\therefore P(\text{spade}) = \frac{13}{52}$

One card is both a king and a spade, $\therefore P(\text{king and a spade}) = \frac{1}{52}$

$$P(\text{king or a spade}) = P(\text{king}) + P(\text{spade}) - P(\text{king and a spade})$$
$$= \frac{4}{42} + \frac{13}{52} - \frac{1}{52}$$
$$= \frac{16}{52}$$
$$= \frac{4}{13}$$

$$P(\text{not a king or a spade}) = 1 - P(\text{a king or a spade})$$
$$= 1 - \frac{4}{13} = \frac{9}{13}$$

Exercise 12.9 ▼

1. An unbiased die is thrown.
   Find the probability that the number obtained is:
   (i) even   (ii) prime   (iii) even or prime.

2. The probability that a woman will hit the target with a single shot at a rifle range is $\frac{3}{5}$.
   If she fires one shot, find the probability that she will miss the target.

3. A bag contains three blue discs, five white discs and four red discs.
   A disc is chosen at random.
   Find the probability that the disc chosen is:
   (i) red   (ii) blue or white   (iii) red or white   (iv) not red or white.

4. A number is chosen at random from the whole numbers 1 to 12 inclusive.
   What is the probability that it is:
   (i) even   (ii) divisible by 3   (iii) even or divisible by 3   (iv) not even or divisible by 3?

5. A number is chosen at random from the whole numbers 1–30 inclusive.
   What is the probability that it is divisible by:
   (i) 3   (ii) 5   (iii) 3 or 5   (iv) not 3 or 5?

6. A letter is selected at random from the word *EXERCISES*.
   Find the probability that the letter is:
   (i) *I*   (ii) *S*   (iii) a vowel   (iv) a vowel or an *S*   (v) not a vowel or an *S*.

7. In a class of 20 students, 4 of the 9 girls and 3 of the 11 boys play on the school hockey team.
   A student from the class is chosen at random. What is the probability that the student chosen is:
   (i)   on the hockey team   (ii)   a boy
   (iii)   a boy or on the hockey team   (iv)   a girl or not on the hockey team?

8. In lotto, there are 42 numbers, numbered from 1 to 42.
   Find the probability that the first number drawn is:
   (i)   an even number
   (ii) a number greater than 24
   (iii) an odd number or a number greater than 24
   (iv) a number divisible by 6
   (v)   a number divisible by 4
   (vi) a number divisible by 6 or 4
   (vii) not a number divisible by 6 or 4.

9. A card is selected at random from a pack of 52.
   Find the probability that the card is:
   (i)   a spade or a club
   (ii) a queen or a red card
   (iii) a heart or a red picture card
   (iv) not a heart or a red picture card.

10. Two unbiased dice, one red and the other blue, are thrown together.
    Calculate the probability that:
    (i)   the numbers are the same or the sum of the numbers is 10
    (ii) the sum of the numbers is 8 or the difference between the two numbers is 2.

Multiplication Rule (AND)

Successive events

> The probability that two events, A and then B, both happen, and in that order is given by:
> $$P(A \text{ and } B) = P(A) \times P(B)$$
> where $P(B)$ has been worked out assuming that A has already occurred.

Order must be taken into account. Also, be very careful where the outcome at one stage does affect the outcome at the next stage.

> When the question says **and**, then multiply

The multiplication rule helps reduce the need to make out a sample space diagram.

Example ▼

An unbiased die is thrown and a fair coin is tossed. Find the probability of getting a 5 and a head.

Solution:
$$P(5) = \tfrac{1}{6}, \qquad P(H) = \tfrac{1}{2}$$
$$P(5 \text{ and an } H) = P(5) \times P(H) \qquad \text{('and' means multiply)}$$
$$= \tfrac{1}{6} \times \tfrac{1}{2}$$
$$= \tfrac{1}{12}$$

Two unbiased dice are thrown. What is the probability of getting two 4s?

Solution:

$$P(\text{4 on the first die}) = \tfrac{1}{6} \qquad\qquad P(\text{4 on the second die}) = \tfrac{1}{6}$$

$$P(\text{two 4s}) = P(\text{4 on the first die}) \times P(\text{4 on the second die})$$

$$= \tfrac{1}{6} \times \tfrac{1}{6} \quad (\text{'and' means multiply})$$

$$= \tfrac{1}{36}$$

Note: A sample space diagram could have been used instead on the last two examples.

Aideen and Bernadette celebrate their birthdays in a particular week (Monday to Sunday inclusive). Assuming that the birthdays are equally likely to fall on any day of the week, what is the probability that:

(i) both people were born on a Wednesday

(ii) one was born on a Monday and the other was born on a Friday?

Solution:

Method 1: Represent the situation with a sample space diagram.

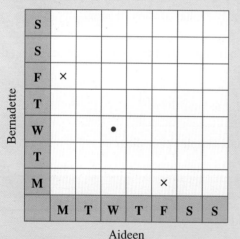

There are $7 \times 7 = 49$ possible outcomes.

● represents both people born on Wednesday.

× represents one person born on Monday and the other person born on Friday.

(i) $P(\text{both people born on Wednesday}) = \tfrac{1}{49}$

(ii) $P(\text{one person born on Monday and the other born on Friday}) = \tfrac{2}{49}$

266

Method 2: Using the rules of probability.

P(any person was born on a particular day of the week) $= \frac{1}{7}$.

Let A_M stand for Aideen was born on Monday, B_F stand for Bernadette was born on Friday, etc.

(i) P(both people were born on a Wednesday)

$= P(A_W \text{ and } B_W)$

$\downarrow$

$= P(A_W) \times P(B_W)$ (and means multiply)

$= \frac{1}{7} \times \frac{1}{7}$

$= \frac{1}{49}$

(ii) P(one was born on Monday and the other was born on Friday)

$= P(A_M \text{ and } B_F)$ or $A_F \text{ and } B_M$

$= P(A_M \text{ and } B_F)$ or $P(A_F \text{ and } B_M)$

$\qquad \downarrow \qquad\qquad \downarrow \qquad\qquad \downarrow$

$= P(A_M) \times P(B_F)$ $+$ $P(A_F) \times P(B_M)$ ('and' means multiply, 'or' means add)

$= \frac{1}{7} \times \frac{1}{7}$ $+$ $\frac{1}{7} \times \frac{1}{7}$

$= \frac{1}{49} + \frac{1}{49}$

$= \frac{2}{49}$

In the next example, the first event affects the outcome of the second event.

Example ▼

A bag contains 4 blue discs and 2 red discs. A disc is chosen at random from the bag and not replaced. A second disc is then chosen from the bag. Find the probability that:

(i)   both discs are blue

(ii)   the first disc is red and the second disc is blue

(iii)   one disc is blue and the other red (in any order).

Solution:

Let B_1 represent that a blue disc is chosen first and R_2 represent that a red disc is chosen second and so on.

(i) P(both discs are blue)

$= P(B_1 \text{ and } B_2)$

$\downarrow$

$= P(B_1) \times P(B_2)$

$= \frac{4}{6} \times \frac{3}{5}$ ('and' means multiply)

$= \frac{12}{30} = \frac{2}{5}$

$P(B_1) = \dfrac{4}{6}$

$P(B_2) = \dfrac{3}{5}$ $\left(\begin{array}{c} \text{1 blue has been removed,} \\ \text{3 blue and 2 red left} \end{array} \right)$

(ii) P(the first disc is red and the second disc is blue)

$= P(R_1 \text{ and } B_2)$

$\downarrow$

$= P(R_1) \times P(B_2)$

$= \frac{2}{6} \times \frac{4}{5}$ ('and' means multiply)

$= \frac{8}{30} = \frac{4}{15}$

$$P(R_1) = \frac{2}{6}$$

$$P(B_2) = \frac{4}{5} \left(\begin{matrix} 1 \text{ red has been removed,} \\ 4 \text{ blue and 1 red left} \end{matrix} \right)$$

(iii) P(one disc is blue and the other is red)

$= P$(blue first **and** a red second **or** a red first and a blue second)

$= P(B_1 \text{ and } R_2 \qquad \text{or} \qquad R_1 \text{ and } B_2)$

$= P(B_1 \text{ and } R_2) \qquad \text{or} \qquad P(R_1 \text{ and } B_2)$

$\qquad\qquad \downarrow \qquad\qquad\qquad \downarrow \qquad\qquad\qquad \downarrow$

$= P(B_1) \times P(R_2) \quad + \quad P(R_1) \times P(B_2)$ ('and' means multiply, 'or' means add)

$= \frac{4}{6} \times \frac{2}{5} \qquad\qquad + \qquad \frac{2}{6} \times \frac{4}{5}$

$= \frac{8}{30} + \frac{8}{30}$

$= \frac{16}{30} = \frac{8}{15}$

Exercise 12.10 ▼

1. A fair coin is tossed and an unbiased die is thrown.
   Find the probability of:
   (i)   a head and a 4   (ii)   a tail and an odd number
   (iii) a tail and a number greater than 2   (iv) a head and a number divisible by 3.

2. Two unbiased dice are thrown, one red and the other blue. What is the probability of:
   (i)   a score of 5 on the red die and a score of 3 on the blue die
   (ii)   a score of 4 on the blue die and an odd score on the red die
   (iii) an odd score on the blue die and an even score on the red die?

3. A bag contains 4 red discs and 2 blue discs. A disc is selected at random and not replaced.
   A second disc is then selected.
   Find the probability that:
   (i)   both discs are red   (ii)   both discs are blue
   (iii) the first disc is red and the second disc is blue   (iv) both discs are of different colours.

4. The letters in the word *ARRANGER* are written on individual cards and the cards are then put into
   a box. A card is selected at random and then replaced. A second card is then selected.
   Find the probability of obtaining:
   (i)   the letter A twice   (ii)   the letter R twice
   (iii) the letter R and N, in that order   (iv) the letter R and N, in any order.

5. A fair coin is tossed and a fair five-sided spinner, with sides A, A, B, B, B, is spun.

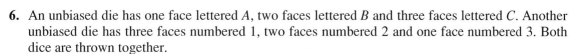

Find the probability of:

(i) a head and an A

(ii) a tail and a B

(iii) a head and an A or a tail and a B

(iv) a tail and a A or a head and a A.

6. An unbiased die has one face lettered A, two faces lettered B and three faces lettered C. Another unbiased die has three faces numbered 1, two faces numbered 2 and one face numbered 3. Both dice are thrown together.

Calculate the probability of obtaining:

(i) a C and a 2

(ii) a B and a 1

(iii) an A and a 3 or a C and a 1

(iv) a B and a 2 or a C and a 3.

7. Box 1 has 4 red cones and 1 blue cone.
Box 2 has 1 red cone and 3 blue cones.
A cone is chosen at random from box 1 and then a cone is chosen at random from box 2.

Find the probability that:

(i) both are red

(ii) both are blue

(iii) the first is red and the second is blue

(v) the first is blue and the second is red

(v) one is red and the other is blue (in any order).

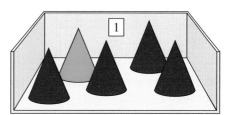
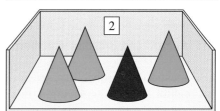

8. A bag contains 6 red and 2 yellow counters.

(i) A counter is drawn at random from the bag and replaced. Then a second counter is drawn at random.

Find the probability that:

(a) the first is yellow

(b) the first is red and the second is yellow

(c) one is red and the other is yellow

(d) both are the same colour.

(ii) If the first counter drawn is not replaced, find the probability that:

(a) the first is yellow and the second is red

(b) one is yellow and the other is red, in any order

(c) both are the same colour.

9. A bag contains 5 black beads and 3 yellow beads. A bead is chosen at random from the bag and not replaced. A second bead is then chosen from the bag.

   Find the probability that:

   (i) both beads are black

   (ii) both beads are yellow

   (iii) the first bead is yellow and the second bead is black

   (iv) both beads are of different colours.

10. A group of people in a room consists of 5 girls and 4 boys. When the door is open they leave the room one at a time in random order.

    Find the probability that:

    (i) the first person is a girl

    (ii) the first person is a boy

    (iii) the first person is a girl and the second person is a girl

    (iv) the first person is a boy and the second person is a girl

    (v) the first two are of different gender.

11. Andrew and Brendan celebrate their birthdays in a particular week (Monday to Sunday inclusive). Assuming that the birthdays are equally likely to fall on any day of the week, what is the probability that:

    (i) Andrew is born on Monday

    (ii) Brendan is born on Tuesday

    (iii) both were born on Thursday

    (iv) one was born on Wednesday and the other was born on Sunday

    (v) both were born on the same day

    (vi) Andrew and Brendan were born on different days?

Note: In questions on probability, selecting two objects at random is equivalent to selecting one object at random and not replacing it, then selecting a second object at random.

12. A bag contain 10 discs. Five are red, three are blue and the remainder are yellow. Two discs are selected at random from the bag.

    Find the probability that:

    (i) the two discs are red

    (ii) one is blue and the other is yellow, in any order

    (iii) one is red and the other is blue, in any order

    (iv) the two discs are the same colour.

13. A committee of two people is chosen at random from five men and four women.

    What is the probability that there will be one man and one woman or two women on the committee?

14. A bag contains 10 identical marbles, except for colour, four of which are white and the remainder black. Three marbles are removed at random, one at a time, without replacement.

    Find the probability that:

    (i) all are black

    (ii) the first is black and the second and third are white.

TRIGONOMETRY

Trigonometric Ratios and Right-angled Triangles

In a right-angled triangle, special ratios exist between the angles and the lengths of the sides. We look at three of these ratios.

Consider the right-angled triangle below with the acute angle θ:

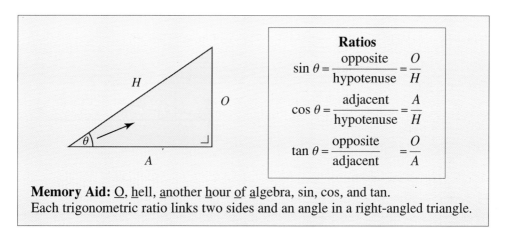

Ratios

$$\sin \theta = \frac{\text{opposite}}{\text{hypotenuse}} = \frac{O}{H}$$

$$\cos \theta = \frac{\text{adjacent}}{\text{hypotenuse}} = \frac{A}{H}$$

$$\tan \theta = \frac{\text{opposite}}{\text{adjacent}} = \frac{O}{A}$$

Memory Aid: <u>O</u>, <u>h</u>ell, <u>a</u>nother <u>h</u>our <u>o</u>f <u>a</u>lgebra, sin, cos, and tan.
Each trigonometric ratio links two sides and an angle in a right-angled triangle.

Notes:

1. The side opposite the right angle is called the **hypotenuse, H**. The side opposite the angle θ is called the **opposite, O**. The other side near the angle θ is called the **adjacent, A**.
2. If the lengths of any two sides are known, the third side can be found using Pythagoras's theorem: $A^2 + O^2 = H^2$, where A, O and H are the lengths of the sides.
3. The three angles of a triangle add up to $180°$.
4. Sin, cos and tan are short for sine, cosine, and tangent, respectively.
5. The arrow points to the side opposite the angle under consideration.
6. θ is a Greek letter, pronounced theta, often used to indicate an angle.

We can write trigonometric ratios for the two acute angles in a right-angled triangle. Make sure you know which angle you are using and which sides are the opposite and adjacent (the hypotenuse is always opposite the right angle). A good idea is to draw an arrow from the angle under consideration to indicate the opposite side to the angle. If we are given one trigonometric ratio we can find the other two trigonometric ratios by representing the situation with a right-angled triangle and using Pythagoras's theorem to find the missing side.

Example ▼

$\sin \theta = \dfrac{5}{13}$, where $0° < \theta < 90°$.

(i) Find, as fractions, the value of $\cos \theta$ and the value of $\tan \theta$.

(ii) Show that $\cos^2 \theta + \sin^2 \theta = 1$.

(iii) Find the measurement of angle θ, correct to the nearest degree.

Solution:

(i) From the trigonometric ratio given, sketch a right-angled triangle to represent the situation and use Pythagoras's theorem to find the missing side.

Given: $\sin \theta = \dfrac{5}{13}$

Opposite = 5, Hypotenuse = 13, let the Adjacent = x.

$x^2 + 5^2 = 13^2$ (Pythagoras's Theorem)

$x^2 + 25 = 169$

$x^2 = 144$

$x = \sqrt{144} = 12$

$\cos \theta = \dfrac{A}{H} = \dfrac{12}{13}$

$\tan \theta = \dfrac{O}{A} = \dfrac{5}{12}$

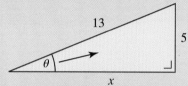

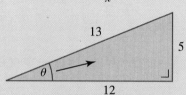

(ii) $\cos^2 \theta + \sin^2 \theta$

$= \left(\dfrac{12}{13}\right)^2 + \left(\dfrac{5}{13}\right)^2$

$= \dfrac{144}{169} + \dfrac{25}{169}$

$= \dfrac{169}{169} = 1$

(iii) Given: $\sin \theta = \dfrac{5}{13}$

$\theta = \sin^{-1} \dfrac{5}{13}$

$\theta = 22.61986495°$

$\theta = 23°$ (nearest degree)

([⌨] [2nd F] [sin] 5 [$a\frac{b}{c}$] 13 [=])

Notes:

1. $\cos^2 \theta = (\cos \theta)^2$, $\sin^2 \theta = (\sin \theta)^2$ and $\tan^2 \theta = (\tan \theta)^2$

2. If $\frac{5}{13}$ is keyed in as 5 [÷] 13 then brackets must be used: [⌨] [2nd F] [sin] [(] 5 [÷] 13 [)] [=]

In each case of the right-angled triangles, write down the value of the ratios:

(i) sin A **(ii)** cos A **(iii)** tan A **(iv)** sin B **(v)** cos B **(vi)** tan B

1.
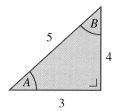

2.
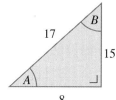

3.
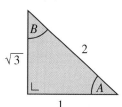

Evaluate each of the following:

4. $3^2 + 1^2$ **5.** $1^2 + (\sqrt{3})^2$ **6.** $2^2 - (\sqrt{3})^2$ **7.** $(\sqrt{13})^2 - 3^2$

Use Pythagoras's theorem to find x, the length of the missing side, in surd form where necessary, and express sin θ, cos θ and tan θ as simple fractions or as surd fractions in each of the following:

8.
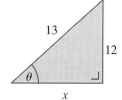

9.
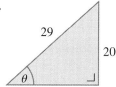

10.
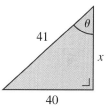

11.
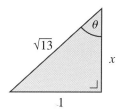

12.
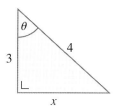

13.
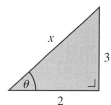

In each of the following, find the measure of the angle θ, where $0° < \theta < 90°$, correct to the nearest degree:

14. $\sin \theta = \dfrac{2}{3}$ **15.** $\cos \theta = \dfrac{4}{7}$ **16.** $\tan \theta = \dfrac{1}{8}$ **17.** $\sin \theta = 0.3$

18. $\tan \theta = 2$ **19.** $\cos \theta = \dfrac{3}{5}$ **20.** $\sin \theta = \dfrac{7}{10}$ **21.** $\tan \theta = \dfrac{1}{\sqrt{10}}$

22. $\cos \theta = \frac{4}{5}$, where $0° < \theta < 90°$.
  (i) Find, as fractions, the value of sin θ and the value of tan θ.
  (ii) Show that: **(a)** $\cos^2 \theta + \sin^2 \theta = 1$ **(b)** $\cos \theta + \sin \theta > \tan \theta$.
  (iii) Find the measure of the angle θ, correct to the nearest degree.

23. $\tan A = \frac{8}{15}$, where $0° < A < 90°$.
  (i) Find, as fractions, the value of sin A and the value of cos A.
  (ii) Show that cos A + sin A > tan A.
  (iii) Find the measure of the angle A, correct to the nearest degree.

24. $\sin \theta = \frac{7}{25}$, where $0° < \theta < 90°$.

   (i) Find, as fractions, the value of $\cos \theta$ and the value of $\tan \theta$.

   (ii) Show that $\cos^2 \theta + \sin^2 \theta = 1$.

25. $29 \sin \theta = 21$, where $0° < \theta < 90°$.

   If $\tan \theta = \dfrac{21}{k}$, find the value of k, $\quad k \in \mathbf{N}$.

26. The diagram shows a triangle with lengths of sides 3, 4 and 5.

   (i) Verify that $\dfrac{\sin \theta}{\cos \theta} = \tan \theta$.

   (ii) Evaluate $\sqrt{\dfrac{\sin \theta \tan \theta}{\cos \theta}}$

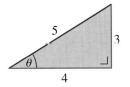

Notation

The diagram shows the **usual notation** for a triangle in trigonometry:

Vertices:	a, b, c
Angles:	A, B, C
Length of sides:	a, b, c

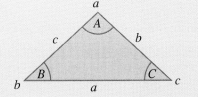

The lengths of the sides are denoted by a lower-case letter, and named after the angle they are opposite, i.e., a is opposite angle A, b is opposite angle B, and c is opposite angle C.

Using the terminology, we also have the following:

$$A = |\angle bac|, \quad B = |\angle abc|, \quad C = |\angle acb|$$
$$a = |bc|, \quad b = |ac|, \quad c = |ab|$$

Solving Right-angled Triangles

We can use a trigonometric ratio to calculate the length of a side in a right-angled triangle if we know the length of one side and one angle (other than the right angle). We can also find the size of an angle in a right-angled triangle if we know the lengths of two of its sides.

Summary of which trigonometric ratio to choose linking the given sides and angles:

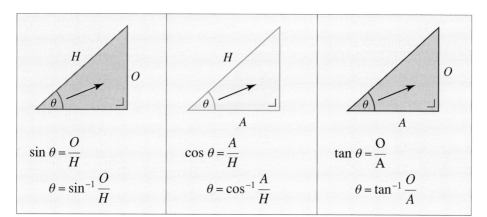

$$\sin \theta = \frac{O}{H}$$

$$\theta = \sin^{-1} \frac{O}{H}$$

$$\cos \theta = \frac{A}{H}$$

$$\theta = \cos^{-1} \frac{A}{H}$$

$$\tan \theta = \frac{O}{A}$$

$$\theta = \tan^{-1} \frac{O}{A}$$

Example ▼

In the diagram, $pr \perp qs$, $|\angle pqr| = 34°$,

    $|qr| = 15$ and $|rs| = 8$.

(i) Calculate $|pr|$, correct to two decimal places.

(ii) Hence, calculate $|\angle psr|$, correct to the nearest degree.

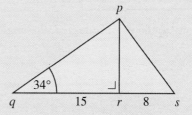

Solution:

Split the diagram up into two right-angled triangles.

(i) We require the opposite and know the adjacent.

Therefore, use the tan ratio.

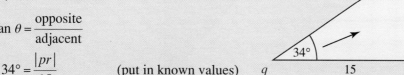

$$\tan \theta = \frac{\text{opposite}}{\text{adjacent}}$$

$$\tan 34° = \frac{|pr|}{15}$$ (put in known values)

$$15 \tan 34° = |pr|$$ (multiply both sides by 15)

$$10.11762775 = |pr|$$ (⌨ 15 ⊗ tan 34 =)

$$10.12 = |pr|$$ (correct to two decimal places)

(ii) We know the opposite, from part **(i)**, and the adjacent. Therefore, use the tan ratio. Let $S = |\angle psr|$.

$$\tan \theta = \frac{\text{opposite}}{\text{adjacent}}$$

$$\tan S = \frac{10.12}{8} \qquad \text{(put in known values)}$$

$$S = \tan^{-1}\left(\frac{10.12}{8}\right)$$

$$S = 51.67314168° \qquad (\boxed{\text{📠}}\ \boxed{\text{2nd F}}\ \boxed{\text{tan}}\ \boxed{(}\ 10.12\ \boxed{÷}\ 8\ \boxed{)}\boxed{=})$$

$$\therefore\ |\angle psr| = 52° \qquad \text{(correct to the nearest degree)}.$$

Note: In part **(ii)**, the question uses the word '**hence**'. Therefore, we must use the value $|pr| = 10.12$.

Exercise 13.2 ▼

Calculate, to the nearest degree, the angles marked with a letter:

1.
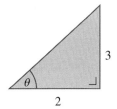
3
θ
2

2.
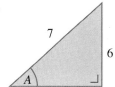
7
6
A

3.
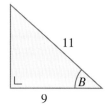
11
B
9

4.
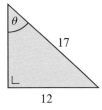
θ
17
12

5.
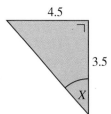
4.5
3.5
X

6.
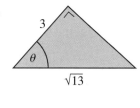
3
θ
$\sqrt{13}$

In each of the following calculate the length of the sides marked with a letter, correct to two decimal places:

7.
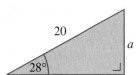
20
a
28°

8.
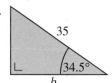
35
34.5°
b

9.
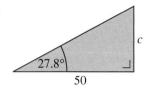
c
27.8°
50

10. In triangle abc, $|\angle abc| = 90°$,

$|ab| = 2$, and $|bc| = 1.5$.

Find:

(i) $|ac|$

(ii) $|\angle bac|$, correct to the nearest degree.

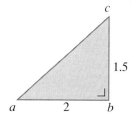

11. In the diagram, $xw \perp yz$,

$|xy| = 10$, $|\angle xyw| = 30°$ and $|wz| = \frac{2}{5}|xy|$.

Calculate:

(i) $|xw|$

(ii) $|\angle wxz|$, correct to the nearest degree.

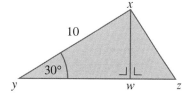

12. In the diagram, $|ab| = 16$ cm, and $|\angle abc| = 90°$.

The point d is on $[bc]$.

$|bd| = 30$ cm and $|ad| = |dc|$

Find:

(i) $|ad|$ **(ii)** $|bc|$

(iii) $|\angle acb|$, correct to the nearest degree.

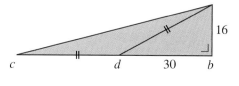

13. In the diagram, $|\angle abc| = 90°$, $|ac| = 17$,

$|bc| = 15$ and $|\angle bda| = 18°$.

Calculate:

(i) $|ab|$

(ii) $|cd|$, correct to two decimal places.

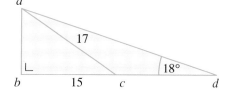

Practical Applications

Many practical problems in navigation, surveying, engineering and geography involve solving a triangle. In this section we will restrict the problems to those that involve right-angled triangles. When solving practical problems using trigonometry in this section, represent each situation with a right-angled triangle.

Mark on your triangle the angles and lengths you know, and label what you need to calculate, using the correct ratio to link the angle or length required with the known angle or length.

Angles of elevation, depression and compass directions

Angle of elevation

The **angle of elevation** of an object as seen by an observer is the angle between the horizontal line from the object to the observer's eye (upwards from the horizontal).

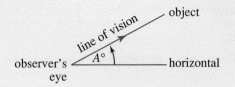

$A° =$ angle of elevation of object

Angle of depression

If the object is below the level of the observer, the angle between the horizontal and the observer's line of vision is called the **angle of depression** (downwards from the horizontal).

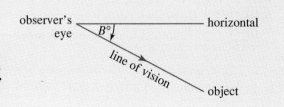

$B° =$ angle of depression of object

Note: An angle of elevation has an equal angle of depression. The angle of elevation from a to b is equal to the angle of depression from b to a. The angles are alternate angles, as the horizontal lines are parallel.

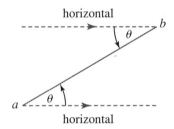

Compass directions

The direction of a point is stated as a number of degrees East or West of North and South.

A is N 60° E

B is N 40° W

C is S 45° W (or SW)

D is S 70° E

Note: N 60° E means start at North and turn 60° towards East.

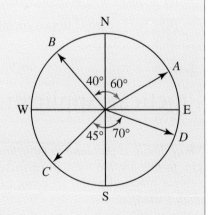

The diagram shows a ladder, 8 m in length, which leans against a vertical wall on level ground. The ladder makes an angle of 58° with the ground. Calculate the distance from the point where the ladder meets the wall, correct to two decimal places.

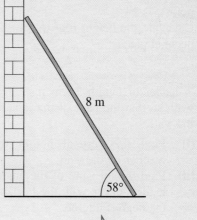

Solution:

Represent the situation with a right-angled triangle. Let d represent the distance from the point where the ladder meets the ground to the wall. We know the hypotenuse and require the adjacent. Therefore, use the cos ratio.

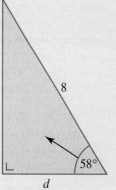

$$\cos\theta = \frac{\text{adjacent}}{\text{hypotenuse}}$$

$\cos 58° = \dfrac{d}{8}$ (put in known values)

$8\cos 58° = d$ (multiply both sides by 8)

$4.239354114 = d$ (🖩 8 × cos 58 =)

$4.24 = d$ (correct to two decimal places)

Therefore, the distance from the point where the ladder meets the ground to the wall is 4.24 m (correct to two decimal places).

1. From a point 12 m from the bottom of a wall, the angle of elevation to the top of the wall is 22°. Calculate the height of the wall, correct to two decimal places.

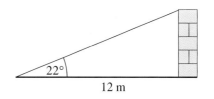

2. When the angle of elevation of the sun is 15°, an upright flagpole casts a shadow of length 18 m. Calculate the height of the pole, correct to one place of decimals.

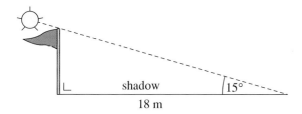

3. This distance of the point p, the top of a wall, from the point q on level ground, is 24 m.
The angle of elevation of the point p from the point q is 29°.
Calculate the height h of the wall, correct to two decimal places.

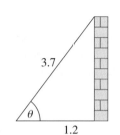

4. A ladder of length 3.7 m rests against a vertical wall, so that the base of the ladder is 1.2 m from the wall.

   (i) Find the vertical height that the ladder reaches on the wall.

   (ii) Find the measure of the angle, θ, which the ladder makes with the horizontal, correct to the nearest degree.

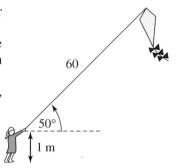

5. A girl is flying a kite. The length of string from her hand to the top of the kite is 60 m.
The string, which is being held 1 m above the ground, makes an angle of elevation of 50° with the horizontal.
Calculate the height of the kite above the ground, correct to the nearest metre.

6. From a boat at sea, the angle of elevation to the top of a vertical cliff, 200 m above sea level, is 14°.
After the boat has sailed directly towards the cliff, the angle of elevation of the cliff is found to be 28°. How far did the boat sail towards the cliff, correct to the nearest metre?

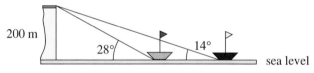

7. When a person stands on level ground at a point 100 m from the foot of a vertical cliff, the angle of elevation of the top of the cliff is 40°.
Calculate the height of the cliff, correct to the nearest metre.
If the person moves to a different point on level ground, 244 m from the foot of the cliff, what will then be the measure of the angle of elevation? Give your answer correct to the nearest degree.

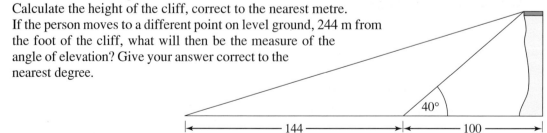

8. Copy the diagram and on it indicate the following directions:

   (i)   N 20° E

   (ii) S 60° W

   (iii) S 50° E

   (iv) N 70° W

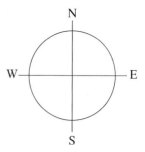

9. Two ships, *p* and *q*, leave a harbour *h* at the same time. *p*, the faster ship, sails in a direction S 70° E at 31 km/h. *q* sails in the direction S 20° W at *x* km/h. After two hours' sailing, the ships are 61 km apart. Calculate the distance travelled by ship *q*.

10. Two ships, *x* and *y*, left a harbour *o* at the same time. *x* travelled due north at 20 km/h while *y* travelled in the direction N 60° E. After one hour *y* was directly east of *x*. Calculate:

   (i)   the distance travelled by *y*

   (ii) the distance between the ships, correct to the nearest km.

11. On leaving a port *p*, a fishing boat sails in the direction South 30° East for 3 hours at 10 km/h, as shown.
What distance has the boat then sailed? The boat next sails in the direction North 60° East, at 10 km/h, until it is due East of the port *p*.
Calculate how far the boat is from the port *p*.

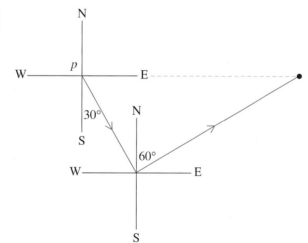

Solving Non-right-angled Triangles

Area of a Triangle

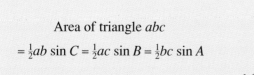

Area of triangle *abc*

$= \frac{1}{2}ab \sin C = \frac{1}{2}ac \sin B = \frac{1}{2}bc \sin A$

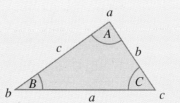

To use this formula to find the area of a triangle we need:
The length of two sides **and** the size of the angle between these sides.

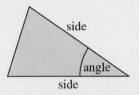

Area of triangle
$= \frac{1}{2}$ (length of side) × (length of side) × (sine of the angle between these sides)

Example ▼

In the triangle abc, $|ab| = 3$ cm, $|bc| = 10$ cm and $|\angle abc| = 62°$.
Calculate the area of triangle abc, correct to one decimal place.

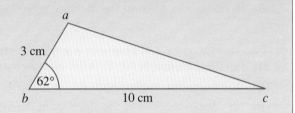

Solution:

Let $B = |\angle abc|$, $a = |bc|$ and $c = |ab|$.

$$\text{Area of triangle } abc = \tfrac{1}{2}ac \sin B$$
$$= \tfrac{1}{2}(10)(3)(\sin 62°)$$
$$= 13.24421389 \qquad (\boxed{\ } \; 1 \; \boxed{a\tfrac{b}{c}} \; 2 \; \boxed{\times} \; 10 \; \boxed{\times} \; 3 \; \boxed{\times} \; \boxed{\sin} \; 62 \; \boxed{=} \;)$$
$$= 13.2 \text{ cm}^2 \qquad \text{(correct to one decimal place)}$$

In some questions we are given an equation in disguise.

Example ▼

In the triangle abc, $|bc| = 25$ m and $|ac| = 14$ m.

If the area of triangle abc is 65 m^2, find $|\angle acb|$, correct to one decimal place.

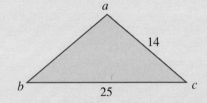

Solution:

Let $C = |\angle acb|$, $a = |bc|$ and $b = |ac|$.

Equation given in disguise:

$$\text{Area of triangle } abc = 65 \text{ m}^2$$
$$\therefore \quad \tfrac{1}{2}ab \sin C = 65$$
$$\tfrac{1}{2}(25)(14)\sin C = 65 \qquad \text{(put in known values)}$$
$$175 \sin C = 65$$
$$\sin C = \tfrac{65}{175} \qquad \text{(divide both sides by 175)}$$
$$\sin C = \tfrac{13}{35} \qquad (\tfrac{65}{175} = \tfrac{13}{35})$$
$$C = \sin^{-1} \tfrac{13}{35}$$
$$C = 21.80374799° \qquad (\boxed{\ } \; \boxed{\text{2nd F}} \; \boxed{\sin} \; 13 \; \boxed{a\tfrac{b}{c}} \; 35 \; \boxed{=} \;)$$
$$\therefore \quad |\angle acb| = 21.8° \qquad \text{(correct to one decimal place)}$$

Find, correct to two decimal places, the area of each of the following triangles, where the lengths of the sides are in cm:

1.
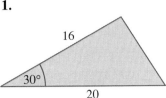

2.
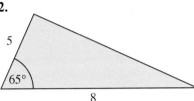

3.
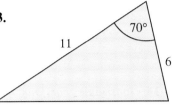

4.
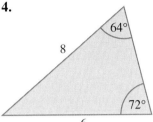

5.
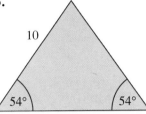

6.
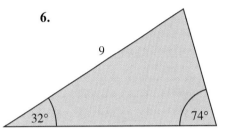

In the following questions a rough diagram may help:

7. In the triangle pqr, $|pr| = 8$ m, $|pq| = 7$ m and $|\angle qpr| = 54°$.
Calculate the area of triangle pqr.

8. In the triangle abc, $|bc| = 8$ cm, $|ac| = 10$ cm and $|\angle abc| = 48°$.
Calculate the area of triangle abc.

9. In the triangle pqr, $|qr| = 6$ m, $|pr| = 16$ m, $|\angle rpq| = 40°$ and $|\angle pqr| = 30°$.
Calculate the area of triangle pqr.

10. In the triangle abc, $|ac| = 14$ cm, $|\angle abc| = 70°$ and $|\angle bac| = 40°$.
Calculate the area of triangle abc.

11. The diagram shows the quadrilateral $pqsr$.
$qp \perp pr$, $|pq| = 2.4$ cm, $|pr| = 1.8$ cm, $|rs| = 2$ cm and $|\angle qrs| = 70°$.

Calculate:

(i) $|pq|$

(ii) the area of triangle pqr

(iii) the area of $pqsr$, correct to two places of decimals.

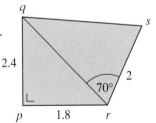

12. opq is a sector of a circle with a radius of 10 cm and $|\angle poq| = 36°$.

(i) Calculate the area of the sector opq.

Calculate, correct to one decimal place:

(ii) the area of triangle opq

(iii) the area of the shaded segment
(assume $\pi = 3.14$).

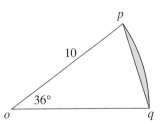

13. *oab* is a sector of a circle with a radius of 6 cm and $|\angle aob| = 150°$.

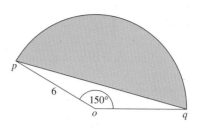

   (i)   Calculate the area of the sector *opq*.

   (ii) Calculate the area of the triangle *opq*.

   (iii) Calculate the area of the shaded segment (assume $\pi = 3.14$).

14. In triangle *pqr*, $|pq| = 8$ cm, $|\angle pqr| = 30°$.

   If the area of triangle *pqr* = 48 cm^2, calculate $|qr|$.

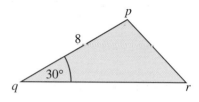

15. (i) Calculate sin 34° correct to two decimal places.

   (ii) In triangle *abc*, $|ab| = 20$ m, and $|\angle bac| = 34°$.

         If the area of triangle *abc* = 145.6 m^2, find $|ac|$, using the value of sin 34° obtained in part (i).

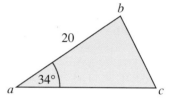

16. (i) Calculate sin 125°, correct to two decimal places.

   (ii) In triangle *pqr*, $|pq| = 20$ cm and $|\angle pqr| = 125°$.

         If the area of triangle *pqr* = 147.6 cm^2, find $|pr|$, using the value of sin 125° obtained in part (i).

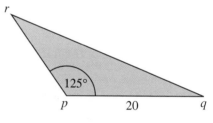

17. In the triangle *pqr*, $|pr| = 14$ m and $|qr| = 10$ m.

   If the area of triangle *pqr* is 45 m^2, calculate $|\angle prq|$, correct to the nearest degree.

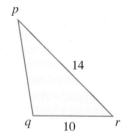

18. In the triangle *xyz*, $|xz| = 40$ cm and $|yz| = 50$ cm.

   If the area of triangle *xyz* is 940 cm^2, calculate $|\angle xzy|$, correct to the nearest degree.

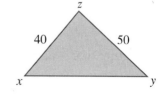

284

Sine Rule

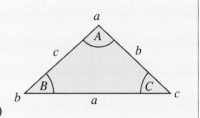

In any triangle *abc*:

$$\frac{a}{\sin A} = \frac{b}{\sin B} = \frac{c}{\sin C}$$

or:

$$\frac{\sin A}{a} = \frac{\sin B}{b} = \frac{\sin C}{c}$$

(The first form is given on page 9 of the tables)

This is known as the '**sine rule**' and it applies to any triangle, including a right-angled triangle.

The sine rule can be used to:

1. Find an unknown side, *a*. Using the sine rule we need: Two angles and one side. 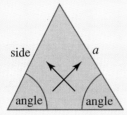 If we know two angles we can calculate the third angle, as the three angles add up to 180°.	**2.** Find an unknown angle, *A*°. Using the sine rule we need: Two sides and the size of one angle opposite one of these sides. 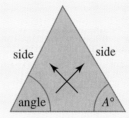 The unknown angle, *A*°, must be opposite a known side.

The sine rule connects each side with the angle opposite in a triangle.

Notes: 1. In practice we put only two fractions equal to each other, e.g.:

$$\frac{a}{\sin A} = \frac{b}{\sin B}$$

2. Put the required quantity, side or angle, on the top of the first fraction.

To find *a*, use $\dfrac{a}{\sin A} = \dfrac{b}{\sin B}$

To find *B*, use $\dfrac{\sin B}{b} = \dfrac{\sin A}{a}$

Example ▼

In the triangle abc, $|ac| = 7$ cm, $|\angle abc| = 30°$ and $|\angle acb| = 80°$.

Find $|ab|$, correct to two decimal places.

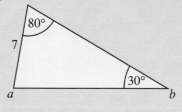

Solution:

Let $c = |ab|$, $b = |ac|$, $B = |\angle abc|$ and $C = |\angle acb|$.

Using the sine rule:

$$\frac{c}{\sin C} = \frac{b}{\sin B} \qquad \text{(c missing, so put that first)}$$

$$\frac{c}{\sin 80°} = \frac{7}{\sin 30°} \qquad \text{(put in known values)}$$

$$c = \frac{7 \sin 80°}{\sin 30°} \qquad \text{(multiply both sides by $\sin 80°$)}$$

$$c = 13.78730854 \qquad (\boxed{⊞}\; 7\; \boxed{×}\; \boxed{\sin}\; 80\; \boxed{÷}\; \boxed{\sin}\; 30\; \boxed{=}\;)$$

$$\therefore \quad |ab| = 13.79 \text{ cm} \qquad \text{(correct to two decimal places)}$$

Example ▼

In the triangle pqr, $|qr| = 10$ m, $|pr| = 8$ m and $|\angle pqr| = 42°$.

Find $|\angle qpr|$, correct to the nearest degree.

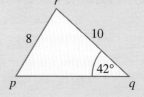

Solution:

Let $p = |qr|$, $q = |pr|$, $Q = |\angle pqr|$ and $P = |\angle qpr|$.

Using the sine rule:

$$\frac{\sin P}{p} = \frac{\sin Q}{q} \qquad \text{(P missing, so put that first)}$$

$$\frac{\sin P}{10} = \frac{\sin 42°}{8} \qquad \text{(put in known values)}$$

$$\sin P = \frac{10 \sin 42°}{8} \qquad \text{(multiply both sides by 10)}$$

$$P = \sin^{-1}\left(\frac{10 \sin 42°}{8}\right)$$

$$P = 56.76328432 \qquad (\boxed{⊞}\; \boxed{\text{2nd F}}\; \boxed{\sin}\; \boxed{(}\; 10\; \boxed{×}\; \boxed{\sin}\; 42\; \boxed{÷}\; 8\; \boxed{)}\; \boxed{=}\;)$$

$$\therefore \quad |\angle qpr| = 57° \qquad \text{(correct to the nearest degree)}$$

In Q1 to Q6, find the value of *a*, correct to two decimal places, and find the value of *A*, correct to the nearest degree.

1.

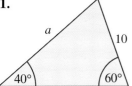

2.

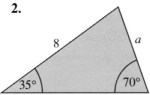

3.

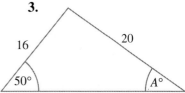

4.

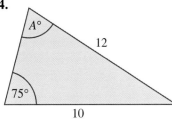

5.

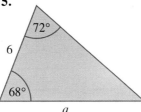

6.

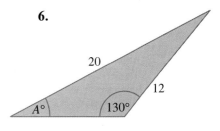

7. In the triangle *pqr*, $|qr| = 7$ cm, $|\angle qpr| = 30°$
and $|\angle pqr| = 84°$.
Calculate:
(i) $|pr|$
(ii) $|pq|$
correct to two decimal places.

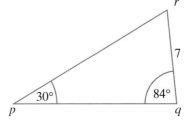

8. In the triangle *pqr*, $|pr| = 10$ cm, $|\angle qpr| = 70°$
and $|\angle pqr| = 45°$.
(i) Find $|\angle prq|$.
Calculate, correct to two decimal places,
(ii) $|qr|$
(iii) $|pq|$.

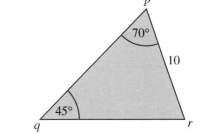

9. In the triangle *abc*, $|ac| = 4$ cm, $|ab| = 6$ cm
and $|\angle acb| = 37°$.
(i) Calculate $|\angle abc|$, correct to the nearest
degree.
(ii) Calculate $|bc|$, correct to the nearest cm.

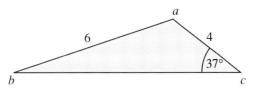

10. In the diagram, $pq \perp qr$, $|pq| = 8$ m, $|qr| = 15$ m.

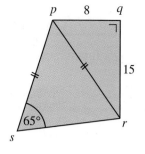

   (i) Find $|pr|$.

$|ps| = |pr|$ and $|\angle psr| = 65°$

   (ii) Find $|\angle spr|$.

   (iii) Find the area of triangle *prs*, correct to the nearest m².

   (iv) Find $|sr|$, correct to two decimal places.

11. In the diagram, $pq \perp sq$, $|sr| = 60$ m,
$|\angle psr| = 42°$ and $|\angle prq| = 65°$.

Calculate:

   (i) $|\angle spr|$

   (ii) $|pr|$, correct to the nearest m.

Hence, or otherwise, calculate $|pq|$, correct to the nearest m.

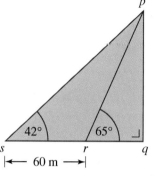

Cosine Rule

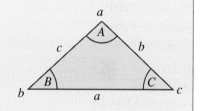

In any triangle *abc*:

    $a^2 = b^2 + c^2 - 2bc \cos A$

or $b^2 = a^2 + c^2 - 2ac \cos B$

or $c^2 = a^2 + b^2 - 2ab \cos C$

(The first form is given on page 9 of the tables)

This is known as the '**cosine rule**' and it applies to any triangle, including a right-angled triangle.

The cosine rule can be used to:

1. Find the length of the third side, *a*, of a triangle when given the lengths of the other two sides and the angle contained between these sides.

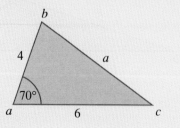

2. Find the measure of an angle, *A*, of a triangle when given the lengths of the three sides.

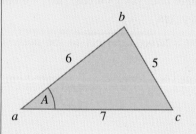

Note: In 1 and 2 above the sine rule would not work.
If the unknown angle is between 90° and 180° its cosine is negative.

For example, $\cos 120° = -\frac{1}{2}$

The largest angle of a triangle is opposite the largest side and the smallest angle is opposite the shortest side. There can be only one obtuse angle in a triangle.

Example ▼

In the triangle abc, $|bc| = 16$ cm, $|ac| = 12$ cm and $|\angle acb| = 43°$.

Calculate $|ab|$, correct to two decimal places.

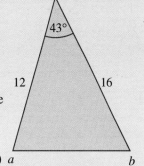

Solution:

Let $c = |ab|$, $a = |bc|$, $b = |ac|$ and $C = |\angle acb|$.
Using the cosine rule:

(**Note:** Because we want to find c, write down the form of the cosine rule that has c^2 on its own)

$$c^2 = a^2 + b^2 - 2ab \cos C$$
$$c^2 = (16)^2 + (12)^2 - 2(16)(12) \cos 43° \qquad \text{(put in known values)}$$
$$c^2 = 256 + 144 - 2(16)(12)(0.7313537016)$$
$$c^2 = 119.1601786$$
$$c = \sqrt{119.1601786}$$
$$c = 10.91605142$$
$$\therefore \ |ab| = 10.92 \text{ cm} \qquad \text{(correct to two decimal places)}$$

Example ▼

In the triangle pqr, $|qr| = 3$ cm, $|pr| = 5$ cm and $|pq| = 7$ cm.

Calculate $|\angle qpr|$, correct to the nearest degree.

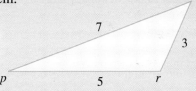

Solution:

Let $p = |qr|$, $q = |pr|$, $r = |pq|$ and $P = |\angle qpr|$.
Using the cosine rule:

(**Note:** Because we want to find the angle P, write down the form of the cosine rule that contains $\cos P$)

$$p^2 = q^2 + r^2 - 2qr \cos P$$
$$3^2 = 5^2 + 7^2 - 2(5)(7) \cos P \qquad (p = 3, q = 5, r = 7)$$
$$9 = 25 + 49 - 70 \cos P$$
$$9 = 74 - 70 \cos P$$
$$70 \cos P = 65$$
$$\cos P = \frac{65}{70} \qquad \text{(divide both sides by 70)}$$
$$\cos P = \frac{13}{14} \qquad \left(\frac{65}{70} = \frac{13}{14}\right)$$
$$P = \cos^{-1} \frac{13}{14}$$
$$P = 21.7867893 \qquad (\boxed{} \ \boxed{\text{2nd F}} \ \boxed{\cos} \ 13 \ \boxed{a \frac{b}{c}} \ 14 \ \boxed{=})$$
$$\therefore \ |\angle qpr| = 22° \qquad \text{(correct to the nearest degree)}$$

Use the cosine rule to calculate, in the triangles below:

(i) *a*, correct to two decimal places **(ii)** *A*, correct to the nearest degree:

1.

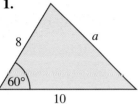

2.

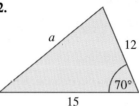

3.

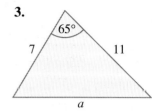

4.

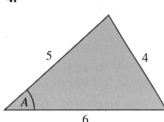

5.

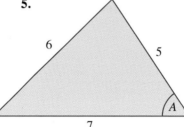

6.

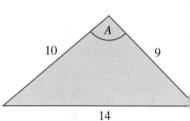

7. In the triangle *abc*, $|ab| = 7$ cm, $|ac| = 4$ cm and $|bc| = 9$ cm.

Calculate the measure of the greatest angle, correct to one decimal place.

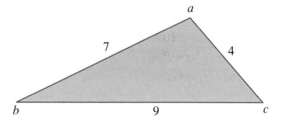

8. In the triangle *xyz*, $|xy| = 6$ cm, $|xz| = 8$ cm and $|yz| = 4$ cm.

Calculate the measure of the smallest angle, correct to the nearest degree.

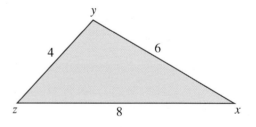

9. In the diagram, $|ab| = 5$ cm, $|ac| = 3$ cm, $|bd| = 8$ cm, $|cd| = 4$ cm and $|\angle bac| = 120°$.
  (i) Calculate $|bc|$
  (ii) Find the measure of $|\angle bdc|$, correct to the nearest degree.

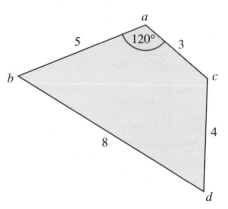

More Difficult Problems and Practical Applications

In more advanced problems, it is usual that one, or more, preliminary steps are necessary before the required side or angle is found. In many cases two triangles are linked. It is good practice in these cases to redraw the situation so as to have two separate triangles. As a general rule, if you cannot use the sine rule then use the cosine rule, and vice versa.

Example ▼

In the diagram, $|pq| = 6$ cm, $|pr| = 5$ cm, $|qr| = 4$ cm and $|\angle psr| = 22°$.

Calculate, correct to one decimal place:

(i) $|\angle qpr|$ **(ii)** $|rs|$.

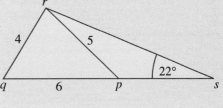

Solution:

Two triangles are linked. Therefore, we redraw the two triangles separately.

1. Consider triangle pqr:

Let $p = |qr|$, $q = |pr|$, $r = |pq|$ and $P = |\angle qpr|$.

We use the cosine rule to calculate P.

$$p^2 = q^2 + r^2 - 2qr \cos P$$
$$4^2 = 5^2 + 6^2 - 2(5)(6) \cos P \quad \text{(put in known values)}$$
$$16 = 25 + 36 - 60 \cos P$$
$$16 = 61 - 60 \cos P$$
$$60 \cos P = 45$$
$$\cos P = \tfrac{45}{60} \quad \text{(divide both sides by 60)}$$
$$\cos P = \tfrac{3}{4} \quad \left(\frac{45}{60} = \frac{3}{4}\right)$$
$$P = \cos^{-1} \tfrac{3}{4}$$
$$P = 41.40962211 \quad (\boxed{⌨}\ \boxed{\text{2nd F}}\ \boxed{\cos}\ 3\ \boxed{a\tfrac{b}{c}}\ 4\ \boxed{=})$$

$\therefore \quad |\angle qpr| = 41.4°$ (correct to one decimal place)

$\therefore \quad |\angle rps| = 180° - 41.4°$

$\quad\quad\quad\quad = 138.6°$

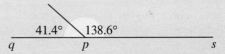

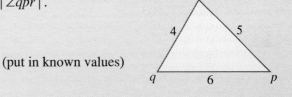

2. Consider triangle prs:

Let $p = |rs|$, $s = |pr|$, $P = |\angle rps|$ and $S = |\angle rsp|$.

We now use the sine rule to find p.

$$\frac{p}{\sin P} = \frac{s}{\sin S}$$
$$\frac{p}{\sin 138.6°} = \frac{5}{\sin 22°} \quad \text{(put in known values)}$$
$$p = \frac{5 \sin 138.6°}{\sin 22°} \quad \text{(multiply both sides by } \sin 138.6°\text{)}$$
$$p = 8.826751543 \quad (\boxed{⌨}\ 5\ \boxed{\times}\ \boxed{\sin}\ 138.6\ \boxed{\div}\ \boxed{\sin}\ 22\ \boxed{=})$$

$\therefore \quad |rs| = 8.8$ cm (correct to one decimal place)

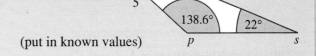

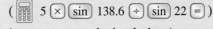

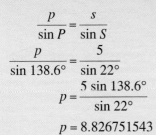

Example ▼

Two ships, a and b, leave a port c at noon.
a is travelling due East and b is travelling East 56° South.
Calculate, to the nearest km, the distance between a and b
when a is 6 km from c and b is 9 km from c.

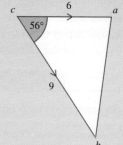

Solution:

Let $c = |ab|$, $b = |ac|$, $a = |bc|$ and $C = |\angle acb|$.
We have two sides and the included angle
∴ use the cosine rule.

$$c^2 = a^2 + b^2 - 2bc \cos C$$
$$c^2 = 9^2 + 6^2 - 2(9)(6) \cos 56° \qquad \text{(put in known values)}$$
$$c^2 = 81 + 36 - 108(0.559192903) \qquad (\cos 56° = 0.559192903)$$
$$c^2 = 117 - 60.39283357$$
$$c^2 = 56.60716643$$
$$c = \sqrt{56.60716643}$$
$$c = 7.523773417$$

∴ $|ab| = 8$ km   (correct to the nearest km)

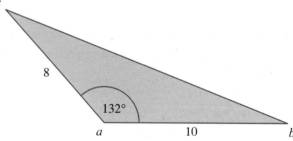

Exercise 13.7 ▼

1. In the triangle xyz, $|xy| = 4$ cm, $|yz| = 6$ cm and $|\angle xyz| = 55°$.
Calculate:

   (i) area of triangle xyz, correct to one decimal place

   (ii) $|xz|$, correct to the nearest cm

   (iii) $|\angle yzx|$, correct to the nearest degree.

2. In the triangle abc, $|ab| = 10$ cm,
$|ac| = 8$ cm and $|\angle bac| = 132°$.
Calculate:

   (i) area of triangle abc, correct to the
   nearest cm^2

   (ii) $|bc|$, correct to one decimal place

   (iii) $|\angle acb|$, correct to the nearest
   degree.

3. In the quadrilateral $pqrs$, $|pr| = 6$ units, $|qr| = 5$ units, $|\angle qrp| = 105°$, $|\angle prs| = 38°$ and $|\angle psr| = 62°$.

Calculate, correct to two decimal places:

(i) $|pq|$

(ii) $|rs|$

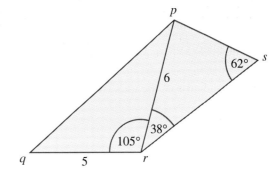

4. $pqrs$, is a quadrilateral, $|pq| = 4.8$ cm, $|qr| = 3.6$ cm, $|rs| = 4$ cm and $|\angle prs| = 54°$.

Calculate:

(i) $|pr|$

(ii) the area of triangle prs, correct to one decimal place

(iii) $|ps|$, correct to two decimal places.

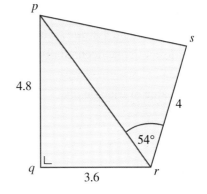

5. In the diagram, the triangle abc is right-angled. $|ab| = 5$, $|bc| = 12$, $|ac| = |ad|$ and ad is parallel to bc.

(i) Find the value of $|ac|$.

Calculate, correct to one decimal place:

(ii) $|\angle bac|$

(iii) $|dc|$.

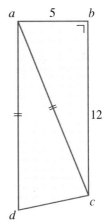

6. A garden, $pqrs$, is in the shape of a quadrilateral with $sp \perp pq$. $|pq| = 22.5$ m and $|ps| = 12$ m, $|sr| = 18$ m and $|\angle qsr| = 42°$.

Calculate:

(i) $|qs|$

(ii) $|rq|$, correct to the nearest m

(iii) the area of the field, correct to the nearest m^2.

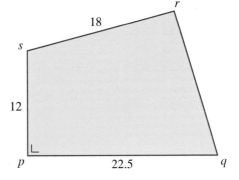

7. *pqrs* is a quadrilateral. $|qr| = 8$ cm, $|sr| = 6$ cm, $|\angle qrs| = 38.7°$ and $|\angle qps| = 75°$.

Calculate, correct to the nearest integer:

(i) $|qs|$

(ii) the area of the quadrilateral *pqrs*.

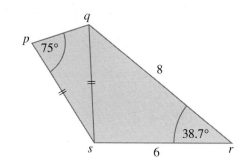

8. *abc* is a triangle and *d* is a point on [*bc*], as shown. $|bd| = 5$ cm, $|ac| = 8$ cm, $|\angle acd| = 70°$ and $|\angle dac| = 62°$.

Find, correct to one decimal place:

(i) $|dc|$

(ii) the area of triangle *abc*.

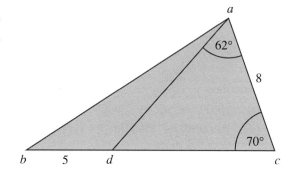

9. The goal posts on a soccer field are 8 m apart. A player kicks for a goal when he is 30 m from one post and 25 m from the other.

Find the angle opposite the goal line, measured from both goal posts to where the ball is positioned, correct to the nearest degree.

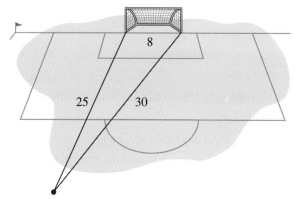

10. The 3rd hole on a golf course is 470 m from the tee. A ball is driven from the tee a distance of 260 metres. However, the drive is 10° off the line to the hole, as shown.

How far from the hole is the ball, correct to the nearest m?

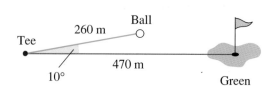

11. Two ships, h and k, set sail from a port, p, at the same time. h sails N 25° W at a steady speed. k sails N 55° E at a speed of 30 km/h. After two hours' sailing, h is directly west of k.

Calculate:

(i) the distance between the ships after two hours, correct to one decimal place

(ii) the average speed of ship h, correct to the nearest km/h.

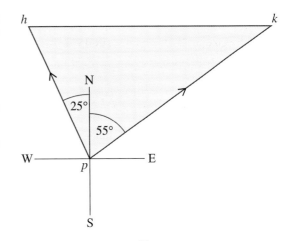

12. A ship, q, is 37 km from a port, p. The direction of q from p is N 45° E. A second ship, r, is 53 km from p. The direction of r from q is S 75° E.

Calculate:

(i) $|\angle qrp|$, correct to one decimal place

(ii) $|qr|$, correct to two decimal places.

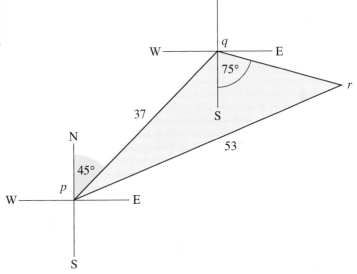

13. A surveyor wishes to measure the height of a church. Measuring the angle of elevation, she finds that the angle increases from 30° to 40° after walking 25 metres towards the church.

What is the height of the church? (Give your answer correct to the nearest m)

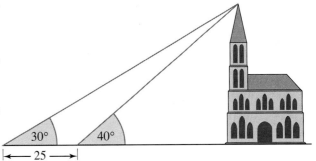

Special Angles: 45°, 30° and 60°

There are three special angles whose sine, cosine and tangent ratios can be expressed as simple fractions or surds.

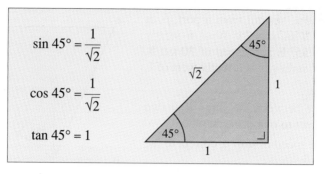

$$\sin 45° = \frac{1}{\sqrt{2}}$$

$$\cos 45° = \frac{1}{\sqrt{2}}$$

$$\tan 45° = 1$$

$$\sin 60° = \frac{\sqrt{3}}{2} \qquad \sin 30° = \frac{1}{2}$$

$$\cos 60° = \frac{1}{2} \qquad \cos 30° = \frac{\sqrt{3}}{2}$$

$$\tan 60° = \sqrt{3} \qquad \tan 30° = \frac{1}{\sqrt{3}}$$

These ratios can be used instead of a calculator.

These ratios are tabulated on page 9 of the maths tables. However, on this page the angles are measured in radians. To use this table we can convert radians to degrees by using the fact that:

$$\pi \text{ radians} = 180°$$

Thus

$\frac{\pi}{2}$ radians = 90°	$\frac{\pi}{3}$ radians = 60°	$\frac{\pi}{4}$ radians = 45°	$\frac{\pi}{6}$ radians = 30°

Example ▼

Without using a calculator, find the value of:

(i) $\tan 45° + \sin 30°$ **(ii)** $\sin^2 60° + \cos^2 45°$

Solution:

(i) $\tan 45° + \sin 30°$

$= 1 + \frac{1}{2}$

$= \frac{3}{2}$

(ii) $\sin^2 60° + \cos^2 45°$

$= \left(\frac{\sqrt{3}}{2}\right)^2 + \left(\frac{1}{\sqrt{2}}\right)^2$

$= \frac{3}{4} + \frac{1}{2} = \frac{5}{4}$

Note: $\sin^2 A = (\sin A)^2$, $\cos^2 A = (\cos A)^2$ and $\tan^2 A = (\tan A)^2$

1. Complete the following tables:

A	30°	45°	60°
cos A			
sin A		$\dfrac{1}{\sqrt{2}}$	
tan A			

A	30°	45°	60°
$\cos^2 A$			
$\sin^2 A$			
$\tan^2 A$		1	

Without using a calculator, evaluate each of the following exactly:

2. $\cos 60° + \sin 30°$

3. $\cos^2 45° + \sin 30°$

4. $1 + \tan^2 60°$

5. $\cos^2 45° + \tan 45°$

6. $\tan 45° - \tan^2 30°$

7. $2 \cos 30° \sin 60°$

8. $1 - \cos^2 30°$

9. $\cos^3 60° + \cos^2 45°$

10. $3 \tan^2 30° - 2 \cos 60°$

11. Verify that: **(i)** $\dfrac{1 + \tan 60° \tan 30°}{\cos^2 45°} = 4$ **(ii)** $\tan^2 30° \sin^2 60° = \tfrac{1}{4}$.

12. If $A = 30°$, verify that:
  (i) $\sin 2A = 2 \sin A \cos A$
  (ii) $\cos 2A = \cos^2 A - \sin^2 A$.

13. If $\theta = 60°$, verify that:
  (i) $\cos^2 \theta + \sin^2 \theta = 1$
  (ii) $\dfrac{\sin \theta}{\cos \theta} = \tan \theta$.

Compound Angles

A **compound angle** is an angle which is written as the sum or difference of two angles.
For example, $(A + B)$ and $(A - B)$ are compound angles.

Compound angle formulas:

> **1.** $\cos(A + B) = \cos A \cos B - \sin A \sin B$
>
> **2.** $\cos(A - B) = \cos A \cos B + \sin A \sin B$
>
> **3.** $\sin(A + B) = \sin A \cos B + \cos A \sin B$
>
> **4.** $\sin(A - B) = \sin A \cos B - \cos A \sin B$

1 and 3 are on page 9 of the tables.

A and B are acute angles where $\sin A = \frac{4}{5}$ and $\cos B = \frac{5}{13}$.

Find, as fractions, the value of:

(i) $\cos A$ **(ii)** $\sin B$ **(iii)** $\cos(A + B)$ **(iv)** $\sin 2A$ **(v)** $\cos 2A$

Solution:

Draw two right-angled triangles from the given information and use Pythagoras' theorem to find the missing sides.

(i)

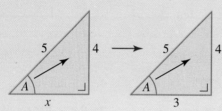

Given: $\sin A = \frac{4}{5}$

$$x^2 + 4^2 = 5^2$$
$$x^2 + 16 = 25$$
$$x^2 = 25 - 16$$
$$x^2 = 9$$
$$x = 3$$
$$\therefore \quad \cos A = \frac{3}{5}$$

(ii)

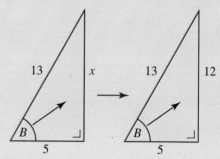

Given: $\cos B = \frac{5}{13}$

$$x^2 + 5^2 = 13^2$$
$$x^2 + 25 = 169$$
$$x^2 = 169 - 25$$
$$x^2 = 144$$
$$x = 12$$
$$\therefore \quad \sin B = \frac{12}{13}$$

(iii) From page 9

$$\cos(A + B) = \cos A \cos B - \sin A \sin B$$
$$= \frac{3}{5} \times \frac{5}{13} - \frac{4}{5} \times \frac{12}{13}$$
$$= \frac{15}{65} - \frac{48}{65} = -\frac{33}{65}$$

(iv) From page 9

$$\sin 2A = 2 \sin A \cos A$$
$$= \frac{2}{1} \times \frac{4}{5} \times \frac{3}{5}$$
$$= \frac{24}{25}$$

(v) From page 9

$$\cos 2A = \cos^2 A - \sin^2 A$$
$$= \left(\tfrac{3}{5}\right)^2 - \left(\tfrac{4}{5}\right)^2 = \frac{9}{25} - \frac{16}{25} = -\frac{7}{25}$$

Write sin 75° in surd form.

Solution:

We first express 75° as a combination of 30°, 45° or 60° and use page 9 of the tables.
$75° = 45° + 30°$

$$\sin(A + B) = \sin A \cos B + \cos A \sin B$$

$$\sin 75° = \sin(45° + 30°) = \sin 45° \cos 30° + \cos 45° \sin 30° \qquad \text{(let } A = 45° \text{ and } B = 30°)$$

$$= \frac{1}{\sqrt{2}} \times \frac{\sqrt{3}}{2} + \frac{1}{\sqrt{2}} \times \frac{1}{2}$$

$$= \frac{\sqrt{3}}{2\sqrt{2}} + \frac{1}{2\sqrt{2}}$$

$$= \frac{\sqrt{3} + 1}{2\sqrt{2}} \qquad \text{(same denominator)}$$

Exercise 13.9 ▼

1. θ is an acute angle where $\tan \theta = \frac{3}{4}$.
   Find, as fractions, the value of:
   (i) $\sin \theta$ (ii) $\cos \theta$ (iii) $\sin 2\theta$ (iv) $\cos 2\theta$.

2. A and B are acute angles where $\sin A = \frac{12}{13}$ and $\cos B = \frac{3}{5}$.
   Find, as fractions, the value of:
   (i) $\cos A$ (ii) $\sin B$ (iii) $\sin (A + B)$ (iv) $\cos (A + B)$.

3. A and B are acute angles where $\cos A = \frac{4}{5}$ and $\sin B = \frac{7}{25}$.
   Find, as fractions, the value of:
   (i) $\sin A$ (ii) $\cos B$ (iii) $\cos (A - B)$ (iv) $\cos 2B$.

4. A is an acute angle where $12 \tan A = 5$.
   Find, as fractions, the value of:
   (i) $\cos A$ (ii) $\sin A$ (iii) $\sin 2A$ (iv) $\cos^2 A$ (v) $\cos 2A$.

5. A and B are acute angles where $\tan A = \frac{7}{24}$ and $\tan B = \frac{8}{15}$.
   Find, as fractions, the value of:
   (i) $\sin A$ (ii) $\cos A$ (iii) $\sin B$ (iv) $\cos B$
   (v) $\sin(A + B)$ (vi) $\sin(A - B)$ (vii) $\cos(A + B)$ (viii) $\cos(A - B)$
   (ix) $\sin 2A$ (x) $\sin 2B$ (xi) $\cos 2A$ (xii) $\cos 2B$.

6. $\sin(A - B) = \sin A \cos B - \cos A \sin B$.

Use the $\sin(A - B)$ formula with $A = 60°$, $B = 45°$ to show that $\sin 15° = \dfrac{\sqrt{3} - 1}{2\sqrt{2}}$.

Write each of the following in surd form:

7. $\cos 75°$ **8.** $\sin 105°$ **9.** $\cos 15°$ **10.** $\cos 105°$

Verify that:

11. $\sin(A + B) + \sin(A - B) = 2 \sin A \cos B$ **12.** $\cos(45° - A) - \sin(45° + A) = 0$

Unit Circle

The unit circle has its centre at the origin $(0, 0)$ and the length of the radius is 1.

Take any point $p(x, y)$ on the circle, making an angle of θ at the centre.

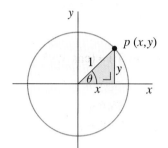

$$\cos \theta = \frac{x}{1} = x$$

$$\sin \theta = \frac{y}{1} = y$$

$$\tan \theta = \frac{y}{x} = \frac{\sin \theta}{\cos \theta}$$

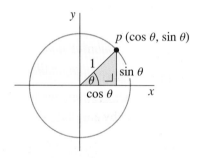

This very important result indicates that the coordinates of any point on the unit circle can be represented by $p(\cos \theta, \sin \theta)$, where θ is any angle.

As the point p rotates, θ changes. These definitions of $\cos \theta$ and $\sin \theta$ in terms of the coordinates of a point rotating around the unit circle apply for **all** values of the angle $\theta°$.

Memory Aid: (christian name, surname) = $(\cos \theta, \sin \theta) = (x, y)$.

Note: Using Pythagoras's theorem $\cos^2 \theta + \sin^2 \theta = 1$.

Values of sin, cos and tan for 0°, 90°, 180°, 270° and 360°

Both diagrams following represent the unit circle, but using two different notations to describe any point p on the circle.

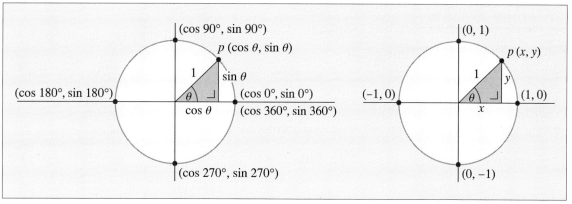

By comparing corresponding points on both unit circles, the values of sin, cos and tan for 0°, 90°, 180°, 270° and 360° can be read directly.

$(\cos 0°, \sin 0°) = (\cos 360°, \sin 360°) = (1, 0)$	$(\cos 90°, \sin 90°) = (0, 1)$
$\cos 0° = \cos 360° = 1$	$\cos 90° = 0$
$\sin 0° = \sin 360° = 0$	$\sin 90° = 1$
$\tan 0° = \tan 360° = \frac{0}{1} = 0$	$\tan 90° = \frac{1}{0}$ (undefined)
$(\cos 180°, \sin 180°) = (-1, 0)$	$(\cos 270°, \sin 270°) = (0, -1)$
$\cos 180° = -1$	$\cos 270° = 0$
$\sin 180° = 0$	$\sin 270° = -1$
$\tan 180° = \frac{0}{-1} = 0$	$\tan 270° = \frac{-1}{0}$ (undefined)

Note: Division by zero is undefined.

Example ▼

(i) Find the value of A for which $\cos A = -1$, $0° \leqslant A \leqslant 360°$.

(ii) If $0° \leqslant A \leqslant 360°$, find the value of A for which $\sin A = 1$.

(iii) If $0° \leqslant A \leqslant 360°$, find the values of A for which $\cos A = 0$.

(iv) Evaluate $\sin^2 270°$.

Solution:

Draw the unit circle.
Remember: (christian name, surname) = $(\cos \theta, \sin \theta) = (x, y)$.

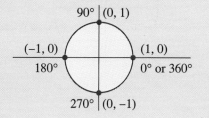

(i) $\cos A = -1$
      $A = 180°$

(ii) $\sin A = 1$
      $A = 90°$

(iii) $\cos A = 0$
      $A = 90°$ or $270°$

(iv) $\sin^2 270°$
      $= (\sin 270°)^2$
      $= (-1)^2 = 1$

Evaluate each of the following:

1. $\cos 90°$

2. $\sin 180°$

3. $\cos 0°$

4. $\sin 90°$

5. $\cos 180°$

6. $\sin 270°$

7. $\sin 360°$

8. $\cos 270°$

9. $\tan 180°$

10. $\dfrac{2\cos 180°}{\sin 90°}$

11. $\dfrac{3\sin 270°}{\cos^2 180°}$

12. $\dfrac{\sin^2 270° + \cos^2 180°}{2\cos 0°}$

13. $\sin 180° \cos 90° + \cos 180° \sin 90°$

14. $(\sin 90° - \cos 180°)^2$

Solve for A, where $0° \leqslant A \leqslant 360°$:

15. $\cos A = 1$

16. $\sin A = 1$

17. $\sin A = -1$

18. $\cos A = -1$

19. $\cos A = 0$

20. $\sin A = 0$

21. $\tan A = 0$

22. If $\cos A = 0$, find the two values of $\sin A$, when $0° \leqslant A \leqslant 360°$.

Trigonometric Ratios for Angles Between 0° and 360°

The x- and y-axes divide the plane into four quadrants. Consider the unit circle on the right:

$$\cos \theta = x \qquad \sin \theta = y$$

$$\tan \theta = \frac{\sin \theta}{\cos \theta} = \frac{y}{x}$$

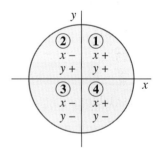

By examining the signs of x and y in the four quadrants, the signs of $\sin \theta$, $\cos \theta$, and $\tan \theta$ for any value of θ can be found.

Summary of signs

1st quadrant: sin, cos and tan are all positive.
2nd quadrant: sin is positive, cos and tan are negative.
3rd quadrant: tan is positive, sin and cos are negative.
4th quadrant: cos is positive, sin and tan are negative.

A very useful memory aid, *CAST*, in the diagram on the right, shows the ratios that are positive for the angles between 0° and 360°.

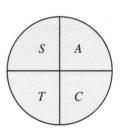

Method for finding the trigonometric ratio for any angle between 0° and 360°:

1. Draw a rough diagram of the angle.

2. Determine in which quadrant the angle lies and use to find its sign.

3. Find its **related** angle (the acute angle to the nearest horizontal).

4. Use the trigonometric ratio of the related angle with the sign in step 2.

Example ▼

Find sin 240°, leaving your answer in surd form.

Solution:

Surd form,   ∴ cannot use calculator.

1. The diagram shows the angle 240°.

2. 240° is in the 3rd quadrant.
   sin is negative in the 3rd quadrant.

3. Related angle is 60°.

4.   ∴ sin 240°

   $= -\sin 60°$

   $= -\dfrac{\sqrt{3}}{2}$

   (or use tables page 9)

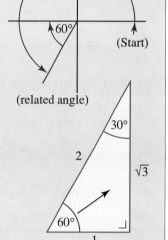

Exercise 13.11 ▼

Without using a calculator, evaluate each of the following exactly:

1. cos 120°   **2.** sin 150°   **3.** tan 240°

4. sin 210°   **5.** tan 135°   **6.** cos 135°

7. sin 300°   **8.** tan 210°   **9.** sin 315°

10. tan 330°   **11.** cos 150°   **12.** cos 225°

Solving Trigonometric Equations

Between 0° and 360° there may be two angles with the same trigonometric ratios.
For example, $\cos 120° = -\frac{1}{2}$ and $\cos 240° = -\frac{1}{2}$.

To solve a trigonometric equation, do the following:

1. Ignore the sign and calculate the related angle.

2. From the sign of the given ratio, decide in which quadrants the angles lie.

3. Using a rough diagram, state the angles between 0° and 360°.

Example ▼

If $\cos \theta = -\dfrac{1}{\sqrt{2}}$, find two values of θ between 0° and 360°.

Solution:

1. Find the related angle (ignore sign).

   If $\cos \theta = \dfrac{1}{\sqrt{2}}$,

   $\theta = 45°$

   The related angle is 45°.

   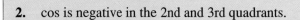

2. cos is negative in the 2nd and 3rd quadrants.

3. Rough diagram:

   $\theta =$ in the 2nd quadrant $\qquad\qquad$ $\theta =$ in the 3rd quadrant

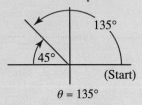

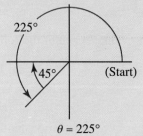

$\qquad\qquad$ Thus, if $\cos \theta = -\dfrac{1}{\sqrt{2}}$, $\qquad$ $\theta = 135°, 225°$

Find all the values of θ between $0°$ and $360°$ if:

1. $\sin \theta = \dfrac{1}{2}$

2. $\sin \theta = \dfrac{\sqrt{3}}{2}$

3. $\tan \theta = \dfrac{1}{\sqrt{3}}$

4. $\cos \theta = \dfrac{1}{2}$

5. $\sin \theta = \dfrac{1}{\sqrt{2}}$

6. $\tan \theta = \sqrt{3}$

7. $\tan \theta = 1$

8. $\cos \theta = \dfrac{\sqrt{3}}{2}$

9. $\sin \theta = -\dfrac{\sqrt{3}}{2}$

10. $\cos \theta = -\dfrac{\sqrt{3}}{2}$

11. $\sin \theta = -\dfrac{1}{\sqrt{2}}$

12. $\tan \theta = -\dfrac{1}{\sqrt{3}}$

13. $\sin \theta = -\dfrac{1}{2}$

14. $\tan \theta = -\sqrt{3}$

15. $\cos \theta = \dfrac{1}{\sqrt{2}}$

In questions 16–21, give your answers correct to the nearest degree:

16. $\sin \theta = 0.4$

17. $\cos \theta = 0.12$

18. $\tan \theta = 1.6$

19. $\cos \theta = -\dfrac{4}{5}$

20. $\tan \theta = -\dfrac{8}{15}$

21. $\sin \theta = -\dfrac{2}{3}$

SEQUENCES AND SERIES

Sequence

> A sequence is a set of numbers, separated by commas, in which each number after the first is formed by some definite rule.

Note: Each number in the set is called a **term** of the sequence.

1. 3, 7, 11, 15, ...

    Each number after the first is obtained by adding 4 to the previous number.

    In this example, 3 is called the **first term**, 7 the **second term** and so on.

2. 1, 3, 9, 27, ...

    Each number after the first is obtained by multiplying the previous number by 3.

    In this example, 1 is called the **first term**, 3 the **second term** and so on.

General Term, T_n

Very often a sequence is given by a **rule** which defines the **general term**. We use the symbol T_n to denote the general term of the sequence. T_n may be used to obtain any term of a sequence. T_1 will represent the first term, T_2 the second term and so on.

Notes:

1. The general term, T_n, is often called the nth term.

2. n used with this meaning must always be positive, a whole number.

    It can never be fractional or negative.

3. A sequence is often called a progression.

Consider the sequence whose general term is: $T_n = 3n + 2$.
We can find the value of any term of the sequence by putting in the appropriate value for n on both sides:

$$T_1 = 3(1) + 2 = 3 + 2 = 5 \quad \text{(first term, put in 1 for } n\text{)}$$
$$T_2 = 3(2) + 2 = 6 + 2 = 8 \quad \text{(second term, put in 2 for } n\text{)}$$
$$T_5 = 3(5) + 2 = 15 + 2 = 17 \text{ (fifth term, put in 5 for } n\text{)}$$

In each case n is replaced with the same number on both sides.
The notation $T_n = 3n + 2$ is very similar to function notation when n is the input and T_n is the output, i.e. (input, output) = (n, T_n).

The nth term of a sequence is given by $T_n = n^2 + 3$.

(i) Write down the first three terms of the sequence.

(ii) Show that: **(a)** $\dfrac{T_5}{T_2} = T_1$ **(b)** $2T_4 = T_6 - 1$.

Solution:

(i) $T_n = n^2 + 3$

$T_1 = 1^2 + 3 = 1 + 3 = 4$ (put in 1 for n)

$T_2 = 2^2 + 3 = 4 + 3 = 7$ (put in 2 for n)

$T_3 = 3^2 + 3 = 9 + 3 = 12$ (put in 3 for n)

Thus, the first three terms are 4, 7, 12.

(ii) $T_n = n^2 + 3$

(a) From (i), $T_1 = 4$ and $T_2 = 7$

$T_5 = 5^2 + 3 = 25 + 3 = 28$

$\dfrac{T_5}{T_2} = \dfrac{28}{7} = 4$

$T_1 = 4$

$\therefore \dfrac{T_5}{T_2} = T_1$

(b) $T_4 = 4^2 + 3 = 16 + 3 = 19$

$T_6 = 6^2 + 3 = 36 + 3 = 39$

$2T_4 = 2(19) = 38$

$T_6 - 1 = 39 - 1 = 38$

$\therefore \ 2T_4 = T_6 - 1$

Write down the next four terms in each of the following sequences:

1. 1, 5, 9, 13, ...

2. 40, 35, 30, 25, ...

3. −11, −9, −7, −5, ...

4. 13, 10, 7, 4, ...

5. 2.5, 2.9, 3.3, 3.7, ...

6. 2.8, 2.2, 1.6, 1, ...

7. 1, 2, 4, 8, ...

8. 2, 6, 18, 54, ...

9. 81, 27, 9, 3, ...

10. 3, −6, 12, −24, ...

Write down the first four terms of the sequence whose nth term is given by:

11. $T_n = 2n + 3$

12. $T_n = 3n + 1$

13. $T_n = 4n - 1$

14. $T_n = 5n - 3$

15. $T_n = 1 - 2n$

16. $T_n = 3 - 4n$

17. $T_n = n^2 + 5$

18. $T_n = n^2 + 2n$

19. $T_n = \dfrac{n+1}{n}$

20. $T_n = \dfrac{2n}{n+1}$

21. $T_n = 2^n$

22. $T_n = 3^n$

23. The nth term of a sequence is given by $T_n = 5n + 2$.

    (i) Write down the first three terms of the sequence.

    (ii) Show that: **(a)** $2T_5 = T_4 + T_6$ **(b)** $6(T_7 - 1) = T_2(T_3 + 1)$.

24. The nth term of a sequence is given by $T_n = n^2 + 2$.

    (i) Write down the first three terms of the sequence.

    (ii) Show that: **(a)** $\dfrac{T_4}{T_2} = T_1$ **(b)** $\dfrac{T_6 - 2}{T_4} = \dfrac{T_2}{T_1}$.

25. The nth term of a sequence is given by $T_n = \dfrac{n \mid 2}{n + 1}$.

    (i) Write down T_1, T_2 and T_3, the first, second and third terms.

    (ii) Show that $T_1 + T_2 > 2T_3$.

Arithmetic Sequence I

Consider the sequence of numbers 2, 5, 8, 11, …
Each term, after the first, can be found by adding 3 to the previous term.
This is an example of an arithmetic sequence.

> A sequence in which each term, after the first, is found by adding a constant number is called an **arithmetic sequence**.

The first term of an arithmetic sequence is denoted by a.
The constant number, which is added to each term, is called the **common difference** and is denoted by d.
Consider the arithmetic sequence 3, 5, 7, 9, 11, …

$$a = 3 \text{ and } d = 2$$

Each term after the first is found by adding 2 to the previous term.
Consider the arithmetic sequence 7, 2, –3, –8, …

$$a = 7 \text{ and } d = -5$$

Each term after the first is found by subtracting 5 from the previous term.
In an arithmetic sequence the difference between any two consecutive terms is always the same.

> Any term – Previous term $= T_n - T_{n-1} = $ constant $= d$

General term of an arithmetic sequence

In an arithmetic sequence a is the first term and d is the common difference.
Thus in an arithmetic sequence:

$T_1 = a$

$T_2 = a + d$

$T_3 = a + 2d$

$T_4 = a + 3d$, etc.

Notice the coefficient of d is always one less than the term number.	E.g: $T_{10} = a + 9d$ $T_{15} = a + 14d$

To go from one term to the next, just add on another d.

$$T_n = a + (n-1)d$$

Note: Once we find a and d we can answer any question about an arithmetic sequence.

Example ▼

The first three terms of an arithmetic sequence are $5, 8, 11, \ldots$

(i) Find the first term, a, and the common difference, d.

(ii) Find, in terms of n, an expression for T_n, the nth term and, hence or otherwise, find T_{17},

(iii) Which term of the sequence is 122?.

Solution:

(i) Find a and d.
The first three terms are $5, 8, 11, \ldots$

$$a = T_1 = 5$$
$$d = T_2 - T_1 = 8 - 5 = 3$$

(**Note:** Don't make the mistake: $d = T_1 - T_2$)

(ii) Find an expression for T_n.

$$\begin{aligned} T_n &= a + (n-1)d \\ &= 5 + (n-1)3 \qquad \text{(put in } a = 5 \text{ and } d = 3\text{)} \\ &= 5 + 3n - 3 \\ &= 3n + 2 \end{aligned}$$

Find T_{17}.

Method 1:

$$T_n = a + (n-1)d$$
$$T_{17} = 5 + (17-1)3$$
(put in $a = 5$, $d = 3$ and $n = 17$)
$$T_{17} = 5 + 16(3)$$
$$T_{17} = 5 + 48 = 53$$

Method 2:

$$T_n = 3n + 2 \text{ (from (ii))}$$
$$T_{17} = 3(17) + 2$$
(put in $n = 17$)
$$T_{17} = 51 + 2$$
$$T_{17} = 53$$

(iii) Which term of the sequence is equal to 122?

Method 1:

Equation given in disguise:

$$T_n = 122$$
$$a + (n-1)d = 122$$

(we know a and d, find n)

$$5 + (n-1)3 = 122$$
$$5 + 3n - 3 = 122$$
$$3n + 2 = 122$$
$$3n = 120$$
$$n = 40$$

Thus, the 40th term is 122.

Method 2:

Equation given in disguise:

$$T_n = 122$$
$$3n + 2 = 122$$

($T_n = 3n + 2$, find n)

$$3n = 120$$
$$n = 40$$

Example ▼

The first three terms in an arithmetic sequence are $k + 2$, $2k + 3$, $5k - 2$, where k is a real number. Find the value of k and write down the first three terms.

Solution:

We use the fact that in an arithmetic sequence the difference between any two consecutive terms is always the same. We are given the first three terms.

$$\therefore \qquad T_3 - T_2 = T_2 - T_1 \qquad \text{(common difference)}$$

$$(5k - 2) - (2k + 3) = (2k + 3) - (k + 2) \qquad \text{(put in given values)}$$
$$5k - 2 - 2k - 3 = 2k + 3 - k - 2$$
$$3k - 5 = k + 1$$
$$2k = 6$$
$$k = 3$$

$$T_1 = k + 2 = 3 + 2 = 5$$
$$T_2 = 2k + 3 = 2(3) + 3 = 6 + 3 = 9$$
$$T_3 = 5k - 2 = 5(3) - 2 = 15 - 2 = 13$$

Thus, the first three terms are 5, 9, 13.

Exercise 14.2 ▼

Find a and d for each of the following arithmetic sequences and in each case find, in terms of n, an expression for T_n, the nth term:

1. 1, 3, 5, ...

2. 2, 5, 8, ...

3. 3, 7, 11, ...

4. 6, 11, 16, ...

5. 9, 7, 5, ...

6. 4, 1, –2, ...

7. 8, 3, –2, ...

8. 4, –2, –8, ...

9. –5, –3, –1, ...

10. The first three terms of an arithmetic sequence are 1, 4, 7, ...
- **(i)** Find the first term, a, and the common difference, d.
- **(ii)** Find, in terms of n, an expression for T_n, the nth term and, hence or otherwise, find T_{50}.
- **(iii)** Which term of the sequence is 88?

11. The first three terms of an arithmetic sequence are 4, 9, 14, ...
- **(i)** Find the first term, a, and the common difference, d.
- **(ii)** Find, in terms of n, an expression for T_n, the nth term and, hence or otherwise, find T_{45}.
- **(iii)** Which term of the sequence is equal to 249?

12. The first three terms of an arithmetic sequence are 40, 36, 32.
- **(i)** Find the first term a and the common difference d.
- **(ii)** Find, in terms of n, an expression for T_n, the nth term and, hence or otherwise, find T_{15}.
- **(iii)** Which term of the sequence is 0?

13. 2, 5, 8, 11, ... is an arithmetic sequence. Which term of the sequence is 179?

14. 3, 8, 13, 18, ... is an arithmetic sequence. Which term of the sequence is 198?

15. The first three terms in an arithmetic sequence are $2k - 1$, $2k + 1$, $3k$, where k is a real number. Find the value of k and write down the first three terms.

16. The first three terms in an arithmetic sequence are $k - 1$, $2k - 1$, $4k - 5$, where k is a real number. Find the value of k and write down the first three terms.

17. The first three terms in an arithmetic sequence are $k + 6$, $2k + 1$, $k + 18$, where k is a real number. Find the value of k and write down the first four terms.

18. The first three terms in an arithmetic sequence are $k - 2$, $2k + 1$, $k + 14$, where k is a real number.
- **(i)** Find the value of k and write down the first four terms.
- **(ii)** Find, in terms of n, an expression for T_n and, hence or otherwise, find T_{21}.
- **(iii)** Which term of the sequence is 243?

Arithmetic Sequence 2

In some questions we are given two terms of an arithmetic sequence. In this case, we use the method of simultaneous equations to find a and d.

In an arithmetic sequence, the fifth term, T_5, is 19 and the eighth term, T_8, is 31. Find the first term, a, and the common difference, d.

Solution:

We are given two equations in disguise and we use these to find a and d.

$$T_n = a + (n - 1)d$$

Given: $T_5 = 19$ Given: $T_8 = 31$

$\therefore$ $a + 4d = 19$ ① $\therefore$ $a + 7d = 31$ ②

Now solve the simultaneous equations ① and ② to find the value of a and the value of d.

$$a + 7d = 31 \qquad ②$$
$$\underline{-a - 4d = -19 \qquad ① \times -1}$$
$$3d = 12$$
$$d = 4$$

Put $d = 4$ into ① or ②

$$a + 4d = 19 \qquad ①$$
$$\downarrow$$
$$a + 4(4) = 19$$
$$a + 16 = 19$$
$$a = 3$$

Thus, $a = 3$ and $d = 4$.

Exercise 14.3 ▼

1. In an arithmetic sequence, the third term, T_3, is 7 and the fifth term, T_5, is 11. Find the first term, a, and the common difference, d.

2. In an arithmetic sequence, the fifth term, T_5, is 13 and the eighth term, T_8, is 22. Find the first term, a, and the common difference, d.

3. In an arithmetic sequence, the fourth term, T_4, is 19 and the seventh term, T_7, is 31. Find the first term, a, and the common difference, d.

4. In an arithmetic sequence, the fifth term, T_5, is 23 and the ninth term, T_9, is 43. Find the first term, a, and the common difference, d.

5. In an arithmetic sequence, the sixth term, T_6, is 35 and the eighth term, T_8, is 47. Find the first term, a, and the common difference, d.

6. In an arithmetic sequence, the first term, T_1, is 7 and the fifth term, T_5, is 19.
    (i)   Find the common difference d.
    (ii) Find, in terms of n, an expression for T_n, the nth term and, hence or otherwise, find T_{20}.
    (iii) Which term of the sequence is 100?

7. In an arithmetic sequence the sum of the third term, T_3 and the seventh term, T_7, is 38, and the sixth term, T_6, is 23.
   (i) Find the first term, a, and the common difference d.
   (ii) Find, in terms of n, an expression for T_n, the nth term.
   (iii) Show that $T_{19} = 5T_4$.
   (iv) For what value of n is $T_n = 99$?

8. The first four terms of an arithmetic sequence are $5, p, q, 11$.
   (i) Find the value of p and the value of q.
   (ii) Find T_{10}, the tenth term.

9. The first five terms of an arithmetic sequence are $p, q, 4, r, -2$. Find:
   (i) the value of p, the value of q and the value of r
   (ii) T_{20}, the twentieth term.

Arithmetic Sequence 3

To verify that a sequence is arithmetic we must show the following:

$$T_n - T_{n-1} = \text{constant}$$

To show that a sequence is **not arithmetic**, it is only necessary to show that the difference between any two consecutive terms is not the same. In practice, this usually involves showing that $T_3 - T_2 \neq T_2 - T_1$ or similar.

Example ▼

(i) T_n, the nth term, of a sequence is given by $T_n = 5n + 2$. Verify that the sequence is arithmetic.

(ii) T_n, the nth term, of a sequence is given by $T_n = n^2 + 3n$. Verify that the sequence is not arithmetic.

Solution:

(i) $T_n = 5n + 2$ $\qquad\qquad T_{n-1} = 5(n-1) + 2$ $\qquad\qquad$ [replace n with $(n-1)$]
$$= 5n - 5 + 2$$
$$= 5n - 3$$

$T_n - T_{n-1}$

$= (5n + 2) - (5n - 3) = 5n + 2 - 5n + 3 = 5$ $\qquad$ (a constant)

$T_n - T_{n-1} = $ a constant

Thus, the sequence is arithmetic.

$$T_n = n^2 + 3n$$

$T_1 = (1)^2 + 3(1)$	$T_2 = (2)^2 + 3(2)$	$T_3 = (3)^2 + 3(3)$
$= 1 + 3$	$= 4 + 6$	$= 9 + 9$
$= 4$	$= 10$	$= 18$

$$T_3 - T_2 = 18 - 10 = 8 \qquad T_2 - T_1 = 10 - 4 = 6$$

$$T_3 - T_2 \neq T_2 - T_1$$

Thus, the sequence is not arithmetic.

Note: We could also have shown $T_n - T_{n-1} \neq$ a constant to show that the sequence is not arithmetic.

Exercise 14.4 ▼

The following shows the nth term, T_n, of a sequence. In each case, show that the sequence is arithmetic:

1. $T_n = 2n + 3$
2. $T_n = 3n + 1$
3. $T_n = 4n + 5$
4. $T_n = 5n$
5. $T_n = 2n$
6. $T_n = 3n - 2$
7. $T_n = n - 4$
8. $T_n = 2n - 5$
9. $T_n = 7n + 1$
10. $T_n = 3 - n$
11. $T_n = 5 - 2n$
12. $T_n = 4 - 3n$

The following shows the nth term, T_n, of a sequence. In each case, show that the sequence is not arithmetic:

13. $T_n = n^2 + 2n$
14. $T_n = n^2 + 5n$
15. $T_n = n^2 - 3n$
16. $T_n = 2n^2 + n$
17. $T_n = 2n^2 - 1$
18. $T_n = n^2 - 4n + 3$

Series

When we add together the terms of a sequence, we get a series.

For example:

Sequence:	$1, 4, 7, 10, \ldots$
Series:	$1 + 4 + 7 + 10 + \cdots$

The commas are replaced by plus signs to form the series.
The sum of the series is the result of adding the terms.
The sum of the first n terms of a series is denoted by S_n.

$$\therefore \quad S_n = T_1 + T_2 + T_3 + \cdots + T_n$$

From this we have:

$$S_1 = T_1$$
$$S_2 = T_1 + T_2$$
$$S_3 = T_1 + T_2 + T_3, \text{ etc.}$$

Arithmetic Series 1

An **arithmetic series** is the sum (added up) of the terms of an arithmetic sequence.

The sum of the first n terms of an arithmetic series is denoted by S_n.
The formula for S_n can be written in terms of a and d.

$$S_n = \frac{n}{2}[2a + (n-1)d]$$

Note: Once we find a and d we can answer any question about an arithmetic series.

Example ▼

The first three terms of an arithmetic series are $4 + 7 + 10 + \cdots$

(i) Find, in terms of n, an expression for S_n, the sum to n terms.

(ii) Find S_{20}, the sum of the first 20 terms.

Solution:

(i) $4 + 7 + 10 + \cdots$

Note: Even though each term is separated by a plus sign rather than a comma, we still write
$T_1 = 4, T_2 = 7, T_3 = 10$, etc.

$$a = T_1 = 4 \qquad d = T_2 - T_1 = 7 - 4 = 3$$

$$S_n = \frac{n}{2}[2a + (n-1)d]$$

$$S_n = \frac{n}{2}[2(4) + (n-1)3] \qquad \text{(put in } a = 4 \text{ and } d = 3)$$

$$S_n = \frac{n}{2}[8 + 3n - 3]$$

$$S_n = \frac{n}{2}(3n + 5)$$

(ii) Find S_{20}

Method 1:	**Method 2:**
$S_n = \dfrac{n}{2}[2a + (n-1)d]$	$S_n = \dfrac{n}{2}(3n + 5)$ (from part **(i)**)
$S_{20} = \dfrac{20}{2}[2(4) + (19)(3)]$	$S_{20} = \dfrac{20}{2}[3(20) + 5]$
(put in $n = 20$, $a = 4$ and $d = 3$)	(put in $n = 20$)
$S_{20} = 10(8 + 57)$	$S_{20} = 10(60 + 5)$
$S_{20} = 10(65)$	$S_{20} = 10(65)$
$S_{20} = 650$	$S_{20} = 650$

In some questions we are given values of S_n and T_n for two values of n. In this case, we use the method of simultaneous equations to find a and d.

Example ▼

In an arithmetic series, the fifth term, T_5, is 14 and the sum of the first six terms, S_6, is 57.

(i) Find the first term a, and the common difference, d.

(ii) Show that: **(a)** $T_n = 3n - 1$ **(b)** $2S_n = 3n^2 + n$.

Solution:

(i) We are given two equations in disguise and we use them to find a and d.

$T_n = a + (n-1)d$	$S_n = \dfrac{n}{2}[2a + (n-1)d]$
Given: $T_5 = 14$	**Given:** $S_6 = 57$
$\therefore \quad a + (5-1)d = 14 \qquad (n = 5)$	$\therefore \quad \dfrac{6}{2}[2a + (6-1)d] = 57 \qquad (n = 6)$
$a + 4d = 14 \qquad ①$	$3(2a + 5d) = 57$
	$2a + 5d = 19 \qquad ②$
	(divide both sides by 3)

Now solve the simultaneous equations ① and ② to find the value of a and the value of d.

$2a + 8d = 28 \qquad ① \times 2$	$a + 4d = 14 \qquad ①$
$\underline{-2a - 5d = -19 \qquad ② \times -1}$	$\downarrow$
$3d = 9$	$a + 4(3) = 14$
$d = 3$	$a + 12 = 14$
put $d = 3$ into ① or ②.	$a = 2$

Thus, $a = 2$ and $d = 3$.

(ii) Show that $T_n = 3n - 1$ and $2S_n = 3n^2 + n$.

What we do is replace a with 2 and d with 3 in the formulas for T_n and S_n.

(a)
$$T_n = a + (n-1)d$$
$$T_n = 2 + (n-1)3$$
(put in $a = 2$ and $d = 3$)
$$T_n = 2 + 3n - 3$$
$$T_n = 3n - 1$$

(b)
$$S_n = \frac{n}{2}[2a + (n-1)d]$$
$$S_n = \frac{n}{2}[2(2) + (n-1)3]$$
(put in $a = 2$ and $d = 3$)
$$S_n = \frac{n}{2}[4 + 3n - 3]$$
$$S_n = \frac{n}{2}(3n + 1)$$
$$2S_n = n(3n + 1)$$
(multiply both sides by 2)
$$2S_n = 3n^2 + n$$

In some questions we have to solve an equation in disguise to find the value of n.

Example ▼

Find the sum of the arithmetic series $7 + 9 + 11 + \cdots + 55$.

Solution:

The first step is to find the number of terms, n, that there are in the series.

$$a = T_1 = 7 \qquad\qquad d = T_2 - T_1 = 9 - 7 = 2$$

Equation given in disguise:

$$T_n = 55$$
$$\therefore \quad a + (n-1)d = 55$$
$$7 + (n-1)2 = 55$$
(put in $a = 7$ and $d = 2$)
$$7 + 2n - 2 = 55$$
$$2n + 5 = 55$$
$$2n = 50$$
$$n = 25$$

$$S_n = \frac{n}{2}[2a + (n-1)d]$$
$$S_{25} = \frac{25}{2}[2(7) + (24)(2)]$$
(put in $n = 25$, $a = 7$ and $d = 2$)
$$= \frac{25}{2}[14 + 48]$$
$$= \frac{25}{2}(62)$$
$$= 775$$

Thus, there are 25 terms.

1. The first three terms of an arithmetic series are $3 + 5 + 7 + \cdots$.
   Find S_{10}, the sum of the first 10 terms.

2. The first three terms of an arithmetic series are $4 + 7 + 10 + \cdots$.
   Find S_{12}, the sum of the first 12 terms.

3. The first three terms of an arithmetic series are $1 + 5 + 9 + \cdots$.
   Find S_{18}, the sum of the first 18 terms.

4. The first three terms of an arithmetic series are $3 + 8 + 13 + \cdots$.
   - **(i)** Find, in terms of n, an expression for S_n, the sum to n terms.
   - **(ii)** Find S_{20}, the sum of the first 20 terms.

5. The first three terms of an arithmetic series are 10, 13, 16, ...
   - **(i)** Find, in terms of n, an expression for S_n, the sum to n terms.
   - **(ii)** Find S_{30}, the sum of the first 30 terms.

6. The nth term of an arithmetic series is given by $2n + 3$.
   - **(i)** Write down the first four terms.
   - **(ii)** Write down the common difference.
   - **(iii)** Find S_{16}, the sum of the first 16 terms.

7. In an arithmetic series, the fifth term, T_5, is 22 and the sum of the first four terms, S_4, is 38.
   - **(i)** Find the first term, a, and the common difference, d.
   - **(ii)** Show that: **(a)** $T_n = 5n - 3$ **(b)** $2S_n = 5n^2 - n$.

8. In an arithmetic series, the eighth term, T_8, is 21 and the sum of the first six terms, S_6, is 18.
   - **(i)** Find the first term, a, and the common difference, d.
   - **(ii)** Show that: **(a)** $T_n = 4n - 11$ **(b)** $S_n = 2n^2 - 9n$.
   - **(iii)** Find: **(a)** T_{20} **(b)** S_{30}.

9. In an arithmetic series, the seventh term, T_7, is 20 and the sum of the first five terms, S_5, is 40.
   - **(i)** Find the first term, a, and the common difference, d.
   - **(ii)** Show that: **(a)** $T_n = 3n - 1$ **(b)** $2S_n = 3n^2 + n$.
   - **(iii)** Find: **(a)** T_{30} **(b)** S_{30}.

10. In an arithmetic series, the eighth term, T_8, is 27 and the sum of the first ten terms, S_{10}, is 120.
    - **(i)** Find the first term, a, and the common difference, d.
    - **(ii)** Show that: **(a)** $T_n = 3(2n - 7)$ **(b)** $S_n = 3(n^2 - 6n)$.
    - **(iii)** Find: **(a)** T_{25} **(b)** S_6.

11. In an arithmetic series, the sum of the first four terms, S_4, is 44 and the sum of the first six terms, S_6, is 102.
    - **(i)** Find the first term, a, and the common difference, d.
    - **(ii)** Find **(a)** T_{20} **(b)** S_{20}.

12. Find the sum of the arithmetic series $2 + 5 + 8 + \cdots + 59$.

13. Find the sum of the arithmetic series $1 + 5 + 9 + \cdots + 117$.

14. Find the sum of the arithmetic series $3 + 8 + 13 + \cdots + 248$.

15. The nth term of a series is given by $T_n = 3n + 2$.
    (i) Write down, in terms of n, an expression for T_{n-1}, the $(n-1)$st term.
    (ii) Show that the series is arithmetic.
    (iii) Find S_{20}, the sum of the first 20 terms.

16. The first three terms of an arithmetic series are $10 + 20 + 30 + \cdots$
    (i) Find, in terms on n, an expression for T_n, the nth term.
    (ii) Find, in terms of n, an expression for S_n, the sum to n terms.
    (iii) Using your expression for S_n, find the sum of the natural numbers that are both multiples of 10 and smaller than 2001.

17. The first three terms in an arithmetic series are $1 + 3 + 5 + \cdots$
    (i) Show that: **(a)** $T_n = 2n - 1$ **(b)** $S_n = n^2$.
    (ii) Hence, or otherwise, evaluate: **(a)** T_{20} **(b)** S_{20}.
    (iii) How many terms need to be added to give a sum of 225?

18. The first three terms of an arithmetic series are $3a + 4a + 5a + \ldots$ where a is a real number.
    (i) Find, in terms of a, an expression for T_{10}, the tenth term.
    (ii) Find, in terms of a, an expression for S_{10}, the sum of the first 10 terms.
    (iii) If $S_{10} - T_{10} = 126$, find the value of a.

    (iv) Write down the first four terms of the series.
    (v) Write down, in terms of n, expressions for: **(a)** T_n **(b)** S_n.
    (vi) Hence, or otherwise, evaluate: **(a)** T_{20} **(b)** S_{20}.

19. The general term, T_n, of an arithmetic series is given by $T_n = 2n + 5$.
    (i) Find the first term, a, and the common difference d.
    (ii) For what value of n is the sum of the first n terms, S_n, equal to 160?

Given S_n of an Arithmetic Series in Terms of n

In many problems we are given an expression for S_n in terms of n and we need to find a and d. In this type of problem we use the fact that for all types of series:

$$T_n = S_n - S_{n-1} \qquad \text{and} \qquad T_1 = S_1$$

(e.g. $T_2 = S_2 - S_1$ $T_3 = S_3 - S_2$ $T_{11} = S_{11} - S_{10}$ etc).

Example ▼

The sum of the first n terms, S_n, of an arithmetic series is given by $S_n = 2n^2 + n$.

Find the first term, a, and the common difference, d.

Solution:

$$S_n = 2n^2 + n$$

$S_1 = 2(1)^2 + (1)$
$\quad = 2 + 1$
$\quad = 3$

$S_2 = 2(2)^2 + (2)$
$\quad = 2(4) + (2)$
$\quad = 8 + 2$
$\quad = 10$

$a = T_1 = S_1 = 3$

$T_2 = S_2 - S_1 = 10 - 3 = 7$

$$d = T_2 - T_1 = 7 - 3 = 4$$
$$\text{Thus, } a = 3 \text{ and } d = 4.$$

Exercise 14.6 ▼

1. The sum of the first n terms, S_n, of an arithmetic series is given by $S_n = n^2 + 2n$.
   Use S_1 and S_2 to find the first term, a, and the common difference, d.

2. The sum of the first n terms, S_n, of an arithmetic series is given by $S_n = n^2 + 3n$.
   Find the first term, a, and the common difference, d.

3. The sum of the first n terms, S_n, of an arithmetic series is given by $S_n = 3n^2 - 2n$.
   Find the first term, a, and the common difference, d.

4. The sum of the first n terms, S_n, of an arithmetic series is given by $S_n = 2n^2 - 3n$.
   Find the first term, a, and the common difference, d.

5. The sum of the first n terms, S_n, of an arithmetic series is given by $S_n = \dfrac{n(3n + 1)}{2}$.
   (i) Calculate the first term of the series.
   (ii) By calculating S_8 and S_7, find T_8, the eighth term of the series.

6. The sum of the first n terms, S_n, of an arithmetic series is given by $S_n = 2n^2 + n$.
   (i) Calculate the first term of the series and the common difference.
   (ii) Find, in terms of n, an expression for T_n, the nth term.
   (iii) Hence, calculate T_{10}.
   (iv) Show that $T_{10} = S_{10} - S_9$.

7. The sum of the first n terms, S_n, of an arithmetic series is given by $S_n = 2n^n - 4n$.
   (i) Find the first term, a, and the common difference, d.
   (ii) Find, in terms of n, an expression for T_n, the nth term.
   (iii) Find T_{20} and verify that $T_{20} = S_{20} - S_{19}$.
   (iv) Starting with the first term, how many terms of the series must be added to give a sum of 160?

Geometric Sequence 1

Consider the sequence of numbers 4, 12, 36, 108, … .
Each term, after the first, can be found by multiplying the previous term by 3.
This is an example of a geometric sequence.

> A sequence in which each term, after the first, is found by multiplying the
> previous term by a constant number is called a **geometric sequence**.

The first term in a geometric sequence is denoted by a.
The constant number, by which each term is multiplied, is called the **common ratio** and is denoted by r.

Consider the geometric series 3, 6, 12, 24, …

$$a = 3 \text{ and } r = 2$$

Each term, after the first, is found by multiplying the previous term by 2.

Consider the geometric series 27, 9, 3, 1, …

$$a = 27 \text{ and } r = \tfrac{1}{3}$$

Each term, after the first, is found by multiplying the previous term by $\tfrac{1}{3}$.

Note: Multiplying by $\tfrac{1}{3}$ is the same as dividing by 3.

r can be found by dividing any term by the previous term.

$$\frac{\text{Any term}}{\text{Previous term}} = \frac{T_n}{T_{n-1}} = \text{constant} = r$$

General Term of a Geometric Sequence

In a geometric sequence, a is the first term and r is the common ratio.

Thus in a geometric sequence:

$$T_1 = a$$
$$T_2 = ar$$
$$T_3 = ar^2$$
$$T_4 = ar^3, \text{ etc.}$$

$$\left[\begin{array}{l} \text{Notice the index of } r \\ \text{is always one less than the} \\ \text{term number.} \end{array} \right. \quad \left. \begin{array}{l} \text{E.g.} \\ T_7 = ar^6 \\ T_{12} = ar^{11} \end{array} \right]$$

To go from one term to the next, just multiply by r.

$$T_n = ar^{n-1}$$

Note: (any real number)^0 = 1; for example: $\quad 2^0 = 1, \qquad 3^0 = 1, \qquad (\tfrac{1}{2})^0 = 1.$

Example ▼

The first three terms of a geometric sequence are 2, 6, 18, ...

(i) Find the first term, a, and the common ratio, r.

(ii) Find, in terms of n, an expression for T_n, the nth term.

(iii) Find T_6.

Solution:

$$2, 6, 18, ...$$

(i) $a = 2$ (given) $\qquad\qquad\qquad\qquad\qquad r = \dfrac{T_2}{T_1} = \dfrac{6}{2} = 3$

Thus, $a = 2$ and $r = 3$.

(ii) $T_n = ar^{n-1} = 2(3)^{n-1}$

(iii) $T_6 = 2(3)^{6-1} = 2(3)^5 = 2(243) = 486$

Example ▼

The first three terms of a geometric sequence are $k + 1$, $k + 4$, $3k + 2$, ... where k is a real number. Find the two values of k.

Solution:

We use the fact that in a geometric sequence, any term divided by the previous term is always a constant.

$$\therefore \quad \frac{T_3}{T_2} = \frac{T_2}{T_1} \qquad\qquad \text{(common ratio)}$$

$$\frac{3k+2}{k+4} = \frac{k+4}{k+1} \qquad\qquad \text{(put in given values)}$$

$(3k + 2)(k + 1) = (k + 4)(k + 4)$ (multiply both sides by $(k + 4)(k + 1)$)

$3k^2 + 5k + 2 = k^2 + 8k + 16$ (remove brackets)

$2k^2 - 3k - 14 = 0$ (every term on the left)

$(2k - 7)(k + 2) = 0$ (factorise the left-hand side)

$2k - 7 = 0 \quad$ or $\quad k + 2 = 0$ (let each factor = 0)

$2k = 7 \quad$ or $\quad k = -2$

$k = \frac{7}{2} \quad$ or $\quad k = -2$

Thus, the two values of k are $\frac{7}{2}$ and -2.

The first three terms of a geometric sequence are given below. In each case:
(i)   write down the first term, a, and find the common ratio, r
(ii) find, in terms of n, an expression for T_n, the nth term
(iii) find the next two terms.

1 $1, 2, 4, \ldots$ **2.** $3, 6, 12, \ldots$ **3.** $1, 4, 16, \ldots$

4. $4, 12, 36, \ldots$ **5.** $2, 8, 32, \ldots$ **6.** $5, 10, 20, \ldots$

7. $3, 12, 48, \ldots$ **8.** $3, 9, 27, \ldots$ **9.** $1, 5, 25, \ldots$

10. $48, 24, 12, \ldots$ **11.** $54, 18, 6, \ldots$ **12.** $8, 2, \frac{1}{2}, \ldots$

13. The first three terms of a geometric sequence are $2, 10, 50, \ldots$
    (i)   Find the first term, a, and the common ratio, r.
    (ii) Find, in terms of n, an expression for T_n, the nth term.
    (iii) Show that $5T_3 + 4T_4 = T_5$.

14. The first three terms of a geometric sequence are $6, 18, 54, \ldots$
    (i)   Find the first term, a, and the common ratio, r.
    (ii) Find, in terms of n, an expression for T_n, the nth term.
    (iii) Show that $3(T_3 + T_5) = 10T_4$.

15. $T_1, T_2, T_3, \ldots$ is a geometric sequence.
    The first term, T_1, is 5 and the common ratio is 3.
    Show that $T_5 + T_3 = 10T_3$.

16. The nth term, T_n, of a geometric sequence is given by $T_n = 3^n$.
    Find the first term, a, and the common ratio r.

17. The nth term, T_n, of a geometric sequence is given by $T_n = 3.4^{n-1}$.
    Find the first term, a, and the common ratio r.

18. The first four terms of a geometric sequence are $2, 6, a, b, \ldots$.
    Find the value of a and the value of b.

19. The first term, T_1, of a geometric sequence is 1 and the fifth term, T_5, is 16.
    (i)   Find the common ratio, r, $r > 0$.
    (ii) Find T_2, T_3 and T_4.
    (iii) Show that $T_4 = 2T_2 + T_3$.

20. The first four terms of a geometric sequence are $3, p, q, 24, \ldots$
    (i)   Find the common ratio, r.
    (ii) Find the value of p and the value of q.

21. The first three terms of a geometric sequence are $k - 1$, $2k + 1$, $4k + 17$, . . . where k is a real number. Find the value of k.

22. The first three terms of a geometric sequence are $k - 4$, k, $k + 6$, ... where k is a real number. Find the value of k.

23. The first three terms of a geometric sequence are $k - 3$, $k - 1$, $k + 3$, ... where k is a real number. Find the value of k.
Hence, write down the value of each of the first four terms.

24. The first three terms of a geometric sequence are 5, k, 45, ... where k is a real number. Find the two values of k.

25. The first three terms of a geometric sequence are $2k - 4$, $k + 1$, $k - 3$, ... where k is a real number. Find the two values of k.

26. The first three terms of a geometric sequence are $k - 3$, k, $3k + 4$, ... where k is a real number. Find the two values of k.

27. The first two terms of a geometric sequence are 4, $\frac{4}{3}$, ...
   (i) Find r, the common ratio.
   (ii) Write down the third and fourth terms of the sequence.

28. The nth term, T_n, of a geometric sequence is given by $T_n = (\frac{2}{3})^n$.
Find the first four terms of the sequence.

Geometric Sequence 2

To verify that a sequence is geometric, we must show the following:

$$\frac{T_n}{T_{n-1}} = \text{constant}$$

Note: To show that a sequence is **not geometric**, it is only necessary to show that the ratio of any two consecutive terms is not the same. In practice, this usually involves showing that $T_3 \div T_2 \neq T_2 \div T_1$ or similar.

Example ▼

T_n, the nth term of a sequence, is given by $T_n = 5.2^n$. Verify that the sequence is geometric.

Solution:

$$T_n = 5.2^n \qquad\qquad T_{n-1} = 5.2^{n-1} \qquad\qquad [\text{replace } n \text{ with } (n-1)]$$

$$\frac{T_n}{T_{n-1}} = \frac{5.2^n}{5.2^{n-1}}$$

$$= \frac{2^n}{2^{n-1}} \qquad \text{(divide top and bottom by 5)}$$

$$= 2^{n-(n-1)} \qquad \text{(subtract the index on the bottom from the index on the top)}$$

$$= 2^{n-n+1}$$

$$= 2^1$$

$$= 2 \qquad \text{(a constant, i.e. does not contain } n\text{)}$$

$\dfrac{T_n}{T_{n-1}}$ is a constant, thus the sequence is geometric.

Example ▼

In a geometric sequence, the third term, T_3, is 12 and the sixth term, T_6, is 96

(i) Find the first term, a, and the common ratio, r.

(ii) Find, in terms of n, an expression for T_n, the nth term.

(iii) Which term of the sequence is 768?

Solution:

(i)
$$T_n = ar^{n-1}$$

Given: $T_3 = 12$ **Given:** $T_6 = 96$

∴ $ar^2 = 12$ ①   ∴ $ar^5 = 96$ ②

We now divide ② by ① to eliminate a and find r.

$$\frac{②}{①}$$

$$\frac{ar^5}{ar^2} = \frac{96}{12} \qquad\qquad\qquad ar^2 = 12 \qquad ①$$

$$r^3 = 8 \qquad\qquad\qquad\qquad a(2)^2 = 12$$

$$r = 2 \qquad\qquad\qquad\qquad\quad a(4) = 12$$

put $r = 2$ into ① or ② to find a $4a = 12$

                                                 $a = 3$

Thus, $a = 3$ and $r = 2$.

Note: If the index of r is even, we get two values for r, positive and negative.

(ii) $T_n = ar^{n-1} = 3(2)^{n-1}$

(iii)   Equation given in disguise:

$$T_n = 768$$

$\therefore$ $ar^{n-1} = 768$ (we know a and r, find n)

$3(2)^{n-1} = 768$ (put in $a = 3$ and $r = 2$)

$2^{n-1} = 256$ (divide both sides by 3)

$2^{n-1} = 2^8$ (both as powers of 2, $256 = 2^8$)

$n - 1 = 8$ (equate the powers)

$n = 9$

Thus, the 9th term of the sequence is 768.

Exercise 14.8 ▼

Each of the following gives the nth term, T_n, of a sequence. In each case, find, in terms of n, an expression for T_{n-1}, and verify that the sequence is geometric:

1. $T_n = 2^n$

2. $T_n = 3^n$

3. $T_n = 5^n$

4. $T_n = 3.4^n$

5. $T_n = 5(2^n)$

6. $T_n = 3(4)^n$

7. $T_n = 2(3)^{n+1}$

8. $T_n = 4(5)^{n+1}$

9. $T_n = 2(4)^{n+1}$

10. $T_n = 3(2)^{n+1}$

11. $T_n = 4^{n-1}$

12. $T_n = 3(2)^{n-1}$

13. The nth term, T_n, of a sequence is given by $T_n = n^3 + n$.
Verify that the sequence is not geometric.

14. The nth term, T_n, of a sequence is given by $T_n = \dfrac{n+2}{n+1}$.
Verify that the sequence is not geometric.

15. Write each of the following:
   (i)   2, 4, 8, 16, 32, 64, 128, 256 as powers of 2
   (ii)   −2, −8, −32, −128 as powers of −2
   (iii)   3, 9, 27, 81, 243, 729 as powers of 3
   (iv)   4, 16, 64, 256 as powers of 4
   (v)   1, 5, 25, 125, 625 as powers of 5.

16. Solve each of the following equations for r:
   (i) $r^3 = 8$ **(ii)** $r^3 = 27$ **(iii)** $r^3 = 64$ **(iv)** $r^3 = 125$
   (v) $r^2 = 4$ **(vi)** $r^2 = 9$ **(vii)** $r^3 = -8$ **(viii)** $r^3 = -27$

17. In a geometric sequence, the second term, T_2, is 2 and the fifth term, T_5, is 16.
   (i) Find the first term, a, and the common ratio, r.
   (ii) Find, in terms of n, an expression for T_n, the nth term.
   (iii) Evaluate T_{11}.

18. In a geometric sequence, the third term, T_3, is 9 and the sixth term, T_6, is 243.
   (i) Find the first term, a, and the common ratio, r.
   (ii) Find, in terms of n, an expression for T_n, the nth term.
   (iii) Evaluate T_8.

19. In a geometric sequence, the second term, T_2, is 6 and the fifth term, T_5, is 48.
   (i) Find the first term, a, and the common ratio, r.
   (ii) Find, in terms of n, an expression for T_n, the nth term.
   (iii) Which term of the sequence is 384?

20. In a geometric sequence, the third term, T_3, is 16 and the sixth term, T_6, is 128.
   (i) Find the first term, a, and the common ratio, r.
   (ii) Find, in terms of n, an expression for T_n, the nth term.
   (iii) Which term of the sequence is 1,024?

Geometric Series

> A **geometric series** is the sum (added up) of the terms of a geometric sequence.

The sum of the first n terms of a gemetric series is denoted by S_n.
The formula for S_n can be written in terms of a and r.

$$S_n = \frac{a(1 - r^n)}{1 - r}, \text{ when } r < 1$$

$$S_n = \frac{a(r^n - 1)}{r - 1}, \text{ when } r > 1$$

Note: In practice it does not matter which form you use.
Once we find a and r we can answer any question about a geometric series.

The first three terms of a geometric series are $1 + 3 + 9 + \ldots$

(i) Show that $S_n = \dfrac{3^n - 1}{2}$ and, hence or otherwise, find S_{10}.

(ii) Investigate if $2S_n = 3T_n - 1$.

Solution:

(i) $1 + 3 + 9 + \ldots$

Note: Even though each term is separated by a plus sign rather than a comma, we still write
$T_1 = 1, T_2 = 3, T_3 = 9$, etc.

$$a = 1 \text{ (given)} \qquad r = \frac{T_2}{T_1} = \frac{3}{1} = 3$$

$$S_n = \frac{a(r^n - 1)}{r - 1} = \frac{1(3^n - 1)}{3 - 1} = \frac{3^n - 1}{2}$$

Method 1:

$$S_n = \frac{a(r^n - 1)}{r - 1)}$$

$$S_{10} = \frac{1(3^{10} - 1)}{3 - 1} \qquad \text{(put in } a = 1, r = 3, n = 10)$$

$$= \frac{3^{10} - 1}{2}$$

$$= \frac{59{,}049 - 1}{2} = \frac{59{,}048}{2} = 29{,}524$$

Method 2:

$$S_n = \frac{3^n - 1}{2} \qquad \text{(from (i))}$$

$$S_{10} = \frac{3^{10} - 1}{2 - 1} \qquad \text{(put in } n = 10)$$

$$= \frac{59{,}049 - 1}{2}$$

$$= \frac{59{,}048}{2} = 29{,}524$$

(ii)

$$S_n = \frac{3^n - 1}{2}$$

$$2S_n = 2\left(\frac{3^n - 1}{2}\right)$$

$$2S_n = 3^n - 1$$

$$a = 1, \qquad r = 3$$

$$T_n = ar^{n-1} = 1(3)^{n-1} = 3^{n-1}$$

$$3T_n = 3(3)^{n-1} = 3^1 . 3^{n-1} = 3^{1 + n - 1} = 3^n$$

$$\therefore \quad 3T_n - 1 = 3^n - 1$$

$$\therefore \quad 2S_n = 3T_n - 1$$

Example ▼

How many terms of the geometric series $3 + 6 + 12 + \dots$ must be taken so that their sum is 765?

Solution:

$$a = 3 \quad \text{(given)} \qquad r = \frac{T_2}{T_1} = \frac{6}{3} = 2$$

Equation given in disguise:

$$S_n = 765$$

$$\frac{a(r^n - 1)}{r - 1} = 765 \qquad \text{(we know } a \text{ and } r, \text{ find } n)$$

$$\frac{3(2^n - 1)}{2 - 1} = 765 \qquad \text{(put in } a = 3 \text{ and } r = 2)$$

$$3(2^n - 1) = 765$$

$$2^n - 1 = 255 \qquad \text{(divide both sides by 3)}$$

$$2^n = 256$$

$$2^n = 2^8 \qquad \text{(both as powers of 2, } 256 = 2^8)$$

$$n = 8 \qquad \text{(equate the powers)}$$

Thus, the sum of the first 8 terms will give 765.

Exercise 14.9 ▼

1. The first three terms of a geometric series are $2 + 6 + 18 + \dots$ \qquad find S_8.

2. The first three terms of a geometric series are $3 + 12 + 48 + \dots$ \qquad find S_6.

3. The first three terms of a geometric series are $5 + 10 + 20 + \dots$ \qquad find S_9.

4. The first three terms of a geometric series are $4 + 12 + 36 + \dots$
   (i) Find the common ratio, r.
   (ii) Find, in terms of n, expressions for T_n, the nth term, and S_n, the sum of the first n terms.
   (iii) Show that $3T_n = 2(S_n + 2)$.

5. The first two terms of a geometric series are $2 + 10 + \dots$
   (i) Find the common ratio, r.
   (ii) Find, in terms of n, expressions for T_n, the nth term, and S_n, the sum of the first n terms.
   (iii) Find, T_5 and S_5.
   (iv) Investigate if $4S_n + 2 = 5T_n$.

6. **(i)** Evaluate $2°$.

The nth term, T_n, of a geometric series is given by $T_n = 3(2)^{n-1}$.

(ii) Find the first term, a, and the common ratio, r.

(iii) Find S_{10}.

(iv) Show that $T_1(S_{10} + T_1) = T_3 . T_9$.

7. In a geometric series the common ratio is 2 and S_5, the sum of the first five terms, is 124. Find the first term, a.

8. In a geometric series the common ratio is 3 and S_6, the sum of the first six terms, is 728. Find the first term, a.

9. Write: **(i)** 4, 32 and 128 as powers of 2   **(ii)** 9, 81 and 729 as powers of 3.

10. How many terms of the geometric series $2 + 4 + 8 + \ldots$ must be added to give a total of 510?

11. How many terms of the geometric series $3 + 6 + 12 + \ldots$ must be added to give a total of 1533?

12. How many terms of the geometric series $10 + 30 + 90 + \ldots$ must be added to give a total of 3640?

13. **(i)** Write 256 as a power of 2.

The nth term, T_n, of a geometric series is given by $T_n = 3(2)^n$.

(ii) Find the first term and the common ratio.

(iii) Which term of the series is 768?

(iv) Find the sum of the geometric series $6 + 12 + 24 + \ldots + 768$.

(v) How many terms of the geometric series $6 + 12 + 24 + \ldots$ must be taken so that their sum is 6,138?

14. The first three terms of a geometric series are $1 + 2 + 4 + \ldots$

(i) Find the first term, a, and the common ratio, r.

(ii) Find, in terms of n, expressions for T_n, the nth term, and S_n, the sum of the first n terms.

(iii) Find T_{10} and S_{10}.

(iv) Show that $S_{20} < (T_5)^5$.

(v) How many terms of the series must be added together to get a total of 511?

15. The sum to n terms, S_n, of a geometric series is given by $S_n = 5(3^n - 1)$.

(i) Find S_1, S_2 and S_3.

(ii) Find the first term, a, and the common ratio, r.

(iii) Find, in terms of n, an expression for T_n, the nth term and, hence, find T_8.

(iv) Show that $T_8 = S_8 - S_7$.

16. The sum to n terms, S_n, of a geometric series is given by $S_n = 3(2^n - 1)$.

(i) Calculate the first term of the series.

(ii) By calculating S_9 and S_8, find T_9.

17. The sum to n terms, S_n, of a geometric series is given by $S_n = 3(4^n - 1)$.

(i) Find S_1, S_2 and S_3.

(ii) Find the first term, a, and the common ratio, r.

(iii) Find, in terms of n, an expression for T_n, the nth term and, hence, find T_5.

(iv) Show that $T_5 = S_5 - S_4$.

GEOMETRY AND ENLARGEMENTS

Types and Names of Angles

Angles may be considered to be an amount of turning or rotation.
Angles are usually measured in degrees, using the symbol °.

Acute angle	Right angle	Obtuse angle	Straight angle
Less than 90°	Equal to 90°	Between 90° and 180°	Equal to 180°
Reflex angle	**Complementary angles**	**Supplementary angles**	**Angles at a point**
Between 180° and 360°	These add up to 90° $a° + b° = 90°$	These add up to 180° $p° + q° = 180°$	These add up to 360° $a° + b° + c° = 360°$

Vertically opposite angles

$a° = c°$ and $b° = d°$
a and c are vertically opposite angles.
b and d are vertically opposite angles

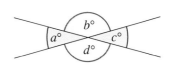

Angles Formed by Parallel Lines

Corresponding angles

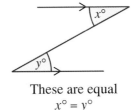

These are equal
$a° = b°$

Alternate angles

These are equal
$x° = y°$

Interior angles

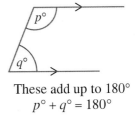

These add up to 180°
$p° + q° = 180°$

Angles in Triangles

Angle sum of a triangle	Exterior angle of a triangle
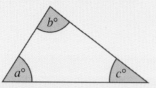	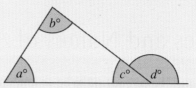
The three angles of a triangle add up to 180°. $a° + b° + c° = 180°$	If one side is produced, the exterior angle is equal to the sum of the two interior opposite angles. $d° = a° + b°$

Special Triangles

Equilateral triangle	Isosceles triangle	Right-angled triangle
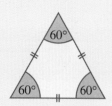	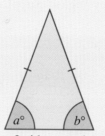	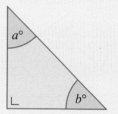
3 sides equal 3 equal angles All angles are equal to 60°	2 sides equal Base angles are equal $a° = b°$ (base angles are the angles opposite the equal sides)	One angle is 90° The other two angles add up to 90° $a° + b° = 90°$

Congruent Triangles

Four cases of congruent triangles

Case 1

three sides of one triangle   =   **three sides of the other triangle**

≡

SSS
(three sides)

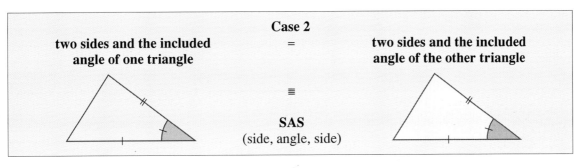

Case 2

two sides and the included
angle of one triangle

=

≡

SAS
(side, angle, side)

two sides and the included
angle of the other triangle

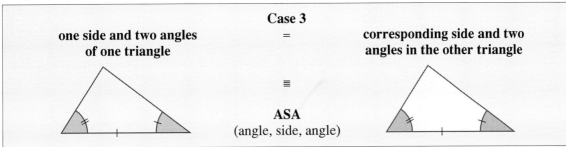

Case 3

one side and two angles
of one triangle

=

≡

ASA
(angle, side, angle)

corresponding side and two
angles in the other triangle

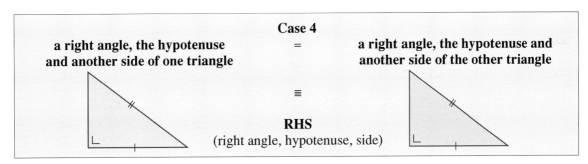

Case 4

a right angle, the hypotenuse
and another side of one triangle

=

≡

RHS
(right angle, hypotenuse, side)

a right angle, the hypotenuse and
another side of the other triangle

Always state which case of congruence is used, i.e., whether SSS, SAS, ASA or RHS.
Justify each statement made, e.g., common side, opp. sides.

Proofs

There are 10 theorems to be proved on our course.
A proof in geometry should consist of five steps:

1. **Diagram**
   Draw a clear diagram, if not given, from the information given in the question.
2. **Given**
   State what is given.
3. **To prove**
   State what is to be proved.
4. **Construction**
   If necessary, state any extra lines that have to be added to the diagram to help in the proof.
   Also at this stage, if necessary, it can simplify the work if the angles are labelled with a number.
5. **Proof**
   Set out each line of the proof, justifying each statement made.

1.

> The sum of the degree-measures of the angles of a triangle is 180°.

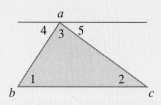

Given:	Triangle *abc* with angles 1, 2 and 3.
To prove:	$\lvert\angle 1\rvert + \lvert\angle 2\rvert + \lvert\angle 3\rvert = 180°$
Construction:	Draw a line through *a*, parallel to *bc*. Label angles 4 and 5.
Proof:	$\lvert\angle 1\rvert = \lvert\angle 4\rvert$ and $\lvert\angle 2\rvert = \lvert\angle 5\rvert$ alternate angles

$\therefore\quad \lvert\angle 1\rvert + \lvert\angle 2\rvert + \lvert\angle 3\rvert = \lvert\angle 4\rvert + \lvert\angle 5\rvert + \lvert\angle 3\rvert$

but $\quad \lvert\angle 4\rvert + \lvert\angle 5\rvert + \lvert\angle 3\rvert = 180°.$ straight angle

$\therefore\quad \lvert\angle 1\rvert + \lvert\angle 2\rvert + \lvert\angle 3\rvert = 180°.$

Corollary 1

> The degree-measure of an exterior angle of a triangle is equal to the sum of the degree-measures of the two remote interior angles.

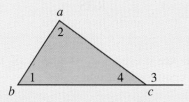

Given:	Triangle *abc* with interior opposite angles 1 and 2 and exterior angle 3.
To prove:	$\lvert\angle 1\rvert + \lvert\angle 2\rvert = \lvert\angle 3\rvert$
Construction:	Label angle 4.
Proof:	$\lvert\angle 1\rvert + \lvert\angle 2\rvert + \lvert\angle 4\rvert = 180°$ three angles in a triangle

$\quad\quad\quad \lvert\angle 3\rvert + \lvert\angle 4\rvert = 180°$ straight angle

$\therefore\quad \lvert\angle 1\rvert + \lvert\angle 2\rvert + \lvert\angle 4\rvert = \lvert\angle 3\rvert + \lvert\angle 4\rvert$

$\therefore\quad \lvert\angle 1\rvert + \lvert\angle 2\rvert = \lvert\angle 3\rvert$

<table>
<tr><td>**Corollary 2**</td><td>An exterior angle of a triangle is greater than either remote (opposite) interior angle.</td></tr>
</table>

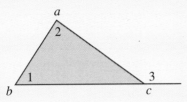

Given:	Triangle abc with interior opposite angles 1 and 2 and exterior angle 3.
To prove:	$\lvert\angle3\rvert>\lvert\angle1\rvert$ and $\lvert\angle3\rvert>\lvert\angle2\rvert$
Proof:	$\lvert\angle3\rvert=\lvert\angle1\rvert+\lvert\angle2\rvert$ exterior angle
but	$\lvert\angle1\rvert>0$ and $\lvert\angle2\rvert>0$
$\therefore$	$\lvert\angle3\rvert>\lvert\angle1\rvert$ and $\lvert\angle3\rvert>\lvert\angle2\rvert$

2.

<table>
<tr><td>Opposite sides of a parallelogram are equal in length.</td></tr>
</table>

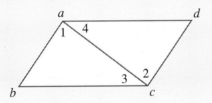

Given:	Parallelogram $abcd$
To prove:	$\lvert ab\rvert=\lvert dc\rvert$ and $\lvert ad\rvert=\lvert bc\rvert$
Construction:	Join a to c. Label angles 1, 2, 3 and 4.
Proof:	Consider triangle abc and triangle adc:
	$\lvert\angle1\rvert=\lvert\angle2\rvert$ and $\lvert\angle3\rvert=\lvert\angle4\rvert$ alternate angles
	$\lvert ac\rvert=\lvert ac\rvert$ common
$\therefore$	triangle $abc \equiv$ triangle adc ASA
$\therefore$	$\lvert ab\rvert=\lvert dc\rvert$ and $\lvert ad\rvert=\lvert bc\rvert$ corresponding sides

3.

> If three parallel lines make intercepts of equal length on a transversal, then they will make intercepts of equal length on any other transversal.

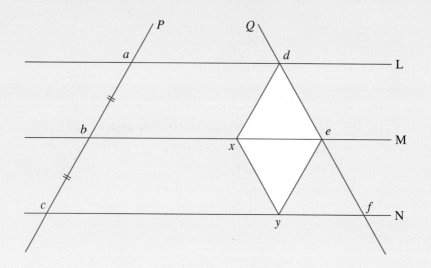

Given:		Three parallel lines L, M and N.
		Transversal P, intersecting the lines at a, b and c such that $|ab| = |bc|$.
		Transversal Q, intersecting the lines at d, e and f.
To prove:		$|de| = |ef|$
Construction:		Complete parallelograms $badx$ and $edxy$.
Proof:		$edxy$ is a parallelogram
	$\therefore$	$|xy| = |de|$
		$xy \parallel ef$
and		$M \parallel N$
	$\therefore$	$fexy$ is a parallelogram.
	$\therefore$	$|xy| = |ef|$
	$\therefore$	$|de| = |ef|$

(right column reasons)

construction
opposite sides
construction
given

opposite sides

4.

A line which is parallel to one side-line of a triangle and cuts a second side will cut the third side in the same proportion as the second.

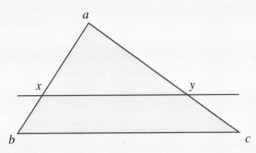

Given: Triangle abc with $xy \parallel bc$.

To prove: $\dfrac{|ax|}{|xb|} = \dfrac{|ay|}{|yc|}$

Proof: Let x divide $[ab]$ in the ratio $m : n$, i.e., $\dfrac{|ax|}{|xb|} = \dfrac{m}{n}$

Let $[ax]$ be divided into m equal parts.

Let $[xb]$ be divided into n equal parts.

Through each point thus obtained on $[ax]$ and $[xb]$ draw lines parallel to bc to meet ac.

$\therefore$ $[ay]$ is divided into m equal parts and $[yc]$ is divided into n equal parts.

$\therefore$ $\dfrac{|ay|}{|yc|} = \dfrac{m}{n}$

$\therefore$ $\dfrac{|ax|}{|xb|} = \dfrac{|ay|}{|yc|}$

5.

> If the three angles of one triangle have degree-measures equal, respectively, to the degree-measures of the angles of a second triangle, then the lengths of the corresponding sides of the two triangles are proportional.

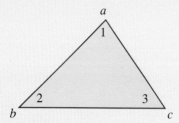 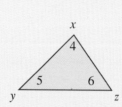 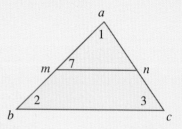

Given:

Equiangular triangles *abc* and *xyz* in which
$|\angle 1| = |\angle 4|$, $|\angle 2| = |\angle 5|$ and $|\angle 3| = |\angle 6|$.

To prove:

$$\frac{|ab|}{|xy|} = \frac{|ac|}{|xz|} = \frac{|bc|}{|yz|}$$

Construction:

Mark the point *m* on [*ab*] such that $|am| = |xy|$.

Mark the point *n* on [*ac*] such that $|an| = |xz|$.

Join *m* to *n*. Label angle 7.

Proof:

Consider triangle *amn* and triangle *xyz*:

$|am| = |xy|$ and $|an| = |xz|$	construction
$|\angle 1| = |\angle 4|$	given
∴ triangle *amn* ≡ triangle *xyz*	SAS
∴ $|\angle 7| = |\angle 5|$	corresponding angles
but $|\angle 2| = |\angle 5|$	given
∴ $|\angle 7| = |\angle 2|$	
∴ *yz* ∥ *bc*	
∴ $\dfrac{|ab|}{|am|} = \dfrac{|ac|}{|an|}$	A line parallel to one side divides the other two sides in the same proportion
∴ $\dfrac{|ab|}{|xy|} = \dfrac{|ac|}{|xz|}$	$|am| = |xy|$ and $|an| = |xz|$

similarly, $\dfrac{|ab|}{|xy|} = \dfrac{|bc|}{|yz|}$

∴ $\dfrac{|ab|}{|xy|} = \dfrac{|ac|}{|xz|} = \dfrac{|bc|}{|yz|}$

Pythagoras's Theorem

6.

In a right-angled triangle, the square of the length of the side opposite to the right angle is equal to the sum of the squares of the lengths of the other two sides.

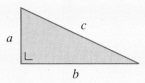

Given: Right-angled triangle with length of sides a, b and c as shown.

To prove: $a^2 + b^2 = c^2$

Construction: Draw a square with sides of length $a + b$.

Draw four congruent right-angled triangles in the square with sides of length a and b and hypotenuse c, as shown.

Label angles 1, 2, 3 and 4.

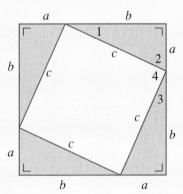

$$|\angle 1| + |\angle 2| = 90° \qquad \text{remaining angles}$$
$$|\angle 1| = |\angle 3| \qquad \text{corresponding angles}$$
$$\therefore \quad |\angle 2| + |\angle 3| = 90°$$
$$\therefore \quad |\angle 4| = 90°$$

Area of square $= (a + b)^2 = 4(\text{area of one triangle}) + c^2$
$$(a + b)^2 = 4(\tfrac{1}{2}ab) + c^2$$
$$a^2 + 2ab + b^2 = 2ab + c^2$$
$$a^2 + b^2 = c^2$$

Note: A difficulty with the proof is trying to draw the diagram. One way to do this is to let $a = 2$ cm, $b = 5$ cm and draw a square with each side 7 cm in length. Then simply mark off 2 cm on each side in clockwise direction. Join these points to construct the smaller square.

6.

In a right-angled triangle, the square of the length of the side opposite to the right angle is equal to the sum of the squares of the lengths of the other two sides.

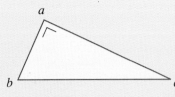

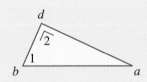

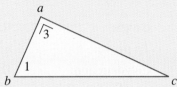

Given:	Triangle abc with $|\angle bac| = 90°$.
To prove:	$|bc|^2 = |ab|^2 + |ac|^2$
Construction:	Draw $ad \perp bc$.
	Label angles 1, 2 and 3.
Proof:	Consider triangle abc and triangle dba:

$$|\angle 1| = |\angle 1| \qquad \text{common angle}$$
$$|\angle 2| = |\angle 3| = 90° \qquad \text{construction}$$

∴ Triangle abc and triangle dba are similar

∴ $$\frac{|ab|}{|bc|} = \frac{|bd|}{|ab|} \qquad \text{corresponding sides are in proportion}$$

$$|ab|^2 = |bc| . |dc| \quad ① \qquad \text{cross-multiply}$$

Similarly, triangle abc and triangle dac are similar

and $|ac|^2 = |bc| . |dc| \quad ②$

Adding ① and ②:

$$|ab|^2 + |ac|^2 = |bc| . |bd| + |bc| . |dc|$$
$$= |bc| (|bd| + |dc|)$$
$$= |bc| . |bc|$$
$$= |bc|^2$$

∴ $|bc|^2 = |ab|^2 + |ac|^2$

Converse of Pythagoras's Theorem

7.

> If the square of the length of one side of a triangle is equal to the sum of the squares of the lengths of the other two sides, then the triangle has a right angle, and this is opposite the longest side.

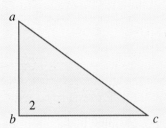

Given: Triangle abc with $[ac]$ the longest side and $|ac|^2 = |ab|^2 + |bc|^2$

To Prove: $|\angle abc| = 90°$

Construction: Draw triangle pqr such that $|\angle pqr| = 90°$,

   $|pq| = |ab|$ and $|qr| = |bc|$.

   Label angles 1 and 2.

Proof: $|ab|^2 + |bc|^2 = |ac|^2$ given

   but $|pq|^2 + |qr|^2 = |pr|^2$ as $|\angle 1| = 90°$

   $\therefore$ $|pr| = |ac|$

   $\therefore$ triangle $abc \equiv$ triangle pqr SSS

   $\therefore$ $|\angle 2| = |\angle 1| = 90°$ corresponding angles

   $\therefore$ $|\angle abc| = 90°$ and is opposite the longest side $[ac]$

8.

> The products of the lengths of the sides of a triangle by the corresponding altitudes are equal.

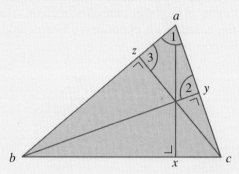

Given:	Triangle abc with altitudes $[ax]$, $[by]$ and $[cz]$.
To Prove:	$\lvert ab \rvert . \lvert cz \rvert = \lvert ac \rvert . \lvert by \rvert = \lvert bc \rvert . \lvert ax \rvert$
Construction:	Mark angles 1, 2 and 3.
Proof:	Consider triangle aby and triangle acz:

$\quad \lvert \angle 1 \rvert = \lvert \angle 1 \rvert$ $\qquad\qquad$ common angle

$\quad \lvert \angle 2 \rvert = \lvert \angle 3 \rvert = 90°$ $\qquad$ given

$\therefore\quad$ triangles aby and acz are equiangular

$\therefore\quad \dfrac{\lvert ab \rvert}{\lvert ac \rvert} = \dfrac{\lvert by \rvert}{\lvert cz \rvert}$ $\qquad$ corresponding sides are in proportion

$\therefore\quad \lvert ab \rvert . \lvert cz \rvert = \lvert ac \rvert . \lvert by \rvert$ $\qquad$ cross-multiply

Similarly, $\lvert ab \rvert . \lvert cz \rvert = \lvert bc \rvert . \lvert ax \rvert$

$\therefore\quad \lvert ab \rvert . \lvert cz \rvert = \lvert ac \rvert . \lvert by \rvert = \lvert bc \rvert . \lvert ax \rvert$

9.

> If the lengths of two sides of a triangle are unequal, then the degree-measures of the angles opposite to them are unequal, with the greater angle opposite the longer side.

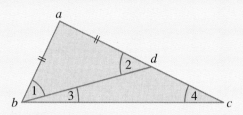

Given:	Triangle abc with $|ac| > |ab|$.
To Prove:	$|\angle abc| > |\angle acb|$
Construction:	Construct point d on $[ac]$ such that $|ad| = |ab|$.
	Join b to d. Mark angles 1, 2, 3 and 4.
Proof:	In triangle abd,

In triangle abd,

$|ab| = |ad|$ construction

$\therefore$ $|\angle 1| = |\angle 2|$ isosceles triangle

In triangle bcd,

$|\angle 2| > |\angle 4|$ exterior angle

$\therefore$ $|\angle 1| > |\angle 4|$

$\therefore$ $|\angle 1| + |\angle 3| > |\angle 4|$

$\therefore$ $|\angle abc| > |\angle acb|$

10.

> The sum of the lengths of any two sides of a triangle is greater than that of the third side.

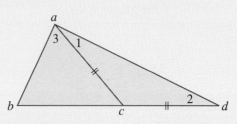

Given:	Triangle abc
To Prove:	$\lvert bc \rvert + \lvert ac \rvert > \lvert ab \rvert$
Construction:	Produce $[bc]$ to d such that $\lvert cd \rvert = \lvert ac \rvert$.
	Join a to d. Mark angles 1, 2 and 3.
Proof:	In triangle acd,

$$\lvert ac \rvert = \lvert cd \rvert \qquad \text{construction}$$
$$\therefore \quad \lvert \angle 1 \rvert = \lvert \angle 2 \rvert \qquad \text{isosceles triangle}$$
$$\therefore \quad \lvert \angle 1 \rvert + \lvert \angle 3 \rvert > \lvert \angle 2 \rvert$$
$$\therefore \quad \lvert bd \rvert > \lvert ab \rvert \qquad \text{side opposite greater angle}$$
$$\text{but} \quad \lvert bd \rvert = \lvert bc \rvert + \lvert cd \rvert$$
$$= \lvert bc \rvert + \lvert ac \rvert$$
$$\therefore \quad \lvert bc \rvert + \lvert ac \rvert > \lvert ab \rvert$$

Exercise 15.1 ▼

1. $tp \parallel qr$, $\lvert qp \rvert = \lvert pr \rvert$ and $\lvert \angle prs \rvert = 140°$.
Find:
   (i) $\lvert \angle qpr \rvert$
   (ii) $\lvert \angle qpt \rvert$.

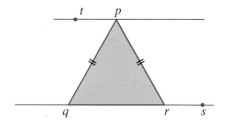

2. L and M are parallel lines.
Find the value of x and the value of y.

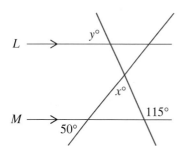

3. A and B are parallel lines.
Find the value of p.

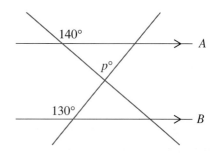

4. In the diagram, $|ab| = |ac|$ and $|\angle bad| = 108°$.

   (i)   Find $|\angle cab|$

   (ii) Find $|\angle abc|$.

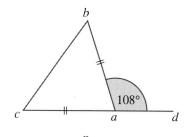

5. $|pr| = |qr| = |rs|$ and $|\angle prq| = 46°$.
Find:

   (i) $|\angle pqr|$

   (ii) $|\angle psr|$.

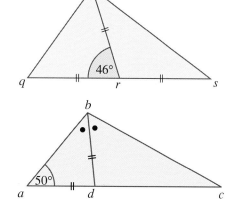

6. In the triangle abc, $|ad| = |bd|$,

   $|\angle abd| = |\angle dbc|$ and $|\angle dab| = 50°$.
Find $|\angle dcb|$.

7. **(i)** $ab \parallel cd$, $|\angle abc| = 40°$, and $|pc| = |pd|$.
   Name another angle that measures $40°$.

         (ii) Calculate the value of   **(a)** a **(b)** b.

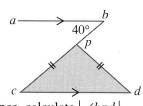

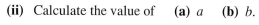

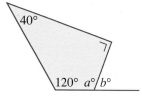

   Hence, calculate $|\angle bpd|$.

8. $|pq| = |qr|$ and
   $|ps| = |pr| = |rs|$.
   Find: **(i)** $|\angle qpr|$ **(ii)** $|\angle psr|$ **(iii)** $|\angle srt|$.

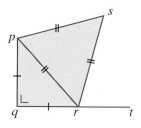

9. Calculate the value of x and the value of y.

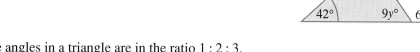

10. The three angles in a triangle are in the ratio $1 : 2 : 3$.
    Find the three angles, in degrees.

11. The supporting wire to the top of a vertical pole is 17 m long and is held to the ground at a distance of 8 m from the foot of the pole.

Calculate h, the height of the pole.

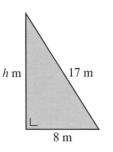

12. In the diagram, $ab \perp bc$ and $ac \perp cd$,
$|ab| = 3$, $|bc| = 4$, and $|ad| = 13$.
Using Pythagoras's theorem twice, calculate:
(i) $|ac|$ **(ii)** $|cd|$.

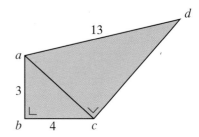

13. In the diagram, $ab \perp bc$ and $ad \perp dc$,
$|ab| = 15$, $|bc| = 20$ and $|cd| = 7$.
Find: **(i)** $|ac|$ **(ii)** $|ad|$.

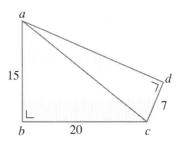

14. In the diagram, $|\angle abd| = 90°$,
$|ab| = 5$, $|ad| = 13$, and $|bc| = 7$.
Calculate:
(i) $|bd|$ **(ii)** $|cd|$
(iii) $|ac|$ (correct to one decimal place).

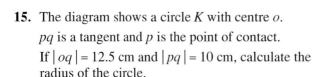
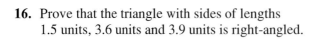

15. The diagram shows a circle K with centre o.
pq is a tangent and p is the point of contact.
If $|oq| = 12.5$ cm and $|pq| = 10$ cm, calculate the radius of the circle.

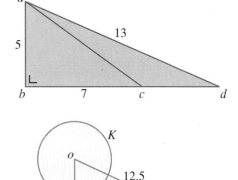

16. Prove that the triangle with sides of lengths 1.5 units, 3.6 units and 3.9 units is right-angled.

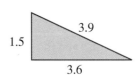

17. In triangle pqr, $|\angle pqr| = 90°$, $|pr| = 7$ cm and $|qr| = 3$ cm.
Calculate $|pq|$, correct to one decimal place.

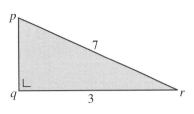

18. In triangle abc, $|\angle abc| = 90°$, $|ab| = 16$ cm and
$|ac| = 34$ cm.
Find:

(i) $|bc|$

(ii) the area of triangle abc.

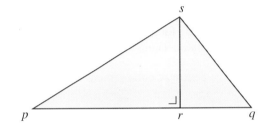

19. In the diagram, $pq \perp rs$, $|pq| = 10$ cm
and the area of triangle $pqs = 40$ cm^2.
Calculate $|rs|$.

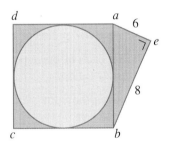

20. In the diagram, $|\angle aeb| = 90°$, $|ae| = 6$ cm and $|be| = 8$ cm.
Calculate the area of the circle inscribed in the square $abcd$
(assume $\pi = 3.14$).

Enlargements

Ray Method

In the diagram below, the triangle abc is the **object** (the starting shape) and the triangle $a'b'c'$ is the
image (the enlarged shape) under an enlargement, centre o and scale factor 3.

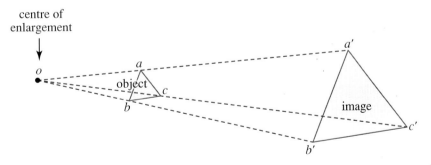

The rays have been drawn from the centre of enlargement, o, to each vertex and beyond. The distance
from the centre of enlargement, o, to each vertex on triangle abc was measured and multiplied by 3.
Thus, $|oa'| = 3|oa|$, $|ob'| = 3|ob|$ and $|oc'| = 3|oc|$.

Note: All measurements are made from the centre of enlargement, o.

Properties of Enlargements

1. The shape of the image is the same as the shape of the object (only size has changed).

2. The amount by which a figure is enlarged is called the 'scale factor' and is denoted by k.

3. image length = k(object length)   or $k = \dfrac{\text{image length}}{\text{object length}}$

4. area of image = k^2(area object)   or $k^2 = \dfrac{\text{area of image}}{\text{area of object}}$

Notes:

1. The scale factor can be less than one (i.e. $0 < k < 1$). In these cases, the image will be smaller than the object. Though smaller, the image is still called an enlargement.

2. The centre of enlargement can be a vertex on the object figure or inside it.

To find the centre of enlargement, do the following:

1. Choose two points on the image and their corresponding points on the original figure.

2. From each of these points on the larger figure draw a line to the corresponding point on the smaller figure.

3. Produce these lines until they intersect at the point which is the centre of enlargement.

Example ▼

The triangle pqr is the image of the triangle abc under an enlargement. $|ab| = 8$ and $|pr| = 24$.
The scale factor of enlargement is 1.5.

(i) Copy the diagram and show how to find the centre of enlargement, o.

(ii) Find: (a) $|pq|$ (b) $|ac|$.

(iii) If the area of triangle abc is 16.4 square units, calculate the area of triangle pqr.

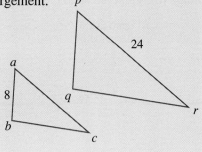

Solution:

(i) Join p to a and continue beyond.
Join r to c and continue beyond.
Continue these lines until they meet.
This is the centre of enlargement, o.

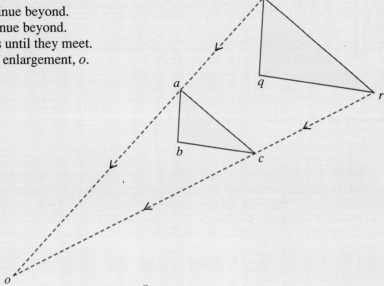

(ii)

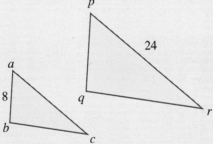

image length = k(object length)

(a) $|pq| = k|ab|$

$|pq| = 1.5(8)$

(put in known values)

$|pq| = 12$

(b) $|pr| = k|ac|$

$24 = 1.5|ac|$

(put in known values)

$16 = |ac|$

(divide both sides by 1.5)

(iii)   area of image = k^2 (area of object)

$\therefore$ area of triangle $pqr = (1.5)^2$ (area of triangle abc)

$= (2.25)(16.4)$

$= 36.9$

Example ▼

The triangle *ors* is the image of the triangle *opq* under an enlargement.
$|op| = 6$ and $|pr| = 7.5$.

(i) Write down the centre of enlargement.

(ii) Find k, the scale factor of enlargement.

(iii) If $|oq| = 8$, find $|qs|$.

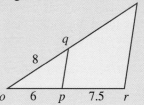

Solution:

(i) The centre of enlargement is the point *o* (as *o* is common to both triangles).
Divide the figure into two separate similar triangles. Mark in known lengths.

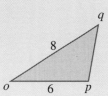

(ii) Scale factor = $k = \dfrac{\text{image length}}{\text{object length}}$

$$= \frac{|or|}{|op|}$$

$$= \frac{13.5}{6}$$

$$= 2.25$$

(iii) image length = k(object length)

$$|os| = k|oq|$$

$$= 2.25(8) = 18$$

$$|qs| = |os| - |oq| = 18 - 8 = 10$$

Example ▼

The rectangle *pqrs* is the image of the rectangle *abcd*,
under an enlargement, centre *o*. If the area of *pqrs*
is 121 cm^2 and the area of *abcd* is 25 cm^2,
find the scale factor of enlargement, k.

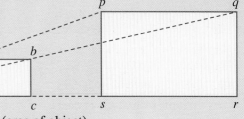

Solution:

(area of image) = k^2	(area of object)
∴ area of rectangle $pqrs$ = k^2	(area of rectangle $abcd$)
$121 = k^2(25)$	(put in known values)
$4.84 = k^2$	(divide both sides by 25)
$\sqrt{4.84} = k$	(take the square root of both sides)
$2.2 = k$	

Thus, the scale factor of enlargement is 2.2.

1. The triangle *pqr* is the image of the triangle *abc* under an enlargement.

   $|pr| = 8$, $|ac| = 4$, $|ab| = 3$ and $|qr| = 4$.

   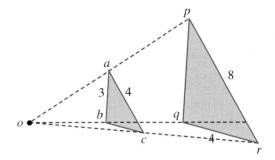

   (i)   Write down the centre of enlargement.

   (ii)   Find the scale factor of enlargement, *k*.

   (iii) Find: (a) $|pq|$ (b) $|bc|$.

   (iv)   If the area of the triangle *abc* is 2.9 square units, find the area of triangle *pqr*.

2. The triangle *pqr* is the image of the triangle *xyz* under the enlargement, centre *o*, with $|xz| = 10$, $|pr| = 15$ and $|pq| = 12$.

   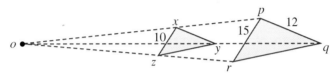

   (i)   Find the scale factor of the enlargement.

   (ii)   Find $|xy|$.

   (iii) The area of the triangle *pqr* is 40.5 square units. Find the area of the triangle *xyz*.

3. The triangle *ors* is the image of the triangle *opq* under an enlargement.

   $|op| = 9$ and $|pr| = 11.25$.

   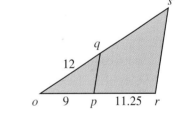

   (i)   Write down the centre of enlargement.

   (ii)   Find *k*, the scale factor of enlargement.

   (iii) If $|oq| = 12$, find $|qs|$.

   (iv)   If the area of triangle *opq* is 32 square units, find the area of triangle *ors*.

   (v)   Find the area of *pqrs*.

4. The triangle *pst* is the image of the triangle *pqr*, under an enlargement.

   $|pq| = 6$, $|qs| = 1\frac{1}{2}$ and $|pr| = 4$.

   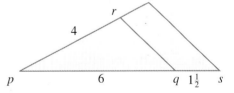

   (i)   Write down the centre of enlargement.

   (ii)   Find *k*, the scale factor of enlargement.

   (iii) Find: (a) $|rt|$ (b) $|pt|:|rt|$.

   (iv)   If the area of triangle *pts* is 9.375 square units, calculate the area of triangle *pqr*.

   (v)   Find the area of *qrts*.

5. The triangle *oab* is the image of the triangle *oxy* under the enlargement, centre *o*, with $|xy| = 8$, $|ox| = 10$ and $|ab| = 18$.

   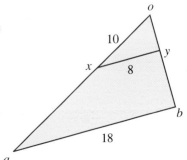

   (i)   Find the scale factor of the enlargement.

   (ii)   Find $|xa|$.

   (iii) The area of the triangle *oab* is 101.25 square units. Find the area of the triangle *oxy*.

6. The triangle *rst* is the image of the triangle *rpq* under an enlargement with centre *r*.

$|pr| = 6$, $|ps| = 4.5$ and $|qr| = 4$.

  (i) Find the scale factor of the enlargement.

  (ii) Find $|qt|$.

  (iii) The area of the triangle *rst* is 24.5 square units.

   Find the area of the triangle *pqs*.

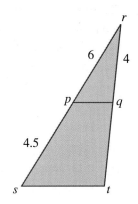

7. The rectangle *aefg* is an enlargement of the rectangle *abcd* with $|ac| = 5$, $|cf| = 3$.

  (i) Write down the centre of enlargement.

  (ii) Find *k*, the scale factor of the enlargement.

  (iii) If the area of the rectangle *aefg* is 62.72 square units, find the area of the rectangle *abcd*.

  (iv) A further enlargement will map rectangle *aefg* back onto rectangle *abcd*.

   Find the scale factor, if the centre of enlargement remains the same.

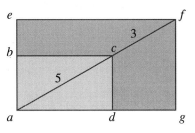

8. The diagram shows a square with sides of 6 cm.

  (i) Copy the diagram and mark, *o*, the point of intersection of the diagonals.

  (ii) Draw the image of the square under the enlargement with centre *o* and scale factor $\frac{2}{3}$.

  (iii) Calculate the area of this image square.

  (iv) Under another enlargement the area of the square with sides 6 cm is 70.56 cm².

   What is the scale factor of this enlargement?

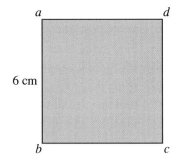

9. The triangle *ors* is the image of the triangle *opq* under an enlargement, centre *o*.

$|rs| = 12$ and $|pq| = 20$.

  (i) Find the scale factor of the enlargement.

  (ii) If the area of triangle *opq* is 150 square units, find the area of triangle *ors*.

  (iii) Write down the area of the region *pqsr*.

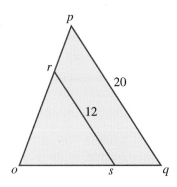

10. The triangle *xyz* is the image of the triangle *abc* under an enlargement, centre *o*.

If the area of triangle *abc* is 40 cm^2 and the area of triangle *xyz* is 122.5 cm^2, find the scale factor of enlargement, *k*.

If $|xy| = 26.25$ cm, find $|ac|$.

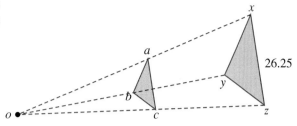

11. The triangle *xyz* is the image of the triangle *abc* under an enlargement.

    (i)   Copy the diagram and show how to find the centre of enlargement.

   (ii) If the area of triangle *abc* is 40 cm^2 and the area of triangle *xyz* is 25.6 cm^2, find the scale factor of enlargement, *k*.

  (iii) If $|bc| = 6.5$ cm, find $|yz|$.

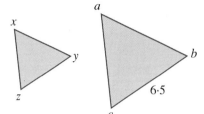

OPTIONS

LINEAR PROGRAMMING

Half-planes

On the right is part of the graph of the line $x + 2y - 2 = 0$.

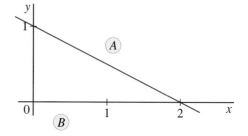

It divides the plane into 3 regions:

1. All the points on the line.

2. All the points in the region A.

3. All the points in the region B.

The regions A and B are called **half-planes**.

Linear Inequalities

All the points on the line are represented by the equation, $x + 2y - 2 = 0$.
All the points on **one** side of the line are represented by the linear inequality, $x + 2y - 2 > 0$.
All the points on the **other** side of the line are represented by the linear inequality, $x + 2y - 2 < 0$.

Note: If the inequality is given in the form $x + 2y - 2 \geqslant 0$, or $x + 2y - 2 \leqslant 0$, then the points **on** the line are also included.

To graph the region (half-plane) represented by a linear inequality of the form $ax + by \geqslant k$ or $ax + by \leqslant k$, do the following:

Step 1: Graph the line $ax + by = k$ by finding two points on the line, and drawing a line through these points.

           The usual points are where the line cuts the x- and y-axes.

           (**Remember:** on the x-axis $y = 0$, on the y-axis $x = 0$).

Step 2: Test a point not on the line, usually $(0, 0)$, in the inequality.

        (a) If the inequality is **true** the arrows point towards the point being tested.

        (b) If the inequality is **false** the arrows point away from the point being tested.

Notes:

1. It is usual to select the point $(0, 0)$ if it is not on the line.

2. The required region is usually indicated by arrows or shading.

3. If both sides of an inequality are multiplied or divided by a **negative** number, the direction of the inequality must be **reversed**.

Graph the inequality, $2x + 3y \geqslant 6$, indicating the correct half-plane.

Solution:

Step 1: Graph the line $2x + 3y = 6$

$2x + 3y = 6$

$y = 0$	$x = 0$
$2x = 6$	$3y = 6$
$x = 3$	$y = 2$
$(3, 0)$	$(0, 2)$

Plot the points $(3, 0)$ and $(0, 2)$ and draw a line through them.

Step 2: Test $(0, 0)$ in $2x + 3y \geqslant 6$

$2(0) + 3(0) \geqslant 6$

$0 \geqslant 6$ **False**

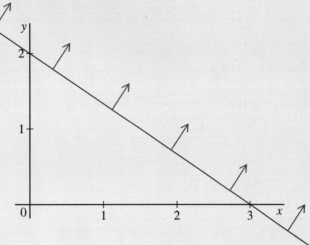

$(0, 0)$ does not satisfy the inequality, hence, all the points on the opposite side of the line $(0, 0)$, indicated by arrows in the diagram, is the required region.

Illustrate, on separate diagrams, the set of points (x, y) which satisfy:

(i) $x \geqslant 0$ **(ii)** $y \geqslant 0$ **(iii)** $x \geqslant 10$ **(iv)** $y \leqslant 8$ $x, y \in \mathbf{R}$.

Solution:

(i) $x \geqslant 0$

$x = 0$ is the equation of the y-axis.
$x \geqslant 0$ is the set of points **on** and to the **right** of the y-axis.

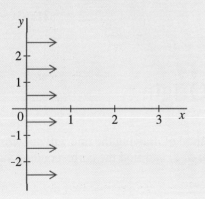

(ii) $y \geqslant 0$

$y = 0$ is the equation of the x-axis.
$y \geqslant 0$ is the set of points **on** and **above** the x-axis.

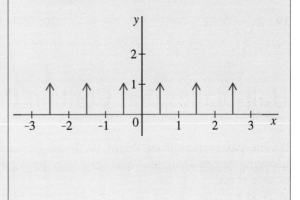

(iii) $x \geqslant 10$

This is the set of points **on** and to the **right** of the line $x = 10$.

(iv) $y \leqslant 8$

This is the set of points **on** and **below** the line $y = 8$.

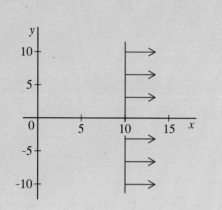

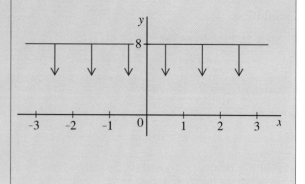

Exercise 16.1 ▼

Illustrate, on separate diagrams, the set of points (x, y) which satisfy each of the following inequalities, $x, y \in \mathbf{R}$:

1. $x + y \leqslant 4$

2. $x + y \geqslant 3$

3. $x + 2y \geqslant 6$

4. $3x + 2y \leqslant 12$

5. $4x + 5y \leqslant 20$

6. $5x + 2y \geqslant 20$

7. $3x + 4y \leqslant 24$

8. $x + 2y \geqslant 10$

9. $3x + 5y \leqslant 30$

10. $x \geqslant 2$

11. $y \geqslant 3$

12. $x \geqslant 5$

13. $y \geqslant 4$

14. $x \leqslant 8$

15. $y \leqslant 10$

16. $2x - y \leqslant 8$

17. $5x - 2y \leqslant 20$

18. $3x - 4y \geqslant 24$

19. $2x + y \geqslant -2$

20. $x - y \leqslant -1$

21. $3x - y \geqslant -6$

Half-planes that Contain the Origin

If a line passes through the origin, $(0, 0)$, the intercept method of drawing the line will not work. If this happens, choose a suitable value for x (e.g. the coefficient of y) and find the corresponding value of y, or vice versa.

Graph the inequality $x - 4y \geqslant 0$, indicating the correct half-plane.

Solution:

Step 1: Graph the line $x - 4y = 0$

One point on this line is $(0, 0)$.
Let $x = 4$ (coefficient of y)

$$x - 4y = 0$$
$$4 - 4y = 0$$
$$-4y = -4$$
$$4y = 4$$
$$y = 1$$
point $(4, 1)$

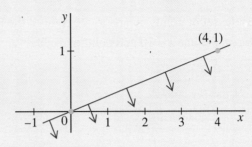

Plot the points $(0, 0)$ and $(4, 1)$ and draw a line through these points.

Step 2: Test $(2, 0)$, not on the line, in $x - 4y \geqslant 0$

$$2 - 4(0) \geqslant 0$$
$$2 \geqslant 0 \quad \textbf{True}$$

$(2, 0)$ satisfies the inequality, hence, all the points on the same side of the line as $(2, 0)$, indicated by arrows in the diagram, is the required region.

Illustrate, on separate diagrams, the set of points (x, y) which satisfy each of the following inequalities, $x, y \in \mathbf{R}$:

1. $x - 2y \geqslant 0$	**2.** $x + 3y \leqslant 0$	**3.** $2x - y \leqslant 0$
4. $3x - y \geqslant 0$	**5.** $2x - 3y \geqslant 0$	**6.** $4x + 3y \geqslant 0$
7. $x + y \geqslant 0$	**8.** $4x - y \geqslant 0$	**9.** $5x - 3y \leqslant 0$

Simultaneous Linear Inequalities

Often it is required to find a region which is common to more than one inequality. This common region is often called the 'feasible region' and is found with the following steps:

Step 1: Complete the calculations to draw the lines and determine the direction of the arrows.

Step 2: Draw a diagram and shade in the common region.

Note: If not given in the question, it is good practice to label each inequality with a capital letter, e.g., A, B, C, D, etc. and put these on your diagram.

Example ▼

Illustrate the set of points (x, y) that simultaneously satisfy the three inequalities:

$$x \geqslant 10 \qquad x + y \leqslant 40 \qquad x + 3y \geqslant 60$$

Solution:

Step 1:

A: $x \geqslant 10$ is the set of points on and to the right of the line $x = 10$,

∴   arrows on the line $x = 10$ and pointing right.

B: $x + y \leqslant 40$	C: $x + 3y \geqslant 60$
Line: $x + y = 40$	Line: $x + 3y = 60$

$$x + y = 40$$

$y = 0$	$x = 0$
$x = 40$	$y = 40$
$(40, 0)$	$(0, 40)$

$$x + 3y = 60$$

$y = 0$	$x = 0$
$x = 60$	$3y = 60$
$(60, 0)$	$y = 20$
	$(0, 20)$

Test $(0, 0)$ in $x + y \leqslant 40$

$$(0) + (0) \leqslant 40$$

$$0 \leqslant 40 \quad \textbf{True}$$

∴   arrows point towards $(0, 0)$

Test $(0, 0)$ in $x + 3y \geqslant 60$

$$(0) + 3(0) \geqslant 60$$

$$0 \geqslant 60 \quad \textbf{False}$$

∴   arrows point away from $(0, 0)$

Step 2:

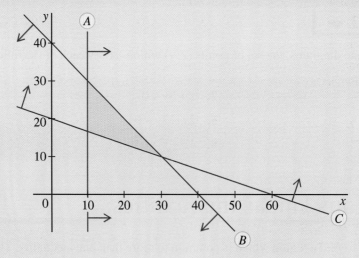

The shaded area is the only region which satisfies the three inequalities simultaneously.

Illustrate the set of points (x, y) that simultaneously satisfy the inequalities:

1. $x \geqslant 0,$ $y \geqslant 0,$ $x + y \leqslant 5$

2. $x \geqslant 0,$ $y \geqslant 0,$ $2x + y \leqslant 6$

3. $x \geqslant 1,$ $y \geqslant 2,$ $3x + 2y \leqslant 12$

4. $x \geqslant 2,$ $y \geqslant 3,$ $5x + 3y \leqslant 30$

5. $x \geqslant 0,$ $y \geqslant 0,$ $x + 2y \leqslant 10,$ $2x + y \leqslant 8$

6. $x \geqslant 0,$ $y \geqslant 0,$ $x + y \leqslant 5,$ $x + 4y \leqslant 8$

7. $y \geqslant 0,$ $x + 2y \leqslant 14,$ $5x + 4y \geqslant 40$

8. $x \geqslant 0,$ $y \geqslant 2,$ $2x + y \leqslant 8,$ $x + y \leqslant 6$

9. $x \geqslant 0,$ $x + 2y \leqslant 4,$ $x - y \leqslant 2$

10. $y \geqslant 1,$ $x + 2y \leqslant 6,$ $4x + y \geqslant -4$

Finding the Inequality

Sometimes we are given the graph of a linear inequality and asked to write down, algebraically, the region that the inequality represents.

When this happens do the following:

Step 1: Find the equation of the line in the form $ax + by + c = 0$ (if not given).

Step 2: Pick a point, not on the line, in the indicated half-plane (indicated by arrows or shading). Pick $(0, 0)$ if possible, otherwise pick a point on the x- or y-axis that you are certain is in the indicated half-plane.

Step 3: Put the coordinates of the point chosen into:
   (a) $ax + by + c \geqslant 0$ **or**   **(b)** $ax + by + c \leqslant 0$

Step 4: Two possibilities arise:
   (a) The inequality chosen is correct. Keep the inequality chosen in step 3.
   (b) The inequality chosen is incorrect. Reverse the inequality in step 3.

Example ▼

The equation of the line M is $x - y + 1 = 0$ and the equation of the line N is $x + y - 6 = 0$.

Write down the three inequalities which define the triangular region indicated in the diagram.

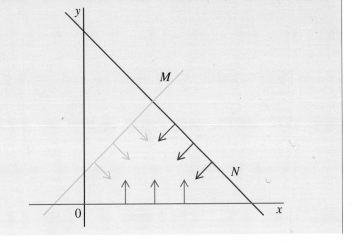

Solution:

The first inequality is $y \geqslant 0$, i.e. on the x-axis and above.

Step 1: Given M: $x - y + 1 = 0$	**Step 1:** Given N: $x + y - 6 = 0$
Step 2: $(0, 0)$ is in the required half-plane.	**Step 2:** $(0, 0)$ is in the required half-plane.
Step 3: Test $(0, 0)$ in $x - y + 1 \geqslant 0$ $\quad 0 - 0 + 1 \geqslant 0$ $\quad 1 \geqslant 0$ **True**	**Step 3:** Test $(0, 0)$ in $x + y - 6 \geqslant 0$ $\quad 0 + 0 - 6 \geqslant 0$ $\quad -6 \geqslant 0$ **False**
Step 4: Keep the inequality chosen in step 3. Thus, the required inequality is: M: $x - y + 1 \geqslant 0$	**Step 4:** Reverse the inequality chosen in step 3. Thus, the required inequality is: N: $x + y - 6 \leqslant 0$

Exercise 16.4 ▼

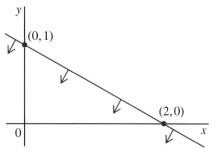

1. The line L passes through the points $(2, 0)$ and $(0, 1)$.
   - **(i)** Find the equation of K.
   - **(ii)** Write down an inequality which defines the region indicated in the diagram.

In each case, find the inequality which defines the region indicated:

2.

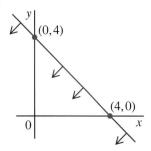

3.

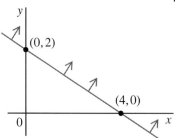

4.

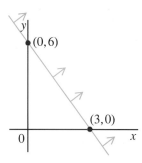

5.

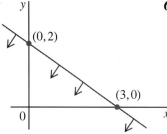

6.

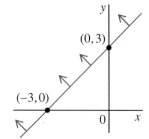

7.

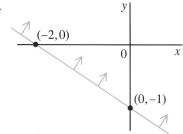

8.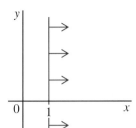

9.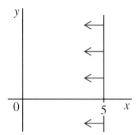

10.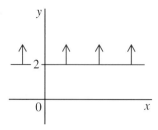

11.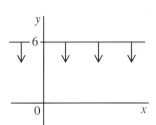

12.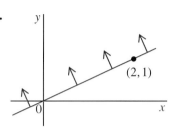

13.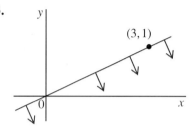

14. The line K passes through the points $(3, 0)$ and $(0, 1)$.

    (i) Find the equation of the line K.

    (ii) Write down three inequalities which define the shaded region in the diagram.

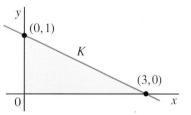

15. The line L passes through the points $(5, 0)$ and $(0, 1)$.

    (i) Find the equation of the line L.

    (ii) Write down three inequalities which define the shaded region in the diagram.

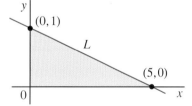

16. The equation of the line is L is $x + y - 6 = 0$.

The equation of the line K is $y - 4 = 0$.

Write down four inequalities which define the shaded region in the diagram.

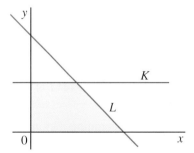

17. The equation of the line K is $x - y + 2 = 0$.

The equation of the line L is $x + y - 6 = 0$.

Write down four inequalities which define the shaded region in the diagram.

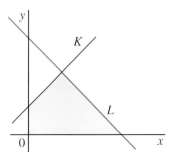

18. The equation of the line K is $x - 2y + 2 = 0$ and the equation of the line L is $3x + y - 6 = 0$.

Write down three inequalities which define the triangular region indicated in the diagram.

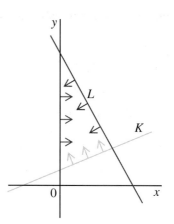

19. The equation of the line M is $x - y - 2 = 0$ and the equation of the line N is $x + 2y - 8 = 0$.

Write down three inequalities which define the triangular region indicated in the diagram.

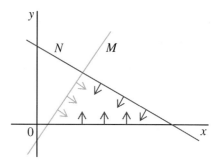

20. The equation of the line L is $8x + 5y - 40 = 0$.
The equation of the line M is $x - y = 0$.

Write down three inequalities which define the shaded region in the diagram.

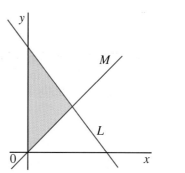

Maximising and Minimising

Having found the common region of three or more inequalities, we may be asked to find the coordinates of the point that will give the maximum or minimum value in the region according to a given rule.

The following is very important:

> The maximum and minimum values of a region bounded by straight lines will **always** occur at one of the vertices of the region.

The maximum or minimum value of the common region is found with the following steps:

Step 1: Do all the calculations to draw the lines and determine the direction of the arrows.

Step 2: Draw a diagram, shade in the common region and label each vertex.

Step 3: Find the coordinates of the vertices of the common region using simultaneous equations (do not read from your graph). However, any vertex which lies on the x- or y-axis can be written down from the graph. Put in the coordinates of each vertex on your diagram.

Step 4: Substitute the coordinates of the vertices of the common region into the given rule, using a table, to find the maximum or minimum values.

Example ▼

(i) Illustrate the set K of points (x, y) that simultaneously satisfy the four inequalities:

$$x \geqslant 0 \qquad y \geqslant 10 \qquad x + y \leqslant 50 \qquad 2x + y \leqslant 60$$

(ii) Find the couple $(x, y) \in K$ for which $10x + 8y$ is **(a)** a maximum **(b)** a minimum, and state this maximum and minimum.

Solution:

Step 1:

A: $x \geqslant 0$ is the set of points on and to the right of the y-axis,
∴   arrows on the y-axis and pointing right.

B: $y \geqslant 10$ is the set of points on and to the right of the y-axis,
∴   arrows on the line $y = 10$ and pointing upwards.

$C: x + y \leqslant 50$		$D: 2x + y \leqslant 60$	
Line: $x + y = 50$		Line: $2x + y \leqslant 60$	
$x + y = 50$		$2x + y = 60$	

$y = 0$	$x = 0$	$y = 0$	$x = 0$
$x = 50$	$y = 50$	$2x = 60$	$y = 60$
$(50, 0)$	$(0, 50)$	$x = 30$	$(0, 60)$
		$(30, 0)$	

Test $(0, 0)$ in $x + y \leqslant 50$
$$(0) + (0) \leqslant 50$$
$$(0) \leqslant 50 \quad \textbf{True}$$
∴   arrows point towards $(0, 0)$.

Test $(0, 0)$ in $2x + y \leqslant 60$
$$2(0) + (0) \leqslant 60$$
$$(0) \leqslant 60 \quad \textbf{True}$$
∴   arrows point towards $(0, 0)$.

Step 2:

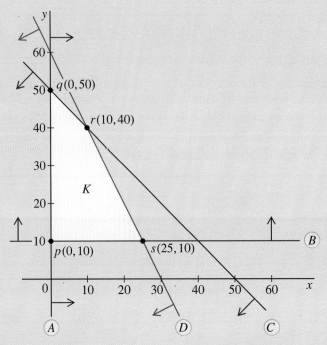

The shaded area K is the only region which satisfies the four inequalities at the same time.

Step 3: Let the coordinates of K be p, q, r and s as shown on the diagram.

From the diagram $p = (0, 10)$ and $q = (0, 50)$

$$r = C \cap D$$

$2x + y = 60$	$\textcircled{D}$	$x + y = 50$ $\textcircled{C}$
$\underline{-x - y = -50}$	$\textcircled{C} \times -1$	$10 + y = 50$
$x = 10$	(add)	$y = 40$
put $x = 10$ into C or D		

$$\therefore \quad r = (10, 40).$$

$$s = B \cap D$$

$y = 10$	$\textcircled{B}$	$2x + y = 60$ $\textcircled{D}$
put $y = 10$ into $\textcircled{D}$		$2x + 10 = 60$
		$2x = 50$
		$x = 25$

$$\therefore \quad s = (25, 10)$$

The coordinates of the vertices of K are $p(0, 10)$, $q(0, 50)$, $r(10, 40)$ and $s(25, 10)$.

Step 4: Using these coordinates, find the maximum and minimum values of $10x + 8y$.

A table is useful for this:

Vertex	$10x$	$8y$	$10x + 8y$	
$p(0, 10)$	0	80	80 ←	minimum value
$q(0, 50)$	0	400	400	
$r(10, 40)$	100	320	420 ←	maximum value
$s(25, 10)$	250	80	330	

From the table,

420 is the maximum value of $10x + 8y$ and it occurs at $(10, 40)$.

80 is the minimum value of $10x + 8y$ and it occurs at $(0, 10)$.

Exercise 16.5 ▼

1. (i) Illustrate the set Q of points (x, y) that simultaneously satisfy the four inequalities:
$$x \geq 0 \qquad y \geq 0 \qquad x + y \leq 8 \qquad 2x + y \leq 12$$

(ii) Calculate the coordinates of the vertices of Q.

(iii) Find the couple $(x, y) \in Q$ for which $3x + 2y$ is a maximum and state this maximum.

2. (i) Illustrate the set P of points (x, y) that simultaneously satisfy the four inequalities:
$$x \geq 0 \qquad y \geq 0 \qquad x + y \leq 12 \qquad 3x + 2y \leq 30$$

(ii) Calculate the coordinates of the vertices of P.

(iii) Find the couple $(x, y) \in P$ for which $10x + 5y$ is a maximum and state this maximum.

3. (i) Illustrate the set K of points (x, y) that simultaneously satisfy the four inequalities:
$$x \geq 0 \qquad y \geq 0 \qquad 2x + y \leq 40 \qquad x + 2y \leq 50$$

(ii) Calculate the coordinates of the vertices of K.

(iii) Find the couple $(x, y) \in K$ for which $15x + 3y$ is a maximum and state this maximum.

4. Illustrate the set S of points (x, y) that simultaneously satisfy the three inequalities:
$$x \geq 5 \qquad 4x + 5y \leq 100 \qquad x + 5y \geq 40$$

(ii) Calculate the coordinates of the vertices of S.

(iii) Find the couple $(x, y) \in S$ for which $100x + 75y$ is a minimum and state this minimum.

5. (i) Illustrate the set S of points (x, y) that simultaneously satisfy the three inequalities:
$$y \geq 0 \qquad x + 2y \leq 140 \qquad 5x + 4y \geq 400$$

(ii) Calculate the coordinates of the vertices of S.

(iii) Find the couple $(x, y) \in S$ for which $30x + 10y$ is **(a)** a maximum **(b)** a minimum, and state this maximum and minimum.

6. (i) Illustrate the set T of points (x, y) that simultaneously satisfy the four inequalities:
$$x \geqslant 0 \qquad y \geqslant 2 \qquad 2x + y \leqslant 8 \qquad x + y \leqslant 6$$

(ii) Calculate the coordinates of the vertices of T.

(iii) Find the couple $(x, y) \in T$ for which $6x + 5y$ is **(a)** a maximum **(b)** a minimum, and state this maximum and minimum.

Linear Programming

Linear inequalities can be used to solve practical problems. When used in this way we call it **Linear Programming**. Linear programming deals with trying to find the best solution, usually the maximum or minimum, to a wide range of problems within certain limitations called **constraints**. When solving a problem in linear programming, read the question carefully a few times and do the following:

1. Let x equal one unknown number and let y equal the other unknown number that is required (unless given in the question).

2. Using the information in the question, convert the constraints into linear inequalities in terms of x and y (using a table can be useful).

3. Graph each of the inequalities and shade in the feasible region.

4. Find the coordinates of the vertices of this common region.

5. Write the objective function, the expression to be maximised or minimised, in terms of x and y.

6. Substitute, separately, the coordinates of the vertices of the feasible region (obtained in **Step 4**) into the objective function, using a table, to find the maximum or minimum values.

Note: In certain questions the inequalities $x \geqslant 0$ and $y \geqslant 0$ will be given in disguise. This is because it is physically impossible for x and y to be negative.

Make sure that both sides of the inequality are measured in the same units.

Example ▼

A firm exports two types of machine, P and Q. Type P occupies $2 \, m^3$ of space and type Q, $4 \, m^3$. Type P weighs $9 \, kg$ and type Q, $6 \, kg$. The available shipping space is $1,600 \, m^3$ and the total weight of the machines cannot exceed $3,600 \, kg$. The profit on type P is €5,000 and the profit on type Q is €4,000.

How many of each machine must be exported to bring a maximum profit and what is the profit?

Solution:

There are two constraints, space and weight.

Step 1: Let x = the number of type P exported
and y = the number of type Q exported.

Step 2: The inequalities given in disguise are:

$$x \geqslant 0 \qquad y \geqslant 0$$

(It is impossible to export a negative number of machines.)

We use a table to help us to write down the other two inequalities.

	x	y	
Space	2	4	$\leqslant 1{,}600$
Weight	9	6	$\leqslant 3{,}600$

Space constraint: $\quad 2x + 4y \leqslant 1{,}600$

$$x + 2y \leqslant 800$$

(divide both sides by 2)

Weight constraint: $\quad 9x + 6y \leqslant 3{,}600$

$$3x + 2y \leqslant 1{,}200$$

(divide both sides by 3)

The four inequalities are:

$$A: x \geqslant 0, \quad B: y \geqslant 0, \quad C: x + 2y \leqslant 800, \quad D: 3x + 2y \leqslant 1{,}200$$

Step 3: $A: x \geqslant 0$, is the set of points on and to the right of the y-axis,

$\therefore$ arrows on the y-axis and pointing right.

$B: y \geqslant 0$, is the set of points on and above the x-axis,

$\therefore$ arrows on the x-axis and pointing upwards.

$C: x + 2y \leqslant 800$

Line: $x + 2y = 800$

$x + 2y = 800$

$y = 0$	$x = 0$
$x = 800$	$2y = 800$
$(800, 0)$	$y = 400$
	$(0, 400)$

Test $(0, 0)$ in $x + 2y \leqslant 800$

$$(0) + 2(0) \leqslant 800$$

$$0 \leqslant 800 \quad \textbf{True}$$

$\therefore$ arrows point towards $(0, 0)$.

$D: 3x + 2y \leqslant 1{,}200$

Line: $3x + 2y = 1{,}200$

$3x + 2y = 1{,}200$

$y = 0$	$x = 0$
$3x = 1{,}200$	$2y = 1{,}200$
$x = 400$	$y = 600$
$(400, 0)$	$(0, 600)$

Test $(0, 0)$ in $3x + 2y \leqslant 1{,}200$

$$3(0) + 2(0) \leqslant 1{,}200$$

$$0 \leqslant 1{,}200 \quad \textbf{True}$$

$\therefore$ arrows point towards $(0, 0)$.

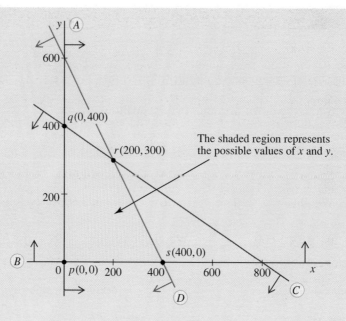

Step 4: Let the vertices of the shaded region be p, q, r and s (as shown).

From the diagram: $p = (0, 0)$, $q = (0, 400)$, $s = (400, 0)$.

We now solve the simultaneous equations $x + 2y = 800$ and $3x + 2y = 1,200$ to find the coordinates of r (cannot be read from the graph).

$-x - 2y = -800$ Ⓒ $\times -1$	$x + 2y = 800$ Ⓒ
$3x + 2y = 1,200$ Ⓓ	$200 + 2y = 800$
$\overline{2x = 400}$ (add)	$2y = 600$
$x = 200$	$y = 300$
put $x = 200$ into C or D.	

$$\therefore \quad r = (200, 300)$$

Step 5: The profit on type P is €5,000 and the profit on type Q is €4,000

$\therefore$ the profit will be €$(5,000x + 4,000y)$

$\therefore$ the objective function is $5,000x + 4,000y$.

Step 6: Using a table, the coordinates of p, q, r and s are substituted, separately, into $5,000x + 4,000y$ to find the maximum value.

Vertex	$5,000x$	$4,000y$	$5,000x + 4,000y$	
$p(0, 0)$	0	0	0	
$q(0, 400)$	0	1,600,000	1,600,000	
$r(200, 300)$	1,000,000	1,200,000	2,200,000 ←	maximum value
$s(400, 0)$	2,000,000	0	2,000,000	

From the table, the firm should export 200 machines of type P and 300 machines of type Q to get a maximum profit of €2,200,000.

370

A ship has space for at most 200 containers, which are of two types – refrigerated and unrefrigerated. Each refrigerated container carries a load of 3 tonnes and each unrefrigerated container carries a load of 8 tonnes. The maximum load the ship can carry is 1,200 tonnes.

Freight charges on each refrigerated container are €100 and on each unrefrigerated container €80.

Graph the set showing the possible numbers of each type of container that the ship can carry. If operating costs on each journey amount to €14,000, calculate the maximum profit if a ready supply of each container is available and state the number of each type of container the ship should carry to achieve this maximum profit.

Indicate by the letter K that region of your graph where the ship is not operating at a loss.

Solution:

There are two constraints, the number of containers and the total weight.

Step 1: Let x = the number of refrigerated containers and
$\qquad$ y = the number of unrefrigerated containers.

Step 2: The inequalities given in disguise are $x \geqslant 0$ and $y \geqslant 0$

$\qquad$ (It is impossible to have a negative number of containers.)

$\qquad$ We use a table to write down the other two inequalities.

	x	y	
Number	1	1	$\leqslant 200$
Weight	3	8	$\leqslant 1200$

Number constraint: $x + y \leqslant 200$ $\qquad\qquad$ Weight constraint: $3x + 8y \leqslant 1200$

The four inequalities are:

$\qquad$ A: $x \geqslant 0$, $\qquad$ B: $y \geqslant 0$, $\qquad$ C: $x + y \leqslant 200$ $\qquad$ D: $3x + 8y \leqslant 1,200$

Step 3: A: $x \geqslant 0$ is the set of points on and to the right of the y-axis,

$\qquad$ ∴ arrows on the y-axis and pointing right.

$\qquad$ B: $y \geqslant 0$ is the set of points on and above the x-axis,

$\qquad$ ∴ arrows on the x-axis and pointing upwards.

C: $x + y \leqslant 200$ $\qquad\qquad\qquad\qquad\qquad$ D: $3x + 8y \leqslant 1,200$

Line: $x + y = 200$ $\qquad\qquad\qquad\qquad\qquad$ Line: $3x + 8y = 1,200$

$x + y = 200$ $\qquad\qquad\qquad\qquad\qquad\qquad$ $3x + 8y = 1,200$

$y = 0$	$x = 0$
$x = 200$	$y = 200$
$(200, 0)$	$(0, 200)$

$y = 0$	$x = 0$
$3x = 1,200$	$8y = 1,200$
$x = 400$	$y = 150$
$(400, 0)$	$(0, 150)$

Test $(0, 0)$ in $x + y \leqslant 200$

$\qquad\qquad$ $0 + 0 \leqslant 200$

$\qquad\qquad\qquad$ $0 \leqslant 200$ $\quad$ **True**

∴ arrows point towards $(0, 0)$.

Test $(0, 0)$ in $3x + 8y \leqslant 1,200$

$\qquad\qquad$ $3(0) + 8(0) \leqslant 1,200$

$\qquad\qquad\qquad\qquad$ $0 \leqslant 1,200$ $\quad$ **True**

∴ arrows point towards $(0, 0)$.

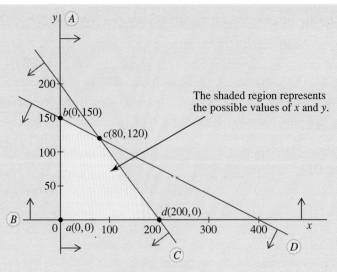

Step 4: Let the vertices of the shaded region be a, b, c and d (as shown).
$a = (0, 0)$ and we have already shown that $b = (0, 150)$ and $d = (200, 0)$.

We now solve the simultaneous equations $x + y = 200$ and $3x + 8y = 1,200$ to find the coordinates of c (cannot be read from the graph).

$x + y = 200$	Ⓒ	Put $y = 120$ into Ⓒ or Ⓓ
$3x + 8y = 1,200$	Ⓓ	$x + y = 200$ Ⓒ
$-3x - 3y = -600$	Ⓒ × − 3	$x + 120 = 200$
$3x + 8y = 1,200$	Ⓒ	$x = 80$
$5y = 600$	(add)	
$y = 120$		

Thus, the coordinates of c are $(80, 120)$.

Step 5: Freight charges (income):
Freight charges on each refrigerated container are €100.
Freight charges on each unrefrigerated container are €80.
∴   Freight charge will be €$(100x + 80y)$
∴   the objective function is $100x + 80y$.

Step 6: Using a table, the coordinates of a, b, c and d are substituted, separately, into $100x + 80y$ to find maximum income.

Vertex	$100x$	$80y$	$100x + 80y$	
$a(0, 0)$	0	0	0	
$b(0, 150)$	0	12,000	12,000	
$c(80, 120)$	8,000	9,000	17,000	
$d(200, 0)$	20,000	0	20,000	⟵ maximum income

Maximum profit = Maximum income − Costs
= €20,000 − €14,000 = €6,000

Thus, the maximum profit is €6,000 and this occurs when the ship carries 200 refrigerated containers and no unrefrigerated containers.

For the ship not to be operating at a loss we require that the freight charges be at least €14,000,

i.e.   Freight charges $\geqslant 14,000$

$\therefore$ $100x + 80y \geqslant 14,000$ (charges are $100x + 80y$)

$$10x + 8y \geqslant 1,400$$

$$5x + 4y \geqslant 700$$

We now graph the inequality $5x + 4y \geqslant 700$.

Line: $5x + 4y = 700$

$5x + 4y = 700$

$y = 0$	$x = 0$
$5x = 700$	$4y = 700$
$x = 140$	$y = 175$
$(140, 0)$	$(0, 175)$

Test $(0, 0)$ in $5x + 4y \geqslant 700$

$$5(0) + 4(0) \geqslant 700$$

$$0 \geqslant 700 \quad \textbf{False}$$

$\therefore$ arrows point away from $(0, 0)$.

The region K, where the freight charges are at least €14,000, is indicated on the graph.

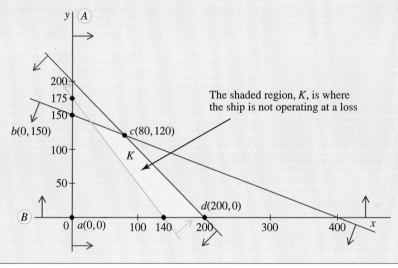

The shaded region, K, is where the ship is not operating at a loss

Exercise 16.6 ▼

1. A manufacturer has a ready-made market for components of two types, type A and type B. The following table shows the time and energy requirements for each component:

	Type A	Type B	Maximum available
Minutes per component	4	4	200
Energy units per component	3	6	240

(i)   Taking x to represent the number of type A and y to represent the number of type B, write down two inequalities in x and y and illustrate these on a graph.

(ii) If the profit on each type of A component is €90 and on each type B component is €100, calculate the number of components of each type that should be made in order to have a maximum profit. What is this profit?

2. A factory can produce two types of bicycle, racing bicycles and mountain bicycles. The following table shows the cost and time requirement for each bicycle:

	Racing bicycle	Mountain bicycle	Maximum available
Cost of materials	€180	€120	€2,160
Labour hours	9	12	144

(i) Taking x to represent the number of racing bicycles and y to represent the number of mountain bicycles, write down two inequalities in x and y and illustrate these on a graph.

(ii) If the profit on each racing bicycle is €240 and the profit on each mountain bicycle is €200, calculate the number of each type of bicycle that should be made in order to have a maximum profit. What is this profit?

3. A floor manager is going to install two types of machine, small and large. The following table shows the number of operators and the space requirements for each machine:

	Small	Large	Maximum available
Number of operators	5	4	40
Space in m²	4	8	56

(i) Taking x to represent the number of small machines and y to represent the number of large machines, write down two inequalities in x and y and illustrate these on a graph.

(ii) If the profit on each small machine is €120 per day and the profit on each large machine is €200 per day, calculate the number of each type of machine that should be installed in order to have a maximum profit. What is this profit?

4. A manufacturer has a ready-made market for products of two types, type P and type Q. The following table shows the cutting and finishing requirement for each component:

	Type P	Type Q	Maximum available
Cutting hours	6	6	180
Finishing hours	3	6	150

(i) Taking x to represent the number of type P and y to represent the number of type Q, write down two inequalities in x and y and illustrate these on a graph.

(ii) If the profit on each type P product is €400 and on each type Q product is €200, calculate the number of products of each type that should be made in order to have a maximum profit. What is this profit?

(iii) Indicate on your graph the region where the profit is greater than or equal to €8,000.

5. A factory produces 2 types of article, type P and type Q. The time it takes to produce each model, the cost of each and the profit on each are given in the following table:

	Type P	**Type Q**
Time, in hours	8	6
Cost, in €	80	120
Profit, in €	400	500

Let x be the number of type P produced and y be the number of type Q produced.
- **(i)** If the total time available to produce the articles is 72 hours and the total amount of money available is €960, write two inequalities in x and y and illustrate these on a graph.
- **(ii)** Find the number of each type that should be produced so as to maximise the profit.
- **(iii)** What is this maximum profit, assuming all articles produced are sold?

6. A tourist car park can accommodate cars and buses. The total number of vehicles must not exceed 54. The parking area required for a car is 20 m^2 and for a bus is 50 m^2. The car park has an area of $1,800 \text{ m}^2$.
- **(i)** If x represents the number of cars and y represents the number of buses parked, write two inequalities in x and y. Illustrate these on a graph.
- **(ii)** The daily parking charge is €10 for a car and €20 for a bus.
  How many of each should be in the parking lot to give a maximum income?
  Calculate this income.

7. A shop intends to buy a number of television sets and DVD players but will buy no more than 60 items. A television costs €600 and a DVD player costs €300.
The maximum amount the shop is prepared to spend is €21,000.
- **(i)** Taking x to represent the number of television sets and y to represent the number of DVD players, write down two inequalities in x and y and illustrate these on a graph.
- **(ii)** If the profit on each television set is €150 and the profit on each DVD player €100, calculate the number of each type the shop should buy in order to have a maximum profit.
  What is this profit?

8. A firm exports two types of machine, P and Q. Type P occupies 5 m^3 of space and type Q, 10 m^3. Type P weighs 4 kg and type Q, 2 kg. The available shipping space is $30,000 \text{ m}^3$ and the total weight of the machines cannot exceed 12,000 kg.
- **(i)** Taking x to represent the number of type P and y to represent the number of type Q, write down two inequalities in x and y and illustrate these on a graph.
- **(ii)** If the profit on each type P machine is €480 and on each type Q machine is €360, calculate the number of machines of each type that should be exported in order to have a maximum profit. What is this profit?

9. A company uses small trucks and large trucks to transport its products in crates. The crates are all of the same size.

On a certain day 8 truck drivers at most are available. Each truck requires one driver only.

Small trucks take 15 minutes each to load and large trucks take 45 minutes each to load. The total loading time must not be more than $4\frac{1}{2}$ hours. Only one truck can be loaded at a time.
- **(i)** If x represents the number of small trucks used and y represents the number of large trucks used, write down two inequalities in x and y. Illustrate these on a graph.
- **(ii)** Each small truck carries 20 crates and each large truck carries 30 crates. How many of each type of truck should be used to maximize the number of crates to be transported that day?

10. A farmer has not more than 2000 m^2 of ground for planting apple trees and blackcurrant bushes. The ground space required for an apple tree is 50 m^2 and for a blackcurrant bush is 5 m^2.

The planting of an apple tree costs €20 and the planting of a blackcurrant bush costs €4. The farmer has at most €1000 to spend on planting.

If the farmer plants x apple trees and y blackcurrant bushes, write two inequalities in x and y and illustrate these on a graph.

When fully grown, each apple tree will produce a crop worth €90 and each blackcurrant bush a crop worth €15.

How many of each should be planted so that the farmer's gross income is a maximum?

Calculate the farmer's maximum profit.

11. A holiday campsite caters for caravans and tents. Each caravan accommodates 8 people and each tent accommodates 5 people. If there are x caravans and y tents on the site and if the site facilities cannot accommodate more than 400 people, write down an inequality to express this information. Each caravan is allotted an are of 60 m^2 and each tent is allotted 50 m^2. The total area available for caravans and tents is 3,600 m^2. Write down an inequality to express this information. Graph the set showing the possible number of caravans and tents on the site.

If there were only caravans on the site, what is the maximum number of caravans which could be catered for?

The charges on the site are €30 per caravan and €20 per tent.

How many caravans and how many tents should be on the site to give a maximum income? What is this income?

Indicate on your graph the region where the income would be less than or equal to €600.

12. A builder is to build at most 10 shopping units on an 8,000 m^2 site. These shopping units are of two types – one will occupy an area of 500 m^2 and the other an area of 1,000 m^2.

Graph the set showing the possible numbers of each type of shopping unit that could be built. The weekly rent from these two types of unit is as follows:

€125 for a 500 m^2 unit;
€200 for a 1000 m^2 unit.

How many of each type should be in the site to give maximum rent?
Indicate on your graph the region where the rent would exceed €1,000 per week.

Note: The next two problems contain inequalities that contain the origin.

13. A company assembles two models of microcomputer – model K and model T. The company must assemble at least 4 times as many of model K as model T. If x of model K and y of model T are assembled, verify that $x \geqslant 4y$.

The assembly time for each model K is 18 hours and for each model T is 36 hours, and a total of 216 hours is available in a given assembly period.

Graph the set showing the possible number of each model assembled in the period. There is a ready market for each model and the company makes a profit of €150 on each model K and €100 on each model T. How many of each type should the company assemble to give a maximum profit?

Indicate on your graph the region where the profit is greater than or equal to €600.

14. A fuel merchant buys coal at €140 per tonne and sells it for €164 per tonne.
He also buys turf at €42 per tonne and sells it for €52 per tonne.
A shortage of space in his yard means that at least one-quarter of his total space must be taken up by coal. Justify the constraint $3x \geqslant y$.
His weekly capital is limited to €2,660.
Write another inequality.
Graph the set showing possible purchases of coal and turf.
Calculate the number of tonnes of coal and turf he should purchase to obtain maximum profit.
Compute this maximum profit.
Indicate on your graph the region where the profit is less than or equal to €240.

VECTORS

Definition of a Vector

A vector is a movement over a certain distance and in a certain direction.
We can represent a vector with a line segment. The length of the line represents the size (magnitude) of the vector and the direction of the line shows which way the vector points, indicated by an arrow.

The diagram on the right shows the movement from p to q, in other words, the vector from p to q.
This is written as $\vec{pq}$.

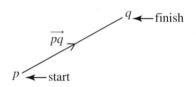

Notice the arrow points from p to q, i.e., from the start to the finish, as indicated in the diagram.

Note: The length of a vector is called the **modulus** or **norm** of the vector.

The modulus of the vector $\vec{pq}$ is written $|\vec{pq}|$.

In the diagram opposite, the length of the vector $\vec{pq}$ is 3 cm.

This is written: $|\vec{pq}| = 3$ cm

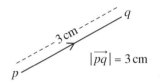

$|\vec{pq}| = 3$ cm

Equality of Vectors

Equal vectors have **three common characteristics:**

| 1. Parallel | 2. Same length | 3. Same direction |

The characteristic 'parallel' can be dropped because 'same direction' implies parallel.
In other words: equal vectors have the same length and direction.

On the right are shown two vectors, $\vec{ab}$ and $\vec{cd}$.

They are **parallel**, have the **same length** and point in the **same direction**.

Therefore they are equal vectors.

Thus we write: $\vec{ab} = \vec{cd}$

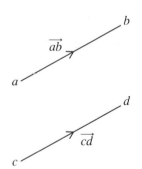

It follows from this that a vector may be represented by any accurate line segment, provided we keep its correct length and direction. Its location does not matter. In other words we can move a vector anywhere, provided we maintain its **original** length and direction.

Inverse of a Vector

The vectors $\overrightarrow{ab}$ and $\overrightarrow{ba}$ are parallel and equal in length but point in opposite directions.

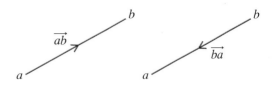

We say $\overrightarrow{ab}$ and $\overrightarrow{ba}$ are the inverse of each other. To get the inverse of a vector, simply change its direction.

The inverse of $\overrightarrow{ab}$ is written $-\overrightarrow{ab}$.

From the diagram it can be seen that, $-\overrightarrow{ab} = \overrightarrow{ba}$

Thus, a negative sign in front of a vector can be changed to a positive sign simply by changing the order of the letters.

$$\text{e.g.,} \qquad -\overrightarrow{pq} = \overrightarrow{qp}, \qquad -\overrightarrow{xy} = \overrightarrow{yx}, \qquad -\overrightarrow{dc} = \overrightarrow{cd}, \qquad \text{etc.}$$

Remember: Equal vectors have the **same** length and direction.

Consider the parallelogram $abcd$ opposite.

$$\overrightarrow{ab} = \overrightarrow{dc}$$
$$\overrightarrow{bc} = \overrightarrow{ad}$$
$$-\overrightarrow{ab} = \overrightarrow{ba} = \overrightarrow{cd}$$
$$-\overrightarrow{ad} = \overrightarrow{da} = \overrightarrow{cb} \qquad \text{etc.}$$

Multiplication by a Scalar (Number)

A scalar is a number. If we multiply a vector by a number, we change its size. If the scalar is a **negative** number, we also change the direction of the vector. However, the new vector will always remain parallel to the original vector.

Example ▼

Given the vector $\overrightarrow{pq}$, construct the vectors:

(i) $2\overrightarrow{pq}$ **(ii)** $\frac{2}{3}\overrightarrow{pq}$ **(iii)** $-3\overrightarrow{pq}$

Solution:

(i) $2\overrightarrow{pq}$

The vector $2\overrightarrow{pq}$ is parallel to and pointing in the same direction as $\overrightarrow{pq}$; however, it is **twice** the length of $\overrightarrow{pq}$.

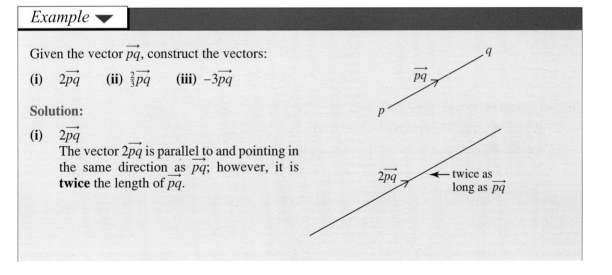

twice as long as $\overrightarrow{pq}$

(ii) $\frac{2}{3}\overrightarrow{pq}$

The vector $\frac{2}{3}\overrightarrow{pq}$ is parallel to and pointing in the same direction as $\overrightarrow{pq}$; however, it is only **two-thirds** the length of $\overrightarrow{pq}$.

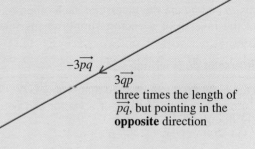

$\frac{2}{3}\overrightarrow{pq}$ ← two-thirds the length of $\overrightarrow{pq}$

(iii) $-3\overrightarrow{pq} = 3\overrightarrow{qp}$ (change sign and change order of letters).

The vector $-3\overrightarrow{pq}$ is parallel to $\overrightarrow{pq}$, **three** times as long; however, it points in the **opposite** direction.

$-3\overrightarrow{pq}$

$3\overrightarrow{qp}$ three times the length of $\overrightarrow{pq}$, but pointing in the **opposite** direction

---

Exercise 17.1 ▼

1. The diagram shows a regular hexagon *abcdef*.

Name a vector equal to:

(i) $\overrightarrow{ab}$ **(ii)** $\overrightarrow{cd}$ **(iii)** $\overrightarrow{fe}$

(iv) $\overrightarrow{db}$ **(v)** $\overrightarrow{fb}$ **(vi)** $-\overrightarrow{bc}$

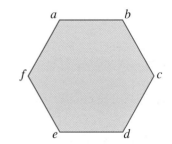

2. *abcd* is a rectangle. *abdx* and *bycd* are parallelograms. Name one other vector equal to:

(i) $\overrightarrow{xd}$ **(ii)** $2\overrightarrow{ab}$ **(iii)** $\frac{1}{2}\overrightarrow{db}$

(iv) $\frac{1}{2}\overrightarrow{ac}$ **(v)** $\frac{1}{2}\overrightarrow{xy}$ **(vi)** $-2\overrightarrow{dc}$

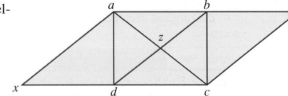

3. $\overrightarrow{ab}$ and $\overrightarrow{ac}$ are two vectors, as shown.

$|\overrightarrow{ab}| = 6$ cm, $|\overrightarrow{ac}| = 4$ cm and $|\angle bac| = 60°$.

Copy the diagram and show on it $\overrightarrow{ar}$ and $\overrightarrow{as}$ such that:

$$\overrightarrow{ar} = -\overrightarrow{ab} \quad \text{and} \quad \overrightarrow{as} = 2\overrightarrow{ac}$$

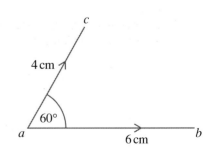

4 cm

60°

6 cm

Adding Vectors

There are two methods of adding vectors:

Triangle Law

To add the two vectors $\vec{ab}$ and $\vec{cd}$, using the Triangle Law, do the following:

1. Place the beginning of the second vector to the end of the first vector.
   (The order chosen is not important.)

2. Join the beginning of the first vector to the end of the second vector.
   This is the required vector (as shown).

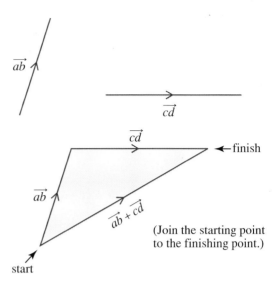

(Join the starting point to the finishing point.)

Parallelogram Law

To add the two vectors $\vec{ab}$ and $\vec{cd}$, using the Parallelogram Law, do the following:

1. Place the starting point of each at the same point.

2. Complete the parallelogram (as shown).

3. Join the common starting point to the opposite vertex.
   This diagonal is the vector required (as shown).

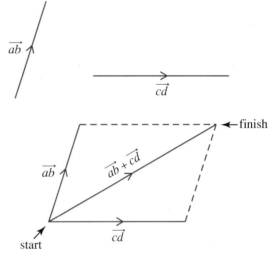

Notes: 1. The Parallelogram Law and the Triangle Law give the same result. However, use one or the other: never use the two methods together.
2. The Triangle Law is easier to use, especially if more than two vectors are to be added or subtracted.
3. The **order** in which vectors are added or subtracted is **not** important.
4. A very useful result is to look for **linkage**:

e.g.
$$\vec{ab} + \vec{bc} = \vec{ac}$$

If the letter at the end of the first vector is equal to the letter at the start of the second vector, the result of adding the two vectors is straightforward to write down. Simply write the letter at the start of the first vector followed by the letter at the end of the second vector together and put an arrow over them.

$$\text{e.g.} \qquad \overrightarrow{pq} + \overrightarrow{qr} = \overrightarrow{pr} \qquad\qquad \overrightarrow{xy} - \overrightarrow{zy} = \overrightarrow{xy} + \overrightarrow{yz} = \overrightarrow{xz}$$

$$-\overrightarrow{pm} + \overrightarrow{qm} = \overrightarrow{mp} + \overrightarrow{qm} = \overrightarrow{qm} + \overrightarrow{mp} = \overrightarrow{qp}$$

(change order of addition)

Any number of vectors can be added in this way. The resultant vector joins the **start** of the **first** vector to the **end** of the **last** vector.

$$\text{i.e.,} \qquad \overrightarrow{ab} + \overrightarrow{bc} + \overrightarrow{cd} + \overrightarrow{de} + \overrightarrow{ef} = \overrightarrow{af}$$

Using a diagram:

Notice that the arrows all **follow** each other. The result is simply obtained by joining the start to the finish.
(Notice the linkage of the vectors.)

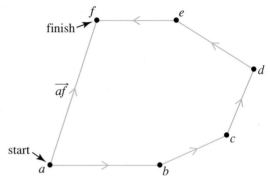

Example ▼

pqrs is a parallelogram. The diagonals intersect at the point *t*. Express each of the following as a single vector:

(i) $\overrightarrow{pq} + \overrightarrow{qt}$ (ii) $\overrightarrow{pq} + \overrightarrow{ps}$

(iii) $\overrightarrow{pr} - \overrightarrow{pq}$ (iv) $\frac{1}{2}\overrightarrow{pr} + \frac{1}{2}\overrightarrow{sq}$

Solution:

Using the Triangle Law:

(i) $\overrightarrow{pq} + \overrightarrow{qt} = \overrightarrow{pt}$

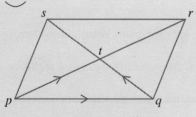

(ii) $\overrightarrow{pq} + \overrightarrow{ps} = \overrightarrow{pq} + \overrightarrow{qr} = \overrightarrow{pr}$

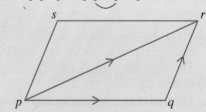

(iii) $\overrightarrow{pr} - \overrightarrow{pq} = \overrightarrow{pr} + \overrightarrow{qp} = \overrightarrow{pr} + \overrightarrow{rs} = \overrightarrow{ps}$

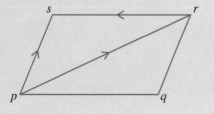

(iv) $\frac{1}{2}\overrightarrow{pr} + \frac{1}{2}\overrightarrow{sq} = \overrightarrow{pt} + \overrightarrow{st} = \overrightarrow{pt} + \overrightarrow{tq} = \overrightarrow{pq}$

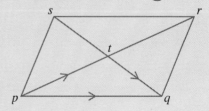

1. *xyzw* is a parallelogram. The diagonals intersect at the point *g*.

   Express each of the following as a single vector:

   (i) $\overrightarrow{xy} + \overrightarrow{yz}$ **(ii)** $\overrightarrow{xw} + \overrightarrow{wg}$

   (iii) $\overrightarrow{xy} + \overrightarrow{xw}$ **(iv)** $\overrightarrow{xz} - \overrightarrow{xy}$

   (v) $\frac{1}{2}\overrightarrow{xz} + \frac{1}{2}\overrightarrow{wy}$ **(vi)** $\overrightarrow{xw} + \overrightarrow{xy} - \overrightarrow{yz}$

   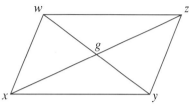

2. *rstu* is a square, and *ustv* is a parallelogram.

   Express each of the following as a single vector:

   (i) $\overrightarrow{sr} + \overrightarrow{ru}$ **(ii)** $\overrightarrow{su} + \overrightarrow{ts}$

   (iii) $\frac{1}{2}\overrightarrow{rv} + \overrightarrow{rs}$ **(iv)** $\overrightarrow{ru} + \overrightarrow{us} - \overrightarrow{vu}$

   (v) $\overrightarrow{su} + \frac{1}{2}\overrightarrow{rv}$

   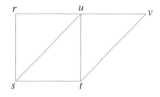

3. *abcd* is a rectangle. The diagonals intersect at the point *z*. *abdx* and *bycd* are parallelograms.

   Express each of the following as a single vector:

   (i) $\overrightarrow{az} + \overrightarrow{zb}$ **(ii)** $\overrightarrow{ac} + \overrightarrow{xa}$

   (iii) $2\overrightarrow{xd} + \overrightarrow{cb}$ **(iv)** $\frac{1}{2}(\overrightarrow{xa} + \overrightarrow{ay})$

   (v) $\overrightarrow{xz} + \overrightarrow{az}$ **(vi)** $\overrightarrow{xa} + \overrightarrow{by} - \overrightarrow{cb}$

   (vii) $\frac{1}{2}\overrightarrow{db} + \frac{1}{2}\overrightarrow{az}$

   Construct the point *k* such that $\overrightarrow{xk} = \overrightarrow{xc} + 2\overrightarrow{cb}$.

   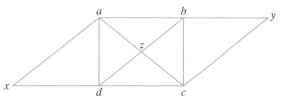

4. The diagram shows two identical squares, *abcd* and *dcef*, with their diagonals intersecting at *x* and *y*, respectively.

   Express each of the following as a single vector:

   (i) $2\overrightarrow{ad} + \overrightarrow{fe}$ **(ii)** $\overrightarrow{ba} - \overrightarrow{da}$

   (iii) $\overrightarrow{bx} + \overrightarrow{xy} - \overrightarrow{ey}$ **(iv)** $\frac{1}{2}\overrightarrow{bd} - \frac{1}{2}\overrightarrow{ed}$

   Construct the point *k* such that $\overrightarrow{ak} = \overrightarrow{af} + \overrightarrow{fe} + \overrightarrow{fc}$.

   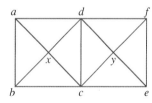

Representing Vectors With Single Letters

We can choose any point in the plane as the origin *o*.

If a vector starts or ends at the origin, we can represent it with a single letter.

Consider the three points *o*, *p*, *q* opposite.

The vector from *o* to *p* is written $\overrightarrow{op}$.

The vector from *q* to *o* is written $\overrightarrow{qo}$ or $-\overrightarrow{oq}$.

The letter *o* **at the beginning** can be dropped.

Thus $\boxed{\overrightarrow{op} = \vec{p}}$ and $\boxed{\overrightarrow{qo} = -\overrightarrow{oq} = -\vec{q}}$

Note: A vector which **starts** from the origin is known as a **position vector**.

Representing any two-letter vectors as a combination of two single-letter vectors

The following results are very useful and should be memorised:

$$\overrightarrow{ab} = \vec{b} - \vec{a}$$

(second letter minus the first letter)

The result can be used to express any two-letter vector as a combination of two single-letter vectors:

e.g., $\quad \overrightarrow{pq} = \vec{q} - \vec{p} \qquad \overrightarrow{xy} = \vec{y} - \vec{x}, \qquad \overrightarrow{dc} = \vec{c} - \vec{d}, \qquad$ etc.

Midpoint

If m is the midpoint of $[ab]$, then $\quad \boxed{\vec{m} = \tfrac{1}{2}\vec{a} + \tfrac{1}{2}\vec{b}}$

These results, which are proved in the next example, can be used directly.

Example ▼

oab is a triangle, where o is the origin and m is the midpoint of $[ab]$.

Prove that: **(i)** $\overrightarrow{ab} = \vec{b} - \vec{a}$

          (ii) $\vec{m} = \tfrac{1}{2}\vec{a} + \tfrac{1}{2}\vec{b}.$

Solution:

(i) Using the Triangle Law:

$$\overrightarrow{ab} = \overrightarrow{ao} + \overrightarrow{ob}$$
$$\overrightarrow{ab} = -\overrightarrow{oa} + \overrightarrow{ob}$$
$$\overrightarrow{ab} = -\vec{a} + \vec{b}$$
$$\overrightarrow{ab} = \vec{b} - \vec{a}$$

(ii) Using the Triangle Law:

$$\overrightarrow{om} = \overrightarrow{oa} + \overrightarrow{am}$$
$$\vec{m} = \vec{a} + \tfrac{1}{2}\overrightarrow{ab}$$
$$\vec{m} = \vec{a} + \tfrac{1}{2}(\vec{b} - \vec{a})$$
$$\vec{m} = \vec{a} + \tfrac{1}{2}\vec{b} - \tfrac{1}{2}\vec{a}$$
$$\vec{m} = \tfrac{1}{2}\vec{a} + \tfrac{1}{2}\vec{b}$$

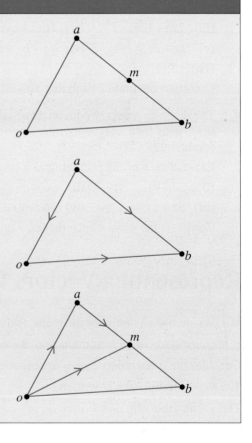

Example ▼

oab is a triangle, *o* is the origin.
p, q are points on [*oa*] and [*ab*], respectively, such that:

$$|op| : |pa| = 2:1 \quad \text{and} \quad |bq| : |qa| = 2:3$$

Express in terms of $\vec{a}$ and $\vec{b}$:

(i) $\vec{p}$ **(ii)** $\vec{bq}$ **(iii)** $\vec{q}$

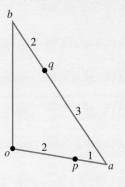

Solution:

(i) $\vec{p} = \vec{op} = \tfrac{2}{3}\vec{a}$

(ii) $\vec{bq} = \tfrac{2}{5}\vec{ba} = \tfrac{2}{5}(\vec{b} - \vec{a}) = \tfrac{2}{5}\vec{b} - \tfrac{2}{5}\vec{a}$

(iii) Using the Triangle Law:

$$\vec{q} = \vec{oq}$$
$$= \vec{ob} + \vec{bq}$$
$$= \vec{b} + \tfrac{2}{5}\vec{a} - \tfrac{2}{5}\vec{b}$$
$$= \tfrac{2}{5}\vec{a} + \tfrac{3}{5}\vec{b}$$

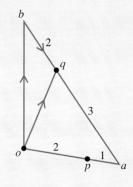

Example ▼

oabc is parallelogram where *o* is the origin.
Write each of the following in terms of $\vec{a}$ and $\vec{c}$:

(i) $\vec{ab}$ **(ii)** $2\vec{cb}$ **(iii)** $\vec{bc}$

(iv) $\vec{b}$ **(v)** $-\vec{ca}$

(vi) Express $\vec{ac} - \vec{cb}$ in terms of $\vec{a}$, $\vec{b}$ and $\vec{c}$.

(vii) Identify the point *k* such that
$(\vec{ob} - \vec{ab}) - \vec{ca} = \vec{ok}$.

Solution:

(i) $\vec{ab} = \vec{oc} = \vec{c}$ **(ii)** $2\vec{cb} = 2\vec{oa} = 2\vec{a}$ **(iii)** $\vec{bc} = \vec{ao} = -\vec{oa} = -\vec{a}$

(iv) $\vec{b} = \vec{ob}$

Using the Triangle Law:

$$\vec{ob} = \vec{oa} + \vec{ab} = \vec{a} + \vec{c}$$

or $\vec{ob} = \vec{oc} + \vec{cb} = \vec{c} + \vec{a}$

(v) $-\vec{ca} = \vec{ac} = \vec{c} - \vec{a}$

(writing a two-letter vector as single vectors)

Or using the Triangle Law:

$$\vec{ac} = \vec{ab} + \vec{bc}$$
$$= \vec{oc} + \vec{ao}$$
$$= \vec{oc} - \vec{oa} = \vec{c} - \vec{a}$$

(vi) $\overrightarrow{ac} - \overrightarrow{cb}$	**(vii)** $(\overrightarrow{ob} - \overrightarrow{ab}) - \overrightarrow{ca} = \overrightarrow{ok}$
$= \overrightarrow{ac} + \overrightarrow{bc}$	$\overrightarrow{ob} - \overrightarrow{ab} - \overrightarrow{ca}$
	$= \overrightarrow{ob} + \overrightarrow{ba} + \overrightarrow{ac}$
$= (\vec{c} - \vec{a}) + (\vec{c} - \vec{b})$	$= \vec{b} + (\vec{a} - \vec{b}) + \vec{c} - \vec{a})$
$= \vec{c} - \vec{a} + \vec{c} - \vec{b}$	$= \vec{b} + \vec{a} - \vec{b} + \vec{c} - \vec{a} = \vec{c} = \overrightarrow{oc}$
$= -\vec{a} - \vec{b} + 2\vec{c}$	$\therefore \quad \overrightarrow{oc} = \overrightarrow{ok}$
	$\therefore \quad k$ is the point c.
	$\left[\text{or using the idea of linkage}\atop \overrightarrow{ob} + \overrightarrow{ba} + \overrightarrow{ac} = \overrightarrow{oc} = \overrightarrow{ok}\right]$

Exercise 17.3 ▼

1. $opqr$ is a square where o is the origin.
 s is the point of intersection of the diagonals and m is the midpoint of $[qr]$.
   (i)   Express $\overrightarrow{pq}$ in terms of $\vec{r}$.
   (ii) Express in terms of $\vec{p}$ and $\vec{r}$ **(a)** $\vec{q}$ **(b)** $\vec{s}$.
   (iii) Express $\vec{p} - \tfrac{1}{2}\overrightarrow{rp}$ in terms of $\vec{q}$.

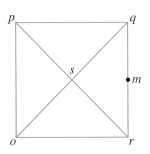

2. $oabc$ is a parallelogram where o is the origin. The diagonals intersect at the point m and d is the midpoint of $[ab]$.
   (i)   Express $\overrightarrow{cb}$ in terms of $\vec{a}$:
   (ii) Express in terms of $\vec{a}$ and $\vec{c}$:
      (a) $\vec{b}$ **(b)** $\vec{m}$ **(c)** $\vec{d}$.
   (ii) Express $\overrightarrow{dm} - \overrightarrow{bm}$ in terms of $\vec{c}$.

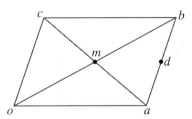

3. opq is a triangle where o is the origin, r is the midpoint of $[oq]$ and s is the midpoint of $[pr]$.
   Express: **(i)** $\vec{r}$ in terms of $\vec{q}$
            (ii) $\vec{s}$ in terms of $\vec{p}$ and $\vec{r}$
            (iii) $\overrightarrow{sq}$ in terms of $\vec{p}, \vec{q}$ and $\vec{r}$.

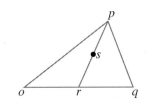

4. $opqr$ is a parallelogram where o is the origin. The point x divides $[pq]$ in the ratio $2:1$.
 y is the midpoint of $[qr]$.
   Express in terms of $\vec{p}$ and $\vec{r}$:
   (i) $\vec{q}$ **(ii)** $\vec{y}$ **(iii)** $\vec{x}$ **(iv)** $\overrightarrow{xy}$.

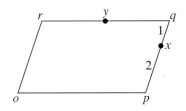

5. *opq* is a triangle where *o* is the origin.

x is the midpoint of [*pq*].

The point *y* divides [*px*] in the ratio 2 : 1.

Express in terms of $\vec{p}$ and $\vec{r}$:

(i) $\overrightarrow{px}$ **(ii)** $\vec{x}$ **(iii)** $\vec{y}$ **(iv)** $\overrightarrow{xy}$.

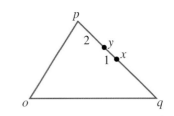

6. *oabc* is a parallelogram where *o* is the origin.

p in the midpoint of [*ab*].

op intersects *cb* at *q*.

Express: **(i)** $\vec{b}$ in terms of $\vec{a}$ and $\vec{c}$

         (ii) $\vec{p}$ in terms of $\vec{a}$ and $\vec{b}$

         (iii) $\vec{p}$ in terms of $\vec{a}$ and $\vec{c}$

         (iv) $\vec{q}$ in terms of $\vec{a}$ and $\vec{c}$.

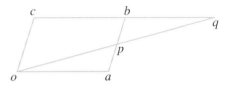

7. In the triangle *abc*,

p is the midpoint of [*ab*],

q is the midpoint of [*bc*],

r is the midpoint of [*ac*].

Express: **(i)** $\vec{p}$ in terms of $\vec{a}$ and $\vec{b}$

         (ii) $\vec{q}$ in terms of $\vec{b}$ and $\vec{c}$

         (iii) $\vec{r}$ in terms of $\vec{a}$ and $\vec{c}$.

Show that $\vec{a} + \vec{b} + \vec{c} = \vec{p} + \vec{q} + \vec{r}$.

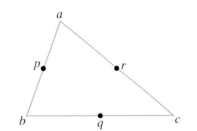

8. *pqrs* is a parallelogram.

The midpoint of [*ps*] is *o*, where *o* is the origin.

(i)   Express $\overrightarrow{pq}$ in terms of $\vec{p}$ and $\vec{q}$.

(ii)   Show that $2\vec{p} = \vec{q} - \vec{r}$.

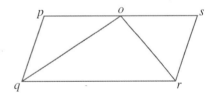

9. *opqr* is a parallelogram with *o* the origin. Copy the diagram and plot the points k_1, k_2, k_3 such that:

$\vec{k}_1 = \vec{p} + \vec{r}$

$\vec{k}_2 = \vec{p} + \frac{1}{2}\vec{r}$

$\vec{k}_3 = \frac{1}{2}\vec{p} + \vec{r}$

Express $\overrightarrow{k_2 k_3}$ in terms of $\vec{p}$ and $\vec{r}$.

10. *oab* is a triangle where *o* is the origin.

$|oa| = 5$ cm, $|ob| = 4$ cm and $|\angle aob| = 45°$.

Copy the diagram and plot separately:

(i) $\vec{k}_1 = \vec{a} - \vec{b}$

(ii) $\vec{k}_2 = \vec{b} - \vec{a}$.

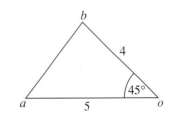

11. *oabc* is a parallelogram, where *o* is the origin.

$|oc| = 6$ cm, $|cb| = 3$ cm and $|\angle aoc| = 60°$.

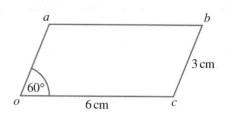

   (i)   Copy the diagram and show on it $\vec{p}$ and $\vec{q}$ such that:

$$\vec{p} = 2\vec{a} + \vec{c} \qquad \text{and} \qquad \vec{q} = 2\vec{c} + \vec{a}.$$

   (ii) Express $\vec{p} + \vec{q}$ in terms of $\vec{b}$.

12. *obca* is a parallelogram, where *o* is the origin.

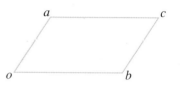

   (i)   Copy the diagram and plot *k* such that $\vec{k} = \vec{a} + \vec{c}$.

   (ii) Express $\vec{k}$ in terms of $\vec{a}$ and $\vec{b}$.

   (iii) Find the value of *k* such that $\vec{a} + \vec{b} + k\vec{c} = 0$.

13. In the diagram *oabc* is a parallelogram.

p is a point on *oa* such that $|op| : |pa| = 2 : 3$.

[*bp*] is produced to *r* such that $|bp| = |pr|$.

Taking $\vec{o}$ as origin:

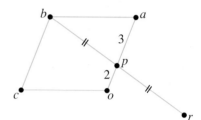

   (i)   Express $\vec{bp}$ in terms of $\vec{a}$ and $\vec{c}$.

   (ii) Find the values of *h* and *k* given

$\vec{r} = h\vec{a} + k\vec{c}$, where $h, k, \in \mathbf{R}$.

14. *opqr* is a parallelogram where *o* is the origin. *y* is the midpoint of [*qr*]. *x* is the point of intersection of [*òq*] and [*py*]. *x* divides [*py*] in the ratio 2 : 1.

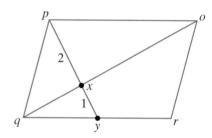

   (i)   Express $\vec{ry}$ in terms of $\vec{p}$.

   (ii) Express in terms of $\vec{p}$ and $\vec{r}$:

       (a) $\vec{y}$ **(b)** $\vec{px}$.

Perpendicular Unit Vectors $\vec{i}$ and $\vec{j}$

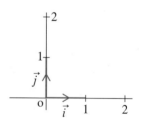

The vector from the origin, $(0, 0)$ to the point $(1, 0)$ on the horizontal axis is called the $\vec{i}$ **vector**.

The vector from the origin, $(0, 0)$ to the point $(0, 1)$ on the vertical axis is called the $\vec{j}$ **vector**.

> The vectors $\vec{i}$ and $\vec{j}$ are called perpendicular unit vectors.

Any vector can be written and represented in terms of $\vec{i}$ and $\vec{j}$.

For example, consider the vectors:

$$\vec{a} = 3\vec{i} + 2\vec{j}$$
$$\vec{b} = -2\vec{i} + \vec{j}$$
$$\vec{c} = -\vec{i} - 2\vec{j}$$
$$\vec{d} = 2\vec{i} - \vec{j}$$
$$\vec{e} = 3\vec{i}$$
$$\vec{f} = 2\vec{j}$$

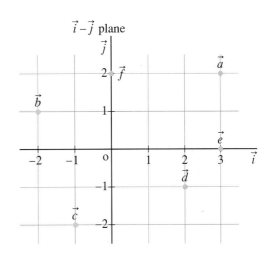

The plane on which these vectors are represented is called the $\vec{i} - \vec{j}$ plane.

It is common practice to represent a vector starting at the origin by its **endpoint only**; however, it must be understood the vector goes from the origin to its endpoint. When we represent vectors by points in this way they are called **position vectors**; for example, $3\vec{i} + 2\vec{j}$ is represented by the point $(3, 2)$.

Note: The vectors $\vec{i}$ and $\vec{j}$ obey all the properties of vectors we met earlier.
If preferred, the origin can be joined to the endpoint with a line.

Example ▼

Let $\vec{p} = 3\vec{i} - 2\vec{j}$ and $\vec{q} = \vec{i} + 3\vec{j}$. Express in terms of $\vec{i}$ and $\vec{j}$:

(i) $\vec{p} + \vec{q}$ (ii) $\vec{pq}$ (iii) $2\vec{p} + 3\vec{q}$

Illustrate the vectors $\vec{p}, \vec{q}, \vec{p} + \vec{q}, \vec{pq}$ and $2\vec{p} + 3\vec{q}$ on a diagram.

Solution:

(i) $\vec{p} + \vec{q}$
$= (3\vec{i} - 2\vec{j}) + (\vec{i} + 3\vec{j})$
$= 3\vec{i} - 2\vec{j} + \vec{i} + 3\vec{j}$
$= 4\vec{i} + \vec{j}$

(ii) $\vec{pq} = \vec{q} - \vec{p}$
$= (\vec{i} + 3\vec{j}) - (3\vec{i} - 2\vec{j})$
$= \vec{i} + 3\vec{j} - 3\vec{i} + 2\vec{j}$
$= -2\vec{i} + 5\vec{j}$

(iii) $2\vec{p} + 3\vec{q}$
$= 2(3\vec{i} - 2\vec{j}) + 3(\vec{i} + 3\vec{j})$
$= 6\vec{i} - 4\vec{j} + 3\vec{i} + 9\vec{j}$
$= 9\vec{i} + 5\vec{j}$

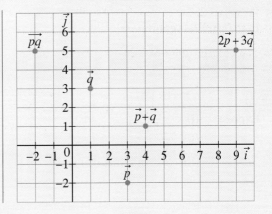

1. Let $\vec{a} = 3\vec{i} + 2\vec{j}$, $\quad \vec{b} = -2\vec{i} + \vec{j}$, $\quad \vec{c} = 2\vec{i}$ $\quad$ and $\quad \vec{d} = -3\vec{j}$.

   Express in terms of $\vec{i}$ and $\vec{j}$:

   (i) $2\vec{a}$ $\qquad$ (ii) $3\vec{b}$ $\qquad$ (iii) $\vec{a} + \vec{b}$ $\qquad$ (iv) $\vec{c} - \vec{d}$ $\qquad$ (v) $\vec{a} + \vec{b} + \vec{c} + \vec{d}$

   (vi) $\overrightarrow{ab}$ $\qquad$ (vii) $\overrightarrow{dc}$ $\qquad$ (viii) $3\vec{a} + 2\vec{b}$ $\qquad$ (ix) $3\vec{c} - 2\vec{a}$ $\qquad$ (x) $2\vec{d} - 3\vec{b}$ $\qquad$ (xi) $2\vec{a} + \overrightarrow{ab}$

2 Let $\vec{a} = 2\vec{i} - \vec{j}$, $\quad \vec{b} = \vec{i} + 2\vec{j}$ $\quad$ and $\quad \vec{c} = -3\vec{i} - 2\vec{j}$.

   Illustrate each of the following on the diagram:

   (i) $\vec{a}$ $\qquad\qquad\qquad$ (ii) $\vec{b}$

   (iii) $\vec{c}$ $\qquad\qquad\qquad$ (iv) $\vec{a} + \vec{b}$

   (v) $\vec{b} - \vec{c}$ $\qquad\qquad\quad$ (vi) $\overrightarrow{ab}$

   (vii) $2\vec{a} - \vec{b}$ $\qquad\qquad$ (viii) $\overrightarrow{ca}$

   (ix) $\vec{a} + \vec{b} - \vec{c}$ $\qquad\quad$ (x) $2\overrightarrow{ba} - \vec{c}$

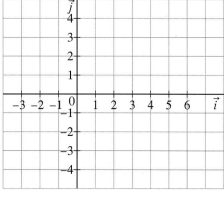

3. If $\vec{a} = 2\vec{i} + 3\vec{j}$ $\quad$ and $\quad \overrightarrow{ab} = 5\vec{i} - \vec{j}$, express $\vec{b}$ in terms of $\vec{i}$ and $\vec{j}$.

4. If $\vec{p} = 5\vec{i} - 3\vec{j}$ $\quad$ and $\quad \overrightarrow{qp} = -\vec{i} + 2\vec{j}$, express $\vec{q}$ in terms of $\vec{i}$ and $\vec{j}$.

5. If $\overrightarrow{xy} = -5\vec{i} + 6\vec{j}$ $\quad$ and $\quad \vec{y} = 2\vec{i} + 3\vec{j}$, express $\vec{x}$ in terms of $\vec{i}$ and $\vec{j}$.

6. abc is a triangle where o is the origin.

   $\vec{a} = \vec{i} + \vec{j}$, $\quad \vec{b} = 13\vec{i} + 7\vec{j}$ $\quad$ and $\quad \vec{c} = 7\vec{i} + 19\vec{j}$.

   p, q, r are the midpoints of the sides, as shown.

   Express, in terms of $\vec{i}$ and $\vec{j}$:

   (i) $\vec{p}$ $\qquad$ (ii) $\vec{q}$ $\qquad$ (iii) $\vec{r}$ $\qquad$ (iv) $\overrightarrow{pq}$

   (v) $\overrightarrow{qr}$ $\qquad$ (vi) $\overrightarrow{pr}$ $\qquad$ (vii) $2\vec{q}$ $\qquad$ (viii) $\vec{q} - 2\vec{r}$.

   Verify that : $\quad \vec{a} + \vec{b} + \vec{c} = \vec{p} + \vec{q} + \vec{r}$.

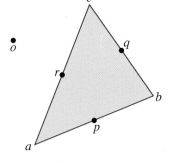

7 In the parallelogram $pqrs$:

   $$\vec{p} = -3\vec{i} - 2\vec{j}$$
   $$\vec{q} = 4\vec{i} + \vec{j}$$
   $$\vec{r} = 6\vec{i} + 5\vec{j}.$$

   Express: (i) $\vec{s}$

   $\qquad\qquad\quad$ (ii) $\overrightarrow{pr}$

   $\qquad\qquad\quad$ (iii) $\overrightarrow{qs}$, in terms of $\vec{i}$ and $\vec{j}$.

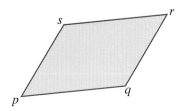

Vector Equations Involving $\vec{i}$ and $\vec{j}$

> If two vectors are equal, then
> their $\vec{i}$ parts are equal and their $\vec{j}$ parts are equal.

For example, if $a\vec{i} + b\vec{j} = c\vec{i} + d\vec{j}$,

then $a = c$ and $b = d$.

Vector equations involving $\vec{i}$ and $\vec{j}$ are solved with the following steps:

> **1.** Remove the brackets.
> **2.** Let the $\vec{i}$ parts equal the $\vec{i}$ parts and the $\vec{j}$ parts equal the $\vec{j}$ parts.
> **3.** Solve these resultant equations.

Note: If one side of the equation does not contain an $\vec{i}$ part or a $\vec{j}$ part, add in $0\vec{i}$ or $0\vec{j}$, respectively.

Example ▼

Find the scalars h and k, such that $h(3\vec{i} - 2\vec{j}) + k(2\vec{i} - \vec{j}) = 5\vec{i} - 4\vec{j}$.

Solution:

$$h(3\vec{i} - 2\vec{j}) + k(2\vec{i} - \vec{j}) = 5\vec{i} - 4\vec{j}$$

Step 1: $3h\vec{i} - 2h\vec{j} + 2k\vec{i} - k\vec{j} = 5\vec{i} - 4\vec{j}$ (remove the brackets)

Step 2:

$\vec{i}$ parts $= \vec{i}$ parts	$\vec{j}$ parts $= \vec{j}$ parts
$3h + 2k = 5$ ①	$-2h - k = -4$ ②

Step 3:   Now solve the simultaneous equations ① and ②:

$3h + 2k = 5$ ①	$3h + 2k = 5$ ①
$-4h - 2k = -8$ ② $\times -2$	$3(3) + 2k = 5$
$-h = -3$ (add)	$9 + 2k = 5$
$h = 3$	$2k = -4$
put $h = 3$ into ① or ②	$k = -2$

Thus, $h = 3$ and $k = -2$.

Exercise 17.5 ▼

1. Find the scalars h and k such that $3h\vec{i} + 2k\vec{j} = 12\vec{i} - 10\vec{j}$.

2. Find the scalars a and b such that $3\vec{i} + 2\vec{j} + a\vec{i} + b\vec{j} = 2\vec{i} + 5\vec{j}$.

3. Find the scalars p and q such that $p\vec{i} + q\vec{j} + 2(\vec{i} - 3\vec{j}) = 7\vec{i} - 8\vec{j}$.

4. Find the scalars h and k such that $2(h\vec{i} + k\vec{j}) - 3(2\vec{i} - \vec{j}) = 2\vec{i} - \vec{j}$.

5. Find the scalars a and b such that $(1 - 4a)\vec{i} - (2b + 1)\vec{j} = 9\vec{i} - 7\vec{j}$.

6. Find the scalars p and q such that $p\vec{i} + p\vec{j} + q\vec{i} - q\vec{j} = 7\vec{i} + 3\vec{j}$.

7. Find the scalars h and k such that $h(2\vec{i} + 3\vec{j}) + k(\vec{i} - 5j) = \vec{i} + 21\vec{j}$.

8. Find the scalars s and t such that $s(3\vec{i} - 4\vec{j}) - t(-2\vec{i} + 3\vec{j}) = -\vec{i} + 3\vec{j}$.

9. Find the scalars k and t such that $2(3\vec{i} + k\vec{j}) + t(\vec{i} - 2\vec{j}) = 4(2\vec{i} + \vec{j})$.

10. Find the scalars a and b such that $3(3\vec{i} + a\vec{j}) + b(6\vec{i} - \vec{j}) = 39\vec{i} - 7\vec{j}$.

11. Let $\vec{u} = 6\vec{i} - 8\vec{j}$ and $\vec{v} = \vec{i} + 4\vec{j}$.
    Find the scalars h and t such that $h\vec{u} + t\vec{v} = 11\vec{i} - 20\vec{j}$.

12. Let $\vec{x} = 3\vec{i} - 2\vec{j}$ and $\vec{y} = -2\vec{i} + \vec{j}$.
    Find the scalars h and k such that $h\vec{x} + k\vec{y} = 13\vec{i} - 8\vec{j}$.

13. Let $\vec{a} = 2\vec{i} - \vec{j}$ and $\vec{b} = 5\vec{i} + 3\vec{j}$. Express $\vec{a} + \vec{b}$ in terms of $\vec{i}$ and $\vec{j}$.
    If $s(\vec{a} + \vec{b}) = 14\vec{i} + (t + 1)\vec{j}$, find the value of the scalar s and the scalar t.

14. **(i)** Let $\vec{a} = 2\vec{i} + 3\vec{j}$ and $\vec{ab} = 5\vec{i} + 10\vec{j}$.
    Express in terms of $\vec{i}$ and $\vec{j}$: **(a)** $\frac{2}{5}\vec{ab}$ **(b)** $\vec{b}$.
    (ii) Let $\vec{a} = 2\vec{i} - 3\vec{j}$ and $\vec{ab} = -3\vec{i} + 7\vec{j}$.
    Find the scalars p and q such that $p\vec{a} + q\vec{b} = 7\vec{i} - 18\vec{j}$.
    (iii) If $\vec{x} = h\vec{i} + 4\vec{j}$ and $\vec{y} = 2\vec{i} + k\vec{j}$, find the scalars h and k such that $\vec{xy} = -\vec{i} + \vec{j}$.

15. oab is a triangle where o is the origin.
    p and q are points such that:
    $$|oq| : |qb| = 2 : 1 = |bp| : |pa|.$$
    If $\vec{a} = 6\vec{i} + 3\vec{j}$ and $\vec{b} = 9\vec{i} + 12\vec{j}$, express $\vec{p}$ and $\vec{q}$
    in terms of $\vec{i}$ and $\vec{j}$ and find $h, k \in \mathbf{R}$, such that
    $h\vec{p} + k\vec{q} = 4\vec{i} + 12\vec{j}$.

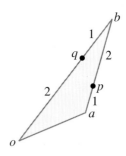

Modulus of a Vector

The **modulus** of the vector $a\vec{i} + b\vec{j}$ is the distance
from the origin to the point (a, b).

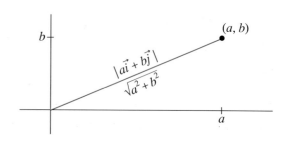

392

The modulus of the vector $a\vec{i} + b\vec{j}$ is denoted by $|a\vec{i} + b\vec{j}|$ and is given by $\sqrt{a^2 + b^2}$ (by Pythagoras's Theorem).

$$|a\vec{i} + b\vec{j}| = \sqrt{a^2 + b^2}$$

Note: The **modulus** of a vector is often called the **length** of the vector.

Before getting the length of a vector, make sure it is written in the form $a\vec{i} + b\vec{j}$.

Example ▼

If $\vec{p} = 3\vec{i} - 4\vec{j}$ and $\vec{q} = -\vec{i} - 6\vec{j}$, verify that $|\vec{p}| + |\vec{q}| > |\vec{pq}|$.

Solution:

$$|\vec{p}| = |3\vec{i} - 4\vec{j}|$$
$$= \sqrt{3^2 + 4^2}$$
$$= \sqrt{9 + 16}$$
$$= \sqrt{25}$$
$$= 5$$

$$|\vec{q}| = |-\vec{i} - 6\vec{j}|$$
$$= \sqrt{1^2 + 6^2}$$
$$= \sqrt{1 + 36}$$
$$= \sqrt{37}$$
$$= 6.08 \text{ (2 decimal places)}$$

$$\therefore \quad |\vec{p}| + |\vec{q}| = 5 + 6.08 = 11.08$$

$\vec{pq}$ must be written in the form $a\vec{i} + b\vec{j}$

$$\vec{pq} = \vec{q} - \vec{p}$$
$$= (-\vec{i} - 6\vec{j}) - (3\vec{i} - 4\vec{j})$$
$$= -\vec{i} - 6\vec{j} - 3\vec{i} + 4\vec{j}$$
$$= -4\vec{i} - 2\vec{j}$$

$$|\vec{pq}| = |-4\vec{i} - 2\vec{j}|$$
$$= \sqrt{4^2 + 2^2}$$
$$= \sqrt{16 + 4}$$
$$= \sqrt{20}$$
$$= 4.47 \text{ (2 decimal places)}$$

$$\text{As } 11.08 > 4.47, |\vec{p}| + |\vec{q}| > |\vec{pq}|.$$

Exercise 17.6 ▼

Evaluate each of the following:

1. $|3\vec{i} + 4\vec{j}|$
2. $|5\vec{i} - 12\vec{j}|$
3. $|-8\vec{i} + 15\vec{j}|$
4. $|-20\vec{i} - 21\vec{j}|$

5. $|2\vec{i} - 3\vec{j}|$
6. $|\vec{i} - 4\vec{j}|$
7. $|-2\vec{i} + 5\vec{j}|$
8. $|-5\vec{i} - 4\vec{j}|$

If $\vec{a} = 2\vec{i} + 3\vec{j}$, $\vec{b} = -\vec{i} + 2\vec{j}$ and $\vec{c} = 5\vec{i} - \vec{j}$ evaluate:

9. $|\vec{a}|$
10. $|\vec{b}|$
11. $|\vec{c}|$
12. $|\vec{a} + \vec{b}|$

13. $|\vec{b} - \vec{c}|$
14. $|\vec{ab}|$
15. $|\vec{ac}|$
16. $|2\vec{a} - 3\vec{b}|$

17. Let $\vec{p} = 3\vec{i} + 4\vec{j}$ and $\vec{q} = -\vec{i} + 2\vec{j}$.

    (i) Express $\overrightarrow{pq}$ in terms of $\vec{i}$ and $\vec{j}$.   **(ii)** Verify that $|\vec{p}| + |\vec{q}| > |\overrightarrow{pq}|$.

18. Let $\vec{a} = -3\vec{i} - 4\vec{j}$ and $\vec{b} = 12\vec{i} - 5\vec{j}$. Show that $|\vec{a}| + |\vec{b}| > |\vec{a} + \vec{b}|$.

19. Let $\vec{u} = -7\vec{i} + 4\vec{j}$ and $\vec{v} = -\vec{i} + 8\vec{j}$. Show that $|\vec{u}| - |\vec{v}| = 0$.

20. Let $\vec{a} = \vec{i} + 2\vec{j}$, $\vec{b} = \vec{i} + 6\vec{j}$ and $\vec{c} = -2\vec{i} + 6\vec{j}$.

    Verify that $|\vec{b} - \vec{a}|^2 + |\vec{b} - \vec{c}|^2 = |\vec{a} - \vec{c}|^2$.

21. If $|k\vec{i} + 10\vec{j}| = |2\vec{i} + 11\vec{j}|$, find two possible values of k, $k \in \mathbf{R}$.

22. If $|t\vec{i} + \vec{j}| = |5\vec{i} + 5\vec{j}|$, find two possible values of t, $t \in \mathbf{R}$.

Dot Product (or Scalar Product)

If $\vec{a}$ and $\vec{b}$ are two vectors, their dot product is defined as:

$$\vec{a} \cdot \vec{b} = |\vec{a}||\vec{b}| \cos \theta$$

where θ is the smaller angle between them.

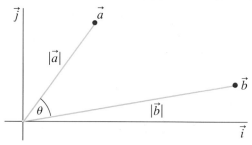

In words:

The length of $\vec{a}$ multiplied by the length of $\vec{b}$ multiplied by the cos of the angle between them. The result of the dot product is a real number **not** a vector.

Note: The **dot product** is also called the **scalar product**.

Properties of the dot product

1.   If two vectors, $\vec{a}$ and $\vec{b}$, are perpendicular, their dot product is zero.

$$\vec{a} \cdot \vec{b} = |\vec{a}||\vec{b}| \cos 90° = 0 \qquad \text{(because } \cos 90° = 0\text{)}.$$

    In particular:

$$\vec{i} \cdot \vec{j} = 0 = \vec{j} \cdot \vec{i}$$

2.   If two vectors, $\vec{a}$ and $\vec{b}$, are parallel, their dot product is $|\vec{a}||\vec{b}|$.

$$\vec{a} \cdot \vec{b} = |\vec{a}||\vec{b}| \cos 0° = |\vec{a}||\vec{b}| \qquad \text{(because } \cos 0° = 1\text{)}.$$

3. The dot product of $\vec{a}$ with $\vec{a}$ is $|\vec{a}|^2$.

$$\vec{a} \cdot \vec{a} = |\vec{a}||\vec{a}| \cos 0° = |\vec{a}||\vec{a}| = |\vec{a}|^2.$$

In particular:

$$\boxed{\vec{i} \cdot \vec{i} = 1 = \vec{j} \cdot \vec{j}}$$

4. $(a\vec{i} + b\vec{j}) \cdot (c\vec{i} + d\vec{j}) = ac + bd$

Multiply the $\vec{i}$ coefficients, multiply the $\vec{j}$ coefficients and add these results.

e.g. If $\vec{a} = 3\vec{i} - 2\vec{j}$ and $\vec{b} = 5\vec{i} + \vec{j}$, then:

$$\vec{a} \cdot \vec{b} = (3\vec{i} - 2\vec{j}) \cdot (5\vec{i} + \vec{j}) = (3)(5) + (-2)(1) = 15 - 2 = 13$$

Note: $2\vec{i} = 2\vec{i} + 0\vec{j}$ and $-3\vec{j} = 0\vec{i} - 3\vec{j}$.

Example ▼

Let $\vec{p} = 2\vec{i} + \vec{j}$ and $\vec{q} = \vec{i} + 3\vec{j}$.

(i) Calculate $\vec{p} \cdot \vec{q}$ **(ii)** Find the measure of the angle between $\vec{p}$ and $\vec{q}$.

Solution:

(i) $\vec{p} \cdot \vec{q}$

$= (2\vec{i} + \vec{j}) \cdot (\vec{i} + 3\vec{j})$

$= (2)(1) + (1)(3) = 2 + 3 = 5$

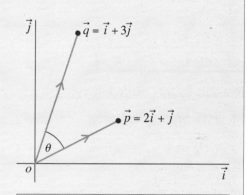

(ii) Let θ be the angle between $\vec{p}$ and $\vec{q}$.

$$\vec{p} \cdot \vec{q} = |\vec{p}||\vec{q}| \cos \theta$$

$$5 = \sqrt{5}\ \sqrt{10} \cos \theta$$

$$\sqrt{5}\ \sqrt{10} \cos \theta = 5 \qquad \text{(swop sides)}$$

$$\cos \theta = \frac{5}{\sqrt{5}\ \sqrt{10}}$$

$$|\vec{p}| = |2\vec{i} + \vec{j}| = \sqrt{2^2 + 1^2} = \sqrt{5}$$

$$|\vec{q}| = |3\vec{i} + \vec{j}| = \sqrt{3^2 + 1^2} = \sqrt{10}$$

$$\theta = \cos^{-1}\left(\frac{5}{\sqrt{5}\ \sqrt{10}}\right)$$

$$\theta = 45°$$

If two vectors, $\vec{a}$ and $\vec{b}$, are perpendicular, then $\vec{a} \cdot \vec{b} = 0$.

Therefore, to show that two vectors are perpendicular, all we need to show is that $\vec{a} \cdot \vec{b} = 0$.

In some questions we have to find the value of a missing coefficient.

Example ▼

(i) If $\vec{a} = \vec{i} - 2\vec{j}$ and $\vec{b} = 6\vec{i} + 3\vec{j}$, verify $\vec{a} \perp \vec{b}$. **(ii)** If $\vec{p} = 3\vec{i} - 4\vec{j}$ and $\vec{q} = -8\vec{i} + k\vec{j}$, find k if $\vec{p} \perp \vec{q}$.

Solution:

(i)

$$\vec{a} \cdot \vec{b}$$
$$= (\vec{i} - 2\vec{j}) \cdot (6\vec{i} + 3\vec{j})$$
$$= (1)(6) + (-2)(3)$$
$$= 6 - 6$$
$$= 0$$
$$\therefore \quad \vec{a} \perp \vec{b}$$

(ii) Given:
$$\vec{p} \perp \vec{q}$$
$$\therefore \quad \vec{p} \cdot \vec{q} = 0$$
$$(3\vec{i} - 4\vec{j}) \cdot (-8\vec{i} + k\vec{j}) = 0$$
$$(3)(-8) + (-4)(k) = 0$$
$$-24 - 4k = 0$$
$$-4k = 24$$
$$4k = -24$$
$$k = -6$$

Exercise 17.7 ▼

Evaluate each of the following:

1. $(3\vec{i} + 2\vec{j}) \cdot (5\vec{i} + 4\vec{j})$ **2.** $(-3\vec{i} - 2\vec{j}) \cdot (4\vec{i} - 3\vec{j})$ **3.** $(-\vec{i} + 4\vec{j}) \cdot (-5\vec{i} + 2\vec{j})$

4. $(-2\vec{i} - 5\vec{j}) \cdot (-4\vec{i} - 8\vec{j})$ **5.** $(7\vec{i} + 6\vec{j}) \cdot (6\vec{i} - 2\vec{j})$ **6.** $(5\vec{i} + 4\vec{j}) \cdot (4\vec{i} - 5\vec{j})$

7. $(5\vec{i} + 3\vec{j}) \cdot 4\vec{i}$ **8.** $-8\vec{j} \cdot (2\vec{i} + 4\vec{j})$ **9.** $\vec{i} \cdot (4\vec{i} - 2\vec{j})$

10. Let $\vec{a} = 3\vec{i} + 4\vec{j}$ and $\vec{b} = 2\vec{i} - \vec{j}$. Calculate $\vec{a} \cdot \vec{b}$.

11. Let $\vec{p} = -2\vec{i} + 5\vec{j}$ and $\vec{q} = 3\vec{i} + 2\vec{j}$. Calculate $\vec{p} \cdot \vec{q}$.

12. Let $\vec{a} = 2\vec{i} + \vec{j}$, $\vec{b} = 4\vec{i} - 2\vec{j}$ and $\vec{c} = \vec{i} + 3\vec{j}$.
Show that: **(i)** $\vec{a} \cdot (\vec{b} + \vec{c}) = \vec{a} \cdot \vec{b} + \vec{a} \cdot \vec{c}$ **(ii)** $\vec{a} \cdot \vec{a} = |\vec{a}|^2$.

13. Let $\vec{x} = 4\vec{i} + \vec{j}$ and $\vec{y} = 2\vec{i} - 5\vec{j}$.
 (i) Express: **(a)** $\vec{x} + \vec{y}$ **(b)** $\overrightarrow{xy}$ in terms of $\vec{i}$ and $\vec{j}$.
 (ii) Calculate: **(a)** $\vec{x} \cdot \vec{y}$ **(b)** $(\vec{x} + \vec{y}) \cdot \overrightarrow{xy}$ **(c)** $3\vec{x} \cdot 2\vec{y}$.

14. Let $\vec{x} = -\vec{i} + 6\vec{j}$ and $\vec{y} = 3\vec{i} + 2\vec{j}$. Express $\overrightarrow{xy}$ in terms of $\vec{i}$ and $\vec{j}$.
 (i) Evaluate $\vec{x} \cdot \overrightarrow{xy}$ **(ii)** Show that $\vec{x} \cdot \overrightarrow{xy} = \vec{x} \cdot \vec{y} - |\vec{x}|^2$.

15. If $|\vec{x}| = 4$, $|\vec{y}| = 5$ and $|\angle xoy| = 60°$, calculate $\vec{x} \cdot \vec{y}$.

16. Let $\vec{p} = 3\vec{i} + \vec{j}$ and $\vec{q} = 2\vec{i} + 4\vec{j}.$
Calculate: **(i)** $\vec{p} \cdot \vec{q}$ **(ii)** $|\vec{p}|$ **(iii)** $|\vec{q}|$.
Hence, find the measure of the angle between $\vec{p}$ and $\vec{q}$.

17. Let $\vec{p} = \vec{i} + 2\vec{j}$ and $\vec{q} = 3\vec{i} + \vec{j}.$
(i) Calculate $\vec{p} \cdot \vec{q}$ **(ii)** Find the measure of the angle between $\vec{p}$ and $\vec{q}$.

18. Let $\vec{a} = -\vec{i} + 2\vec{j}$ and $\vec{b} = -\vec{i} - 3\vec{j}.$ Verify that $|\angle aob| = 135°$, where o is the origin.

19. Let $\vec{x} = 3\vec{i} + 4\vec{j}$ and $\vec{y} = 5\vec{i} + 12\vec{j}.$
(i) Calculate $\vec{x} \cdot \vec{y}$.
(ii) Find the measure of the angle between $\vec{x}$ and $\vec{y}$, correct to two decimal places.

20. Let $\vec{a} = 5\vec{i} + 12\vec{j}$ and $\vec{b} = 15\vec{i} + 8\vec{j}.$
(i) Calculate $\vec{a} \cdot \vec{b}$.
(ii) Find the measure of the angle between $\vec{a}$ and $\vec{b}$, correct to one decimal place.

21. Let $\vec{a} = 4\vec{i} + \vec{j}$ and $\vec{b} = 2\vec{i} + 3\vec{j}.$
Find the measure of the angle between $\vec{a}$ and $\vec{b}$, correct to one decimal place.

22. Let $\vec{p} = 2\vec{i} - 5\vec{j}$ and $\vec{q} = 5\vec{i} + 2\vec{j}.$ Verify that $\vec{p} \perp \vec{q}$.

23. Let $\vec{x} = -3\vec{i} + \vec{j}$ and $\vec{y} = -2\vec{i} - 6\vec{j}.$ Verify that $\vec{x} \perp \vec{y}$.

24. Let $\vec{a} = -2\vec{i} - 5\vec{j}$ and $\vec{b} = -10\vec{i} + 4\vec{j}.$ Verify that $|\angle aob| = 90°$, where o is the origin.

25. Let $\vec{a} = 3\vec{i} + 2\vec{j}$ and $\vec{b} = -8\vec{i} + k\vec{j}.$ If $\vec{a} \perp \vec{b}$, find the value of k.

26. Let $\vec{x} = 2\vec{i} + 5\vec{j}$ and $\vec{y} = -20\vec{i} + h\vec{j}.$ If $\vec{x} \perp \vec{y}$, find the value of h.

27. Let $\vec{p} = \vec{i} + k\vec{j}$ and $\vec{q} = 10\vec{i} + 2\vec{j}.$ If $\vec{p} \perp \vec{q}$, find the value of k.

28. Let $\vec{a} = h\vec{i} + 30\vec{j}$ and $\vec{b} = -6\vec{i} + 2\vec{j}$, find the value of h if:
(i) $\vec{a} \perp \vec{b}$ **(ii)** $\vec{a} \cdot \vec{b} = 12$ **(iii)** $\vec{a} \cdot \vec{b} = 72$

29. Let $\vec{x} = 4\vec{i} - 2\vec{j}$ and $\vec{y} = k\vec{i} - 8\vec{j}.$ If $\vec{x} \perp \vec{xy}$, find the value of k.

Related Perpendicular Vector $r^{\perp}$

If

$$\vec{r} = a\vec{i} + b\vec{j},$$

then:

$$r^{\perp} = -b\vec{i} + a\vec{j}.$$

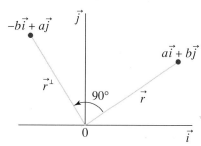

In short: Swop the coefficients and **then** change the sign of the coefficient of $\vec{i}$.
$\vec{r}^{\perp}$ is obtained by rotating $\vec{r}$ anticlockwise, about the origin, through $90°$.

If $\vec{a} = 2\vec{i} + 3\vec{j}$, then $\vec{a}^{\perp} = -3\vec{i} + 2\vec{j}$

If $\vec{p} = -4\vec{i} - 5\vec{j}$, then $\vec{p}^{\perp} = 5\vec{i} - 4\vec{j}$

Note: (i) $\vec{r} \cdot \vec{r}^{\perp} = 0$ (ii) $|\vec{r}| = |\vec{r}^{\perp}|$

Example ▼

Let $\vec{a} = -3\vec{i} + 4\vec{j}$ and $\vec{b} = 2\vec{i} + 6\vec{j}$.

(i)   Write $\vec{a}^{\perp}$ and $\vec{b}^{\perp}$ in terms of $\vec{i}$ and $\vec{j}$.

(ii)   Investigate if $\vec{a}^{\perp} + \vec{b}^{\perp} = (\vec{a} + \vec{b})^{\perp}$.

Solution:

(i) $\vec{a} = -3\vec{i} + 4\vec{j}$,   thus $\vec{a}^{\perp} = -4\vec{i} - 3\vec{j}$

     $\vec{b} = 2\vec{i} + 6\vec{j}$,   thus $\vec{b}^{\perp} = -6\vec{i} + 2\vec{j}$

(ii) $\vec{a}^{\perp} + \vec{b}^{\perp}$ $\vec{a} + \vec{b}$

     $= -4\vec{i} - 3\vec{j} - 6\vec{i} + 2\vec{j}$ $= -3\vec{i} + 4\vec{j} + 2\vec{i} + 6\vec{j}$

     $= -10\vec{i} - \vec{j}$ $= -\vec{i} + 10\vec{j}$

                                   $\therefore \ (\vec{a} + \vec{b})^{\perp} = -10\vec{i} - \vec{j}$

$$\therefore \ \vec{a}^{\perp} + \vec{b}^{\perp} = (\vec{a} + \vec{b})^{\perp}$$

Exercise 17.8 ▼

In each case write down the related perpendicular vector $\vec{r}^{\perp}$:

1. $\vec{r} = 4\vec{i} + 3\vec{j}$ **2.** $\vec{r} = 2\vec{i} + 5\vec{j}$ **3.** $\vec{r} = 4\vec{i} - 2\vec{j}$ **4.** $\vec{r} = 6\vec{i} - 5\vec{j}$

5. $\vec{r} = -2\vec{i} - 3\vec{j}$ **6.** $\vec{r} = -7\vec{i} - \vec{j}$ **7.** $\vec{r} = -3\vec{i} + 4\vec{j}$ **8.** $\vec{r} = -2\vec{i} + 7\vec{j}$

9. Let $\vec{x} = 8\vec{i} + 15\vec{j}$. Express $\vec{x}^{\perp}$ in terms of $\vec{i}$ and $\vec{j}$. Show that $|\vec{x}| = |\vec{x}^{\perp}|$.

10. Let $\vec{a} = 5\vec{i} + 2\vec{j}$. Express $\vec{a}^{\perp}$ in terms of $\vec{i}$ and $\vec{j}$. Show that $|\vec{a}|^2 = |\vec{a}^{\perp}|^2$.

11. Let $\vec{x} = 2\vec{i} - 3\vec{j}$ and $\vec{y} = 5\vec{i} + 4\vec{j}$. Determine if $(\vec{x} + \vec{y})^{\perp} = \vec{x}^{\perp} + \vec{y}^{\perp}$.

12. Let $\vec{p} = -3\vec{i} - 5\vec{j}$ and $\vec{q} = 4\vec{i} - \vec{j}$. Investigate if $(\vec{p} - \vec{q})^{\perp} = \vec{p}^{\perp} - \vec{q}^{\perp}$.

13. Let $\vec{a} = 3\vec{i} - 2\vec{j}$ and $\vec{b} = 4\vec{i} + 5\vec{j}$.

     (i)   Write: **(a)** $\vec{a}^{\perp} + \vec{b}^{\perp}$ **(b)** $\vec{a}^{\perp} - \vec{b}^{\perp}$ in terms of $\vec{i}$ and $\vec{j}$.

     (ii)   Investigate if: **(a)** $(\vec{a}^{\perp} + \vec{b}^{\perp}) \cdot (\vec{a}^{\perp} - \vec{b}^{\perp}) = 0$ **(b)** $(\vec{a}^{\perp})^{\perp} = -\vec{a}$.

14. Let $\vec{a} = -5\vec{i} + 3\vec{j}$ and $\vec{b} = -4\vec{i} + 7\vec{j}$.
Let $\vec{p} = \vec{a}^{\perp}$ and $\vec{q} = \vec{b}^{\perp}$. Investigate if $\overrightarrow{ab} \perp \overrightarrow{pq}$.

15. Let $\vec{x} = t\vec{i} + 3\vec{j}$ and $\vec{y} = -2\vec{i} - \vec{j}$.
Find the value of the scalars t and k such that $2\vec{x}^{\perp} + k\vec{y}^{\perp} = -2(\vec{i} - 4\vec{j})$.

16. Let $\vec{a} = 5\vec{i} + 3\vec{j}$ and $\vec{b} = 2\vec{i} - 4\vec{j}$.
   (i)   Write $\vec{a}^{\perp}$ and $\vec{b}^{\perp}$ in terms of $\vec{i}$ and $\vec{j}$.
   (ii) Find the value of the scalars h and k such that $\vec{a}^{\perp} + h\vec{b}^{\perp} = 5\vec{i} - 3k\vec{j}$.

17. Let $\vec{u} = 2\vec{i} - 3\vec{j}$, $\vec{v} = 2\vec{i} - \vec{j}$ and $\vec{s} = 2\vec{i} - 7\vec{j}$.
   (i)   Write $\vec{u}^{\perp}$, $\vec{v}^{\perp}$ and $\vec{s}^{\perp}$ in terms of $\vec{i}$ and $\vec{j}$.
   (ii) Find the scalars h and k such that $h\vec{u}^{\perp} + k\vec{v}^{\perp} = \vec{s}^{\perp}$.

18. Let $\vec{a} = -3\vec{i} + 4\vec{j}$ and $\vec{b} = 12\vec{i} - 5\vec{j}$.
   (i)   Write down $\vec{a}^{\perp}$ and $\vec{b}^{\perp}$ in terms of $\vec{i}$ and $\vec{j}$.
   Show that:
   (ii) $|\vec{a}| + |\vec{b}^{\perp}| > |\vec{a} + \vec{b}^{\perp}|$ **(iii)** $|\vec{a}|^2 + |\vec{a}^{\perp}|^2 = |\vec{a} - \vec{a}^{\perp}|^2$ **(iv)** $|\vec{b}|^2 + |\vec{b}^{\perp}|^2 = |\vec{b} - \vec{b}^{\perp}|^2$

19. $\vec{a} = -6\vec{i} - x\vec{j}$, $\vec{b} = x\vec{i} - 4\vec{j}$ and $\vec{c} = -2x\vec{i} - \vec{j}$.
Find the two values of the scalar x such that $x\vec{a}^{\perp} + x\vec{b}^{\perp} - 5\vec{j} = 5\vec{c}^{\perp}$.

20. Let $\vec{p} = -12\vec{i} + 5\vec{j}$ and $\vec{q} = 4\vec{i} + 3\vec{j}$.
   (i)   Write down $\vec{p}^{\perp}$ and $\vec{q}^{\perp}$ in terms of $\vec{i}$ and $\vec{j}$.
   (ii) Evaluate $|\vec{p}^{\perp}|$ and $|\vec{q}^{\perp}|$.
   (iii) Find the scalar k such that $|\vec{p}^{\perp} + \vec{q}^{\perp}| = k[|\vec{p}^{\perp}| - |\vec{q}^{\perp}|]$.
   Give your answer in the form $\sqrt{n}$, where $n \in \mathbb{N}$.
   (Hint: $\sqrt{20} = \sqrt{4 \times 5} = \sqrt{4}\sqrt{5} = 2\sqrt{5}$).

C H A P T E R
18

FURTHER SEQUENCES AND SERIES: BINOMIAL THEOREM

Applications of Arithmetic Sequences and Series

Sequences and series have many practical applications.

Arithmetic Sequences and Series

$$a, a + d, a + 2d, a + 3d, \dots$$

$$T_n - T_{n-1} = \text{constant} = \text{common difference} = d$$

$$T_1 = a$$

$$T_n = a + (n - 1)d \qquad S_n = \frac{n}{2}[2a + (n - 1)d]$$

Example ▼

A pupil saves money each week. The pupil saves 50c in the first week, 60c the next week, 70c the next week, continuing the pattern for 30 weeks.

(i) How much will the pupil save in the 30th week?

(ii) How much will the pupil have saved after 30 weeks?

Solution:

(i) 50, 60, 70, 80, …
This is an arithmetic sequence with
$a = 50$ and $d = 10$
Find T_{30}.

$$T_n = a + (n - 1)d$$
$$T_{30} = 50 + (29)(10)$$

(put in $a = 50$, $d = 10$ and $n = 30$)

$$T_{30} = 50 + 290$$
$$T_{30} = 340c = €3.40$$

Thus, the pupil will save €3.40 in the 30th week.

(ii) $50 + 60 + 70 + 80 + \dots + 340$
This is an arithmetic series with
$a = 50$ and $d = 10$
Find S_{30}.

$$S_n = \frac{n}{2}[2a + (n - 1)d]$$

$$S_{30} = \tfrac{30}{2}[2(50) + (29)(10)]$$

(put in $a = 50$, $d = 10$ and $n = 30$)

$$S_{30} = 15(100 + 290)$$
$$S_{30} = 15(390)$$
$$S_{30} = 5850c = €58.50$$

Thus, after 30 weeks the pupil will have saved €58.50.

1. The first three terms of an arithmetic series are $2 + 5 + 8 + \ldots$

    (i) Find the common difference d.

    (ii) Find T_{20}, the 20th term and S_{20}, the sum of the first 20 terms.

    (iii) Which term of the series is 74?

    (iv) How many terms of the series need to be added to give a sum of 155?

2. A pupil saves money each week. The pupil saves 40c in the first week, 60c in the second week, 80c in the next week, continuing this pattern for 50 weeks.

    (i) How much will the pupil save in the 50th week?

    (ii) How much will the pupil have saved after 50 weeks?

3. A woman accepts a post with a starting salary of €30,000. In each following year she received an increase in salary of €2,000. What were her total earnings in the first 12 years?

4.

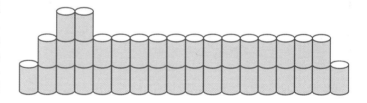

In a potato race, 10 potatoes are placed 8 m apart in a straight line. The object of the race is to pick up the first potato and place it in a basket, 20 m in front of the first potato, then run to the second potato, pick it up and place it in the basket and so on. The race begins at the basket. Find the total distance covered by a contestant who finishes the race.

5. A display in a grocery store will consist of cans stocked as shown. The first row is to have 18 cans and each row after the first is to have 2 cans fewer than the preceding row. How many cans will be needed in the display?

6. A man is given an interest-free loan. He repays the loan in monthly instalments. He repays €40 at the end of the first month, €44 at the end of the second month, €48 at the end of the third month, continuing the pattern of increasing the monthly repayments by €4 a month until the loan is repaid. The final monthly repayment is €228.

    (i) Show that it will take the man 48 months to repay the loan.

    (ii) Calculate the amount of the loan.

7. A ball rolls down a slope. The distances it travels in successive seconds are 2 cm, 6 cm, 10 cm, 14 cm, and so on. How many seconds elapse before it has travelled a total of 18 metres?

Applications of Geometric Sequences and Series

Geometric Sequences and Series

$$a, ar, ar^2, ar^3, \ldots$$

$$\frac{T_n}{T_{n-1}} = \text{constant} = \text{common ratio} = r$$

$$T_1 = a \qquad T_n = ar^{n-1}$$

$$S_n = \frac{a(1-r^n)}{1-r}, \quad (r<1) \qquad \text{or} \qquad S_n = \frac{a(r^n - 1)}{r-1}, \quad (r>1)$$

Example ▼

A company invested €40,000 in new machinery. The machinery depreciated at the rate of 20% per annum. Write down a sequence giving the value of the machinery at the end of each year for the first six years.

Solution:

This is a geometric sequence with $T_1 = a = 40,000$ and $r = 0.8$ (100% − 20% = 80% = 0.8)

$$T_n = ar^{n-1}$$

$T_2 = ar \ = 40,000\,(0.8) \ = 32,000$ (value after one year)
$T_3 = ar^2 = 40,000\,(0.8)^2 = 25,600$ (value after two years)
$T_4 = ar^3 = 40,000\,(0.8)^3 = 20,480$ (value after three years)
$T_5 = ar^4 = 40,000\,(0.8)^4 = 16,384$ (value after four years)
$T_6 = ar^5 = 40,000\,(0.8)^5 = 13,107.20$ (value after five years)
$T_7 = ar^6 = 40,000\,(0.8)^6 = 10,485.76$ (value after six years)

Thus the sequence is:

€32,000, €25,600, €20,480, €16,384, €13,107.20, €10,485.76

A woman accepts a post with a starting salary of €40,000 per annum. Each year after that her salary increases by 8% of the previous year. Calculate, correct to the nearest €:

(i) her salary in the tenth year

(ii) the total amount she earns in the first ten years in the post.

Solution:

Her salary for the first year is €40,000
Her salary for the second year is €40,000 × 1.08 = 43,200
Her salary for the third year is €40,000 × $(1.08)^2$ = 46,656, and so on.

$$40,000 + 43,200 + 46,656 + \ldots$$

This is a geometric series with $a = 40,000$ and $r = 1.08$

(i)
$$T_n = ar^{n-1}$$
$$T_{10} = 40,000(1.08)^9$$
(put in $a = 40,000$, $r = 1.08$ and $n = 10$)
$$T_{10} = 79,960.18508$$
Thus, her salary in the tenth year is
$$€79,960$$
(correct to the nearest €).

(ii)
$$S_n = \frac{a(r^n - 1)}{r - 1}$$
$$S_{10} = \frac{40,000[(1.08)^{10} - 1]}{1.08 - 1}$$
(put in $a = 40,000$, $r = 1.08$ and $n = 10$)
$$S_{10} = 579,462.4986$$
Thus, in the first ten years she earns
$$€579,462$$
(correct to the nearest €).

Exercise 18.2 ▼

1. The first three terms in a geometric series are $3 + 6 + 12 + \ldots$
   (i) Find the common ratio r.
   (ii) Find T_{10}, the tenth term and S_{12}, the sum of the first 12 terms.
   (iii) Which term of the series is 384?
   (iv) How many terms of the series need to be added to give a sum of 381?

2. A man accepts a post with a starting salary of €50,000 per annum. Each year after that his salary increases by 6% of the previous year. Calculate, correct to the nearest €:
   (i) his salary in the tenth year
   (ii) the total amount he earns in the first ten years in the post.

3. The population of a certain town is growing at the rate of 5% each year. If at the beginning of a certain year the population of the town is 12,000, what will it be eight years later, correct to the nearest 100?

4. A father gives his son €10 on his 12th birthday and decides to double his gift each following year. How much did the boy receive on his 21st birthday?

5. (i) The first three terms of a geometric series are $1 + 2 + 4 + \ldots$
   Show that S_n, the sum of the first n terms, is $2^n - 1$.

   (ii) A board consists of 16 squares. €1 is placed on the first square, €2 on the second square, €4 on the third square and so on with each square doubling the amount of money on the square before it.
   Calculate the total amount of money on the board.

6. A side of an equilateral triangle is 72 cm long. A second equilateral triangle is inscribed in it by joining the midpoints of the sides of the first triangle. The process is continued, as shown in the accompanying diagram. Find the perimeter of the fifth inscribed equilateral triangle.

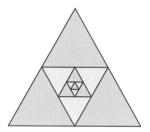

7. A company invested €64,000 in new machinery. The machinery depreciated at the rate of 25% per annum. Write down a sequence giving the value of the machinery at the end of each year for the first five years.

8. A jar contains 5,000 cm³ of air. On its first stroke, an air pump removes 20% of the air from the jar, on the second stroke the pump removes 20% of the remaining air, and so on. How much air is left in the jar after the sixth stroke of the pump?

Series of Investments

If a fixed sum of money is invested at regular intervals and at a constant interest rate, then the total accumulated value of all investments, including interest, can be found by using the formula S_n of a geometric series:

$$S_n = \frac{a(r^n - 1)}{r - 1} \quad (r > 1) \qquad \text{or} \qquad S_n = \frac{a(1 - r^n)}{1 - r} \quad (r < 1)$$

A woman invests €500 at the beginning of each year for ten consecutive years, where the rate is 6% per annum compound interest throughout. Calculate the total value of the investment at the end of ten years, correct to the nearest €.

Solution:

The first €500 is accumulating for 10 years. Thus $A_1 = 500(1.06)^{10}$
The second €500 is accumulating for 9 years. Thus $A_2 = 500(1.06)^9$
The process continues to the last €500, which is accumulating only for 1 year.

$$\text{Thus } A_{10} = 500(1.06)$$

If A is the total accumulated value, then:

$$
\begin{aligned}
A &= A_1 + A_2 + A_3 + \ldots + A_9 + A_{10} \\
&= 500(1.06)^{10} + 500(1.06)^9 + 500(1.06)^8 + \ldots + 500(1.06)^2 + 500(1.06) \\
&= 500(1.06) + 500(1.06)^2 + 500(1.06)^3 + \ldots + 500(1.06)^9 + 500(1.06)^{10} \\
&= 500[(1.06) + (1.06)^2 + (1.06)^3 + \ldots + (1.06)^9 + (1.06)^{10}]
\end{aligned}
$$

(The series in the brackets is a geometric series containing ten terms with $a = 1.06$ and $r = 1.06$)

$$= 500\, S_{10}$$

We need to find S_{10}.

$$S_n = \frac{a(r^n - 1)}{r - 1}$$

$$S_{10} = \frac{a(r^{10} - 1)}{r - 1}$$

$$= \frac{1.06[(1.06)^{10} - 1]}{1.06 - 1} = 13.97164264$$

$$A = 500\, S_{10}$$

$$= 500(13.97164264) = 6{,}985.821319$$

Thus the total accumulated value is €6,986 (correct to the nearest €).

Example ▼

A company invested €x in new equipment at the beginning of each year for three consecutive years. The equipment depreciated at the rate of 10% per annum.

(i)   Write, in terms of x, the total value of all the investments at the end of the third year.

(ii)   If the total value of all the investments is €48,780, find the value of x.

Solution:

$$100\% - 10\% = 90\% = 0.9$$

(i)   After three years, the value of the first investment of $x = (0.9)^3 x = 0.729x$
After two years, the value of the second investment of $x = (0.9)^2 x = 0.81x$
After one year, the value of the third investment of $x = 0.9x$
Thus, at the end of three years the total value, in terms of x, of the investment is:

$$0.729x + 0.81x + 0.9x = 2.439x$$

(ii)   Equation given in disguise:

Total value of all investments = €48,780

$\therefore$ $2.439x = 48,780$

$x = 20,000$ (divide both sides by 2.439)

Thus, $x = 20,000$.

Exercise 18.3 ▼

1. A person invested €5,000 at the beginning of each year for two consecutive years at 4% per annum compound interest.
   Find: **(i)**   the value of the first investment of €5,000 at the end of the second year
   (ii)   the total value of all the investments at the end of the second year.

2. A person invested €40,000 at the beginning of each year for three consecutive years at 6% per annum compound interest.
   Find: **(i)**   the value of the first investment of €40,000 at the end of the third year
   (ii)   the total value of all the investments at the end of the third year.

3. A person invested €20,000 at the beginning of each year for four consecutive years at 5% per annum compound interest.
   Find: **(i)**   the value of the first investment of €20,000 at the end of the fourth year, correct to the nearest cent
   (ii)   the total value of all the investments at the end of the fourth year, correct to the nearest €.

4. €50,000 was invested at the beginning of each year for four consecutive years at 3% per annum compound interest. Find the total value of the investments at the end of the fourth year, correct to the nearest cent.

5. A company invested €1,000 in new machinery at the beginning of each year for three consecutive years. The machinery depreciated at the rate of 10% per annum.

Find: **(i)** the value of the first investment of €1,000 at the end of the third year

   (ii) the total value of all the investments at the end of the third year.

6. A company invested €5,000 in new machinery at the beginning of each year for three consecutive years. The machinery depreciated at the rate of 20% per annum.

Find: **(i)** the value of the first investment of €5,000 at the end of the third year

   (ii) the total value of all the investments at the end of the third year.

7. A person invested €x at the beginning of each year for 2 consecutive years at 8% per annum compound interest. The total value of the investments at the end of the third year was €22,464. Find the value of x.

8. A person invested €x at the beginning of each year for 3 consecutive years at 5% per annum compound interest. The total value of the investments at the end of the third year was €132,405. Find the value of x.

9. A person invested €x at the beginning of each year for 4 consecutive years at 10% per annum compound interest. The total value of the investments at the end of the fourth year was €102,102. Find the value of x.

10. A company invested €x in new equipment at the beginning of each year for three consecutive years. The equipment depreciated at the rate of 20% per annum.
Write, in terms of x, the value of the first investment of €x at the end of the first year.
The value of the first investment of €x at the end of the third year is €15,360.
Find the value of x.
Find the total value of all the investments at the end of the third year.

11. A company invested €x in new equipment at the beginning of each year for three consecutive years. The equipment depreciated at the rate of 30% per annum.

   (i) Write, in terms of x, the total value of all the investments at the end of the third year.

   (ii) If the total value of all the investments is €64,386, find the value of x.

12. A company invested €x in new equipment at the beginning of each year for three consecutive years. The equipment depreciated at the rate of 20% per annum.

   (i) Write, in terms of x, the total value of all the investments at the end of the third year.

   (ii) If the total value of all the investments is €70,272, find the value of x.

13. €1,000 was invested at the beginning of each year for eight consecutive years at 10% per annum compound interest.
Calculate the total value of the investment at the end of the eight years, correct to the nearest €.

14. €2,000 was invested at the beginning of each year for ten consecutive years at 5% per annum compound interest.
Calculate the total value of the investment at the end of the ten years, correct to the nearest €.

15. €100 was invested at the beginning of each year for twelve consecutive years at 3% per annum compound interest.
Calculate the total value of the investment at the end of the twelve years, correct to the nearest €.

16. €500 was invested at the beginning of each year for fifteen consecutive years at 6% per annum compound interest.
Calculate the total value of the investment at the end of the fifteen years, correct to the nearest €.

17. €3,000 was invested at the beginning of each year for twenty consecutive years at 4% per annum compound interest.
Calculate the total value of the investment at the end of the twenty years, correct to the nearest €.

Infinite Geometric Series

When a series has an infinite number of terms, it is called an **infinite series** and the sum of the series is called the **sum to infinity** of the series. We will concentrate our work on the infinite geometric series.

Let us consider the value of a proper fraction (less than 1) if we keep multiplying it by itself. Take for example $\frac{1}{4}$, and keep multiplying it by itself, i.e. $(\frac{1}{4})^n$, as n increases indefinitely. We can represent this situation in a table using a calculator.

n	1	2	3	...	10
$(\frac{1}{4})^n$	0.25	0.0625	0.015625	...	0.0000009537

From the table we can see that the bigger the value of n, the nearer $(\frac{1}{4})^n$ gets to 0.
(This will happen for any proper fraction, positive or negative.)

We say that the limit of $(\frac{1}{4})^n$, as n approaches infinity is 0.

Symbolically

$$\lim_{n \to \infty} (\text{proper fraction})^n = 0$$

$n \to \infty$ means 'as n approaches infinity'.
lim is short for limit.
In general, for the infinite geometric series:

$$a + ar + ar^2 + ar^3 + \dots$$

if r is a proper fraction, then the terms will get closer to zero.
For r to be a proper fraction it must be between -1 and 1, i.e., $-1 < r < 1$.

$$\therefore \quad \text{If } -1 < r < 1$$
$$\text{then } \lim_{n \to \infty} r^n = 0$$

The sum to infinity, S_∞, of a series is denoted by $\lim_{n \to \infty} S_n$.

Let us now develop the general formula for the sum to infinity of a geometric series in which $-1 < r < 1$.

$$S_n = \frac{a(1 - r^n)}{1 - r}$$

The only part of this formula that changes as n increases is r^n.
As $n \to \infty$, $r^n \to 0$, because r is a proper fraction.

$$\therefore S_\infty = \frac{a(1-0)}{1-r} = \frac{a}{1-r}$$

> **Sum to infinity of a geometric series**
>
> $$S_\infty = \frac{a}{1-r} = \frac{\text{first term}}{1-\text{common ratio}}$$
>
> if $-1 < r < 1$.

Note: If $r \geqslant 1$ or $r \leqslant -1$, then a geometric series will have no limit, i.e., it does not exist.

Example ▼

Find the sum to infinity of the geometric series:

(i) $18 + 12 + 8 + \ldots$ 　　　**(ii)** $\frac{3}{5} + \frac{3}{50} + \frac{3}{500} + \ldots$

Solution:

(i) $18 + 12 + 8 + \ldots$

$$a = 18, \quad r = \tfrac{12}{18} = \tfrac{2}{3}$$

$$S_\infty = \frac{a}{1-r}$$

$$= \frac{18}{1-\frac{2}{3}} = \frac{18}{\frac{1}{3}} = 54.$$

(ii) $\frac{3}{5} + \frac{3}{50} + \frac{3}{500} + \ldots$

$$a = \tfrac{3}{5}, \quad r = \frac{\frac{3}{50}}{\frac{3}{5}} = \tfrac{1}{10}$$

$$S_\infty = \frac{a}{1-r}$$

$$= \frac{\frac{3}{5}}{1-\frac{1}{10}} = \frac{\frac{3}{5}}{\frac{9}{10}} = \tfrac{2}{3}.$$

Recurring decimals

An application of the sum of infinite geometric series is expressing non-terminating recurring decimals as rational numbers.

Note: The first five letters in the word 'rational' spell 'ratio'. In other words, a rational number is any number that can be written as a ratio (i.e. a fraction).

Recurring decimals can be expressed neatly by placing a dot over the first and last figures which repeat.
This is called the **dot notation**. For example:

1. $0.\dot{4} = 0.44444 \ldots = \tfrac{4}{9}$ 　　　　　　　　　**2.** $0.1\dot{6} = 0.166666 \ldots = \tfrac{1}{6}$

3. $1.\dot{2}\dot{5} = 1.252525 \ldots = 1 + \tfrac{25}{99} = \tfrac{124}{99}$ 　　　　**4.** $0.\dot{1}8\dot{5} = 0.185185185 \ldots = \tfrac{5}{27}$

(i) Find the sum to infinity of the geometric series $\frac{3}{100} + \frac{3}{1,000} + \frac{3}{10,000} + \ldots$

(ii) Using this series, show that $0.7\dot{3} = \frac{11}{15}$

Solution:

(i) $\frac{3}{100} + \frac{3}{1,000} + \frac{3}{10,000} + \ldots$

$$a = \frac{3}{100} \qquad r = \frac{\frac{3}{1000}}{\frac{3}{100}} = \frac{1}{10}$$

$$S_\infty = \frac{a}{1-r} = \frac{\frac{3}{100}}{1 - \frac{1}{10}} = \frac{\frac{3}{100}}{\frac{9}{10}} = \frac{1}{30}$$

(ii) $$0.7\dot{3} = 0.7 + 0.03 + 0.003 + 0.0003 + \ldots$$

$$= \frac{7}{10} + [\frac{3}{100} + \frac{3}{1,000} + \frac{3}{10,000} + \ldots]$$

(The series in the square brackets forms an infinite geometric series with $a = \frac{3}{100}$ and $r = \frac{1}{100}$, as above.)

$$= \frac{7}{10} + \frac{1}{30} \qquad \text{(from above)}$$

$$= \frac{21}{30} + \frac{1}{30} = \frac{22}{30} = \frac{11}{15}$$

Sometimes we are given an equation in disguise.

The sum to infinity of a geometric series is 3. The common ratio and the first term of the series are equal. Find the common ratio.

Solution:

Given: $\qquad S_\infty = 3$

$$\therefore \quad \frac{a}{1-r} = 3 \qquad \text{(equation given in disguise)}$$

$$\frac{r}{1-r} = 3 \qquad \text{(replace } a \text{ with } r, \text{ as we are given } a = r)$$

$$r = 3 - 3r \qquad \text{(multiply both sides by } (1-r))$$

$$4r = 3$$

$$r = \frac{3}{4}$$

Find the sum to infinity of each of the following geometric series:

1. $1 + \frac{1}{2} + \frac{1}{4} + \dots$

2. $2 + \frac{2}{3} + \frac{2}{9} + \dots$

3. $16 + 4 + 1 + \dots$

4. $1 + \frac{1}{3} + \frac{1}{9} + \dots$

5. $2 + \frac{1}{2} + \frac{1}{8} + \dots$

6. $5 + 1 + \frac{1}{5} + \dots$

7. $\frac{1}{4} + \frac{1}{8} + \frac{1}{16} + \dots$

8. $100 + 20 + 4 + \dots$

9. $75 + 25 + \frac{25}{3} + \dots$

10. The first three terms of a geometric series are $\frac{1}{4} + \frac{1}{12} + \frac{1}{36} + \dots$
Show that the sum to infinity is $\frac{3}{8}$.

11. Find the sum to infinity of the geometric series $\frac{5}{10} + \frac{5}{100} + \frac{5}{1,000} + \dots$
Using this series, show that $1.\dot{5} = \frac{14}{9}$.

12. Find the sum to infinity of the geometric series $\frac{2}{10} + \frac{2}{100} + \frac{2}{1,000} + \dots$
Using this series, show that $2.\dot{2} = \frac{20}{9}$.

13. Find the sum to infinity of the geometric series $\frac{7}{100} + \frac{7}{1,000} + \frac{7}{10,000} + \dots$
Using this series, show that $0.2\dot{7} = \frac{5}{18}$.

14. Find the sum to infinity of the geometric series $\frac{3}{100} + \frac{3}{1,000} + \frac{3}{10,000} + \dots$
Using this series, show that $1.8\dot{3} = \frac{11}{6}$.

15. Find the sum to infinity of the geometric series $\frac{4}{100} + \frac{4}{1,000} + \frac{4}{10,000} + \dots$
Using this series, show that $2.1\dot{4} = \frac{193}{90}$.

16. Find the sum to infinity of the geometric series $\frac{54}{100} + \frac{54}{10,000} + \frac{54}{1,000,000} + \dots$
Using this series, show that $1.\dot{5}\dot{4} = \frac{17}{11}$.

17. Show that $0.\dot{2}\dot{3} = \frac{23}{100} + \frac{23}{10,000} + \frac{23}{1,000,000} + \dots$
Hence, express $0.\dot{2}\dot{3}$ in the form $\frac{a}{b}$, $a, b \in \mathbf{N}$.

18. Show that $0.1\dot{2} = \frac{1}{10} + \frac{2}{100} + \frac{2}{1,000} + \frac{2}{10,000} + \dots$
Hence, express $0.1\dot{2}$ in the form $\frac{p}{q}$, $p, q \in \mathbf{N}$.

19. The sum to infinity of a geometric series is 3 and the first term is 2.
Find the common ratio, r.

20. The sum to infinity of a geometric series is 8 and the common ratio is $\frac{1}{2}$.
Find the first term.

21. The sum to infinity of a geometric series is 6 and the common ratio is $\frac{2}{3}$.
Find the first term.

22. The sum to infinity of a geometric series is 4. The common ratio and the first term of the series are equal. Find the common ratio.

23. The sum to infinity of a geometric series is 5. The common ratio and the first term of the series are equal. Find the common ratio.

24. If the sum to infinity of a geometric series is five times the first term, find the common ratio.

25. Find the first two terms of the geometric series whose third term is 3 and whose sum to infinity is twice its first term.

26. In each week the growth of a plant is two-thirds of the growth in the previous week. If the plant grows 24 cm in the first week calculate the maximum height of the plant.

Binomial Theorem

An expression with two terms is called a binomial.

For example, $1 + x$ and $1 - x$ are binomials.

The Binomial Theorem is used to write down the expansion of a binomial to any power, for example $(1 + x)^6$.

On our course, the binomial expansions are confined to:

$$(1 + x)^n \text{ and } (1 - x)^n, \text{ where } n \in \mathbf{N} \text{ and } n \leqslant 7.$$

The Binomial Expansions of $(1 + x)^n$ and $(1 - x)^n$ are found as follows:

$$(1 + x)^n = \binom{n}{0} + \binom{n}{1}x + \binom{n}{2}x^2 + \binom{n}{3}x^3 + \ldots + \binom{n}{n}x^n$$

$$(1 - x)^n = \binom{n}{0} - \binom{n}{1}x + \binom{n}{2}x^2 - \binom{n}{3}x^3 + \ldots + \binom{n}{n}x^n$$

Notes:

1. The expansion contains $(n + 1)$ terms (one more than the power).
2. The powers of x increase by 1 in each successive term.
3. The power of x is **always** the same as the lower number in the combination bracket.
4. In the expansion of $(1 - x)^n$, the signs are alternately $+, -, +, -, +, - \ldots$

(i) Expand fully: **(a)** $(1 + x)^4$ **(b)** $(1 - x)^4$

(ii) Hence, find the real numbers a, b and c such that:

$$(1 + x)^4 + (1 - x)^4 = a + bx^2 + cx^4$$

(iii) Show that $(1 + \sqrt{3})^4 = 28 + 16\sqrt{3}$.

Solution:

(i) (a) $(1 + x)^4$ (the power is 4, thus there are 5 terms)

$$= \binom{4}{0} + \binom{4}{1}x + \binom{4}{2}x^2 + \binom{4}{3}x^3 + \binom{4}{4}x^4$$

$$= 1 + 4x + 6x^2 + 4x^3 + x^4$$

(b) The only difference between the expansions of $(1 + x)^4$ and $(1 - x)^4$ is that in the expansion of $(1 - x)^4$ the signs alternate $+, -, +, -, +, -$.

Thus, $(1 - x)^4 = 1 - 4x + 6x^2 - 4x^3 + x^4$

(ii) $(1 + x)^4 + (1 - x)^4$

$$= (1 + 4x + 6x^2 + 4x^3 + x^4) + (1 - 4x + 6x^2 - 4x^3 + x^4)$$

$$= 1 + 4x + 6x^2 + 4x^3 + x^4 + 1 - 4x + 6x^2 - 4x^3 + x^4$$

$$= 2 + 12x^2 + 2x^4$$

By comparing $a + bx^2 + cx^4$ to $2 + 12x^2 + 2x^4$

$$a = 2, \qquad b = 12, \qquad c = 2$$

(iii) We use the expansion of $(1 + x)^4$ to show that $(1 + \sqrt{3})^4 = 28 + 16\sqrt{3}$.

Let $(1 + x)^4 = (1 + \sqrt{3})^4$, $\therefore$ $x = \sqrt{3}$

$(1 + x)^4 = 1 + 4x + 6x^2 + 4x^3 + x^4$

$(1 + \sqrt{3})^4 = 1 + 4(\sqrt{3}) + 6(\sqrt{3})^2 + 4(\sqrt{3})^3 + (\sqrt{3})^4$ (replace x with $\sqrt{3}$)

$= 1 + 4(\sqrt{3}) + 6(3) + 4(3\sqrt{3}) + (9)$

$= 1 + 4\sqrt{3} + 18 + 12\sqrt{3} + 9$

$= 28 + 16\sqrt{3}$

$[(\sqrt{3})^2 = 3; \quad (\sqrt{3})^3 = (\sqrt{3})^2(\sqrt{3}) = 3\sqrt{3}; \quad (\sqrt{3})^4 = (\sqrt{3})^2(\sqrt{3})^2 = (3)(3) = 9]$

Evaluate each of the following:

1. $\binom{5}{2}$ 2. $\binom{7}{3}$ 3. $\binom{4}{3}$ 4. $\binom{6}{1}$

5. $\binom{2}{0}$ 6. $\binom{4}{2}$ 7. $\binom{7}{6}$ 8. $\binom{4}{4}$

9. $\binom{5}{5}$ 10. $\binom{5}{0}$ 11. $\binom{6}{4}$ 12. $\binom{7}{4}$

Use the Binomial Theorem to expand fully each of the following:

13. $(1 + x)^3$ 14. $(1 - x)^3$ 15. $(1 + x)^5$ 16. $(1 - x)^5$

17. $(1 + x)^6$ 18. $(1 - x)^6$ 19. $(1 + x)^7$ 20. $(1 - x)^7$

21. If   (i) $(1 + x)^2 + (1 - x)^2 = a(1 + x^2)$ (ii) $(1 + x)^2 - (1 - x)^2 = bx$,
    find the value of the real numbers a and b.

22. Expand fully: (i) $(1 + x)^4$ (ii) $(1 - x)^4$.
    Hence, find the real number a such that $(1 + x)^4 - (1 - x)^4 = ax(1 + x^2)$.

23. Use the Binomial Theorem to show that:
$$(1 + x)^6 - (1 - x)^6 = 4x(3 + 10x^2 + 3x^4).$$

24. Expand $(1 + x)^3$ in ascending powers of x.
    Show that $(1 + \sqrt{5})^3 = 8(2 + \sqrt{5})$.

25. Expand fully: (i) $(1 + x)^3$ (ii) $(1 - x)^3$.
    Hence, find the real numbers p and q such that $(1 + x)^3 - (1 - x)^3 = px + qx^3$.
    Show that $(1 + \sqrt{2})^3 - (1 - \sqrt{2})^3 = 10\sqrt{2}$.

26. Use the Binomial Theorem to show that:
    (i) $(1 + x)^4 + (1 - x)^4 = 2(1 + 6x^2 + x^4)$
    (ii) $(1 + \sqrt{2})^4 + (1 - \sqrt{2})^4 = 34$.

27. Expand fully $(1 + x)^5$. If $(1 + \sqrt{3})^5 = a + b\sqrt{3}$, find the value of a and b, $a, b \in \mathbf{N}$.

28. Expand fully $(1 + x)^4$.
    By letting $x = 0.01$, show that $(1.01)^4 > 1.04$.

29. For what value of x is $(1 + x) = 1.2$?
    Expand fully $(1 + x)^5$. Use your expansion to evaluate $(1.2)^5$.

30. For what value of x is $(1 - x) = 0.9$?
    Expand fully $(1 - x)^4$. Use your expansion to evaluate $(0.9)^4$.

FURTHER GEOMETRY

Circle

The diagrams below show some of the terms we use when dealing with a circle:

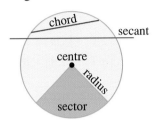

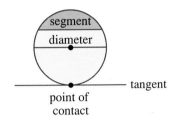

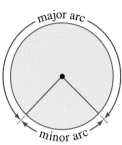

Theorem:	The degree-measure of an angle subtended at the centre of a circle by a chord is equal to twice the degree-measure of any angle subtended by the chord at a point of the arc of the circle which is on the same side of the chordal line as is the centre.

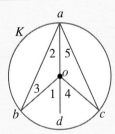

Given: Circle K, centre o, containing points a, b and c.

To prove: $|\angle boc| = 2|\angle bac|$

Construction: Join a to o and continue to d. Label angles 1, 2, 3, 4 and 5.

Proof: Consider triangle aob:

$$|\angle 1| = |\angle 2| + |\angle 3| \qquad \text{exterior angle}$$

but $|\angle 2| = |\angle 3| \qquad\qquad\quad |oa| = |ob|$

∴ $|\angle 1| = 2|\angle 2|$

similarly, $|\angle 4| = 2|\angle 5|$

∴ $|\angle 1| + |\angle 4| = 2|\angle 2| + 2|\angle 5|$

∴ $|\angle 1| + |\angle 4| = 2(|\angle 2| + |\angle 5|)$

i.e. $|\angle boc| = 2|\angle bac|$

Corollaries: Three very important angle properties of a circle can be deduced from this theorem:

1.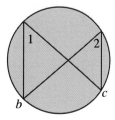

All angles standing on the same arc, or chord, are equal in measure.

Angles 1 and 2 stand on arc bc.

$$|\angle 1| = |\angle 2|$$

2.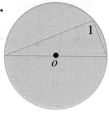

The angle in a semicircle is a right angle.

$$|\angle 1| = 90°$$

3.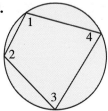

The opposite angles of a cyclic quadrilateral add up to 180°.

$$|\angle 1| + |\angle 3| = 180°$$
$$|\angle 2| + |\angle 4| = 180°$$

Note: A cyclic quadrilateral is a quadrilateral with all of its vertices on the circumference of the same circle.

Corollary 1: | All angles standing on the same arc or chord are equal in measure.

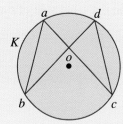   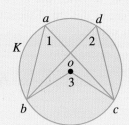

Given: Circle K, centre o, $\angle bac$ and $\angle bdc$ standing on the same arc bc.

To Prove: $|\angle bac| = |\angle bdc|$

Construction: Join b to o and c to o. Mark angles 1, 2 and 3.

Proof: $|\angle 3| = 2|\angle 1|$ angle at the centre is twice the angle on the circumference (both on arc bc)

$|\angle 3| = 2|\angle 2|$ angle at the centre is twice the angle on the circumference (both on arc bc)

∴ $2|\angle 1| = 2|\angle 2|$
∴ $|\angle 1| = |\angle 2|$
∴ $|\angle bac| = |\angle bdc|$

Corollary 2:	The angle at the circle standing on a diameter is a right angle.

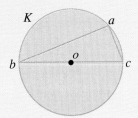 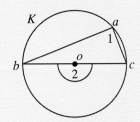

Given:	Circle K, centre o, $\angle bac$ at the circle standing on the diameter $[bc]$.
To Prove:	$\lvert \angle bac \rvert = 90°$
Construction:	Mark angles 1 and 2.

Proof:

$\lvert \angle 2 \rvert = 2\lvert \angle 1 \rvert$	angle at the centre is twice the angle on the circumference (both on arc bc)
but $\lvert \angle 2 \rvert = 180°$	straight angle
$\therefore \quad 2\lvert \angle 1 \rvert = 180°$	
$\therefore \quad \lvert \angle 1 \rvert = 90°$	
$\therefore \quad \lvert \angle bac \rvert = 90°$	

Converse:	In a right-angled triangle, the hypotenuse is the diameter of a circle which will pass through the three vertices of the triangle.

Corollary 3:	The measure of the opposite angles of a cyclic quadrilateral add to 180°.

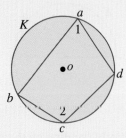 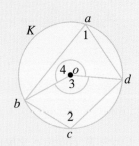

Given:	Circle K, centre o, cyclic quadrilateral $abcd$ with opposite angles 1 and 2
To Prove:	$|\angle 1| + |\angle 2| = 180°$
Construction:	Join b to o and d to o. Mark angles 3 and 4.
Proof:	$|\angle 3| = 2|\angle 1|$ angle at the centre is twice the angle on the circumference (both on arc bd)
	$|\angle 4| = 2|\angle 2|$ angle at the centre is twice the angle on the circumference (both on arc bd)
	$\therefore \quad |\angle 3| + |\angle 4| = 2|\angle 1| + 2|\angle 2|$
	but $|\angle 3| + |\angle 4| = 360°$ angles at a point
	$\therefore \quad 2|\angle 1| + 2|\angle 2| = 360°$
	$\therefore \qquad |\angle 1| + |\angle 2| = 180°$
	Similarly, it can be proved that the other pair of opposite angles add to 180°.
Converse:	If both pairs of opposite angles in a quadrilateral add up to 180°, then the quadrilateral is cyclic.

Example ▼

In the diagram, *pqrs* is a cyclic quadrilateral. *o* is the centre of the circle.

$$|\angle qps| = 61° \quad \text{and} \quad |\angle osr| = 72°,$$

Find: **(i)** $|\angle qos|$, where $\angle qos$ is obtuse

          (ii) $|\angle srq|$

          (iii) $|\angle rqo|$.

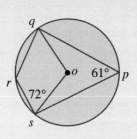

Solution:

(i) $|\angle qos| = 2\,|\angle qps|$ $\left(\begin{array}{l} \text{angle at the centre} \\ = 2(\text{angle at the circumference}) \end{array} \right)$

            $= 2(61°)$

            $= 122°$

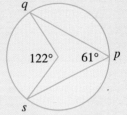

(ii) $|\angle srq| + |\angle qps| = 180°$ $\left(\begin{array}{l} \text{opposite angles of} \\ \text{a cyclic quadrilateral} \end{array} \right)$

         $|\angle srq| + 61° = 180°$

            $|\angle srq| = 119°$

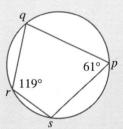

(iii) $|\angle rqo| + 119° + 72° + 122° = 360°$ $\left(\begin{array}{l} \text{four angles in a} \\ \text{quadrilateral add to } 360° \end{array} \right)$

            $|\angle rqo| + 313° = 360°$

              $|\angle rqo| = 47°$

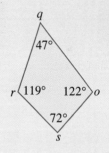

The circle in the diagram has centre *o*.
Find the value of *x* and the value of *y*.

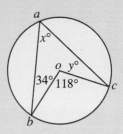

Solution:

$x = \frac{1}{2}(118°)$ $\left(\begin{array}{l} \text{angle at the circumference} \\ = \frac{1}{2} \text{ (angle at the centre)} \end{array} \right)$

$x = 59°$

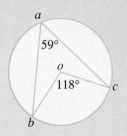

Draw triangles *obc* and *abc* separately and label angles 1 and 2.

In triangle *obc*, $|ob| = |oc|$ (both radii)

$\quad |\angle 1| + |\angle 2| + 118° = 180°$ (3 angles in a triangle)

$\quad\quad |\angle 1| + |\angle 2| = 62°$

$\quad\quad$ but $|\angle 1| = |\angle 2|$ (because $|ob| = |oc|$)

$\quad\quad \therefore \quad |\angle 1| = |\angle 2| = 31°$

In triangle *abc*:

$y + 31 + 31 + 34 + 59 = 180°$ (3 angles in a triangle)

$\quad\quad y + 155 = 180°$

$\quad\quad\quad y = 25°$

Find the value of the letters representing the angles in each of the following circles:

1.

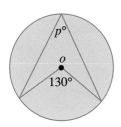

2.

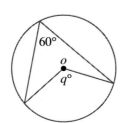

3.

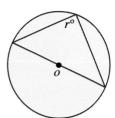

4.

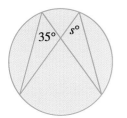

5.

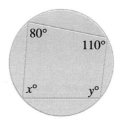

6.

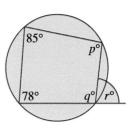

7.

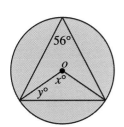

8.

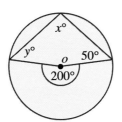

9.

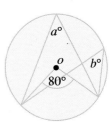

10.

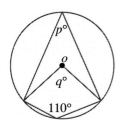

11.

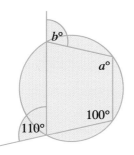

12.

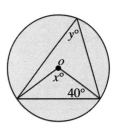

13.

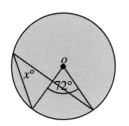

14.

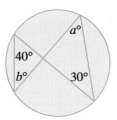

15.

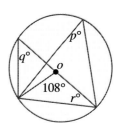

16.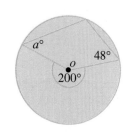

17.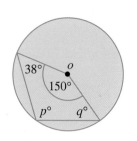

18.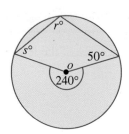

19.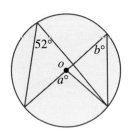

20.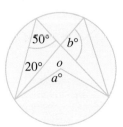

21.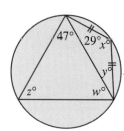

22.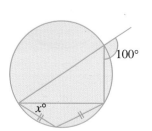

23.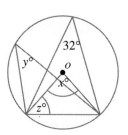

24.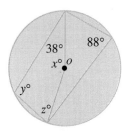

25.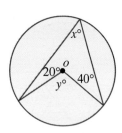

26.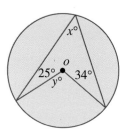

27.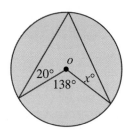

28. In a circle, centre o, oa is parallel to bc.
If $|\angle abc| = 23°$, find:
 (i) $|\angle aoc|$
 (ii) $|\angle oxb|$
 (iii) $|\angle oca|$.

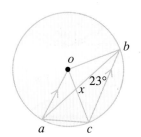

29. In the diagram, $|\angle xcb| = 54°$; o is the centre of the circle.
Calculate $|\angle bod|$, where $\angle bod$ is obtuse.

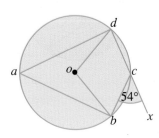

30. The centre of the circle is o.
  If $|\angle aob| = 130°$ and
        $|\angle cao| = 15°$,
  calculate $|\angle obc|$.

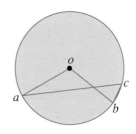

31. p, q, r and s are points of a circle, centre c, as in diagram.
  Name an angle equal in measure to:
  (i) $2|\angle rpq|$
  (ii) $|\angle qsp|$
  (iii) a right angle.
  If $|pq| = |pr|$ and $|\angle qsr| = 36°$, calculate $|\angle prs|$.

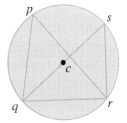

32. In the diagram, $pqrs$ is a cyclic quadrilateral.
  o is the centre of the circle.
  $|\angle qos| = 120°$ and $|\angle osr| = 74°$.
  Find:
  (i) $|\angle qps|$
  (ii) $|\angle srq|$
  (iii) $|\angle rqo|$.

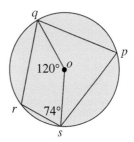

33. r is a point of a circle, centre c, $|\angle cpq| = 40°$.
  Calculate:
  (i) $|\angle pcq|$
  (ii) $|\angle prq|$.
  If $|\angle pcr| = 200°$, calculate $|\angle crp|$.

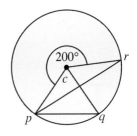

34. Two circles intersect at a and b.
  $[ab]$ is a diameter.
  c is the centre of the other circle.
  Calculate $|\angle bda|$.

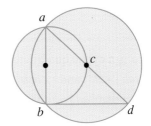

Questions 35 to 44 require a proof.

35. The circles H and K have diameters $[ab]$ and $[ac]$, respectively.
  Prove that eb is parallel to dc.

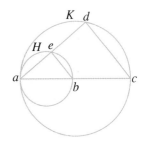

423

36. p, q, r and s are points on a circle.

If $pq \parallel sr$, prove that $|\angle psr| = |\angle qrs|$.

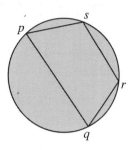

37. p, q, r and s are four points on a circle.

If $|\angle psq| = |\angle rsq|$ and $|\angle pqs| = |\angle rqs|$, prove that $[sq]$ is a diameter of the circle.

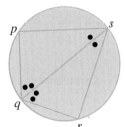

38. (i) $abcd$ is a cyclic quadrilateral.

o is the centre of the circle.

ad is produced to e.

Prove that $|\angle abc| = |\angle cde|$.

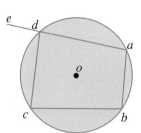

(ii) $abcd$ is a parallelogram and a, b, y, d are points on the circle.

Show that $|dy| = |dc|$.

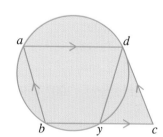

39. $abcd$ is a cyclic quadrilateral.

$|\angle dab| = 80°$ and $|\angle acb| = 50°$.

Prove that $|ad| = |ab|$.

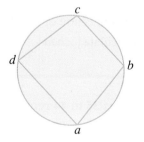

40. [ab] and [pq] are two diameters of a circle, as in diagram.

Prove that:

(i) $|\angle qab| = |\angle qpb|$

(ii) $aq \parallel pb$.

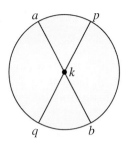

41. The diagram shows a circle, centre o.

a, b, c, d and e are points on the circle such that:

$|\angle aoe| = 2|\angle eod|$.

Prove that $|\angle acd| = 3|\angle ebd|$.

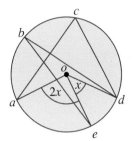

42. k is the centre of the given circle.

$kp \perp bc$ and $|ab| = |ap|$.

Prove that:

(i) $|\angle pab| = |\angle pac|$

(ii) $|\angle abc| = 22\frac{1}{2}°$.

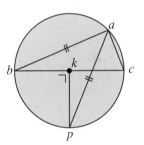

43. $cdts$ is a parallelogram and c is the centre of the circle.

Prove that $|\angle dts| = 120°$.

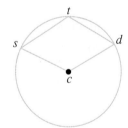

44. c is the centre of the circle.

Prove that $|\angle cpq| + |\angle qrp| = 90°$.

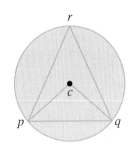

Tangent to a Circle

A line which meets a circle in one, and only one, point is called a **tangent**. A tangent to a circle is perpendicular to a diameter (or radius) drawn from the point of contact.

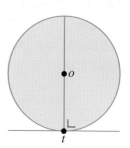

Theorem:	A line is a tangent to a circle at a point t on the circle if, and only if, it passes through t and is perpendicular to the line through t and the centre.

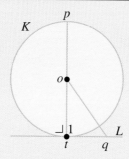

Given: Circle K, centre o, diameter $[pt]$ and a line L such that $pt \perp L$ at t.

To Prove: The line L is a tangent to the circle.

Construction: Let q be any other point on L. Join o to q. Mark angle 1.

Proof: In triangle otq

         $|\angle 1| = 90°$ given

$\therefore$ Triangle otq is a right-angled triangle with hypotenuse $[oq]$

$\therefore$ $|oq| > |ot|$ hypotenuse is the longest side

         $|oq| > $ radius

$\therefore$ q lies outside the circle

         Similarly, it may be shown that any other point on the line L, except t, lies outside the circle.

$\therefore$ The line L meets the circle at only one point, t.

$\therefore$ The line L is a tangent.

Converse: A tangent to a circle is perpendicular to the diameter drawn through the point of contact.

Corollary 1:   The perpendicular to a tangent at its point of contact with the circumference of a circle passes through the centre.

Corollary 2:   At any point on the circumference of a circle, one, and only one, tangent can be drawn.

Corollary 3:   Two tangents can be drawn to a circle from a point outside the circle, and the distance from the point outside the circle to each point of contact is the same. Using the diagram: $|pa| = |pb|$

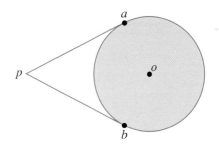

Alternate Segment Theorem

Any chord of a circle divides the circle into two **segments**.
If a tangent is drawn to meet the chord the shaded segment is called the **'alternate segment'**.
If a tangent and a chord meet on the circumference of a circle, then the angle between them is equal to the angle that stands on the chord in the alternate (opposite) segment.

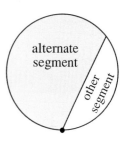

Consider both diagrams below:

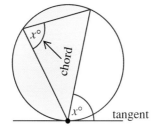 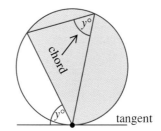

In both cases, the angle opposite the chord is equal to the angle between the tangent and the chord, on the **opposite** side of the chord.

| **Theorem:** | An angle between a tangent *ak* and a chord [*ab*] of a circle has degree-measure equal to that of any angle in the alternate segment. |

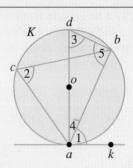

Given:	Circle *K*, centre *o*, chord [*ab*], tangent *ak* and point *c* on the circle in the alternate segment.
To Prove:	$\left\lvert \angle kab \right\rvert = \left\lvert \angle acb \right\rvert$
Construction:	Draw diameter [*ad*]. Join *d* to *b*. Mark angles 1, 2, 3, 4 and 5.

Proof:

$\left\lvert \angle 5 \right\rvert = 90°$	angle in a semi-circle
$\therefore \quad \left\lvert \angle 3 \right\rvert + \left\lvert \angle 4 \right\rvert = 90°$	remaining angles in triangle *abd*.
but $\left\lvert \angle 1 \right\rvert + \left\lvert \angle 4 \right\rvert = 90°$	construction
$\therefore \quad \left\lvert \angle 1 \right\rvert = \left\lvert \angle 3 \right\rvert$	
but $\left\lvert \angle 2 \right\rvert = \left\lvert \angle 3 \right\rvert$	standing on the same chord [*ab*]
$\therefore \quad \left\lvert \angle 1 \right\rvert = \left\lvert \angle 2 \right\rvert$	
$\therefore \quad \left\lvert \angle qab \right\rvert = \left\lvert \angle acb \right\rvert$	

The line *ab* is a tangent to the circle at *p*.
$|\angle apq| = 75°$ and $|\angle pqr| = 50°$.
Find:

(i) $|\angle qrp|$

(ii) $|\angle rpb|$

(iii) $|\angle qpr|$

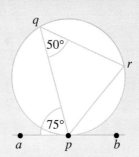

Solution:

(i) $|\angle qrp| = |\angle apq| = 75°$
     (angle in alternate segment)

(ii) $|\angle rpb| = |\angle pqr| = 50°$
     (angle in alternate segment)

(iii) $|\angle qpr| = 180° - |\angle apq| - |\angle rpb|$
     $= 180° - 75° - 50°$
     $= 55°$

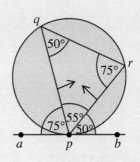

Exercise 19.2 ▼

Find the value of the letter representing the angles in each of the following circles.
In each case *o* is the centre of the circle and *T* is a tangent at *s*.

1.

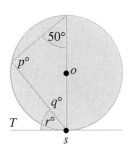

2.

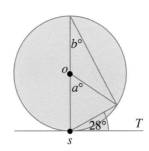

3.

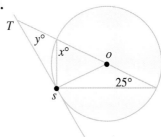

4.

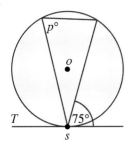

5.

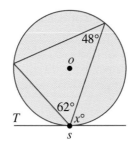

6.

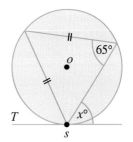

7.

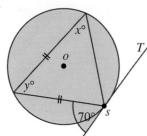

8.

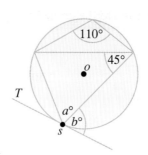

9.

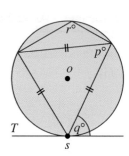

10.

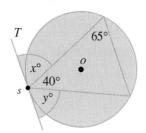

11.

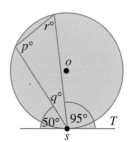

12.

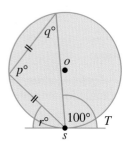

13. In the diagram, o is the centre of the circle.
pt is a tangent, $|pq| = |rq|$, $|\angle spt| = 38°$.
Calculate $|\angle qrs|$.

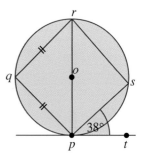

14. In the diagram, ta and tb are tangents at a and b to a
circle of centre o.
tc is a line passing through o and $|\angle atb| = 56°$.
Calculate:

  (i) $|\angle tao|$
  (ii) $|\angle ato|$
  (iii) $|\angle aob|$
  (iv) $|\angle aco|$.

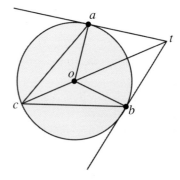

15. In the diagram, pq is a tangent to the circle of centre o,
at q. $[rs]$ is a diameter.
If $|\angle orq| = 34°$, calculate:

  (i) $|\angle qos|$
  (ii) $|\angle oqs|$
  (iii) $|\angle sqp|$.

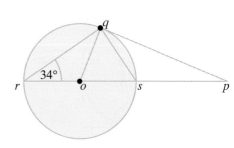

16. In the diagram, *kp* and *kq* are tangents to the circle of centre *o*, at *p* and *q*.

[*rs*] is a diameter and | ∠*pos* | = 120°.

Calculate:

(i) | ∠*kop* |

(ii) | ∠*pkq* |.

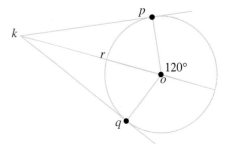

17. In the diagram, *o* is the centre of the circle. *ab* is a tangent and | ∠*brq* | = 28°.

Calculate:

(i) | ∠*soq* |, where ∠*soq* is obtuse

(ii) | ∠*soq* |, where ∠*soq* is reflex

(iii) | ∠*srq* |

(iv) | ∠*ars* |.

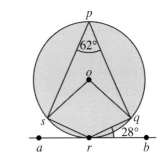

18. In the diagram, *pq*, *pr* and *qr* are tangents to the circle at *a*, *b* and *c*, respectively.

| ∠*pqr* | = 70° and | ∠*qrp* | = 48°.

Calculate:

(i) | ∠*bcr* |

(ii) | ∠*cab* |

(iii) | ∠*abc* |

(iv) | ∠*acb* |.

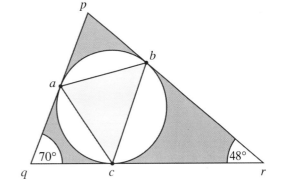

19. *ab* and *ac* are tangents to the circle at *b* and *c*, respectively.

The centre of the circle is *o* and *d* is a point on the circle.

If | ∠*bac* | = 30°, find | ∠*bdc* |.

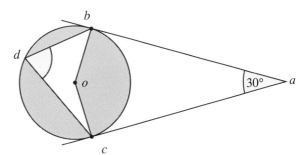

Questions 20 to 26 require a proof.

20. In the diagram, *pr* is a tangent to the circle of centre *o*, at *q*. [*ab*] is a chord and *pq* ∥ *ab*.

Prove that | *qa* | = | *qb* |.

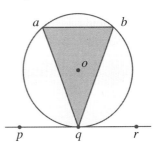

21. In the diagram, *pr* is a tangent to the circle at *q*.
[*qs*] is any chord; *x* and *y* are points on the circle.
xq bisects $\angle pqs$ and *yq* bisects $\angle rqs$.
Prove that [*qs*] is a diameter of the circle.

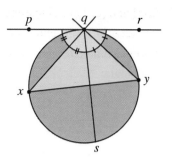

22. In the diagram, [*xy*] is a diameter of the circle of centre *o*.
zt is a tangent at *p* and $xz \perp zt$.
Prove that:
(i) $|\angle xpz| = |\angle opy|$
(ii) $|\angle zxp| = |\angle ypt|$.

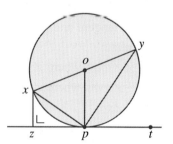

23. In the diagram, *kp* and *kq* are tangents to a circle of centre *o*, at *p* and *q*, respectively.
$|\angle qkp| = 50°$.
Prove that $|\angle qkp| = 2|\angle rps|$.

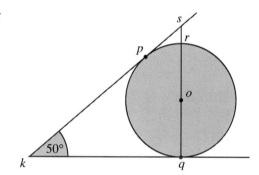

24. In the diagram, *pt* and *ps* are tangents to a circle of centre *o*, at *t* and *s*, respectively.
Prove that:
(i) $|ps| = |pt|$
(ii) $|\angle tpr| = 2|\angle top|$.

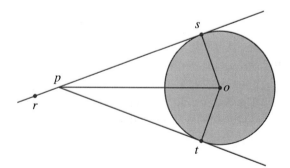

25. *p*, *t* and *u* are points on a circle *K*, centre *o*.
wt is the tangent at *t*.
[*pt*] is a diameter.
Prove that $|\angle wtu| = |\angle tpu|$.

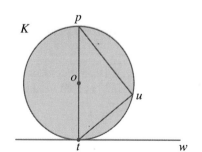

26. $[dm]$ and $[cb]$ are diameters of a circle, centre o.
ab and pm are tangents at b and m respectively.
Show that $|\angle pmc| = |\angle abd|$.

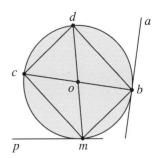

Intersecting Chords

In the circle, $[ab]$ and $[cd]$ are two chords intersecting inside
the circle at k.

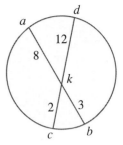

$|ka| = 8$, $|kb| = 3$

$|kc| = 2$, $|kd| = 12$

$|ka|.|kb| = 8 \times 3 = 24$

$|kc|.|kd| = 2 \times 12 = 24$

  i.e., $|ka|.|kb| = |kc|.|kd|$

In the circle, $[ab]$ and $[cd]$ are two chords intersecting outside
the circle at k.

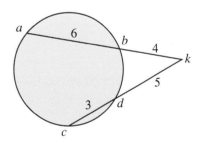

$|ka| = 10$, $|kb| = 4$

$|kc| = 8$, $|kd| = 5$

$|ka|.|kb| = 10 \times 4 = 40$

$|kc|.|kd| = 8 \times 5 = 40$

  i.e., $|ka|.|kb| = |kc|.|kd|$

In both cases the result is the same.
In both cases it is important to note that all four lengths are measured from the point of intersection of
the chordal lines.

Note: When asked to prove these results, they are written $|ak|.|kb| = |ck|.|kd|$.
However, when solving problems it is better to use $|ka|.|kb| = |kc|.|kd|$, always starting from
the point of intersection.

Theorem:	If [ab] and [cd] are chords of a circle and the lines ab and cd meet at the point k which is inside the circle, then $\lvert ak \rvert . \lvert kb \rvert = \lvert ck \rvert . \lvert kd \rvert$.

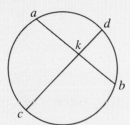 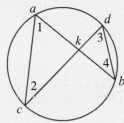

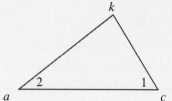

Given:	Two chords of a circle, [ab] and [cd] intersecting inside the circle at k.
To Prove:	$\lvert ak \rvert . \lvert kb \rvert = \lvert ck \rvert . \lvert kd \rvert$
Construction:	Join a to c and d to b. Mark angles 1, 2, 3 and 4.
Proof:	In triangles akc and dkb

$$\lvert \angle 1 \rvert = \lvert \angle 3 \rvert \qquad \text{standing on the same arc } bc$$

$$\lvert \angle 2 \rvert = \lvert \angle 4 \rvert \qquad \text{standing on the same arc } ad$$

∴   triangles akc and dkb are equiangular

∴ $\dfrac{\lvert ak \rvert}{\lvert kd \rvert} = \dfrac{\lvert ck \rvert}{\lvert kb \rvert}$ corresponding sides are in the same ratio

∴ $\lvert ak \rvert . \lvert kb \rvert = \lvert ck \rvert . \lvert kd \rvert$ cross-multiply

Theorem:	If [ab] and [cb] are chords of a circle and the lines ab and cd meet at the point k, where k is outside the circle, then
	$$|ak|.|kb| = |ck|.|kd|.$$

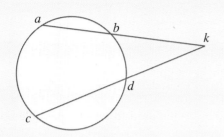 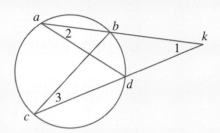

Given:	Two chords of a circle [ab] and [cd] intersecting outside the circle at a point k.

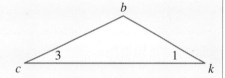

To Prove:	$|ak|.|kb| = |ck|.|kd|$

Construction:	Join a to d and c to b.
	Mark angles 1, 2 and 3.

Proof: In triangles adk and cbk:

$$|\angle 1| = |\angle 1| \qquad \text{common angle}$$

$$|\angle 2| = |\angle 3| \qquad \text{standing on the same arc } bd$$

∴   triangles adk and cbk are equiangular

∴ $\dfrac{|ak|}{|ck|} = \dfrac{|kd|}{|kb|}$ corresponding sides are in the same ratio

∴ $|ak|.|kb| = |ck|.|kd|$ cross-multiply

Converse:

If two line segments [ab] and [cd] intersect at a point k such that $|ak|.|kb| = |ck|.|kd|$, then the points a, b, c and d are concyclic, i.e., the four points are on the circumference of a circle.

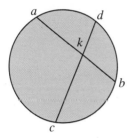 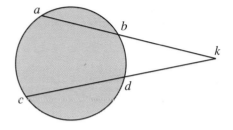

Note: The converses of the two theorems are true and are often used to test for possible concyclic points.

Tangent: Special Case

A special case of the previous theorem arises when from a point p outside a circle, a tangent is drawn to the circle at t and from p a line is drawn to intersect the circle at a and b.
Consider the following diagram.
From the previous theorem it was proved:

$$|pa|.|pb| = |pc|.|pd|$$

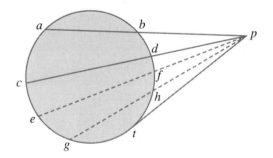

However, if pdc were to rotate about p, in an anti-clockwise direction, c and d would move to e and f, and then to g and h, and so on, and eventually c and d would approach one another and coincide at t.

∴ $|pa|.|pb| = |pt|.|pt|$
∴ $|pa|.|pb| = |pt|^2$

Note: The line segment pba is called a **secant** from p.

| **Corollary:** | If from a point p outside a circle a tangent is drawn to touch the circle at t and from p a line is drawn to intersect the circle at a and b, then $|pa|.|pb| = |pt|^2$. |

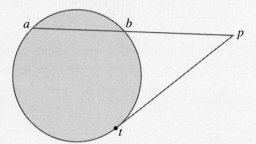 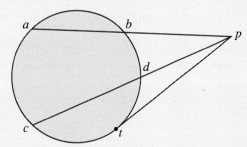

Given:	The tangent from the point p touching the circle at t and a line from p intersecting the circle at a and b.
To Prove:	$|pa|.|pb| = |pt|^2$
Construction:	Draw any other secant from p intersecting the circle at c and d.
Proof:	$|pa|.|pb| = |pc|.|pd|$
	Let the secant pdc rotate, about p, in an anti-clockwise direction until c and d coincide at the point t.
	$\therefore \quad |pa|.|pb| = |pt|.|pt|$
	$\therefore \quad |pa|.|pb| = |pt|^2$
Converse:	If a, b and t are three points on a circle and p is a point on ab outside the circle such that $|pa|.|pb| = |pt|^2$, then pt is a tangent to the circle.

The results of these theorems can be used to find the unknown lengths of line segments connected with a circle. We use the following four steps:

> **1.** Let $x =$ the unknown length.
>
> **2.** Write down the result of the appropriate theorem.
>
> **3.** Substitute in the given values, including x, to form an equation.
>
> **4.** Solve the equation.

Two chords of a circle, $[ab]$ and $[cd]$, intersect
inside the circle at k.

If $|ak| = 6$, $|ck| = 8$ and $|kd| = 5$, find $|kb|$.

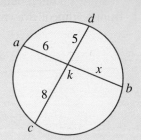

Solution:

1. Let $|kb| = x$

2. $|ka| . |kb| = |kc| . |kd|$ (theorem)

3. $(6)(x) = (8)(5)$ (substitute in values to form equation)

4. $6x = 40$ (simple equation)

    $x = \dfrac{40}{6}$ (divide both sides by 6)

    $x = 6\frac{2}{3}$

    Thus $|kb| = 6\frac{2}{3}$

Two chords of a circle, pq and rs, intersect outside
the circle at t.

If $|tp| = 8$, $|pq| = 6$ and $|rs| = 9$, find $|tr|$.

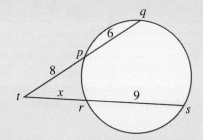

Solution:

1.   Let $|tr| = x$

2. $|ts| . |tr| = |tq| . |tp|$ (theorem)

3. $(x + 9)(x) = (14)(8)$ (substitute in values to form equation)

4. $x^2 + 9x = 112$ (quadratic equation)

    $x^2 + 9x - 112 = 0$ (everything to the left)

    $(x + 16)(x - 7) = 0$ (factorise)

    $x + 16 = 0$ or $x - 7 = 0$ (let each factor = 0)

    $x = -16$ or $x = 7$

    $\therefore$ $x = 7$ ($x = -16$ is rejected as the length cannot be negative)

    Thus, $|tr| = 7$

438

Example ▼

The diagram shows a circle of centre o, diameter $[ab]$ and cd a tangent at d.

If $|bc| = 8$ and $|cd| = 12$, find the radius of the circle.

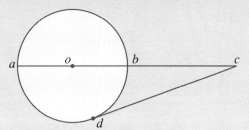

Solution:

1. Let the length of the radius $= x$.

   Thus, $\quad |ao| = |ob| = x$.

2. $\quad |ca| . |cb| = |cd|^2 \quad$ (theorem)

3. $\quad (2x + 8)(8) = 12^2 \quad$ (substitute in values to form equation)

4. $\quad 16x + 64 = 144$

   $\quad\quad 16x = 144 - 64$

   $\quad\quad 16x = 80$

   $\quad\quad\quad x = 5$

   Thus, the radius of the circle is 5.

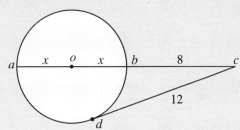

Exercise 19.3 ▼

In each of the following diagrams, find the length of the line segment represented by a letter. Where necessary, the point of tangency is indicated by a dot.

1.

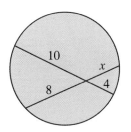

2.

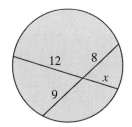

3.

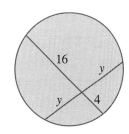

4.

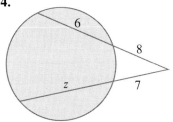

5.

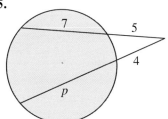

6.

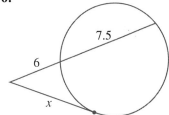

7.

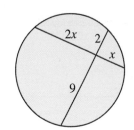

8.

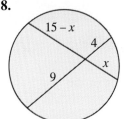

9.

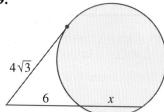

10.

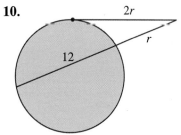

11.

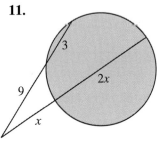

12.

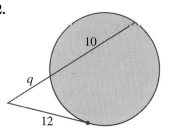

13.

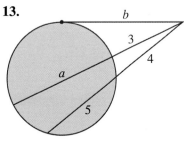

14.

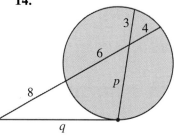

15.

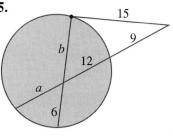

16. pt is a tangent to the circle, as in the diagram.
If $|pt| = 6$ and $|ab| = 5$, find $|ap|$.

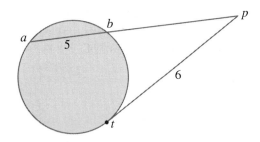

17. o is the centre of the circle K.
If $|rt| = 12.5$, $|ts| = 3.5$ and $|pq| = |qr|$,
find the radius of the circle.

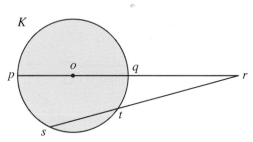

440

18. M is a circle of centre o.

If $|qk| = 9$, $|pq| = 14$ and $|ko| = \frac{1}{7}|pq|$, find the radius of the circle.

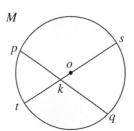

19. $[ab]$ and $[cd]$ are two chords of a circle, centre o and radius 10.

If $|ak| = 6.72$ and $|ab| = 18.72$, find $|ko|$.

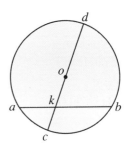

20. The line kt is a tangent to the circle at the point t.

$|kb| = \frac{1}{2}|kt|$ and $|ab| = 12$.

Calculate $|kt|$.

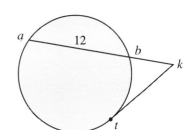

Questions 21 to 25 require proof.

21. $[pq]$ is a common chord of two circles of different radii. r is a point on the line pq. rb and rc are tangents to the circles, the points of contact being b and c, respectively.

Prove that $|rb| = |rc|$.

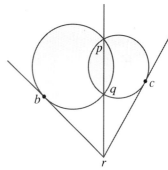

22. Two circles intersect at n and t.

The line pr is a tangent to the circles at p and at r.

Prove that m is the midpoint of $[pr]$.

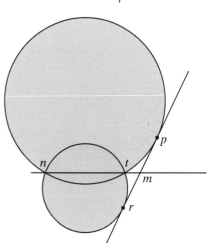

23. *pt* is a tangent to a circle at *t*.
   ps cuts the circle at *r* and *s*.
   $|pr| = |rs|$.
   Show that $|ps|^2 = 2|pt|^2$.

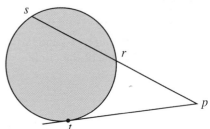

24. [*kp*] cuts the circle at *q*.
   [*kr*] cuts the circle at *s*.
   $|kp| = 2|kr|$.
   Prove that $|ks| = 2|kq|$.

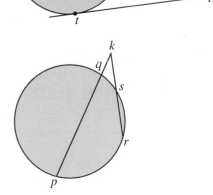

25. *pt* is a tangent, at the point *t*, to a circle of centre
   o, as in the diagram.
   Prove that $|pb|^2 + 2|pb||bo| = |pt|^2$.

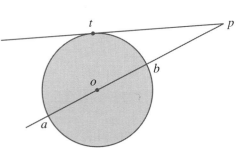

REVISION EXERCISE 1: ARITHMETIC

Paper 1   Question 1

This revision exercise covers chapter 11.

> *Exercise 1R.A* ▼

1. €35 is divided between Peter and Anne in the ratio 3 : 4. How much does each receive?

2. €40 is divided between two pupils in the ratio 7 : 3. How much does each pupil get?

3. €19.50 pocket money is divided between two pupils in the ratio 8 : 5. How much does each get?

4. Copper and zinc are mixed in the ratio 19 : 6. The amount of copper used is 133 kg. How many kilograms of zinc are used?

5. A prize fund of €6,000 is divided as follows:

    the first prize is half the fund;

    the second prize is two-thirds the first prize;

    the third prize is what remains.

    How much is the third prize worth?

6. €105 was shared among three people in the ratio $1 : 2 : \frac{1}{2}$. Calculate the smallest share.

7. A sum of money is divided in the ratio 5 : 6. The smaller amount is €25. What is the total amount of money?

8. A sum of money was divided in the ratio 3 : 2. The larger amount was €39. What was the total amount of money?

9. A sum of money was divided in the ratio 5 : 2. If the larger share was €54 more than the smaller share, calculate the sum.

10. A glass rod falls and breaks into 3 pieces whose lengths are in the ratio 8 : 9 : 5. If the sum of the lengths of the two larger pieces is 119 cm, find the length of the third piece.

11. A cookery book gives the following instruction for calculating the amount of time for which a turkey should be cooked:

    'Allow 15 minutes per 450 grams plus an extra 15 minutes.'

    For how many hours and minutes should a turkey weighing 9 kilograms be cooked?

12. Express 250 m as a fraction of 1 km.

13. Express 400 grams as a fraction of a kilogram. Give your answer in its simplest form.

14. The scale of a map is 1 : 25,000. The length of a wall on the map is 2.8 mm, Calculate the actual length in metres.

15. Express each of the following in hours:
    (i) 2 hours 30 minutes (ii) 3 hours 15 minutes (iii) 1 hour 20 minutes.

16. A train takes 3 hours and 30 minutes to travel a distance of 280 km.
    Calculate the average speed in km/h.

17. How long, in hours and minutes, does it take a bus to travel 168 km at an average speed of 96 km/h?

18. A car travelled at an average speed of 120km/h between the times of 1255 and 1410.
    What distance did it travel?

19. A train travelled 155 km at an average speed of 62 km/h.
    How long did the journey take?

20. An athlete ran 1500 metres in 4 minutes.
    Find the average speed of the athlete in metres per second.

21. A distance of 375 metres is travelled in 25 seconds.
    Find the average speed in kilometres per hour.

22. A cyclist started a journey of 56 km at 1015 and finished the journey at 1135.
    Calculate the average speed of the cyclist in km/h.

23. It takes 4 hours and 20 minutes to travel a journey at an average speed of 120 km/h. How many hours and minutes will it take to travel the same journey if the average speed is reduced to 100 km/h?

24. When a cyclist had travelled a distance of 12.6 km he had completed $\frac{3}{7}$ of his journey.
    What was the length of the journey?

25. A woman bought a car for €28,500 and sold it for €22,800.
    Calculate her percentage loss as a percentage of: (i) the cost price (ii) the selling price.

26. A car was bought for €18,750. At the end of the first year the value of the car had fallen by 20%.
    Find its value at the end of the first year.

27. One litre of water is added to four litres of milk in a container.
    Calculate the percentage of water in the container.

28. Prize money for a race is divided between first, second and third places with the first place getting 60%, the second place getting 25% and the third place getting 15% of the prize money.
    If the first place got €3,600, how much did the second and third places get?

29. A solicitor's fee for the sale of a house is 2% of the selling price.
    If the fee is €6,800, calculate the selling price of the house.

30. An article was priced at €210 + VAT. If a person paid €247.80 for the article, calculate the rate of VAT.

31. A telephone bill, including VAT at 21%, came to €99.22. Calculate the bill without VAT.

32. In a sale the price of a piece of furniture was reduced by 10%. The sale price was €1125. What was the price before the sale?

33. By selling a car for €8,840 a loss of 35% is made on the purchase price. Calculate the purchase price.

34. A sum of money, invested at 6% per annum interest, amounted to €1,590 after one year. What sum of money was invested?

35. Interest of 4% per annum is paid on an investment of €3,500.

Tax at the rate of 20c in the € is paid on the interest.

How much is the investment worth after tax at the end of the first year?

36. On a certain day €1 = US$1.18.
- **(i)** How many dollars would you get for €650?
- **(ii)** How many euros would you get for US$885?

Exercise 1R.B ▼

1. Divide 357 grams in the ratio $\frac{1}{2} : \frac{1}{4} : 1$.

2. (i) Express as a ratio of whole numbers $\frac{1}{2} : \frac{2}{3} : \frac{3}{4}$.
   (ii) Hence, or otherwise, divide €920 in the ratio $\frac{1}{2} : \frac{2}{3} : \frac{3}{4}$.

3. A tourist paid US$2,486 to a travel agent for a holiday in Europe.
The cost to the travel agent of organising the holiday was €1,950.
- **(i)** Calculate, in US$, the profit made by the travel agent, if €1 = US$0.92.
- **(ii)** The travel agent pays tax at 24% on this profit.
Calculate, in US$, the travel agent's profit after tax on this holiday.

4. A car journey of 559 kilometres took 6 hours and 30 minutes.
- **(i)** Calculate the average speed, in km/h, for the journey.
- **(ii)** If the average petrol consumption for the journey was 8.3 kilometres per litre, calculate the number of litres of petrol used, correct to the nearest litre.

5. A tanker delivered heating oil to a school. Before the delivery the meter reading showed 11,360 litres of oil in the tanker. After the delivery, the meter reading was 7,160 litres.

Calculate the cost of the oil delivered, if 1 litre of oil cost 20.5c.

When VAT was added to the cost of the oil delivered, the bill to the school amounted to €1,041.81.

Calculate the rate of VAT added.

6. The answer to 3.58 + 2.47 was given as 6.50.

What was the percentage error, correct to one decimal place?

7. Calculate the percentage error, correct to one decimal place, in taking 50 + 60 as an approximation for 52.47 + 64.87.

8. Four telephone calls cost €3.85, €7.45, €8.40 and €11.55.

   (i) John estimates the total cost of the four calls by ignoring the cent part in the cost of each call. Calculate the percentage error in his estimate.

   (ii) Anne estimates the total cost of the four calls by rounding the cost of each call to the nearest euro. Calculate the percentage error in her estimate.

9. At what rate of interest will €2,000 amount to €2,065 after one year?

10. €5,000 was invested for two years at compound interest.

    (i) The interest at the end of the first year was €275.
    Calculate the rate of interest for the year.

    (ii) At the end of the second year the investment was worth €5,644.25.
    Calculate the rate of interest for the second year.

11. €2,500 was invested for three years at compound interest.

    The rate of interest was 4% per annum for the first year and 3% per annum for the second year.

    Calculate the amount of the investment after two years.

    If the investment amounted to €2,744.95 after three years, calculate the rate of interest per annum for the third year.

12. A person buys 5,400 Canadian dollars when the exchange rate is €1 = $2.25.
    A charge (commission) is made for this service. How much, in €, is this charge if the person pays €2,442? Calculate the percentage commission on the transaction.

13. €2,500 was invested for three years at compound interest. The rate for the first year was 4%, the rate for the second year was 3%, and the rate for the third year was 2.5%.

    Calculate the amount after three years and the compound interest earned.

14. A machine cost €24,000 when new. In the first year it depreciates by 10%. In the second year it depreciates by 8% of its value at the end of the second year. In the third year it depreciates by 5% of its value at the end of the second year. Calculate its value after three years. Calculate its total depreciation after three years.

15. A man borrowed €10,000 at 3% per annum compound interest. He agreed to repay €2,000 after one year and a further €3,000 at the end of two years. How much is outstanding after the second repayment?

16. €2,500 is invested for 8 years at 6% per annum compound interest.

    Find: **(i)** the amount   **(ii)** the compound interest after 8 years, to the nearest cent.

17. A machine bought for €8,000 depreciates at a compound rate of 8% per annum.

    Find its value after 6 years, correct to the nearest €.

18. A sum of money, €40,000, is invested for 3 years at compound interest. The rate for year 1 is 10% and for year 2 is also 10%. Calculate how much the invested money amounts to at the end of year 2.

    At the end of year 3, the invested money amounted to €51,667.
    Calculate the rate of interest for year 3.

19. A person invested €20,000 in a building society. The rate of interest for the first year was $2\frac{1}{2}\%$.

At the end of the first year the person invested a further €2,000. The rate of interest for the second year was 2%.

Calculate the value of the investment at the end of the second year.

At the end of the second year a further sum of €1,050 was invested. At the end of the third year the total value of the investment was €24,720.

Calculate the rate of interest for the third year.

20. €5,000 was invested for 3 years at compound interest.

The rate for the first year was 4%. The rate for the second year was $4\frac{1}{2}\%$.

Find the amount of the investment at the end of the second year.

At the beginning of the third year a further €4,000 was invested.

The rate for the third year was $r\%$.

The total investment at the end of the third year was €9,764.19.

Calculate the value of r.

21. A woman has a gross yearly income of €27,500. She has a standard rate cut-off point of €29,400 and a tax credit of €1,925. The standard rate of tax is 16% of income up to the standard rate cut-off point. Calculate:

(i) the amount of gross tax for the year

(ii) the amount of tax paid for the year

(iii) net income for the year.

Express tax paid for the year as a percentage of gross income for year.

22. Express $\dfrac{1.26 \times 10^9}{2.8 \times 10^{12}}$ in the form $a \times 10^n$, where $1 \leqslant a < 10$ and $n \in \mathbf{Z}$.

23. Express $5 \times 10^{-2} + 1.2 \times 10^{-3}$ in the form $a \times 10^n$, where $1 \leqslant a < 10$ and $n \in \mathbf{Z}$.

24. Express $8.42 \times 10^2 - 42 \times 10^{-1}$ in the form $a \times 10^n$, where $1 \leqslant a < 10$ and $n \in \mathbf{Z}$.

25. Express: **(i)** $(2.25 \times 10^4) \times (1.6 \times 10^3)$ **(ii)** $(3.91 \times 10^3) \div (1.7 \times 10^7)$
                in the form $a \times 10^n$, where $1 \leqslant a < 10$ and $n \in \mathbf{Z}$.

26. Write $2.3 \times 10^{-2} + 3.5 \times 10^{-3}$ as a decimal number.

Say if this number is greater than or less than 0.02.

27. Calculate the value of:

$$\frac{3.1 \times 10^5 - 1.5 \times 10^4}{5.9 \times 10^6}$$

and write your answer as a decimal number.

1. A holiday complex consists of three different types of chalet.

Chalet Type	Number of chalets	Number of people per chalet	Weekly rent per chalet
Type A	12	5	€300
Type B	20	6	€350
Type C	14	8	€450

During one week in July all chalets are fully occupied.

(i) Calculate the number of people staying in the chalets at the holiday complex that week.

(ii) Calculate the total amount of rent paid for that week.

In the last week of September, a 35% discount is offered on the weekly rent of a Type C chalet. Calculate the weekly rent on a Type C chalet for the last week in September.

2. A raffle to raise money for a charity is being held.

The first prize is €100, the second is €85, the third is €65 and the fourth is €50.

The cost of printing tickets is €42 for the first 500 tickets and €6 for each additional 100 tickets. The smallest number of tickets that can be printed is 500.

Tickets are being sold at €1.50 each.

(i) What is the minimum possible cost of holding the raffle?

(ii) If 500 tickets are printed, how many tickets must be sold in order to avoid a loss?

(iii) If 1,000 tickets are printed and 65% of the tickets are sold, how much money will be raised for the charity?

3. Members of a club had two weeks to raise money for their club.

A business person agreed to give 50c to the club for every €5 collected by the members.

(i) In the first week the members collected €2,640. How much did the business person give the club in the first week?

(ii) In the second week the money raised from the members and the business person amounted to €6,930.

How much did the club members collect in the second week?

4. (i) Calculate the value of:

$$\frac{5.1 \times 10^8 + 19 \times 10^7}{1.4 \times 10^{12}}$$

and write your answer as a decimal number.

(ii) Calculate the percentage error if 5 is taken as an approximation of 4.95.

Give your answer correct to two places of decimals.

5. €5,000 was invested for 3 years at compound interest.
   The rate for the first year was 4%. The rate for the second year was $4\frac{1}{2}\%$.

   (i) Find the amount of the investment at the end of the second year.

   At the beginning of the third year a further €4,000 was invested.
   The rate for the third year was $r\%$.
   The total investment at the end of the third year was €9,811.36.

   (ii) Calculate the value of r.

6. A sum of money was invested at compound interest. The interest rate for the first year was 8%, for the second year the rate was 5% and the rate was 4% for the third year. After three years this sum amounted to €53,071.20. Find the sum invested.

7. A man borrowed €10,000. He agreed to repay €2,000 after one year, €3,000 after two years and the balance at the end of the third year. If interest was charged at 8% in the first year, 5% in the second year and 6% in the third year, how much was paid at the end of the third year to clear the debt?

8. A man borrowed €x for three years at compound interest. The rate for the first year was $12\frac{1}{2}\%$ and at the end of the year he repaid €1,000. The rate for the second year was 15% and at the end of that year he repaid €2,000. The rate for the third year was 10% and at the end of that year he repaid €5,073.75, the full amount due. Calculate the value of x.

9. A person invested €50,000 for three years at 8% per annum compound interest.

   At the end of the first year, €9,000 was withdrawn.

   At the end of the second year, another sum of money, €x, was withdrawn.

   At the end of the third year, the person's investment was worth €39,960.

   Calculate the value of x.

10. A man has a gross yearly income of €45,000. He has a standard rate cut-off point of €28,000 and a tax credit of €1,784. The standard rate of tax is 15% of income up to the standard rate cut-off point and 38% on all income above the standard rate cut-off point.
    Calculate:

    (i) the amount of gross tax for the year.

    (ii) the amount of tax paid for the year.

11. A woman has a gross yearly income of €58,000. She has a standard rate cut-off point of €28,000 and a tax credit of €4,500. The standard rate of tax is 18% of income up to the standard rate cut-off point and 40% on all income above the standard rate cut-off point.
    Calculate:

    (i) the amount of gross tax for the year

    (ii) the amount of tax paid for the year.

12. When the standard rate of tax is 20c in the euro, a man with a tax credit of €1,780 pays €3,180 in tax. If his gross income for the year was below his standard rate cut-off point, calculate his gross income for the year.

13. A woman has a gross yearly income of €26,500. She has a standard rate cut-off point of €28,700 and a tax credit of €1,825. If she pays tax of €2,680, calculate the standard rate of tax.

14. The standard rate of income tax is 20% and the higher rate is 42%. For a single person, the annual personal tax credit is €1,520 and the standard rate cut-off point is €28,000.

Brian earns €22,000 per annum and Mary earns €36,000 per annum. Both of them are single and have no tax credits other than the personal tax credit.

(i) Calculate the tax payable by Brian for the year.

(ii) Calculate the tax payable by Mary for the year.

(iii) If Brian and Mary were married to each other, their joint personal tax credit would be €3,040 and their joint standard rate cut-off point would be €56,000.

How much less tax would they have to pay between them in this case?

15. A man paid €11,240 in tax for the year. He had a tax credit of €4,860 and a standard rate cut-off point of €24,000. The standard rate of tax is 18% of income up to the standard rate cut-off point and 38% on all income above the standard rate cut-off point.
Calculate:

(i) the amount of income taxed at the rate of 38%.

(ii) the man's gross income for the year.

16. An antiques dealer bought three chairs at an auction. He sold them later for €301.60, making a profit of 16% on their total cost. Calculate the total cost of the chairs.

The first chair cost €72 and it was sold at a profit of 15%.
Calculate its selling price.

The second chair cost €98 and it was sold for €91.

Find the percentage profit made on the sale of the third chair.

17. Tea served in a canteen is made from a mixture of two different types of tea, type A and type B. Type A costs €4.05 per kg. Type B costs €4.30 per kg. The mixture costs €4.20 per kg.

If the mixture contains 7 kg of type A, how many kilograms of type B does it contain?

(Hint: Let x = the number of kilograms of type B and form an equation.)

REVISION EXERCISE 2: ALGEBRA

Paper 1   Questions 2 and 3

This revision exercise covers chapters 4 and 5.

Exercise 2R.A ▼

1. Find the value of $5x - 3y$ when $x = \frac{5}{2}$ and $y = \frac{2}{3}$.

2. Given that $u^2 + 2as = v^2$, calculate the value of a when $u = 10$, $s = 30$ and $v = 20$.

3. Solve for x:

   (i) $3(2x - 1) = 4x$ (ii) $2(x + 8) = 7x$ (iii) $\dfrac{x-7}{2} = \dfrac{x+3}{6}$

4. Solve for x:

   (i) $2x^2 + 7x + 6 = 0$ (ii) $x^2 - 3x = 0$ (iii) $x^2 - 4 = 0$

5. Solve for x and y:

   (i) $2x - y = 7$ (ii) $3x - 2y = -10$ (iii) $5x - 2y = 13$

        $x + 2y = 6$ $2x + 3y = 2$ $3(x - 4) = 4y$

6. Show that $x = 5$ is a root of the equation $x^3 - x^2 - 17x - 15 = 0$.

7. Show that $x = -3$ is a root of the equation $x^3 - x^2 - 8x + 12 = 0$.

8. (i) If $x - 5$ is a factor of $x^3 - kx^2 - 13x - 10$, find the value of k.

   (ii) If $x + 2$ is a factor of $2x^3 + 5x^2 + kx - 18$, find the value of k.

9. Solve the inequality $3x - 7 < 2$, $x \in \mathbf{R}$ and illustrate your solution on the number line.

10. Solve the inequality $5x + 1 \geqslant 4x - 3$, $x \in \mathbf{R}$ and illustrate your solution on the number line.

11. Find the range of values of $x \in \mathbf{R}$ for which $3(x - 4) > 5(2x - 3) + 17$ and graph your solution on the number line.

12. Find the values of x for which $4x - 11 \leqslant 2x - 7$, $x \in \mathbf{N}$. Graph your solution on the number line.

13. Find the solution set of $11 - 2n \leqslant 3$, $n \in \mathbf{R}$.

14. Express p in terms of t and k when $tp - k = 7k$.

15. Express p in terms of q and t when $2p - q = 3(p - t)$.

16. Express q in terms of p and t when $2(p - 3q) = t$.

17. Express p in terms of q and r when $\dfrac{p-3r}{q} = 5$, $\quad q \neq 0$.

18. Express t in terms of p and q when $p + \dfrac{t}{q} = 1$, $\quad q \neq 0$.

19. Express p in terms of q and t when $q + \dfrac{p}{5t} = 3$, $\quad t \neq 0$.

20. Solve for x: **(i)** $2^x = 8$ **(ii)** $3^{2x} = 9$.

Exercise 2R.B ▼

1. Find the value of $\dfrac{a-b+1}{a+b+1}$ when $a = \tfrac{1}{8}$ and $b = 2$.

2. Express t in terms of p and q when $p = \dfrac{q-t}{3t}$, $\quad t \neq 0$.

Calculate the value of t when $p = 0.5$ and $q = 25$.

3. If $6x^3 - 17x^2 + 22x - 15 = (2x-3)(3x^2 - kx + 5)$, find the value of k.

4. Show that $x = 4$ is a root of $x^3 - 2x^2 - 11x + 12 = 0$, and find the other two roots.

5. **(i)** Show that $x = 2$ is a root of $3x^3 + 8x^2 - 33x + 10 = 0$.
    (ii) Find the other roots of $3x^3 + 8x^2 - 33x + 10 = 0$.

6. **(i)** Show that $x + 2$ is a factor of $2x^3 + 7x^2 + x - 10$.
    (ii) Hence, or otherwise, find the three roots of $2x^3 + 7x^2 + x - 10 = 0$.

7. If $x = -1$ is a root of $2x^3 - 5x^2 + kx + 3 = 0$, find k and the other two roots.

8. If $f(x) = x^3 + 3x^2 - 16x + 12$, verify that $f(2) = 0$ and find the three values of x which satisfies the equation $f(x) = 0$.

9. Solve the equation $2x^3 - 9x^2 + 7x + 6 = 0$.

10. Find the roots of the equation $2x^3 - 5x^2 + x + 2 = 0$.

11. Solve the equation $2x^3 + 3x^2 - 5x - 6 = 0$.

12. **(i)** If $(x-2)$ is a factor of $3x^3 + x^2 + kx + 6$, find the value of k.
    (ii) Write down an equation which has three roots, of values -3, 1 and 5.

13. Form an equation with roots -1, -2 and $\tfrac{1}{2}$.

14. **(i)** Find the solution set E of $2x + 7 \leqslant 19$, $\qquad x \in \mathbf{R}$.
    (ii) Find the solution set H of $3 - 2x < 11$, $\qquad x \in \mathbf{R}$.
    (iii) Find $E \cap H$ and graph your solution on the number line.

15. **(i)** Find the solution set H of $2x + 3 \geqslant -2$, $\quad x \in \mathbf{R}$.

(ii) Find the solution set K of $7 - 3x \geqslant 4$, $\quad x \in \mathbf{R}$.

(iii) Find $H \cap K$ and graph your solution on the number line.

16. **(i)** Find the solution set E of $5x - 6 < 4$,

(ii) Find the solution set H of $-4x \leqslant 3$,

(iii) Find $E \cap H$ and graph your solution on the number line.

17. **(i)** Find the solution set E of $9 - 2x \geqslant 7$, $\quad x \in \mathbf{N}$.

(ii) Find the solution set H of $\frac{1}{4}x - \frac{1}{3} \leqslant \frac{5}{12}$, $\quad x \in \mathbf{N}$.

(iii) Write down the elements of the set $H \backslash E$.

18. Find the value of x for which:

(i) $2^{x-1} = 32$ **(ii)** $9^{x-1} = 81$ **(iii)** $5^{2x-1} = 125$

(iv) $4^{x-1} = 32$ **(v)** $5^{2x+1} = \frac{1}{125}$ **(vi)** $7^{2x+1} = \frac{1}{49}$

19. **(i)** Simplify $(x + \sqrt{x})(x - \sqrt{x})$ when $x > 0$.

(ii) Hence, or otherwise, find the value of x for which $(x + \sqrt{x})(x - \sqrt{x}) = 6$.

20. Solve for x and y:

(i) $y = x + 2$ **(ii)** $x = 3 - 2y$ **(iii)** $y = x - 1$

        $x^2 + y^2 = 10$ $x^2 = y^2 + 24$ $xy = 2x + 4$

(iv) $x = 6 - 2y$ **(v)** $x + 2y = 3$ **(vi)** $x - 3y = 1$

        $x^2 + y^2 = 17$ $x^2 + y^2 = 26$ $x^2 - y^2 = 0$

21. Solve for x and y: $y = 10 - 2x$ and $x^2 + y^2 = 25$.

Hence, find the two possible values for $x^3 + y^3$.

Exercise 2R.C ▼

1. Let $f(x) = x^2 + ax + t$, where $a, t \in \mathbf{R}$.

(i) Find the value of a, given that $f(-5) = f(-1)$.

(ii) Given that there is only one value of x for which $f(x) = 0$, find the value of t.

2. If $(x + 1)$ and $(x - 2)$ are factors of $x^3 + 2x^2 + ax + b$, find the values of $a, b, \in \mathbf{R}$.

3. Let $f(x) = x^3 + ax^2 + bx - 6$, where a and b are real numbers.

Given that $x - 1$ and $x - 2$ are factors of $f(x)$:

(i) find the value of a and the value of b

(ii) hence, find the values of x for which $f(x) = 0$.

4. **(i)** $f(x) = ax^2 + bx - 8$, where a and b are real numbers.

If $f(1) = -9$ and $f(-1) = 3$, find the value of a and the value of b.

(ii) Using your values of a and b from **(i)**, find the two values of x for which:

$$ax^2 + bx = bx^2 + ax.$$

5. Solve for x:

(i) $\quad 4 = \dfrac{12}{x} - \dfrac{5}{x^2}, \quad x \neq 0$

(ii) $\quad \dfrac{3}{2} - \dfrac{1}{x} = \dfrac{1}{x-1}, \quad x \neq 0, x \neq 1.$

(iii) $\quad \dfrac{3}{2x-1} = 1 + \dfrac{2x}{x+2}, \quad x \neq \dfrac{1}{2}$ and $x \neq -2.$

(iv) $\quad \dfrac{x-1}{x} - \dfrac{3x}{x-1} = 2, \quad x \neq 0$ and $x \neq 1.$

6. Solve, correct to two decimal places, the equation $5x^2 + 7x - 2 = 0.$

7. Solve, correct to two decimal places, the equation $\dfrac{4}{x+5} - \dfrac{1}{x+1} = -1 \quad x \neq -5, x \neq -1.$

8. (i) Write $\dfrac{1}{x+1} + \dfrac{2}{x-3}$ as a single fraction, where $x \neq 1$ and $x \neq 3.$

(ii) Hence, or otherwise, find, correct to one place of decimals, the two solutions of:
$$\dfrac{1}{x+1} + \dfrac{2}{x-3} = 1, \quad x \neq -1, x \neq 3.$$

9. Factorise $x^2 - x - 2$. Show that $x^2 - x - 2$ is a factor of $2x^3 - 3x^2 - 3x + 2.$
Hence, or otherwise, find the roots of $2x^3 - 3x^2 - 3x + 2 = 0.$

10. Express as whole numbers: (i) $9^{3/2}$ (ii) $8^{4/3}$ (iii) $32^{2/5}$

11. Express as rational numbers: (i) $100^{-1/2}$ (ii) $8^{-2/3}$ (iii) $16^{-3/4}$

12. (i) Express b in terms of a and c, where $\dfrac{8a-5b}{b} = c.$

(ii) Hence, or otherwise, evaluate b when $a = 2^{5/2}$ and $c = 3^3.$

13. Simplify: (i) $(\sqrt{a})^2$ (ii) $\sqrt{a} \cdot \dfrac{2}{\sqrt{a}}$ (iii) $\dfrac{5}{\sqrt{a}} \cdot \dfrac{5}{\sqrt{a}}$

14. Simplify $\left(\sqrt{x} + \dfrac{3}{\sqrt{x}}\right)\left(\sqrt{x} - \dfrac{3}{\sqrt{x}}\right)$, where $x > 0.$

Hence, solve for x: $\left(\sqrt{x} + \dfrac{3}{\sqrt{x}}\right)\left(\sqrt{x} - \dfrac{3}{\sqrt{x}}\right) = 8$, where $x > 0.$

15. Let $f(x) = (2+x)(3-x), \quad x \in \mathbf{R}.$
Write down the solutions (roots) of $f(x) = 0.$

16. Let $f(x) = (1-x)(2+x), \quad x \in \mathbf{R}.$
Write down the solutions of $f(x) = 0.$
Let $g(x) = f(x) - f(x+1).$
Express $g(x)$ in the form $ax + b, \quad a, b \in \mathbf{R}.$
Find the solution set of $g(x) < 0.$

17. (i) Write in the form 2^n: **(a)** $\sqrt{2}$ **(b)** 8 **(c)** $8^{4/3}$ **(d)** $\sqrt{8}$ **(e)** $\left(\dfrac{16}{\sqrt{8}}\right)$

(ii) Solve for x the equations:

(a) $4^{2x} = 32$

(b) $2^{3x-7} = 2^6 - 2^5$

(c) $2^{2x-1} = \left(\dfrac{16}{\sqrt{8}}\right)^3$

(d) $8^{4/3} = \dfrac{2^{5x-4}}{\sqrt{2}}$

18. (i) Write in the form 3^n: **(a)** 81 **(b)** 243 **(c)** $\sqrt{3}$ **(d)** $\dfrac{81}{\sqrt{3}}$ **(e)** $\sqrt{27}$

(ii) Solve for x the equations:

(a) $3^{2x} = 81$

(b) $9^x = \dfrac{1}{\sqrt{3}}$

(c) $3^{x-2} = \left(\dfrac{81}{\sqrt{3}}\right)^2$

(d) $\sqrt{3}\,(3^x) = \left(\dfrac{243}{\sqrt{27}}\right)^2$

19. (i) Write in the form 5^n: **(a)** 25 **(b)** $\tfrac{1}{5}$ **(c)** $\sqrt{5}$ **(d)** $\dfrac{125}{\sqrt{5}}$ **(e)** $\sqrt{125}$

(i) Solve for x the equations:

(a) $5^{3x-1} = 25$

(b) $5^{2x} = \dfrac{25}{\sqrt{5}}$

(c) $5^{2x+1} = \left(\dfrac{125}{\sqrt{5}}\right)^3$

(d) $\dfrac{5^{2x+1}}{\sqrt{5}} = \left(\dfrac{1}{\sqrt{125}}\right)^3$

REVISION EXERCISE 3: COMPLEX NUMBERS

Paper I   Question 4

This revision exercise covers chapter 2.

Exercise 3R.A ▼

1. Given that $i^2 = -1$, simplify each of the following, writing your answer in the form $x + yi$, where $x, y \in \mathbf{R}$:

   (i) $3(1 + 5i) + i(2 + 3i)$ **(ii)** $2 + 3i(4 + 5i) - 6i$

   (iii) $2(3 - i) + i(4 + 5i)$ **(iv)** $7(2 + i) + i(11 + 9i)$

2. If $z_1 = 2 + 3i$: $z_2 = 1 - 4i$ and $z_3 = -2i$, express:

   (i) $3z_1 - 2z_2$ **(ii)** $5z_2 - 4z_3$ **(iii)** $z_3 z_2$ in the form $a + bi$, where $a, b \in \mathbf{R}$ and $i^2 = -1$.

3. Let $z = 1 - 4i$, where $i^2 = -1$. Plot on the Argand diagram:

   (i) z **(ii)** $z + 2$ **(iii)** $z - 3i$

4. Let $z_1 = 2 + 3i$ and $z_2 = 4 + i$, where $i^2 = -1$. Plot on the Argand diagram:

   (i) z_1 **(ii)** z_2 **(iii)** $z_1 + z_2$ **(iv)** $z_1 - z_2$ **(v)** iz_2 **(vi)** $\dfrac{13}{z_1}$

5. Let $w = 2i$, where $i^2 = -1$. Plot on the Argand diagram:

   (i) iw **(ii)** w^2 **(iii)** w^3

Exercise 3R.B ▼

1. Let $z_1 = 1 + 7i$ and $z_2 = 4 + 3i$.

   Express $\dfrac{z_1}{z_2}$ in the form $a + bi$, where $a, b \in \mathbf{R}$. Calculate $\left| \dfrac{z_1}{z_2} \right|$.

2. Express $\dfrac{2 - i}{1 - 2i}$ in the form $p + qi$, where $p, q \in \mathbf{R}$. Evaluate $p^2 + q^2$.

3. Express $\dfrac{1}{4 + 3i}$ in the form $a + bi$, where $a, b \in \mathbf{R}$. Show that $a^2 + b^2 = 1$.

4. Let $z = 5 + 4i$. Plot z and $\bar{z}$ on the Argand diagram. Calculate $z\bar{z}$.

   Express $\dfrac{z}{\bar{z}}$ in the form $u + vi$, where $u, v \in \mathbf{R}$.

5. Let $z = (1 - 2i)(3 - i)$. Plot z, $z + 3$ and $\bar{z}$ on the Argand diagram. Calculate $|z\bar{z}|$.

6. Let $w = \dfrac{1 + i}{2 - 2i}$. Express w in the form $p + qi$, where $p, q \in \mathbf{R}$.

    (i) Calculate $|w|$ **(ii)** Verify that $|w|^2 = w\bar{w}$.

7. Let $u = 3 - 6i$.   **(i)** Calculate $|u|$ **(ii)** Show that $iu + \dfrac{u}{i} = 0$.

    (iii) Express $\dfrac{u}{u + 3i}$ in the form $p + qi$, where $p, q \in \mathbf{R}$.

8. Let $w = 3 - i$.   **(i)** Plot w and $w + 6i$ on the Argand diagram   **(ii)** Calculate $|w + 6i|$.

    (iii) Express $\dfrac{1}{w + 6i}$ in the form $u + vi$, where $u, v \in \mathbf{R}$.

9. Verify that $4 - 3i$ is a root of $z^2 - 8z + 25 = 0$ and write down the other root.

10. Verify that $-2 + 5i$ is a root of $z^2 + 4z + 29 = 0$ and write down the other root.

11. Solve the equations: **(i)** $z^2 - 4z + 13 = 0$ **(ii)** $z^2 - 10z + 29 = 0$.

12. Investigate if: **(i)** $|5 + 5i| = |1 + 7i|$ **(ii)** $|2 + 14i| = |10(1 - i)|$.

13. For what values of x is $|8 + xi| = 10$, $x \in \mathbf{R}$?

14. For what values of a is $|a + 5i| = 29$, $a \in \mathbf{R}$?

15. Solve for real a and b: $a(7 - 3i) + b(4 - 8i) = 2(1 + 9i)$.

16. Solve for real p and q: $p(2 - i) + qi(4 + 2i) = 1 + p + qi$.

17. Let $z = 4 - 2i$. Solve for real x and y: $\bar{z} - xz = yi$, $x, y \in \mathbf{R}$.

18. Solve $(x + 2yi)(1 - i) = 7 + 5i$, for real x and real y.

19. Let $w = (1 - 3i)(2 + i)$. Express w in the form $p - pi$, where $p \in \mathbf{R}$.

    Verify that $|w + \bar{w}| = |w - \bar{w}|$. For what value of a is $\dfrac{w}{2i} = aw$, where $a \in \mathbf{R}$?

Exercise 3R.C ▼

1. (i)   Solve for real x and real y: $2x + (x + y)i = 4 - 5i$.

    (ii)   Let $z = 3 - 2i$. Solve for real s and t: $\dfrac{s + ti}{1 + 2i} = \bar{z}$

2. Let $w = i - 2$. Express w^2 in the form $a + bi$, where $a, b \in \mathbf{R}$.
Hence, solve $kw^2 = 2w + 1 + ti$ for real k and real t.

3. Let $z = 1 + i$. Express $\dfrac{z}{\bar{z}}$ in the form $x + yi$, where $x, y \in \mathbf{R}$.

Hence, solve $k\left(\dfrac{z}{\bar{z}}\right) + tz = -3 - 4i$ for real k and real t.

4. Let $u = 2 - i$. Express $u + \dfrac{1}{u}$ in the form $a + bi$, where $a, b \in \mathbf{R}$.

Hence, solve $k\left(u + \dfrac{1}{u}\right) + ti = 18$ for real k and real t.

5. Let $w = 3 - 4i$. **(i)** Solve for real x and real y: $x + w = 3yi$.

   (ii) Solve for real s and real t: $|w|(s + ti) = \dfrac{5}{w}$.

6. Find the values of $x, y \in \mathbf{R}$ such that $(x - yi) + (y + xi) = 1 - 5i$.

Using these values of x and y, express $\dfrac{x - yi}{y + xi}$ in the form $a + bi$, and hence, or otherwise,

find the value of $\left| \dfrac{x - yi}{y + xi} \right|$.

7. Solve for x and $y \in \mathbf{R}$: $(x + yi) - (4 - i) = 2(1 - i) + i(x + yi) + i$.

Using these values of x and y, find the value of $\left| \dfrac{\sqrt{x}}{2} - \dfrac{x}{y}i \right|$.

8. p and k are real numbers such that $p(2 + i) + 8 - ki = 5k - 3 - i$.
   (i) Find the value of p and the value of k.
   (ii) Investigate if $p + ki$ is a root of the equation $z^2 - 4z + 13 = 0$.

9. Solve for x: $2x^2 + 2x + 1 = 0$.

10. If $3 - 4i$ is a root of $x^2 + ax + b = 0$, $a, b \in \mathbf{R}$, find the values of a and b.

11. Let $z = 2 - i$ be one root of the equation $z^2 + pz + q = 0$, $p, q \in \mathbf{R}$.
Find the value of p and the value of q.

12. Let $z_1 = 3 + 4i$ and $z_2 = 12 - 5i$.
$\bar{z}_1$ and $\bar{z}_2$ are the complex conjugates of z_1 and z_2, respectively.
   (i) Show that $z_1\bar{z}_2 + \bar{z}_1 z_2$ is a real number.
   (ii) Investigate if $|z_1| + |z_2| = |z_1 + z_2|$.

13. $u = 1 - 2i$, $v = 2 + 5i$, $x = 6 + 4i$ and $y = a + bi$.
If u, v, x and y are the vertices of the parallelogram $uvxy$, find the values of a and b.

14. Let $z = 2 + 4i$.

    (i)   Express $z^2 + 28$ in the form $p + pi$, where $p \in \mathbf{R}$.

    (ii) Solve for real k: $k(z^2 + 28) = |z|(1 + i)$.

           Express your answer in the form $\dfrac{\sqrt{a}}{b}$, where $a, b \in \mathbf{N}$ and a is a prime number.

15. Let $u = 6 - 5i$. Solve for real a and b: $u + ai = 2b$.

    Solve for real s and real t: $s(2 - i) + ti(4 + 2i) = 1 + s + ti$.

    If $z = x + iy$, where $x, y \in \mathbf{R}$, what type of curve is represented by $|z|^2 = |s + it|^2$?

16. Show that $x = 2$ is a root of $x^3 - 8x^2 + 46x - 68 = 0$ and find the other two roots, expressing your answer in the form $a + bi$.

REVISION EXERCISE 4: SEQUENCES AND SERIES

Paper 1   Question 5

This revision exercise covers chapter 14.

Exercise 4R.A ▼

1. Write down the next three terms in each of the following arithmetic sequences:
    (i) $-10, -8, -6, \ldots$ **(ii)** $4.1, 4.7, 5.3, \ldots$

2. The first two terms of an arithmetic sequence are $17, 13, \ldots$
    Find: **(i)** d, the common difference   **(ii)** T_7, the seventh term.

3. The nth term of a sequence is given by $T_n = n^2 + 1$.
    (i)   Write down the first three terms of the sequence.
    (ii)   Show that $T_1 + T_2 + T_3 = T_4$.

4. The nth term of a sequence is given by $T_n = \dfrac{n}{n+1}$.
    (i) Find T_2, the second term.   **(ii)** Show that $T_2 + T_3 > 1$.

5. The first two terms of an arithmetic sequence are $5, 0, \ldots$
    Find: **(i)** d, the common difference   **(ii)** T_{11}, the eleventh term.

6. The first term T_1, of an arithmetic sequence is 9 and the common difference is 4.
    Find T_5, the fifth term and T_n, the nth term.

7. $T_1 + T_2 + T_3 + \ldots$ is a geometric series.
    The first term, T_1, is 1 and the common ratio is 2.
    Show that $T_3 + T_5 = 2(T_2 + T_4)$.

8. The first three terms of a geometric sequence are $2, 6, 18, \ldots$
    Find: **(i)** T_5 **(ii)** T_{10}.

Exercise 4R.B ▼

1. The first two terms of an arithmetic series are given as $2 + 8 + \ldots$ Find:
    (i) d, the common difference   **(ii)** T_{10}, the tenth term
    (iii)   the value of n such that $T_n = 200$ **(iv)** S_{16}, the sum to 16 terms.

2. The first two terms of a geometric series are $32 + 16 + \ldots$ Find:
    (i) r, the common ratio   **(ii)** T_n the nth term
    (iii) S_n, the sum to n terms   **(iv)**   the value of $S_n + T_n$ when $n = 4$.

3. The first term of a geometric series is 1 and the common ratio is $\frac{11}{10}$.
- **(i)** Write down the second, third and fourth terms of the series.
- **(ii)** Calculate S_4, the sum of the first four terms. Give your answer as a decimal.

4. The first two terms of a geometric series are $2 + \frac{2}{3} + \ldots$
- **(i)** Find r, the common ratio.
- **(ii)** Write down the third and fourth terms of the series.
- **(iii)** Show that S_6, the sum to 6 terms, is $3 - \dfrac{1}{3^5}$.

5. The nth term of a geometric sequence is $T_n = \dfrac{2^n}{3^n}$.
- **(i)** Find the first three terms of the sequence.
- **(ii)** Show that S_5, the sum of the first five terms, is $\frac{422}{243}$.

6. The nth term of a geometric series is given by $T_n = 3^n$.
- **(i)** What is the value of a, the first term?
- **(ii)** What is the value of r, the common ratio?
- **(iii)** Show that S_{10}, the sum of the first 10 terms, is $\frac{3}{2}(3^{10} - 1)$.

7. The first three terms of a geometric sequence are $\frac{1}{2}, 1, 2, \ldots$ Find:
- **(i)** r, the common ratio
- **(ii)** T_n, the nth term
- **(iii)** S_6, the sum to six terms.

8. The nth term, T_n, of an arithmetic sequence is $T_n = 52 - 4n$. Find:
- **(i)** T_1, the first term
- **(ii)** d, the common difference
- **(iii)** the term which is zero
- **(iv)** the sum of the terms which are positive.

9. The first three terms of an arithmetic sequence are $3, 8, 13, \ldots$
- **(i)** Find the value of a, the first term, and d, the common difference.
- **(ii)** Calculate the value of $T_{13} + S_{10}$.
- **(iii)** Which term of the sequence is equal to 148?

10. The general term, T_n, of an arithmetic sequence is given by $T_n = 2n + 5$. Find the first term, a, and the common difference, d. For what value of n is $S_n = 160$?
Show that $S_{n+3} - S_{n+1} = 4(n + 5)$.

11. The first three terms of a geometric sequence are $5, 15, 45, \ldots$
- **(i)** Find the values of a and r.
- **(ii)** Write down an expression for T_n and, hence, calculate T_9.
- **(iii)** Calculate S_6, the sum to six terms.
- **(iv)** Which term of the sequence is equal to 10,935?

12. The first three terms in an arithmetic sequence are $2x + 1, 3x - 2, 3x + 1$.
Calculate the value of x and write down the first three terms.

13. The first three terms in an arithmetic sequence are $k + 6, 2k + 1, k + 18$.
Calculate the value of k and write down the first three terms.

14. The first three terms of a geometric sequence are $x - 3, x, x + 6$.
Find the value of x.

15. The first three terms of a geometric sequence are $3x - 5$, $x - 1$ and $x - 2$.
Find the value of x.

16. In an arithmetic sequence, the first term, T_1, is 18, and the ninth term, T_9, is -14.
Express T_n in its simplest form and use this to find T_{30}.

17. In an arithmetic sequence $T_6 = 20$ and $4T_2 = T_{10}$. Find the values of a and d.

18. The first four terms of an arithmetic sequence are given as a, -4, b, 6, ...
Find: **(i)** the value of a and the value of b **(ii)** T_5, the fifth term.

19. The nth term, T_n, of a geometric series is $T_n = 3^{n-1}$. Find:
   (i) T_1, the first term
   (ii) r, the common ratio
   (iii) S_n, the sum to n terms.
   Investigate if $2S_n - T_n = 2T_n - 1$.

20. The sum of the first n terms of an arithmetic sequence is given by $S_n = \dfrac{3n}{2}(n + 3)$.
   (i) Calculate the first term of the series.
   (ii) By calculating S_9 and S_{10}, find T_{10} (the tenth term of the series).

Exercise 4R.C ▼

1. The first three terms of a geometric sequence are $k - 3$, $2k - 4$, $4k - 3$, ... where k is a real number.
   (i) Find the value of k.
   (ii) Hence, write down the value of each of the first four terms of the sequence.

2. The first three terms of a geometric series are $1 + 2 + 4 + ...$
   (i) Write down the values of a and r.
   (ii) How many terms of the series must be added together to get a total of 2,047?
   (iii) Show that $S_{33} < 2^{33}$.

3. T_n of a sequence is $5n + 3$. Verify that the sequence is arithmetic.

4. T_n of a sequence is $n^2 + 3n + 2$. Verify that the sequence is not arithmetic.

5. T_n of a sequence is 3.5^n. Verify that the sequence is geometric.

6. T_n of a sequence is $3n^2$. Verify that the sequence is not geometric.

7. The nth term of a series is given by $T_n = 4n + 1$.
   (i) Write down, in terms of n, an expression for T_{n-1}, the $(n - 1)$th term.
   (ii) Show that the series is arithmetic.
   (iii) Find S_{20}, the sum of the first 20 terms of the series.

8. In a certain sequence $T_n = 3 - 4n$. Verify that $T_{n+1} - T_{n-1} > T_3$.

9. The sum of the first n terms of an arithmetic series is given by $S_n = 4n^2 - 8n$.
   (i) Use S_1 and S_2 to find the first term and the common difference.
   (ii) Starting with the first term, how many terms of the series must be added to give a sum of 252?

10. In an arithmetic sequence, S_n, the sum to n terms is $S_n = 5n - 2n^2$.
Find T_1 and the common difference.

11. In an arithmetic series $S_n = n^2 + n$. Write down:
(i) S_{11} (ii) S_{10} (iii) T_{11}.

12. In an arithmetic series, $S_n = 2n^2 - 3n$.
Find the first term, a, and the common difference, d.
Find, in terms of n, an expression for T_n, the nth term.
Show that $S_n - S_{n-1} = T_n$.

13. The first three terms of an arithmetic series are $1 + 3 + 5 + \ldots$
Show that: (i) $T_n = 2n - 1$ (ii) $S_n = n^2$ (iii) $S_{n+1} - S_n = T_{n+1}$.

14. The sum of the first n terms of an arithmetic series is given by $S_n = n^2 - 3n$.
(i)   Use S_1 and S_2 to find the first term and the common difference.
(ii)   Find, in terms of n, an expression for T_n.
(iii) Show that $S_n - S_{n-1} = T_n$.
(iv)   Show that $S_{n+3} - S_n = 3(T_n + 4)$.

15. In an arithmetic series, the tenth term, T_{10}, is 19 and the sum to ten terms, S_{10}, is 55.
Find the first term and the common difference.
Show that $2S_n = 3n^2 - 19n$.

16. In an arithmetic series, T_3, the third term is 12 and the common difference is -3.
(i)   Find, in terms of n, an expression for T_n.
(ii)   If $S_n = 33$, find two values of n.
       Explain why there are two possible values of n.

17. The first three terms of an arithmetic series are $5 + 10 + 15 + \ldots$
(i)   Find, in terms of n, an expression for T_n, the nth term.
(ii)   Find, in terms of n, an expression for S_n, the sum to n terms.
(iii) Using your expression for S_n, find the sum of the natural numbers that are both multiples of 5 and smaller than 1000.

18. The first three terms of an arithmetic series are $2d + 3d + 4d + \ldots$ where d is a real number.
(i)   Find, in terms of d, an expression for T_{10}, the tenth term.
(ii)   Find, in terms of d, an expression for S_{10}, the sum to 10 terms.
(iii) If $S_{10} - T_{10} = 162$, find the value of d and write down the first four terms of the series.

19. In a geometric sequence, T_2, the second term is 6 and T_5, the fifth term is 48. Find:
(i)   the first term, a (ii) the common ratio, r (iii) T_n, the nth term
(iv) S_n, the sum to n terms   (v) T_{10} (vi) S_{10}

20. The sum of the first n terms of a geometric series is given by $S_n = 5(3^n - 1)$.
(i)   Use S_1 and S_2 to find the first term and the common ratio.
(ii)   Find, in terms of n, an expression for T_n and find T_6.

REVISION EXERCISE 5:
FUNCTIONS AND DIFFERENTIATION

Paper I   Questions 6, 7 and 8

This revision exercise covers chapters 8, 9 and 10.

Exercise 5R.A ▼

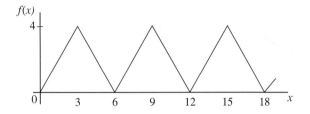

1. The graph shows a portion of a periodic function $f : x \rightarrow f(x)$.

   Write down the period and range of the function.

   Evaluate $f(3)$, $f(6)$ and $f(21)$.

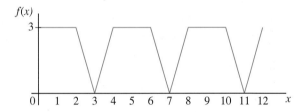

2. The graph shows a portion of a periodic function $f : x \rightarrow f(x)$.

   Write down the period and range of the function.

   Evaluate $f(3)$, $f(5)$ and $f(9)$.

3.

   The graph shows a portion of a periodic function $f : x \rightarrow f(x)$.
   Write down the period and range of the function.
   What is the value of $f(77.5)$?

4. Let $f(x) = 5x - 10$.
   (i) Find $f(3)$ **(ii)** Find the value of x for which $f(x) = 0$.

5. Let $f(x) = \frac{1}{3}(x - 8)$. Evaluate $f(5)$.

6. Let $f(x) = 2(3x - 1)$, $x \in \mathbf{R}$. Find the value of x for which $f(x) = 0$.

7. Let $p(x) = 3x - 12$. For what values of x is $p(x) < 0$, where x is a positive whole number?

8. Let $g(x) = \dfrac{1}{x^2 + 1}$. Evaluate: **(i)** $g(2)$ **(ii)** $g(3)$, writing your answers as decimals.

9. Let $f(x) = 3x + k$, $\quad x \in \mathbf{R}$. If $f(5) = 0$, find the value of k.

10. The function f is defined by $f : x \rightarrow 4x - 5$. Find $f(3)$ and $f(10)$.
Hence, find the value of k for which $kf(3) = f(10)$.

11. The function f is defined by $f : x \rightarrow 7 - 3x$.
Find $f(-2)$ and find a number k such that $kf(-2) = f(24)$.

12. If $f(x) = 5x - 8$ and $g(x) = 13 - 2x$, find the value of x for which $f(x) = g(x)$.

13. Differentiate with respect to x:

  (i) x^3 **(ii)** $-x^2$ **(iii)** $4x^2 + 5$ **(iv)** $9x - x^3$

  (v) $6 - 5x^3$ **(vi)** $3x^4 - 2x + 1$ **(vii)** $x^2 - 3x$ **(viii)** $6x^5 + x^2$

  (ix) $x(5 - 3x^2)$ **(x)** $(x - 3)(x + 3)$ **(xi)** $\dfrac{1}{x^2}$ **(xii)** $\dfrac{1}{x^3}$

14. (i) Find $\dfrac{ds}{dt}$ when $s = 6t^2 - 3t + 7$. **(ii)** If $s = t^3 - 4t^2$, find $\dfrac{ds}{dt}$ when $t = 2$.

15. Let $f(x) = x^2 - 4x$, for $x \in \mathbf{R}$.
  (i) Find $f'(x)$, the derivative of $f(x)$. **(ii)** For what value of x is $f'(x) = 0$?

16. Let $g(x) = x^4 - 32x$ for $x \in \mathbf{R}$.
  (i) Write down $g'(x)$, the derivative of $g(x)$. **(ii)** For what value of x is $g'(x) = 0$?

17. Differentiate from first principles with respect to x:
  (i) $4x + 3$ **(ii)** $7x + 2$ **(iii)** $3x - 7$ **(iv)** $2x - 1$.

Exercise 5R.B ▼

1. The graph shows a portion of a periodic function $f : x \rightarrow f(x)$ which is defined for $x \in \mathbf{R}$.

  (i) Write down the period and the range of $f(x)$.

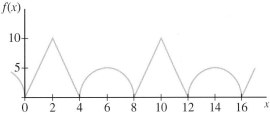

  (ii) Complete the following table:

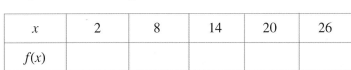

x	2	8	14	20	26
$f(x)$					

2. Shown opposite is part of the graph of the periodic function $y = f(x)$.

State its period and range.

Evaluate:

(i) $f(2)$ **(ii)** $f(3)$

(iii) $f(6)$ **(iv)** $f(-2)$

(v) $f(18)$ **(vi)** $f(-6)$

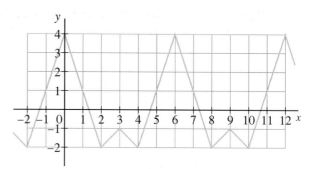

Find the number of times $f(x)$ reaches its minimum value in the domain $18 \leqslant x \leqslant 42$.

3. Find $\dfrac{dy}{dx}$ if:

(i) $y = (x^3 - 3)(x^2 - 4)$ **(ii)** $y = (x^2 - 3)(1 - x)$ **(iii)** $y = \dfrac{2x}{x+1}$

(iv) $y = \dfrac{2x - 7}{x - 1}$ **(v)** $y = (x^2 + 3x)^4$ **(vi)** $y = (x^2 + 5x - 1)^3$

(vii) $y = (x^3 + 3)(5x^2 - 1)$ **(viii)** $y = (2x - 3)^7$ **(ix)** $y = \dfrac{3x + 1}{x + 2}$

(x) $y = (3 - 7x)^5$ **(xi)** $y = x^5 - 17x + \dfrac{1}{x^5}$ **(xii)** $y = \left(1 - \dfrac{1}{x}\right)^{10}$

4. Find $\dfrac{dy}{dx}$ when $y = \dfrac{2x}{x^2 + 1}$.

5. Differentiate $\left(x^5 - \dfrac{1}{x^2}\right)^7$ with respect to x, $x \neq 0$.

6. Find $\dfrac{dy}{dx}$ where $y = (x - 1)^7$ and evaluate your answer at $x = 2$.

7. Find the value of $\dfrac{dy}{dx}$ at $x = -1$ when $y = (3x + 1)^4$.

8. Find $\dfrac{dy}{dx}$ when $y = \dfrac{x^2}{1 - x}$, $x \neq 1$. Show that $\dfrac{dy}{dx} = 0$ at $x = 0$.

9. Find the value of $\dfrac{dy}{dx}$ at $x = 2$ when $y = (1 - x^2)^3$.

10. (i)   Find $\dfrac{dy}{dx}$ when $y = \dfrac{x^2}{x - 4}$, $x \neq 4$.

(ii)   Find the value of $\dfrac{dy}{dx}$ at $x = 0$ when $y = (x^2 - 7x + 1)^5$.

11. Differentiate from first principles with respect to x:

(i) $x^2 + 5x$ **(ii)** $x^2 - 6x + 4$ **(iii)** $3x^2 - 2$ **(iv)** $2x^2 + 3x$

12. Using calculus, find the coordinates of the local maximum and the local minimum of the curves:
- **(i)** $y = 2x^3 - 3x^2 - 12x + 18$
- **(ii)** $y = x^3 - 9x^2 + 24x - 20$
- **(iii)** $y = 2x^3 - 15x^2 + 36x - 24$
- **(iv)** $y = x^3 - 3x + 7$

13. Find, using calculus, the coordinates of the local maximum of the curve $y = 3x^2 - x^3$, given that the curve has a local minimum at $(0, 0)$.

14. Find the coordinates of the local maximum and minimum points of the curve $y = 5 + 18x + 6x^2 - 2x^3$.

15. Find the equation of the tangent to the curve $y = x^3 - 4x + 7$ at the point where $x = 1$.

16. Find the equation of the tangent to the curve $f(x) = \dfrac{x-1}{x+2}$ at the point $(-1, -2)$.

17. Let $y = x^2 - 5x + 6, \qquad x \in \mathbf{R}$.

Find the slopes of the tangents to the graph of y at the points $(2, 0)$ and $(3, 0)$, and investigate if these two tangents are at right angles to each other.

18. $f : x \rightarrow x^2 - 1$ and $g : x \rightarrow 1 - 2x$.

Find the values of x for which $3f(x) = 5g(x)$.

19. On the right is part of the graph of the function
$f : x \rightarrow -x^2 - 2x + 8, \qquad x \in \mathbf{R}$.

Find the coordinates of p, q, r and s, where q is the turning point of the curve.

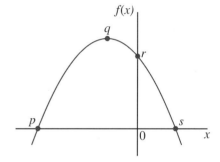

20. Let $g(x) = x(x - 2)$ for $x \in \mathbf{R}$.

Find $g(0)$, $g(4)$, $g(-2)$.

Show that $g(1 + t) = g(1 - t)$ for $t \in \mathbf{R}$.

Find the derivative, $g'(x)$, and show that $g'(x) > 0$ for $x > 1$.

21. Let $g(x) = \dfrac{1}{x}$, for $x \in \mathbf{R}$ and $x \neq 0$.

Find $g(\frac{1}{4})$, $g(\frac{1}{2})$, $g(1)$, $g(2)$, $g(4)$.

Under the central symmetry in the origin, find the image of each of the points $(1, 1)$ and $(4, \frac{1}{4})$.

22. Let $f(x) = 2 - 9x + 6x^2 - x^3$ for $x \in \mathbf{R}$.
- **(i)** Find $f(-1), f(2)$ and $f(5)$.
- **(ii)** Find $f'(x)$, the derivative of $f(x)$.
- **(iii)** Find the coordinates of the local maximum and the local minimum of $f(x)$.
- **(iv)** Draw the graph of $f(x)$ in the domain $-1 \leqslant x \leqslant 5$.
- **(v)** Use your graph to find the range of real values of k for which $f(x) = k$ has more than one solution.

23. (i) Draw the graph of $g(x) = \dfrac{1}{x}$ for $-3 \leqslant x \leqslant 3$, $x \in \mathbf{R}$ and $x \neq 0$.

(ii) Using the same axes and the same scales, draw the graph of $h(x) = x + 1$ for $-3 \leqslant x \leqslant 3$, $x \in \mathbf{R}$.

(iii) Use your graphs to estimate the values of x for which $\dfrac{1}{x} = x + 1$.

24. The speed, v, in metres per second of an engine moving along a track is related to time, t, in seconds by:
$$v = \tfrac{1}{3}(2t + 5).$$

(i) Draw the straight-line graph of this relation, putting t on the horizontal axis, for $0 \leqslant t \leqslant 8$.

(ii) Use your graph to estimate the speed when $t = 2.5$ seconds.

(iii) Use your graph to estimate the time at which the speed reaches 6 metres per second.

Exercise 5R.C ▼

1. The air resistance, R, to a body moving with speed v metres per second is given by $R = \dfrac{v^2}{100}$.

Find the rate of change of the air resistance with respect to the speed.

Calculate this rate of change when $v = 16$ m/s.

2. $f(x) = (x + k)(x - 2)^2$, where k is a real number.

(i) If $f(3) = 7$, find the value of k.

(ii) Using this value for k, find the coordinates of the local maximum and of the local minimum of $f(x)$.

3. Let $f(x) = x^3 - ax + 7$ for all $x \in \mathbf{R}$ and for $a \in \mathbf{R}$.

(i) The slope of the tangent to the curve $y = f(x)$ at $x = 1$ is -9.

Find the value of a.

(ii) Hence, find the coordinates of the local maximum point and the local minimum point on the curve $y = f(x)$.

4. Let $y = \dfrac{5 + x^2}{2 - x}$, $x \neq 2$. Find the values of x for which $\dfrac{dy}{dx} = 0$.

5. Find $\dfrac{dy}{dx}$ when $y = \dfrac{2x}{4 - x^2}$, for $x \in \mathbf{R}$ and $x \neq \pm 2$. Show that $\dfrac{dy}{dx} > 0$.

6. Find $\dfrac{dy}{dx}$ when $y = \dfrac{1 - x^2}{x}$. Show that $\dfrac{dy}{dx} < 0$ for all $x \neq 0$, $x \in \mathbf{R}$.

7. If $y = \dfrac{4x + 1}{x - 3}$, $x \in \mathbf{R}$, show that $\dfrac{dy}{dx} < 0$ for all $x \neq 3$.

8. Let $f(x) = 6x^2 - x^3$ for $x \in \mathbf{R}$.
   (i)   Find $f'(x)$, the derivative of $f(x)$.
         Hence, calculate the coordinates of the local maximum and the local minimum of $f(x)$.
   (ii) Draw the graph of $f(x) = 6x^2 - x^3$ for $-2 \leqslant x \leqslant 6$.
   (iii) Find the solution set for which $f(x)$ is decreasing.

9. Let $f(x) = x^3 - 3x^2$, for $x \in \mathbf{R}$.
   (i)   Find $f'(x)$, the derivative of $f(x)$.
         Hence, calculate the coordinates of the local maximum and the local minimum of $f(x)$.
   (ii) Draw the graph of $f(x) = x^3 - 3x^2$ in the domain $-1 \leqslant x \leqslant 3$.
   (iii) Use your graph to estimate the values of x for which $f(x) + 2 = 0$.
   (iv) Use your graph to estimate the range of values of x for which $f'(x) < 0$.

10. Let $f(x) = 2x^3 - 5x^2 - 4x + 3$ for $x \in \mathbf{R}$.
    (i)   Complete the table:

x	-1.5	-1	0	1	2	3	3.5
$f(x)$	-9						13.5

    (ii) Find the derivative of $f(x)$.
          Calculate the coordinates of the local minimum and show that the coordinates of the local maximum are $\left(-\frac{1}{3}, \frac{100}{27}\right)$.
    (iii) Draw the graph of $f(x) = 2x^3 - 5x^2 - 4x + 3$ for $-1.5 \leqslant x \leqslant 3.5$.
    (iv) Write the equation $2x^3 - 5x^2 - 6x + 6 = 0$ in the form $2x^3 - 5x^2 - 4x + 3 = ax + b$, $\quad a, b \in \mathbf{Z}$.
          Hence, use your graph to estimate the solutions of the equation $2x^3 - 5x^2 - 6x + 6 = 0$.

11. On the same axes and scales, graph the functions:
    $$g : x \longrightarrow \frac{1}{x+2} \text{ and } h : x \longrightarrow x - 2 \text{ in the domain } 0 \leqslant x \leqslant 4, \qquad x \in \mathbf{R}.$$
    Show how your graphs may be used to estimate the value of $\sqrt{5}$.

12. Let $f(x) = \dfrac{1}{x+2}$.
    (i)   Find $f(-6), f(-3), f(-1), f(0)$ and $f(2)$.
    (ii) For what real value of x is $f(x)$ not defined?
    (iii) Draw the graph of $f(x) = \dfrac{1}{x+2}$ for $-6 \leqslant x \leqslant 2$.
    (iv) Find $f'(x)$, the derivative of $f(x)$.
    (v)   Find the two values of x at which the slope of the tangent to the graph is $-\frac{1}{9}$.
    (vi) Show that there is no tangent to the graph of f that is parallel to the x-axis.

13. Let $f(x) = \dfrac{1}{x-1}$, for $x \in \mathbf{R}$ and $x \neq 1$.

    (i)   Find the value of $f(-2), f(0), f(\tfrac{3}{2})$ and $f(5)$.

    (ii)   Find $f'(x)$, the derivative of $f(x)$.

    (iii)   Prove that the tangents to $f(x)$ at $(2, 1)$ and $(0, -1)$ are parallel to each other.

    (iv)   Draw the graph of $f(x)$ for $-2 \leqslant x \leqslant 5$.

    (v)   Find the equation of the tangent T to the curve at the point $(0, -1)$.

    (vi)   Find the coordinates of the other point on the graph of $f(x)$ at which the tangent to the curve is parallel to T.

14. **(i)**   Find $\tan 135°$.

    (ii)   Let $f(x) = \dfrac{1}{x-2}$ for $x \in \mathbf{R}$ and $x \neq 2$. Find the derivative of $f(x)$.

    (iii)   Tangents to $f(x)$ make an angle of $135°$ with the x-axis.

    Find the coordinates of the points on the curve of $f(x)$ at which this occurs.

15. **(i)**   Write down the slope of the line $x + y - 5 = 0$.

    (ii)   Let $f(x) = 2x^3 - 3x^2 - 13x + 2$ for $x \in \mathbf{R}$. Find the derivative of $f(x)$.

    Find the coordinates of the points on the curve $f(x)$ at which the tangents to the curve are parallel to the line $x + y - 5 = 0$. Find the equations of the tangents at these points.

16. **(i)**   Write down the slope of the x-axis.

    (ii)   Let $f(x) = x^3 - 6x^2 + 12$ for $x \in \mathbf{R}$. Find the derivative of $f(x)$.

    (iii)   At the two points (x_1, y_1) and (x_2, y_2), the tangents to the curve $y = f(x)$ are parallel to the x-axis, where $x_2 > x_1$.

    Show that: **(a)** $x_2 - x_1 = 4$ **(b)** $y_2 = y_1 - 32$.

17. Let $g(x) = (2x + 3)(x^2 - 1)$ for $x \in \mathbf{R}$. Find $g'(x)$, the derivative of $g(x)$.

    (i)   For what two values of x is the slope of the tangent to the curve of $g(x)$ equal to 10?

    (ii)   Find the equations of the two tangents to the curve of $g(x)$ which have slope 10.

18. Let $f(x) = 2x^3 - 7x^2 + 7x - 2$ for $x \in \mathbf{R}$. Find the derivative of $f(x)$.

    Find the equation of one of the tangents to the curve of $f(x)$ which is parallel to the line $y = 3x - 8$.

19. Let $f(x) = \dfrac{1}{x+1}$ for $x \in \mathbf{R}$ and $x > -1$. Find $f'(x)$.

    Find the coordinates of the point on the curve of $f(x)$ at which the tangent has slope of $-\tfrac{1}{4}$.

    Find the equation of the tangent to the curve which has slope of $-\tfrac{1}{4}$.

20. Let $f(x) = x^3 - 3x^2 + ax + 1$ for all $x \in \mathbf{R}$ and for $a \in \mathbf{R}$.

    $f(x)$ has a turning point (a local maximum or a local minimum) at $x = -1$.

    (i)   Find the value of a.

    (ii)   Is this turning point a local maximum or a local minimum?

    Give a reason for your answer.

    (iii)   Find the coordinates of the other turning point of $f(x)$.

21. The graph of the quadratic function $x \rightarrow f(x)$, $x \in \mathbf{R}$ is as shown.

Express $f(x)$ in the form $x^2 + bx + c$.

$g(x) = px + q$, where $g(0) = -3$ and $g(1) = 0$.

Find the value of p and the value of q.

Find the values of x for which $g(x) = f(x)$.

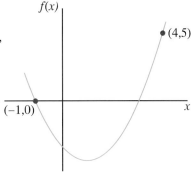

22. Let $f(x) = x^2 + bx + c$, $\quad x \in \mathbf{R}$.

The solutions of $f(x) = 0$ are -3 and 1. Find the value of b and the value of c.

If $f(-1) = k$, find the value of k. Solve the equation $f(x) - k = 0$.

23. Let $f(x) = ax^3 + bx + c$, for all $x \in \mathbf{R}$ and for $a, b, c \in \mathbf{R}$.

Use the information which follows to find the value of a, of b and of c:

(i) $f(0) = 3$

(ii) the slope of the tangent to the curve of $f(x)$ at $x = 1$ is -18

(iii) the curve of $f(x)$ has a local minimum at $x = 2$.

24. Let $g(x) = x^2 + bx + c$, $\quad x \in \mathbf{R}$.

The solutions of $g(x) = 0$ are symmetrical about the line $x = 1$.

If $x = -3$ is one solution of $g(x) = 0$, find the other solution.

Find the value of b and the value of c.

25. A marble rolls along the top of a table. It starts to move at $t = 0$ seconds.

The distance that it has travelled at t seconds is given by $s = 14t - t^2$, where s is in centimetres.

(i)   What distance has the marble travelled when $t = 2$ seconds?

(ii) What is the speed of the marble when $t = 5$ seconds?

(iii) When is the speed of the marble equal to zero?

(iv) What is the acceleration of the marble?

26. Two fireworks were fired straight up in the air at $t = 0$ seconds.

The height, h metres, which each firework reached above the ground t seconds after it was fired, is given by $h = 80t - 5t^2$.

The first firework exploded 5 seconds after it was fired.

(i)   At what height was the first firework when it exploded?

(ii) At what speed was the first firework travelling when it exploded?

The second firework failed to explode and it fell back to the ground.

(iii) After how many seconds did the second firework reach its maximum height?

27. A car, starting at $t = 0$ seconds, travels a distance of s metres in t seconds, where $s = 30t - \frac{9}{4}t^2$.

(i)   Find its speed after t seconds

(ii) Find the speed of the car after 2 seconds.

(iii) After how many seconds is the speed of the car equal to zero?

(iv) Find the distance travelled by the car up to the time when its speed is zero.

28. A stone is dropped from a height of 80 metres.

Its height h metres above the ground after t seconds is given by $h = 80 - 10t^2$.

Find:

(i) its speed after t seconds

(ii) its speed after 2.5 seconds

(iii) the time it takes to fall the first 14.4 metres.

29. The speed, v, in metres per second, of a body after t seconds is given by $v = 3t(4 - t)$.

Find the acceleration at each of the two instants when the speed is 9 metres per second.

Find the speed at the instant when the acceleration is zero.

30. The volume of water, V, in cm^3, that remains in a leaking tank after t seconds is given by:

$$V = 45,000 - 300t + 0.5t^2$$

(i) After how many seconds will the tank be empty?

(ii) Find the rate of change of the volume with respect to t when $t = 50$ seconds.

REVISION EXERCISE 6:
PERIMETER, AREA AND VOLUME

Paper 2   Question 1

This revision exercise covers chapter 7.

> *Exercise 6R.A* ▼

1. Two squares have sides of length 4 cm and 10 cm, respectively.
   Find, in its simplest form, the ratio of their areas.

2. The area of a square is 36 cm^2. Find the length of a side of the square.

3. Each side of a square is increased in length from 5 cm to 7 cm.
   Calculate the percentage increase in the area of the square.

4. Calculate the area of the shaded region in the diagram.

   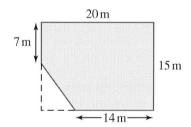

5. The lengths of the four sides of a rectangle add up to 53 cm. One of the sides measures 9 cm.
   Find the area of the rectangle.

6. The area of triangle *abc* is 10.125 cm^2.
   The length of [*bc*] is 8.1 cm.
   The height of the triangle is *h* cm.
   Calculate the value of *h*.

   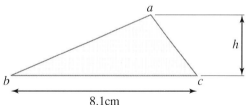

7. The length of the radius of the large circle in the diagram is 8 cm.
   The length of the radius of the small circle is 1 cm.
   Find the area of the shaded region, assuming $\pi = \frac{22}{7}$.

8. A rectangular piece of metal measures 7 cm by 14 cm.

   A semicircular section with radius of length 7 cm is removed.

   Calculate the area of the remaining piece of metal.

   (Assume $\pi = \frac{22}{7}$.)

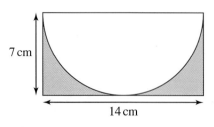

9. A bicycle wheel, including the tyre, has a diameter of 70 cm. How many revolutions of the wheel occur in a journey of 11 km? (Assume $\pi = \frac{22}{7}$.)

10. A running track is made up of two straight parts and two semicircular parts, as shown in the diagram.

    The length of each of the straight parts is 90 metres.

    The diameter of each of the semicircular parts is 70 metres.

    Calculate the length of the track correct to the nearest metre. (Assume $\pi = \frac{22}{7}$.)

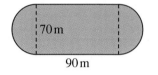

11. A window is in the shape of a rectangle and a semicircle, as shown. The rectangular part of the window is 70 cm wide and 90 cm high.

    Find the area of the window in cm². (Assume $\pi = \frac{22}{7}$.)

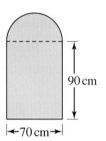

12. In the diagram, o is the centre of the circle of radius length 4 cm.

    $|\angle poq| = 90°$.

    Find, in terms of π, the area of the shaded sector.

13. A pizza in the shape of a circle has a piece missing from it, as shown in the diagram.

    The radius of the pizza is 10 cm and $|\angle pqr| = 135°$.

    Find the area of the pizza left. (Assume $\pi = 3.14$.)

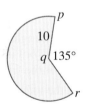

14. A piece of wire of length 154 cm is in the shape of a semicircle.

    Find the radius length of the semicircle. (Assume $\pi = \frac{22}{7}$.)

474

1. A rectangular block has volume 720 cm³.

   The width and length of the block are 9 cm and 20 cm, respectively. Its height is h cm.

   Calculate:

   (i) the value of h

   (ii) the sum of the areas of the four vertical sides.

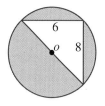

2. A triangle is enclosed in a circle, centre o.

   The lengths of two of the sides are 8 cm and 6 cm, as shown.

   (i) Find the radius of the circle.

   (ii) Calculate the area of the shaded region. (Assume $\pi = 3.14$.)

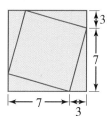

3. Calculate the area of the smaller square in the diagram, given the lengths 3 cm and 7 cm, as shown.

4. A square is inscribed in a circle. The diameter of the circle is 4 cm in length. Find the area of the square.

5. Find the slant height, l, of a cone which has perpendicular height of 4 cm and a base with radius of length 3 cm.

   Write down the curved surface area of the cone in terms of π.

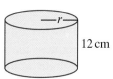

6. The volume of a cylinder is 3,768 cm³.

   The height of the cylinder is 12 cm.

   Calculate the radius, r of the cylinder. (Assume $\pi = 3.14$.)

7. The volume of a right circular cone is 1,884 cm³. Its height measures 8 cm.

   Find:

   (i) the length of the base radius   **(ii)** its curved surface area. (Assume $\pi = 3.14$.)

8. Three tennis balls fit exactly in a cylindrical container, as shown in the diagram. The radius of a tennis ball is 21 mm.

Find, assuming $\pi = \frac{22}{7}$:

(i)   the volume of a tennis ball

(ii) the volume of the cylindrical container

(iii) the difference between the capacity of the container and the volume of the three tennis balls.

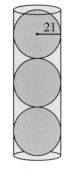

9. (i)   Soup is contained in a cylindrical saucepan which has internal radius 14 cm. The depth of the soup is 20 cm.

Calculate, in terms of π, the volume of soup in the saucepan.

(ii) A ladle in the shape of a hemisphere with internal radius of length 6 cm is used to serve the soup.

Calculate, in terms of π, the volume of soup contained in one full ladle.

(iii) The soup is served into cylindrical cups, each with internal radius of length of 4 cm. One ladleful is placed in each cup. Calculate the depth of the soup in each cup.

(iv) How many cups can be filled from the contents of the saucepan if each cup must contain exactly one full ladle?

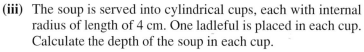
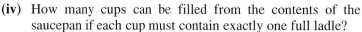

6 cm

10. A machine part consists of a solid sphere submerged in a closed cylindrical container full of oil. The radius of the cylinder is 4 cm, the radius of the sphere is 3 cm and the volume of oil contained in the cylinder is 108π cm^3.

Calculate the height of the cylinder.

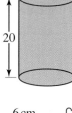

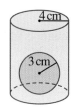

11. A toy is made of a cone which fits exactly on top of a hemisphere, as shown in the diagram. The radius length of the hemisphere is 6 cm and the total height of the toy is 21 cm.

(i)   Write down the height of the cone and, hence, find the volume of the cone in terms of π.

(ii) Find the volume of the hemisphere in terms of π.

(iii) Express the volume of the cone as a percentage of the total volume of the toy. (Give your answer correct to one place of decimals.)

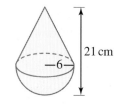

12. A container is in the shape of a cone on top of a hemisphere (as shown). The hemisphere has a diameter of 12 cm.

Find the volume of the container, in terms of π, given that the height of the cone is $2\frac{1}{2}$ times the length of its radius.

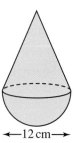

476

13. The diagram shows a sector of a circle, centre *o*. The length of the arc *pq* is $16\frac{1}{2}$ cm, and $|\angle poq| = 63°$.

Find: **(i)** the length of the radius

(ii) the area of the sector *opq*. (Assume $\pi = \frac{22}{7}$.)

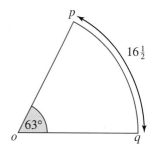

14. The front face of a stone wall of a ruined castle is shown in the diagram.

All distances are measured in metres. The heights are measured at intervals of 2.4 m along the base line.

Use Simpson's Rule to calculate the area of the front face of the stone wall.

15. The diagram opposite shows a site for sale.

The offsets of lengths 6, 9, 14, 11, 17, 15 and 4 metres are measured at intervals of 5 metres along [*ab*].

Using Simpson's Rule, calculate the area of this site, correct to the nearest square metre.

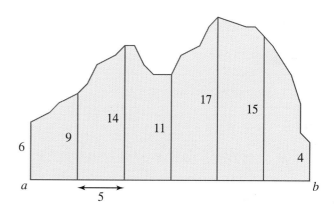

16. A sketch of a piece of land *abcd* is shown.

At equal intervals of 15 m along [*bc*], perpendicular measurements of 40 m, 60 m, 50 m, 70 m, 60 m, 30 m and 20 m are made to the top boundary.

Use Simpson's Rule to estimate the area of the piece of land.

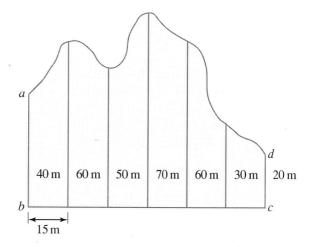

17. The sketch shows a piece of land covered by forest which lies on one side of a straight road.

At equal intervals of 50 m along the road, perpendicular measurements of 130 m, 185 m, 200 m, 210 m, 190 m, 155 m and 120 m are made to the forest boundary.

Use Simpson's Rule to estimate the area of land covered by the forest.

Give your answer in hectares.

[Note: 1 hectare = 10,000 m².]

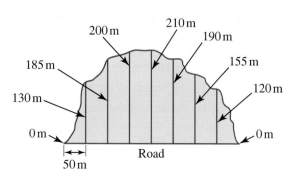

18. The diagram shows the curve $y = x^2 + 1$ in the domain $0 \leqslant x \leqslant 4$.

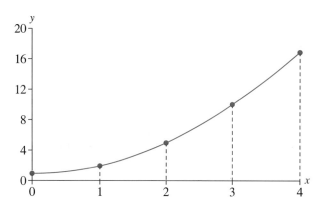

(i) Copy the following table. Then complete it, using the equation of the curve:

x	0	1	2	3	4
y					

(ii) Hence, use Simpson's Rule to estimate the area between the curve and the x-axis.

19. The sketch shows a field $abcd$ which has one uneven edge. At equal intervals of 6 m along [bc] perpendicular measurements of 7 m, 8 m, 10 m, 11 m, 13 m, 15 m and x m are made to the top of the field.

Using Simpson's Rule, the area of the field is calculated to be 410 m².

Calculate the value of x.

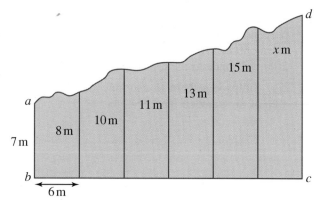

20. The diagram shows a sketch of a piece of paper *abcd* with one uneven edge. At equal intervals of *h* cm along [*bc*], perpendicular measurements of 12 cm, 8 cm, 9 cm, 6 cm, 5 cm, 7 cm and 11 cm are made to the top edge.

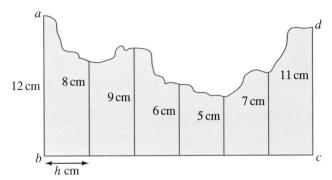

Using Simpson's Rule, the area of the piece of paper is estimated to be 180 cm².

Calculate the value of *h*.

21. The sketch shows a flood caused by a leaking underground pipe that runs from *a* to *b*.

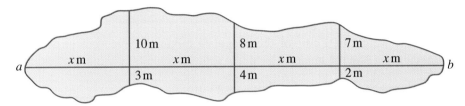

At equal intervals of *x* m along [*ab*] perpendicular measurements are made to the edges of the flood. The measurements to the top edge are 10 m, 8 m and 7 m. The measurements to the bottom edge are 3 m, 4 m and 2 m. At *a* and *b* the measurements are 0 m.

Using Simpson's Rule, the area of the flood is estimated to be 672 m².

Find *x* and, hence, write down the length of the pipe.

Exercise 6R.C ▼

1. A wax sphere has surface area 1,017.36 cm². Assuming $\pi = 3.14$, calculate:
   (i) the radius of the sphere   **(ii)** the volume of the sphere.

2. A candle is in the shape of a cylinder surmounted by a cone, as in the diagram.

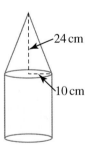

   (i)   The cone has height 24 cm and the length of the radius of its base is 10 cm. Find the volume of the cone in terms of π.
   (ii) The height of the cylinder is equal to the slant height of the cone. Find the volume of the cylinder in terms of π.
   (iii) A solid spherical ball of wax with radius of length *r* cm was used to make the candle.
   Calculate *r*, correct to one decimal place.

3. Wax in the shape of a cylinder with radius of length 4 cm and height 36 cm is melted down. The resulting wax is formed into cone-shaped candles. Each candle has height 6 cm and base of radius length 2 cm.

    (i) Calculate the number of candles that can be made, assuming that no wax is lost.

    (ii) The candles are placed, base down and in rows of three, in the smallest possible rectangular box. Calculate, in cm^3, the volume (internal capacity) of the box.

    (iii) What percentage of the volume of the box is empty? (Take $\pi = 3.14$.)

    Give your answer correct to the nearest whole number.

4. Sweets, made from a chocolate mixture, are in the shape of solid spherical balls. The diameter of each sweet is 3 cm.

    36 sweets fit exactly in a rectangular box which has internal height 3 cm.

    (i) The base of the box is a square. How many sweets are there in each row?

    (ii) What is the internal volume of the box?

    (iii) The 36 sweets weigh 675 grammes.

    What is the weight of 1 cm^3 of the chocolate mixture? Give your answer correct to one decimal place. (Assume $\pi = 3.14$.)

5. The diagram shows a prism-shaped building on a farm.

    One of the end walls is *abcd*.

    ab and *dc* are perpendicular to *bc*.

    The internal length is $|ck|$. *ck* is the perpendicular to *bc*.

    The internal measurements of the building are $|ab| = 3$ m, $|bc| = |dc| = 2$ m and $|ck| = 4$ m.

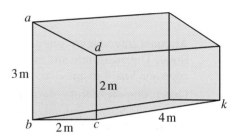

    (i) Find the area of the end wall *abcd*.

    (ii) Find the internal volume of the building.

6. The internal height of a cylinder is 20 cm. 50 identical solid metal cubes, each of edge 2 cm, are placed in the cylinder. Water is then poured into the cylinder until it is full. If the volume of water needed is 1.17 litres, calculate the radius length of the cylinder. (Assume $\pi = 3.14$.)

7. Find the volume of a solid sphere which has radius of length 2.1 cm. Give your answer correct to the nearest cm^3. (Assume $\pi = \frac{22}{7}$.)

    This sphere and a solid cube with edge of length 3 cm are completely submerged in water in a cylinder. The cylinder has a radius of length r cm.

    Both the sphere and the cube are then removed from the cylinder. The water level drops by 4 cm. Find r, correct to one place of decimals. (Assume $\pi = \frac{22}{7}$.)

8. Find the volume of a solid sphere with a diameter of length 3 cm. Give your answer in terms of π.

    A cylindrical vessel with internal diameter of length 15 cm contains water. The surface of the water is 11 cm from the top of the vessel.

    How many solid spheres, each with diameter of length 3 cm, must be placed in the vessel in order to bring the surface of the water to 1 cm from the top of the vessel?

    (Assume that all the spheres are submerged in the water.)

9. A solid cylinder, made of lead, has a radius of length 15 cm and a height of 135 cm. Find its volume in terms of π.

The solid cylinder is melted down and recast to make four identical right circular solid cones. The height of each cone is equal to twice the length of its base radius. Calculate the base radius length of the cones.

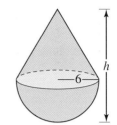

10. A toy is made of a cone which fits exactly on top of a hemisphere, as shown in the diagram. The radius length of the hemisphere is 6 cm and the volume of the cone is half the volume of the hemisphere. Calculate h, the total height of the toy.

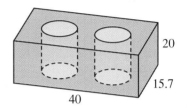

11. Calculate the volume of a solid metal block with dimensions 40 cm by 15.7 cm by 20 cm. Two identical solid cylinders are cut out of the block from top to bottom, as shown in the diagram.

This reduces the volume of the block by 25%.
Find the radius of each of the cylinders.

(Assume $\pi = 3.14$.)

12. An egg timer consists of two identical cones, as shown in the diagram. Sand in the upper cone falls into the lower cone at a rate such that it empties in 3 minutes. If the height of sand in the upper cone at the beginning of the 3 minutes' interval is 3.6 cm and the diameter of the top surface of the sand is 6 cm, find the rate, in terms of π cm^3/s, at which the sand is falling.

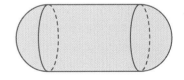

13. (i) Write down, in terms of π and r, the volume of a hemisphere with radius of length r.

(ii) A fuel storage tank is in the shape of a cylinder with a hemisphere at each end, as shown.

The capacity (internal volume) of the tank is 81π m^3.

The ratio of the capacity of the cylindrical section to the sum of the capacities of the hemispherical ends is $5 : 4$.

Calculate the internal radius length of the tank.

14. A solid is in the shape of a hemisphere surmounted by a cone, as in the diagram.

(i) The volume of the hemisphere is 18π cm^3.
Find the radius of the hemisphere.

(ii) The slant height of the cone is $3\sqrt{5}$ cm.
Show that the vertical height of the cone is 6 cm.

(iii) Show that the volume of the cone equals the volume of the hemisphere.

(iv) The solid is melted down and recast in the shape of a solid cylinder. The height of the cylinder is 9 cm. Calculate its radius.

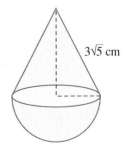

15. (i) A container is in the shape of a cylinder on top of a hemisphere, as shown in the diagram. The cylinder has a radius length of 6 cm and the container has a total height of 22 cm.

Calculate the volume of the container in terms of π.

(ii) If two-fifths of the volume of the container is filled with water, calculate the depth, d, of water in the container.

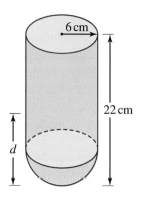

REVISION EXERCISE 7:
COORDINATE GEOMETRY OF THE LINE

Paper 2   Question 2

This revision exercise covers chapter 1.

> *Exercise 7R.A* ▼

1. Find the distance between the two points $(-5, 1)$ and $(7, -4)$.

2. Find the coordinates of the midpoint of the line segment which joins the points $(2, -3)$ and $(-8, -6)$.

3. If $m(4, 5)$ is the midpoint of $[pq]$, and $p = (-2, 8)$, find the coordinates of q.

4. Find the equation of the line through the point $(3, -2)$ with slope $-\frac{2}{5}$.

5. $p(1, -2)$ and $q(5, 1)$ are two points. Find:
   (i) the slope of pq **(ii)** the equation of the line pq.

6. $L : 3x + 2y - 7 = 0$ and $K : 2x - 3y - 1 = 0$ are the equations of two lines. Prove that $L \perp K$.

7. L is the line $x + 2y - 1 = 0$. The line K contains the point $(-1, 4)$ and $K \perp L$.
   Find the equation of K.

8. Find the coordinates of the point of intersection of the line $4x + y = 5$ and the line $3x - 2y = 12$.

9. Find the image of the point $(-1, 2)$ under the central symmetry in the point $(3, -1)$.

10. Find the image of the point $(2, -3)$ under the translation $(1, -1) \rightarrow (-2, 1)$.

11. $p(-3, -2)$, $q(1, -1)$ and $r(3, 5)$ are three vertices of the parallelogram $pqrs$.
    Find the coordinates of the fourth vertex s.

12. The point $(-3, 4)$ is on the line whose equation is $5x + y + k = 0$. Find the value of k.

13. The point $(k, 1)$ lies on the line $4x - 3y + 15 = 0$. Find the value of k.

14. The point $(t, 2t)$ lies on the line $3x + 2y + 7 = 0$. Find the value of t.

15. Find the coordinates of p, the point of intersection of L and K.
    The equation of the line K is $3x - 2y - 12 = 0$.
    K intersects the x-axis at a and the y-axis at b.
    (i)   Find the coordinates of a and the coordinates of b.
    (ii) Graph the line K.
    (iii) Calculate the area of triangle aob, where o is the origin.

16. $a(1, 2)$, $b(6, 6)$ and $c(4, 8)$ are three points. Find the area of triangle abc.

1. The line L has equation $4x - 5y = -40$.

   $a(0, 8)$ and $b(-10, 0)$ are two points.

   (i) Verify that a and b lie on L.

   (ii) What is the slope of L?

   (iii) The line K is perpendicular to L and it contains b. Find the equation of K.

   (iv) K intersects the y-axis at the point c. Find the coordinates of c.

   (v) d is another point such that $abcd$ is a rectangle. Calculate the area of $abcd$.

   (vi) Find the coordinates of d.

2. The equation of the line L is $2x - y + 4 = 0$.

   L intersects the x-axis at p and the y-axis at q.

   Find the coordinates of p and the coordinates of q. Show L on a diagram.

   The line K passes through $(1, 1)$ and is perpendicular to L.

   Find the equation of K.

   Find the coordinates of the point where K cuts the x-axis.

   Find the coordinates of r, the point of intersection of L and K.

   Find the area of the triangle enclosed by L, K and the x-axis.

3. $a(2, -1)$, $b(-2, 3)$, $c(-1, 1)$ and $d(4, -6)$ are four points.

   (i) Show that ab is parallel to cd.

   (ii) Investigate if $abcd$ is a parallelogram.

   Give a reason for your answer.

4. $p(4, 3)$, $q(-1, 0)$ and $r(10, 3)$ are three points.

   (i) Find the slope of pq.

   (ii) Find the equation of the line through r which is parallel to pq.

   (iii) Find the equation of the line which is perpendicular to pq and which contains the origin.

5. $a(4, 2)$, $b(-2, 0)$ and $c(0, 4)$ are three points.

   (i) Prove that $ac \perp bc$.

   (ii) Prove that $|ac| = |bc|$.

   (iii) Calculate the area of the triangle bac.

   (iv) The diagonals of the square $bahg$ intersect at c.

   Find the coordinates of h and the coordinates of g.

   (v) Find the equation of the line bc and show that h lies on this line.

6. $p(4, -1)$ and $q(-6, 5)$ are two points.

   Find the coordinates of r, the midpoint of $[pq]$.

   Find the equation of the perpendicular bisector of $[pq]$.

   Calculate the ratio $\dfrac{\text{area of triangle } pro}{\text{area of triangle } pqo}$, where o is the origin.

7. **(i)** Explain why $\sqrt{18} = 3\sqrt{2}$.

    (ii) $a(-2, -1)$, $b(1, 0)$ and $c(-5, 2)$ are three points.

        (a) Show that $|ab| = \sqrt{10}$.

        (b) Find $|bc|$.

        (c) Hence, find the ratio $|ab| : |bc|$.

            Give your answer in the form $m : n$, where m and n are whole numbers.

Exercise 7R.C ▼

1. The equation of the line M is $y - 4x - c = 0$.

    M contains the point $p(1, 6)$.

    (i) Find the value c.

    (ii) The origin is the midpoint of $[pq]$.
         Find the equation of the line K, if K is parallel to M and K contains the point q.

    (iii) Find the equation of the line L, if L is perpendicular to M and L contains the point q.

2. The equation of the line L is $x - 2y + 10 = 0$. L contains the point $t(2, 6)$.

    (i) Find the equation of the line N which passes through t and which is perpendicular to L.

    (ii) The line N cuts the x-axis at r and it cuts the y-axis at s.

        Calculate the ratio $\dfrac{|rt|}{|ts|}$.

        Give your answer in the form $\dfrac{p}{q}$, where p and q are whole numbers.

3. **(i)** The line L has the equation $3x - 4y + 20 = 0$.
        K is the line through $p(0, 5)$ which is perpendicular to L.
        Find the equation of K.

    (ii) L cuts the x-axis at the point t. Find the coordinates of t.
        K cuts the x-axis at the point r. Find the coordinates of r.
        Calculate the area of the triangle ptr. Give your answer as a fraction.

4. K is the line which contains the points $a(0, 4)$ and $b(3, 0)$.

    Find the equation of K.

    N is the line which is perpendicular to K and which contains the origin.

    Find the equation of N.

    Investigate if b is the image of a under the axial symmetry in N.

5. $pqrs$ is a parallelogram in which the opposite vertices are $p(2, 1)$ and $r(4, 4)$.

    If the slope of pq is $\frac{1}{3}$ and the slope of $ps = -2$, find:

    (i) the equation of pq

    (ii) the equation of qr.

    (iii) Hence, or otherwise, find the coordinates of q and s.

6. $x(1, 2)$, $y(-2, 1)$ and $z(k, 5)$ are three points.
If $|xy|^2 = |xz|^2$, find the two possible values of k.

7. $c(1, 6)$ and $d(-3, -1)$ are two points. The point r has coordinates $(2, y)$ such that $|cd| = |cr|$.
Find the two possible values of y.

8. $a(0, 5)$, $b(x, 10)$ and $c(2x, x)$ are three points.
Find $|ab|$ in terms of x.
If $|ab| = |bc|$, calculate the two possible values of x.

REVISION EXERCISE 8:
COORDINATE GEOMETRY OF THE CIRCLE

Paper 2   Question 3

This revision exercise covers chapter 6.

Exercise 8R.A ▼

1. The equation of a circle is $x^2 + y^2 = 25$. Write down its centre and radius.

2. C is a circle with centre $(0, 0)$ passing through the point $(8, 6)$.
   Find: **(i)** the radius length of C **(ii)** the equation of C.

3. C is a circle centre $(0, 0)$ and passing through the point $(3, 1)$.
   Find: **(i)** the radius length of C **(ii)** the equation of C.

4. The equation of a circle is $x^2 + y^2 = 36$.
   (i) Write down its radius length.
   (ii) Verify, by calculation, that the point $(2, 3)$ is inside the circle.

5. The circle C has equation $x^2 + y^2 = 16$.
   (i) Write down the length of the radius of C.
   (ii) Show, by calculation, that the point $(3, 1)$ is inside the circle.

6. A circle C, with centre $(0, 0)$, passes through the point $(4, -3)$.
   (i) Find the length of the radius of C.
   (ii) Show, by calculation, that the point $(6, -1)$ lies outside C.

7. Find the equation of the circle, C, with centre $(3, -2)$ and radius $\sqrt{5}$.

8. Find the centre and radius of the circle, K: $(x - 4)^2 + (y + 5)^2 = 9$.

9. The point $(k, 5)$ is on the circle $x^2 + y^2 = 29$. Find the two real values of k.

10. The circle S has equation $(x - 3)^2 + (y - 4)^2 = 25$.
    (i) Write down the centre and the radius of S.
    (ii) The point $(k, 0)$ lies on S. Find the two real values of k.

11. The equation of a circle is $x^2 + y^2 = 49$
    Write down the coordinates of the points where it intersects the x- and y-axes.

12. Write down the coordinates of any three points that lie on the circle with equation $x^2 + y^2 = 100$.

1. The points $(-1, -1)$ and $(3, -3)$ are the end points of a diameter of a circle S.
   Find the: (i) coordinates of the centre of S (ii) radius length of S (iii) equation of S.

2. A circle K has centre $(2, -4)$ and radius length 5.
   (i)   Find the equation of K.
   (ii)   Show, by calculation, that the point $(3, 2)$ lies outside K.
   (iii) Find the coordinates of a and b, the points where K intersects the x-axis.
   (iv)   Find $|ab|$.

3. $a(3, 5)$ and $b(-1, -1)$ are the end points of a diameter of a circle K.
   (i)   Find the centre and radius length of K.
   (ii)   Find the equation of K.
   (iii) K intersects the x-axis at p and q.
          Find the coordinates of p and q.

4. (i)   Find the slope of the tangent to the circle $x^2 + y^2 = 29$ at the point $(2, 5)$.
   (ii)   Hence, find the equation of the tangent.

5. The circle C has equation $(x - 2)^2 + (y + 1)^2 = 8$.
   (i)   Find the coordinates of the two points at which C cuts the y-axis.
   (ii)   Find the equation of the tangent to C at the point $(4, 1)$.

6. The equation of the circle K is $(x - 3)^2 + (y + 2)^2 = 29$.
   (i)   Write down the radius length and the coordinates of the centre of K.
   (ii)   Find the coordinates of the two points where K intersects the x-axis.

7. State the centre and radius length of the circle $K : (x + 1)^2 + (y - 3)^2 = 4$.
   Find the equation of the image of K under the central symmetry in the point $(2, 1)$.

8. State the centre and radius length of the circle $K: (x + 2)^2 + (y - 4)^2 = 25$.
   Find the equation of the image of K under the central symmetry in the point $(-1, 2)$.

9. Prove that the line $x - 3y = 10$ is a tangent to the circle with equation $x^2 + y^2 = 10$ and find the co-ordinates of the point of contact.

10. Prove that line $x - 2y + 10 = 0$ is a tangent to the circle whose equation is $x^2 + y^2 = 20$ and find the coordinates of the point of contact.

11. A circle K has equation $x^2 + y^2 = 10$ and a line L has equation $x + y - 4 = 0$.
    L intersects K at two points, p and q.
    Find the coordinates of p and q.

12. The point $(2, \sqrt{21})$ is on a circle K, centre $(0, 0)$.
    Find the equation of K.
    The line $L : 2x - y + 5 = 0$ meets K at p and q. Calculate the coordinates of p and q.

13. The points $(1, 0)$ and $(4, 4)$ are the end points of a diameter of a circle C.

    (i)   Find the coordinates of the centre of C.

    (ii)   Find the radius length of C.

    (iii) Find the equation of C.

14. The vertices of a square are $a(1, 3)$, $b(5, 3)$, $c(5, -1)$ and $d(1, -1)$.
A circle K touches the four sides of $abcd$.

    (i)   Write down the coordinates of the centre, and length of the radius, of K.

    (ii)   Hence write down the equation of K.

The circle C passes through the four points a, b, c and d.

    (iii) Find the equation of C.

    (iv) Calculate the ratio $\dfrac{\text{area of } K}{\text{area of } C}$.

Exercise 8R.C ▼

1. A circle K has equation $x^2 + y^2 = 25$.

    (i) T is a tangent to K at $(3, 4)$.

         Find the equation of T.

    (ii)   Find the equation of the other tangent to K which is parallel to T.

2. A circle K has equation $x^2 + y^2 = 17$.

    (i) T is a tangent to K at $(-4, -1)$.

         Find the equation of T.

    (ii)   Find the equation of the other tangent to K which is parallel to T, and the distance between T and K.

3. The equation of the circle, C, is $(x + 1)^2 + (y - 1)^2 = 13$.

    Find the centre and radius of C.

    Show that the point $(2, -1)$ is on C and represent C on a diagram.

    T is a tangent to C at $(2, -1)$.

    Find the equation of T.

    K is a second tangent to C and $K \parallel T$.

    Find the equation of K and the distance between T and K.

4. The line with equation $3x - y + 10 = 0$ is a tangent to the circle which has equation $x^2 + y^2 = 10$.

    (i)   Find the coordinates of a, the point at which the line touches the circle.

    (ii)   The origin is the midpoint of $[ab]$.

         Find the equation of the tangent to the circle at b.

5. (i) The end points of a diameter of a circle are $(-2, -3)$ and $(-4, 3)$.
Find the equation of the circle.

(ii) The circle cuts the y-axis at the points a and b.
Find $|ab|$.

(iii) c and d are points on the circle such that $abcd$ is a rectangle.
Find the area of the rectangle $abcd$.

6. $a(-5, 1)$, $b(3, 7)$ and $c(9, -1)$ are three points.

(i) Show that the triangle abc is right-angled at b.

(ii) Find the coordinates of the midpoint of $[ac]$ and find the equation of the circle that passes through a, b and c.

7. C is the circle with centre $(-1, 2)$ and radius 5. Write down the equation of C.
The circle K has equation $(x - 8)^2 + (y - 14)^2 = 100$.
Prove that the point $p(2, 6)$ is on C and on K.
Show that p lies on the line which joins the centres of the two circles.

8. $a(-1, 0)$ and $b(5, 0)$ are the end points of a diameter of a circle K with centre c.

(i) Write down the coordinates of c and the radius length of K.

(ii) Find the equation of K.

(iii) T is a tangent to K and T is parallel to the x-axis. Find the two possible equations for T.

(iv) If $cq \perp ac$, where $q \in K$, find the area of the shaded region in terms of π.

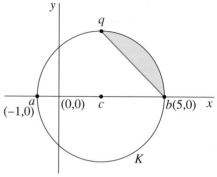

9. C is a circle with centre $(0, 0)$. It passes through the point $(1, -5)$.

(i) Write down the equation of C.

(ii) The point (p, p) lies inside C, where $p \in \mathbf{Z}$.
Find all the possible values of p.

10. Points $o(0, 0)$, $p(12, 0)$ and $q(6, 8)$ form a triangle in which $|qp| = |qo|$.

Circles S_1, S_2 and S_3, each of radius length 5, have o, p and q, respectively, as centres. S_1, S_3 and S_2, S_3 touch as shown.

Write the equations of:

(i) S_1

(ii) S_2

(iii) S_3.

Find the equation of T, the tangent common to S_1 and S_3.

Find the equation of K, the tangent common to S_1 and S_3.
Find the point of intersection of T and K.

11. Write down the equations of the circles:

    (i) K_1, centre $(0, 0)$, radius length 10

    (ii) K_2, centre $(3, 4)$, when K_2 contains $(0, 0)$

    (iii) K_3, centre $(-3, -4)$, when K_3 contains $(0, 0)$.

Find:

    (iv) the equation of the tangent T through $(0, 0)$ and common to K_2 and K_3

    (v) the coordinates of the points p and q, the point of intersection of T and K.

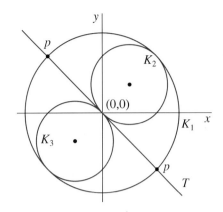

12. (i) The circle S_1 has equation $x^2 + y^2 = 20$.

    Write down the radius of S_1.

  (ii) The line T has equation $x + 2y - 10 = 0$.

    Find the coordinates of r, the point of intersection of T and S_1.

  (iii) The circle S_2 is the image of the circle S_1 under an axial symmetry in T.

    Write down the equation of S_2.

  (iv) Find the coordinates of p and q, points in which S_2 intersects the y-axis.

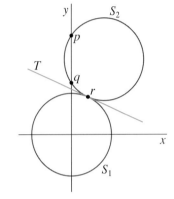

REVISION EXERCISE 9: GEOMETRY

Paper 2   Question 4

This revision exercise covers chapter 15.

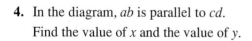
Exercise 9R.A ▼

1. The lines *L* and *M* are parallel.
Find the value of:

(i)   *p*

(ii)   *q*

(iii)   *r*

(iv)   *s*.

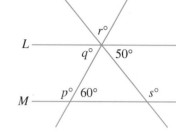

2. Lines *P* and *Q* in the diagram are parallel.
Find the value of:

(i)   *t*

(ii)   *s*.

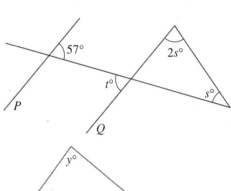

3. The diagram shows a triangle.
Find the value of *x* and the value of *y*.

4. In the diagram, *ab* is parallel to *cd*.
Find the value of *x* and the value of *y*.

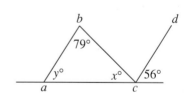

5. In the triangle *abc*, | *ad* | = | *bd* |,
| ∠*abd* | = | ∠*dbc* | and | ∠*dab* | = 48°.
Find | ∠*dcb* |.

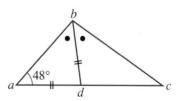

6. $|pr| = |qr| = |rs|$ and $|\angle prq| = 50°$.
Find:
   (i) $|\angle pqr|$
   (ii) $|\angle psr|$.

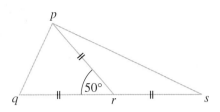

7. pqr is a triangle and ts is a line parallel to qr.
$|\angle tpq| = 56°$, $|\angle spr| = 33°$.
Find:
   (i) $|\angle pqr|$ **(ii)** $|\angle rpq|$.

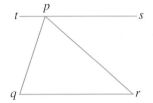

8. **(i)** Find the value of x and y.   **(ii)** Evaluate $X + Y + Z$.

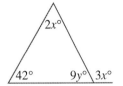 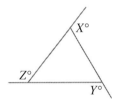

9. From the parallelogram shown, find the value of x and the value of y.

10. The diagram shows a parallelogram.
Find the value of:
   (i) p
   (ii) q
   (iii) r
   (iv) s.

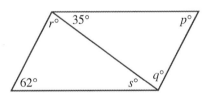

11. From the parallelogram shown, find the value of:
   (i) x
   (ii) y
   (iii) s
   (iv) t.

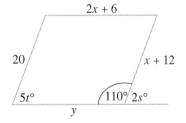

12. $[pq]$ is a diameter of the circle, centre c, and
$|pr| = |rq|$.
Calculate the value of:
   (i) y
   (ii) x.

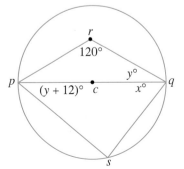

13. [*mn*] is the diameter of a circle, centre *o*.
|*no*| = |*ok*| = |*kn*|. Find:

   (i) |∠*nko*|

   (ii) |∠*okm*|

   (iii) |∠*mok*|.

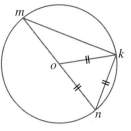

14. Prove that the triangle with sides of lengths 10 units, 24 units and 26 units is right-angled.

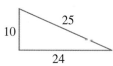

15. Find the values of *x* and *y*.

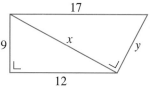

16. In the diagram, |∠*abc*| = 90°, |*ab*| = 23.2 and |*bc*| = 17.4. Calculate |*ac*|.

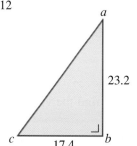

17. In the diagram, *pt* is a tangent to the circle of centre *o*, at *t*. |*op*| = 17 cm and |*pt*| = 15 cm. Calculate the radius of the circle.

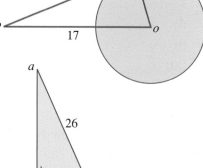

18. Find the area of the triangle *abc* if |∠*abc*| = 90°, |*ac*| = 26 and |*bc*| = 10.

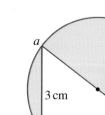

19. *a*, *b* and *c* are points on a circle with centre *o*. [*ac*] is a diameter of the circle.
|*ab*| = 3 cm, |*bc*| = 4 cm and |∠*acb*| = 37°.

   (i) Give a reason why ∠*abc* is a right angle.

   (ii) Find |∠*bac*|.

   (iii) Calculate the length of the diameter [*ac*].

   (iv) Calculate the area of the shaded region. (Assume π = 3.14.)

20. abc is a triangle with $|ab| = 8$, $|bc| = 4$ and $|\angle acb| = 90°$.
Calculate $|ac|$, correct to two places of decimals.

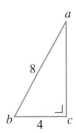

1. Prove that the sum of the degree-measures of the angles of a triangle is 180°.
Hence:

   (i) Prove that the degree-measure of an exterior angle of a triangle is equal to the sum of the degree-measures of the two remote interior angles.

   (ii) Prove that an exterior angle of a triangle is greater than either remote (opposite) interior angle.

2. Prove that opposite sides of a parallelogram have equal lengths.

3. Prove that if three parallel lines make intercepts of equal length on a transversal, then they will also make intercepts of equal length on any other transversal.

4. Prove that a line which is parallel to one side-line of a triangle, and cuts a second side, will cut the third side in the same proportion as the second.

5. Prove that if the three angles of one triangle have degree-measures equal, respectively, to the degree-measures of the angles of a second triangle, then the lengths of the corresponding sides of the two triangles are proportional.

6. Prove that in a right-angled triangle, the square of the length of the side opposite to the right-angle is equal to the sum of the squares of the lengths of the other two sides.

7. Prove that if the square of the length of one side of a triangle is equal to the sum of the squares of the lengths of the other two sides, then the triangle has a right angle, and this is opposite the longest side.

8. Prove that the products of the lengths of the sides of a triangle by the corresponding altitudes are equal.

9. Prove that if the lengths of the two sides of a triangle are unequal, then the degree-measures of the angles opposite to them are unequal, with the greater angle opposite to the longer side.

10. Prove that the sum of the lengths of any two sides of a triangle is greater than that of the third side.

1. The triangle xyz is the image of the triangle abc under the enlargement, centre o, with $|ab| = 4$ and $|xz| = 12$. The scale factor of the enlargement is 1.5.

   (i) Find $|xy|$.

   (ii) Find $|ac|$.

   (iii) If the area of triangle abc is 12.2 square units, calculate the area of triangle xyz.

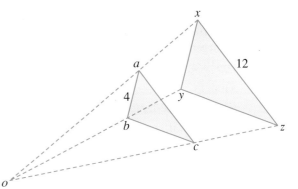

2. The triangle *xzy* is the image of the triangle *dgh* under the enlargement, centre *o*, with $|dg| = 8$, $|xz| = 12$ and $|xy| = 9$.

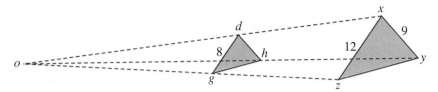

(i) Find the scale factor of the enlargement.

(ii) Find $|dh|$.

(iii) The area of the triangle *xzy* is 27 square units. Find the area of triangle *dgh*.

3. The triangle *ors* is the image of the triangle *opq* under an enlargement, centre *o*.

$|op| = 4$, $|pr| = 6$.

(i) Find the scale factor of the enlargement.

(ii) Given the area of triangle *opq* to be 6 square units, find the area of the triangle *ors*.

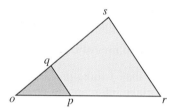

4. The triangle *ocd* is the image of the triangle *opq* under the enlargement, centre *o*, with $|pq| = 4$, $|op| = 5$ and $|cd| = 9$.

(i) Find the scale factor of the enlargement.

(ii) Find $|pc|$.

(iii) The area of the triangle *ocd* is 60.75 square units. Find the area of the triangle *opq*.

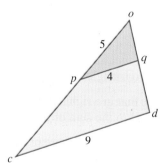

5. The triangle *odc* is the image of the triangle *oab* under an enlargement, centre *o*.

$|cd| = 9$ and $|ab| = 15$.

(i) Find the scale factor of the enlargement.

(ii) If the area of triangle *oab* is 87.5 square units, find the area of triangle *odc*.

(iii) Write down the area of the region *abcd*.

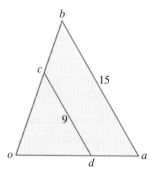

6. The triangle *ors* is the image of the triangle *opq* under an enlargement, centre *o*.

$|op| = 4$, $|pr| = 10$.

Find:

(i) the scale factor of the enlargement

(ii) $|qs|$, if $|oq| = 3.2$

(iii) $|pq| : |rs|$

(iv) the area of the triangle *ors*, given the area of triangle *opq* to be 4 square units.

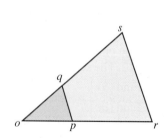

7. The rectangle *aefg* is an enlargement of the rectangle *abcd* with $|ac| = 5$, $|cf| = 3$.

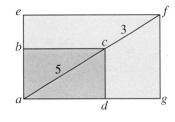

    (i) Write down the centre of enlargement.

    (ii) Find k, the scale factor of the enlargement.

    (iii) If the area of the rectangle *aefg* is 62.72 square units, find the area of the rectangle *abcd*.

    (iv) A further enlargement will map rectangle *aefg* back onto the rectangle *abcd*.

    Find the scale factor, if the centre of enlargement remains the same.

8. Triangle *xyz* is the image of triangle *abc*, under an enlargement, centre *o*.

If the area of triangle *abc* = 40 cm^2 and the area of triangle *xyz* = 25.6 cm^2, find:

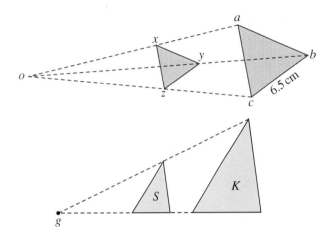

    (i) the scale factor of enlargement, k

    (ii) $|yz|$ if $|bc| = 6.5$ cm.

9. A large triangle, *K*, is the image of a small triangle, *S*, under an enlargement, centre *g*. If area $K = 97.28$ cm^2 and area $S = 38$ cm^2, calculate the scale factor of the enlargement.

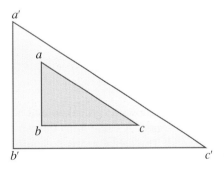

10. A photograph has area 80 cm^2.

This photograph is enlarged to give a photograph of area 288.8 cm^2.

Find the scale factor of the enlargement.

In the original photograph, a door was 2.4 cm wide.

How wide will the door measure in the enlarged photograph?

11. The triangle *a'b'c'* is the image of the triangle *abc* under an enlargement.

    (i) Find, by measurement, the scale factor of the enlargement.

    (ii) Copy the diagram and show how to find the centre of the enlargement.

    (iii) Units are chosen so that $|bc| = 8$ units. How many of these units is $|b'c'|$?

    (iv) Find the area of triangle *abc*, given that the area of *a'b'c'* is 84 square units.

12. **(i)** Draw a square with sides 7 cm and mark *o*, the point of intersection of the diagonals.

    (ii) Draw the image of the square under the enlargement with centre *o* and scale factor $\frac{1}{2}$.

    (iii) Calculate the area of the image square.

    (iv) Under another enlargement the area of the image of the square with sides 7 cm is 196 cm^2. What is the scale factor of this enlargement?

REVISION EXERCISE 10: TRIGONOMETRY

Paper 2   Question 5

This revision exercise covers chapter 13.

Exercise 10R.A ▼

1. *abc* is a right-angled triangle with $|\angle acb| = 90°$, $|ab| = 13$, $|bc| = 5$ and $|ac| = 12$.
   Find, as fractions, the value of $\sin \angle abc$ and the value of $\tan \angle bac$.

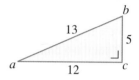

2. Sin $\theta = \frac{3}{5}$, where $0° < 0 < 90°$.
   Find, without using the Tables or a calculator, the value of:
   (i) $\cos \theta$
   (ii) $\cos 2\theta$. [Note: $\cos 2\theta = \cos^2 \theta - \sin^2 \theta$.]

3. Use the information given in the diagram to show that
   $\sin \theta + \cos \theta > \tan \theta$.

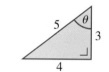

4. If $\tan A = \frac{8}{15}$, $0° \leqslant A \leqslant 90°$, express $\sin A$ and $\cos A$ as fractions.
   (i) Show that $\cos 2A = \frac{161}{289}$ $[\cos 2A = \cos^2 A - \sin^2 A]$
   (ii) Verify that $\sin^2 A + \cos^2 A = 1$.

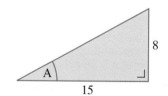

5. The diagram shows a vertical pole of height 12 m, which stands on level ground. A cable joins the top of the pole to a point on the ground. The cable makes an angle of 59° with the ground. Find the length of the cable, correct to the nearest metre.

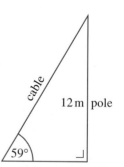

6. $|ad| = 6$ cm, $|db| = 9$ cm, $|\angle cad| = 35°$ and $cd \perp ab$.
   Find:
   (i) $|cd|$, correct to one decimal place
   (ii) $|\angle cbd|$, correct to the nearest degree.

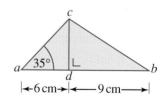

7. In the triangle abc, $|ab| = 7$ m, $|bc| = 8$ m and $|\angle abc| = 42°$.

Calculate the area of the triangle, correct to one place of decimals.

8. In the triangle xyz, $|xy| = 3$ cm, $|yz| = 4$ cm and $|\angle xyz| = 60°$.

Use the cosine rule to find $|xz|$, correct to one place of decimals.

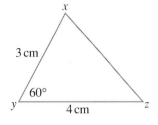

9. In the diagram, o is the centre of the circle of radius length 14 cm.

Assuming $\pi = \frac{22}{7}$, calculate the length of the minor arc pq, given $|\angle poq| = 45°$.

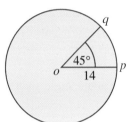

10. The angle at the centre of a sector of a disc measures 140°.

The radius of the disc measures 6 cm.

Find, in terms of π, the area of the minor sector.

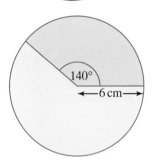

11. Find the length of an arc of a circle of radius length 6 cm subtending an angle of 120° at the centre.

Give your answer in terms of π.

12. Find the length of an arc of a circle of radius length 3 cm subtending an angle of 60° at the centre. Give your answer in terms of π.

Exercise 10R.B ▼

1. The diagram shows a vertical pole which stands on level ground.

A cable joins the top of the pole to a point on the ground which is 50 m from the base of the pole.

The cable makes an angle of 66.3° with the ground.

(i) Find the height of the pole, correct to the nearest metre.

(ii) Find the length of the cable, correct to the nearest metre.

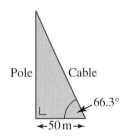

2. In the diagram, o is the centre of the circle with radius length 5 and p and q are points on the circle. $|\angle poq| = 80°$.

Find, correct to two places of decimals:

(i) the area of triangle poq

(ii) the area of the shaded region, assuming, $\pi = 3.14$.

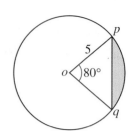

3. opq is a sector of a circle of radius 18 cm where $|\angle poq| = 40°$.

Calculate the area of the shaded region, correct to two decimal places. (Assume $\pi = 3.14$.)

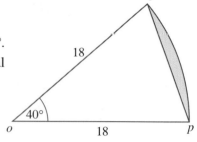

4. A is an acute angle such that $\tan A = \frac{21}{20}$

(i) Find, as fractions, the value of cos A and the value of sin A.

(ii) Find the measurement of angle A, correct to the nearest degree.

5. θ is an acute angle such that $\tan \theta = \frac{5}{12}$

Find, as a fraction, the value of $\cos 2\theta$. (Note: $\cos 2\theta = \cos^2 \theta - \sin^2 \theta$)

6. A and B are acute angles where $\sin A = \frac{3}{5}$ and $\cos B = \frac{5}{13}$

(i) Find, as fractions, the value of cos A and the value of sin B.

(ii) Find, as fractions, the values of:

(a) $\sin(A + B)$ **(b)** $\cos(A + B)$ **(c)** $\sin 2A$ **(d)** $\cos 2A$

(Note: $\sin 2A = 2 \sin A \cos A$ and $\cos 2A = \cos^2 A - \sin^2 A$)

7. In the triangle abc, $|ab| = 3$ units, $|bc| = 7$ units and $|\angle abc| = 67°$.

(i) Calculate the area of the triangle abc, correct to one decimal place.

(ii) Calculate $|ac|$, correct to the nearest whole number.

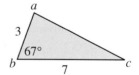

8. A plot of land has a triangular shape pqr, as shown, where $|pq| = 40$ m and $|pr| = 60$ m.

Find:

(i) the area of triangle pqr, correct to the nearest m^2

(ii) $|qr|$, correct to the nearest metre.

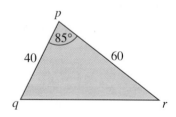

9. In triangle abc, $|ac| = 7$ cm, $|\angle abc| = 30°$ and $|\angle abc| = 80°$.

Calculate $|ab|$, correct to one decimal place.

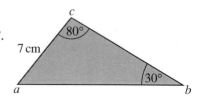

10. pqs is a triangle in which $|pq| = 8$ cm, $|ps| = 5$ cm, $|\angle spq| = 75°$.
Calculate $|sq|$, correct to one decimal place.

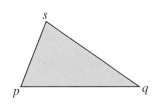

11. Find the size of the greatest angle of the triangle which has sides of length 3, 5 and 7.

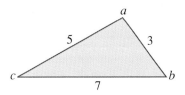

12. A garden $pqrs$ is in the shape of a quadrilateral.
$|pq| = 15$ m, $|ps| = 8$ m, $|rs| = 9$ m, $|\angle spq| = 90°$ and $|\angle qrs| = 80°$.
Find the value of:

(i) $|qs|$

(ii) $|\angle rqs|$, to the nearest degree.

Find $|pr|$, correct to one decimal place.

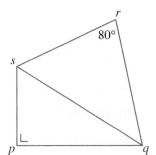

13. In the triangle rst, $|rs| = 15$, $|rt| = 9$ and $|\angle rts| = 120.69°$.
Calculate $|\angle srt|$, giving your answer correct to two decimal places.

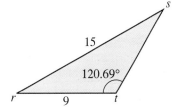

14. A ship, q, is 7 km from a port, p.
The direction of q from p is N 45° E.
A second ship, r, is 4.2 km from q.
The direction of r from q is S 75° E.

Calculate the distance from the port p to the ship r.

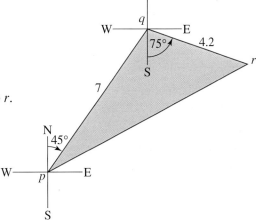

15. (i) θ is an acute angle such that $\cos \theta = \frac{2}{5}$. Find the value of $\sin \theta$ in surd form.

(ii) In a triangle xyz, $|xy| = 10$, $|yz| = 7$ and $\cos \angle xyz = \frac{2}{5}$.
Find the area of triangle xyz, giving your answer in the form $a\sqrt{b}$, where $a, b \in \mathbf{N}$.

501

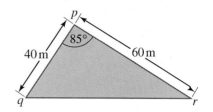

1. A plot of land has a triangular shape *pqr*, as shown.
Find:

   (i) the area of triangle *pqr*, correct to the nearest m^2

   (ii) $|qr|$, correct to the nearest metre.

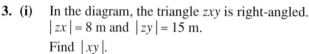

2. *xyz* is a triangle where $|xy| = 15$ cm, $|yz| = 22$ cm and $|\angle xyz| = 74°$.

Find:

   (i) the area of triangle *xyz*, correct to the nearest cm^2

   (ii) $|xz|$, correct to the nearest cm

   (iii) $|\angle yxz|$, correct to the nearest degree.

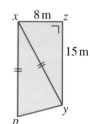

3. (i) In the diagram, the triangle *zxy* is right-angled.
$|zx| = 8$ m and $|zy| = 15$ m.
Find $|xy|$.

   (ii) *xp* is parallel to *zy*.
$|xp| = |xy|$, as shown.
Calculate $|py|$, correct to the nearest metre.

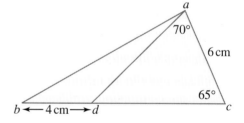

4. *abc* is a triangle and $d \in [bc]$, as shown.
If $|bd| = 4$ cm, $|ac| = 6$ cm, $|\angle acd| = 65°$
and $|\angle dac| = 70°$, find:

   (i) $|dc|$, correct to the nearest cm

   (ii) the area of triangle *abc*, correct to the nearest cm^2.

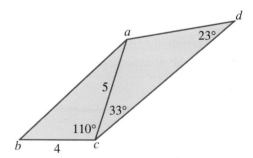

5. In the quadrilateral *abcd*, $|ac| = 5$ units,
$|bc| = 4$ units, $|\angle bca| = 110°$, $|\angle acd| = 33°$
and $|\angle cda| = 23°$.

   (i) Calculate $|ab|$, correct to two decimal places.

   (ii) Calculate $|cd|$, correct to two decimal places.

6. Three ships are situated in a straight line at points a, b and c.

p is a port such that
$|\angle bap| = 55°$, $|\angle abp| = 110°$,
$|ab| = 10$ km and $|bc| = 20$ km.

Calculate:

(i) $|bp|$, correct to the nearest km

(ii) $|cp|$, correct to the nearest km.

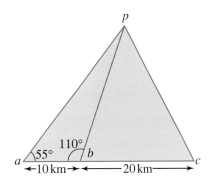

7. Two ships, A and B, leave port k at noon. A is travelling due East and B is travelling East 70° South, as shown.

Calculate, to the nearest km, the distance between A and B when A is 8 km from k and B is 12 km from k.

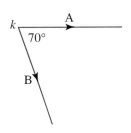

8. A ship leaves a port p and sails in a direction S 36° E to reach a port q. It then sets out from the port q on a course S 52° W to reach another port r, which is directly south of p. If the distance from p to r is 80 km, calculate the distance sailed by the ship, correct to the nearest km.

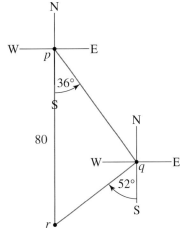

9. s and t are two points 300 m apart on a straight path due north.

From s the bearing of a pillar is N 40° E.
From t the bearing of the pillar is N 70° E.

(i) Show that the distance from t to the pillar is 386 m, correct to the nearest metre.

(ii) Find the shortest distance from the path to the pillar, correct to the nearest metre.

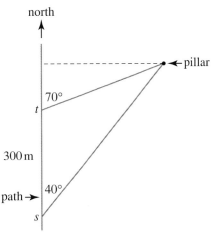

10. (i) Calculate sin 43°, correct to two decimal places.

(ii) In triangle abc, $|ab| = 16$ cm, and $|\angle bac| = 43°$. If the area of triangle $abc = 81.6$ cm², find $|ac|$, using the value of sin 43° obtained in part **(i)**.

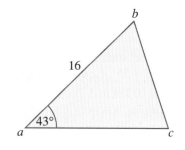

11. In the triangle xyz, $|xz| - 40$ cm and $|yz| = 50$ cm. If the area of triangle xyz is 940 cm², calculate $|\angle xyz|$, correct to the nearest degree.

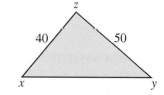

12. Find, in surd form: **(i)** cos 210° **(ii)** tan 150°.

13. Write cos 75° in surd form.

14. (i) Find the value of A for which $\sin A = -1$, $0° \leqslant A \leqslant 360°$.

(ii) If $0° \leqslant A \leqslant 360°$, find the two values of A for which $\cos A = 1$.

(iii) Evaluate $\cos^2 180°$.

(iv) If $\sin A = 0$, find the three values of A, $0° \leqslant A \leqslant 360°$.

15. If $\sin \theta = -\dfrac{1}{\sqrt{2}}$, find the two values of θ, $0° \leqslant A \leqslant 360°$.

16. $\text{Sin } \theta = \dfrac{\sqrt{3}}{2}$

Write two values for θ in $0° \leqslant \theta \leqslant 180°$.

Hence, write the two corresponding values for $\cos \theta$.

17. If $\cos A = -0.7914$, find the two values of A in $0° \leqslant A \leqslant 360°$, correct to the nearest degree.

18. An arc of length 48 cm subtends an angle A at o. Calculate A, correct to the nearest degree.

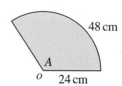

REVISION EXERCISE 11: PERMUTATIONS, COMBINATIONS AND PROBABILITY

Paper 2   Question 6

This revision exercise covers chapter 12.

Exercise 11R.A ▼

1. A letter is selected at random from the letters of the word $M\,I\,S\,S\,I\,S\,S\,I\,P\,P\,I$.
   Find the probability that the letter is:
   (i) M **(ii)** S or P **(iii)** a vowel.

2. A bag contains 24 beads of which 12 are red, 8 are blue and 4 are white.
   A bead is taken at random from the bag.
   What is the probability that the colour of the bead is:
   (i)   blue?   **(ii)** red or white?

3. A hat contains 40 tickets. 11 of these tickets are red, 9 are green and 20 are white.
   One ticket is picked at random from the hat.
   Find the probability that it is: **(i)** red   **(ii)** green   **(iii)** not green.

4. The place-name $B\,A\,L\,L\,Y\,N\,A\,H\,I\,N\,C\,H$ is printed on a card. The first 6 letters are printed in red and the rest are printed in green. The card is cut so that each letter is on a separate piece. The pieces are put in a bag.
   When one piece is taken out at random, what is the probability that it is:
   (i)   a green letter?   **(ii)** the letter A in red?   **(iii)** the letter N or a red letter?

5. One hundred students, girls and boys, took an examination and the grades achieved are recorded in the following table:

Grade	A	B	C	D	E
Number of girls	8	20	18	10	4
Number of boys	4	16	10	6	4

   If a student is selected at random, what is the probability that the student is a:
   (i)   boy who got grade A?
   (ii) boy or girl who got grade B?
   (iii) girl who got grade A or grade B?

6. A number is chosen at random from the whole numbers 1 to 24.

   What is the probability that the number is:

   (i) even? **(ii)** divisible by 6? **(iii)** even or divisible by 6?

   (iv) odd? **(v)** divisible by 3? **(vi)** even or divisible by 3?

7. A card is drawn at random from a pack of 52. What is the probability that:

   (i) it is a club? **(ii)** it is a king?

   (iii) it is a queen or a king? **(iv)** it is a spade or an ace?

8. A class of 29 students wins a prize. Two members of the class are chosen to receive the prize. How many different pairs of students can be chosen?

9. **(i)** In how many ways can a team of 5 players be chosen from a panel of 8 players?

   (ii) If a certain player must be on the team, in how many ways can the team then be chosen?

10. There are eight questions on an examination paper.

    (i) In how many different ways can a candidate select six questions?

    (ii) In how many different ways can a candidate select six questions if one particular question must always be selected?

11. To go to work, a woman can walk or travel by bus or travel by car with a neighbour.

    To return home, she can walk or travel by bus.

    (i) In how many different ways can the woman go to and return from work on any one day?

    (ii) List all of these different ways.

12. Three cards, numbered 3, 4 and 5 respectively, are to be shuffled and placed in a row so that the numbers are visible.

    List the six possible outcomes.

    Find the probability that:

    (i) the numbers are 3, 4, 5 in that order

    (ii) the middle number is 4

    (iii) the number on the right is less than the middle number

    (iv) the first and second numbers are each odd.

Exercise 11R.B ▼

1. There are three balls in a bag, one green, one red, one blue. When a fair die is rolled a ball is also taken from the bag at random. What is the probability of:

   (i) a red ball and a six?

   (ii) a green ball and an even number?

2. A meeting is attended by 23 men and 21 women.

   Of the men, 14 are married and the others are single.

   Of the women, 8 are married and the others are single.

   (i) A person is picked at random. What is the probability that the person is a woman?

   (ii) A person is picked at random. What is the probability that the person is married?

(iii) A man is picked at random. What is the probability that he is married?

(iv) A woman is picked at random. What is the probability that she is single?

3. A coin and a die are thrown.

   Write down the probability of obtaining:

   (i) a tail and an odd number **(ii)** a head or a number greater than or equal to 5.

4. A 'spinner' used in a game has 10 sections, of which 5 are coloured red, 3 green and 2 blue.

   The spinner is spun once. What is the probability of obtaining:

   (i) a blue?

   (ii) a green?

   (iii) a red?

   (iv) a red or a green?

   (v) a blue or a red?

   If the spinner is spun twice, calculate the probability of obtaining:

   (vi) two reds

   (vii) two blues

   (viii) a red and a blue (in that order).

5. In a class, there are 15 boys and 13 girls. Four boys wear glasses and three girls wear glasses.

   A pupil is picked at random from the class.

   (i) What is the probability that the pupil is a boy?

   (ii) What is the probability that the pupil wears glasses?

   (iii) What is the probability that the pupil is a boy who wears glasses?

   A girl is picked at random from the class.

   (iv) What is the probability that she wears glasses?

6. There are 40 people in a club, 24 male, 16 female.

   Four of the males and two of the females wear glasses.

   When a person is selected at random what is the probability that the person is a:

   (i) male?

   (ii) female not wearing glasses?

   (iii) female wearing glasses or a male not wearing glasses?

   (iv) male, given that the person wears glasses?

7. Sarah and Jim celebrate their birthdays in a particular week (Monday to Sunday inclusive).

   Assuming that the birthdays are equally likely to fall on any day of the week, what is the probability that:

   (i) Sarah's birthday is on Friday?

   (ii) Sarah's birthday and Jim's birthday are both on Friday?

8. Seven people take part in a chess competition. How many games will be played if every person must play each of the others?

9. In how many ways can a selection of 5 books be made from 12?
    (i)   If a certain book must always be chosen, in how many ways can the selection be made?
    (ii) If a certain book must never be chosen, in how many ways can the selection be made?

10. A committee of 4 people is to be formed from a group of 7 men and 6 women.
    (i)   How many different committees can be formed?
    (ii) On how many of these committees is there an equal number of men and of women?

11. How many different arrangements, taking 3 letters at a time, can be formed from the word *PHOENIX*?

12. A number-plate is to consist of three letters of the English alphabet and two digits. If no letter or digit can be repeated and 0 can never be used as the first digit, how many different plates can be manufactured?

(an example)

13. There are 5 horses — *A*, *B*, *C*, *D* and *E* — in a race. Each horse takes a different time to complete the race. On completing the race:
    (i)   in how many different placing arrangements can the 5 horses finish?
    (ii) if *A* is placed first and *B* last, in how many different placing arrangements can the other horses finish?

14. (i)   How many different arrangements can be made using all the letters of the word *IRELAND*?
    (ii) How many arrangements begin with the letter *I*?
    (iii) How many arrangements end with the word *LAND*?
    (iv) How many begin with *I* and end with *LAND*?

15. (i)   In how many different ways can the 5 letters of the word *A N G L E* be arranged?
    (ii) How many of these arrangements begin with a vowel?
    (iii) In how many of the arrangements do the two vowels come together?

16. (i)   How many different permutations can be made using all of the letters of the word *SQUARE*?
    (ii) How many begin with the letter *S*?
    (iii) How many begin with the letter *S* and end with the letter *E*?
    (iv) In how many of these permutations are the three vowels the first three letters?

17. How many different arrangements can be made from the letters *V, W, X, Y, Z*, taking all the letters at a time, if *V* must be second and *Z* can never be last?

18. How many different five-digit numbers can be formed from the digits, 1, 2, 3, 4 and 5, if no digit can be repeated and:
    (i)   there are no restrictions on digits?
    (ii) the number is odd?
    (iii) the number is even?
    (iv) the number is greater than 30,000?

19. How many different four-digit numbers can be formed from the digits 2, 4, 6 and 8, if no digit can be used more than once in a number?
    How many of these numbers:
    (i)   are greater than 6,000?   (ii) end with 8?

508

1. Two unbiased dice are thrown, one red and the other black, and the scores are added.

   The faces of the red die are numbered 1, 2, 3, 4, 5 and 6.

   The faces of the black die are numbered 1, 1, 2, 3, 3 and 4.

   Find the probability of obtaining:

   (i) a score of 5   **(ii)** a score of 6 or more   **(iii)** a score of less than 4.

2. A game consists of spinning an unbiased arrow on a square board and throwing an unbiased die.

   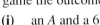

   The board contains the letters *A*, *B*, *C* and *D*. The board is so designed that when the arrow stops spinning it can point only at one letter and it is equally likely to point at *A* or *B* or *C* or *D*.

   List all possible outcomes of the game, that is, of spinning the arrow and throwing the die. Find the probability that in any one game the outcome will be:

   (i) an *A* and a 6

   (ii) a *B* and an even number

   (iii) an *A* and an even number or a *B* and an odd number

   (iv) a *C* and a number ⩾ 4 or a *D* and a number ⩽ 2.

3. A bag contains 5 red and 3 yellow discs only. When a disc is drawn from the bag, it is returned before the next draw. What is the probability that two draws will yield:

   (i) both discs yellow?   **(ii)** both discs the same colour?

4. Twelve blood samples are tested in a laboratory. Of these it is found that five blood samples are of type A, four of type B and the remaining three are of type O.

   Two blood samples are selected at random from the twelve.

   What is the probability that:

   (i) the two samples are of type A?

   (ii) one sample is of type B and the other sample is of type O?

   (iii) the two samples are of the same blood type?

5. **(i)** How many different numbers, each with 3 digits or fewer, can be formed from the digits 1, 2, 3, 4, 5? Each digit can be used only once in each number.

   (ii) How many of the above numbers are even?

6. The digits 0, 1, 2, 3, 4, 5 are used to form four-digit codes. A code cannot begin with 0 and no digit is repeated in any code.

   (i) Write down the largest possible four-digit code.

   (ii) Write down the smallest possible four-digit code.

   (iii) How many four-digit codes can be formed?

   (iv) How many of the four-digit codes are greater than 4,000?

7. (i) How many different five-digit numbers can be formed from the digits 2, 3, 4, 5, 6? Each digit can be used once only in each number.

(ii) How many of the numbers are even?

(iii) How many of the numbers are less than 40,000?

(iv) How many of the numbers are both even and less than 40,000?

8. (i) Eight points lie on a circle, as in the diagram.

How many different lines can be drawn by joining any two of the eight points?

(ii) Find the value of the natural number n such that $\binom{n}{2} = 105$.

9. Two people are chosen at random from a large crowd. Each person names the day of the week on which he or she was born. Assuming that each day is equally likely, what is the probability that:

(i) both people were born on a Friday?

(ii) one person was born on a Tuesday and the other was born on a Thursday?

(iii) the two people were born on different days?

10. A committee of two people is chosen at random from 4 men and 5 women.

What is the probability that there will be either one woman or two women on the committee?

11. A bag contains 5 red buttons, 3 black buttons and 7 pink buttons. A button is removed at random from the bag and not replaced. Then a second button is removed.

Find the probability that:

(i) both buttons are pink

(ii) the first button is black and the second is red

(iii) both buttons are the same colour.

REVISION EXERCISE 12: STATISTICS

Paper 2   Question 7

This revision exercise covers chapter 3.

Exercise 12R.A ▼

1. Calculate the mean of the following numbers: 1, 0, 1, 5, 2, 3, 9.

2. Find the median of the following array of numbers: 5, 4, 8, 7, 4, 3.

3. Find the mean and the median of the following array of numbers: 2, 5, 7, 11, 15, 3, 6.

4. **(i)**   Calculate the mean of the following numbers: 2, 3, 5, 7, 8.
   (ii) Hence, calculate the standard deviation of the numbers, correct to one decimal place.

5. Calculate: **(i)** the median   **(ii)** the mean   **(iii)** the standard deviation,
   correct to two decimal places, of the array of numbers: 2, 6, 1, 8, 3.

6. Four people have a meal in a restaurant. The average cost of the meal per person is €12.50, excluding the service charge. What is the total bill for the four people if a 10% service charge is added?

7. The table shows the distribution of ages of a group of 100 people.

Age (in years)	0–10	10–20	20–30	30–50	50–80
Number of people	10	19	25	30	16

   [Note that 10–20 means that 10 is included but 20 is not, etc.]
   Taking 5, 15, etc. as mid-interval values, estimate the mean age of the people in the group.

8. Find the weighted mean of 11, 15, 19 and 21 if the weights are 2, 3, 1 and 2 respectively.

9.

Subject	Physics	Chemistry	Mathematics	Irish
Mark	74	65	82	58
Weight	3	4	5	2

   The table shows a student's marks and the weights given to these marks.
   Calculate the weighted mean mark for the student.

10. Two people A and B scored marks as shown:

Subject		English	Irish	Mathematics
Marks	A	40	74	90
	B	50	60	90

If weights of 4, 3, 3, respectively, are assigned to English, Irish and Mathematics, find which of A or B scored higher overall.

11. The mean of the six numbers 5, x, 3, 9, 8, 7 is 7. Find x.

12. The numbers 3, 5, 6, x, 9, 2 have a mean of 6. Find x.

13. The mean of the six numbers 8, $2x + 1$, 7, $3x$, 4 and 2 is 7. Calculate the value of x.

14. The mean of eight numbers is 9. When one of the numbers is taken away the mean is increased by 1. Find the number that was taken away.

15. The table below shows the distribution of the number of goals scored by a certain school team in each of the matches played during the season.

Goals scored	0	1	2	3	4	5
Number of matches	4	7	6	3	3	2

Find the mean of the distribution.

Exercise 12R.B ▼

1. Show that 4 is the mean of the array of numbers: 2, 5, 6, 4.5, 2.5.

Hence, calculate the standard deviation, correct to one place of decimals.

2. Calculate the:　　**(i)** median　　**(ii)** mean　　**(iii)** standard deviation, correct to two decimal places, of the following frequency distribution:

Number	2	5	8	11	14
Frequency	2	5	6	5	2

3. 20 pupils were given a problem to solve. The following grouped frequency distribution table gives the numbers of pupils who solved the problem in the given time interval:

Time (minutes)	0–4	4–12	12–24	24–40
Frequency	3	8	7	2

Assuming the data can be taken at the mid-interval values, calculate:
(i) the mean　　**(ii)** the standard deviation, correct to two places of decimals.

4. The intelligence quotients (I.Q.) of 50 children are recorded and grouped in the following table:

I.Q.	90–100	100–110	110–120	120–130
Number of children	11	22	12	5

[Note that 90–100 means that 90 is included but 100 is not, etc.]

Taking 95, 105, etc. as mid-interval values, calculate for this data:

(i) the mean, correct to the nearest integer

(ii) the standard deviation, correct to the nearest integer.

5. The table shows the number of people who have saved money in a School Credit Union.

Amount saved in €	0–20	20–40	40–60	60–80	80–100	100–120
Number of people	10	24	44	32	22	8

[Note that 20–40 means 20 is included but 40 is not, etc.]

Construct a cumulative frequency table. Draw a cumulative frequency curve.

Use the curve to estimate:

(i) the median amount of money saved per person, correct to the nearest €

(ii) the interquartile range.

6. The following cumulative frequency table refers to the ages of 70 guests at a wedding:

Age (in years)	<20	<40	<60	<90
Number of guests	6	23	44	70

(i) Copy and complete the following frequency table:

Age (in years)	0–20	20–40	40–60	60–90
Number of guests				

[Note that 20–40 means 20 years old or more but less than 40, etc.]

(ii) Using mid-interval values, calculate the mean age of the guests.

(iii) What is the greatest number of guests who could have been over 65 years of age?

7. The cumulative frequency table below shows the ages of people attending a swimming pool on a particular day:

Ages of people (years)	<10	<20	<40	<50	<70
Number of people	2	4	19	39	50

(i) Represent the data with a cumulative frequency curve (ogive) putting the number of people on the vertical axis.

Use your graph to estimate:

(ii) the number of people aged less than 32

(iii) the percentage of people between the ages of 48 and 56.

(iv) Complete the corresponding grouped frequency distribution:

Ages of people (years)	0–10	10–20	20–40	40–50	50–70
Number of people					

(v) Using the mid-interval values, calculate the mean age of the swimmers.

8. The following table shows the distribution of the amounts spent by 40 customers in a shop:

Amount spent	€0–€8	€8–€12	€12–€16	€16–€20	€20–€32
Number of customers	2	9	13	10	6

[Note that €8–€12 means €8 or over but less than €12, etc.]

(i) Taking mid-interval values, estimate the mean amount spent by the customers.

(ii) Copy and complete the following cumulative frequency table:

Amount spent	<€8	<€12	<€16	<€20	<€32
Number of customers					

(iii) Draw a cumulative frequency curve (ogive).

(iv) Use your curve to estimate the number of customers who spent €25 or more.

9. The cumulative frequency table below shows the distribution of ages of 110 people living in an estate:

Age in years	≤5	≤10	≤20	≤35	≤50	≤60
Number of people	5	15	40	90	105	110

(i) Draw the cumulative frequency curve, putting number of people on the vertical axis.

(ii) Use your curve to estimate the median age.

(iii) Use your curve to estimate the number of people who are more than 15 years of age.

10. The table shows the distribution of points obtained by 50 people who took a driving test:

Points obtained	0–20	20–40	40–80	80–100
Number of people	4	8	28	10

   (i) Draw a histogram to illustrate the data.

   (ii) To pass the driving test a person must obtain 65 points or more. What is the greatest possible number of people who passed the test?

11. The following frequency distribution gives the contributions, in €, of people to a fund:

Amount contributed	€0–€20	€20–€40	€40–€60	€60–€100	€100–€160
Number of people	12	16	24	16	12

   (i) Draw a histogram to illustrate the data.

   (ii) Taking mid-interval values, estimate the mean amount contributed.

   (iii) Calculate the standard deviation, correct to two decimal places.

12. The distribution of percentage marks awarded to a group of 200 Leaving Certificate students in a particular subject is shown in the histogram below:

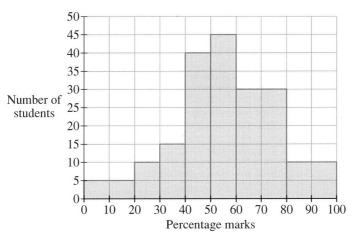

   (i) If 45 students obtained between 50% and 60%, copy and complete the frequency table below:

Marks (%)	0–20	20–30	30–40	40–50	50–60	60–80	80–100
Frequency					45		

   (ii) What is the greatest possible number of students who could have obtained a grade C or better (i.e. mark ⩾ 55)?

1. The table below refers to the number of emergency calls recorded at a fire station each week for 52 weeks:

Number of emergency calls	0–10	11–20	21–30	31–40	41–50	51–60	61–70
Number of weeks	6	8	11	12	7	5	3

(i) Copy and complete the following cumulative frequency table:

Number of emergency calls	⩽10	⩽20	⩽30	⩽40	⩽50	⩽60	⩽70
Number of weeks	6						52

(ii) Draw the cumulative frequency curve.

(iii) Use your graph to estimate the interquartile range.

(iv) Use your graph to estimate the number of weeks during which more than 56 emergency calls were recorded.

2. A new shop opened at 0900 hours. During the first hour of trading, customers were counted as they entered the shop. The following cumulative frequency table shows the number of customers who had entered before the given times:

Time	Before 0910 hours	Before 0920 hours	Before 0930 hours	Before 0940 hours	Before 0950 hours	Before 1000 hours
No. of customers who had entered	45	69	95	120	144	250

(i) Draw a cumulative frequency curve.

(ii) A photograph was taken of the 100th customer as he or she entered the shop.
    Use your curve to estimate the time at which the photograph was taken.

(iii) Use your curve to estimate the number of customers who entered the shop during the 15 minutes immediately after the photograph was taken.

3. The grouped frequency table below shows the minutes spent in a shopping complex by a number of people:

Minutes	5–15	15–25	25–35	35–65
Number of people	10	50	80	60

[Note that 5–15 means that 5 is included but 15 is not, etc.]

(i) Draw a histogram to illustrate the data.

(ii) Calculate the mean number of minutes spent per person in the shopping complex, taking 10, 20, etc. as mid-interval values.

4. The number of minutes taken by 20 pupils to answer a short question is shown in the following distribution table:

Minutes	2–4	4–6	6–8	8–10
Number of pupils	6	9	4	1

By taking the data at mid-interval values, calculate:

(i) the mean number of minutes taken per pupil

(ii) the standard deviation, correct to one place of decimals.

5. The following table shows the sizes, in hectares, of 20 farms in a particular area:

Number of hectares	15–45	45–75	75–105	105–195
Number of farms	1	4	8	7

By taking the data at mid-interval values, calculate:

(i) the mean number of hectacres per farm

(ii) the standard deviation, correct to the nearest hectare.

6. The histogram shows the distribution of the distances, in km, that some students have to travel to school:

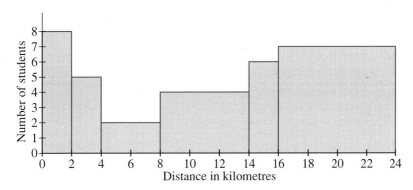

(i) Complete the corresponding frequency distribution table:

Distances (km)	0–2	2–4	4–8	8–14	14–16	16–24
No. of students				24		

(ii) Calculate the total number of students.

(iii) Taking mid-interval values, calculate the mean, correct to two decimal places.

7. The cumulative frequency table below shows the marks obtained by 100 students in a school test.

Marks	⩽20	⩽40	⩽60	⩽80	⩽100
Number of students	9	19	57	92	100

Draw a cumulative frequency curve.
(i) Use the curve to estimate the number of students who got fewer than 50 marks.
(ii) The school decides that the 15 highest marked students will each receive a prize.
Use the curve to estimate the least mark a student must obtain in order to qualify for a prize.
(iii) Complete the corresponding frequency table:

Marks	0–20	20–40	40–60	60–80	80–100
Number of students					

(iv) Taking mid-interval values, calculate the mean mark.

8. The grouped frequency table below refers to the marks obtained by 85 students in a test:

Marks	0–40	40–55	55–70	70–100
Number of students	16	18	27	24

[Note that 40–55 means 40 marks or more but less than 55, etc.]
(i) What percentage of students obtained 55 marks or higher?
(ii) Name the interval in which the median lies.
(iii) Draw an accurate histogram to represent the data.

9. Calculate the mean, in terms of k, of the numbers, 1, k, $3k - 2$, 9.

10. The mean of the following frequency distribution is 13. Find the value of x.

Number	10	12	14	16
Frequency	5	6	x	4

11. The table below shows the frequency of 0, 1, 2 or 3 goals scored in a number of football matches:

Number of goals scored	0	1	2	3
Number of matches	1	x	1	5

If the mean number of goals scored per match is 2, find the value of x.

12. People attending a course were asked to choose one of the whole numbers from 1 to 12. The results were recorded as follows:

Number	1–3	4–6	7–9	10–12
Number of people	3	x	2	8

Using mid-interval values, 6.5 was calculated as the mean of the numbers chosen.

Find the value of x.

REVISION EXERCISE 13 OPTION 1: FURTHER GEOMETRY

Paper 2   Question 8

This revision exercise covers chapter 19.

> *Exercise 13R.A* ▼

1. The points *f*, *g*, *h* and *m* lie on a circle with centre *o*.
   Given that $|\angle foh| = 80°$, find:
   (i) $|\angle fgh|$
   (ii) $|\angle fmh|$.

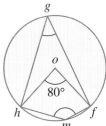

2. In the diagram, *o* is the centre of the circle and $|\angle xoy| = 210°$.
   Find $|\angle xzy|$.

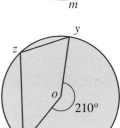

3. The centre of the circle is *o* and $|\angle prq| = 50°$.
   Find:
   (i) $|\angle poq|$
   (ii) $|\angle opq|$.

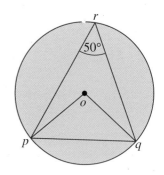

4. *p* is a point of a circle, centre *o*.
   If $|\angle pao| = 10°$: find $|\angle aox|$.

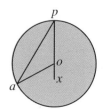

5. x and y are two points on a circle with centre o.

px and py are tangents to the circle, as shown.

  (i)   Write down $|\angle pxo|$.

  (ii) Given that $|\angle xoy| = 135°$, find $|\angle ypx|$.

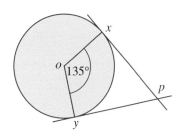

6. In the diagram, o is the circle's centre and pq is a straight line. $|\angle qro| = 28°$.

Find $|\angle orp|$ and $|\angle rpo|$.

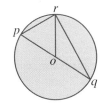

7. The line rs is a tangent to the circle K at the point t.

The obtuse angle between the tangent rs and the chord $[td]$ measures $120°$.

The point c is on the circle K and $|dc| = |tc|$.

Find $|\angle cdt|$.

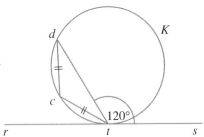

8. In the diagram, $[pt]$ is a diameter of the circle.

sr is parallel to pt and $|\angle ptr| = 56°$.

  (i)   Write down the value of $|\angle prt|$.

  (ii) Find the value of $|\angle prs|$.

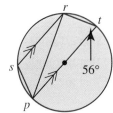

9. In the diagram, o is the centre of the circle.

If $|dc| = 6$ cm, $|ce| = 3$ cm and $|xc| = 9$ cm, find:

  (i) $|cy|$

  (ii) the length of the radius of the circle.

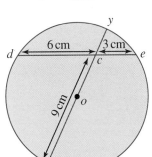

10. pq and rs intersect at k.

If $|rs| = 6$, $|sk| = 4$ and $|qk| = 5$, calculate $|pq|$.

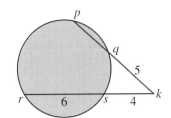

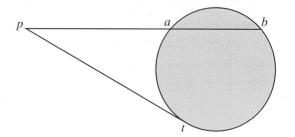

11. In the diagram, $|pt|$ is a tangent.
$|pa| = 5$ and $|ab| = 2.2$.
Calculate $|pt|$.

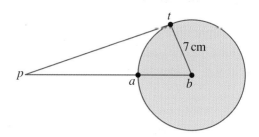

12. In the given diagram, pt is a tangent to the circle of radius 7 cm.

If $|pa| = 18$ cm, find $|pt|$.

Exercise 13R.B ▼

1. Prove that the degree-measure of an angle subtended at the centre of a circle by a chord is equal to twice the degree-measure of any angle subtended by the chord at a point of the arc of the circle which is on the same side of the chordal line as is the centre.

Hence:

(i) Prove that all angles standing on the same arc, or chord, are equal in measure.

(ii) Prove that the angle at the circle standing on a diameter is a right angle.

(iii) Prove that the measures of the opposite angles of a cyclic quadrilateral add to 180°.

2. Prove that a line is a tangent to a circle at point t of the circle if, and only if, it passes through t and is perpendicular to the line through t and the centre.

3. Prove that an angle between a tangent ak and a chord $[ab]$ of a circle has a degree-measure equal to that of any angle in the alternate segment.

4. Prove that if $[ab]$ and $[cd]$ are chords of a circle and the lines ab and cd meet at the point k, which is inside the circle, then $|ak|.|kb| = |ck|.|kd|$.

5. Prove that if $[ab]$ and $[cd]$ are chords of a circle and the lines ab and cd meet at the point k, where k is outside the circle, the $|ak|.|kb| = |ck|.|kd|$.

Hence:

Prove that if from a point p outside a circle a tangent is drawn to touch the circle at t and from p a line is drawn to intersect the circle at a and b, then $|pa|.|pb| = |pt|^2$.

1. In the diagram, o is the centre of the circle.
   a, b, c and d are points on the circle.
   $|da| = |dc|$ and $|\angle abc| = 62°$.
   (i) Find $|\angle aoc|$, where $\angle aoc$ is obtuse.
   (ii) Find $|\angle adc|$.
   (iii) Find $|\angle oad|$.

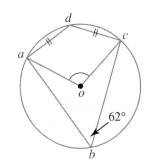

2. $[ab]$ is a diameter of the circle with centre o.
   The line pq is a tangent to the circle at q.

   The point r on qa is joined to b.
   If $|\angle apq| = 40°$ and $|\angle arb| = 22°$, find:
   (i) $|\angle abq|$
   (ii) $|\angle qab|$
   (iii) $|\angle abr|$.

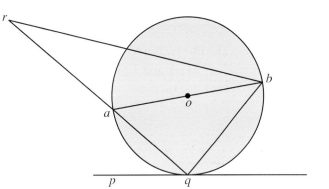

3. **(i)** The centre of the circle is o.
   $|\angle qps| = 50°$ and $|\angle qor| = |\angle ros|$.
   Find $|\angle qrs|$.

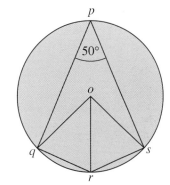

   (ii) The centre of the circle is k.
   $|\angle akc| = 140°$ and $|\angle kab| = 20°$.
   Find $|\angle akb|$.
   Find $|\angle kcb|$.

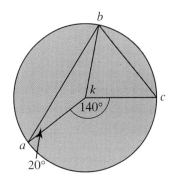

4. In the diagram, o is the centre of the circle and
$|ps| = |sr|$. $|\angle pqr| = 56°$.

Find:

(i) $|\angle qpr|$

(ii) $|\angle qps|$.

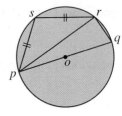

5. The centre of a circle is o.

If $|\angle aob| = 130°$ and $|\angle cao| = 15°$,
calculate $|\angle obc|$.

6. (i) The line pq is a tangent to the circle at t.
$|rs| = |rt|$ and $|\angle srt| = 72°$.
Find $|\angle stp|$.
Find $|\angle rtq|$.

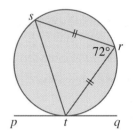

(ii) A circle, with centre o, has tangents
uv and uw at v and w, respectively.
kv is parallel to wu. $|\angle zvk| = 82°$.
Find $|\angle kwv|$.
Find $|\angle vwu|$.

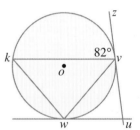

7. The line kd is a tangent to the circle at a.
$|\angle kab| = 75°$ and $|\angle abc| = 49°$.

Find:

(i) $|\angle bca|$

(ii) $|\angle bac|$

(iii) $|\angle cad|$.

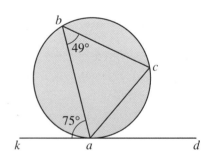

8. In the diagram, tangents from v to the circle
are drawn at t and w. $|\angle wyt| = 70°$.

Give reasons for the following:

(i) $|\angle wtv| = 70°$

(ii) $|\angle tvw| = 40°$.

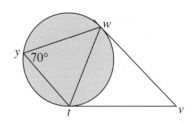

9. The lines *kd* and *kr* are tangents to a circle at *d* and *r*, respectively. *s* is a point on the circle as shown.

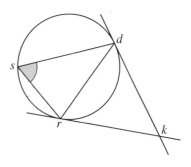

(i) Name two angles in the diagram equal in measure to $\angle dsr$.

(ii) Find $|\angle rkd|$, given that $|\angle dsr| = 65°$.

(iii) Is $|dk| = |rk|$? Give a reason for your answer.

10. Two circles K_1 and K_2 intersect at *x* and *y* and *dxe* is a straight line. The tangents to the circles at *d* and *e* meet at *f*.

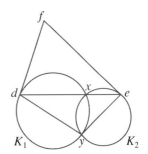

Given $|\angle fde| = 74°$ and $|\angle dye| = 118°$:

(i) Find: **(a)** $|\angle dy\hat{x}|$ **(b)** $|\angle def|$ **(c)** $|\angle dfe|$, giving brief reasons for your answers.

(ii) Explain why *fdye* is a cyclic quadrilateral.

(iii) Find: **(a)** $|\angle fyd|$ **(b)** $|\angle fyx|$, giving brief reasons for your answers.

11. In the diagram, *xy* is a tangent to the circle at *p* and *qp* is parallel to *rs*.

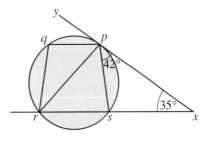

$|\angle spx| = 42°$ and $|\angle sxp| = 35°$. Find:

(i) $|\angle prs|$

(ii) $|\angle ypr|$

(iii) $|\angle pqr|$.

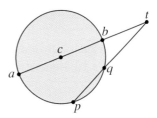

12. The centre of the circle is *c* and $|cb| = |bt|$.

If $|pq| = 3$ and $|qt| = 9$, calculate the length of the radius of the circle.

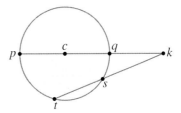

13. *c* is the centre of the circle, as in the diagram, and *q* is the midpoint of [*kp*]. If $|ks| = 10$ and $|st| = 2.8$, calculate the length of the radius of the circle.

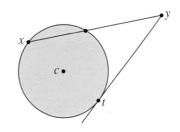

14. The diagram shows a circle, centre *c*, and a tangent *yt* to the circle. If $|xy| = 9$ cm, $|cx| = 5$ cm and *c* is 3 cm from *xy*, calculate $|yt|$.

15. The line *pt* is a tangent to the circle *C* at the point *t*.

[*xt*] is a diameter of the circle.

[*px*] cuts the circle at *y*.

If $|py| = 6$ and $|pt| = 4\sqrt{3}$, calculate $|xy|$.

Hence, calculate $|xt|$.

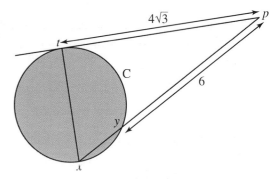

16. [*xy*] and [*rs*] are chords of a circle which intersect at a point *p* outside the circle.

pt is a tangent to the circle at the point *t*.

Given that $|py| = 8$, $|xy| = 3$ and $|ps| = 10$:

(i) Write down $|px|$.

(ii) Calculate $|rs|$.

(iii) Calculate $|pt|$, giving your answer in surd form.

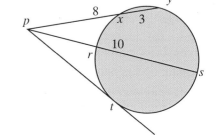

17. The diagram shows a piece of metal which has broken off from a disc, where *ptq* is part of the original circle.

If $|pq| = 36$ cm, $|tm| = 12$ cm, where $|pm| = |mq|$, calculate the length of the radius of the disc.

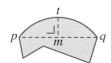

18. *ab* is a common tangent to two circles as shown and the common chord [*cd*] cuts *ab* in *e*.

Prove that *e* is the midpoint of [*ab*].

If $|ab| = |ec| = 16$, find $|de|$.

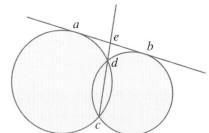
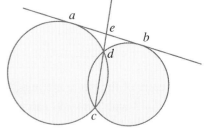

19. In the diagram, *pt* is a tangent to the circle of centre *o*. $|pt| = 8$ and $|po| = 10$.

Find the length of the radius of the circle.

(Hint: let the radius have length *r*.)

20. *pq* and *pr* are two tangents to the given circle of centre *o*.

Prove that $|pq| = |pr|$.

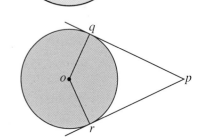

21. Through any point x in the common chord $[pq]$ of the circles as shown, two chords $[ab]$ and $[cd]$ are drawn.

Prove that $|ax|.|xb| = |cx|.|xd|$.

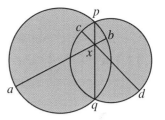

22. Two circles have a common chord $[mn]$ as shown.

k is a point outside both circles.

Prove that:
$$|kp|.|kq| = |kr|.|ks|.$$

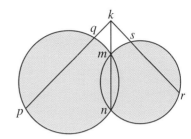

23. In the diagram, ea is a tangent to the circle at a, $|\angle abc| = |\angle aed|$. Prove that:

(i) $|ac| = |ae|$

(ii) $|\angle abc| = |\angle ade|$.

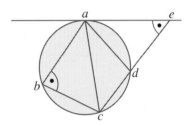

REVISION EXERCISE 14 OPTION 2: VECTORS

Paper 2   Question 9

This revision exercise covers chapter 17.

> *Exercise 14R.A* ▼

1. Let $\vec{x} = 3\vec{i} + 2\vec{j}$ and $\vec{y} = 4\vec{i} - \vec{j}$. Express, in terms of $\vec{i}$ and $\vec{j}$:   **(i)** $\vec{x} + \vec{y}$ **(ii)** $3\vec{y} - 4\vec{x}$.

2. Let $\vec{p} = -\vec{i} + 2\vec{j}$ and $\vec{w} = 3\vec{i} - 4\vec{j}$. Express, in terms of $\vec{i}$ and $\vec{j}$:   **(i)** $2\vec{w}$ **(ii)** $2\vec{w} - \vec{p}$.

3. Given that $\vec{p} = 5\vec{i} - 12\vec{j}$:   **(i)** calculate $|\vec{p}|$ **(ii)** write down $\vec{p}^{\perp}$ in terms of $\vec{i}$ and $\vec{j}$.

4. Let $\vec{x} = \vec{i} + \vec{j}$ and $\vec{y} = 2\vec{i} + 5\vec{j}$. Express, in terms of $\vec{i}$ and $\vec{j}$:   **(i)** $3\vec{x} + \vec{y}$ **(ii)** $\overrightarrow{xy}$.

5. Let $\vec{x} = 4\vec{i} + 3\vec{j}$ and $\overrightarrow{xy} = 4\vec{i} + 12\vec{j}$.
   (i)   Express $\vec{y}$ in terms of $\vec{i}$ and $\vec{j}$.
   (ii) Evaluate   **(a)** $|\vec{x}|$ **(b)** $|\vec{y}|$.
   (iii) Evaluate $|\vec{y}| - 3|\vec{x}|$.

6. *pqro* is a rectangle, where *o* is the origin.
   The midpoint of [*rq*] is *m*.
   Express in terms of $\vec{p}$ and $\vec{r}$:
   (i) $\vec{q}$
   (ii) $\vec{m}$
   (iii) $\overrightarrow{mp}$.

7. *oabc* is a square, where *o* is the origin.
   m is the midpoint of [*oa*].
   Express in terms of $\vec{a}$ and $\vec{c}$:
   (i) $\vec{b}$
   (ii) $\overrightarrow{cm}$.

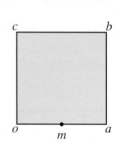

8. *abcd* is a parallelogram. The midpoint of [*ad*] is *o*,
   where *o* is the origin.
   (i)   Express $\overrightarrow{ab}$ in terms of $\vec{a}$ and $\vec{b}$.
   (ii) Show that $\vec{c} = \vec{b} - 2\vec{a}$.

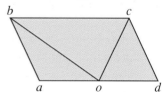

9. Copy the diagram and show, on separate diagrams, o being the origin:

    (i) the point k_1, so that $\vec{k}_1 = 2\vec{q}$

    (ii) the point k_2, so that $\vec{k}_2 = \vec{p} + \vec{q}$

    (iii) the point k_3, so that $\vec{k}_3 = \vec{p} - \vec{q}$.

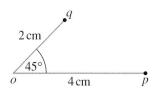

10. The diagram shows $\vec{x}$ and $\vec{y}$ with respect to the origin at o.

    Copy the diagram and show on it $\vec{r}$ and $\vec{s}$ such that:

$$\vec{r} = -\vec{x}$$
$$\vec{s} = 2\vec{y}.$$

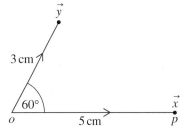

Exercise 14R.B ▼

1. $\vec{a} = 2\vec{i} + 2\vec{j}$ and $\vec{b} = -\vec{i} - 2\vec{j}$.

    Express $\vec{a} + \vec{b}$ and $\vec{ab}$ in terms of $\vec{i}$ and $\vec{j}$.

    Illustrate $\vec{a}$, $\vec{b}$, $\vec{a} + \vec{b}$ and $\vec{ab}$ on a diagram.

    Evaluate $|\vec{ab}|$.

    Verify that $|\vec{ab}| < |\vec{a}| + |\vec{b}|$.

2. Let $\vec{p} = 3\vec{i} + \vec{j}$ and $\vec{q} = 2\vec{i} - 3\vec{j}$.

    (i) Express $\vec{p} + \vec{q}$ in terms of $\vec{i}$ and $\vec{j}$.

    (ii) Calculate $|\vec{p} + \vec{q}|$.

    (iii) Calculate $\vec{p} \cdot \vec{q}$.

3. Let $\vec{p} = 6\vec{i} - 2\vec{j}$ and $\vec{q} = 2\vec{i} + 3\vec{j}$.

    (i) Express $\vec{q} - \vec{p}$ in terms of $\vec{i}$ and $\vec{j}$.

    (ii) Calculate $|\vec{q} - \vec{p}|$.

    (iii) Calculate $\vec{p} \cdot \vec{q}$.

4. Find scalars h and k such that $h(2\vec{i} + 3\vec{j}) + k(\vec{i} + 3\vec{j}) = 4\vec{i} + 3\vec{j}$.

5. Find scalars p and q such that $3(p\vec{i} - 3\vec{j}) - q(2\vec{i} + 4\vec{j}) = 7(p\vec{i} + \vec{j})$.

6. If $a\vec{i} - b\vec{j} + b\vec{i} + a\vec{j} = 7\vec{i} - \vec{j}$, find the value of a and the value of b.

7. If $\vec{u} = 6\vec{i} - 8\vec{j}$ and $\vec{v} = \vec{i} + 4\vec{j}$, calculate $|\vec{uv}|$.

    If $5\vec{i} - 12\vec{j} = m\vec{u} + n\vec{v}$, find the value of m and the value of n, where m and n are scalars.

8. If $\vec{a} = 5\vec{i} + 7\vec{j}$ and $\vec{b} = 3\vec{i} - \vec{j}$:

    (i) express $\vec{a} + \vec{b}$ in terms of $\vec{i}$ and $\vec{j}$

    (ii) illustrate the vectors $\vec{a}$, $\vec{b}$, $\vec{a} + \vec{b}$ on a diagram

    (iii) evaluate $|\vec{a} + \vec{b}|$

    (iv) find k and t where $k(\vec{a} + \vec{b}) = 16\vec{i} + (t + 2)\vec{j}$.

9. (i) Find the scalars k and t such that $2(3\vec{i} - t\vec{j}) + k(-\vec{i} + 2\vec{j}) = t\vec{i} - 8\vec{j}$.

(ii) $oacb$ is a parallelogram, where o is the origin.
p is the point of intersection of the diagonals.
m is the midpoint of $[ac]$.
Express $\vec{p}$ and $\vec{m}$ in terms of $\vec{a}$ and $\vec{b}$.

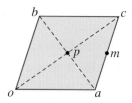

10. Let $\vec{p} = 3\vec{i} - 2\vec{j}$ and $\vec{q} = \vec{i} + 3\vec{j}$.

(i) Express $\vec{pq}$ in terms of $\vec{i}$ and $\vec{j}$.

(ii) Calculate $|\vec{pq}|$.

(iii) Find the value of the scalar k and the value of scalar n for which $k(\vec{pq}) = (n + 3)\vec{i} + 2\vec{j}$.

11. $ocba$ is a parallelogram, where o is the origin.
The point r divides $[ab]$ in the ratio $1:2$ and
the point s divides $[bc]$ in the ratio $1:2$.
Express in terms of $\vec{a}$ and $\vec{c}$:

(i) $\vec{b}$

(ii) $\vec{r}$

(iii) $\vec{s}$

(iv) $\vec{rs}$.

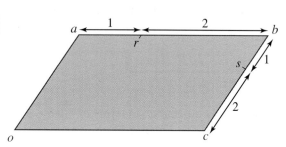

12. $abcd$ is a parallelogram. The diagonals intersect at the point m.
Express each of the following as a single vector:

(i) $\vec{ab} + \vec{bm}$

(ii) $\vec{ab} + \vec{ad}$

(iii) $\vec{ac} - \vec{ab}$

(iv) $\frac{1}{2}\vec{ac} + \frac{1}{2}\vec{db}$.

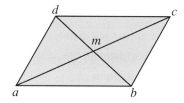

13. The diagram shows vectors $\vec{p}$ and $\vec{q}$ with respect to an origin at o.
Show on separate diagrams the points k_1 and k_2 such that:

$$\vec{k_1} = \vec{q} + \tfrac{1}{2}\vec{p}$$
$$\vec{k_2} = \vec{p} - \vec{q}.$$

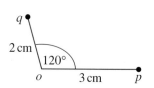

14. $osrp$ is a parallelogram, where o is the origin.

(i) Copy the diagram and show on it $\vec{k}$ and $\vec{m}$ such that
$\vec{k} = \vec{s} + 2\vec{p}$ and $\vec{m} = 2\vec{s} + \vec{p}$.

(ii) Express $\vec{k} + \vec{m}$ in terms of $\vec{r}$.

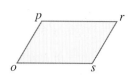

Exercise 14R.C ▼

1. $\vec{p} = 2\vec{i} - 5\vec{j}$, $\vec{q} = 10\vec{i} + k\vec{j}$. If $\vec{p} \perp \vec{q}$, find k.

2. $\vec{x} = 3\vec{i} + 4\vec{j}$ and $\vec{y} = 4\vec{i} - \vec{j}$.

Verify that: **(i)** $|\vec{x}| + |\vec{y}| > |\vec{x} + \vec{y}|$ **(ii)** $\left|\dfrac{\vec{x}}{|\vec{x}|}\right| = 1$ **(iii)** $\vec{x}.\vec{y} = 8$.

3. If $|\vec{x}| = 5$, $|\vec{y}| = 8$ and $|\angle xoy| = 120°$, calculate $\vec{x} \cdot \vec{y}$.

4. Let $\vec{x} = \vec{i} + 2\vec{j}$ and $\vec{y} = 6\vec{i} + 2\vec{j}$.
   (i) Calculate $\vec{x} \cdot \vec{y}$.   (ii) Hence, find the measure of the smaller angle between $\vec{x}$ and $\vec{y}$.

5. Let $\vec{p} = 3\vec{i} + k\vec{j}$, $\vec{q} = t\vec{i} + 3\vec{j}$. If $\vec{pq} = -5\vec{i} - 2\vec{j}$, find the values of k and t and, hence, calculate $\vec{p} \cdot \vec{q}$.

6. If $\vec{p} = -\vec{i} + 2\vec{j}$ and $\vec{q} = \vec{p}^{\perp}$, where o is the origin, express $\vec{q}$ in terms of $\vec{i}$ and $\vec{j}$. Verify that $|\vec{p}| = |\vec{q}|$.

7. Let $\vec{u} = -2\vec{i} - \vec{j}$ and $\vec{v} = \vec{i} + 3\vec{j}$.
   Write $\vec{u}^{\perp}$ and $\vec{v}^{\perp}$ in terms of $\vec{i}$ and $\vec{j}$.
   Find the value of the scalar k and the value of the scalar p for which $k(\vec{u}^{\perp}) + p(\vec{v}^{\perp}) = 5(\vec{i} - \vec{j})$.

8. Let $\vec{x} = 8\vec{i} - 2\vec{j}$ and $\vec{y} = 2\vec{i} + 4\vec{j}$.
   Write $\vec{x}^{\perp}$ and $\vec{y}^{\perp}$ in terms of $\vec{i}$ and $\vec{j}$.
   Find the value of the scalar m and the value of the scalar n for which $\vec{x}^{\perp} + m\vec{y}^{\perp} = 3\vec{i} - n\vec{j}$.

9. Let $\vec{x} = 3\vec{i} - 2\vec{j}$ and $\vec{y} = 5\vec{i} + 8\vec{j}$.
   (i)   Express $\vec{x} + \vec{y}$ in terms of $\vec{i}$ and $\vec{j}$.
   (ii) Calculate $|\vec{x} + \vec{y}|$.
   (iii) Find the value of the scalar k and the value of the scalar n for which $k(\vec{x} + \vec{y}) = 16\vec{i} + (n - 2)\vec{j}$.
   (iv) Investigate whether or not $\vec{x} \perp \vec{y}$.
   (v)   Determine if $(\vec{x} + \vec{y})^{\perp} = \vec{x}^{\perp} + \vec{y}^{\perp}$.

10. Let $\vec{x} = 3\vec{i} + 4\vec{j}$ and $\vec{y} = 5\vec{i} + 12\vec{j}$.
   (i) Show that $|\vec{x}| + |\vec{y}| > |\vec{x} + \vec{y}|$.
   (ii) Write down $\vec{x}^{\perp}$ in terms of $\vec{i}$ and $\vec{j}$ and, hence, show that $|\vec{x}|^2 + |\vec{x}^{\perp}|^2 = |\vec{x} - \vec{x}^{\perp}|^2$.

11. Let $\vec{x} = 3\vec{i} + 5\vec{j}$ and $\vec{y} = 7\vec{i} + 4\vec{j}$.
   Find $\vec{x}^{\perp} - \vec{y}^{\perp}$ in terms of $\vec{i}$ and $\vec{j}$.
   If $\vec{u} = \vec{x}^{\perp}$ and $\vec{v} = \vec{y}^{\perp}$, investigate if $\vec{vu} \perp \vec{xy}$.

12. $\vec{a} = 5\vec{i} + 12\vec{j}$ and $\vec{b} = 3\vec{i} - 4\vec{j}$.
   (i)   Write down $\vec{a}^{\perp}$ and $\vec{b}^{\perp}$ in terms of $\vec{i}$ and $\vec{j}$.
   (ii) Evaluate $|\vec{a}^{\perp}|$ and $|\vec{b}^{\perp}|$.
   (iii) Find the scalar k such that $|\vec{a}^{\perp} + \vec{b}^{\perp}| = k(|\vec{a}^{\perp}| - |\vec{b}^{\perp}|)$.
          Give your answer in the form $\sqrt{n}$, where $n \in \mathbf{N}$.

13. Let $\vec{u} = 3\vec{i} + 2\vec{j}$, $\vec{w} = -\vec{i} + 4\vec{j}$. The vector $t\vec{w} + \vec{u}$ is on the $\vec{j}$-axis; find the value of the scalar t.

14. Let $\vec{h} = 6\vec{i} - 8\vec{j}$ and $\vec{k} = 4\vec{i} - 3\vec{j}$.
   (i) If $ohkm$ is a parallelogram, o being the origin, express $\vec{m}$ in terms of $\vec{i}$ and $\vec{j}$.
   (ii) If $\vec{p} = \vec{k} + a\vec{m}$, $a \in \mathbf{R}$, and $\vec{p}$ is a point on the $\vec{j}$-axis, calculate the value of a.
         Express $\vec{p}$ in terms of $\vec{i}$ and $\vec{j}$ and calculate $|\vec{pm}|$.

15. *abo* is a triangle where *o* is the origin.

$|od| = |db|$ and $|cd| = \frac{1}{2}|ac|$.

Express:

(i) $\vec{d}$ in terms of $\vec{b}$

(ii) $\vec{dc}$ in terms of $\vec{da}$

(iii) $\vec{c}$ in the form $k(\vec{a} + \vec{b})$, where $k \in \mathbf{Q}$.

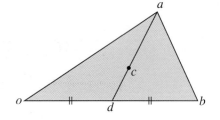

16. *opqr* is a square.

$|ps| = \frac{1}{3}|op|$. $rs \cap qp = \{t\}$.

Taking *o* as origin, express in terms of $\vec{p}$ and/or $\vec{r}$:

(i) $\vec{os}$ **(ii)** $\vec{rs}$.

Taking $\vec{i}$ and $\vec{j}$ as unit vectors along and perpendicular to *os*, respectively, and given $\vec{p} = 4\vec{i}$ and $\vec{r} = 4\vec{j}$, calculate $|\vec{tr}|$, given $|pt| = \frac{1}{4}|pq|$.

Find $\vec{p} \cdot \vec{q}$, the scalar product of $\vec{p}$ and $\vec{q}$.

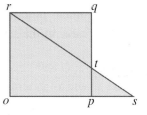

17. *oab* is a triangle, *o* is the origin. *p*, *q* are points on [*oa*] and [*ab*], respectively, such that $|ap| : |po| = |bq| : |qa| = 1 : 2$.

Express in terms of $\vec{a}$ and $\vec{b}$:

(i) $\vec{bq}$

(ii) $\vec{oq}$

(iii) $\vec{qp}$.

If $\vec{a} = 6\vec{i} - 3\vec{j}$ and $\vec{b} = 3\vec{i} + 9\vec{j}$ find:

(iv) $\vec{a} \cdot \vec{b}$

(v) $|\vec{qp}|$.

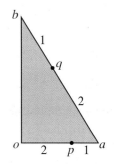

REVISION EXERCISE 15 OPTION 3: FURTHER SEQUENCES AND SERIES – BINOMIAL THEOREM

Paper 2   Question 10

....

This revision exercise covers chapter 18.

Exercise 15R.A ▼

1. A pupil saves money each day in the month of November. The pupil saves 10c on the 1st of November, 15c on the 2nd, 20c on the 3rd, continuing this pattern until the last day of November. How much will the pupil have saved at the end of the 30 days?

2. Find the sum to infinity of the geometric series $1 + \frac{1}{2} + \frac{1}{4} + \frac{1}{8} + \ldots$

3. Find the sum to infinity of the geometric series $9 + 3 + 1 + \frac{1}{3} + \frac{1}{9} + \ldots$

4. Find the sum to infinity of the geometric series $3 + 2 + \frac{4}{3} + \frac{8}{9} + \ldots$

5. The first three terms of an infinite geometric series are $\frac{5}{6} + \frac{2}{3} + \frac{8}{15} + \ldots$
    Find **(i)** the common ratio   **(ii)** the sum to infinity of the series.

6. $0.\dot{5}$ written as an infinite geometric series is $\frac{5}{10} + \frac{5}{100} + \frac{5}{1,000} + \ldots$
    By finding the sum to infinity of the series, express $0.\dot{5}$ as a fraction.

7. $0.\dot{8}$ written as an infinite geometric series is $\frac{8}{10} + \frac{8}{100} + \frac{8}{1,000} + \ldots$
    By finding the sum to infinity of the series, express $1.\dot{8}$ as a fraction.

8. **(i)**   Calculate each of the following correct to three decimal places:
    $$\left(\frac{1}{2}\right)^6, \quad \left(\frac{1}{2}\right)^7, \quad \left(\frac{1}{2}\right)^8, \quad \left(\frac{1}{2}\right)^9.$$

    (ii)   Hence, write down $\lim_{n \to \infty} \left(\frac{1}{2}\right)^n$.

9. Expand:
    (i) $(1 + x)^4$ **(ii)** $(1 - x)^4$ in ascending powers of x.
    (iii) Show that $(1 + x)^4 + (1 - x)^4 = 2(1 + 6x^2 + x^4)$.
    (iv) Show that $(1 + \sqrt{2})^4 = 17 + 12\sqrt{2}$.

10. (i) Expand: **(a)** $(1+x)^3$ **(b)** $(1-x)^3$ in ascending powers of x.

(ii) Hence, find the real numbers a and k such that $(1+x)^3 + (1-x)^3 = a + kx^2$.

(iii) Show that $(1+\sqrt{3})^3 = 10 + 6\sqrt{3}$.

Exercise 15R.B ▼

1. (i) Find the sum to infinity of the geometric series $\frac{7}{10} + \frac{7}{100} + \frac{7}{1,000} + \ldots$

(ii) Using this, show that $1.\dot{7} = \frac{16}{9}$.

2. (i) Find the sum to infinity of the geometric series $\frac{63}{100} + \frac{63}{10,000} + \frac{63}{1,000,000} + \ldots$

(ii) Using this series, show that $1.\dot{6}\dot{3} = \frac{18}{11}$.

3. (i) Find the sum to infinity of the geometric series $\frac{3}{100} + \frac{3}{1,000} + \frac{3}{10,000} + \ldots$

(ii) Using this infinite series, show that $0.1\dot{3} = \frac{2}{15}$.

4. (i) Find the sum to infinity of the geometric series $\frac{2}{100} + \frac{2}{1,000} + \frac{2}{10,000} + \ldots$

(ii) Using this infinite series, show that $0.6\dot{2} = \frac{28}{45}$.

5. (i) Find the sum to infinity of the geometric series $\frac{4}{5} + \frac{4}{50} + \frac{4}{500} + \ldots$

(ii) Hence, show that $1.\dot{8} = \frac{17}{9}$.

6. The sum of the first 21 terms of an arithmetic series is 735.
The common difference between each term is 1.
Find the first term of the series.

7. The first term of a geometric series is 3. The second term of the series is 12.

(i) Write down the common ratio.

(ii) What is the fifth term of the series?

(iii) Calculate the sum of the first nine terms of the series.

8. The first term of a geometric series is 12. The sum to infinity is 18.

(i) Find the common ratio.　　**(ii)** Find the second term.

9. The second term of a geometric series is 16. The sum to infinity is twice the first term.

(i) Find the common ratio.　　**(ii)** Find the third term.

10. The nth term of a geometric series is given by $T_n = 27(\frac{2}{3})^n$.

(i) Write out the first three terms of the series.

(ii) Find an expression for the sum of the first five terms.

(iii) Find the sum to infinity of the series.

11. The general term of a series is given by $T_n = \dfrac{1}{3^{n-1}}$.

(i) Verify that the series is geometric.

(ii) Explain why the series has a sum to infinity.

(iii) Show that the sum to infinity of the series is $\frac{3}{2}$.

12. (i) Write the terms of the expansion of $(1 + x)^5$ in ascending powers of x.

(ii) Use this expansion to express $(1 + \sqrt{3})^5$ as a number in the form $a + b\sqrt{3}$, where $a, b \in \mathbf{N}$.

(iii) Show that $(1 + x)^5 - (1 - x)^5 = 2x(5 + 10x^2 + x^4)$.

(iv) By putting $x = 0.01$, use the expansion to show that $(1.01)^5 > 1.05$.

(v) By putting $x = 1$, show that $\binom{5}{0} + \binom{5}{1} + \binom{5}{2} + \binom{5}{3} + \binom{5}{4} + \binom{5}{5} = 32$.

13. Expand $(1 + x)^7$ fully.
By letting $x = -1$, show that $\binom{7}{0} + \binom{7}{2} + \binom{7}{4} + \binom{7}{6} = \binom{7}{1} + \binom{7}{3} + \binom{7}{5} + \binom{7}{7}$

14. A group of children arrange themselves in the form of a triangle with one child in the first row, 3 children in the second row, 5 children in the third row and so on.

(i) If there are 15 rows, how many children are there altogether?

(ii) If there are 1,225 children, how many rows do they form?

15. Three children agree to divide a rectangular cake equally. They cut the cake into four equal rectangles and take one each. The remaining quarter is then divided into four equal rectangles and they again take one part each. The process continues until the amount left is negligible.

Write down a series for the amount of cake each child receives, and, by finding its sum to infinity, show that the method of sharing the cake is fair.

Exercise 15R.C ▼

1. Expand $(1 + x)^6$ in ascending powers of x. Express $(1 + \sqrt{5})^6$ in the form $a + b\sqrt{5}$, $a, b \in \mathbf{N}$.
If $(1 + x)^6 - (1 - x)^6 = ax(b + cx^2 + 3)$, find the values of a, b and c, $a, b, c \in \mathbf{N}$.

2. The sum to infinity of a geometric series is 2. The common ratio and the first term of the series are equal. Find the common ratio.

3. On Jane's fifth birthday her uncle decides to put aside for her, then and on each subsequent birthday, a number of € equal to twice her age, until she reaches the age of 21 years.
How much money accumulates, without interest?

4. A ball rolls down a slope. The distances it travels in successive seconds are 3 cm, 9 cm, 15 cm, 21 cm and so on. Show that the total distance it travels in n seconds is given by $3n^2$.
How many seconds elapse before it has travelled a total of 48 m?

5. €100 is invested at 10% compound interest per annum.
Show that the value of the investment is less than €1,000 after 24 years and more than €1,000 after 25 years.

6. A man's salary is increased each year by 3% of the previous year's salary. Explain briefly why this means it is multiplied by 1.03 each year. If his salary is €50,000 on 1 January 2003, write down a series in terms of his salary in the succeeding years up to 1 January 2013.
Hence, calculate, to the nearest €, his total earnings in the 10 years 2003–2013.

7. (i) Calculate the sum of the first four terms of the geometric series $1.2 + (1.2)^2 + \ldots$

(ii) A person deposited €1,000 in a bank on 1 June each year, for 4 consecutive years. The bank rate of 20% per annum remained steady throughout.
When the fourth €1,000 had remained at interest for a full year, the person withdrew all four deposits and their interests.
How much was withdrawn?

8. A person invested €750 at the beginning of each year for four consecutive years at 6% per annum compound interest.

Find:

(i) the value of the first investment of €750 at the end of the fourth year, correct to the nearest cent.

(ii) the total value of all the investments at the end of the fourth year, correct to the nearest €.

9. €100 was invested at the beginning of each year for twenty consecutive years at 4% per annum compound interest.

Calculate the total value of the investment at the end of the twenty years, correct to the nearest €.

10. A person invests €1,000 at the beginning of each year for 3 consecutive years at 8% per annum compound interest. Tax at 24% is deducted at the end of each year from the interest earned.

Find:

(i) the value of the first investment at the end of the third year, correct to the nearest cent

(ii) the total value of all the investments at the end of the third year, correct to the nearest cent.

11. A company invested €10,000 in new machinery at the beginning of each year for three consecutive years. The machinery depreciated at the rate of 10% per annum.

Find:

(i) the value of the first investment of €10,000 at the end of the third year

(ii) the total value of all the investments at the end of the third year.

12. A person invested €x at the beginning of each year for 4 consecutive years at 10% per annum compound interest. The total value of the investments at the end of the fourth year was €51,051. Find the value of x.

13. A company invested €x in new equipment at the beginning of each year for three consecutive years. The equipment depreciated at the rate of 20% per annum.

(i) Write, in terms of x, the value of the first investment of €x at the end of the first year.

(ii) The value of the first investment of €x at the end of the third year is €10,240.

Find the value of x.

(ii) Find the total value of all the investments at the end of the third year.

14. The odd natural numbers are 1, 3, 5, 7, 9, …

Prove that n^2 is the sum of the first n odd natural numbers.

If the odd numbers are arranged as follows:

$\{1\}, \{3, 5\}, \{7, 9, 11\}, \{13, 15, 17, 19\}, …$

and $O_1 = \{1\}$, $O_2 = \{1, 3, 5\}$, $O_3 = \{1, 3, 5, 7, 9, 11\}$, list the elements of O_4.

Find: **(i)** the number of elements in O_{20} **(ii)** the sum of all the numbers in O_{20}

15. A ball is dropped from a height of 128 cm. If the ball bounces $\frac{3}{4}$ of its previous height on each bounce, what is the total vertical distance the ball has travelled when it strikes the ground for the 6th time?

What vertical distance has the ball travelled after it comes to a stop?

REVISION EXERCISE 16 OPTION 4: LINEAR PROGRAMMING

Paper 2   Question 11

This revision exercise covers chapter 16.

> *Exercise 16R.A* ▼

1. The line L passes through the points (3, 0) and (0, 2).
   - **(i)** Find the equation of the line L.
   - **(ii)** Write down an inequality which defines the region indicated in the diagram.

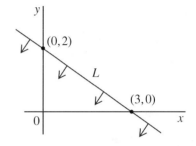

2. The line K passes through the points (–2, 0) and 0, 2).
   - **(i)** Find the equation of the line K.
   - **(ii)** Write down an inequality which defines the region indicated in the diagram.

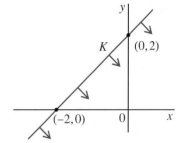

3. The line K passes through the points (5, 0) and (0, 1).
   - **(i)** Find the equation of the line K.
   - **(ii)** Write down an inequality which defines the region indicated in the diagram.

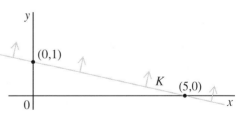

4. The equation of the line L is $x - 2y = 0$.
   Write down an equality which defines the region indicated in the diagram.

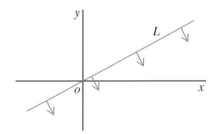

5. The line K passes through the points $(2, 0)$ and $0, 4)$.

    (i) Find the equation of the line K.

    (ii) Write down three inequalities which define the shaded region in the diagram.

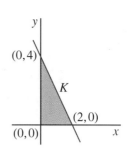

6. The line L passes through the points $(4, 0)$ and $(0, 3)$.

    (i) Find the equation of the line L.

    (ii) Write down three inequalities which define the shaded region in the diagram.

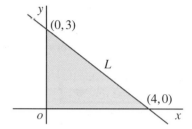

Exercise 16R.B ▼

1. On a diagram, illustrate the set of points (x, y) that simultaneously satisfy the four inequalities:

$$x \geqslant 0 \qquad y \geqslant 0 \qquad x + y \leqslant 6 \qquad 2x + y \leqslant 10$$

2. On a diagram, illustrate the set of points (x, y) that simultaneously satisfy the three inequalities:

$$y \geqslant 0 \qquad x + y \leqslant 7 \qquad 2x + y \geqslant 8$$

3. On a diagram, illustrate the set of points (x, y) that simultaneously satisfy the three inequalities:

$$x \geqslant 3 \qquad y \geqslant 2 \qquad 2x + 3y \leqslant 18$$

4. On a diagram, illustrate the set of points (x, y) that simultaneously satisfy the three inequalities:

$$y \geqslant 2 \qquad x + 2y \leqslant 8 \qquad 5x + y \geqslant -5$$

5. The equation of the line M is $2x + y = 10$.

The equation of the line N is $4x - y = 8$.

Write down the three inequalities that define the shaded region in the diagram.

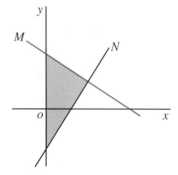

6. The equation of the line M is $x - y - 1 = 0$ and the equation of the line N is $x + 2y - 6 = 0$.

Write down the three inequalities which define the triangular region indicated in the diagram.

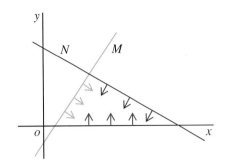

7. The equation of the line M is $x - y + 1 = 0$ and the equation of the line N is $x + y - 6 = 0$.

Write down the three inequalities which define the triangular region indicated in the diagram.

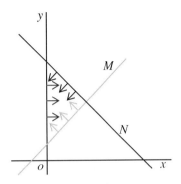

8. The equation of the line K is $y - x = 0$ and the equation of the line N is $y - 4 = 0$.

 (i) Write down the three inequalities which define the triangular region indicated in the diagram.

 (ii) In a diagram, illustrate the set of points (x, y) that satisfy $y - 4 \geqslant 0$, $y - x \leqslant 0$ and $x - 6 \leqslant 0$.

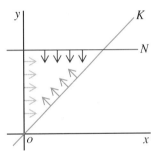

9. Write down the four inequalities which define the shaded region in the diagram.

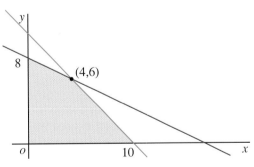

10. Write down the four inequalities which define the shaded region in the diagram.

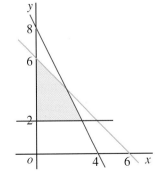

11. On the same diagram. graph the three inequalities:

$$A: y \geqslant 0 \qquad B: x + 2y \leqslant 14 \qquad C: 5x + 4y \geqslant 40$$

Shade in the region $D = A \cap B \cap C$ (the region common to all three inequalities).

Calculate the coordinates of the vertices of D (it is not sufficient to read these coordinates from your graph).

Find the couple $(x, y) \in D$ for which $30x + 10y$ is a maximum and write down this maximum.

Exercise 16R.C ▼

1. Two types of machine, type A and type B, can be purchased for a new factory. Each machine of type A costs €1,600. Each machine of type B costs €800. The purchase of the machines can cost, at most, €27,200.

Each machine of type A needs 90 m^2 of floor space in the factory.

Each machine of type B needs 54 m^2 of floor space.

The maximum amount of floor space available for the machines is 1,620 m^2.

(i) If x represents the number of machines of type A and y represents the number of machines of type B, write down two inequalities in x and y and illustrate these on a graph.

(ii) The daily income from the use of each machine of type A is €75. The daily income from the use of each machine of type B is €42. How many of each type of machine should be purchased so as to maximise daily income?

(iii) What is the maximum daily income?

2. A factory, which manufactures television sets, makes two types of set – a wide-screen model and a standard model.

In any week, 500 sets at most can be manufactured.

Each wide-screen model costs €200 to produce. Each standard model costs €150 to produce. Total weekly production costs must not be greater than €90,000.

(i) If the factory manufactures x of the wide-screen model and y of the standard model, write down two inequalities in x and y and illustrate these on a graph.

(ii) If the profit on a wide-screen model is €100 and the profit on a standard model is €70, how many of each type of set should be manufactured in order to maximise profit?

3. A property developer wishes to construct a business centre consisting of shops and offices. The floor space required for each shop is 60 m^2 and for each office is 20 m^2. The total floor space for the business centre cannot exceed 960 m^2.

The construction of each shop takes 5 working days to complete and each office 3 working days to complete. The developer has at most 120 working days to complete the construction.

(i) If the developer constructs x shops and y offices, write two inequalities in x and y and illustrate these on a graph.

(ii) If the rental charge is €200 per m^2 for a shop and €140 per m^2 for an office, how many of each type should be built so as to maximize the developer's rental income?

Find this maximum rental income.

(iii) If each shop provides 7 jobs and each office 3 jobs, write an expression in x and y for the total number of jobs to be provided. How many of each type should be built so as to maximize the number of jobs?

4. A parking lot has an area of 1500 m^2. The parking area required for a car is 15 m^2 and for a bus is 60 m^2. Not more than 46 vehicles can be accommodated at any one time.

   (i) If x represents the number of cars and y represents the number of buses parked, write two inequalities in x and y. Illustrate these on a graph.

   (ii) The daily parking charge is €5 for a car and €15 for a bus.

   How many of each should be in the parking lot to give a maximum income?

   Calculate this income.

5. A farmer has not more than 2000 m^2 of ground for planting apple trees and blackcurrant bushes. The ground space required for an apple tree is 50 m^2 and for a blackcurrant bush is 5 m^2.

   The planting of an apple tree costs €20 and the planting of a blackcurrant bush costs €4. The farmer has at most €1000 to spend on planting.

   (i) If the farmer plants x apple trees and y blackcurrant bushes, write two inequalities in x and y and illustrate these on a graph.

   When fully grown, each apple tree will produce a crop worth €90 and each blackcurrant bush a crop worth €15.

   (ii) How many of each should be planted so that the farmer's gross income is a maximum?

   (iii) Calculate the farmer's maximum profit.

6. A new ship is being designed. It can have two types of cabin accommodation for passengers – type A and type B cabins.

   Each type A cabin accommodates 6 passengers and each type B cabin accommodates 3 passengers. The maximum number of passengers that the ship can accommodate is 330.

   Each type A cabin occupies 50 m^2 of floor space. Each type B cabin occupies 10 m^2 of floor space. The total amount of floor space occupied by cabins cannot exceed 2300 m^2.

   (i) Taking x to represent the number of type A cabins and y to represent the number of type B cabins, write down two inequalities in x and y and illustrate these on a graph.

   (ii) The income on each voyage from renting the cabins to passengers is €600 for each type A cabin and €180 for each type B cabin. How many of each type of cabin should the ship have so to maximise income, assuming that all cabins are rented?

   (iii) What is the maximum possible income on each voyage from renting the cabins?

7. A company uses small trucks and large trucks to transport its products in crates. The crates are all of the same size.

   On a certain day 10 truck drivers at most are available. Each truck requires one driver only.

   Small trucks take 10 minutes each to load and large trucks take 30 minutes each to load. The total loading time must not be more than 3 hours. Only one truck can be loaded at a time.

   (i) If x represents the number of small trucks used and y represents the number of large trucks used, write down two inequalities in x and y.

   Illustrate these on a graph.

   (ii) Each small truck carries 30 crates and each large truck carries 70 crates. How many of each type of truck should be used to maximize the number of crates to be transported that day?

8. A company produces two products, A and B.

   Each unit of the two products must be processed on two assembly lines, the red line and the blue line, for a certain length of time.

   Each unit of A requires 3 hours on the red line and 1 hour on the blue line.

   Each unit of B requires 1 hour on the red line and 2 hours on the blue line.

   Each week, the maximum time available on the red line is 60 hours and the maximum time available on the blue line is 40 hours.

   (i) If x represents the number of units of A produced in a week and y represents the number of units of B produced in a week, write down two inequalities in x and y.

   Illustrate these on a graph.

   (ii) The profit made on each unit of A is twice the profit made on each unit of B. How many units of each product must be manufactured in a week so as to maximise profit?

   (iii) If the maximum profit that can be made in a week is €1,980, calculate the profit made on each unit of A and on each unit of B.

9. Houses are to be built on 9 hectares of land.

   Two types of house, bungalows and semi-detached houses, are possible.

   Each bungalow occupies one-fifth of a hectare.

   Each semi-detached house occupies one-tenth of a hectare.

   The cost of building a bungalow is €80,000.

   The cost of building a semi-detached house is €50,000.

   The total cost of building the houses cannot be greater than €4 million.

   (i) Taking x to represent the number of bungalows and y to represent the number of semi-detached houses, write down two inequalities in x and y and illustrate these on a graph.

   (ii) The profit on each bungalow is €10,000. The profit on each semi-detached house is €7,000. How many of each type of house should be built so as to maximise profit?

ANSWERS

Exercise 1.1 ▼

1. 5   **2.** 10   **3.** $\sqrt{5}$ **4.** $\sqrt{65}$ **5.** 3   **6.** 6   **7.** $\sqrt{40}$ **8.** $\sqrt{50}$

9. $\sqrt{40}$ **10.** $\sqrt{72}$ **11.** $\sqrt{\dfrac{5}{2}}$ or $\dfrac{\sqrt{10}}{2}$ **12.** $\sqrt{\dfrac{9}{2}}$ or $\dfrac{\sqrt{18}}{2}$ **14.** 5   **16.** −4; 2

Exercise 1.2 ▼

1. $(4, 3)$ **2.** $(5, 3)$ **3.** $(9, -3)$ **4.** $(-6, 5)$ **5.** $(-8, -3)$

6. $(-2, 2)$ **7.** $(3, 3)$ **8.** $(1, -\tfrac{3}{2})$ **9.** $(\tfrac{7}{2}, -2)$ **10.** $(3, 1)$

11. $(2, -\tfrac{1}{2})$ **12.** $(\tfrac{3}{2}, \tfrac{5}{2})$ **13.** $(5, 2)$ **14.** $(-5, -1)$ **15.** $p = 10, q = -5$

16. $a = -2, b = 5$ **17.** 9   **18.** $p = 6, q = -3$ **19.** $(3, 1)$

20. $p(1, -1), q(5, -4); 5 = \tfrac{1}{2}(10)$

Exercise 1.3 ▼

1. 1   **2.** $\tfrac{3}{2}$ **3.** 1   **4.** $\tfrac{5}{3}$ **5.** −1   **6.** $-\tfrac{8}{11}$ **7.** −1   **8.** 10

9. $-\tfrac{11}{4}$ **10.** 2   **16.** $\tfrac{4}{3}$ **17.** $-\tfrac{3}{5}$ **18.** $-\tfrac{1}{3}$ **19.** −4   **20.** $\tfrac{1}{3}$ **21.** 8

22. 6   **23.** 2

Exercise 1.4 ▼

12. 7   **13.** 2   **14.** 3   **15.** −5   **16.** 4

Exercise 1.5 ▼

1. $2x - y - 7 = 0$ **2.** $3x - y - 1 = 0$ **3.** $x + y + 2 = 0$

4. $5x + y - 22 = 0$ **5.** $4x - y = 0$ **6.** $3x - 5y - 47 = 0$

7. $4x + 3y + 15 = 0$ **8.** $5x - 4y - 30 = 0$ **9.** $x + 6y + 15 = 0$

10. $5x + 7y + 17 = 0$ **11.** $2x - 5y - 9 = 0$ **12.** $x + 2y + 1 = 0$

1. $x - y + 3 = 0$ **2.** $2x + y - 10 = 0$ **3.** $3x - y - 18 = 0$ **4.** $5x + 7y - 19 = 0$

5. $3x - 5y + 13 = 0$ **6.** $x + 2y + 9 = 0$ **7.** $5x - 2y - 14 = 0$ **8.** $4x + 2y + 3 = 0$

9. (i) $4x - 3y - 18 = 0$ **10. (i)** $2x - y - 6 = 0$ **11.** $2x + 3y - 7 = 0$ **12.** $3x - 2y + 14 = 0$
  (ii) $3x + 4y - 1 = 0$ **(ii)** $x + 2y + 2 = 0$

1. -2 **2.** 3 **3.** 2 **4.** -3 **5.** $-\frac{2}{3}$ **6.** $\frac{4}{3}$ **7.** $-\frac{1}{4}$ **8.** $\frac{1}{3}$ **9.** $\frac{4}{3}$

10. $\frac{5}{7}$ **11.** $\frac{3}{2}$ **12.** $\frac{7}{10}$ **16.** 6 **17.** 5 **18.** $-\frac{5}{2}; -\frac{a}{10}$ **(i)** 25 **(ii)** -4

1. $2x - y - 3 = 0$ **2.** $2x + 3y = 0$ **3.** $5x + 4y + 21 = 0$ **4.** $3x + 4y - 14 = 0$

5. $5x - 3y + 10 = 0$ **6.** $x + 2y + 5 = 0$ **7.** $5x - 2y - 13 = 0$

1. $(2, 1)$ **2.** $(3, 2)$ **3.** $(1, 0)$ **4.** $(-4, 3)$ **5.** $(-3, -1)$ **6.** $(0, -5)$ **7.** $(1, 2)$

8. $(6, -1)$ **9.** $(-3, 7)$ **10.** $\left(\frac{3}{5}, \frac{4}{5}\right)$ **11.** $\left(\frac{3}{2}, -\frac{3}{2}\right)$ **12.** $\left(\frac{6}{5}, \frac{2}{5}\right)$ **13.** $\left(\frac{4}{5}, \frac{6}{5}\right)$ **14.** $\left(\frac{5}{2}, \frac{1}{2}\right)$

15. $\left(\frac{10}{3}, \frac{10}{3}\right)$ **16.** $(-3, -3)$ **17.** $(-2, -4)$ **18.** $4x - y - 7 = 0$ **19.** $a = 2; b = 4$

1. 7 **2.** 13 **3.** 19 **4.** 9 **5.** $\frac{11}{2}$ **6.** 0 **7.** 20 **8.** 19 **9.** $\frac{27}{2}$

10. 12 **11.** 10 **12.** 6 **13.** 12 **14.** 7 **15.** 9 **16.** 36 **17.** 37 **18.** 72

Exercise 1.14 ▼

1. (i) $\sqrt{20}$ **(ii)** $(0, 3)$ **(iii)** 5   **(iv)** $-\frac{1}{2}$ **(v)** $x + 2y - 6 = 0$ **(vi)** $2x - y - 7 = 0$ **(vii)** $(4, 1)$

2. (ii) 3   **4.** $(3, -5)$ **5. (i)** $a(4, 0), b(0, -6)$ **(iii)** 12   **6.** $a(1, 3), b(-5, 0), c(2, 0); \frac{21}{2}$

7. (i) $4x - 3y + 23 = 0$ **(ii)** $d(-2, 5)$ **(iii)** $m(5, 3)$ **(iv)** 34   **(v)** 5

8. (iii) $q(-4, 1)$ **(iv)** $r(0, 9)$ **(vi)** 40

9. (i) $r(0, \frac{5}{2})$ **(ii)** $2x + y - 5 = 0$ **(iii)** $q(1, 3)$ **(iv)** 5

10. (ii) $b(5, 3)$ **(iii)** no   **(iv)** $2x - y - 10 = 0$ **(v)** $d(5, 0)$ **(vi)** $\frac{15}{2}$

11. (ii) $(0, -8)$ **(iii)** $x + 3y - 6 = 0$ **(iv)** $(0, 2)$ **(v)** $(3, 1)$ **(vi)** 15

12. 5; 11

Exercise 1.15 ▼

1. $(5, 6)$

2. (i) $(4, 5)$ **(ii)** $(1, 2)$ **(iii)** $(-6, 0)$ **(iv)** $(-8, 3)$

3. (i) $(7, -3)$ **(ii)** $(1, 4)$ **(iii)** $(-2, -4)$ **(iv)** $(12, 3); (-2, 3)$

4. (i) $(1, 6)$ **(ii)** $(6, 2)$ **(iii)** $(0, 1)$ **(iv)** $(-1, -1)$

5. $h = 1, k = -1$ **6.** $(5, -8)$ **7.** $(-8, 7)$

8. $(10, -2)$ **9. (i)** $(6, -9)$ **(ii)** $(0, 3)$ **10.** $c(11, 5), d(3, 4)$

11. (i) $b(5, -1)$ **(ii)** $(5, 0)$

12. (i) $(4, -3)$ **(ii)** $(-4, 3)$ **(iii)** $(-4, -3)$

13. (i) $(5, -1)$ **(ii)** $(-5, 1)$ **(iii)** $(-5, -1)$

14. (i) $(-2, 3)$ **(ii)** $(2, -3)$ **(iii)** $(2, 3)$

15. (i) $(-1, -5)$ **(ii)** $(1, 5)$ **(iii)** $(1, -5)$

16. (i) $(-3, -4)$ **(ii)** $(3, 4)$ **(iii)** $(3, -4)$

17. (ii) $q(-3, 5)$ **(iv)** $t(-4, 2)$ **(v)** $r(1, 6)$ **(vi)** $3x - y + 3 = 0$

18. (ii) $(2, 1)$ **(iv)** $r(8, 5)$

Exercise 1.16 ▼

1. (i) $p(-1, 2), q(-4, -2)$ **(ii)** $4x - 3y + 10 = 0$ **(iii)** yes, slope of ab = slope of $pq = \frac{4}{3}$

2. $2x + 3y - 8 = 0$ **3.** $5x - 2y - 11 = 0$ **4.** $7x - 2y + 19 = 0$

5. $3x + 5y + 15 = 0$ **6.** $3x - 4y - 2 = 0$ **7. (i)** $\frac{2}{5}$ **(ii)** $(0, -3)$ **(iii)** $2x - 5y + 8 = 0$

Exercise 2.1 ▼

1. $3i$ **2.** $4i$ **3.** $5i$ **4.** $2i$ **5.** $7i$ **6.** $8i$ **7.** $10i$ **8.** $11i$ **9.** $12i$

Exercise 2.3 ▼

1. $9 + 8i$ **2.** $8 + 5i$ **3.** $6 + 5i$ **4.** $3 + 4i$ **5.** $14 - i$ **6.** $-3 + 8i$

7. $-3 - 3i$ **8.** $22 - 24i$ **9.** $-5 - 21i$ **10.** $31 - 12i$ **11.** $8 - 3i$ **12.** 19

13. $-1 - 9i$ **14.** $-11 - 13i$ **15.** $17 - 2i$ **16.** $28 + 18i$ **17.** $2 - i$ **18.** $2 - 5i$

19. $-25 - 17i$

Exercise 2.4 ▼

1. $6 + 17i$ **2.** $1 + 13i$ **3.** $16 + 11i$ **4.** $-4 + 7i$ **5.** $18 - 26i$

6. $1 - 3i$ **7.** $-5 + 5i$ **8.** $7 + 11i$ **9.** $12 - 7i$ **10.** $14 + 22i$

11. $8 - 64i$ **12.** $66 - 8i$ **13.** $8 + 12i$ **14.** $-8 + 6i$ **15.** $16 + 4i$

16. $-5 + 12i$ **17.** $9 + 24i$ **18.** $20 - 16i$ **19.** $18 + 12i$ **20.** $-34 - 12i$

Exercise 2.5 ▼

9. (i) 8 **(ii)** $10i$ **(iii)** 41 **10. (i)** 6 **(ii)** $-4i$ **(iii)** 13

11. (i) -8 **(ii)** $4i$ **(iii)** 20 **12. (i)** -2 **(ii)** $-2i$ **(iii)** 2

13. (i) 0 **(ii)** $10i$ **(iii)** 25 **14. (i)** 8 **(ii)** 0 **(iii)** 16

15. (i) -6 **(ii)** 0 **(iii)** 9 **16. (i)** 0 **(ii)** $-12i$ **(iii)** 36

Exercise 2.6

1. $2 + 2i$ **2.** $2 + 3i$ **3.** $2 + i$ **4.** $-2 + i$ **5.** $5 + 2i$

6. $3 - 4i$ **7.** $3 - 5i$ **8.** $2 - 3i$ **9.** $4 + 0i$ **10.** $0 - i$

11. $\frac{1}{2} + \frac{3}{2}i$ **12.** $\frac{6}{5} - \frac{8}{5}i$ **13.** $a = 3, b = 1$ **14.** 1 **15.** $2u$

16. **(i)** $2 + 3i$ **(ii)** $3 - i$ **(iii)** $2 + i$

Exercise 2.7

1. $x = 4, y = 3$ **2.** $x = 5, y = 4$ **3.** $x = 2, y = 1$ **4.** $x = 2, y = 3$

5. $x = 7, y = 7$ **6.** $x = 1, y = 2$ **7.** $x = 3, y = 2$ **8.** $x = -4, y = 3$

9. $x = -2, y = 5$ **10.** $x = -7, y = 15$ **11.** $x = 2, y = -3$ **12.** $x = 15, y = -21$

13. $k = 3, l = 2$ **14.** $a = 2, b = -4$ **15.** $h = 3, k = 2$ **16.** $p = 4, q = -1$

17. $t = \frac{3}{5}, k = 7$ **18.** $k = 2, t = 10$ **19.** $a = -\frac{4}{3}, b = \frac{4}{3}$ **20.** $l = -2, k = -3$

21. $l = -2, p = 7$ **22.** $x = 0, y = 5$ **23.** **(i)** $x = 1, y = 1$ **(ii)** $x = 1, y = -2$

Exercise 2.9

1. 5 **2.** 10 **3.** 13 **4.** 17 **5.** 41 **6.** 7

7. $\sqrt{34}$ **8.** $\sqrt{61}$ **9.** 15 **10.** 13 **11.** 1 **12.** $\sqrt{13}$

15. yes **16.** **(i)** $\sqrt{50}$ **(ii)** 50 **17.** $3 - 3i;$ **(i)** $\sqrt{18}$ **(ii)** $a = -\frac{1}{2}$

18. $3 - 4i; \dfrac{\sqrt{50}}{\sqrt{2}} = \sqrt{\frac{50}{2}} = \sqrt{25} = 5; h = 2; k = -\frac{2}{5}$ **19.** **(ii)** ± 4 **20.** ± 6 **21.** ± 2

22. ± 5 **23.** ± 4

Exercise 2.10 ▼

1. $3 \pm 2i$ **2.** $1 \pm 3i$ **3.** $-2 \pm i$ **4.** $-5 \pm 3i$ **5.** $-2 \pm 3i$ **6.** $5 \pm 4i$

7. $-1 \pm i$ **8.** $1 \pm 2i$ **9.** $-7 \pm 2i$ **10.** $-4 \pm i$ **11.** $\pm 4i$ **12.** $\pm 5i$

13. $\frac{1}{2} \pm \frac{1}{2}i$ **14.** $\frac{3}{2} \pm \frac{1}{2}i$ **15.** $-1 - 2i$ **16.** $3 + 2i$ **17.** $2 + 5i$ **18.** $-4 + 6i$

19. $-5 + i$ **20.** $-5 - 4i$ **21.** $z^2 + 4z + 5 = 0$ **22.** $z^2 - 8z + 25 = 0$

23. $z^2 + 2z + 10 = 0$ **24.** $z^2 - 2z + 5 = 0$ **25.** $z^2 - 2z + 2 = 0$ **26.** $z^2 + 10z + 29 = 0$

27. $z^2 + 1$ **28.** $z^2 + 9 = 0$ **29.** $p = -6, q = 34$ **30.** $a = -14, b = 50$

31. $m = 6, n = 18$ **32.** $h = 2, k = 26, \sqrt{34}$ **33.** 144   **34.** $z^2 + 4z + 20 = 0$

Exercise 3.1 ▼

1. 4; 3   **2.** 4; 4   **3.** 6; 5   **4.** 6.3; 6.4   **5.** 4.7; 4.35   **6.** €5.06; €5.15

7. 45   **8.** $x = 9$; 8   **9.** 2   **10.** 11   **11.** $3a + 5$

Exercise 3.2 ▼

1. 2; 2   **2.** 3; 3   **3.** 8; 7   **4.** 14; 14   **5.** 3; 2   **6.** 12.75; 12.5

7. (i) 3   **(ii)** 3.25   **(iii)** 3.3   **8. (ii)** 4   **(iii)** 4   **(iv)** 40%   **(v)** 200   **(vi)** 6

Exercise 3.3 ▼

1. 3; 2 – 4   **2.** 10; 9 – 13   **3.** 54; 40 – 60   **4.** 10; 6 – 12

5. 29; 15 – 35   **6.** 22; 20 – 35   **7.** 117; 60 – 120   **8.** 20; 15 – 25

10. (i) 36   **(ii)** 31   **(iii)** 90   **(iv)** 30 – 40

Exercise 3.4 ▼

1. 5   **2.** 7   **3.** 6.8   **4.** A; B   **5.** 105.5   **6.** S_2; S_1 **7.** 17; B; A

Exercise 3.5

1. 1.41   **2.** 3.06   **3.** 1.87   **4.** 1.63   **5.** 2.45   **6.** 4.24   **7.** 3.87

8. 2.65   **9.** 2.55   **10.** $k = 2$ **11.** $\sqrt{5.2} = \sqrt{5.2}$ **13.** 1.5

Exercise 3.6

1. 3; 1.21   **2.** 8; 3.02   **3.** 6; 4.02   **4.** 16; 1.36   **5.** 11; 4.36   **6.** 35; 20.37   **7.** 8; 4.95

8. 49; 26.95   **9. (i)** 4 – 12   **(iii)** 13   **(iv)** 8.54

Exercise 3.7

8. (ii) 6 – 12   **(iii)** 10; 5.9   **9. (ii)** 42   **(iii)** 11.87   **(iv)** 54

Exercise 3.8

1. 290   **2.** 30 – 60   **3. (i)** 13   **(ii)** 7.25   **4. (i)** 36   **(ii)** 21.77

Exercise 3.9

1. (i) 17   **(ii)** 19   **(iii)** 13   **(iv)** 6

2. (i) 42   **(ii)** 52   **(iii)** 28   **(iv)** 24

3. (i) 52   **(ii)** 65   **(iii)** 39   **(iv)** 26

4. (i) 57   **(ii)** 64   **(iii)** 51   **(iv)** 13

5. (i) $5\frac{1}{2}$ mins   **(ii)** 2 mins   **(iii)** 5   **(iv)** 5

6. (i) 16   **(ii)** 34

7. (i) 08.51   **(ii)** 23   **(iii)** 25%

8. (i) €32; €12.08   **(v)** €33   **(vi)** €13   **(vii)** 12   **(viii)** 8

9. (ii) 51   **(iii)** 20.89   **(vi)** 52   **(vii)** 29   **(viii)** 45

10. (i) 66 mins   **(v)** 27 mins   **(vi) (a)** 15 **(b)** 10

11. (i) 10 years   **(ii)** 4 years   **(iii)** 5   **(v)** 67%

Exercise 3.10

1. 5   **2.** 2   **3.** 7   **4.** 6   **5.** 8; 30   **6.** 3   **7.** 2   **8.** 4   **9.** 3; 7   **10.** 76

1. 23   **2.** −2   **3.** −3   **4.** −5   **5.** −8   **6.** 3

7. 5   **8.** 6   **9.** $\frac{2}{3}$ **10.** $\frac{1}{2}$ **11.** $\frac{5}{8}$ **12.** $\frac{7}{4}$

13. $\frac{25}{12}$ **14.** $\frac{19}{30}$ **15.** 2   **16.** $\frac{25}{36}$ **17.** $\frac{7}{8}$ **18.** 1

19. 1   **20.** −2   **21.** 3   **22.** 0   **23.** 2   **24.** $\frac{2}{3}$

25. 10   **26.** 20   **27.** 9   **28.** 4   **29.** 2   **30.** −2

31. 5   **32.** 2   **33.** 4   **34.** 5   **35.** $\frac{1}{5}$

1. $8x$ **2.** $-3x$ **3.** $-7x$ **4.** $3x$ **5.** $-6x$ **6.** $-4x^2$

7. $2a^2$ **8.** $3x-1$ **9.** x^2+2x-3 **10.** $6x^2$ **11.** $-10x^2$ **12.** $-12x^3$

13. $5x^3$ **14.** $-24x^3$ **15.** $6a^2b^2$ **16.** $-10p^2q$ **17.** $12a^3b^3$ **18.** a^2

19. $2ab$ **20.** $2x$ **21.** $6x^2$ **22.** $3q^2$ **23.** 0   **24.** x^2+5x+6

25. x^2+x-12 **26.** x^2-3x+2 **27.** $2x^2-5x-3$ **28.** $6x^2+11x-10$

29. $10x^2-7x+1$ **30.** x^2+6x+9 **31.** $4x^2-4x+1$ **32.** $9x^2-12x+4$

33. $4a^2-12ab+9b^2$ **34.** $2x^3+5x^2+9x+6$ **35.** $2x^3+11x^2+13x+4$

36. $6x^3-11x^2-12x+5$ **37.** $3x^3-19x^2+32x-16$ **38.** 0   **39.** 7   **40.** −2

1. 3   **2.** 2   **3.** 4   **4.** −6   **5.** 1   **6.** 2   **7.** 5   **8.** 6   **9.** 1   **10.** 5

11. 1   **12.** 3   **13.** 7   **14.** 4   **15.** 4   **16.** 7   **17.** 2   **18.** 3   **19.** $\frac{13}{2}$ **20.** −2

1. $x \geqslant 3$ **2.** $x \leqslant 1$ **3.** $x \geqslant 4$ **4.** $x = 0, 1, 2, 3$ **5.** $x < -2$

6. $x \leqslant -4$ **7.** $x < -2$ **8.** $x < 2$ **9.** $x > -6$ **10.** $x = 0, 1, 2$

11. $x \leqslant 3, \quad x \geqslant -2, \quad -2 \leqslant x \leqslant 3$ **12.** $x \leqslant 4, \quad x \geqslant -1, \quad -1 \leqslant x \leqslant 4$

13. (i) $x < 1$ (ii) $x \geqslant -3$ (iii) $-3 \leqslant x < 1$ **14.** (i) $x \leqslant 2$ (ii) $x \geqslant -\frac{7}{2}$ (iii) $-\frac{7}{2} \leqslant x \leqslant 2$

15. (i) $x \geqslant -2$ (ii) $x \leqslant 5$ (iii) $a = -2, b = 5$ **16.** (i) 0, 1   (ii) 0, 1, 2, 3   (iii) 2, 3

17. 0, 1, 2, 3, 4; 4

Exercise 4.5 ▼

1. $x = 2, y = 1$ **2.** $x = 4, y = 2$ **3.** $x = 5, y = 3$ **4.** $x = 5, y = 2$

5. $x = -2, y = -3$ **6.** $x = 2, y = 3$ **7.** $x = 7, y = 3$ **8.** $x = 3, y = -1$

9. $x = 3, y = 2$ **10.** $x = -1, y = 1$ **11.** $x = 1, y = -4$ **12.** $x = -1, y = -1$

13. $x = -2, y = -1$ **14.** $x = 3, y = 4$ **15.** $x = -1, y = 1$ **16.** $x = 2, y = 3$

17. $x = 2, y = -3$ **18.** $x = 3, y = 3$ **19.** $x = 5, y = -1$ **20.** $x = 2, y = -2$

21. $x = -1, y = -3$ **22.** $x = 1, y = \frac{1}{3}$ **23.** $x = \frac{3}{2}, y = \frac{5}{2}$ **24.** $x = \frac{5}{2}, y = \frac{4}{3}$

25. $x = \frac{3}{5}, y = \frac{4}{5}$ **26.** $x = \frac{5}{2}, y = 1$ **27.** $x = \frac{3}{2}, y = \frac{1}{2}$

Exercise 4.6 ▼

1. $(2x + 3)(x + 1)$ **2.** $(3x - 1)(x + 3)$ **3.** $(2x - 3)(x - 2)$ **4.** $(3x - 7)(x + 1)$

5. $(2x + 1)(x - 5)$ **6.** $(5x - 1)(x + 2)$ **7.** $(2x - 3)(x + 5)$ **8.** $(3x + 4)(x - 5)$

9. $(7x - 2)(x + 1)$ **10.** $(x - 3)(x - 4)$ **11.** $(x + 3)(x - 5)$ **12.** $(x - 3)(x - 7)$

13. $(3x + 2)(x + 3)$ **14.** $(2x + 7)(x + 2)$ **15.** $(3x + 2)(x - 1)$ **16.** $(2x - 3)(x + 2)$

17. $(3x - 2)(x + 4)$ **18.** $(5x - 1)(x - 4)$ **19.** $(2x + 1)(2x + 3)$ **20.** $(4x + 1)(x - 3)$

21. $(3x - 2)(2x + 1)$ **22.** $(6x - 1)(x - 2)$ **23.** $(4x + 5)(2x - 1)$ **24.** $(5x - 3)(2x + 1)$

25. $x(x + 2)$ **26.** $x(x - 4)$ **27.** $x(x + 5)$ **28.** $x(x - 7)$

29. $x(x + 1)$ **30.** $x(x - 1)$ **31.** $x(2x - 1)$ **32.** $x(2x - 3)$

33. $x(3x + 5)$ **34.** $(x - 3)(x + 3)$ **35.** $(x - 2)(x + 2)$ **36.** $(x - 1)(x + 1)$

37. $(x - 7)(x + 7)$ **38.** $(x - 10)(x + 10)$ **39.** $(x - 6)(x + 6)$ **40.** $(2x - 3)(2x + 3)$

41. $(5x - 6)(5x + 6)$ **42.** $(3x - 2)(3x + 2)$ **43.** $(4x - 5)(4x + 5)$ **44.** $(2x - 1)(2x + 1)$

45. $(3x - 1)(3x + 1)$

Exercise 4.7 ▼

1. $2, -5$ **2.** $-\frac{2}{3}, 7$ **3.** $0, 6$ **4.** $0, \frac{2}{3}$ **5.** $2, -2$ **6.** $\frac{5}{3}, -\frac{5}{3}$

7. $\frac{1}{2}, 5$ **8.** $1, -\frac{5}{3}$ **9.** $\frac{1}{5}, -1$ **10.** $\frac{3}{2}, -1$ **11.** $\frac{2}{5}, -1$ **12.** $2, -\frac{5}{3}$

13. $3, \frac{2}{5}$ **14.** $3, -5$ **15.** $-3, 9$ **16.** $0, 3$ **17.** $0, -2$ **18.** $0, 5$

19. $0, -7$ **20.** $0, \frac{3}{2}$ **21.** $0, -\frac{4}{3}$ **22.** ± 2 **23.** ± 5 **24.** ± 6

25. $\pm \frac{3}{2}$ **26.** $\pm \frac{4}{3}$ **27.** $\pm \frac{1}{2}$ **28.** $-\frac{1}{4}, 3$ **29.** $\frac{1}{2}, \frac{5}{2}$ **30.** $\frac{1}{2}, -\frac{2}{3}$

31. $\frac{1}{3}, -\frac{5}{2}$ **32.** $\frac{1}{4}, \frac{3}{2}$ **33.** $\frac{2}{3}$ **34.** $2x^2 - x - 15; (2x + 5)(x - 3); -\frac{5}{2}, 3$

35. $-\frac{3}{2}, -2$ **36.** $-3, -4$ **37.** $3, -1$

1. $\dfrac{17x}{6}$ **2.** $\dfrac{7x}{12}$ **3.** $\dfrac{3x+7}{20}$ **4.** $\dfrac{10}{3x}$ **5.** $\dfrac{9}{20x}$

6. $\dfrac{3x+38}{12x}$ **7.** $\dfrac{5x+8}{(x+2)(x+1)}$ **8.** $\dfrac{5x+21}{(x+3)(x+5)}$ **9.** $\dfrac{3x-6}{(x-4)(x+2)}$ **10.** $\dfrac{8x+9}{(3x+4)(2x+1)}$

11. $\dfrac{18x+1}{(2x-1)(2x+1)}$ **12.** $\dfrac{13x+4}{(3x-2)(2x+5)}$ **13.** $\dfrac{3-x}{2x(3x-1)}$ **14.** $\dfrac{11-5x}{(2x-5)(x-3)}$ **15.** $\dfrac{x+8}{(3x-1)(2x+1)}$

16. $\dfrac{x^2+12x+16}{4x(x+4)}$ **17.** $\dfrac{5x^2+15x+6}{2x(x+1)}$ **18.** $\dfrac{4x^2-6x-10}{x(x-2)}$ **19.** $p=7,\ q=-2$

1. 2, 4 **2.** −2, −3 **3.** −3, 5 **4.** −1, 2 **5.** −1, 5 **6.** $\frac{3}{2}$, 1 **7.** 0, 4

8. −1, 3 **9.** 4, −5 **10.** −3, 4 **11.** $\frac{2}{3}$, 1 **12.** −2, 3 **13.** $\frac{1}{2}$, −3 **14.** −3, 4

15. 1, 3 **16.** $-\frac{7}{3}$, 4 **17.** $-\frac{2}{5}$, 4 **18.** $-\frac{1}{3}$, 3 **19.** 1, 8 **20.** $-\frac{1}{2}$, −1 **21.** $-\frac{1}{2}$, 5

1. −2, 4 **2.** 3, 4 **3.** −2, $\frac{1}{2}$ **4.** $-\frac{3}{5}$, 2 **5.** $\frac{4}{3}$, −3 **6.** $\frac{2}{3}$, −4

7. −1.39, 2.89 **8.** 0.38, −1.58 **9.** 0.53, −7.53 **10.** 2.47, −0.14

11. 0.39, −0.64 **12.** −0.23, −1.43 **13.** 0.77, −0.43 **14.** 1.69, −0.44

15. 1.85, −1.35 **16.** −0.31, −1.29 **17.** −0.46, −2.87 **18.** 1.58, 0.42

19. $2x^2+x-5=0$; 1.4, −1.9 **20.** $x^2-3x+1=0$; 2.6, 0.4 **21.** $2x^2+3x-8=0$; 1.4, −2.9

22. $4x^2+x-2=0$; 0.6, −0.8 **23.** $2x^2-7x+2=0$; 3.2, 0.3 **24.** $3x^2+6x+2=0$; −0.4, −1.6

25. $x^2-7x+4=0$; 6.4, 0.6 **26.** $x^2-5x-9=0$; 6.4, −1.4 **27.** $2x^2-4x-3=0$; 2.6, −0.6

28. (i) $\dfrac{3x-1}{(x+1)(x-3)}$ (ii) 5.4, −0.4

1. $x^2 + 2x + 1$ **2.** $y^2 - 4y + 4$ **3.** $x^2 + 6x + 9$ **4.** $y^2 - 8y + 16$

5. $4x^2 - 4x + 1$ **6.** $9y^2 - 6y + 1$ **7.** $4x^2 + 12x + 9$ **8.** $25y^2 - 20y + 4$

9. $x = 0, y = 1$ or $x = -1, y = 0$ **10.** $x = 1, y = 3$ or $x = -3, y = -1$

11. $x = 1, y = 2$ or $x = 2, y = 1$ **12.** $x = 5, y = 0$ or $x = -3, y = -4$

13. $x = 4, y = 2$ or $x = -4, y = -2$ **14.** $x = 0, y = -4$ or $x = 5, y = 1$

15. $x = -1, y = -2$ or $x = 2, y = 1$ **16.** $x = -2, y = -3$ or $x = 3, y = 2$

17. $x = \frac{1}{3}, y = 3$ or $x = 1, y = 1$ **18.** $x = 1, y = 2$

19. $x = 0, y = -4$ or $x = 5, y = 1$ **20.** $x = 2, y = -2$ or $x = -2, y = 2$

21. $x = -\frac{1}{2}, y = 0$ or $x = -1, y = -1$ **22.** $x = -1, y = 3$ or $x = 2, y = -3$

22. $x = -\frac{3}{2}, y = -\frac{1}{6}$ or $x = 5, y = 2$

1. x^2 **2.** $2x$ **3.** x^2 **4.** 1

5. $4x$ **6.** $-2x$ **7.** $2x$ **8.** $-3x$

9. -3 **10.** 1 **11.** $x^2 + 4x + 3$ **12.** $x^2 + 3x + 2$

13. $x^2 + 3x + 1$ **14.** $x^2 + 2x + 1$ **15.** $x^2 - 2x - 3$ **16.** $x^2 - 2x - 15$

17. $x^2 - x + 2$ **18.** $x^2 + 2x + 15$ **19.** $x^2 - 4x - 3$ **20.** $x^2 - 2x - 1$

21. $x^2 + 3x + 2$ **22.** $3x^2 - 8x + 4$ **23.** $a = 1, b = 4, c = 3; 6; (x+1)(x+3)$ **24.** $(x-2)(x-3)$

7. -2 **8.** 5 **9.** 6 **10.** 1 **11.** -2 **12.** 3 **13.** $8, -4$ **14.** $-2, 6$ **15.** $3, 10$ **16.** $2, 7$

1. $1, 2, -5$ **2.** $(x+3)(x+4); -2, -3, -4$ **3.** $(x-2)(x+4)(x+3); 2, -3, -4$

4. $(x-2)(x+1)(x+3); 2, -1, -3$ **5.** $(x-4)(2x-3)(x-2); 4, \frac{3}{2}, 2$ **6.** $(x-1)(x-2)(x+3); 1, 2, -3$

7. $1, -1, 4$ **8.** $1, -2, 3$ **9.** $1, 3, 4$ **10.** $1, -2, 5$ **11.** $1, 3, 5$

12. $2, 3, -4$ **13.** $-1, -\frac{1}{2}, -2$ **14.** $-1, \frac{1}{3}, 2$ **15.** $-2, \frac{1}{2}, -\frac{1}{2}$ **16.** $-2, \frac{1}{3}, -\frac{3}{2}$

17. $2.35, -0.85$ **18.** $k = 26; 3, 4$ **19.** $k = 5; 1, -4$ **20.** $h = -5, k = -6; -3$ **21.** $a = -4, b = 3$

1. $x^2 - 5x + 6 = 0$ **2.** $x^2 + x - 2 = 0$ **3.** $x^2 + 8x + 15 = 0$

4. $x^2 - 3x - 4 = 0$ **5.** $x^2 + 2x - 15 = 0$ **6.** $x^2 + 6x - 16 = 0$

7. $x^2 - 9 = 0$ **8.** $x^2 - 1 = 0$ **9.** $x^2 + 2x = 0$

10. $x^2 - 4x = 0$ **11.** $2x^2 - 7x + 3 = 0$ **12.** $3x^2 - 5x - 2 = 0$

13. $m = -4; n = -21$ **14.** $a - 2, b - -9, c - -5$ **15.** $x^3 + 6x^2 + 11x + 6 = 0$

16. $x^3 - 2x^2 - 19x + 20 = 0$ **17.** $x^3 + 5x^2 - x - 5 = 0$ **18.** $x^3 - x^2 - 14x + 24 = 0$

19. $x^3 - 7x^2 + 2x + 40 = 0$ **20.** $x^3 + 5x^2 - 2x - 24 = 0$ **21.** $2x^3 + 3x^2 - 8x + 3 = 0$

22. $3x^3 + 16x^2 + 3x - 10 = 0$ **23.** $a = -6, b = 3, c = 10$ **24.** $a = 2, b = -1, c = -25, d = -12$

1. $\dfrac{q+r}{2}$ **2.** $\dfrac{c-b}{3}$ **3.** $\dfrac{c+d}{a}$ **4.** $\dfrac{v-u}{a}$ **5.** $\dfrac{5c-2b}{3}$

6. $\dfrac{4p+2r}{3}$ **7.** $\dfrac{2r+q}{2}$ **8.** $\dfrac{ac+d}{a}$ **9.** $2a - 2c$ **10.** $3r - 3p$

11. $\dfrac{6c-2b}{3}$ **12.** $2r - q$ **13.** $\dfrac{b-3a}{2}$ **14.** $p - 2r$ **15.** $yz - xy$

16. $\dfrac{sr-2pr}{3}$ **17.** $\dfrac{2a-c}{b}$ **18.** $\dfrac{t-a+d}{d}$ **19.** $\dfrac{3V}{\pi r^2}$ **20.** $\dfrac{V^2-u^2}{25}$

21. $\dfrac{25-2ut}{t^2}$ **22.** $\dfrac{p+r}{s}$ **23.** $\dfrac{q-pr}{p}$ **24.** $\dfrac{mx-n}{m}$ **25.** $\dfrac{1}{r-t}$

26. $\dfrac{t}{r-p}$ **27.** $\dfrac{y}{x-u}$ **28.** $\dfrac{b^2}{a-bd}$ **29.** $\dfrac{b}{2-c}$ **30.** $\dfrac{2a}{b+2}$

31. $\dfrac{ab}{b-a}$ **32.** $\dfrac{pr}{p-2r}$ **33.** $\dfrac{p-r}{r+1}$ **34.** $\dfrac{pq-q}{p+1}$ **35.** $\dfrac{c^2}{b}$

36. $\dfrac{p}{a^2}$ **37.** $\dfrac{s^2+r}{q}$ **38.** $\dfrac{u-s}{uv^2}$ **39.** $\dfrac{x+2t^2}{t^2}; 3$ **40.** $\dfrac{4+4p^2}{p^2}; 5$

Exercise 5.6 ▼

1. 7 **2.** 10 **3.** 4 **4.** 2 **5.** 3 **6.** −2 **7.** 6 **8.** 10 **9.** 18 **10.** −2

11. −3 **12.** 2 **13.** $\frac{1}{2}$ **14.** 2 **15.** $\frac{3}{2}$ **16.** 3 **17.** 5 **18.** 10 **19.** 2 **20.** 3

21. 4 **22.** 5 **23.** 2 **24.** 3 **25.** 10 **26.** 8 **27.** 4 **28.** 125 **29.** 8 **30.** 25

31. 16 **32.** 16 **33.** 8 **34.** 243 **35.** 32 **36.** $\frac{1}{2}$ **37.** $\frac{1}{3}$ **38.** $\frac{1}{9}$ **39.** $\frac{1}{16}$ **40.** $\frac{1}{16}$

41. $\frac{2}{3}$ **42.** $\frac{4}{25}$ **43.** $\frac{16}{9}$ **44.** $\frac{3}{2}$ **45.** $\frac{27}{64}$ **46.** $\frac{1}{9}$ **47.** $\frac{9}{8}$ **48.** $\frac{4}{3}$ **49.** $\frac{1}{125}$ **50.** $\frac{1}{32}$

51. (i) 2^3 (ii) $3^{3/2}$

52. (i) 2^3 (ii) 2^4 (iii) 2^5 (iv) $2^{1/2}$ (v) $2^{3/2}$ (vi) $2^{5/2}$ (vii) $2^{3/2}$ (viii) 2^3 (ix) $2^{5/2}$ (x) 2^{-5} (xi) 2^{-1}

53. (i) 3^2 (ii) 3^3 (iii) 3^4 (iv) 3^5 (v) $3^{1/2}$ (vi) $3^{3/2}$ (vii) $3^{5/2}$ (viii) 3^5 (ix) 3^5 (x) 3^{-3}

54. (i) 5^2 (ii) 5^3 (iii) $5^{1/2}$ (iv) $5^{3/2}$ (v) $5^{-1/2}$ (vi) 5^{-1} (vii) 5^{-3} (viii) 5^{-3}

Exercise 5.7 ▼

1. 2^3 **2.** 3^2 **3.** 2^5 **4.** 3^3 **5.** 5^3 **6.** 3^4 **7.** 7^2 **8.** 2^6 **9.** 5^4 **10.** 3^5

11. 2^7 **12.** 7^3 **13.** 2^{-4} **14.** 2^{-5} **15.** 3^{-5} **16.** $3^{5/2}$ **17.** $5^{-3/2}$ **18.** 2^3 **19.** $5^{3/2}$ **20.** $3^{1/2}$

21. $3^{-3/2}$ **22.** 3^{-3} **23.** $5^{-3/2}$ **24.** 5^{-3} **25.** 4 **26.** 3 **27.** 2 **28.** 3 **29.** 6 **30.** 2

31. 1 **32.** $\frac{7}{2}$ **33.** $\frac{1}{4}$ **34.** −3 **35.** −2 **36.** −1 **37.** $-\frac{5}{2}$ **38.** 2 **39.** 3 **40.** $4^2; \frac{3}{2}$

41. 3 **42.** (i) 5^3 (ii) $5^{1/2}$ (iii) $5^{5/2}; 3$ **43.** (i) $2^{1/2}$ (ii) $2^4; \frac{9}{4}$

44. (i) $3^{1/2}$ (ii) 3^3 (iii) $3^{3/2}$ (iv) 2 (v) $-\frac{3}{2}$

Exercise 6.1 ▼

1. $x^2 + y^2 = 4$ **2.** $x^2 + y^2 = 9$ **3.** $x^2 + y^2 = 16$ **4.** $x^2 + y^2 = 100$ **5.** $x^2 + y^2 = 5$

6. $x^2 + y^2 = 13$ **7.** $x^2 + y^2 = 17$ **8.** $x^2 + y^2 = 23$ **9.** $x^2 + y^2 = 25$ **10.** $x^2 + y^2 = 13$

11. $x^2 + y^2 = 26$ **12.** $x^2 + y^2 = 16$ **13.** $x^2 + y^2 = 2$ **14.** $x^2 + y^2 = 29$ **15.** 4

16. 3 **17.** 1 **18.** $\sqrt{13}$ **19.** $\sqrt{5}$ **20.** $\sqrt{29}$

21. $(3, 0), (-3, 0), (0, 3), (0, -3)$ **22.** $(4, 0), (-4, 0), (0, 4), (0, -4)$ **23.** $(7, 0), (-7, 0), (0, 7), (0, -7)$

24. $x^2 + y^2 = 25$ **25.** $x^2 + y^2 = 37$ **26.** $(-6, 3)$ **27.** 40π

1. on   **2.** outside   **3.** on   **4.** inside   **5.** on   **6.** on

7. inside   **8.** on   **9.** inside   **10.** outside   **11.** on   **12.** on

14. ±2   **15.** ±6   **16. (i)** $x^2 + y^2 = 37$ **(ii)** $0, ±1, ±2, ±3, ±4$

Exercise 6.3 ▼

1. $(2, -1), (1, -2)$ **2.** $(4, -1), (1, -4)$ **3.** $(-4, 3), (-3, 4)$ **4.** $(3, 1), (-3, -1)$

5. $(3, 1), (-1, 3)$ **6.** $(-3, -2), (2, -3)$ **7.** $(-3, 2), (2, -3)$ **8.** $(3, 4), (5, 0)$

9. $(-1, 2), (2, 1)$ **10.** $(-6, -2), (-2, -6)$ **11.** $\sqrt{80}$ **12.** $\sqrt{10}$

13. $x - 2y - 5 = 0; (5, 0), (-3, -4)$

Exercise 6.4 ▼

1. $(-1, 1)$ **2.** $(2, -2)$ **3.** $(2, -1)$ **4.** $(-1, 3)$ **5.** $(3, 1)$ **6.** $(1, -4)$ **7.** $(5, -1)$

8. $(1, 7)$ **9.** $x^2 + y^2 = 5; (-2, 1)$ **10.** $\sqrt{20}; x^2 + y^2 = 20; x - 2y + 10 = 0; (-2, 4)$

Exercise 6.5 ▼

1. $(x - 2)^2 + (y - 3)^2 = 16$ **2.** $(x - 1)^2 + (y - 4)^2 = 25$ **3.** $(x - 2)^2 + (y + 1)^2 = 4$

4. $(x + 5)^2 + (y - 2)^2 = 1$ **5.** $(x + 4)^2 + (y + 3)^2 = 17$ **6.** $(x + 3)^2 + y^2 = 13$

7. $x^2 + (y - 2)^2 = 5$ **8.** $(x + 2)^2 + (y + 6)^2 = 29$ **9.** $(x + 1)^2 + (y + 1)^2 = 10$

10. $(x + 4)^2 + (y - 2)^2 = 12$ **11.** $(x - 1)^2 + (y - 2)^2 = 10$ **12.** $(x - 2)^2 + (y + 1)^2 = 41$

13. $(x - 4)^2 + (y + 3)^2 = 80$ **14.** $(x + 2)^2 + (y + 5)^2 = 50$ **15.** $(x - 1)^2 + (y + 1)^2 = 26$

16. $(x + 4)^2 + (y + 2)^2 = 20$ **17.** $(3, 2); 4$ **18.** $(-4, -5); 3$

19. $(1, -3); 5$ **20.** $(3, 5); 2$ **21.** $(2, 2); 7$

22. $(8, 7); 1$ **23.** $(5, -2); 5$ **24.** $(1, -5); 6$

25. $(0, 2); 8$ **26.** $(3, 0); 2$ **27.** $(x - 3)^2 + (y - 3)^2 = 5$

28. $(x + 1)^2 + (y - 2)^2 = 13$ **29.** $(x - 2)^2 + (y - 9)^2 = 25$ **30.** $(1, 0), (-5, 0), (0, -1), (0, 5)$

31. $p(2, 0), q(8, 0)$ **32. (i)** $(x + 2)^2 + (y - 1)^2 = 20$ **(ii)** 8

33. (i) $(1, 2); \sqrt{13}$ **(ii)** $(x - 1)^2 + (y - 2)^2 = 13$ **(iii)** $(-2, 0), (4, 0)$

Exercise 6.6

1. outside   **2.** outside   **3.** inside   **4.** inside   **5.** outside   **6.** outside

7. on   **8.** inside   **9.** inside   **10.** inside   **11.** outside   **12.** on

13. on   **14.** inside   **15.** $-6; 4$ **16.** $1; 7$

Exercise 6.7

1. $3x + y - 10 = 0$ **2.** $2x - y - 5 = 0$ **3.** $5x + y + 26 = 0$ **4.** $3x - 2y + 13 = 0$

5. $x - 7y + 50 = 0$ **6.** $x - 4y + 17 = 0$ **7.** $2x + y - 10 = 0$ **8.** $5x + 2y + 29 = 0$

9. $2x - 3y - 27 = 0$ **10.** $2x + y + 4 = 0$ **11.** $3x - y - 25 = 0$ **12.** $6x - 7y + 41 = 0$

13. $x + y = 0$ **14.** $3x + 4y - 16 = 0$ **15.** $5x - 2y - 19 = 0$ **16.** $x + 3y = 0$

17. $5x + 2y + 25 = 0$ **18.** $3x - 4y - 15 = 0$

Exercise 6.8

1. $(x - 4)^2 + (y + 2)^2 = 20$ **2.** $(x + 5)^2 + (y + 4)^2 = 25$ **3.** $(x - 4)^2 + (y + 4)^2 = 9$

4. $(x + 1)^2 + (y - 2)^2 = 9$ **5.** $(5, -6); 8; (x - 5)^2 + (y - 6)^2 = 64$ **6.** $(x + 5)^2 + (y - 2)^2 = 36$

7. **(i)** $(10, 6)$ **(iii)** $2x + y - 16 = 0$ **(iv)** $r(8, 0)$ **(v)** $(x - 2)^2 + (y - 2)^2 = 20$ **(vi)** $(-2, 0), (6, 0)$

8. $\sqrt{20}; r(-2, 4); (x + 4)^2 + (y - 8)^2 = 20; p(0, 10), q(0, 6); (x - 6)^2 + (y - 8)^2 = 40$

Exercise 7.1

1. **(i)** 64 cm   **(ii)** 240 cm^2 **2.** **(i)** 60 cm   **(ii)** 225 cm^2

3. **(i)** 24 cm   **(ii)** 24 cm^2 **4.** **(i)** 94.2 cm   **(ii)** 706.5 cm^2

5. **(i)** 35.7 cm   **(ii)** 78.5 cm^2 **6.** **(i)** 52.56 cm   **(ii)** 125.6 cm^2

7. **(i)** 56 cm   **(ii)** 144 cm^2 **8.** **(i)** 68 cm   **(ii)** 290 cm^2

9. **(i)** 80 cm   **(ii)** 280 cm^2

10. 150 cm^2 **11.** 2,206.5 cm^2 **12.** 977 cm^2 **13.** 108 cm^2 **14.** 251.cm^2

15. 86 cm^2 **16.** 927 cm^2 **17.** 2,016 cm^2 **18.** 1,438.5 cm^2 **19.** 1,134 cm^2

20. 115.5 cm^2 **21.** $1 : 16$ **22.** 200 cm^2 **23.** 56 cm^2

24. **(i)** 352 m   **(ii)** 525   **25.** **(i)** 500 m   **(ii)** 20   **(iii)** 18 km/h

Exercise 7.2

1. (i) 8 cm   **(ii)** 96 cm   **2. (i)** 81 cm^2 **(ii)** 20 cm   **3.** 8 cm

4. 15   **5.** 8 cm; 96 cm^2 **6.** 675 m^2 **7.** 16 m by 8 m   **18.** 49 cm

19. 21 cm   **20.** 39π cm^2 **21.** 10 cm   **22.** 6 cm

Exercise 7.3

1. (i) 120 cm^3 **(ii)** 148 cm^2 **2. (i)** 576 m^3 **(ii)** 432 m^2 **3. (i)** 1,260 mm^3 **(ii)** 766 mm^2

4. (i) 5 cm   **(ii)** 392 cm^2 **5.** 525   **6. (i)** 8 cm   **(ii)** 860 cm^2

7. 576   **8.** 54cm^2 **9.** 96 cm^2 **10.** 8 cm^3

11. 125 cm^3 **12.** 8 cm by 12 cm by 28 cm; 1,312 cm^2 **13. (i)** 9 cm   **(ii)** 270 cm^3

Exercise 7.4

1. 400 cm^3 **2.** 8,160 cm^3 **3.** 864 cm^3 **4.** 400 cm^3 **5.** 1,350 cm^3

6. 3,840 cm^3 **7. (i)** 240 cm^2 **(ii)** 96,000 cm^3 **8.** 1.44 m^3

9. (i) 3,480 m^3 **(ii)** 5 hours 48 minutes   **(iii)** €41.76   **10. (i)** 6 cm^2 **(ii)** 20

Exercise 7.5

17. 24,492 cm^3 **18.** 9   **19. (i)** 19,800 cm^3 **(ii)** 4,851 cm^3 **(iii)** 14,949 cm^3

Exercise 7.6

11. (i) 123$\frac{1}{5}$ cm^3 **(ii)** 316$\frac{4}{5}$ cm^2 **12. (i)** 5,510.7 cm^3 **(ii)** 2,387.97 cm^2

Exercise 7.7

2. 36π cm^3 **3. (i)** 936π m^3 **(ii)** 360π m^2

4. 1,944π cm^3; 549π cm^2 **5. (i)** 795.048 cm^3 **(ii)** 431.436 cm^2

Exercise 7.8

1. (i) 20 cm   **(ii)** 240π cm^2 **2. (i)** 6 cm   **(ii)** 288π cm^3 **3.** 15 cm

4. (i) 3 cm   **(ii)** 36π cm^2 **5. (i)** 4 cm   **(ii)** 80π cm^2

6. (i) 20 cm   **(ii)** 1,570 cm^3 **7. (i)** 3$\frac{1}{2}$ **(ii)** 341 m^2

8. (i) 10 cm   **(ii)** 96π cm^3 **9.** 10 cm

10. (i) 2 cm   **(ii)** 35.2 cm^2 **11. (i)** 4 m   **(ii)** 301.44 m^2

1. $h = 9$ cm   **2.** $r = 2$ cm   **3.** $r = 6$ cm   **4.** $h = 18$ cm

5. $r = 5$ cm   **6.** $h = 7\frac{1}{2}$ cm   **7.** 20 cm   **8.** 8 cm

9. 36π cm^3; 6 cm   **10.** 400   **11.** $3\frac{1}{2}$ cm   **12.** 3.2 cm

13. 36 cm   **14.** 25 cm   **15.** 2 cm   **16.** 1.28 cm; 6 cm

17. $1{,}152\pi$ cm^3; 18 cm   **18.** $\frac{9}{2}\pi$ cm^3; 125   **19.** 90π cm^3/s; 6 minutes   **20.** 5,652 cm^3; 5 cm

21. **(i)** 1.5 cm   **(ii)** 2π cm^3; 4 cm   **22.** **(i)** $3{,}920\pi$ cm^3 **(ii)** 144π cm^3 **(iii)** 9 cm   **(iv)** 27

23. 100π cm^3; 500 seconds; 4 cm   **24.** **(i)** **(a)** 2   **(b)** 5   **(c)** 1.5   **(d)** 2.5   **(ii)** 4.5 cm; 5 cm

1. 228 m^2 **2.** 780 m^2 **3.** 416 m^2 **4.** 564 m^2 **5.** 200 m^2 **6.** 318 m^2

7. 259.6 m^2 **8.** 29.2 m^2 **9.** 77 cm^2 **10.** $k = 4$ **11.** $k = 8$ **12.** $h = 5$

1. **(i)** 10   **(ii)** 19   **(iii)** 1   **(iv)** 4   **(v)** 6

2. **(i)** 13   **(ii)** −12   **(iii)** −2   **(iv)** −7   **(v)** 0; 4

3. **(i)** 18   **(ii)** 4   **(iii)** 0   **(iv)** −2   **(v)** 12; −5, 2

4. **(i)** **(a)** 10   **(b)** 5   **(ii)** $k = 2$

5. $k = 3$

6. **(i)** 3   **(ii)** −1   **(iii)** 8   **(iv)** −6; −5, 3

7. **(i)** −1   **(ii)** −2   **(iii)** $\frac{1}{4}$ or 0.25   **(iv)** $\frac{11}{56}$ or 0.56; 0, −2

8. **(i)** $\frac{1}{2}$ **(ii)** −1   **(iii)** 2; $x = 1$

9. **(i)** 0.2   **(ii)** 0.5   **(iii)** 0.3125; $x = -4$; −1

10. **(i)** **(a)** 15   **(b)** 8   **(c)** 3   **(ii)** −4   **(iii)** ± 2

11. **(i)** 4; 2   **(ii)** 2   **(iii)** 1

Exercise 8.2 ▼

1. $k = 2$ **2.** $h = 4$ **3.** $a = 3$ **4.** $b = -10$ **5.** $a = 2$ **6.** $k = -4$

7. $a = 2$ or $a = \frac{3}{2}$ **8. (i)** $a = 2$ **(ii)** $b = -3$ **9.** $a = 3; b = -4$

10. $a = -7; b = -1$ **11. (i)** $a = 2; b = -3$ **(ii)** $-1; 5$ **(iii)** $-\frac{3}{2}; 4$

12. (i) $a = 5; b = -17$ **(ii)** $0, 1, 2, 3, 4$ **13.** $a + b = 1; a - b = 5; a = 3, b = -2$

14. $p + q = 7; p - q = -3; p = 2, q = 5; -3, \frac{1}{2}$

15. (i) $a + b = -1; 2a + b = 1$ **(ii)** $a = 2, b = -3$ **(iii)** $0; 1$

16. $c = -3, a = 4, b = -5$ **17. (i)** $q = -6$ **(ii)** $-8; -3$ **18.** $a = 2; b = -3$

19. $b = 1, c = -2, k = -2$ **20.** $p = -3, q = -4; a = -1, b = 4, c = 6; \frac{3}{5}, 4$

21. $a = 2, b = -5; h = -\frac{1}{2}, k = 3; -2, 3$ **22.** $b = -2, c = 4; p = 2, q = -1; -5, 1$

23. $b = 3, c = -10; k = -10; 0, -3$ **24.** $-3; b = 2, c = -3$

Exercise 9.1 ▼

1. (i) $(2, -4)$

Exercise 9.2 ▼

10. (i) $(-1, 4), (2, -5)$ **(ii)** $x = -1, x = 2$

Exercise 9.3 ▼

12. $(-3, 0), (-2, 3), (1, 0)$ **13.** $(-1, 5), (3, -7)$

Exercise 9.4 ▼

1. (i) $-\frac{1}{4}, -\frac{1}{2}, -2, 2, 1, \frac{1}{3}$ **(ii)** $x = 5$

1. **(i)** −1, 2   **(ii)** max (0, 4); min (2, 0)   **(iii)** max value = 4, min value = 0
   (iv) 10.1   **(v)** $0 < x < 2$ **(vi)** $2 \leqslant x < 0$; $2 < x \leqslant 4$
   (vii) $-2 \leqslant x < -1$ **(viii)** $0 \leqslant k \leqslant 4$ **(ix) (a)** −0.7, 1, 2.7   **(b)** $-0.7 \leqslant x \leqslant 1$; $2.7 \leqslant x \leqslant 4$

2. **(i)** −3, −2, 1   **(ii)** $-3 \leqslant x \leqslant -2$; $1 \leqslant x \leqslant 2$ **(iii)** $-4 \leqslant n \leqslant -3$; $-2 \leqslant x \leqslant 0$; 6

3. **(i)** −2, 1, 3   **(ii) (a)** $-2 < x < 1$; $3 < x < 4$ **(b)** $-3 < x < -2$; $1 < x - 3$ **(iii)** −1.6, 0.2, 3.4

4. **(iii)** max (−1, 11); min (2, −16)
   (iv) (a) $-2.5 \leqslant x \leqslant -1$; $2 < x < 3.5$ **(b)** $-1 < x < 2$ **(c)** $-2 < x < -1$ **(v)** −2, 0.3, 3.2

5. −1, 1, 2.5   **(i)** −3   **(ii)** −0.4, 0, 2.9

6. **(i)** (0, 5)   **(ii)** −1, 1.4, 3.6   **(iii)** −0.7, 0.8, 3.9; $-20 \leqslant h \leqslant 4.5$

7. **(i)** −1.8, 0, 3.3   **(ii)** −1.9, 0.2, 3.3   **(iii)** $3.3 \leqslant x \leqslant 3.5$
   (iv) max (2, 20); min (−1, −7)   **(v) (a)** $-7 \leqslant k \leqslant 4$ **(b)** $4 < k \leqslant 20$

8. **(i)** −2, 2, 3   **(ii)** −1, 0, 4   **(iii)** −1, 1, 3   **(iv)** $-1 \leqslant x \leqslant 1$; $3 \leqslant x \leqslant 4$ **(v)** $-2 \leqslant x \leqslant -1$; $1 \leqslant x \leqslant 3$

9. **(i)** 1, 3.5   **(ii)** $1 \leqslant x \leqslant 3.5$ **(iii)** $-2 \leqslant x \leqslant 1$; $3.5 \leqslant x \leqslant 4$

10. **(i)** −1, 0.5, 2   **(ii)** −1.1, 0, 2.6   **(iii)** $-1.1 \leqslant x \leqslant 0$; $2.6 \leqslant x \leqslant 3$

11. **(i)** max (2, 6); min (0, 2)   **(ii)** 3.2   **(iii)** $2 + 3x - x^3 = 2x + 2$ **(iv)** 0, 1, 2

12. **(iii)** −3.7, −0.3, 2   **(iv)** −6   **(v)** 6   **(vi)** −3, −1, 2

13. **(i)** −1, 4   **(ii)** −1, 2, 4   **(iii)** $x^3 - 5x^2 + 2x + 8 = 8 - 2x$ **(v)** 0, 1, 4   **(vi)** $0 \leqslant x \leqslant 1$; $4 \leqslant x \leqslant 5$

14. $x(x^2 - 4)$; −2, 0, 2   **(i)** −2.4, 0.4, 2   **(ii)** −2.2, 0, 2.2; 2.2

15. **(i)** max = 4; min = 0   **(ii)** max (−1, 4); min (1, 0)
   (iii) (a) $-1 < x < 1$ **(b)** $-3 \leqslant x \leqslant -2$ **(b)** $-2 < x < -1$; $1 < x \leqslant 3$ **(iv)** $0 < k < 4$; −1.7, 0, 1.7; 1.7

16. **(iv)** −1.6   **17.** 1.44

1. **(i)** Period = 8; Range = [0, 6]   **(ii)** 6; 0; 3; 6

2. **(i)** Period = 3; Range = [0, 4]   **(ii)** 4; 0; 4; 0

3. **(i)** Period = 6; Range = [1, 5]

4. **(i)** Period = 8; Range = [−3, 3]

5. **(i)** Period = 20; Range = [0, 4]   **(iii)** 40, 50, 60   **(iv) (a)** 75   **(b)** $60 \leqslant x < 65$; $70 \leqslant x < 75$

6. **(i)** Period = 12; Range = [−8, 8]   **(iii)** 48, 52, 56, 60
   (iv) (a) 42   **(b)** $38 < x < 42$ **(c)** $36 < x < 38$

7. $k = 2$; $a = -2$, $b = 3$

1. (ii) $\frac{88}{3}$　　**2.** 78　　　**3.** 36　　　**4.** 32　　　**5.** 90　　　**6.** 54

Exercise 10.2 ▼

1. $4x^3$　　　　**2.** $6x^5$　　　　**3.** $6x$　　　　**4.** $-20x^3$　　　　**5.** 4

6. -3　　　**7.** 0　　　**8.** 0　　　**9.** $-3x^{-4}$ or $-\dfrac{3}{x^4}$　　**10.** x^{-2} or $\dfrac{1}{x^2}$

11. $4x^3 + 6x^2$　　**12.** $6x^2 + 10x$　　**13.** $6x + 4$　　**14.** $4x - 6$　　**15.** $5 - 4x$　　**16.** 3

17. $3x^2 + 4x + 5$　　**18.** $1 - 6x - 12x^2$　　**19.** $-10x - 24x^3$　　**20.** $2x - 1$　　**21.** $3x^2 - 6x$

22. $20 - 4x$　　**23.** $6x^2 - 16x + 7$　　**24.** $3x^2 - 4x + 4$　　**25.** $2 - 6x - 3x^2$

26. $3x^2 - 3x^{-4}$ or $3x^2 - \dfrac{3}{x^4}$　　**27.** $6x - 2x^{-3}$ or $6x - \dfrac{2}{x^3}$　　**28.** $4x^3 - 4x^{-5}$ or $4x^3 - \dfrac{4}{x^5}$

Exercise 10.3 ▼

1. 10　　**2.** 43　　**3.** 23　　**4.** -5　　**5.** 6　　**6.** 13　　**7.** -37　　**8.** -20　　**9.** 10π　　**10.** 36π

Exercise 10.4 ▼

1. $12x + 22$　　　　**2.** $8x^3 + 22x$　　　**3.** $6x^2 + 18x + 17$　　　**4.** $5x^4 + 12x^3 - 9x^2 - 10x + 12$

5. $27x^2 - 42x + 19$　　**6.** $2x + 1$　　　**7.** $-8x^3 + 9x^2 + 8x - 6$　　**8.** $4x^3 - 12x^2 - 5$

9. $3x^2 - 2x - 1$　　**10.** $-6x^5 - 5x^4 + 12x^3 + 15x^2 - 6$　　　**11.** $6x^5 - 5x^4 + 4x^3 - 6x^2 - 4x$

12. $25x^4 - 60x^3 - 33x^2 + 36x + 6$　　　**13.** $9x^2 - 8x - 4$　　　**14.** $-5x^4 + 8x^3 + 2x - 2$

15. -2　　　　**16.** -8　　　**17.** 7　　　　**18.** -16

Exercise 10.5 ▼

1. $\dfrac{1}{(x+1)^2}$　　**2.** $\dfrac{5}{(x+3)^2}$　　**3.** $\dfrac{-1}{(x-1)^2}$　　**4.** $\dfrac{18}{(x+4)^2}$　　**5.** $\dfrac{-1}{(x+2)^2}$

6. $\dfrac{-1}{(x-3)^2}$　　**7.** $\dfrac{-3}{(x+4)^2}$　　**8.** $\dfrac{x^2 - 2x}{(x-1)^2}$　　**9.** $\dfrac{-23}{(5x-4)^2}$　　**10.** $\dfrac{-2x^2 + 6x + 2}{(x^2+1)^2}$

11. $\dfrac{-4x}{(3x^2-1)^2}$　　**12.** $\dfrac{12x}{(4-x^2)^2}$　　**13.** -8　　**14.** 1　　**15.** 4

Exercise 10.6 ▼

1. $5(2x + 3)^4(2)$ or $10(2x + 3)^4$

2. $4(5x - 1)^3(5)$ or $20(5x - 1)^3$

3. $3(x^2 + 3x)^2(2x + 3)$

4. $7(x^2 - 5x - 6)^6(2x - 5)$

5. $6(4 - 5x)^5(-5)$ or $-30(4 - 5x)^5$

6. $5(3 - 2x)^4(-2)$ or $-10(3 - 2x)^4$

7. $4(1 + x^2)^3(2x)$ or $8x(1 + x^2)^3$

8. $7(5 - 2x^2)^6(-4x)$ or $-28x(5 - 2x^2)^6$

9. $8(4 - 3x - x^2)^7(-3 - 2x)$

10. $5\left(x^2 + \dfrac{1}{x^2}\right)^4(2x - 2x^{-3})$ or $5\left(x^2 + \dfrac{1}{x^2}\right)^4\left(2x - \dfrac{2}{x^3}\right)$

11. $4\left(x^3 - \dfrac{1}{x^3}\right)^3(3x^2 + 3x^{-4})$ or $4\left(x^3 - \dfrac{1}{x^3}\right)^3\left(3x^2 + \dfrac{3}{x^4}\right)$

12. $10\left(1 + \dfrac{1}{x}\right)^9(-x^{-2})$ or $10\left(1 + \dfrac{1}{x}\right)^9\left(\dfrac{-1}{x^2}\right)$

13. 0 **14.** -30 **15.** 2 **16.** 24 **17.** -40 **18.** 0

Exercise 10.7 ▼

1. -1 **2.** -7 **3.** 0 **4.** $3x - y - 6 = 0$ **5.** $3x - y + 5 = 0$

6. $6x - y + 5 = 0$ **7.** $x + y - 10 = 0$ **8.** $3x - y + 1 = 0$ **9.** $x + y - 2 = 0$; $x - y - 3 = 0$; yes

Exercise 10.8 ▼

1. $(1, 1)$ **2.** $(-2, 13)$ **3.** $(4, -1)$

4. $(3, 0)$; $(-1, -4)$ **5.** $(2, -20)$; $(-1, 10)$ **6.** $(1, 5)$

7. $(3, -9)$; $(-2, -4)$ **8.** $(0, 0)$; $(-2, 2)$; $x - y = 0$; $x - y + 4 = 0$ **9.** **(i)** 0 **(iii)** 3 **(iv)** $-1, 2$

10. -4 **11.** -3 **12.** **(i)** $-2; 4$ **(ii)** $20x - y + 28 = 0$; $20x - y - 80 = 0$

Exercise 10.9 ▼

1. $(2, -1)$ **2.** $(-3, -8)$ **3.** $(2, -5)$ **4.** $(-3, 16)$ **5.** $(-2, 9)$ **6.** $(-2, 13)$

7. max$(-1, 9)$; min$(3, -23)$ **8.** max$(1, 3)$; min$(3, -1)$ **9.** max$(1, 6)$; min$(2, 5)$

10. max$(1, 13)$; min$(-3, -19)$ **11.** max$(-1, 10)$; min$(-2, 9)$ **12.** max$(-2, 20)$; min$(2, -12)$

13. **(ii)** $3x^2 - 18x + 24$ **(iii)** max$(2, 3)$; min$(4, -1)$ **(v)** $2 < x < 4$

14. **(ii)** $a(-1, 0)$, $b(0, 25)$, $c(1, 32)$, $d(5, 0)$

15. **(i)** $a = -3$; $(2, -2)$ **(ii)** $(0, 2)$ **(iv)** $-2 < k < 2$

16. $2px + q$ **17.** $a = 2, b = -6, c = -3$

563

Exercise 10.10 ▼

1. **(i)** $x < 1$ **(ii)** $x > 1$ **2.** **(i)** $x < -3$ **(ii)** $x > -3$

Exercise 10.11 ▼

1. **(i)** 15   **(ii)** 8

2. **(i)** 0   **(ii)** 12

3. **(i)** $3t^2 - 12t + 9$; $6t - 12$ **(ii)** 9 m/s   **(iii)** 6 m/s^2 **(iv)** $t = 1$ or $t = 3$ **(v)** $t = 2$
    (vi) $t = 3$ **(vii)** $t = 5$

4. **(i)** $3t^2 - 18t + 24$; $6t - 18$ **(ii)** 24 m/s   **(iii)** $t = 2$ or $t = 4$ **(iv)** 6 m/s
    (v) $t = 3$ **(vi)** $t = 4$

5. **(i)** 30 m   **(ii)** $18 - 3t$ **(iii)** 6 m/s   **(iv)** $t = 6$ **(v)** 54 m   **(vi)** -3 m/s^2

6. $\dfrac{d^2 s}{dt^2} = -2$ (a constant)   **(i)** 10 m/s   **(ii)** 25 m

7. **(i)** 24 m   **(ii)** $16 - 4t$ **(iii)** 4 m/s   **(iv)** 14 m   **(v)** $t = 4$; 32 m

8. **(i)** $30 - 10t$ **(ii)** 15 m/s   **(iii)** -10 m/s^2 **(iv)** $t = 3$; 46 m

9. **(i)** 8 m/s^2 or -8 m/s^2 **(ii)** 18 m/s

10. **(i)** 9 m/s^2 or -9 m/s^2 **(ii)** 18.75 m/s

11. **(i)** $8 - 2t$ **(ii)** -4 **(iii)** $t = 4$ **(iv) (a)** 6   **(b)** 3

12. **(i)** $-20p^{-2}$ or $-\dfrac{20}{p^2}$ **(ii)** $-\frac{1}{5}$

Exercise 11.1 ▼

1. **(i)** €56; €24   **(ii)** 250 g; 200 g

2. **(i)** €120; €160; €200   **(ii)** €1,000; €1,600; €1,400

3. **(i)** 119 g; 34 g; 85 g   **(ii)** 72 cm; 54 cm; 36 cm

4. **(i)** €126; €168; €210   **(ii)** 48 cm; 120 cm; 168 cm

5. **(i)** €102; €119; €153   **(ii)** 960 g; 120 g; 480 g

6. $3 : 4$ **7.** $1 : 3$ **8.** $2 : 1 : 4$ **9.** $3 : 2 : 4$ **10.** **(i)** €28; €14   **(ii)** 56 g; 224 g

11. **(i)** €60; €120; €30   **(ii)** 39 cm; 156 cm; 390 cm

12. **(i)** 252 g; 168 g; 126 g   **(ii)** €240; €320; €360   **13.** A received €15,750; B received €12,250

14. €178,800   **15.** €120   **16.** 100 cm   **17.** 162 cm

18. **(i)** €30   **(ii)** €165   **19.** €10,160   **20.** 35 cm   **21.** €9,500

22. $k = 5$ **23.** 27.2 km

1. (i) €9.60   (ii) €25.92   (iii) €26.04   2. €4,573.80

3. €288;   (a) €244.80   (b) 2%   4. 20%   5. 60%   6. €82

7. €10.08   8. €1,200; €1,452   9. €72.80   10. €3,267   11. 700

12. 160   13. €14,000   14. €232,000   15. €1,560   16. €350,000

17. 2.8 litres   18. 400; 700   19. €20   20. €1,533; 18%

21. €260; €82.80; 42%

7. (i) 0.15 m   (ii) 9.1%   8. (i) 2.5 kg   (ii) 3.7%

9. (i) 5 km   (ii) $\frac{5}{105}$ or $\frac{1}{21}$ (iii) 4.8%   10. 5%   11. 5.44%   12. 2.3%

13. 1.64%   14. 4.5%   15. 10.3%   16. (i) 4%   (ii) 0.8%

1. (i) $257.50   (ii) €600   2. 50   3. (i) ¥72,960   (ii) €380

4. South Africa by €30   5. R11,000; R750   6. €8.10; $1\frac{1}{2}$%

7. €3,587.50   8. €48; 2%   9. $2\frac{1}{2}$%

10. $880   11. (i) 30%   (ii) 24.8%

1. €1,996.80   2. €2,173.50   3. €2,837.25   4. €6,492.80

5. €3,709.08   6. €3,745.92   7. €248.25   8. €306.04

9. €1,664.39   10. €6,151.25   11. €368   12. €1,755.52

13. €8,234.85   14. €22,604.40   15. €18,423.75   16. €36,085.50

17. €85,000, €78,200, €74,290; €25,710   18. €26,644.40   19. €44,896.41

20. €62,318.70   21. €118,320.65   22. $P = \dfrac{A}{\left(1 + \dfrac{R}{100}\right)^{T}}$; €50,000

1. €24,812.48   **2.** €26,981.76   **3.** €12,624.60

4. 3%   **5.** 4%   **6.** $3\frac{1}{2}$%

7. $2\frac{1}{2}$%   **8.** (i) 5%   (ii) $4\frac{1}{2}$%   **9.** (i) €62,400   (ii) 3%

10. (i) €43,056   (ii) $2\frac{1}{2}$%   **11.** €22,950; 3%   **12.** (i) €10,868   (ii) 3%

13. (i) €68,500   (ii) $3\frac{1}{2}$%   **14.** (i) €33,075   (ii) €8,075   **15.** €7,120

16. €5,600   **17.** €4,450

Exercise 11.7 ▼

1. (i) €11,100   (ii) €7,300   **2.** (i) €9,960   (ii) €7,470

3. (i) €9,370   (ii) €6,130   **4.** (i) €11,876.50   (ii) €8,726.50

5. 20%   **6.** 18%

7. (i) €19,000   (ii) €48,000   **8.** (i) €23,500   (ii) €52,000

Exercise 11.8 ▼

13. 4.2×10^3 **14.** 7.8×10^4 **15.** 3.2×10^{-2} **16.** 4.5×10^{-3}

17. $n = 3$ **18.** $n = 4$ **19.** $n = -2$

Exercise 11.9 ▼

1. 3.2×10^3 **2.** 2.8×10^6 **3.** 5.2×10^5 **4.** 2.3×10^4 **5.** 7.8×10^{-3}

6. 2.94×10^{-4} **7.** 7.2×10^7 **8.** 3.6×10^7 **9.** 7.48×10^5 **10.** 9.54×10^6

11. 2.3×10^3 **12.** 1.4×10^5 **13.** 2.4×10^3 **14.** 5.8×10^3 **15.** 1.5×10^5

16. 2.8×10^{-4} **17.** 3.51×10^6 **18.** 5.4×10^3 **19.** 3×10^3 **20.** 5×10^2

21. 1.52×10^2 **22.** 2.8×10^3 **23.** 0.078; less than 0.8

24. 0.2; greater than 0.19   **25.** $k = 20$

Exercise 12.1 ▼

1. (i) 120   (ii) 120   (iii) 60   (iv) 20   **2.** 24;   (i) 6   (ii) 6

3. 120;   (i) 24   (ii) 6   **4.** 6

5. (i) 720   (ii) 24   **6.** (i) 120   (ii) (a) 12   (b) 12

7. 720;   (i) 120   (ii) 24   (iii) 240   (iv) 48   (v) 6   (vi) 2

8. 260; 189   **9.** 4,536

10. (i) 120   (ii) 72   (iii) 48   (iv) 72   (v) 24   **11.** 1,263,600

12. (i) 9,876   (ii) 1,023   (iii) 4,536   (iv) 1,512   **13.** (i) 85   (ii) 34

14. 24;   (i) 12   (ii) 2   (iii) 12

15. 120;   (i) 12   (ii) 12   (iii) 36   (iv) 84

Exercise 12.2 ▼

1. 120   **2.** 720   **3.** 40,320   **4.** 362,880   **5.** 479,001,600   **6.** 30

7. 336   **8.** 5,040   **9.** 28   **10.** 120   **11.** 576   **12.** 64

13. 12,996   **14.** 126   **15.** 4   **16.** 20   **17.** 116   **18.** 1,329

19. 42

Exercise 12.3 ▼

1. 10   **2.** 28   **3.** 35   **4.** 120   **5.** 35   **6.** 126   **7.** 1   **8.** 4   **9.** 8

10. 84   **11.** 190   **12.** 4,060   **13.** 93   **14.** 220   **15.** 315   **21.** 3   **22.** 8

Exercise 12.4 ▼

1. 5   **2.** 6   **3.** 8   **4.** 10   **5.** 4   **6.** 11   **7.** 6   **8.** 3   **9.** 8

Exercise 12.5 ▼

1. 56   **2.** 66   **3.** 190   **4.** 495   **5.** 126

6. 35   **7.** (i) 126   (ii) 70   (iii) 56   **8.** 1,365; 1,001; 66

9. (i) 210   (ii) 84   (iii) 126   (iv) 70

10. (i) 35   (ii) 20   (iii) 15   (iv) 10   (v) 10   **11.** 45; 120

Exercise 12.6 ▼

1. 60   **2.** 588   **3.** 2,450   **4.** 84   **5.** 150

6. (i) 210   **(ii)** 90   **(iii)** 170   **7.** 165, 95   **8.** 245

9. (i) 120   **(ii)** 66   **10.** 224

Exercise 12.7 ▼

1. (i) $\frac{1}{3}$ **(ii)** $\frac{5}{12}$ **(iii)** $\frac{1}{12}$ **(iv)** $\frac{1}{6}$

2. (i) $\frac{1}{12}$ **(ii)** $\frac{1}{6}$ **(iii)** $\frac{1}{2}$ **(iv)** $\frac{1}{2}$

3. $\frac{3}{8}$ **4.** $\frac{1}{20}$

5. (i) $\frac{1}{2}$ **(ii)** $\frac{1}{5}$ **(iii)** $\frac{1}{5}$ **(iv)** $\frac{1}{10}$ **(v)** $\frac{7}{10}$ **(vi)** $\frac{1}{6}$ **(vii)** $\frac{1}{3}$

6. (i) $\frac{1}{8}$ **(ii)** $\frac{1}{4}$ **(iii)** $\frac{1}{2}$

7. (i) $\frac{1}{52}$ **(ii)** $\frac{1}{2}$ **(iii)** $\frac{1}{4}$ **(iv)** $\frac{1}{13}$ **(v)** $\frac{3}{13}$ **(vi)** $\frac{3}{26}$ **(vii)** $\frac{4}{13}$ **(viii)** $\frac{12}{13}$ **(ix)** 0

8. 20   **9.** 200   **10.** $\frac{2}{5}$; 4

11. (i) $\frac{7}{15}$ **(ii)** $\frac{7}{30}$ **(iii)** $\frac{18}{25}$ **(iv)** $\frac{4}{25}$ **(v)** $\frac{1}{5}$ **(vi)** $\frac{1}{3}$ **(vii)** $\frac{1}{4}$ **(viii)** $\frac{9}{10}$

12. (i) $\frac{2}{5}$ **(ii)** $\frac{3}{5}$ **(iii)** $\frac{3}{10}$ **(iv)** $\frac{2}{5}$ **(v)** $\frac{2}{3}$ **(vi)** $\frac{1}{4}$

13. (i) $\frac{2}{5}$ **(ii)** $\frac{3}{5}$ **(iii)** $\frac{3}{20}$ **(iv)** $\frac{1}{2}$ **(v)** $\frac{1}{20}$ **(vi)** $\frac{1}{8}$ **(vii)** $\frac{2}{3}$

Exercise 12.8 ▼

1. (i) $\frac{1}{6}$ **(ii)** $\frac{1}{9}$ **(iii)** $\frac{5}{6}$ **(iv)** $\frac{1}{3}$ **(v)** $\frac{2}{9}$ **(vi)** $\frac{1}{9}$ **(vii)** $\frac{1}{12}$

2. (i) $\frac{1}{5}$ **(ii)** 0   **(iii)** $\frac{6}{25}$ **3.** 20; **(i)** $\frac{3}{20}$ **(ii)** $\frac{1}{5}$ **(iii)** $\frac{3}{10}$ **(iv)** $\frac{1}{2}$

4. (i) $\frac{1}{12}$ **(ii)** $\frac{7}{12}$ **(iii)** $\frac{1}{4}$ **5. (i)** $\frac{1}{4}$ **(ii)** $\frac{1}{2}$ **(iii)** $\frac{3}{8}$ **(iv)** $\frac{5}{8}$

6. (i) $\frac{4}{9}$ **(ii)** $\frac{5}{9}$ **(iii)** $\frac{4}{9}$ **7. (i)** $\frac{1}{30}$ **(ii)** $\frac{1}{10}$ **(iii)** $\frac{1}{5}$ **(iv)** $\frac{2}{15}$

8. 20;   **(i)** $\frac{1}{5}$ **(ii)** $\frac{1}{5}$ **(iii)** $\frac{3}{10}$

Exercise 12.9 ▼

1. (i) $\frac{1}{2}$ **(ii)** $\frac{1}{2}$ **(iii)** $\frac{5}{6}$ **2.** $\frac{2}{5}$ **3. (i)** $\frac{1}{3}$ **(ii)** $\frac{2}{3}$ **(iii)** $\frac{3}{4}$ **(iv)** $\frac{1}{4}$

4. (i) $\frac{1}{2}$ **(ii)** $\frac{1}{3}$ **(iii)** $\frac{2}{3}$ **(iv)** $\frac{1}{3}$ **5. (i)** $\frac{1}{3}$ **(ii)** $\frac{1}{5}$ **(iii)** $\frac{7}{15}$ **(iv)** $\frac{8}{15}$

6. (i) $\frac{1}{9}$ **(ii)** $\frac{2}{9}$ **(iii)** $\frac{4}{9}$ **(iv)** $\frac{2}{3}$ **(v)** $\frac{1}{3}$ **7.** (i) $\frac{7}{20}$ **(ii)** $\frac{11}{20}$ **(iii)** $\frac{3}{4}$ **(iv)** $\frac{17}{20}$

8. (i) $\frac{1}{2}$ **(ii)** $\frac{3}{7}$ **(iii)** $\frac{5}{7}$ **(iv)** $\frac{1}{6}$ **(v)** $\frac{5}{21}$ **(vi)** $\frac{1}{3}$ **(vii)** $\frac{2}{3}$

9. (i) $\frac{1}{2}$ **(ii)** $\frac{7}{13}$ **(iii)** $\frac{4}{13}$ **(iv)** $\frac{9}{13}$ **10.** (i) $\frac{2}{9}$ **(ii)** $\frac{11}{36}$

Exercise 12.10 ▼

1. (i) $\frac{1}{12}$ **(ii)** $\frac{1}{4}$ **(iii)** $\frac{1}{3}$ **(iv)** $\frac{1}{6}$

2. (i) $\frac{1}{36}$ **(ii)** $\frac{1}{12}$ **(iii)** $\frac{1}{4}$

3. (i) $\frac{2}{5}$ **(ii)** $\frac{1}{15}$ **(iii)** $\frac{4}{15}$ **(iv)** $\frac{8}{15}$

4. (i) $\frac{1}{16}$ **(ii)** $\frac{9}{64}$ **(iii)** $\frac{3}{64}$ **(iv)** $\frac{3}{32}$

5. (i) $\frac{1}{5}$ **(ii)** $\frac{3}{10}$ **(iii)** $\frac{1}{2}$ **(iv)** $\frac{2}{5}$

6. (i) $\frac{1}{6}$ **(ii)** $\frac{1}{6}$ **(iii)** $\frac{5}{18}$ **(iv)** $\frac{7}{16}$

7. (i) $\frac{1}{5}$ **(ii)** $\frac{3}{20}$ **(iii)** $\frac{3}{5}$ **(iv)** $\frac{1}{20}$ **(v)** $\frac{3}{4}$

8. (i) **(a)** $\frac{1}{4}$ **(b)** $\frac{3}{16}$ **(c)** $\frac{3}{8}$ **(d)** $\frac{5}{8}$ **(ii) (a)** $\frac{3}{14}$ **(b)** $\frac{3}{7}$ **(c)** $\frac{4}{7}$

9. (i) $\frac{5}{14}$ **(ii)** $\frac{3}{28}$ **(iii)** $\frac{5}{28}$ **(iv)** $\frac{15}{28}$

10. (i) $\frac{5}{9}$ **(ii)** $\frac{4}{9}$ **(iii)** $\frac{5}{18}$ **(iv)** $\frac{5}{18}$ **(v)** $\frac{5}{9}$

11. (i) $\frac{1}{7}$ **(ii)** $\frac{1}{7}$ **(iii)** $\frac{1}{49}$ **(iv)** $\frac{2}{49}$ **(v)** $\frac{1}{7}$ **(vi)** $\frac{6}{7}$

12. (i) $\frac{2}{9}$ **(ii)** $\frac{2}{15}$ **(iii)** $\frac{1}{3}$ **(iv)** $\frac{14}{45}$

13. $\frac{13}{18}$ **14.** (i) $\frac{1}{6}$ **(ii)** $\frac{1}{10}$

Exercise 13.1 ▼

4. 10   **5.** 4   **6.** 1   **7.** 4

8. 5; $\frac{12}{13}$; $\frac{5}{13}$; $\frac{12}{5}$ **9.** 21; $\frac{20}{29}$; $\frac{21}{29}$; $\frac{20}{21}$ **10.** 9; $\frac{40}{41}$; $\frac{9}{41}$; $\frac{40}{9}$ **11.** 4; $\frac{1}{\sqrt{17}}$; $\frac{4}{\sqrt{17}}$; $\frac{1}{4}$

12. $\sqrt{7}$; $\frac{\sqrt{7}}{4}$; $\frac{3}{4}$; $\frac{\sqrt{7}}{3}$ **13.** $\sqrt{13}$; $\frac{3}{\sqrt{13}}$; $\frac{2}{\sqrt{13}}$; $\frac{3}{2}$ **14.** $42°$ **15.** $55°$

16. $7°$ **17.** $17°$ **18.** $63°$ **19.** $53°$

20. $44°$ **21.** $18°$ **22.** (i) $\frac{3}{5}$; $\frac{3}{4}$ **(ii)** $37°$ **23.** (i) $\frac{8}{17}$; $\frac{15}{17}$ **(ii)** $28°$

24. (i) $\frac{24}{25}$; $\frac{7}{24}$ **25.** $k = 20$ **26.** (ii) $\frac{3}{4}$ or 0.75

Exercise 13.2

1. 56° **2.** 59° **3.** 35° **4.** 45° **5.** 52°

6. 34° **7.** 9.39 **8.** 28.84 **9.** 26.36

10. (i) 2.5 **(ii)** 37° **11. (i)** 5 **(ii)** 39°

12. (i) 34 cm **(ii)** 64 cm **(ii)** 14° **13. (i)** 8 **(ii)** 9.62

Exercise 13.3

1. 4.85 m **2.** 4.8 m **3.** 11.64 m **4. (i)** 3.5 m **(ii)** 71°

5. 47 m **6.** 426 m **7.** 84 m; 19° **9.** 11 km

10. (i) 40 km **(ii)** 35 km **11.** 30 km; 60 km

Exercise 13.4

1. 80.00 cm^2 **2.** 18.13 cm^2 **3.** 31.01 cm^2 **4.** 16.67 cm^2 **5.** 47.55 cm^2

6. 21.46 cm^2 **7.** 22.65 m^2 **8.** 29.73 cm^2 **9.** 45.11 m^2 **10.** 62.99 cm^2

11. (i) 3 cm **(ii)** 2.16 cm^2 **(iii)** 4.98 cm^2 **12. (i)** 31.4 cm^2 **(ii)** 29.4 cm^2 **(iii)** 2.0 cm^2

13. (i) 47.1 cm^2 **(ii)** 9 cm^2 **(iii)** 38.1 cm^2 **14.** 24 cm **15.** 26 cm

16. 18 cm **17.** 40° **18.** 70°

Exercise 13.5

1. 13.47 **2.** 4.88 **3.** 38° **4.** 54° **5.** 8.88 **6.** 27°

7. (i) 13.92 cm **(ii)** 12.79 cm **8. (i)** 65° **(ii)** 13.29 cm **(iii)** 12.82 cm

9. (i) 24° **(ii)** 9 cm **10. (i)** 17 m **(ii)** 50° **(iii)** 111 m^2 **(iv)** 14.37 m

11. (i) 23° **(ii)** 103 m; 93 m

Exercise 13.6

1. 9.17 **2.** 15.68 **3.** 10.24 **4.** 41° **5.** 57° **6.** 95°

7. 106.6° **8.** 29° **9. (i)** 7 cm **(ii)** 61°

Exercise 13.7 ▼

1. (i) 9.8 cm^2 (ii) 5 cm   (iii) 41°   **2.** (i) 30 cm^2 (ii) 16.5 cm   (iii) 27°

3. (i) 8.75   (ii) 6.69   **4.** (i) 6 cm   (ii) 9.7 cm^2 (iii) 4.88 cm

5. (i) 13   (ii) 67.4°   (iii) 5.1   **6.** (i) 25.5 m   (ii) 17 m   (iii) 289 m^2

7. (i) 5 m   (ii) 21 m^2 **8.** (i) 9.5 cm   (ii) 54.5 cm^2

9. 13°   **10.** 219 m

11. (i) 65.2 km   (ii) 19 km/h   **12.** (i) 37.2°   (ii) 23.72 km   (iii) 46 m

Exercise 13.8 ▼

2. 1   **3.** 1   **4.** 4   **5.** $\frac{3}{2}$ or $1\frac{1}{2}$ **6.** $\frac{2}{3}$ **7.** $\frac{3}{2}$ or $1\frac{1}{2}$ **8.** $\frac{1}{4}$ **9.** $\frac{5}{8}$ **10.** 0

Exercise 13.9 ▼

1. (i) $\frac{3}{5}$ (ii) $\frac{4}{5}$ (iii) $\frac{24}{25}$ (iv) $\frac{7}{25}$

2. (i) $\frac{5}{13}$ (ii) $\frac{4}{5}$ (iii) $\frac{56}{65}$ (iv) $-\frac{33}{65}$

3. (i) $\frac{3}{5}$ (ii) $\frac{24}{25}$ (iii) $\frac{117}{125}$ (iv) $\frac{527}{625}$

4. (i) $\frac{12}{13}$ (ii) $\frac{5}{13}$ (iii) $\frac{120}{169}$ (iv) $\frac{144}{169}$ (v) $\frac{119}{169}$

5. (i) $\frac{7}{25}$ (ii) $\frac{24}{25}$ (iii) $\frac{8}{17}$ (iv) $\frac{15}{17}$ (v) $\frac{297}{425}$ (vi) $-\frac{87}{425}$ (vii) $\frac{304}{425}$ (viii) $\frac{416}{425}$

     (ix) $\frac{336}{625}$ (x) $\frac{240}{289}$ (xi) $\frac{527}{625}$ (xii) $\frac{161}{289}$

7. $\dfrac{\sqrt{3}-1}{2\sqrt{2}}$ **8.** $\dfrac{\sqrt{3}+1}{2\sqrt{2}}$ **9.** $\dfrac{\sqrt{3}+1}{2\sqrt{2}}$ **10.** $\dfrac{1-\sqrt{3}}{2\sqrt{2}}$

Exercise 13.10 ▼

1. 0   **2.** 0   **3.** 1   **4.** 1   **5.** −1

6. −1   **7.** 0   **8.** 0   **9.** 0   **10.** −2

11. −3   **12.** 1   **13.** −1   **14.** 4   **15.** 0° or 360°

16. 90°   **17.** 270°   **18.** 180°   **19.** 90° or 270°

20. 0°, 180°, 360°   **21.** 0°, 180°, 360°   **22.** 1, −1

Exercise 13.11 ▼

1. $-\frac{1}{2}$ **2.** $\frac{1}{2}$ **3.** $\sqrt{3}$ **4.** $-\frac{1}{2}$ **5.** -1 **6.** $-\frac{1}{\sqrt{2}}$

7. $-\frac{\sqrt{3}}{2}$ **8.** $\frac{1}{\sqrt{3}}$ **9.** $-\frac{1}{\sqrt{2}}$ **10.** $-\frac{1}{\sqrt{3}}$ **11.** $-\frac{\sqrt{3}}{2}$ **12.** $-\frac{1}{\sqrt{2}}$

Exercise 13.12 ▼

1. $30°, 150°$ **2.** $60°, 120°$ **3.** $30°, 210°$ **4.** $60°, 300°$

5. $45°, 135°$ **6.** $60°, 240°$ **7.** $45°, 225°$ **8.** $30°, 330°$

9. $240°, 300°$ **10.** $150°, 210°$ **11.** $225°, 315°$ **12.** $150°, 330°$

13. $210°, 330°$ **14.** $120°, 300°$ **15.** $45°, 315°$ **16.** $24°, 156°$

17. $83°, 277°$ **18.** $58°, 238°$ **19.** $143°, 217°$ **20.** $152°, 332°$

21. $222°, 318°$

Exercise 14.1 ▼

11. 5, 7, 9, 11   **12.** 4, 7, 10, 13   **13.** 3, 7, 11, 15   **14.** 2, 7, 12, 17

15. −1, −3, −5, −7   **16.** −1, 5, −9, −13   **17.** 6, 9, 14, 21   **18.** 3, 8, 15, 24

19. $2, \frac{3}{2}, \frac{4}{3}, \frac{5}{4}$ **20.** $1, \frac{4}{3}, \frac{3}{2}, \frac{8}{5}$ **21.** 2, 4, 8, 16   **22.** 3, 9, 27, 81

23. (i) 7, 12, 17   **24. (i)** 3, 6, 11   **25. (i)** $\frac{3}{2}, \frac{4}{3}, \frac{5}{4}$

Exercise 14.2 ▼

1. $1, 2; 2n - 1$ **2.** $2, 3; 3n - 1$ **3.** $3, 4; 4n - 1$ **4.** $6, 5; 5n + 1$

5. $9, -2; 11 - 2n$ **6.** $4, -3; 7 - 3n$ **7.** $8, -5; 13 - 5n$ **8.** $4, -6; 10 - 6n$

9. $-5, 2; 2n - 7$ **10. (i)** $1; 3$ **(ii)** $3n - 2; 148$ **(iii)** T_{30}

11. (i) $4; 5$ **(ii)** $5n - 1; 224$ **(iii)** T_{50} **12. (i)** $40; -4$ **(ii)** $44 - 4n; -16$ **(iii)** T_{11}

13. T_{60} **14.** T_{40} **15.** $k = 3; 5, 7, 9$ **16.** $k = 4; 3, 7, 11$

17. $k = 11; 17, 23, 29, 35$ **18. (i)** $k = 5; 3, 11, 19, 27$ **(ii)** $8n - 5; 163$ **(iii)** T_{31}

Exercise 14.3 ▼

1. 3; 2   **2.** 1; 3   **3.** 7; 4   **4.** 3; 5   **5.** 5; 6

6. (i) 3   **(ii)** $3n+4$; 32   **(iii)** T_{32} **7. (i)** 3; 4   **(ii)** $4n-1$ **(iv)** T_{25}

8. (i) $p=7$, $q=9$ **(ii)** 23   **9. (i)** $p=10$, $q=7$, $r=1$ **(ii)** -47

Exercise 14.5 ▼

1. 120   **2.** 246   **3.** 630

4. (i) $\dfrac{n(5n+1)}{2}$ **(ii)** 1010   **5. (i)** $\dfrac{n(3n+17)}{2}$ **(ii)** 1605

6. (i) 5, 7, 9, 11   **(ii)** 2   **(iii)** 320   **7. (i)** 2; 5

8. (i) -7; 4   **(iii) (a)** 69   **(b)** 1,530   **9. (i)** 2; 3   **(iii) (a)** 89   **(b)** 1,365

10. (i) -15; 6   **(iii) (a)** 129   **(b)** 0   **11. (i)** 2; 6   **(ii) (a)** 116   **(b)** 1,180

12. 610   **13.** 1,770   **14.** 6,275

15. (i) $3n-1$ **(iii)** 670   **16. (i)** $10n$ **(ii)** $5n^2+5n$ **(iii)** 201,000

17. (ii) (a) 39   **(b)** 400   **(iii)** 15

18. (i) $12a$ **(ii)** $75a$ **(iii)** $a=2$ **(iv)** 6, 8, 10, 12   **(v) (a)** $2n+4$ **(b)** n^2+5n
   (vi) (a) 44   **(b)** 500

19. (i) 7; 2   **(ii)** $n=10$

Exercise 14.6 ▼

1. 3; 2   **2.** 4; 2   **3.** 1; 6   **4.** -1; 4   **5. (i)** 2   **(ii)** 23

6. (i) 3; 4   **(ii)** $4n-1$ **(iii)** 39   **(iv)** $39=210-171$

7. (i) -2; 4   **(ii)** $4n-6$ **(iii)** 74; $74=720-646$ **(iv)** 10

Exercise 14.7 ▼

1. (i) 1; 2   **(ii)** 2^{n-1} **(iii)** 8, 16   **2. (i)** 3; 2   **(ii)** $3(2)^{n-1}$ **(iii)** 24, 48

3. (i) 1; 4   **(ii)** 4^{n-1} **(iii)** 64, 256   **4. (i)** 4; 3   **(ii)** $4(3)^{n-1}$ **(iii)** 108, 324

5. (i) 2; 4   **(ii)** $2(4)^{n-1}$ **(iii)** 128, 512   **6. (i)** 5; 2   **(ii)** $5(2)^{n-1}$ **(iii)** 40, 80

7. (i) 3; 4   **(ii)** $3(4)^{n-1}$ **(iii)** 192, 768   **8. (i)** 3; 3   **(ii)** $3(3)^{n-1}$ or 3^n; 81, 243

9. (i) 1; 5   **(ii)** 5^{n-1} **(iii)** 125, 625   **10. (i)** 48; $\frac{1}{2}$ **(ii)** $48(\frac{1}{2})^{n-1}$ **(iii)** 6, 3

11. (i) $54; \frac{1}{3}$ (ii) $54(\frac{1}{3})^{n-1}$ (iii) $2, \frac{2}{3}$ **12.** (i) $8; \frac{1}{4}$ (ii) $8(\frac{1}{4})^{n-1}$ (iii) $\frac{1}{8}, \frac{1}{32}$

13. (i) $2; 5$ (ii) $2(5)^{n-1}$ **14.** (i) $6; 3$ (ii) $6(3)^{n-1}$

16. $3; 3$ **17.** $3; 4$ **18.** $a = 18, b = 54$ **19.** (i) $r = 2$ (ii) $2, 4, 8$

20. (i) $r = 2$ (ii) $p = 6, q = 12$ **21.** $k = 2$ **22.** $k = 12$ **23.** $k = 5; 2, 4, 8, 16$

24. $k = \pm 15$ **25.** $k = 11$ or $k = 1$ **26.** $k = 4$ or $k = -\frac{3}{2}$

27. (i) $r = \frac{1}{3}$ (ii) $\frac{4}{9}, \frac{4}{27}$ **28.** $\frac{2}{3}, \frac{4}{9}, \frac{8}{27}, \frac{16}{81}$

Exercise 14.8 ▼

17. (i) $1; 2$ (ii) 2^{n-1} (iii) $1,024$ **18.** (i) $1; 3$ (ii) 3^{n-1} (iii) $2,187$

19. (i) $3; 2$ (ii) $3(2)^{n-1}$ (iii) T_8 **20.** (i) $4; 2$ (ii) $4(2)^{n-1}$ or 2^{n+1} (iii) T_9

Exercise 14.9 ▼

1. $6,560$ **2.** $4,095$ **3.** $2,555$

4. (i) $r = 3$ (ii) $4(3)^{n-1}; 2(3^n - 1)$ **5.** (i) $r = 5$ (ii) $2(5)^{n-1}; \dfrac{5^n - 1}{2}$ (iii) $1,250; 1,562$

6. (i) 1 (ii) $3; 2$ (iii) $3,069$

7. $a = 4$ **8.** $a = 2$ **10.** 8 **11.** 9 **12.** 6

13. (i) 2^8 (ii) $6; 2$ (iii) T_8 (iv) $1,530$ (v) 10

14. (i) $1; 2$ (ii) $2^{n-1}; 2^n - 1$ (iii) $512; 1,023$ (iv) $4,095 < 4,096$ (v) 9

15. (i) $10; 40; 130$ (ii) $10; 3$ (iii) $21,870$ (iv) $21,870 = 32,800 - 10,930$

16. (i) 3 (ii) 768

17. (i) $9; 45; 189$ (ii) $9; 4$ (iii) $9(4)^{n-1}; 2,304$ (iv) $2,304 = 3,069 - 765$

Exercise 15.1 ▼

1. (i) $100°$ (ii) $40°$ **2.** $x = 65, y = 65$ **3.** $p = 90$ **4.** (i) $72°$ (ii) $54°$

5. (i) $67°$ (ii) $23°$ **6.** $30°$

7. (i) $\angle pcd$ or $\angle pdc; 80°$ (ii) (a) $a = 110$ (b) $b = 70$

8. (i) $45°$ (ii) $60°$ (iii) $75°$ **9.** $x = 21; y = 6$ **10.** $30°, 60°, 90°$

11. 15 m   **12.** (i) 5 (ii) 12 **13.** (i) 25 (ii) 24

14. (i) 12 (ii) 5 (iii) 8.6 **15.** 7.5 cm   **16.** $(1.5)^2 + (3.6)^2 = (3.9)^2$

17. 6.3 cm   **18.** (i) 30 cm (ii) 240 cm   **19.** 8 cm   **20.** 78.5 cm^2

Exercise 15.2 ▼

1. (i) 0   (ii) 2   (iii) (a) 6   (b) 2   (iv) 11.6 square units

2. (i) 1.5   (ii) 8   (iii) 18 square units

3. (i) 0   (ii) 2.25 or $\frac{9}{4}$ (iii) 15   (iv) 162 square units   (v) 130 square units

4. (i) p (ii) 1.25 or $\frac{5}{4}$ (iii) 1   (iv) 5 : 1   (v) 6 square units   (vi) 3.375 square units

5. (i) 2.25 or $\frac{9}{4}$ (ii) 12.5 or $\frac{25}{2}$ (iii) 20

6. (i) 1.75 or $\frac{7}{4}$ (ii) 3   (iii) 8 square units

7. (i) a (ii) 1.6 or $\frac{8}{5}$ (iii) 24.5 square units   (iv) $\frac{5}{8}$ or 0.625

8. (iii) 16 cm^2 (iv) 1.4 or $\frac{7}{5}$

9. (i) 0.6 or $\frac{3}{5}$ (ii) 54 square units   (iii) 96 square units

10. 1.75 or $\frac{7}{4}$; 15 cm

11. (ii) 0.8 or $\frac{4}{5}$ (iii) 5.2 cm

Exercise 16.4 ▼

1. (i) $x + 2y = 2$ (ii) $x + 2y \leqslant 2$ **2.** $x + y \leqslant 4$ **3.** $x + 2y \geqslant 4$

4. $2x + y \geqslant 6$ **5.** $2x + 3y \leqslant 6$ **6.** $x - y \leqslant -3$ **7.** $x + 2y \geqslant -2$

8. $x \geqslant 1$ **9.** $x \leqslant 5$ **10.** $y \geqslant 2$ **11.** $y \leqslant 6$

12. $x - 2y \leqslant 0$ **13.** $x - 3y \geqslant 0$ **14.** (i) $x + 3y = 3$ (ii) $x \geqslant 0; y \geqslant 0; x + 3y \leqslant 3$

15. (i) $x + 5y = 5$ (ii) $x \geqslant 0; y \geqslant 0; x + 5y \leqslant 5$ **16.** $x \geqslant 0; y \geqslant 0; y \leqslant 4; x + y - 6 \leqslant 0$

17. $x \geqslant 0; y \geqslant 0; x - y + 2 \geqslant 0; x + y - 6 \leqslant 0$ **18.** $x \geqslant 0; x - 2y + 2 \leqslant 0; 3x + y - 6 \leqslant 0$

19. $y \geqslant 0; x - y - 2 \geqslant 0; x + 2y - 8 \leqslant 0$ **20.** $x \geqslant 0; 8x + 5y - 40 \leqslant 0; x - y \leqslant 0$

Exercise 16.5 ▼

1. (ii) $(0, 0), (0, 8), (4, 4), (6, 0)$ (iii) $(4, 4)$; 20

2. (ii) $(0, 0), (0, 12), (6, 6), (10, 0)$ (iii) $(10, 0)$; 100

3. (ii) $(0, 0), (0, 25), (10, 20), (20, 0)$ (iii) $(20, 0)$; 300

4. (ii) $(5, 7), (5, 16), (20, 4)$ (iii) $(5, 7)$; 1,025

5. (ii) $(80, 0), (40, 50), (140, 0)$ (iii) (a) $(140, 0)$; 4,200   (b) $(40, 50)$; 1,700

6. (ii) $(0, 2), (0, 6), (2, 4), (3, 2)$ (iii) (a) $(2, 4)$; 32   (b) $(0, 2)$; 10

575

Exercise 16.6 ▼

1. (i) $x + y \leqslant 50$; $x + 2y \leqslant 80$ **(ii)** 20 type A and 30 type B; €4,800

2. (i) $3x + 2y \leqslant 36$; $3x + 4y \leqslant 48$ **(ii)** 8 racing and 6 mountain; €3,120.

3. (i) $5x + 4y \leqslant 40$; $x + 2y \leqslant 14$ **(ii)** 4 small and 5 large; €1,480

4. (i) $x + y \leqslant 30$; $x + 2y \leqslant 50$ **(ii)** 30 type P and 0 type Q; €12,000

5. (i) $4x + 3y \leqslant 36$; $2x + 3y \leqslant 24$ **(ii)** 6 type P and 4 type Q   **(iii)** €4,400

6. (i) $x + y \leqslant 54$; $2x + 5y \leqslant 180$ **(ii)** 30 cars and 24 buses; €780

7. (i) $x + y \leqslant 60$; $2x + y \leqslant 70$ **(ii)** 10 television sets and 50 DVD players; €6,500

8. (i) $x + 2y \leqslant 6{,}000$; $2x + y \leqslant 6{,}000$ **(ii)** 2,000 type P and 2,000 type Q; €1,680,000

9. (i) $x + y \leqslant 8$; $x + 3y \leqslant 18$ **(ii)** 3 small and 5 large; 210

10. $10x + y \leqslant 400$; $5x + y \leqslant 250$; 30 apple trees and 100 blackcurrant bushes; €4,200

11. $8x + 5y \leqslant 400$; $6x + 5y \leqslant 360$; 50 caravans; 20 caravans and 48 tents; €1,560

12. 4 of the 500 m^2 and 6 of 1000 m^2

13. 12 type K and O type T

14. $10x + 3y \leqslant 190$; 10 tonnes of coal and 30 tonnes of turf; €540

Exercise 17.1 ▼

1. (i) $\overrightarrow{ed}$ **(ii)** $\overrightarrow{af}$ **(iii)** $\overrightarrow{bc}$ **(iv)** $\overrightarrow{ea}$ **(v)** $\overrightarrow{ec}$ **(vi)** $\overrightarrow{ef}$

2. (i) $\overrightarrow{dc}$ or $\overrightarrow{ab}$ or $\overrightarrow{by}$ **(ii)** $\overrightarrow{ay}$ or $\overrightarrow{xc}$ **(iii)** $\overrightarrow{dz}$ or $\overrightarrow{zb}$ **(iv)** $\overrightarrow{az}$ or $\overrightarrow{zc}$ **(v)** $\overrightarrow{xz}$ or $\overrightarrow{zy}$ **(vi)** $\overrightarrow{cx}$ or $\overrightarrow{ya}$

Exercise 17.2 ▼

1. (i) $\overrightarrow{xz}$ **(ii)** $\overrightarrow{xg}$ or $\overrightarrow{gz}$ **(iii)** $\overrightarrow{xz}$ **(iv)** $\overrightarrow{yz}$ or $\overrightarrow{xw}$ **(v)** $\overrightarrow{xy}$ or $\overrightarrow{wz}$ **(vi)** $\overrightarrow{xy}$ or $\overrightarrow{wz}$

2. (i) $\overrightarrow{su}$ or $\overrightarrow{tv}$ **(ii)** $\overrightarrow{sr}$ or $\overrightarrow{tu}$ **(iii)** $\overrightarrow{rt}$ **(iv)** $\overrightarrow{rt}$ **(v)** $\overrightarrow{sv}$

3. (i) $\overrightarrow{ab}$ or $\overrightarrow{by}$ or $\overrightarrow{xd}$ or $\overrightarrow{dc}$ **(ii)** $\overrightarrow{ay}$ or $\overrightarrow{xc}$ **(iii)** $\overrightarrow{xb}$ **(iv)** $\overrightarrow{xz}$ or $\overrightarrow{zy}$ **(v)** $\overrightarrow{xc}$ or $\overrightarrow{ay}$
 (vi) $\overrightarrow{xc}$ or $\overrightarrow{ay}$ **(vii)** $\overrightarrow{dc}$ or $\overrightarrow{xd}$ or $\overrightarrow{ab}$ or $\overrightarrow{by}$

4. (i) $\overrightarrow{ae}$ **(ii)** $\overrightarrow{bd}$ or $\overrightarrow{cf}$ **(iii)** $\overrightarrow{be}$ or $\overrightarrow{af}$ **(iv)** $\overrightarrow{bc}$ or $\overrightarrow{ce}$ or $\overrightarrow{ad}$ or $\overrightarrow{df}$

1. (i) $\vec{r}$ (ii) (a) $\vec{p}+\vec{r}$ (b) $\frac{1}{2}\vec{p}+\frac{1}{2}\vec{r}$ (iii) $\frac{1}{2}\vec{q}$

2. (i) $\vec{a}$ (ii) (a) $\vec{a}+\vec{c}$ (b) $\frac{1}{2}\vec{a}+\frac{1}{2}\vec{c}$ (c) $\vec{a}+\frac{1}{2}\vec{c}$ (iii) $\frac{1}{2}\vec{c}$

3. (i) $\frac{1}{2}\vec{q}$ (ii) $\frac{1}{2}\vec{p}+\frac{1}{2}\vec{r}$ (iii) $-\frac{1}{2}\vec{p}+\vec{q}-\frac{1}{2}\vec{r}$

4. (i) $\vec{p}+\vec{r}$ (ii) $\frac{1}{2}\vec{p}+\vec{r}$ (iii) $\vec{p}+\frac{2}{3}\vec{r}$ (iv) $-\frac{1}{2}\vec{p}+\frac{1}{3}\vec{r}$

5. (i) $\frac{1}{2}\vec{q}+\frac{1}{2}\vec{p}$ (ii) $\frac{1}{2}\vec{p}+\frac{1}{2}\vec{q}$ (iii) $\frac{2}{3}\vec{p}+\frac{1}{3}\vec{q}$ (iv) $\frac{1}{6}\vec{p}-\frac{1}{6}\vec{q}$

6. (i) $\vec{a}+\vec{c}$ (ii) $\frac{1}{2}\vec{a}+\frac{1}{2}\vec{b}$ (iii) $\vec{a}+\frac{1}{2}\vec{c}$ (iv) $2\vec{a}+\vec{c}$

7. (i) $\frac{1}{2}\vec{a}+\frac{1}{2}\vec{b}$ (ii) $\frac{1}{2}b+\frac{1}{2}c$ (iii) $\frac{1}{2}\vec{a}+\frac{1}{2}\vec{c}$

8. (i) $\vec{q}-\vec{p}$ **9.** $\frac{1}{2}\vec{r}-\frac{1}{2}\vec{p}$ **11.** (ii) $3\vec{b}$ **12.** (ii) $2\vec{a}+\vec{b}$ (iii) $k=-1$

13. (i) $-\frac{3}{5}\vec{a}-\vec{c}$ (ii) $h=-\frac{1}{5}, k=-1$ **14.** (i) $\frac{1}{2}\vec{p}$ (ii) (a) $\vec{r}+\frac{1}{2}\vec{p}$ (b) $\frac{2}{3}\vec{r}-\frac{1}{3}\vec{p}$

1. (i) $6\vec{i}+4\vec{j}$ (ii) $-6\vec{i}+3\vec{j}$ (iii) $\vec{i}+3\vec{j}$ (iv) $2\vec{i}+3\vec{j}$ (v) $3\vec{i}$ (vi) $-5\vec{i}-\vec{j}$

     (vii) $2\vec{i}+3\vec{j}$ (viii) $5\vec{i}+8\vec{j}$ (ix) $-4\vec{j}$ (x) $6\vec{i}-9\vec{j}$ (xi) $\vec{i}+3\vec{j}$

3. $7\vec{i}+2\vec{j}$ **4.** $6\vec{i}-5\vec{j}$ **5.** $7\vec{i}-3\vec{j}$

6. (i) $7\vec{i}+4\vec{j}$ (ii) $10\vec{i}+13\vec{j}$ (iii) $4\vec{i}+10\vec{j}$ (iv) $3\vec{i}+9\vec{j}$ (v) $-6\vec{i}-3\vec{j}$ (vi) $-3\vec{i}+6\vec{j}$

     (vii) $20\vec{i}+26\vec{j}$ (viii) $2\vec{i}-7\vec{j}$ **7.** (i) $-\vec{i}+2\vec{j}$ (ii) $9\vec{i}+7\vec{j}$ (iii) $-5\vec{i}+\vec{j}$

1. $h=4, k=-5$ **2.** $a=-1, b=3$ **3.** $p=5, q=-2$ **4.** $h=4, k=-2$

5. $a=-2, b=3$ **6.** $p=5, q=2$ **7.** $h=2, k=-3$ **8.** $s=3, t=-5$

9. $k=4, t=2$ **10.** $a=4, b=5$ **11.** $h=2, t=-1$ **12.** $h=3, k=-2$

13. $7\vec{i}+2\vec{j}; s=2, t=3$ **14.** (i) (a) $2\vec{i}+4\vec{j}$ (b) $7\vec{i}+13\vec{j}$ (ii) $p=2, q=-3$ (iii) $h=3, k=5$

15. $\vec{p}=7\vec{i}+6\vec{j}; \quad \vec{q}=6\vec{i}+8\vec{j}; \quad h=-2, k=3$

1. 5   **2.** 13   **3.** 17   **4.** 29   **5.** $\sqrt{13}$ **6.** $\sqrt{17}$ **7.** $\sqrt{29}$ **8.** $\sqrt{41}$ **9.** $\sqrt{13}$ **10.** $\sqrt{5}$

11. $\sqrt{26}$ **12.** $\sqrt{26}$ **13.** $\sqrt{45}$ **14.** $\sqrt{10}$ **15.** 5   **16.** 7   **17.** (i) $-4\vec{i}-2\vec{j}$ **21.** $k=\pm5$ **22.** $t=\pm7$

Exercise 17.7 ▼

1. 23   **2.** –6   **3.** 13   **4.** 48   **5.** 30   **6.** 0   **7.** 20   **8.** –32   **9.** 4   **10.** 2

11. 4   **13.** (i) (a) $6\vec{i} - 4\vec{j}$ (b) $-2\vec{i} - 6\vec{j}$ (ii) (a) 3   (b) 12   (c) 18

14. $4\vec{i} - 4\vec{j}$;   (i) –28   **15.** 10

16. (i) 10   (ii) $\sqrt{10}$ (iii) $\sqrt{20}$; 45°   **17.** (i) 5   (ii) 45°

19. (i) 63   (ii) 14.25°   **20.** (i) 171   (ii) 39.3°

21. 42.3°   **25.** 12   **26.** 8   **27.** –5

28. (i) 10   (ii) 8   (iii) –2   **29.** $k = 1$

Exercise 17.8 ▼

1. $-3\vec{i} + 4\vec{j}$ **2.** $-5\vec{i} + 2\vec{j}$ **3.** $2\vec{i} + 4\vec{j}$ **4.** $5\vec{i} + 6\vec{j}$ **5.** $3\vec{i} - 2\vec{j}$

6. $\vec{i} - 7\vec{j}$ **7.** $-4\vec{i} - 3\vec{j}$ **8.** $-7\vec{i} - 2\vec{j}$ **9.** $-15\vec{i} + 8\vec{j}$ **10.** $-2\vec{i} + 5\vec{j}$

11. yes   **12.** yes   **13.** (i) (a) $-3\vec{i} + 7\vec{j}$ (b) $7\vec{i} - \vec{j}$ (ii) (a) no   (b) yes

14. yes   **15.** $t = 8, k = 4$ **16.** (i) $-3\vec{i} + 5\vec{j}$; $4\vec{i} + 2\vec{j}$ (ii) $h = 2, k = -3$

17. (i) $3\vec{i} + 2\vec{j}$; $\vec{i} + 2\vec{j}$; $7\vec{i} + 2\vec{j}$ (ii) $h = 3, k = -2$ **18.** (i) $-4\vec{i} - 3\vec{j}$; $5\vec{i} + 12\vec{j}$

19. $x = -5$ or $x = 1$ **20.** (i) $-5\vec{i} - 12\vec{j}$; $-3\vec{i} + 4\vec{j}$ (ii) 13; 5   (iii) $\sqrt{2}$

Exercise 18.1 ▼

1. (i) 3   (ii) 59; 610   (iii) 25th   (iv) 10   **2.** (i) €10.20   (ii) €265

3. €492,000   **4.** 1,120 m   **5.** 90   **6.** (ii) €6,432   **7.** 30

Exercise 18.2 ▼

1. (i) 2   (ii) 1,536; 12,285   (iii) 8   (iv) 7   **2.** (i) €84,474   (ii) 659,040

3. 17,700   **4.** €5,120   **5.** (ii) €65,535   **6.** 13.5 cm

7. €48,000; €36,000; €27,000; €20,250; €15,187.50   **8.** 1,310.72 cm^3

1. (i) €5,408   (ii) €10,608   **2.** (i) €47,640.64   (ii) €134,984.64

3. (i) €24,310.13   (ii) €90,513   **4.** €215,456.79

5. (i) €729   (ii) €2,439   **6.** (i) €2,560   (ii) €9,760

7. 10,000   **8.** 40,000   **9.** 20,000   **10.** 0.8x; 30,000; €58,560

11. (i) 1.533x (ii) 42,000   **12.** (i) 1.952x (ii) 36,000

13. €12,579   **14.** €26,414   **15.** €1,462   **16.** €12,336   **17.** €92,908

1. 2   **2.** 3   **3.** $\frac{64}{3}$ **4.** $\frac{3}{2}$ **5.** $\frac{8}{3}$ **6.** $\frac{25}{4}$ **7.** $\frac{1}{2}$ **8.** 125   **9.** $\frac{225}{2}$ **11.** $\frac{5}{9}$

12. $\frac{2}{9}$ **13.** $\frac{7}{90}$ **14.** $\frac{1}{30}$ **15.** $\frac{2}{45}$ **16.** $\frac{6}{11}$ **17.** $\frac{23}{99}$ **18.** $\frac{101}{90}$ **19.** $\frac{1}{3}$ **20.** 4   **21.** 2

22. $\frac{4}{5}$ **23.** $\frac{5}{6}$ **24.** $\frac{4}{5}$ **25.** 12; 6   **26.** 72 cm

1. 10   **2.** 35   **3.** 4   **4.** 6   **5.** 1   **6.** 6   **7.** 7   **8.** 1

9. 1   **10.** 1   **11.** 15   **12.** 35   **13.** $1 + 3x + 3x^2 + x^3$ **14.** $1 - 3x + 3x^2 - x^3$

15. $1 + 5x + 10x^2 + 10x^3 + 5x^4 + x^5$ **16.** $1 - 5x + 10x^2 - 10x^3 + 5x^4 - x^5$

17. $1 + 6x + 15x^2 + 20x^3 + 15x^4 + 6x^5 + x^6$ **18.** $1 - 6x + 15x^2 - 20x^3 + 15x^4 - 6x^5 + x^6$

19. $1 + 7x + 21x^2 + 35x^3 + 35x^4 + 21x^5 + 7x^6 + x^7$ **20.** $1 - 7x + 21x^2 - 35x^3 + 35x^4 - 21x^5 + 7x^6 - x^7$

21. $a = 2$; $b = 4$ **22.** (i) $1 + 4x + 6x^2 + 4x^3 + x^4$ (ii) $1 - 4x + 6x^2 - 4x^3 + x^4$; $a = 8$

24. $1 + 3x + 3x^2 + x^3$ **25.** (i) $1 + 3x + 3x^2 + x^3$ (ii) $1 - 3x + 3x^2 - x^3$; $p = 6$; $q = 2$

27. $1 + 5x + 10x^2 + 10x^3 + 5x^4 + x^5$; $a = 76$; $b = 44$ **28.** $1 + 4x + 6x^2 + 4x^3 + x^4$

29. 0.2; $1 + 5x + 10x^2 + 10x^3 + 5x^4 + x^5$; 2.48832   **30.** 0.1; $1 - 4x + 6x^2 - 4x^3 + x^4$; 0.6561

Exercise 19.1 ▼

1. $p = 65$ **2.** $q = 120$ **3.** $r = 90$ **4.** $s = 35$ **5.** $x = 70, y = 100$

6. $p = 102, q = 95, r = 85$ **7.** $x = 112, y = 34$ **8.** $x = 100, y = 50$

9. $a = 40, b = 40$ **10.** $p = 70, q = 140$ **11.** $a = 110, b = 100$

12. $x = 100, y = 50$ **13.** $x = 36$ **14.** $a = 40, b = 30$

15. $p = q = 54, r = 36$ **16.** $a = 52$ **17.** $p = 105, q = 67$

18. $r = 120, s = 70$ **19.** $a = 104, b = 52$ **20.** $a = 100, b = 110$

21. $x = 122, y = 29, z = 58, w = 75$ **22.** $x = 40$ **23.** $x = 64, y = 32, z = 58$

24. $x = 176, y = 92, z = 54$ **25.** $x = 60, y = 120$ **26.** $x = 59, y = 118$

27. $x = 49$ **28. (i)** $46°$ **(ii)** $69°$ **(iii)** $67°$

29. $108°$ **30.** $80°$ **31. (i)** $\angle rcq$ **(ii)** $\angle qrp$ **(iii)** $\angle qrs$; $18°$

32. (i) $60°$ **(ii)** $120°$ **(iii)** $46°$ **33. (i)** $100°$ **(ii)** $50°$; $10°$ **34.** $45°$

Exercise 19.2 ▼

1. $p = 90, q = 40, r = 50$ **2.** $a = 56, b = 28$ **3.** $x = 65, y = 40$

4. $p = 75$ **5.** 70 **6.** 50 **7.** $x = 70, y = 40$

8. $a = 70, b = 65$ **9.** $p = 60, q = 60, r = 120$ **10.** $x = 75, y = 65$

11. $p = 95, q = 35, r = 50$ **12.** $p = 100, q = 40, r = 40$ **13.** $83°$

14. (i) $90°$ **(ii)** $28°$ **(iii)** $124°$ **(iv)** $31°$ **15. (i)** $68°$ **(ii)** $56°$ **(iii)** $34°$

16. (i) $60°$ **(ii)** $60°$ **17. (i)** $124°$ **(ii)** $236°$ **(iii)** $118°$ **(iv)** $34°$

18. (i) $66°$ **(ii)** $66°$ **(iii)** $55°$ **(iv)** $59°$ **19.** $75°$

Exercise 19.3 ▼

1. $x = 5$ **2.** $x = 6$ **3.** $y = 8$ **4.** $z = 9$

5. $p = 11$ **6.** $x = 9$ **7.** $x = 3$ **8.** $x = 12$ or 3

9. $x = 2$ **10.** $r = 4$ **11.** $x = 6$ **12.** $q = 8$

13. $a = 9, b = 6$ **14.** $p = 8, q = 12$ **15.** $a = 4, b = 8$ **16.** 9

17. 5 **18.** 7 **19.** 4.4 **20.** 8

Exercise 1R.A ▼

1. €15; €20 **2.** €28; €12 **3.** €12; €7.50 **4.** 42 **5.** €1,000

6. €15 **7.** €55 **8.** €65 **9.** €126 **10.** 35 cm

11. 5 hours and 15 mins **12.** $\frac{1}{4}$ **13.** $\frac{2}{5}$ **14.** 70 m

15. (i) $2\frac{1}{2}$ hours **(ii)** $3\frac{1}{4}$ hours **(iii)** $1\frac{1}{3}$ hours **16.** 80 km/h **17.** 1 hour 45 mins

18. 150 km **19.** $2\frac{1}{2}$ hours **20.** $6\frac{1}{4}$ m/s **21.** 54 km/h **22.** 42 km/h

23. 5 hours 12 mins **24.** 29.4 km **25. (i)** 20% **(ii)** 25%

26. €15,000 **27.** 20% **28.** €1,500; €900 **29.** €340,000 **30.** 18%

31. €82 **32.** €1,250 **33.** €13,600 **34.** €1,500 **35.** €3,612

36. (i) US$767 **(ii)** €750

Exercise 1R.B ▼

1. 102 g; 51 g; 204 g **2. (i)** $6 : 8 : 9$ **(ii)** €240; €320; €360

3. (i) US$692 **(ii)** US$529.92 **4. (i)** 86 km/h **(ii)** 67 litres

5. €861; 21% **6.** 7.4% **7.** 6.3% **8. (i)** 7.2% **(ii)** 0.8%

9. 3.25% **10. (i)** 5.5% **(ii)** 7% **11.** €2,678; 2.5% **12.** €42; 1.75%

13. €2,744.95; €244.95 **14.** €18,875.40; €5,121.60 **15.** €5,549

16. (i) €3,984.62 **(ii)** €1,484.62 **17.** €4,851 **18.** €48,400; 6.75% **19.** €22,950; 3%

20. €5,434; 3.5 **21. (i)** €4,400 **(ii)** €2,475 **(iii)** €25,025; 9% **22.** 4.5×10^{-4}

23. 5.12×10^{-2} **24.** 8.383×10^{2} **25. (i)** 3.6×10^{7} **(ii)** 2.3×10^{-4}

26. 0.0265; 0.0265 > 0.02 **27.** 0.05

Exercise 1R.C ▼

1. (i) 292 **(ii)** €16,900; €292.50 **2. (i)** €342 **(ii)** 228 **(iii)** €603

3. (i) €264 **(ii)** €6,300 **4. (i)** 0.0005 **(ii)** 1.01%

5. (i) €5,434 **(ii)** 4 **6.** €45,000 **7.** €6,614.40

8. 6,000 **9.** 11,600 **10. (i)** €10,660 **(ii)** €8,876

11. (i) €17,040 **(ii)** €12,540 **12.** €24,800 **13.** 17c in the €

14. (i) €2,880 **(ii)** €7,440 **(iii)** €1,320 **15. (i)** €31,000 **(ii)** €55,000

16. €260; €82.80; 42% **17.** $10\frac{1}{2}$

581

1. $\frac{21}{2}$ **2.** 5   **3.** (i) $\frac{3}{2}$ (ii) $\frac{16}{5}$ (iii) 12

4. (i) $-\frac{3}{2}, -2$ (ii) 0, 3   (iii) ± 2 **5.** (i) $x = 4, y = 1$ (ii) $x = -2, y = 2$ (iii) $x = 2, y = -\frac{3}{2}$

8. (i) 2   (ii) -7 **9.** $x < 3$ **10.** $x \geqslant -4$ **11.** $x < -2$ **12.** 0, 1, 2

13. 0, 1, 2, 3   **14.** $\dfrac{8k}{t}$ **15.** $3t - q$ **16.** $\dfrac{2p - t}{6}$ **17.** $3r + 5q$

18. $q - pq$ **19.** $15t - 5qt$ **20.** (i) 3   (ii) 1

1. $-\frac{7}{25}$ **2.** $\dfrac{q}{3p + 1}$; 10   **3.** 4   **4.** $-3, 1$ **5.** $-5, \frac{1}{3}$

6. $-\frac{5}{2}, -2, 1$ **7.** $k = -4; \frac{1}{2}, 3$ **8.** $-6, 1, 2$ **9.** $-\frac{1}{2}, 2, 3$ **10.** $-\frac{1}{2}, 1 \, 2$

11. $-2, -1, \frac{3}{2}$ **12.** (i) -17 (ii) $x^3 - 3x^2 - 13x + 15 = 0$ **13.** $2x^3 + 5x^2 + x - 2 = 0$

14. (i) $x \leqslant 6$ (ii) $x > -4$ (iii) $-4 < x \leqslant 6$ **15.** (i) $x \geqslant -\frac{5}{2}$ (ii) $x \leqslant 1$ (iii) $-\frac{5}{2} \leqslant x \leqslant 1$

16. (i) $x < 2$ (ii) $x \geqslant -\frac{3}{4}$ (iii) $-\frac{3}{4} \leqslant x < 2$ **17.** (i) 0, 1   (ii) 0, 1, 2, 3   (iii) 2, 3

18. (i) 6   (ii) 3   (iii) 2   (iv) $\frac{7}{2}$ (v) -2 (vi) $-\frac{3}{2}$

19. (i) $x^2 - x$ (ii) $x = 3$ or $x = -2$

20. (i) $x = 1, y = 3$ or $x = -3, y = -1$ (ii) $x = -7, y = 5$ or $x = 5, y = -1$
    (iii) $x = 4, y = 3$ or $x = -1, y = -2$ (iv) $x = 4, y = 1$ or $x = -\frac{8}{5}, y = \frac{19}{5}$
    (v) $x = 5, y = -1$ or $x = -\frac{19}{5}, y = \frac{17}{5}$ (vi) $x = \frac{1}{4}, y = -\frac{1}{4}$ or $x = -\frac{1}{2}, y = -\frac{1}{2}$

21. $x = 5, y = 0$ or $x = 3, y = 4$; 125, 91

1. (i) $a = 6$ (ii) $t = 9$ **2.** $a = -5, b = -6$ **3.** (i) $a = -6, b = 11$ (ii) 1, 2, 3

4. (i) $a = 5, b = -6$ (ii) 0, 1   **5.** (i) $\frac{1}{2}, \frac{5}{2}$ (ii) $\frac{1}{3}, 2$ (iii) $-1, \frac{4}{3}$ (iv) $\pm \frac{1}{2}$

6. $-1.64, 0.24$ **7.** $-0.47, -8.53$ **8.** (i) $\dfrac{3x - 1}{(x + 1)(x - 3)}$ (ii) $-0.4, 5.4$

9. $(x - 2)(x + 1)$; $-1, \frac{1}{2}, 2$ **10.** (i) 27   (ii) 16   (iii) 4

11. (i) $\frac{1}{10}$ (ii) $\frac{1}{4}$ (iii) $\frac{1}{8}$ **12.** (i) $\dfrac{8a}{c + 5}$ (ii) $\sqrt{2}$ or $2^{1/2}$

13. (i) a (ii) 2   (iii) $\dfrac{25}{a}$ **14.** $x - \dfrac{9}{x}$; $x = 9$

15. $-2, 3$ **16.** $1, -2;\ g(x) = 2x + 2;\ x < -1$

17. (i) (a) $2^{1/2}$ **(b)** 2^3 **(c)** 2^4 **(d)** $2^{3/2}$ **(e)** $2^{5/2}$ **(ii) (a)** $\frac{5}{4}$ **(b)** 4 **(c)** $\frac{17}{4}$ **(d)** $\frac{17}{10}$

18. (i) (a) 3^4 **(b)** 3^5 **(c)** $3^{1/2}$ **(d)** $3^{7/2}$ **(e)** $3^{3/2}$ **(ii) (a)** 2 **(b)** $-\frac{1}{4}$ **(c)** 9 **(d)** $\frac{13}{2}$

19. (i) (a) 5^2 **(b)** 5^{-1} **(c)** $5^{1/2}$ **(d)** $5^{5/2}$ **(e)** $5^{3/2}$ **(ii) (a)** 1 **(b)** $\frac{3}{4}$ **(c)** $\frac{13}{4}$ **(d)** $-\frac{5}{2}$

Exercise 3R.A ▼

1. (i) $0 + 17i$ **(ii)** $-13 + 6i;\ 1$ **(iii)** $1 + 2i$ **(iv)** $5 + 18i$

2. (i) $4 + 17i$ **(ii)** $5 - 12i$ **(iii)** $-8 - 2i$

Exercise 3R.B ▼

1. $1 + i;\ \sqrt{2}$ **2.** $\frac{4}{5} + \frac{3}{5}i;\ 1$ **3.** $\frac{4}{25} - \frac{3}{25}i$ **4.** $41;\ \frac{9}{41} + \frac{40}{41}i$ **5.** 50

6. $0 + \frac{1}{2}i$ **(i)** $\frac{1}{2}$ **(ii)** both $= \frac{1}{4}$ **7. (i)** $\sqrt{45}$ **(iii)** $\frac{3}{2} - \frac{1}{2}i$

8. (ii) $\sqrt{34}$ **(iii)** $\frac{3}{34} - \frac{5}{34}i$ **9.** $4 + 3i$ **10.** $-2 - 5i$

11. (i) $2 \pm 3i$ **(ii)** $5 \pm 2i$ **12. (i)** yes   **(ii)** yes   **13.** ± 6

14. ± 2 **15.** $a = 2, b = -3$ **16.** $p = 3, q = 1$ **17.** $x = 1, y = 4$

18. $x = 1, y = 3$ **19.** $5 - 5i;\ \frac{1}{2}$

Exercise 3R.C ▼

1. (i) $x = 2, y = -7$ **(ii)** $s = -1, t = 8$ **2.** $3 - 4i;\ k = -1, t = -6$

3. $0 + i;\ k = -1, t = -3$ **4.** $\frac{12}{5} - \frac{4}{5}i;\ k = 7\frac{1}{2}, t = 6$

5. (i) $x = -3, y = -\frac{4}{3}$ **(ii)** $s = \frac{3}{25}, t = -\frac{4}{25}$ **6.** $x = -2, y = 3;\ 0 - i;\ 1$

7. $x = 4, y = 2;\ \sqrt{5}$ **8. (i)** $p = 2, k = 3$ **(ii)** yes

9. $-\frac{1}{2} \pm \frac{1}{2}i$ **10.** $a = -6, b = 25$

11. $p = -4, q = 5$ **12. (i)** 32 (real number)   **(ii)** no, $18 \neq \sqrt{226}$

13. $a = 5, b = -3$ **14. (i)** $16 + 16i$ **(ii)** $\dfrac{\sqrt{5}}{8}$

15. $a = 5, b = 3;\ t = 1, s = 3;\ x^2 + y^2 = 10$, circle, centre $(0, 0)$ and radius $\sqrt{10}$ **16.** $3 \pm 5i$

1. (i) $-4, -2, 0$ **(ii)** $5.9, 6.5, 7.1$ **2. (i)** -4 **(ii)** -7 **3. (i)** $2, 5, 10$

4. (i) $\frac{2}{3}$ **5. (i)** -5 **(ii)** -45 **6.** $25; 4n + 5$

8. (i) 162 **(ii)** $39,366$

Exercise 4R.B ▼

1. (i) 6 **(ii)** 56 **(iii)** 34 **(iv)** 752

2. (i) $\frac{1}{2}$ **(ii)** $32(\frac{1}{2})^{n-1}$ **(iii)** $64[1 - (\frac{1}{2})^n]$ **(iv)** 64

3. (i) $\frac{11}{10}, \frac{121}{100}, \frac{1,331}{1,000}$ **(ii)** 4.641 **4. (i)** $\frac{1}{3}$ **(ii)** $\frac{2}{9}, \frac{2}{27}$

5. (i) $\frac{2}{3}, \frac{4}{9}, \frac{8}{27}$ **6. (i)** 3 **(ii)** 3

7. (i) 2 **(ii)** $\frac{1}{2}(2)^{n-1}$ **(iii)** $\frac{63}{2}$ **8. (i)** 48 **(ii)** -4 **(iii)** T_{13} **(iv)** 312

9. (i) $3; 5$ **(ii)** 318 **(iii)** T_{30} **10.** $7; 2; 10$

11. (i) $5; 3$ **(ii)** $5(3)^{n-1}; 32,805$ **(iii)** $1,820$ **(iv)** 8

12. $x = 6; 13, 16, 19$ **13.** $k = 11; 17, 23, 29$ **14.** $x = 6$ **15.** $\frac{3}{2}; 3$

16. $22 - 4n; -98$ **17.** $5; 3$ **18. (i)** $a = -9, b = 1$ **(ii)** 11

19. (i) 1 **(ii)** 3 **(iii)** $\dfrac{3^n - 1}{2}$; yes   **20. (i)** 6 **(ii)** 33

Exercise 4R.C ▼

1. (i) 7 **(ii)** $4, 10, 25, 62.5$ **2. (i)** $1; 2$ **(ii)** 11

4. (i) $4n - 3$ **(ii)** 860 **9. (i)** $-4; 8$ **(ii)** 9 **10.** $3; -4$

11. (i) 132 **(ii)** 110 **(iii)** 22 **12.** $-1; 4; 4n - 5$

14. (i) $-2; 2$ **(ii)** $2n - 4$ **15.** $-8; 3$

16. (i) $21 - 3n$ **(ii)** $2, 11$ **17. (i)** $5n$ **(ii)** $\dfrac{n}{2}(5n + 5)$ **(iii)** $99,500$

18. (i) $11d$ **(ii)** $65d$ **(iii)** $d = 3; 6, 9, 12, 15$

19. (i) 3 **(ii)** 2 **(iii)** $3(2)^{n-1}$ **(iv)** $3(2^n - 1)$ **(v)** $1,536$ **(vi)** $3,069$

20. (i) $10; 3$ **(ii)** $10(3)^{n-1}; 2,430$

1. 6; [0, 4]; 4, 0, 4   **2.** 4; [0, 3]; 0, 3, 3   **3.** 10; [0, 3]; 3   **4. (i)** 5   **(ii)** 2

5. -1 **6.** $\frac{1}{3}$ **7.** 1, 2, 3   **8. (i)** 0.2   **(ii)** 0.1

9. -15 **10.** 7; 35; 5   **11.** 13, -5 **12.** 3

13. (i) $3x^2$ **(ii)** $-2x$ **(iii)** $8x$ **(iv)** $9 - 3x^2$ **(v)** $-15x^2$ **(vi)** $12x^3 - 2$ **(vii)** $2x - 3$

     (viii) $30x^4 + 2x$ **(ix)** $5 - 9x^2$ **(x)** $2x$ **(xi)** $-2x^{-3}$ or $\dfrac{-2}{x^3}$ **(xii)** $-3x^{-4}$ or $\dfrac{-3}{x^4}$

14. (i) $2t - 3$ **(ii)** -4 **15. (i)** $2x - 4$ **(ii)** 2   **16. (i)** $4x^3 - 32$ **(ii)** 2

1. (i) 8; [0, 10]   **(ii)** 10, 0, 5, 0, 10

2. 6; [-2, 4];   **(i)** -2 **(ii)** -1 **(iii)** 4   **(iv)** -2 **(v)** 4   **(vi)** 4; 8

3. (i) $5x^4 - 12x^2 - 6x$ **(ii)** $-3x^2 + 2x + 3$ **(iii)** $\dfrac{2}{(x+1)^2}$ **(iv)** $\dfrac{5}{(x-1)^2}$

     (v) $4(x^2 + 3x)^3(2x + 3)$ **(vi)** $3(x^2 + 5x - 1)^2(2x + 5)$

     (vii) $25x^4 - 3x^2 + 30x$ or $(x^3 + 3)(10x) + (5x^2 - 1)(3x^2)$

     (viii) $7(2x - 3)^6(2)$ or $14(2x - 3)^6$ **(ix)** $\dfrac{5}{(x+2)^2}$

     (x) $5(3 - 7x)^4(-7)$ or $-35(3 - 7x)^4$ **(xi)** $5x^4 - 17 - 5x^{-6}$ or $5x^4 - 17 - \dfrac{5}{x^6}$

     (xii) $10\left(1 - \dfrac{1}{x}\right)^9(x^{-2})$ or $10\left(1 - \dfrac{1}{x}\right)^9\left(\dfrac{1}{x^2}\right)$

4. $\dfrac{-2x^2 + 2}{(x^2 + 1)^2}$ **5.** $7\left(x^5 - \dfrac{1}{x^2}\right)^6\left(5x^4 + \dfrac{2}{x^3}\right)$ **6.** $7(x - 1)^6$; 7   **7.** -96 **8.** $\dfrac{-x^2 + 2x}{(1 - x)^2}$

9. -108 **10. (i)** $\dfrac{x^2 - 8x}{(x - 4)^2}$ **(ii)** -35

12. (i) max $(-1, 25)$, min $(2, -2)$ **(ii)** max $(2, 0)$, min $(4, -4)$ **(iii)** max $(2, 4)$, min $(3, 3)$
     (iv) max $(-1, 9)$, min $(1, 5)$

13. $(2, 4)$ **14.** max $(3, 59)$, min $(-1, -5)$ **15.** $x + y - 5 = 0$ **16.** $3x - y + 1 = 0$

17. -1 and 1; they are perpendicular as $-1 \times 1 = -1$ **18.** $-4, \frac{2}{3}$

19. $p(-4, 0)$, $q(-1, 9)$, $r(0, 8)$, $s(2, 0)$ **20.** 0, 8, 8; $2x - 2$ **21.** 4, 2, 1, $\frac{1}{2}$, $\frac{1}{4}$; $(-1, -1)$, $(-4, -\frac{1}{4})$

22. (i) 18, 0, -18 **(ii)** $-9 + 12x - 3x^2$ **(iii)** max $(3, 2)$, min $(1, -2)$ **(v)** $-2 \leqslant k \leqslant 2$

23. (iii) $-1.6, 0.6$ **24. (i)** $\frac{10}{3}$ m/s   **(iii)** $\frac{13}{2}$ seconds

1. $\frac{V}{50}$; $\frac{8}{25}$

2. (i) 4   **(ii)** max $(-2, 32)$, min $(2, 0)$

3. (i) $a = 12$ **(ii)** max $(-2, 23)$, min $(2, -9)$

4. $-1, 5$

5. $\dfrac{2x^2 + 8}{(4 - x^2)^2}$

6. $\dfrac{-x^2 - 1}{x^2}$

8. (i) $12x - 3x^2$; max $(4, 32)$, min $(0, 0)$ **(iii)** $-2 \leqslant x < 0$ and $4 < x \leqslant 6$

9. (i) $3x^2 - 6x$; max $(0, 0)$, min $(2, -4)$ **(iii)** $-0.7, 1, 2.7$ **(iv)** $0 < x < 2$

10. (ii) $6x^2 - 10x - 4$; min $(2, -9)$ **(iii)** $2x^3 - 5x^2 - 4x + 3 = 2x - 3$ **(iv)** $-1.35, 0.7, 3.15$

11. point of intersection of $g(x)$ and $h(x)$

12. (i) $-\frac{1}{4}, -1, 1, \frac{1}{2}, \frac{1}{4}$ **(ii)** -2 **(iv)** $\dfrac{-1}{(x + 2)^2}$ **(v)** -5 or 1

13. (i) $-\frac{1}{3}, -1, 2, \frac{1}{4}$ **(ii)** $\dfrac{-1}{(x - 1)^2}$ **(iii)** both slopes $= -1$ **(v)** $x + y + 1 = 0$ **(vi)** $(2, 1)$

14. (i) -1 **(ii)** $\dfrac{1}{(x - 2)^2}$ **(iii)** $(1, -1). (3, 1)$

15. (i) -1 **(ii)** $(2, -20), (-1, 10)$; $x + y + 18 = 0, x + y - 9 = 0$

16. (i) 0 **(ii)** $3x^2 - 12x$

17. $6x^2 + 6x - 2$ **(i)** $-2, 1$ **(ii)** $10x - y - 10 = 0, 10x - y + 17 = 0$

18. $6x^2 - 14x + 7$; $3x - y - 6, 81x - 27y - 37 = 0$ **19.** $\dfrac{-1}{(x + 1)^2}$; $(1, \frac{1}{2})$; $x + 4y - 3 = 0$

20. (i) -9 **(ii)** $(3, -26)$ **21.** $f(x) = x^2 - 2x - 3$; $p = 3, q = -3$; $0, 5$

22. $b = 2, c = -3$; $k = -4$; -1 **23.** $a = 2, b = -24, c = 3$ **24.** $b = -2, c = -15$

25. (i) 24 cm   **(ii)** 4 cm/s   **(iii)** 7 seconds   **(iv)** -2 cm/s^2

26. (i) 275 m   **(ii)** 30 m/s   **(iii)** 8 seconds

27. (i) $30 - \frac{9}{2}t$ **(ii)** 21 m/s   **(iii)** $\frac{20}{3}$ seconds   **(iv)** 100 m

28. (i) $-20t$ **(ii)** -50 m/s   **(iii)** 1.2 seconds

29. 6 m/s^2 and -6 m/s^2; 12 m/s   **30. (i)** 300   **(ii)** -250 cm^3/s

1. $4 : 25$ **2.** 6 cm   **3.** 96%   **4.** 276 m^2 **5.** 157.5 cm^2 **6.** 2.5

7. 198 cm^2 **8.** 21 cm^2 **9.** 5,000   **10.** 400 m   **11.** 8,225 cm^2 **12.** 4π cm^2

13. 196.25 cm^2 **14.** 49 cm

Exercise 6R.B

1. (i) 4   **(ii)** 232 cm^2 **2. (i)** 5 cm   **(ii)** 54.5 cm^2 **3.** 58 cm^2

4. 8 cm^2 **5.** 5 cm; 15π cm^2 **6.** 10 cm

7. (i) 15 cm   **(ii)** 800.7 cm^2

8. (i) 38,808 mm^3 **(ii)** 174,636 mm^3 **(iii)** 52,212 mm^3

9. (i) 3,920π cm^3 **(ii)** 144π cm^3 **(iii)** 9 cm   **(iv)** 27

10. 9 cm

11. (i) 15 cm; 180π cm^3 **(ii)** 144π cm^3 **(iii)** 55.6%

12. 324π cm^3 **13. (i)** 15 cm   **(ii)** 123.75 cm^2

14. 40.72 m^2 **15.** 353 m^2 **16.** 4,600 m^2

17. 6.1 hectares   **18. (i)** 1, 2, 5, 10, 17   **(ii)** $\frac{76}{3}$ **19.** 16

20. 4   **21.** $x = 18$; 72 m

Exercise 6R.C

1. (i) 9 cm   **(ii)** 3,052.08 cm^3 **2. (i)** 800π cm^3 **(ii)** 2,600π cm^3 **(iii)** 13.7 cm

3. (i) 72   **(ii)** 6,912 cm^3 **(iii)** 74%   **4. (i)** 6   **(ii)** 972 cm^3 **(iii)** 1.3 g

5. (i) 5 m^2 **(ii)** 20 m^3 **6.** 5 cm   **7.** 39 cm^3; 2.3 cm

8. $\frac{9}{2}\pi$ cm^3; 125   **9.** 30,375π cm^3; 22.5 cm   **10.** 12 cm

11. 12,560 cm^3; 5 cm   **12.** 0.06π cm^3/s   **13. (i)** $\frac{2}{3}\pi r^3$ **(ii)** 3 cm

14. (i) 3 cm   **(iv)** 2 cm   **15. (i)** 720π cm^3 **(ii)** 10 cm

Exercise 7R.A

1. 13   **2.** $(-3, -4\frac{1}{2})$ **3.** (10, 2)

4. $2x + 5y + 4 = 0$ **5. (i)** $\frac{3}{4}$ **(ii)** $3x - 4y - 11 = 0$ **7.** $2x - y + 6 = 0$

8. (2, −3)   **9.** (7, −4)   **10.** (−1, −1)

11. 5(−1, 4)   **12.** 11   **13.** −3

14. −1   **15. (i)** $a(4, 0), b(0, -6)$ **(iii)** 12   **16.** 9

587

1. (ii) $\frac{4}{5}$ (iii) $5x + 4y + 50 = 0$ (iv) $(0, -\frac{25}{2})$ (v) 205 (vi) $(10, -\frac{9}{2})$

2. $p(-2, 0), q(0, 4); k : x + 2y - 3 = 0; (3, 0); (-1, 2); 5$

3. (ii) no, as $bc \nparallel ad$

4. (i) $\frac{3}{5}$ (ii) $3x - 5y - 15 = 0$ (iii) $5x + 3y = 0$

5. (iii) 10 (iv) $h(2, 8), g(-4, 6)$ (v) $2x - y + 4 = 0$

6. $r(-1, 2); 5x - 3y + 11 = 0; 1 : 2$

7. (ii) (b) $\sqrt{40}$ (c) $1 : 2$

1. (i) 2 (ii) $4x - y - 2 = 0$ (iii) $x + 4y + 25 = 0$

2. (i) $2x + y - 10 = 0$ (ii) $\frac{3}{2}$

3. (i) $4x + 3y - 15 = 0$ (ii) $t(-\frac{20}{3}, 0), r(\frac{15}{4}, 0); \frac{625}{24}$

4. $4x + 3y - 12 = 0; 3x - 4y = 0;$ no

5. (i) $x - 3y + 1 = 0$ (ii) $2x + y - 12 = 0$ (iii) $q(5, 2), s(1, 3)$

6. 0 or 2 **7.** $-2, 14$ **8.** $\sqrt{x^2 + 5}; 5, 15$

1. centre $(0, 0)$ and radius 5 **2.** (i) 10 (ii) $x^2 + y^2 = 100$ **3.** (i) $\sqrt{10}$ (ii) $x^2 + y^2 = 10$

4. (i) 6 **5.** (i) 4 **6.** (i) 5

7. $(x - 3)^2 + (y + 2)^2 = 5$ **8.** centre $(4, -5)$ and radius 3 **9.** ± 2

10. (i) centre $(3, 4)$ and radius 5 (ii) $0, 6$ **11.** $(7, 0), (-7, 0), (0, 7), (0, -7)$

1. (i) $(1, -2)$ (ii) $\sqrt{5}$ (iii) $(x - 1)^2 + (y + 2)^2 = 5$

2. (i) $(x - 2)^2 + (y + 4)^2 = 25$ (ii) $a(-1, 0), b(5, 0)$ (iv) 6

3. (i) centre $(1, 2)$, radius $\sqrt{13}$ (ii) $(x - 1)^2 + (y - 2)^2 = 13$ (iii) $p(-2, 0), q(4, 0)$

4. (i) $-\frac{2}{5}$ (ii) $2x + 5y - 29 = 0$ **5.** (i) $(0, 1), (0, -3)$ (ii) $x + y - 5 = 0$

6. (i) radius $\sqrt{29}$, centre $(3, -2)$ (ii) $(8, 0), (-2, 0)$

7. centre $(-1, 3)$, radius 2; $(x - 5)^2 + (y + 1)^2 = 4$

8. centre $(-2, 4)$, radius 5; $x^2 + y^2 = 5$ **9.** $(1, -3)$ **10.** $(-2, 4)$ **11.** $(1, 3), (3, 1)$

12. $x^2 + y^2 = 25$; $p(0, 5)$, $q(-4, -3)$ **13. (i)** $(\frac{5}{2}, 2)$ **(ii)** $\frac{5}{2}$ **(iii)** $(x - \frac{5}{2})^2 + (y - 2)^2 = \frac{25}{4}$

14. (i) centre $(3, 1)$, radius 2   **(ii)** $(x - 3)^2 + (y - 1)^2 = 4$ **(iii)** $(x - 3)^2 + (y - 1)^2 = 8$ **(iv)** $1 : 2$

Exercise 8R.C ▼

1. (i) $3x + 4y - 25 = 0$ **(ii)** $3x + 4y + 25 = 0$

2. (i) $4x + y + 17 = 0$ **(ii)** $4x + y - 17 = 0$; $2\sqrt{17}$ or $\sqrt{68}$

3. centre $(-1, 1)$, radius $\sqrt{13}$; $3x - 2y - 8 = 0$; $3x - 2y + 18 = 0$; $2\sqrt{13}$ or $\sqrt{52}$

4. (i) $(-3, 1)$ **(ii)** $3x - y - 10 = 0$

5. (i) $(x + 3)^2 + y^2 = 10$ **(ii)** 2   **(iii)** 12

6. (ii) $(2, 0)$ **(iii)** $(x - 2)^2 + y^2 = 50$

8. (i) $c(2, 0)$; 3   **(ii)** $(x - 2)^2 + y^2 = 9$ **(iii)** $y = 3$ or $y = -3$ **(iv)** $\dfrac{9\pi}{4} - \dfrac{9}{2}$

9. (i) $x^2 + y^2 = 26$ **(ii)** $0, \pm 1, \pm 2, \pm 3$

10. $S_1 : x^2 + y^2 = 25$; $S_2 : (x - 12)^2 + y^2 = 25$; $S_3 : (x - 6)^2 + (y - 8)^2 = 25$; $T : 3x + 4y - 25 = 0$;
     $K : 3x - 4y - 11 = 0$; $(6, \frac{7}{4})$

11. $K_1 : x^2 + y^2 = 100$; $K_2 : (x - 3)^2 + (y - 4)^2 = 25$; $K_3 : (x + 3)^2 + (y + 4)^2 = 25$; $T : 3x + 4y = 0$;
     $(-8, 6), (8, -6)$

12. (i) $\sqrt{20}$ **(ii)** $(2, 4)$ **(iii)** $(x - 4)^2 + (y - 8)^2 = 20$ **(iv)** $p(0, 10), q(0, 6)$

Exercise 9R.A ▼

1. (i) $p = 120$ **(ii)** $q = 60$ **(iii)** $r = 70$ **(iv)** $s = 130$ **2. (i)** $t = 57$ **(ii)** $s = 41$

3. $x = 45, y = 85$ **4.** $x = 45, y = 56$ **5.** $36°$

6. (i) $65°$ **(ii)** $25°$ **7. (i)** $56°$ **(ii)** $91°$ **8. (i)** $x = 42, y = 6$ **(ii)** $360°$

9. $x = 127, y = 53$ **10. (i)** $p = 62$ **(ii)** $q = 83$ **(iii)** $r = 83$ **(iv)** $s = 35$

11. (i) $x = 8$ **(ii)** $y = 22$ **(iii)** $s = 35$ **(iv)** $t = 14$

12. (i) $x = 30$ **(ii)** $y = 48$ **13. (i)** $60°$ **(ii)** $30°$ **(iii)** $120°$

15. $x = 15, y = 8$ **16.** 29   **17.** 8 cm   **18.** 120

19. (i) $53°$ **(ii)** 5 cm   **(iii)** 13.625 cm^2 **20.** 6.93

Exercise 9R.C ▼

1. (i) 6   (ii) 8   (iii) 27.45 sq. units   **2.** (i) $\frac{3}{2}$ or 1.5   (ii) 6   (iii) 12 sq. units

3. (i) $\frac{5}{2}$ or 2.5   (ii) $\frac{75}{2}$ sq. units   **4.** (i) $\frac{9}{4}$ or 2.25   (ii) $\frac{25}{4}$ or 6.25   (iii) 12 sq. units

5. (i) $\frac{3}{5}$ or 0.6   (ii) $\frac{63}{2}$ or 31.5 sq. units   (iii) 56 sq. units

6. (i) $\frac{7}{2}$ or 3.5   (ii) 8   (iii) $2:7$ (iv) 49 sq. units

7. (i) a (ii) $\frac{8}{5}$ or 1.6   (iii) $\frac{49}{2}$ or 24.5 sq. units   (iv) $\frac{5}{8}$ or 0.625

8. (i) $\frac{4}{5}$ or 0.8   (ii) 5.2 cm   **9.** $\frac{8}{5}$ or 1.6   **10.** $\frac{19}{10}$ or 1.9; 4.56 cm

11. (i) 2   (iii) 16   (iv) 21 sq. units   **12.** (iii) 12.25 cm^2 (iv) 2

Exercise 10R.A ▼

2. (i) $\frac{4}{5}$ or 0.8   (ii) $\frac{7}{25}$ or 0.28   **4.** $\frac{8}{17}$; $\frac{15}{17}$ **5.** 14 m   **6.** (i) 4.2 cm   (ii) 25°

7. 18.7 m^2 **8.** 3.6 cm   **9.** 11 cm   **10.** 14π cm^2 **11.** 4π cm   **12.** π cm

Exercise 10R.B ▼

1. (i) 114 m   (ii) 124 m   **2.** (i) 12.31   (ii) 5.13

3. 8.91 cm^2 **4.** (i) $\cos A = \frac{20}{29}$, $\sin A = \frac{21}{29}$ (ii) 46°

5. $\frac{119}{169}$ **6.** (i) $\cos A = \frac{4}{5}$, $\sin B = \frac{12}{13}$ (ii) (a) $\frac{63}{65}$ (b) $-\frac{16}{65}$ (c) $\frac{24}{25}$ (d) $\frac{7}{25}$

7. (i) 9.7   (ii) 6   **8.** (i) 1195 m^2 (ii) 69 m

9. 13.8 cm   **10.** 8.3 cm   **11.** 120°

12. (i) 17 m   (ii) 31°; 15.5 m   **13.** 28.25°   **14.** 9.8 km

15. (i) $\dfrac{\sqrt{21}}{5}$ (ii) $7\sqrt{21}$

Exercise 10R.C ▼

1. (i) 1195 m^2 (ii) 69 m   **2.** (i) 159 cm^2 (ii) 23 cm   (iii) 67°

3. (i) 17 m   (ii) 8 m   **4.** (i) 8 cm   (ii) 33 cm^2

5. (i) 7.39   (ii) 10.61   **6.** (i) 32 km   (ii) 31 km

7. 12 km   **8.** 110 km

9. (i) 363 m   **10.** (i) 0.68   (ii) 15 cm

11. 70°

12. (i) $-\dfrac{\sqrt{3}}{2}$ (ii) $-\dfrac{1}{\sqrt{3}}$

13. $\dfrac{\sqrt{3}-1}{2\sqrt{2}}$

14. (i) 270°   (ii) 0°, 360°   (iii) 1   (iv) 0°, 180°, 360°

15. 225°, 315°

16. 60°, 120°; $\pm\dfrac{1}{2}$

17. 142°, 218°

18. 115°

$\boxed{Exercise\ 11R.A\ \blacktriangledown}$

1. (i) $\dfrac{1}{11}$ (ii) $\dfrac{6}{11}$ (iii) $\dfrac{4}{11}$ **2.** (i) $\dfrac{1}{3}$ (ii) $\dfrac{2}{3}$

3. (i) $\dfrac{11}{40}$ (ii) $\dfrac{9}{40}$ (iii) $\dfrac{31}{40}$ **4.** (i) $\dfrac{1}{2}$ (ii) $\dfrac{1}{12}$ (iii) $\dfrac{7}{12}$

5. (i) $\dfrac{1}{25}$ (ii) $\dfrac{9}{25}$ (iii) $\dfrac{7}{25}$ **6.** (i) $\dfrac{1}{2}$ (ii) $\dfrac{1}{6}$ (iii) $\dfrac{1}{2}$ (iv) $\dfrac{1}{2}$ (v) $\dfrac{1}{3}$ (vi) $\dfrac{2}{3}$

7. (i) $\dfrac{1}{4}$ (ii) $\dfrac{1}{13}$ (iii) $\dfrac{2}{13}$ (iv) $\dfrac{4}{13}$ **8.** 406

9. (i) 56   (ii) 35   **10.** (i) 28   (ii) 21

11. (i) 6   (ii) WW, WB, BW, BB, CW, CB **12.** (i) $\dfrac{1}{6}$ (ii) $\dfrac{1}{3}$ (iii) $\dfrac{1}{2}$ (iv) $\dfrac{1}{3}$

$\boxed{Exercise\ 11R.B\ \blacktriangledown}$

1. (i) $\dfrac{1}{18}$ (ii) $\dfrac{1}{6}$ **2.** (i) $\dfrac{21}{44}$ (ii) $\dfrac{1}{2}$ (iii) $\dfrac{14}{23}$ (iv) $\dfrac{13}{21}$ **3.** (i) $\dfrac{1}{4}$ (ii) $\dfrac{2}{3}$

4. (i) $\dfrac{1}{5}$ (ii) $\dfrac{3}{10}$ (iii) $\dfrac{1}{2}$ (iv) $\dfrac{4}{5}$ (v) $\dfrac{7}{10}$ (vi) $\dfrac{1}{4}$ (vii) $\dfrac{1}{25}$ (viii) $\dfrac{1}{10}$

5. (i) $\dfrac{15}{28}$ (ii) $\dfrac{1}{4}$ (iii) $\dfrac{1}{7}$ (iv) $\dfrac{3}{13}$

6. (i) $\dfrac{3}{5}$ (ii) $\dfrac{7}{20}$ (iii) $\dfrac{11}{20}$ (iv) $\dfrac{2}{3}$ **7.** (i) $\dfrac{1}{7}$ (ii) $\dfrac{1}{49}$ **8.** 21

9. 792;   (i) 330   (ii) 462   **10.** (i) 715   (ii) 315   **11.** 210

12. 1,263,600   **13.** (i) 120   (ii) 6

14. (i) 7! or 5,040   (ii) 6! or 720   (iii) 6   (iv) 2

15. (i) 120   (ii) 48   (iii) 48

16. (i) 6! or 720   (ii) 5! or 120   (iii) 4! or 24   (iv) 36

17. 18   **18.** (i) 120   (ii) 72   (iii) 48   (iv) 72   **19.** 24;   (i) 12   (ii) 6

Exercise 11R.C

1. (i) $\frac{1}{6}$ (ii) $\frac{5}{9}$ (iii) $\frac{5}{16}$ **2.** (i) $\frac{1}{24}$ (ii) $\frac{1}{8}$ (iii) $\frac{1}{4}$ (iv) $\frac{5}{24}$

3. (i) $\frac{9}{64}$ (ii) $\frac{17}{32}$ **4.** (i) $\frac{5}{33}$ (ii) $\frac{2}{11}$ (iii) $\frac{19}{66}$

5. (i) 85   (ii) 34   **6.** (i) 5,432   (ii) 1,023   (iii) 300   (iv) 120

7. (i) 120   (ii) 72   (iii) 48   (iv) 30   **8.** (i) 28   (ii) 15

9. (i) $\frac{1}{49}$ (ii) $\frac{2}{49}$ (iii) $\frac{6}{7}$ **10.** $\frac{5}{6}$ **11.** (i) $\frac{1}{5}$ (ii) $\frac{1}{14}$ (iii) $\frac{34}{105}$

Exercise 12R.A

1. 3   **2.** 4.5   **3.** 7; 6   **4.** (i) 5   (ii) 2.3   **5.** 3; 4; 2.61

6. €55   **7.** 32   **8.** 16   **9.** 72   **10.** A

11. 10   **12.** 11   **13.** 4   **14.** 2   **15.** 2

Exercise 12R.B

1. 1.5   **2.** (i) 8   (ii) 8   (iii) 3.42

3. (i) 13   (ii) 8.54   **4.** (i) 107   (ii) 9

5. (i) €57   (ii) €35   **6.** (i) 6, 17, 21, 26   (ii) 51   (iii) 26

7. (ii) 12   (iii) 22%   (iv) 2, 2, 15, 20, 11   (v) 41

8. (i) €15.40   (ii) 2, 11, 24, 34, 40   (iv) 1

9. (ii) 24   (iii) 83   **10.** (ii) 38

11. (ii) 58   (iii) 37.36   **12.** (i) 10, 10, 15, 40, 45, 60, 20   (ii) 125

Exercise 12R.C

1. (iii) 24 calls   (iv) 5 weeks   **2.** (ii) 09.32   (iii) 36

3. 32.5 minutes   **4.** (i) 5   (ii) 1.7

5. (i) 102 hectares   (ii) 38 hectares   **6.** (i) 16, 10, 8, 24, 12, 56   (ii) 126   (iii) 13.16

7. (i) 33   (ii) 76   (iii) 9, 10, 38, 35, 8   (iv) 54.6

8. (i) 60%   (ii) 55–70   **9.** $k + 2$ **10.** 9   **11.** 3   **12.** 17

Exercise 13R.A ▼

1. (i) 40°   **(ii)** 140°   **2.** 105°   **3. (i)** 100°   **(ii)** 40°   **4.** 20°

5. (i) 90°   **(ii)** 45°   **6.** 62°; 62°   **7.** 30°   **8. (i)** 90°   **(ii)** 34°

9. (i) 2 cm   **(ii)** $\frac{11}{2}$ cm   **10.** 3   **11.** 6   **12.** 24 cm

Exercise 13R.C ▼

1. (i) 124°   **(ii)** 118°   **(iii)** 59°   **2. (i)** 40°   **(ii)** 50°   **(iii)** 28°

3. (i) 130°   **(ii)** 140°; 50°   **4. (i)** 34°   **(ii)** 62°   **5.** 80°

6. (i) 72°; 54°   **(ii)** 82°; 49°   **7. (i)** 75°   **(ii)** 56°   **(iii)** 49°

9. (i) ∠krd or ∠kdr   **(ii)** 50°   **(iii)** yes

10. (i) (a) 74°   **(b)** 44°   **(c)** 62°   **(ii) (a)** 44°   **(b)** 30°

11. (i) 42°   **(ii)** 77°   **(iii)** 103°   **12.** 6   **13.** 4   **14.** 3 cm   **15.** 2; 4

16. (i) 5   **(ii)** 6   **(iii)** $\sqrt{40}$ or $2\sqrt{10}$ **17.** $19\frac{1}{2}$ cm   **18.** 4   **19.** 6

Exercise 14R.A ▼

1. (i) $7\vec{i} + \vec{j}$ **(ii)** $0\vec{i} - 11\vec{j}$ **2. (i)** $6\vec{i} - 8\vec{j}$ **(ii)** $7\vec{i} - 10\vec{j}$

3. (i) 13   **(ii)** $12\vec{i} + 5\vec{j}$ **4. (i)** $5\vec{i} + 8\vec{j}$ **(ii)** $\vec{i} + 4\vec{j}$

5. (i) $8\vec{i} + 15\vec{j}$ **(ii) (a)** 5   **(ii)** 17   **(iii)** 2   **6. (i)** $\vec{p} + \vec{r}$ **(ii)** $\frac{1}{2}\vec{p} + \vec{r}$ **(iii)** $\frac{1}{2}\vec{p} - \vec{r}$

7. (i) $\vec{a} + \vec{c}$ **(ii)** $\frac{1}{2}\vec{a} - \vec{c}$ **8. (i)** $\vec{b} - \vec{a}$

Exercise 14R.B ▼

1. $\vec{i} + 0\vec{j}$; $-3\vec{i} + 4\vec{j}$;   5

2. (i) $5\vec{i} - 2\vec{j}$ **(ii)** $\sqrt{29}$ **(iii)** 3   **3. (i)** $-4\vec{i} + 5\vec{j}$ **(ii)** $\sqrt{41}$ **(iii)** 6

4. $h = 3, k = -2$ **5.** $p = 2, q = -4$ **6.** $a = 3, b = 4$ **7.** 13; $m = 1, n = -1$

8. (i) $8\vec{i} + 6\vec{j}$ **(iii)** 10   **(iv)** $k = 2, t = 10$ **9. (i)** $k = 1, t = 5$ **(ii)** $\vec{p} = \frac{1}{2}\vec{a} + \frac{1}{2}\vec{b}$; $\vec{m} = \vec{a} + \frac{1}{2}\vec{b}$

10. (i) $-2\vec{i} + 5\vec{j}$ **(ii)** $\sqrt{29}$ **(iii)** $k = \frac{2}{5}, n = -\frac{19}{5}$

11. (i) $\vec{a} + \vec{c}$ **(ii)** $\vec{a} + \frac{1}{3}\vec{c}$ **(iii)** $\vec{c} + \frac{2}{3}\vec{a}$ **(iv)** $\frac{2}{3}\vec{c} - \frac{1}{3}\vec{a}$

12. (i) $\overrightarrow{am}$ or $\overrightarrow{mc}$ **(ii)** $\overrightarrow{ac}$ **(iii)** $\overrightarrow{ad}$ or $\overrightarrow{bc}$ **(iv)** $\overrightarrow{ab}$ or $\overrightarrow{dc}$ **14. (ii)** $3\vec{r}$

1. 4   **3.** −20   **4. (i)** 10   **(ii)** $45°$ or $\frac{\pi}{4}$ **5.** $k = 5, t = -2; 9$ **6.** $-2\vec{i} - \vec{j}$

7. $\vec{i} - 2\vec{j};$ $-3\vec{i} + \vec{j};$ $p = -1, k = 2$ **8.** $2\vec{i} + 8\vec{j};$ $-4\vec{i} + 2\vec{j};$ $m = -\frac{1}{4}, n = -\frac{15}{2}$

9. (i) $8\vec{i} + 6\vec{j}$ **(ii)** 10   **(iii)** $k = 2, n = 14$ **(iv)** no   **(v)** yes

10. (ii) $-4\vec{i} + 3\vec{j}$ **11.** $-\vec{i} - 4\vec{j};$ yes

12. (i) $-12\vec{i} + 5\vec{j}; 4\vec{i} + 3\vec{j}$ **(ii)** 13; 5   **(iii)** $\sqrt{2}$ **13.** $t = 3$

14. (i) $-2\vec{i} + 5\vec{j}$ **(ii)** $a = 2;$ $\vec{p} = 0\vec{i} + 7\vec{j};$ $\sqrt{8}$ or $2\sqrt{2}$ **15. (i)** $\frac{1}{2}\vec{b}$ **(ii)** $\frac{1}{3}\vec{da}$ **(iii)** $\frac{1}{3}(\vec{a} + \vec{b})$

16. (i) $\frac{4}{3}\vec{p}$ **(ii)** $\frac{4}{3}\vec{p} - \vec{r};$ 5; 16   **17. (i)** $\frac{1}{3}\vec{a} - \frac{1}{3}\vec{b}$ **(ii)** $\frac{1}{3}\vec{a} + \frac{2}{3}\vec{b}$ **(iii)** $\frac{1}{3}\vec{a} - \frac{2}{3}\vec{b}$ **(iv)** −9   **(v)** 7

1. €24.75   **2.** 2   **3.** $\frac{27}{2}$ **4.** 9   **5. (i)** $\frac{4}{5}$ **(ii)** $\frac{25}{6}$ **6.** $\frac{5}{9}$ **7.** $\frac{17}{9}$

8. (i) 0.016; 0.008; 0.004; 0.0002   **(ii)** 0

9. (i) $1 + 4x + 6x^2 + 4x^3 + x^4;$ **(ii)** $1 - 4x + 6x^2 - 4x^3 + x^4$

10. (i) (a) $1 + 3x + 3x^2 + x^3$ **(b)** $1 - 3x + 3x^2 - x^3$ **(ii)** $a = 2, k = 6$

1. (i) $\frac{7}{9}$ **2. (i)** $\frac{7}{11}$ **3. (i)** $\frac{1}{30}$ **4. (i)** $\frac{1}{45}$ **5. (i)** $\frac{8}{9}$ **6.** 25

7. (i) 4   **(ii)** 768   **(iii)** 262,143   **8. (i)** $\frac{1}{3}$ **(ii)** 4   **9. (i)** $\frac{1}{2}$ **(ii)** 8

10. (i) 18, 12, 8   **(ii)** $\dfrac{18[1 - (\frac{2}{3})^5]}{\frac{1}{3}}$ or $54[1 - (\frac{2}{3})^5]$ **(iii)** 54

12. (i) $1 + 5x + 10x^2 + 10x^3 + 5x^4 + x^5$ **(ii)** $76 + 44\sqrt{3}$

13. $1 + 7x + 21x^2 + 35x^3 + 35x^4 + 21x^5 + 7x^6 + x^7$

14. (i) 225   **(ii)** 35   **15.** $\frac{1}{4} + \frac{1}{16} + \frac{1}{64} + \cdots = \frac{1}{3}$

1. $1 + 6x + 15x^2 + 20x^3 + 15x^4 + 6x^5 + x^6;$ $576 + 256\sqrt{5};$ $a = 4, b = 3\ c = 10$

2. $\frac{2}{3}$ **3.** €442   **4.** 40   **5.** 24 years = €984.97; 25 years = €1,083.47

6. $50{,}000[(1.03) + (1.03)^2 + \cdots + (1.03)^{10}]$; €590,390   **7. (i)** 6.4416   **(ii)** €6,441.60

8. (i) €946.86   **(ii)** €3,478   **9.** €3,097   **10. (i)** €1,193.71   **(ii)** €3,379.81

11. (i) €7,290   **(ii)** €24,390   **12.** 10,000   **13. (i)** €0.8x **(ii)** 20,000   **(iii)** €39,040

14. $\{1, 3, 5, 7, 9, 11, 13, 15, 17, 19\}$;   **(i)** 210   **(ii)** 44,100

15. $713\frac{3}{4}$ cm; 896 cm

Exercise 16R.A ▼

1. (i) $2x + 3y - 6 = 0$ **(ii)** $2x + 3y - 6 \leqslant 0$ **2. (i)** $x - y + 2 = 0$ **(ii)** $x - y + 2 \geqslant 0$

3. (i) $x + 5y - 5 = 0$ **(iii)** $x + 5y - 5 \geqslant 0$ **4.** $x - 2y \geqslant 0$

5. (i) $2x + y - 4 = 0$ **(ii)** $x \geqslant 0, y \geqslant 0, 2x + y - 4 \leqslant 0$

6. (i) $3x + 4y - 12 = 0$ **(ii)** $x \geqslant 0, y \geqslant 0, 3x + 4y - 12 \leqslant 0$

Exercise 16R.B ▼

5. $x \geqslant 0$; $2x + y \leqslant 10$; $4x - y \leqslant 8$ **6.** $y \geqslant 0$; $x - y - 1 \geqslant 0$; $x + 2y - 6 = 0$

7. $x \geqslant 0$; $x - y \leqslant -1$; $x + y \leqslant 6$ **8. (i)** $x \geqslant 0$; $y \leqslant 4$; $x - y \leqslant 0$

9. $x \geqslant 0$; $y \geqslant 0$; $x + y \leqslant 10$; $x + 2y \leqslant 16$ **10.** $x \geqslant 0$; $y \geqslant 2$; $2x + y \leqslant 8$; $x + y \leqslant 6$

11. $(8, 0), (4, 5), (14, 0)$; $(14, 0)$, 420

Exercise 16R.C ▼

1. (i) $2x + y \leqslant 34$; $5x + 3y \leqslant 90$ **(ii)** 12A and 10B   **(iii)** €1,320

2. (i) $x + y \leqslant 500$; $4x + 3y \leqslant 1{,}800$ **(ii)** 450 wide-screen and no standard models

3. (i) $3x + y \leqslant 48$; $5x + 3y \leqslant 120$ **(ii)** no shops and 40 offices   **(iii)** 6 shops and 30 offices

4. (i) $x + y \leqslant 46$; $x + 4y \leqslant 100$ **(ii)** 28 cars and 18 buses; €410

5. (i) $10x + y \leqslant 400$; $5x + y \leqslant 250$ **(ii)** 30 apple trees and 100 blackberry bushes   **(iii)** €3,200

6. (i) $2x + y \leqslant 110$; $5x + y \leqslant 230$ **(ii)** 40 type A and 30 type B   **(iii)** €29,400

7. (i) $x + y \leqslant 10$; $x + 3y \leqslant 18$ **(ii)** 6 small trucks and 4 large trucks

8. (i) $3x + y \leqslant 60$; $x + 2y \leqslant 40$ **(ii)** 16A and 12B   **(iii)** Profit on A = €90; Profit on B = €45

9. (i) $\frac{1}{5}x + \frac{1}{10}y \leqslant 9$ or $2x + y \leqslant 90$; $8x + 5y \leqslant 400$
(ii) no bungalows and 80 semi-detached houses